THE STORY SO FAR...

Batman is gone, but his secrets live on. Bruce Wayne has lost his memory, and in his absence, Jim Gordon has taken over as the new Batman in Gotham. Dick Grayson, Batman's first Robin, returned to Gotham on a mission for secret espionage organization Spyral, but immediately found himself targeted by assassins, all sent by the mysterious "Mother," a deadly human trafficker who creates "custom humans."

Dick was rescued by a silent, mysterious martial artist—Cassandra Cain. She gave Dick a valuable lead: a drive containing a message from Bruce along with a list of names of "Mother's children." A list that includes Dick and his fellow former Robins—Jason Todd (now the Red Hood) and Tim Drake (now Red Robin)!

Following Mother's deadly assassin the Orphan, the Robins met up with another name on Mother's list, Harper Row, a.k.a. Bluebird, and Harper's roommate, Stephanie Brown, a.k.a. the Spoiler. When Cassandra and Harper—who have formed a special bond—discovered a training ground in an abandoned church with ties to one of Dick's first missions as Robin, Dick decided to follow the same trail that he and Batman did chasing Scarecrow many years ago—to Prague.

Tim and Jason, meanwhile, tracked Mother's influence to Santa Prisca, former site of the world's most infamous super-prison, now home to religious zealots, the Order of St. Dumas. Tim and Jason are joined by Bane, who wants to take his former home back from the Order. They battled yet another of Mother's "children," Azrael, and barely escaped with their lives.

Back in Prague, Cassandra fled after a confrontation with Mother, but Harper and Dick continued the trail and uncovered the Sculptor, a psychic woman who conditioned Mother's children. Wanting to atone for her role in the organization, the Sculptor revealed valuable information on Mother and her children. First, that Orphan is really David Cain, Cassandra's father, who raised her in isolation to be the ultimate assassin. And second, that when Bruce and Dick were in Prague chasing Scarecrow years ago, Bruce made a deal with Mother for a child—a new Robin to replace Dick. And the price was that Batman had to murder the child's parents himself...

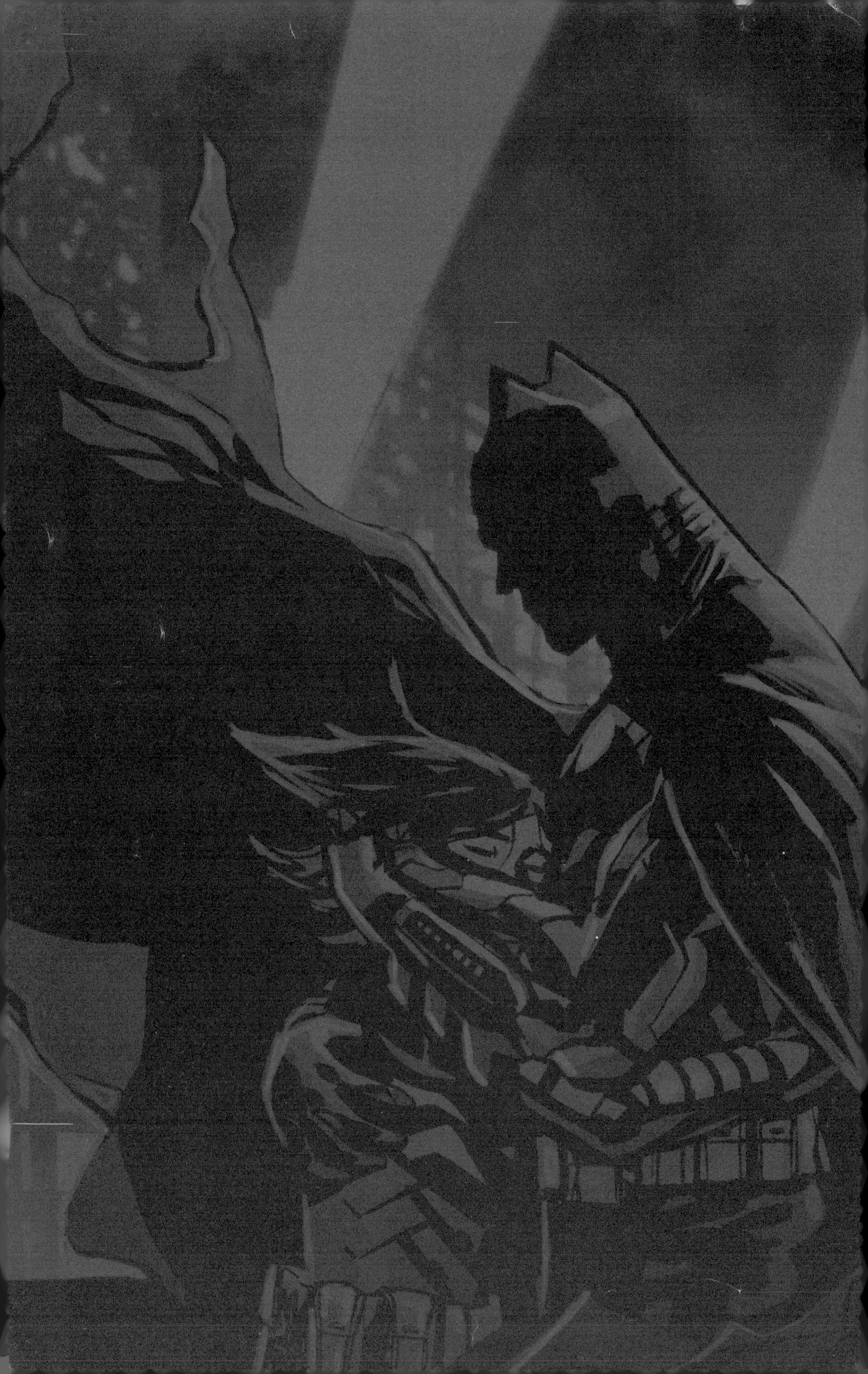

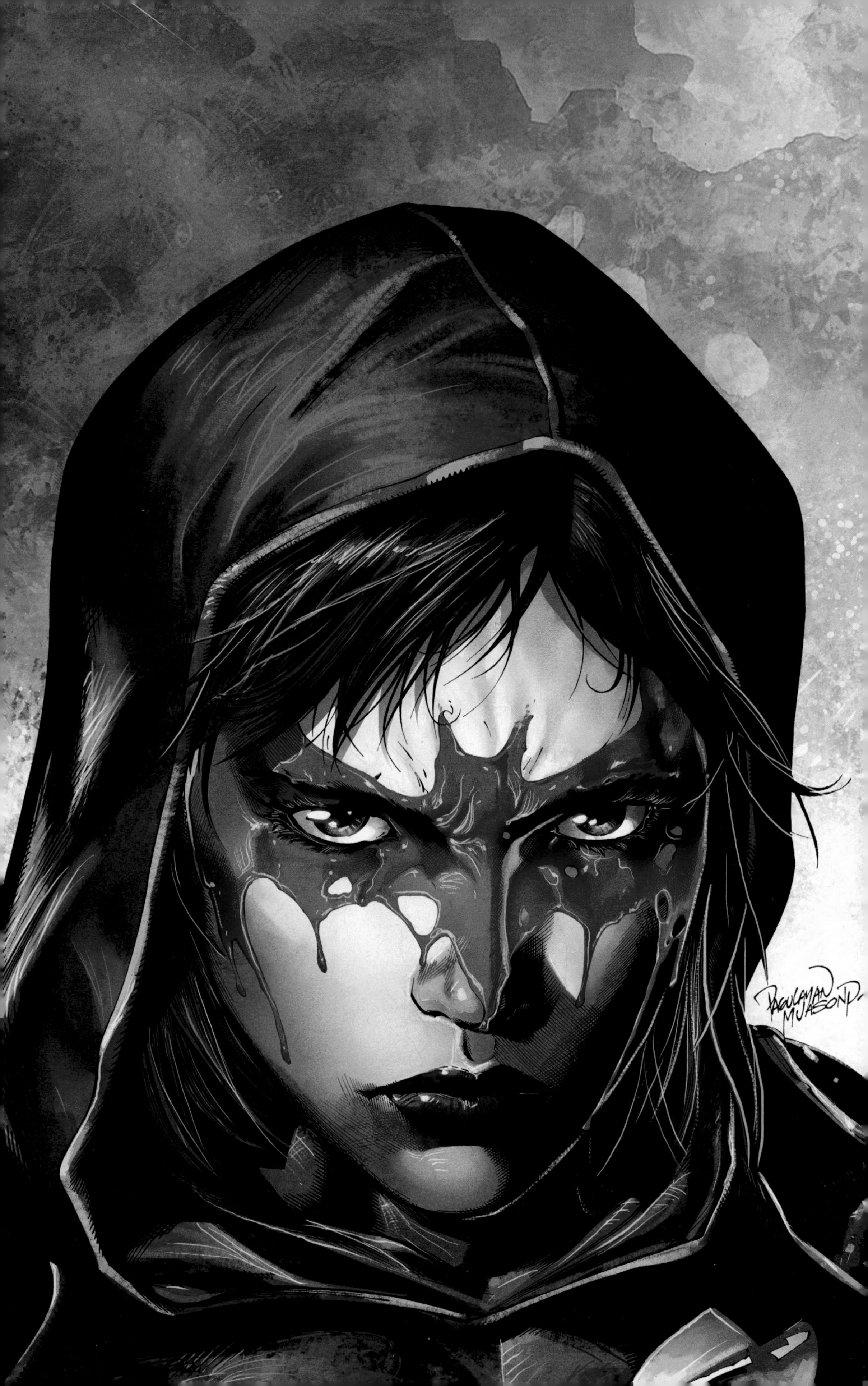

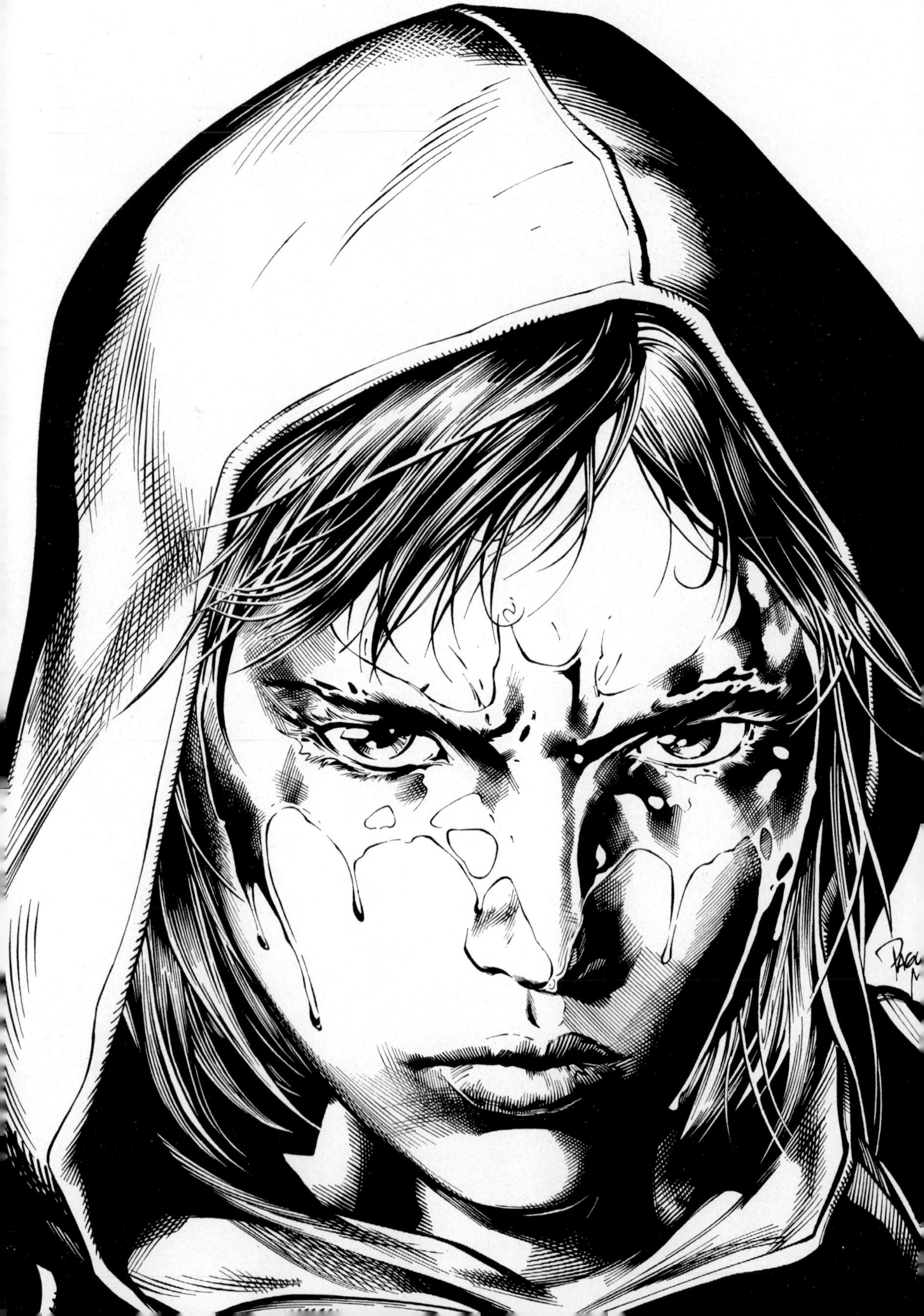

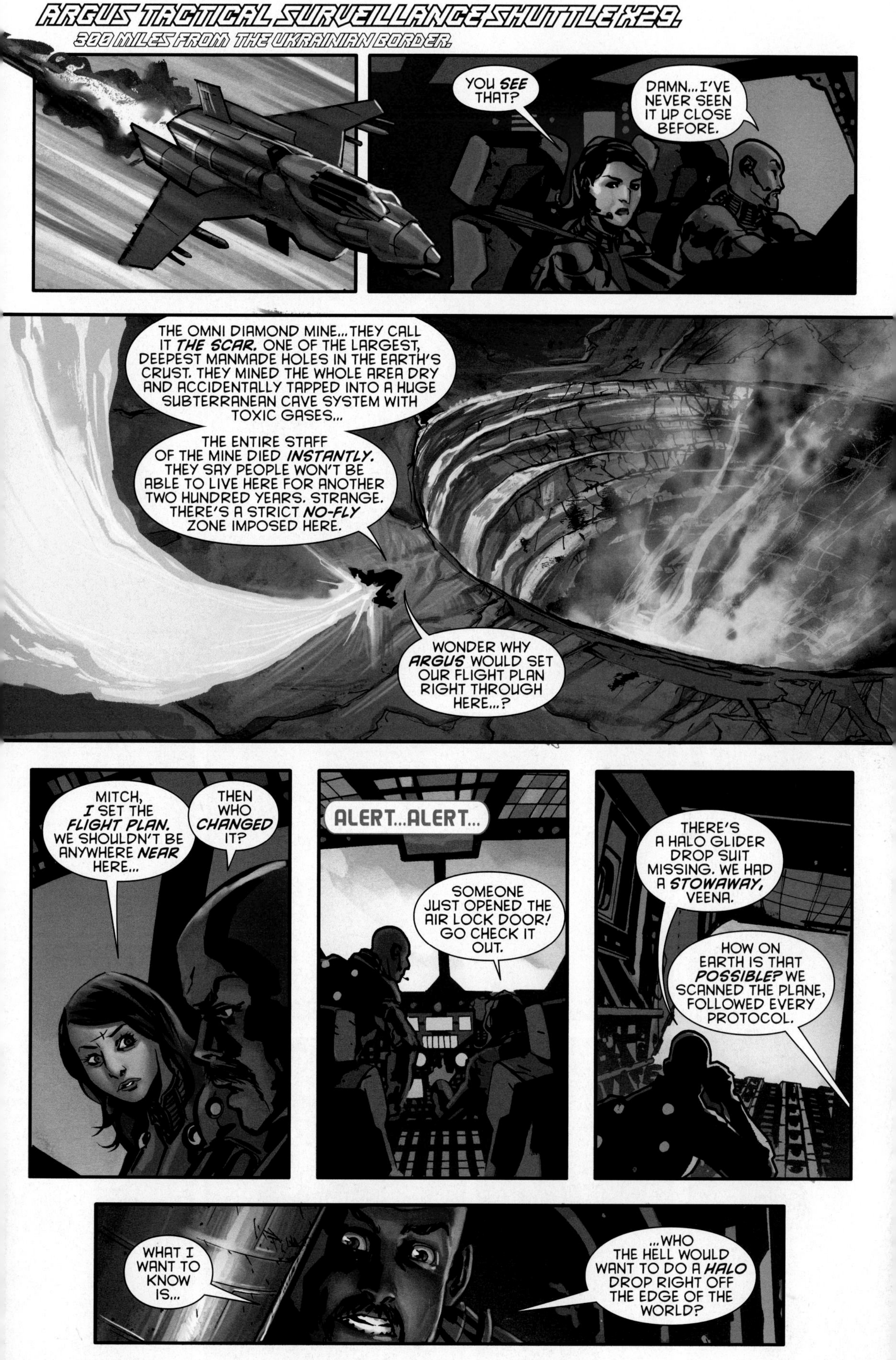
ARGUS TACTICAL SURVEILLANCE SHUTTLE X29.
300 MILES FROM THE UKRAINIAN BORDER.
YOU SEE THAT?
DAMN...I'VE NEVER SEEN IT UP CLOSE BEFORE.
THE OMNI DIAMOND MINE...THEY CALL IT THE SCAR. ONE OF THE LARGEST, DEEPEST MANMADE HOLES IN THE EARTH'S CRUST. THEY MINED THE WHOLE AREA DRY AND ACCIDENTALLY TAPPED INTO A HUGE SUBTERRANEAN CAVE SYSTEM WITH TOXIC GASES...
THE ENTIRE STAFF OF THE MINE DIED INSTANTLY. THEY SAY PEOPLE WON'T BE ABLE TO LIVE HERE FOR ANOTHER TWO HUNDRED YEARS. STRANGE. THERE'S A STRICT NO-FLY ZONE IMPOSED HERE.
WONDER WHY ARGUS WOULD SET OUR FLIGHT PLAN RIGHT THROUGH HERE...?
MITCH, I SET THE FLIGHT PLAN. WE SHOULDN'T BE ANYWHERE NEAR HERE...
THEN WHO CHANGED IT?
ALERT...ALERT...
SOMEONE JUST OPENED THE AIR LOCK DOOR! GO CHECK IT OUT.
THERE'S A HALO GLIDER DROP SUIT MISSING. WE HAD A STOWAWAY, VEENA.
HOW ON EARTH IS THAT POSSIBLE? WE SCANNED THE PLANE, FOLLOWED EVERY PROTOCOL.
WHAT I WANT TO KNOW IS...
...WHO THE HELL WOULD WANT TO DO A HALO DROP RIGHT OFF THE EDGE OF THE WORLD?

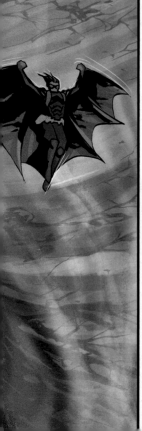

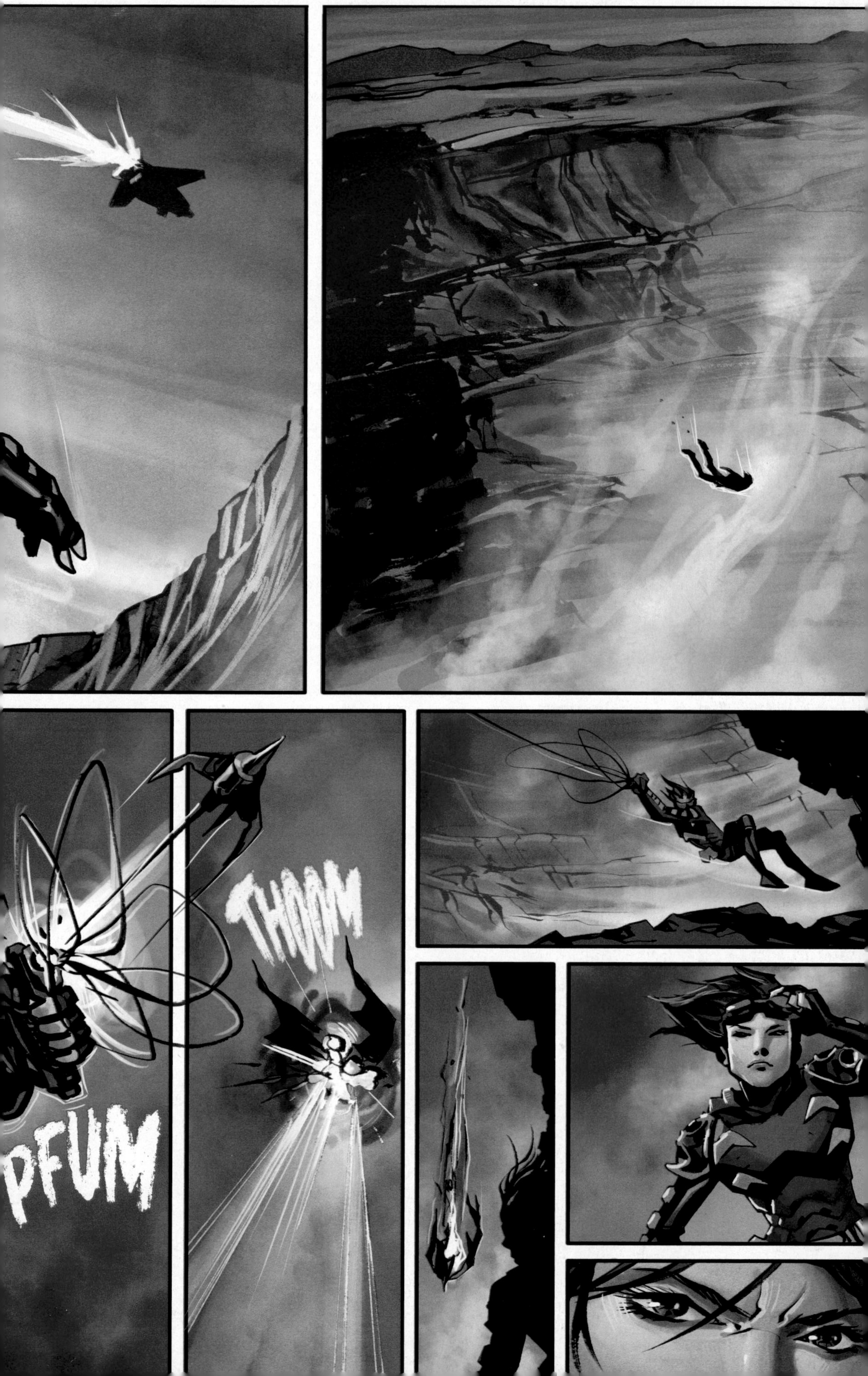
PFUM
THOOM

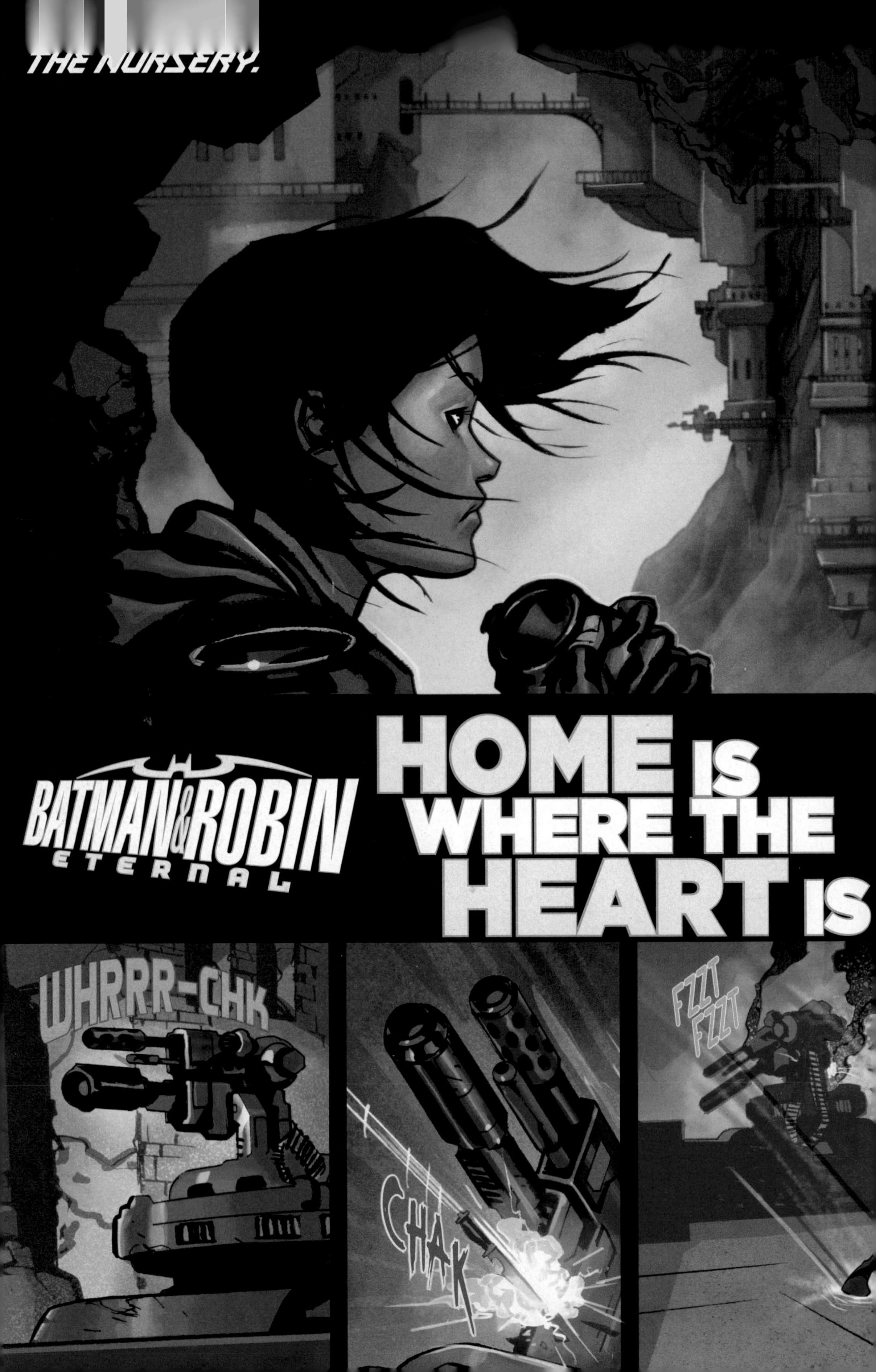
THE NURSERY.
BATMAN & ROBIN ETERNAL
HOME IS WHERE THE HEART IS
WHRRR-CHK
CHAK
FZZT FZZT

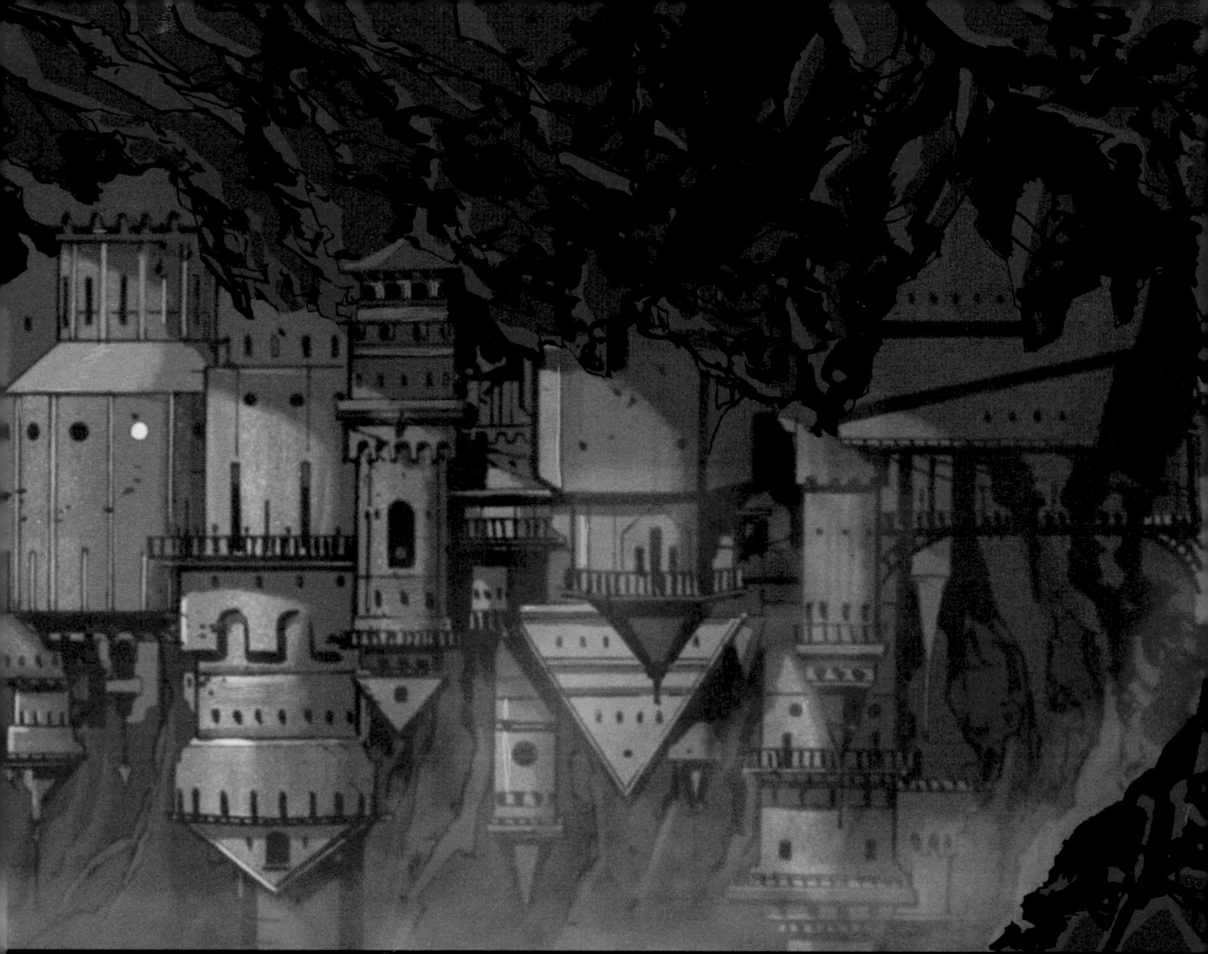

JAMES TYNION IV & SCOTT SNYDER Story
JAMES TYNION IV Script **MARCIO TAKARA** Artist
DEAN WHITE Colors **SAIDA TEMOFONTE** Letters
CARLO PAGULAYAN, JASON PAZ & ROMULO FAJARDO JR Cover

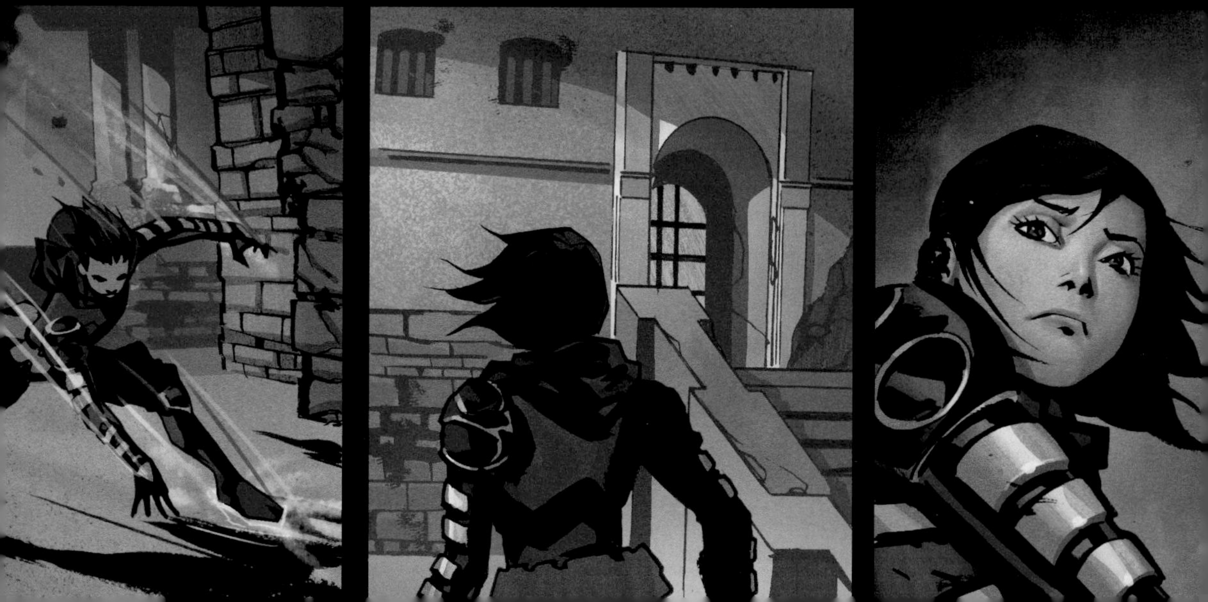

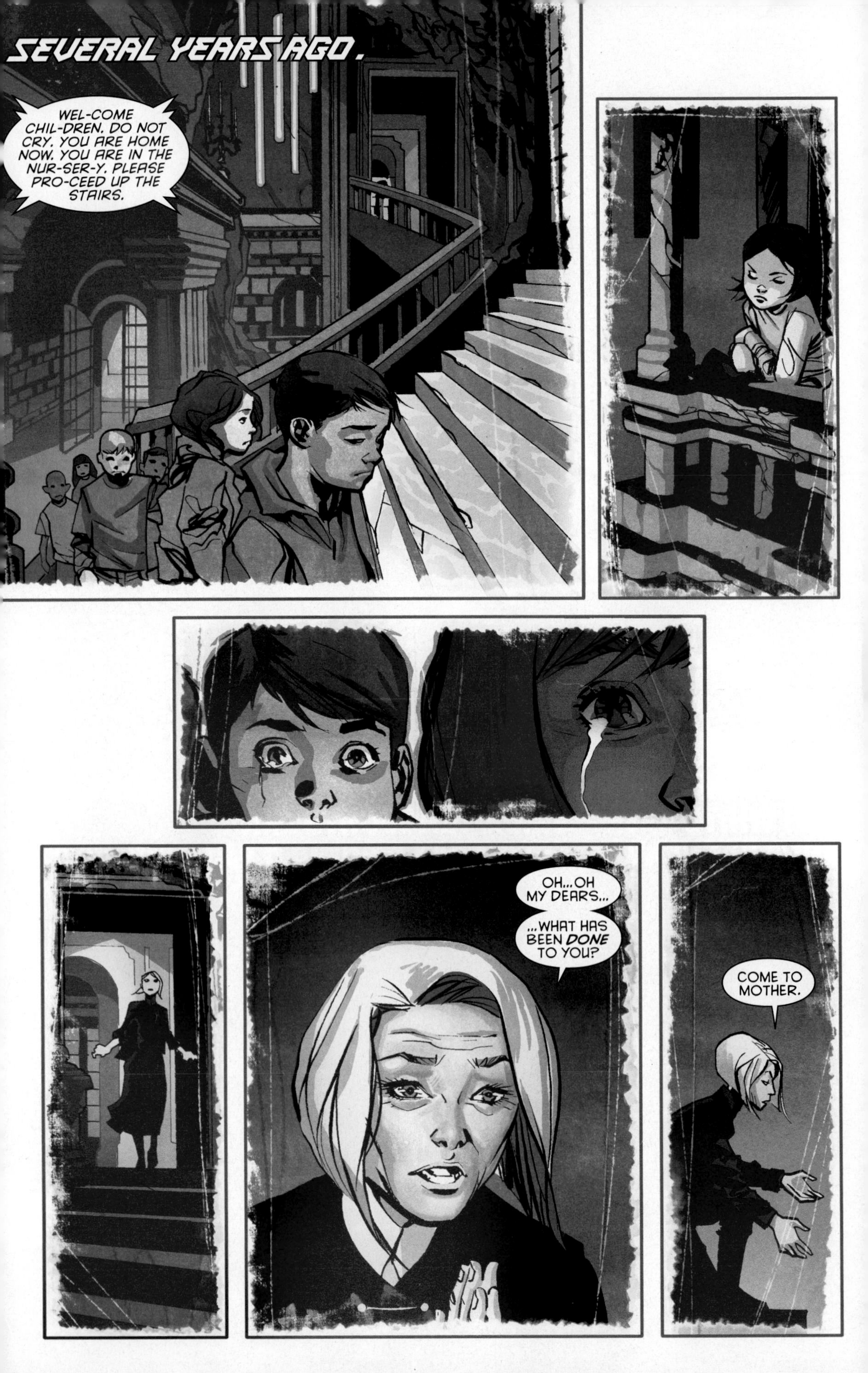
SEVERAL YEARS AGO.
WEL-COME CHIL-DREN. DO NOT CRY. YOU ARE HOME NOW. YOU ARE IN THE NUR-SER-Y. PLEASE PRO-CEED UP THE STAIRS.
OH...OH MY DEARS...
...WHAT HAS BEEN DONE TO YOU?
COME TO MOTHER.

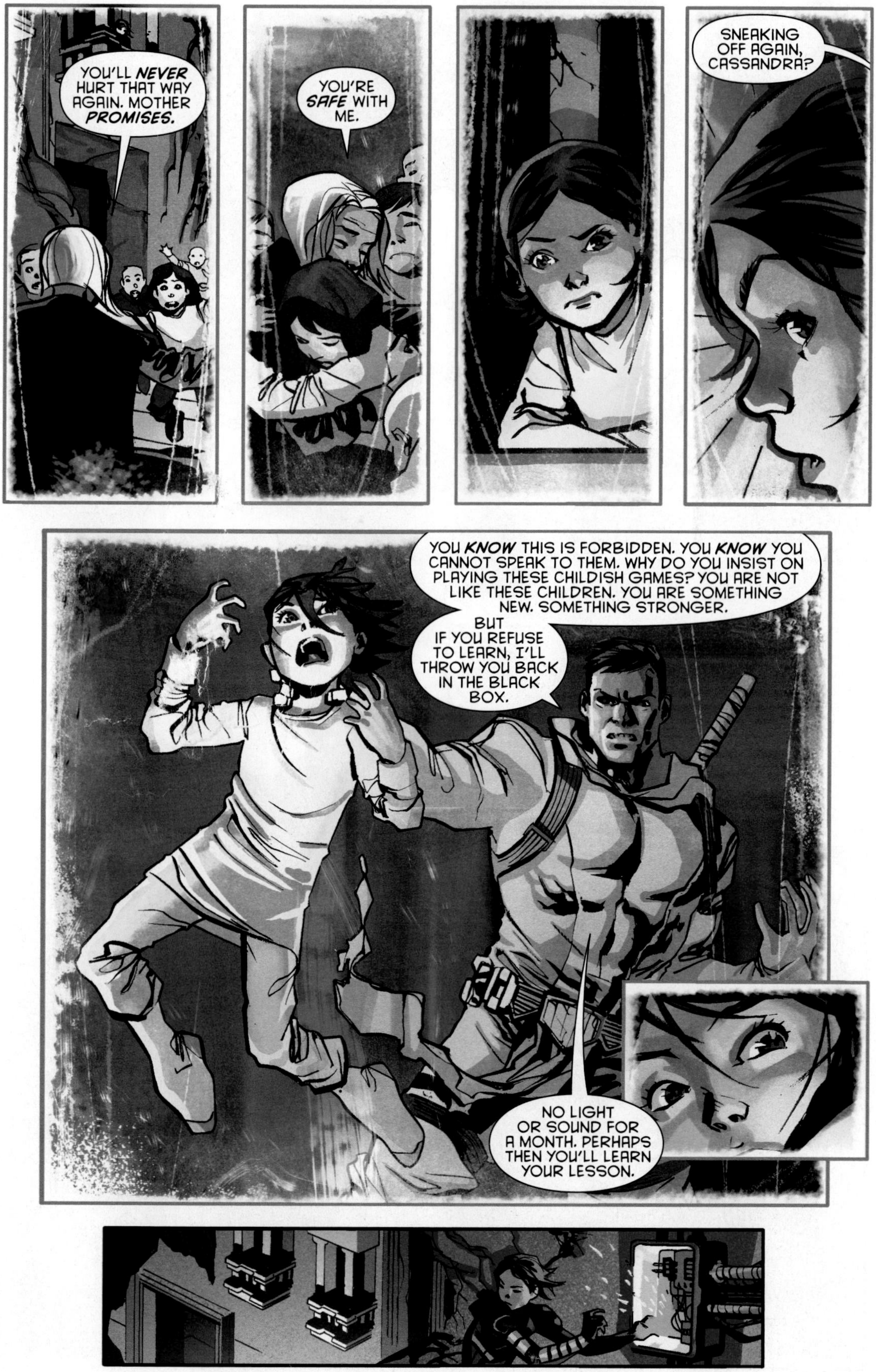
YOU'LL NEVER HURT THAT WAY AGAIN. MOTHER PROMISES.
YOU'RE SAFE WITH ME.
SNEAKING OFF AGAIN, CASSANDRA?
YOU KNOW THIS IS FORBIDDEN. YOU KNOW YOU CANNOT SPEAK TO THEM. WHY DO YOU INSIST ON PLAYING THESE CHILDISH GAMES? YOU ARE NOT LIKE THESE CHILDREN. YOU ARE SOMETHING NEW. SOMETHING STRONGER.
BUT IF YOU REFUSE TO LEARN, I'LL THROW YOU BACK IN THE BLACK BOX.
NO LIGHT OR SOUND FOR A MONTH. PERHAPS THEN YOU'LL LEARN YOUR LESSON.

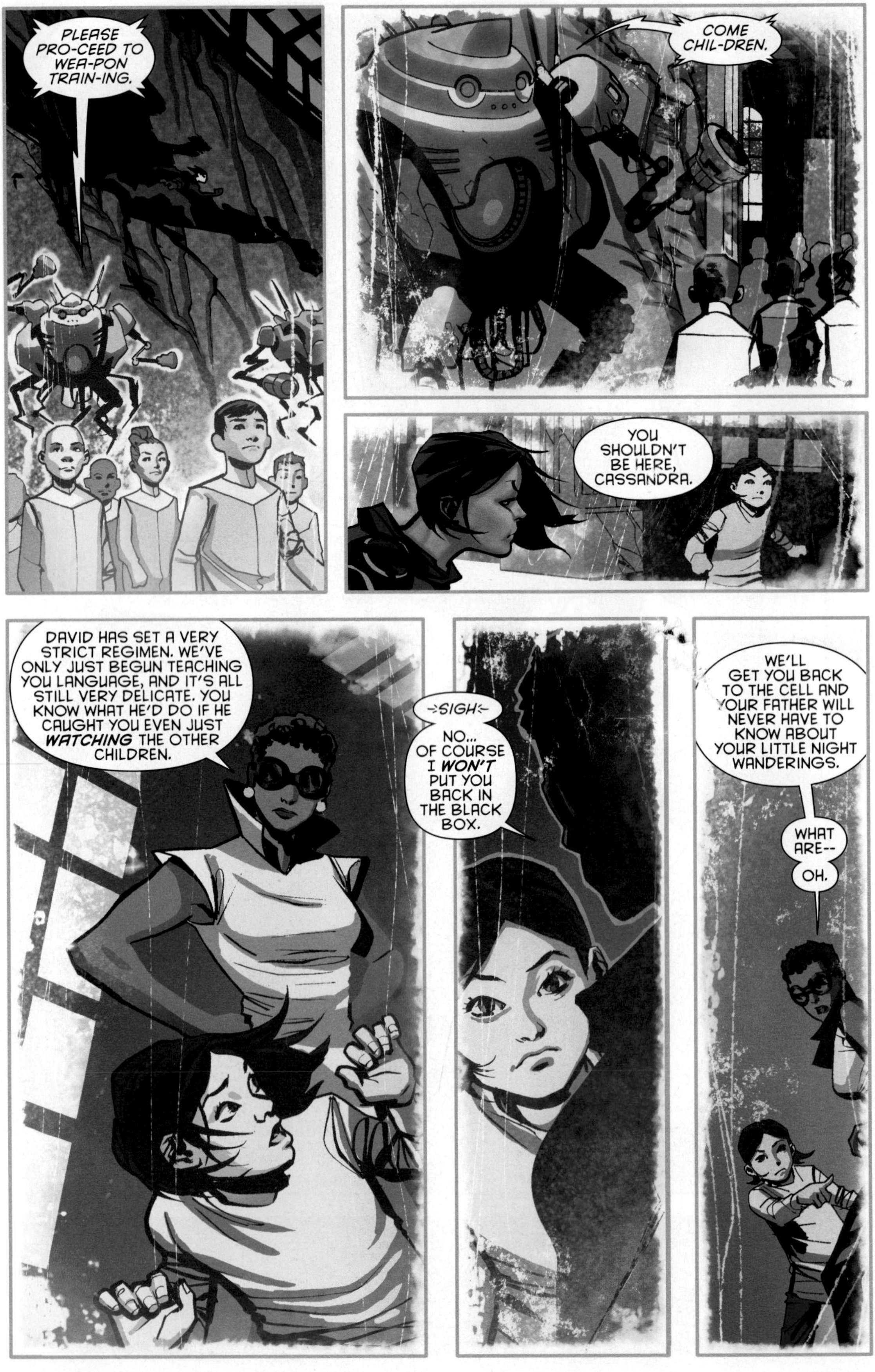
PLEASE PRO-CEED TO WEA-PON TRAIN-ING.
COME CHIL-DREN.
YOU SHOULDN'T BE HERE, CASSANDRA.
DAVID HAS SET A VERY STRICT REGIMEN. WE'VE ONLY JUST BEGUN TEACHING YOU LANGUAGE, AND IT'S ALL STILL VERY DELICATE. YOU KNOW WHAT HE'D DO IF HE CAUGHT YOU EVEN JUST WATCHING THE OTHER CHILDREN.
SIGH
NO... OF COURSE I WON'T PUT YOU BACK IN THE BLACK BOX.
WE'LL GET YOU BACK TO THE CELL AND YOUR FATHER WILL NEVER HAVE TO KNOW ABOUT YOUR LITTLE NIGHT WANDERINGS.
WHAT ARE--
OH.

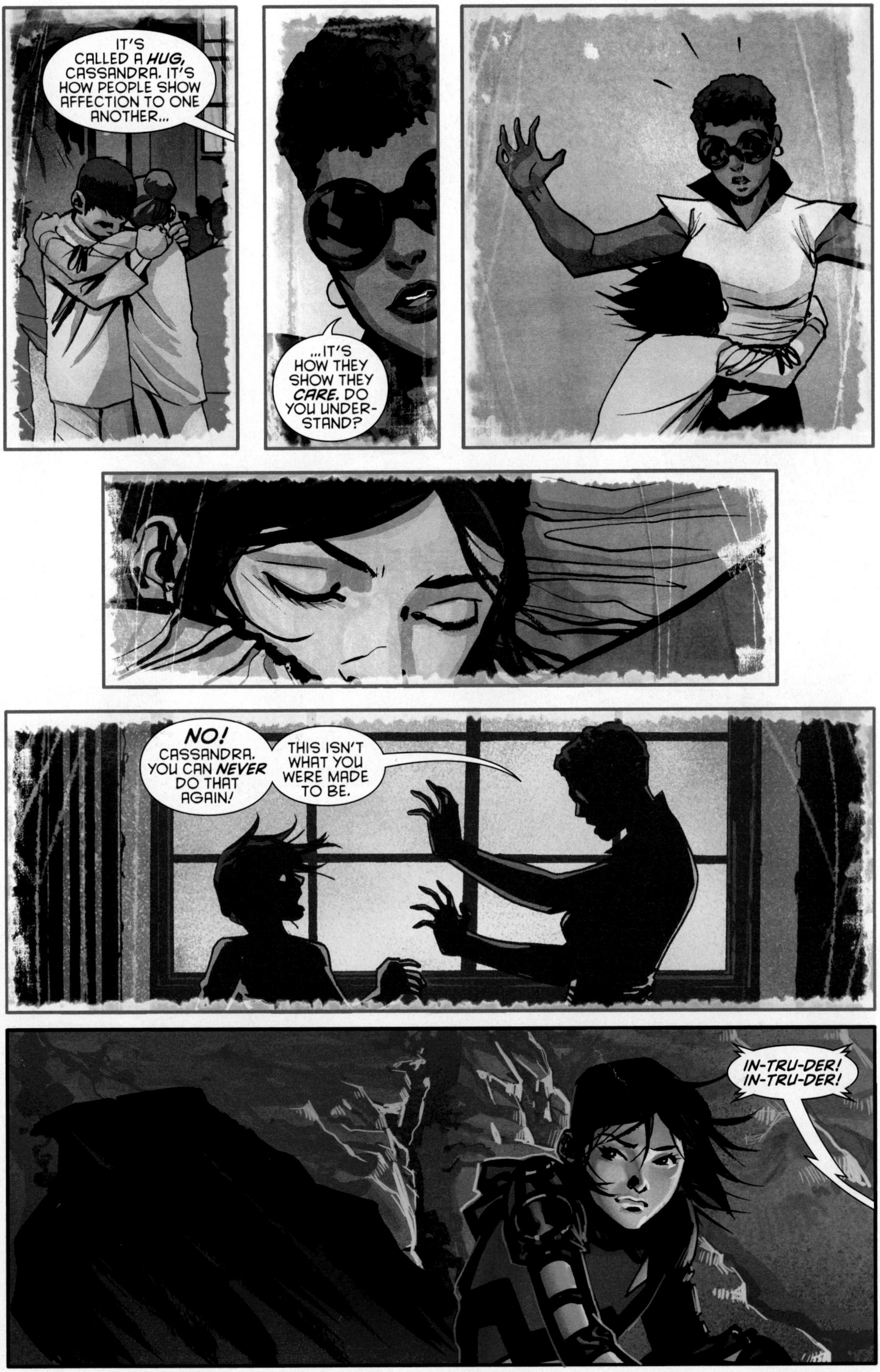
IT'S CALLED A HUG, CASSANDRA. IT'S HOW PEOPLE SHOW AFFECTION TO ONE ANOTHER...
...IT'S HOW THEY SHOW THEY CARE. DO YOU UNDERSTAND?
NO! CASSANDRA. YOU CAN NEVER DO THAT AGAIN!
THIS ISN'T WHAT YOU WERE MADE TO BE.
IN-TRU-DER! IN-TRU-DER!

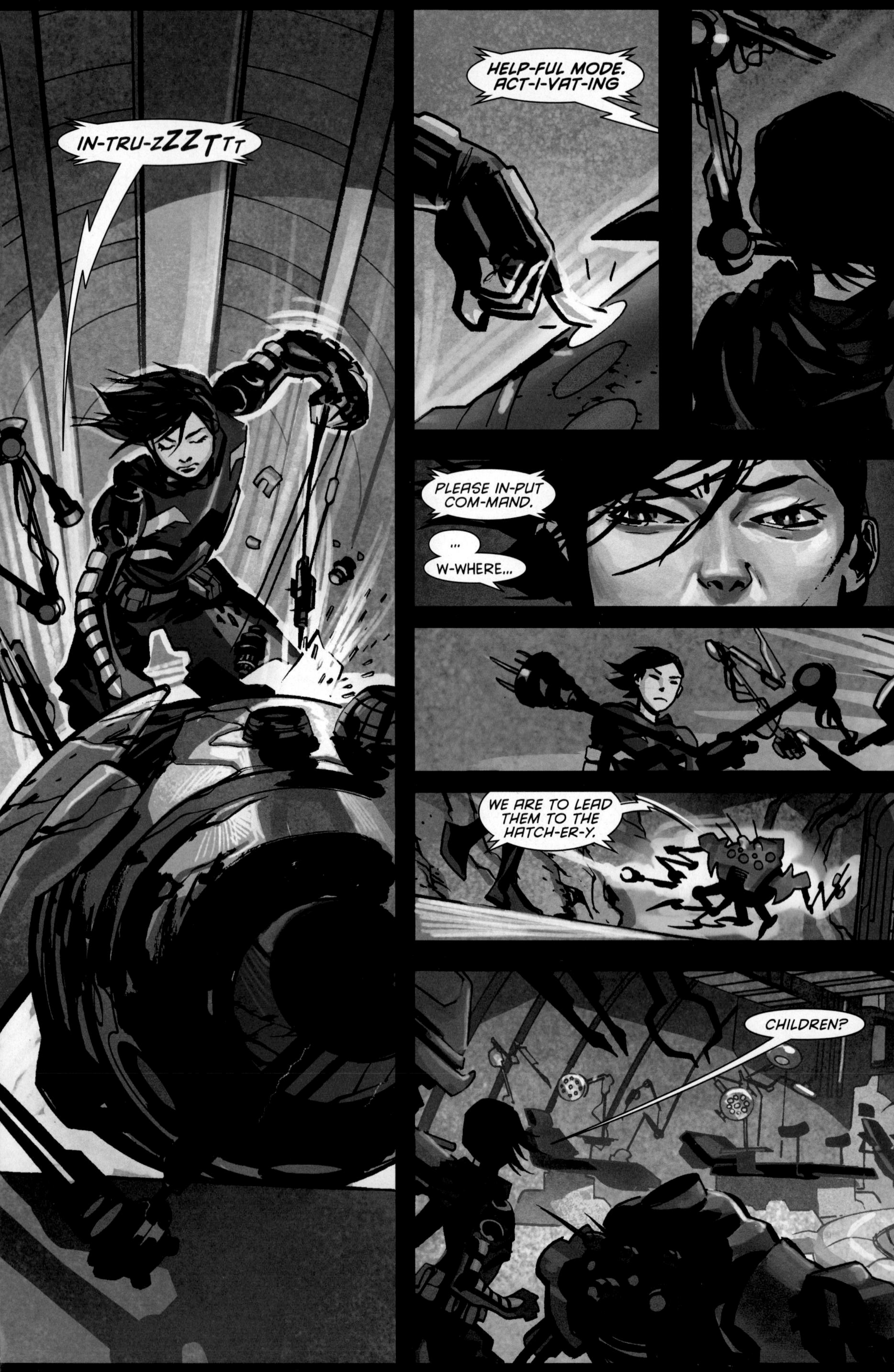

IN-TRU-zZZTTT
HELP-FUL MODE. ACT-I-VAT-ING
PLEASE IN-PUT COM-MAND.
...
W-WHERE...
WE ARE TO LEAD THEM TO THE HATCH-ER-Y.
CHILDREN?

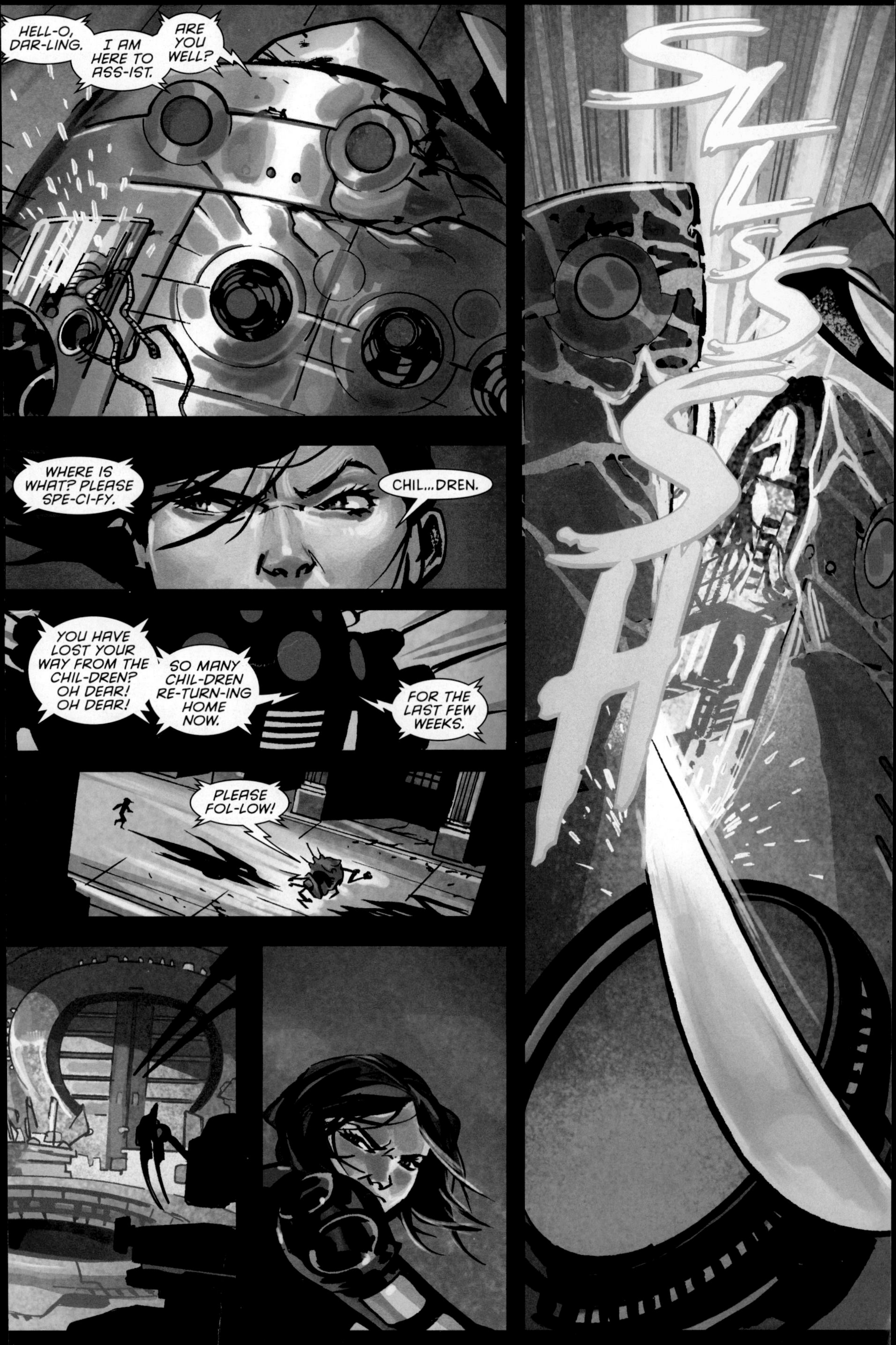
HELL-O, DAR-LING.
I AM HERE TO ASS-IST.
ARE YOU WELL?
WHERE IS WHAT? PLEASE SPE-CI-FY.
CHIL...DREN.
YOU HAVE LOST YOUR WAY FROM THE CHIL-DREN? OH DEAR! OH DEAR!
SO MANY CHIL-DREN RE-TURN-ING HOME NOW.
FOR THE LAST FEW WEEKS.
PLEASE FOL-LOW!
SZZSSSH

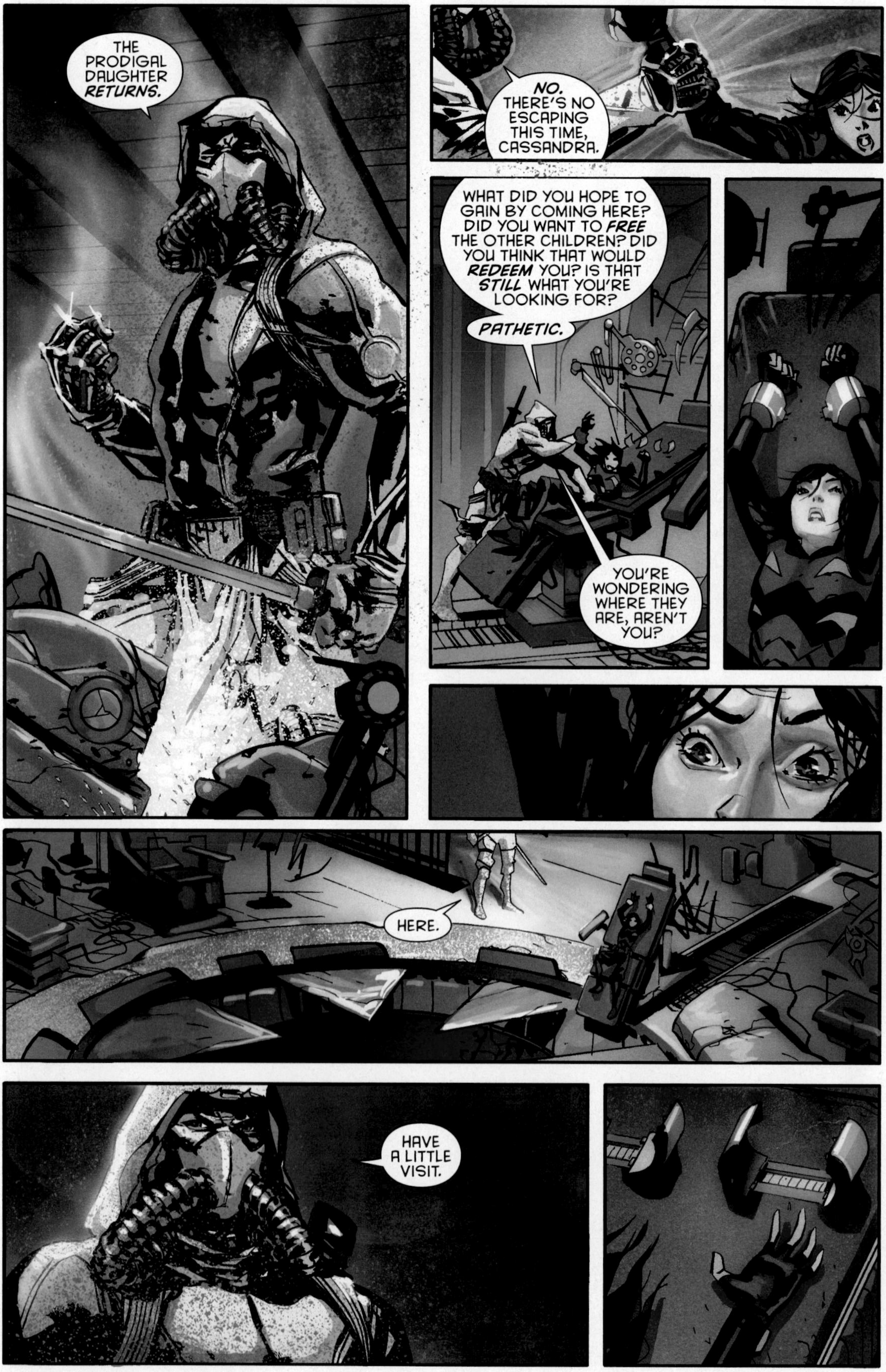
THE PRODIGAL DAUGHTER *RETURNS.*
NO. THERE'S NO ESCAPING THIS TIME, CASSANDRA.
WHAT DID YOU HOPE TO GAIN BY COMING HERE? DID YOU WANT TO *FREE* THE OTHER CHILDREN? DID YOU THINK THAT WOULD *REDEEM* YOU? IS THAT *STILL* WHAT YOU'RE LOOKING FOR?
PATHETIC.
YOU'RE WONDERING WHERE THEY ARE, AREN'T YOU?
HERE.
HAVE A LITTLE VISIT.

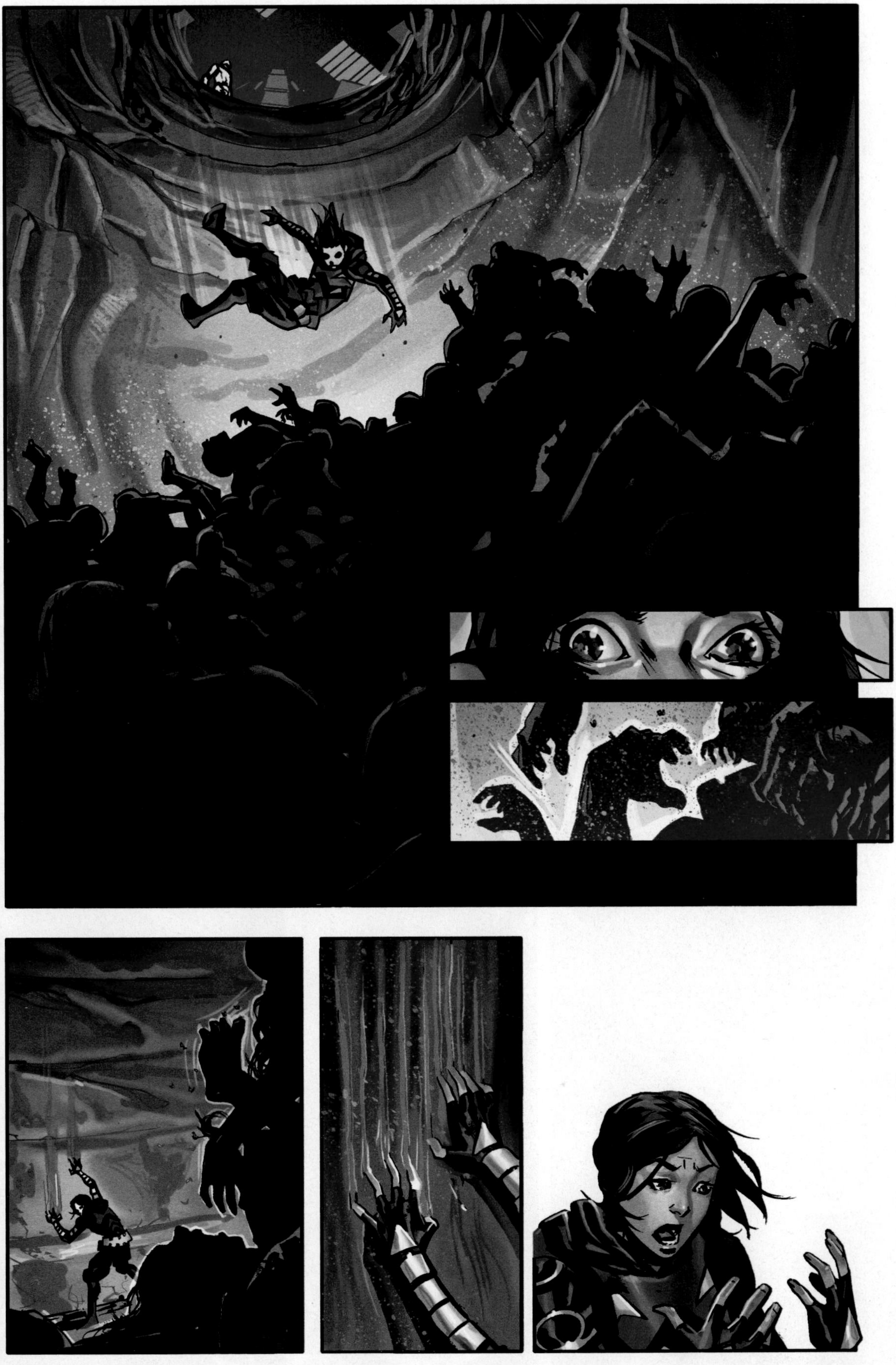

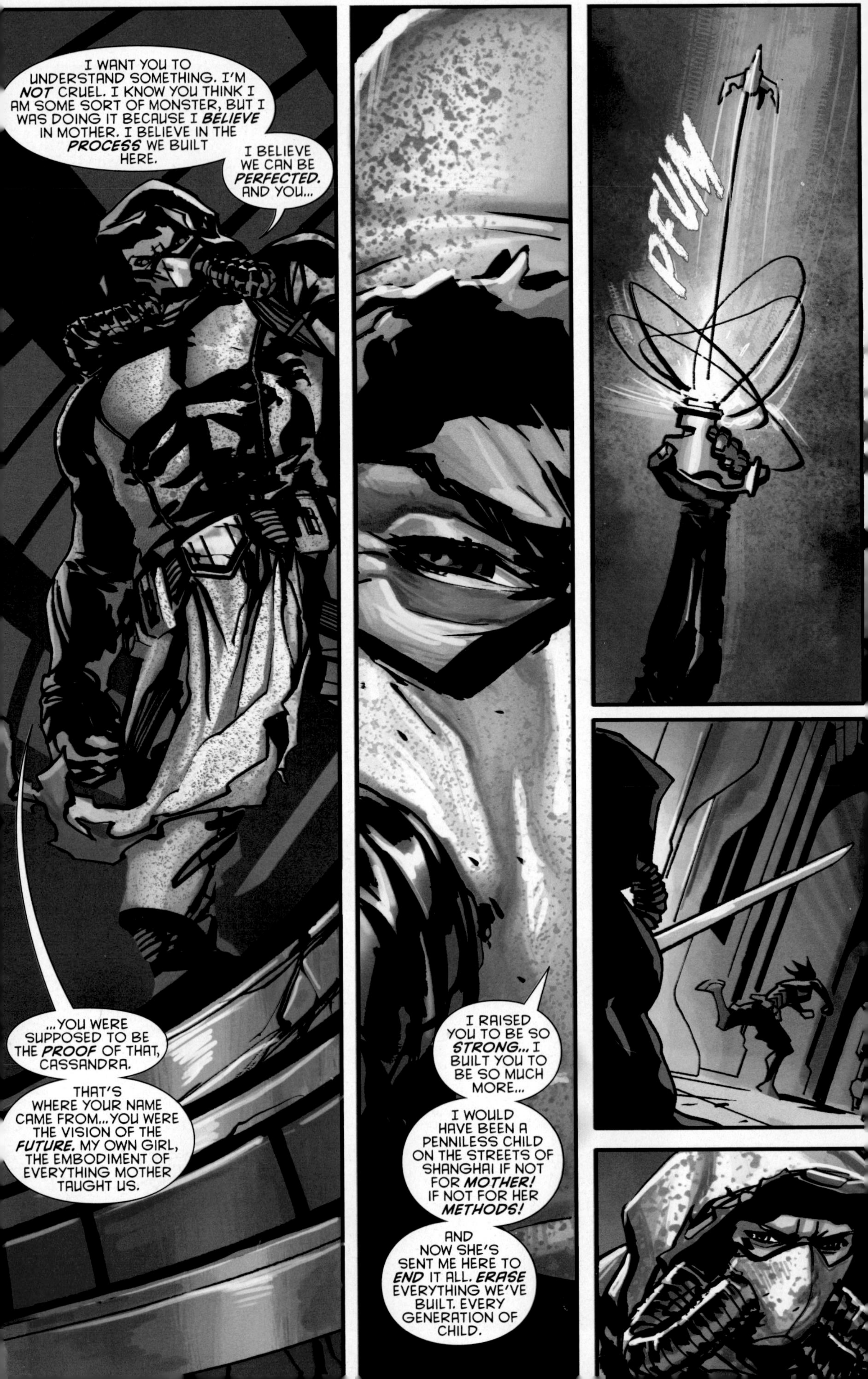
I WANT YOU TO UNDERSTAND SOMETHING. I'M NOT CRUEL. I KNOW YOU THINK I AM SOME SORT OF MONSTER, BUT I WAS DOING IT BECAUSE I BELIEVE IN MOTHER. I BELIEVE IN THE PROCESS WE BUILT HERE.
I BELIEVE WE CAN BE PERFECTED. AND YOU...
...YOU WERE SUPPOSED TO BE THE PROOF OF THAT, CASSANDRA.
THAT'S WHERE YOUR NAME CAME FROM... YOU WERE THE VISION OF THE FUTURE. MY OWN GIRL, THE EMBODIMENT OF EVERYTHING MOTHER TAUGHT US.
I RAISED YOU TO BE SO STRONG... I BUILT YOU TO BE SO MUCH MORE...
I WOULD HAVE BEEN A PENNILESS CHILD ON THE STREETS OF SHANGHAI IF NOT FOR MOTHER! IF NOT FOR HER METHODS!
AND NOW SHE'S SENT ME HERE TO END IT ALL. ERASE EVERYTHING WE'VE BUILT. EVERY GENERATION OF CHILD.
PFUM

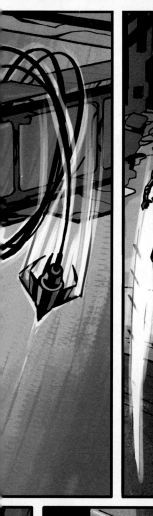

I WANT YOU TO KNOW, YOU COULD HAVE SAVED ALL OF THEM.

IF YOU HADN'T *ESCAPED*...

...IF YOU HADN'T CONVINCED MOTHER TO TO *SHUT DOWN* THE WHOLE PROGRAM AND TAKE THIS NEWER, DARKER PATH.

IF YOU HADN'T *RUN*...

...TO *HIM*.

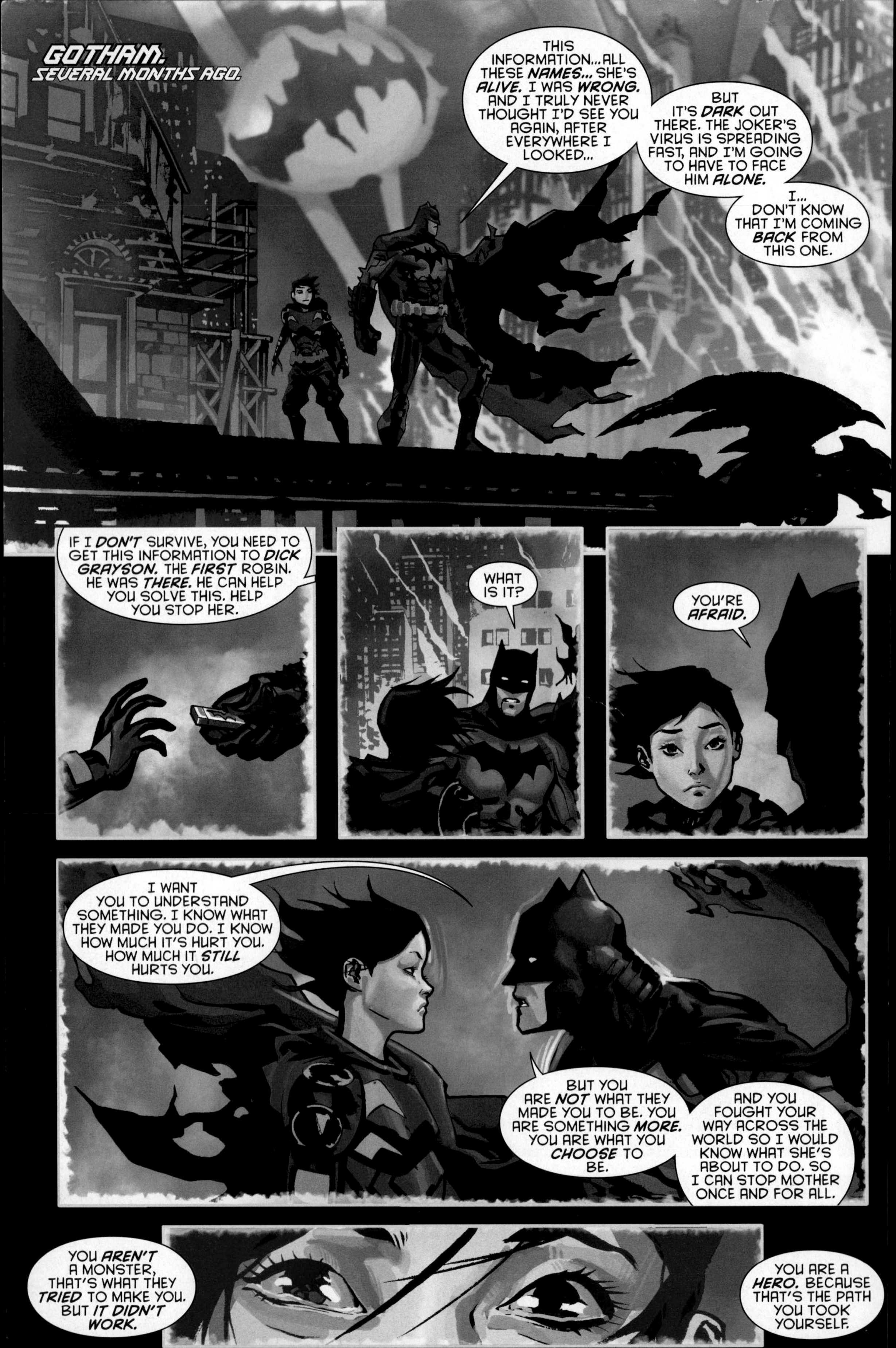
GOTHAM.
SEVERAL MONTHS AGO.
THIS INFORMATION... ALL THESE NAMES... SHE'S ALIVE. I WAS WRONG. AND I TRULY NEVER THOUGHT I'D SEE YOU AGAIN, AFTER EVERYWHERE I LOOKED...
BUT IT'S DARK OUT THERE. THE JOKER'S VIRUS IS SPREADING FAST, AND I'M GOING TO HAVE TO FACE HIM ALONE.
I... DON'T KNOW THAT I'M COMING BACK FROM THIS ONE.
IF I DON'T SURVIVE, YOU NEED TO GET THIS INFORMATION TO DICK GRAYSON. THE FIRST ROBIN. HE WAS THERE. HE CAN HELP YOU SOLVE THIS. HELP YOU STOP HER.
WHAT IS IT?
YOU'RE AFRAID.
I WANT YOU TO UNDERSTAND SOMETHING. I KNOW WHAT THEY MADE YOU DO. I KNOW HOW MUCH IT'S HURT YOU. HOW MUCH IT STILL HURTS YOU.
BUT YOU ARE NOT WHAT THEY MADE YOU TO BE. YOU ARE SOMETHING MORE. YOU ARE WHAT YOU CHOOSE TO BE.
AND YOU FOUGHT YOUR WAY ACROSS THE WORLD SO I WOULD KNOW WHAT SHE'S ABOUT TO DO. SO I CAN STOP MOTHER ONCE AND FOR ALL.
YOU AREN'T A MONSTER, THAT'S WHAT THEY TRIED TO MAKE YOU. BUT IT DIDN'T WORK.
YOU ARE A HERO. BECAUSE THAT'S THE PATH YOU TOOK YOURSELF.

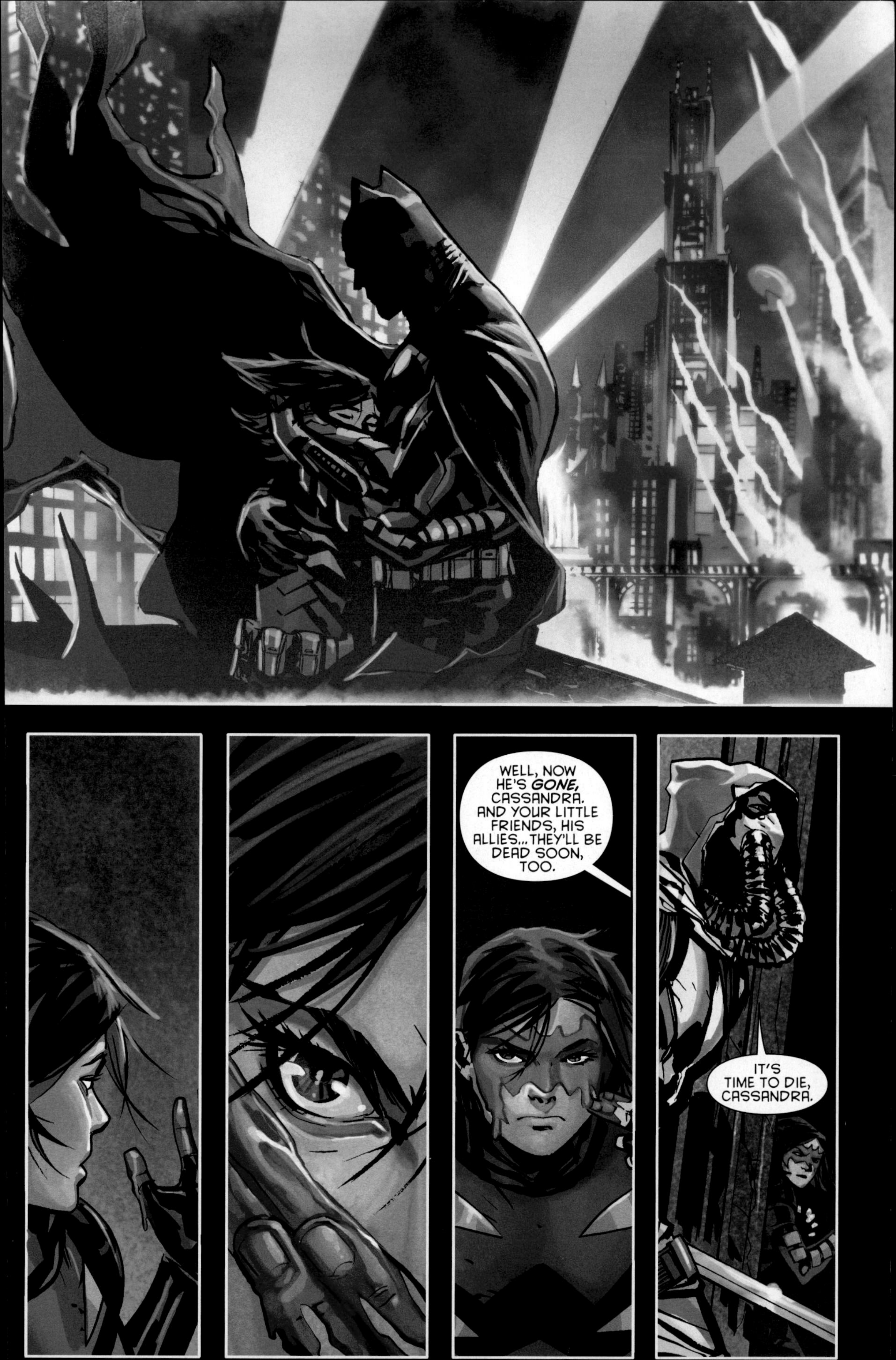
WELL, NOW HE'S GONE, CASSANDRA. AND YOUR LITTLE FRIENDS, HIS ALLIES...THEY'LL BE DEAD SOON, TOO.
IT'S TIME TO DIE, CASSANDRA.

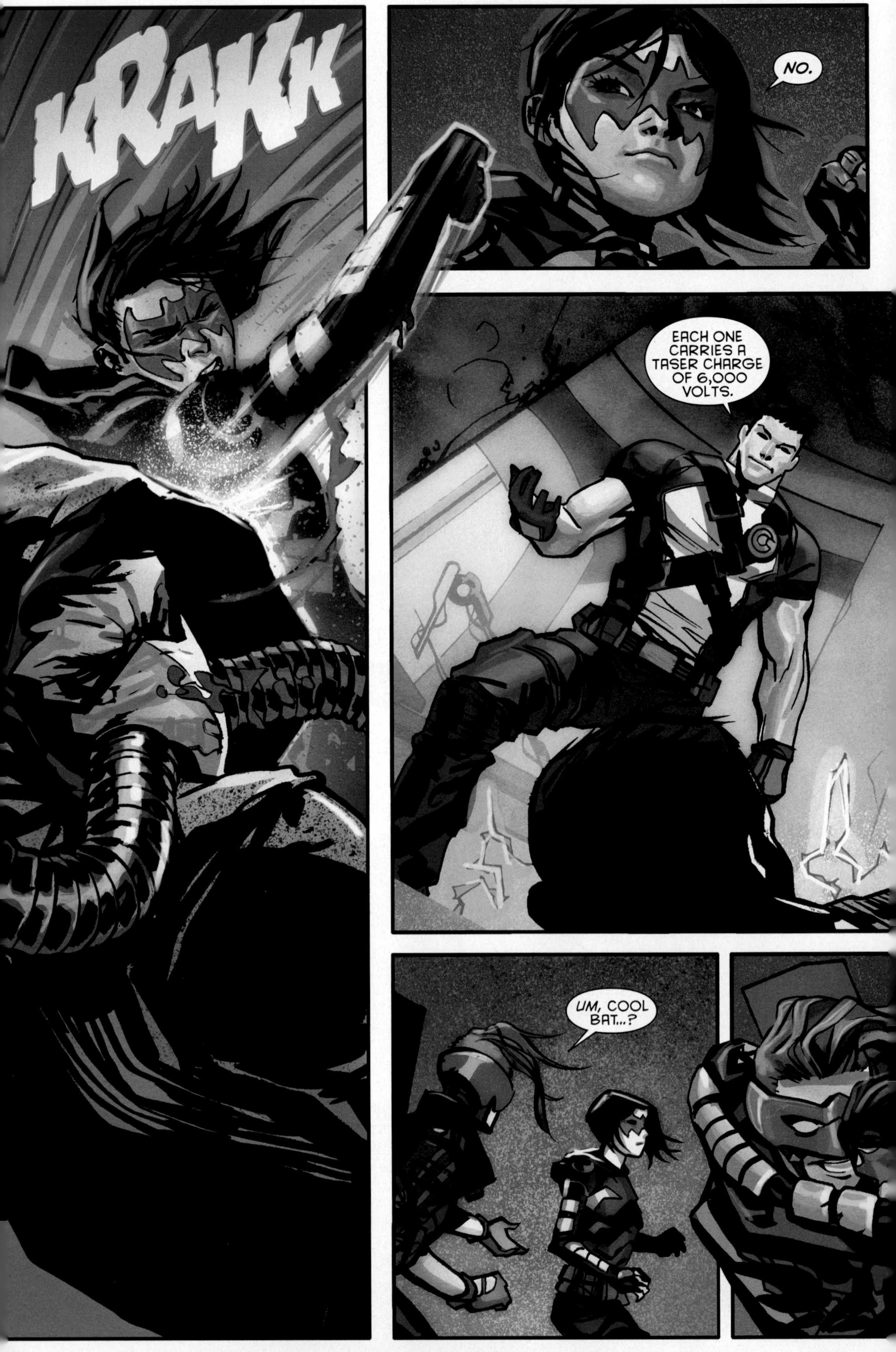
KRAKK
NO.
EACH ONE CARRIES A TASER CHARGE OF 6,000 VOLTS.
UM, COOL BAT...?

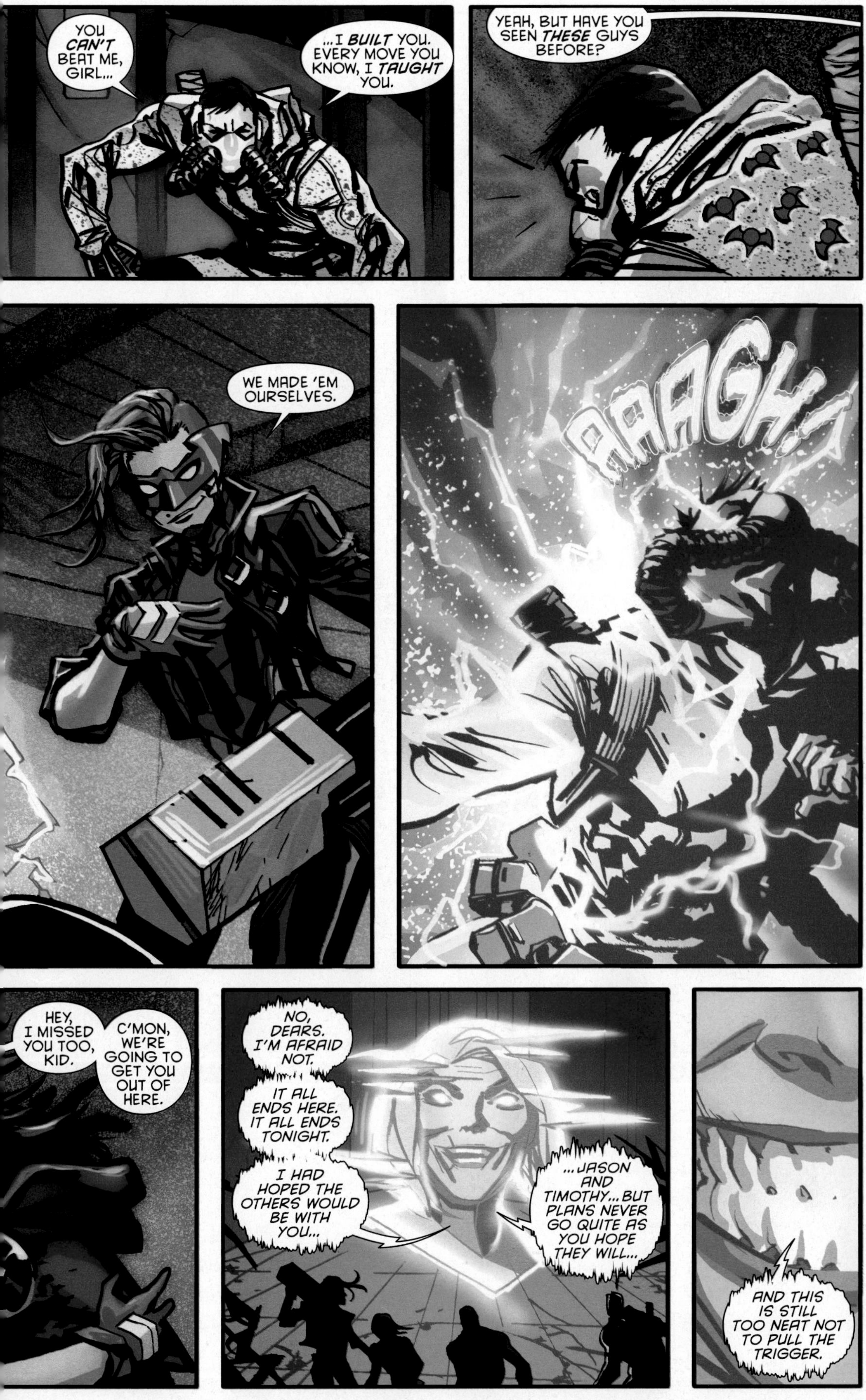
YOU CAN'T BEAT ME, GIRL...
...I BUILT YOU. EVERY MOVE YOU KNOW, I TAUGHT YOU.
YEAH, BUT HAVE YOU SEEN THESE GUYS BEFORE?
WE MADE 'EM OURSELVES.
RAAAGH!!
HEY, I MISSED YOU TOO, KID.
C'MON, WE'RE GOING TO GET YOU OUT OF HERE.
NO, DEARS. I'M AFRAID NOT.
IT ALL ENDS HERE. IT ALL ENDS TONIGHT.
I HAD HOPED THE OTHERS WOULD BE WITH YOU...
...JASON AND TIMOTHY...BUT PLANS NEVER GO QUITE AS YOU HOPE THEY WILL...
AND THIS IS STILL TOO NEAT NOT TO PULL THE TRIGGER.

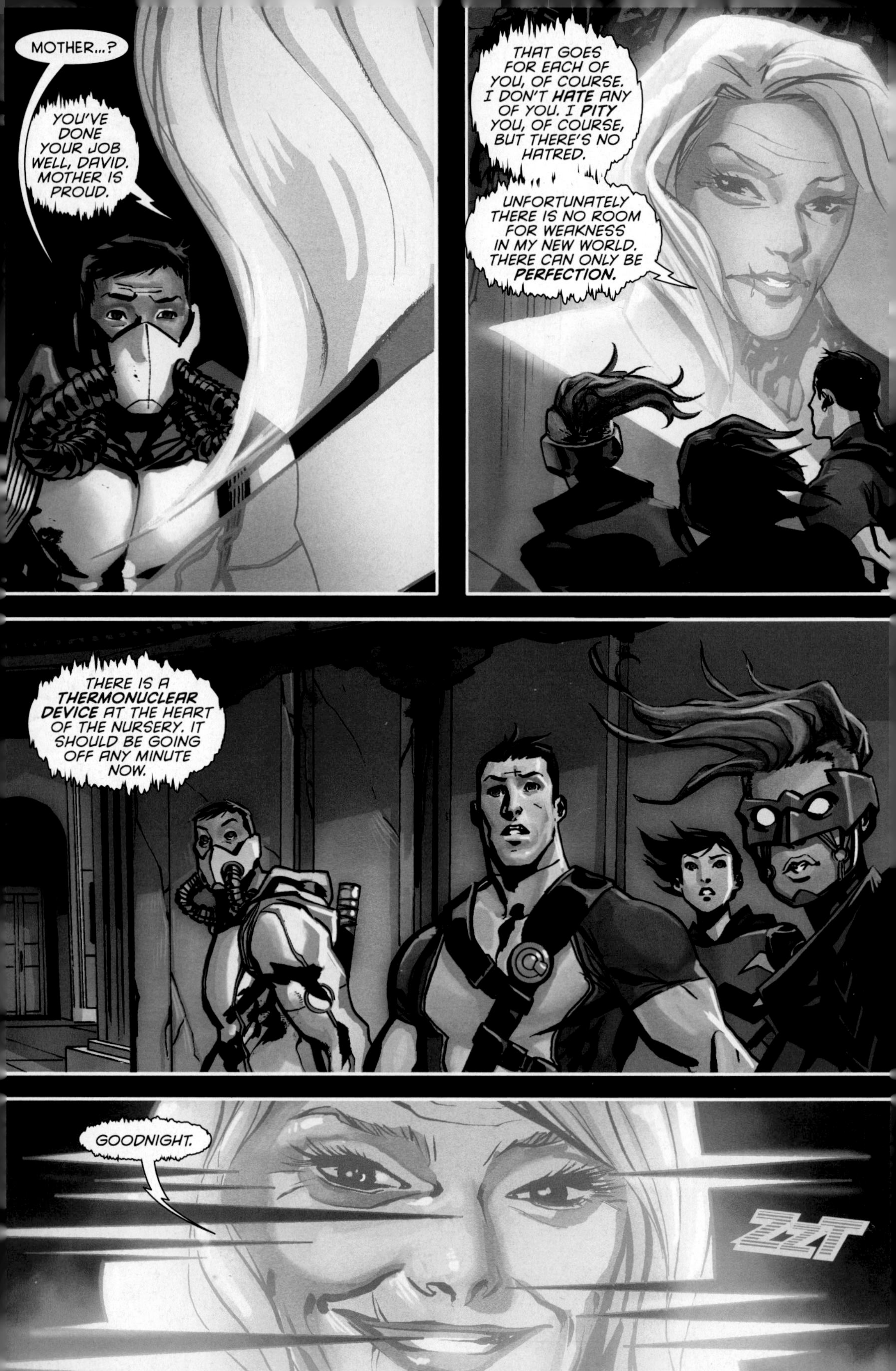
MOTHER...?
YOU'VE DONE YOUR JOB WELL, DAVID. MOTHER IS PROUD.
THAT GOES FOR EACH OF YOU, OF COURSE. I DON'T HATE ANY OF YOU. I PITY YOU, OF COURSE, BUT THERE'S NO HATRED.
UNFORTUNATELY THERE IS NO ROOM FOR WEAKNESS IN MY NEW WORLD. THERE CAN ONLY BE PERFECTION.
THERE IS A THERMONUCLEAR DEVICE AT THE HEART OF THE NURSERY. IT SHOULD BE GOING OFF ANY MINUTE NOW.
GOODNIGHT.
ZZT

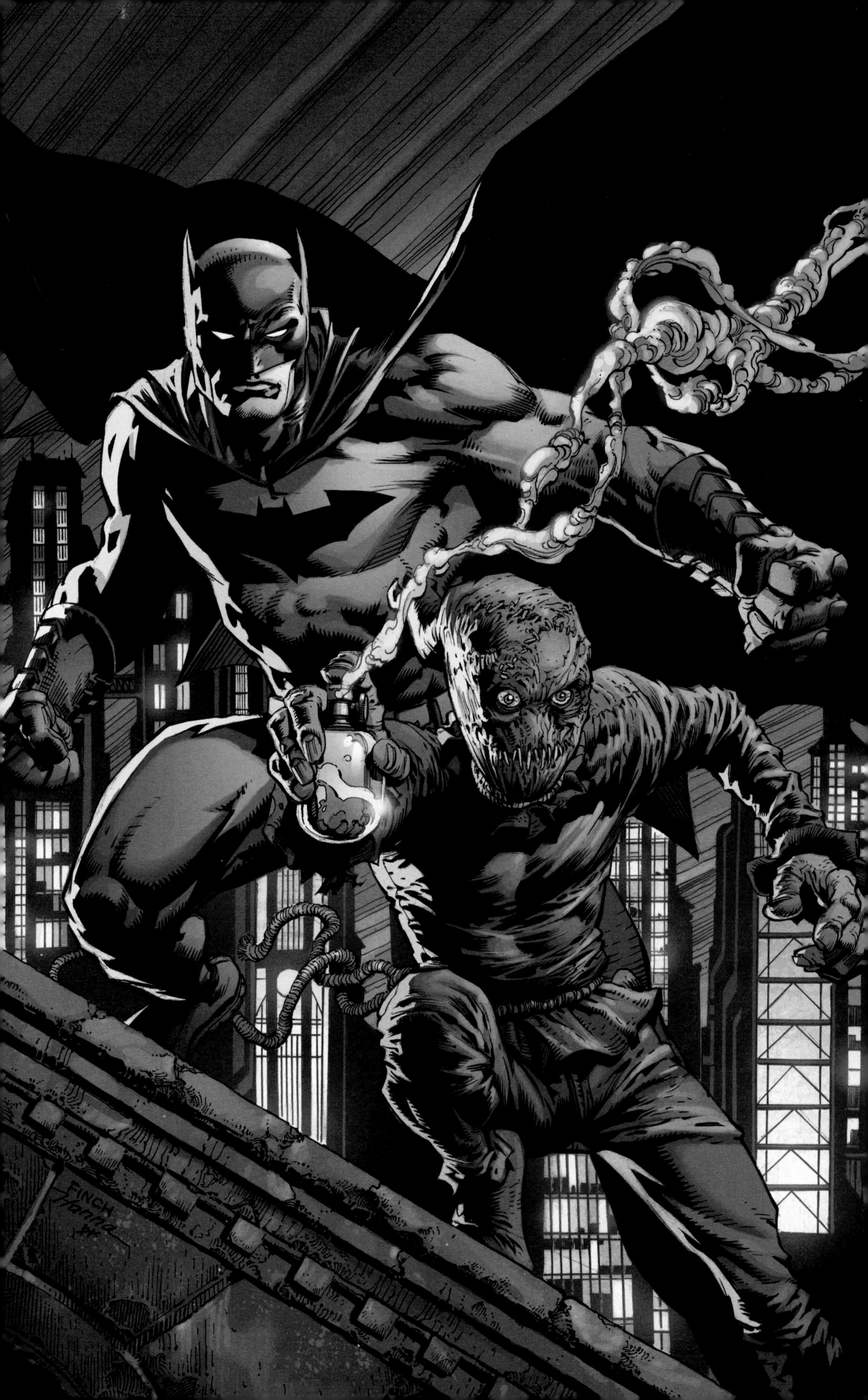
FINCH

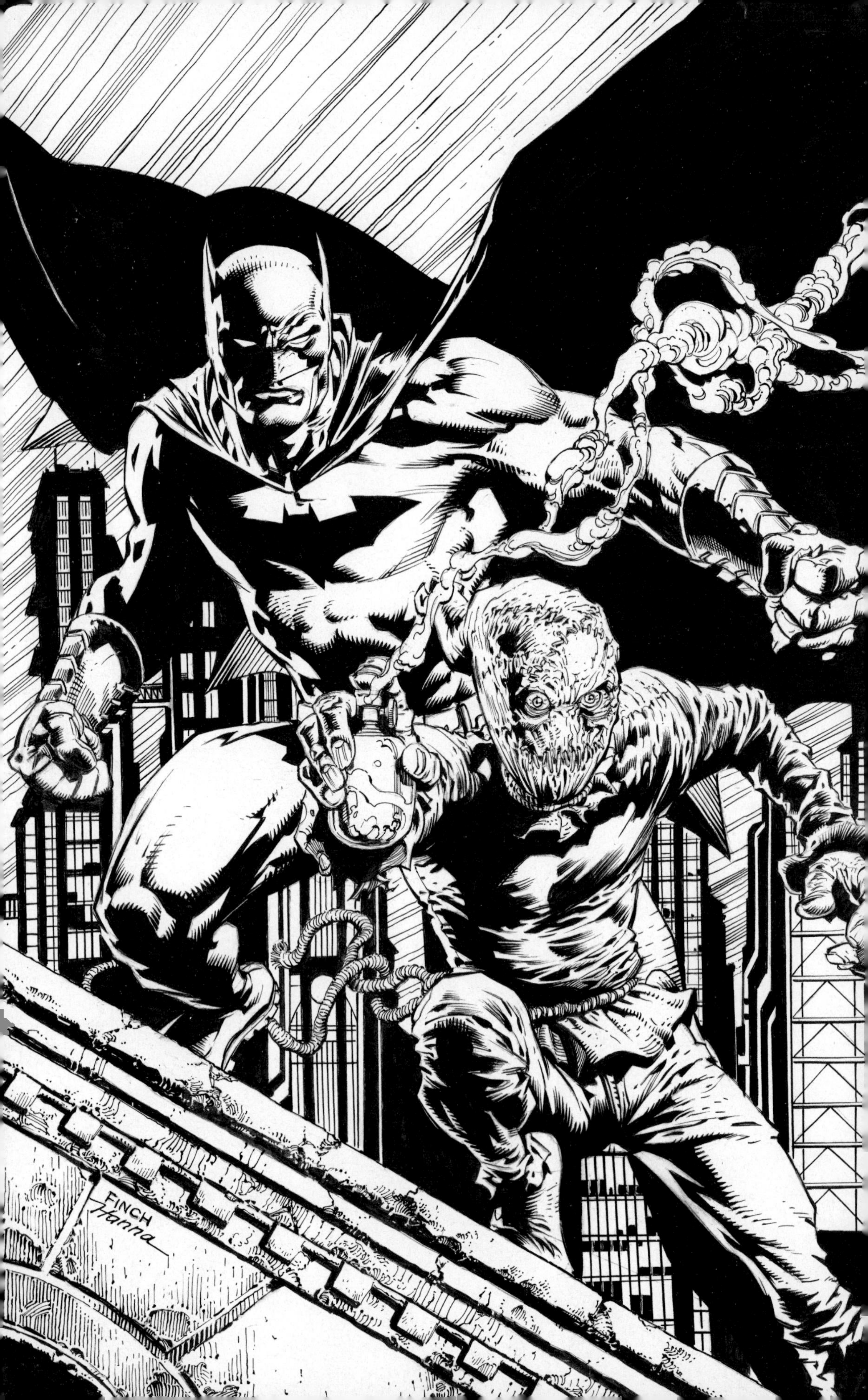
FINCH
Hanna

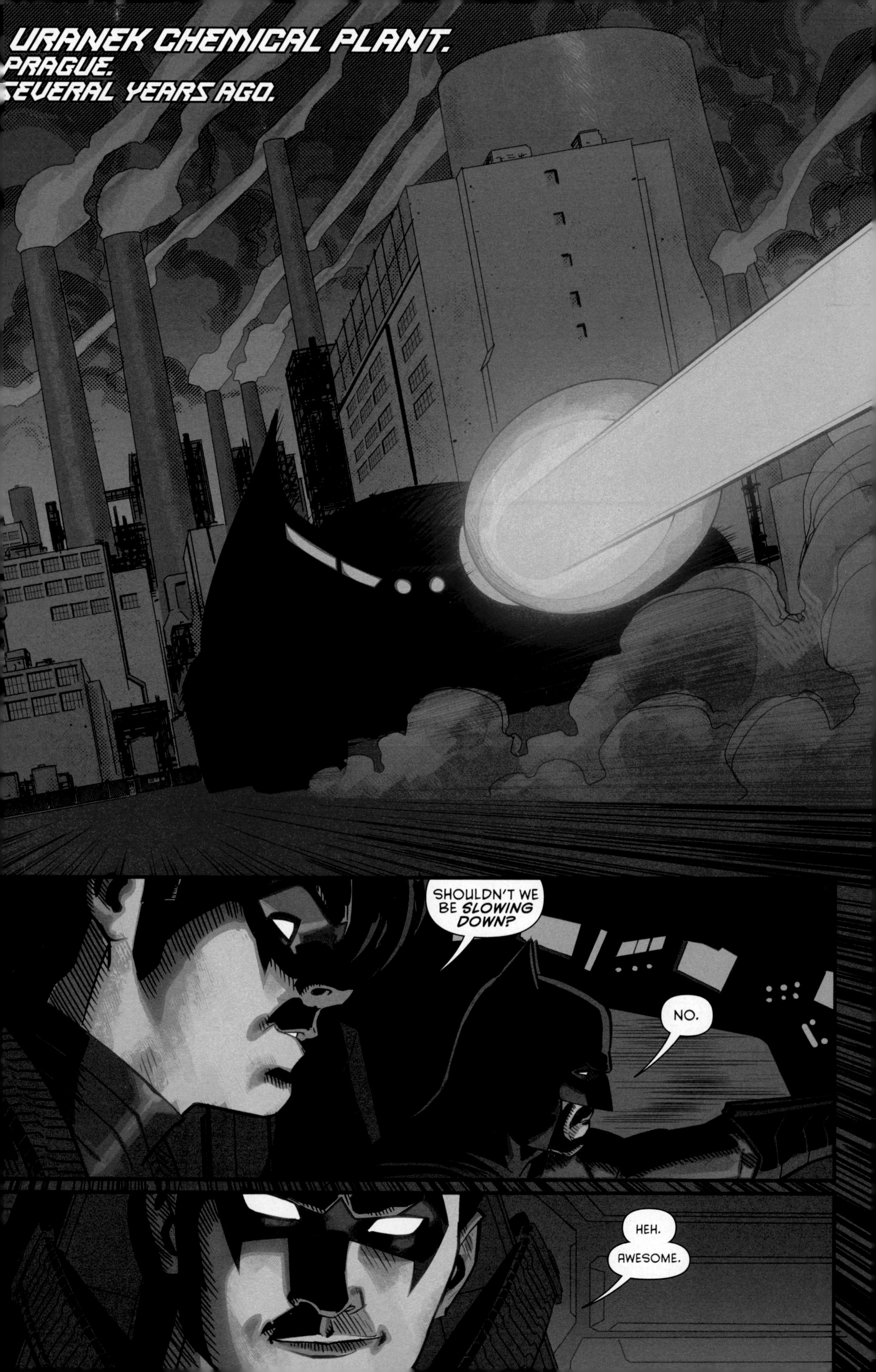
URANEK CHEMICAL PLANT.
PRAGUE.
SEVERAL YEARS AGO.
SHOULDN'T WE BE SLOWING DOWN?
NO.
HEH.
AWESOME.

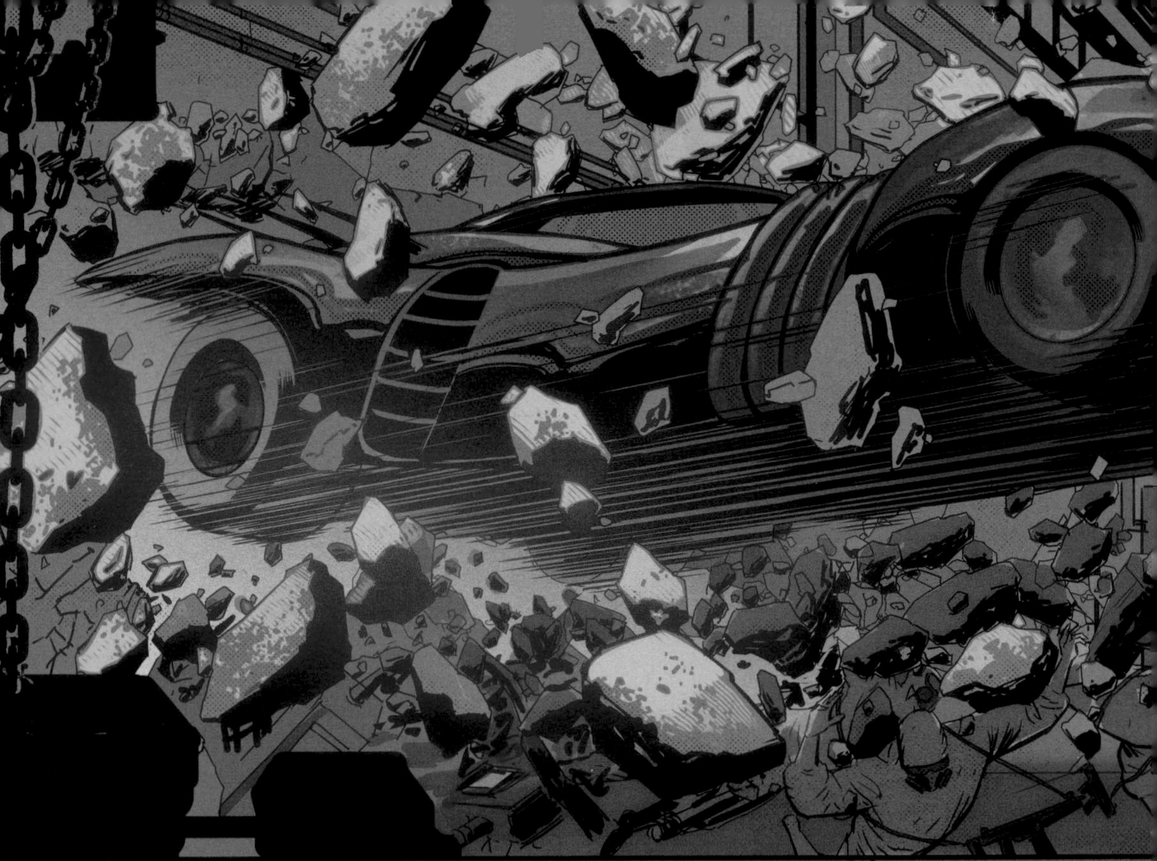

JAMES TYNION IV & SCOTT SNYDER Story
JAMES TYNION IV Script
FERNANDO BLANCO & ROGER ROBINSON Art
JOHN RAUCH Colors

BATMAN & ROBIN ETERNAL

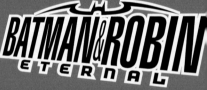

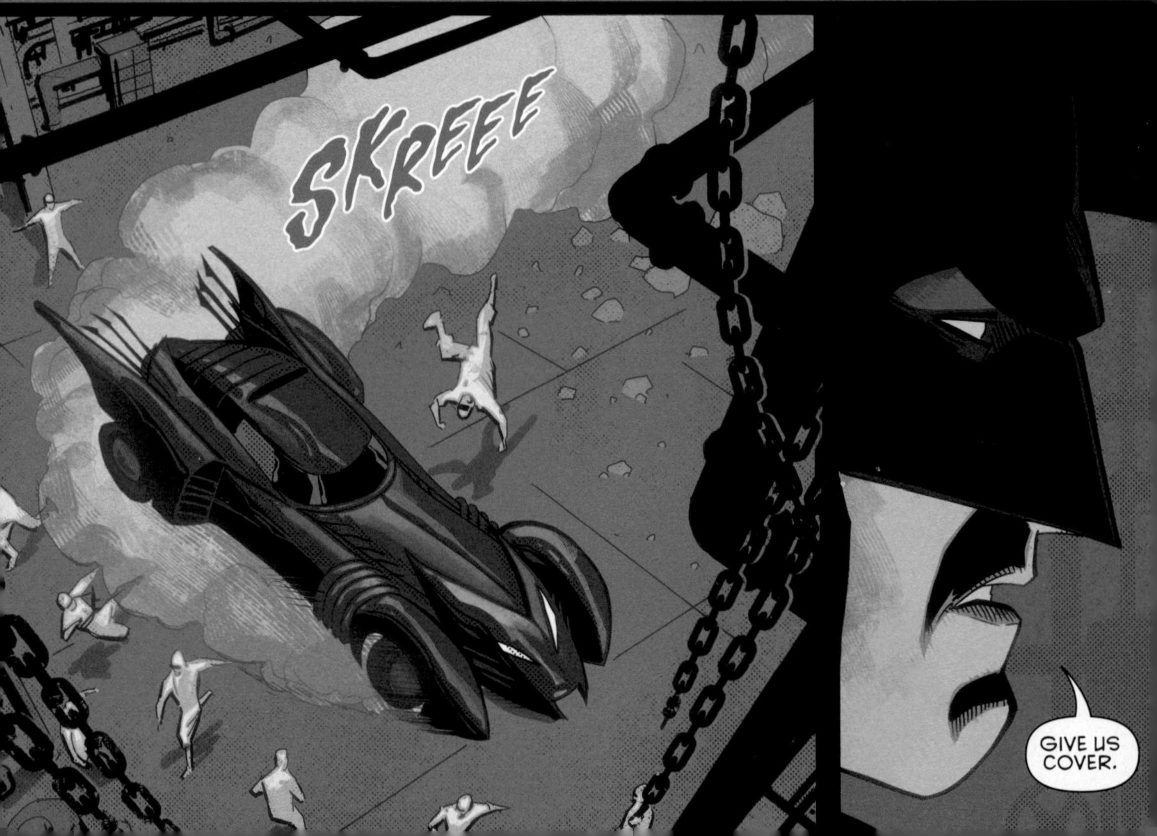
SKREEE
GIVE US COVER.

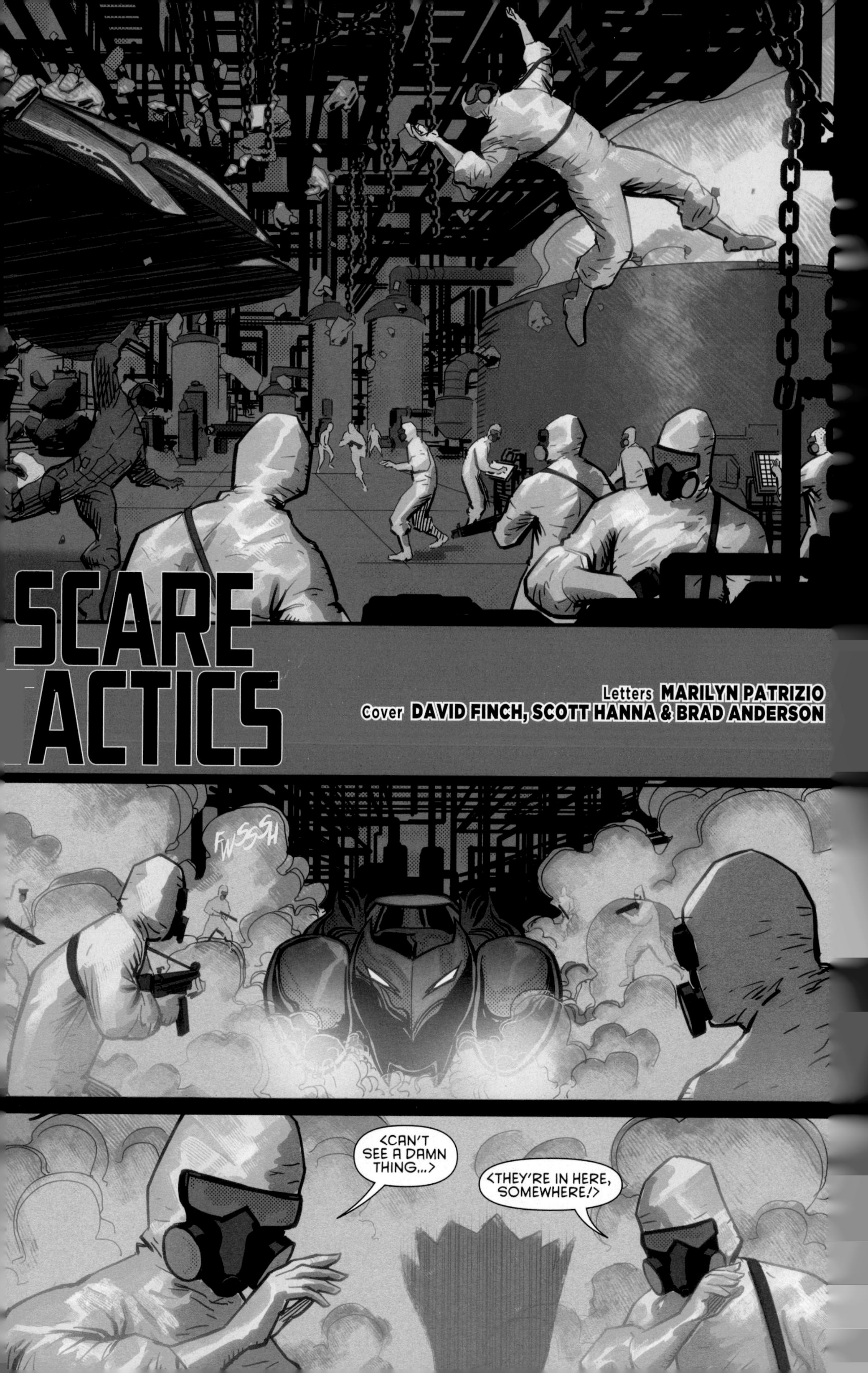
SCARE TACTICS
Letters MARILYN PATRIZIO
Cover DAVID FINCH, SCOTT HANNA & BRAD ANDERSON
FWSSSH
<CAN'T SEE A DAMN THING...>
<THEY'RE IN HERE, SOMEWHERE!>

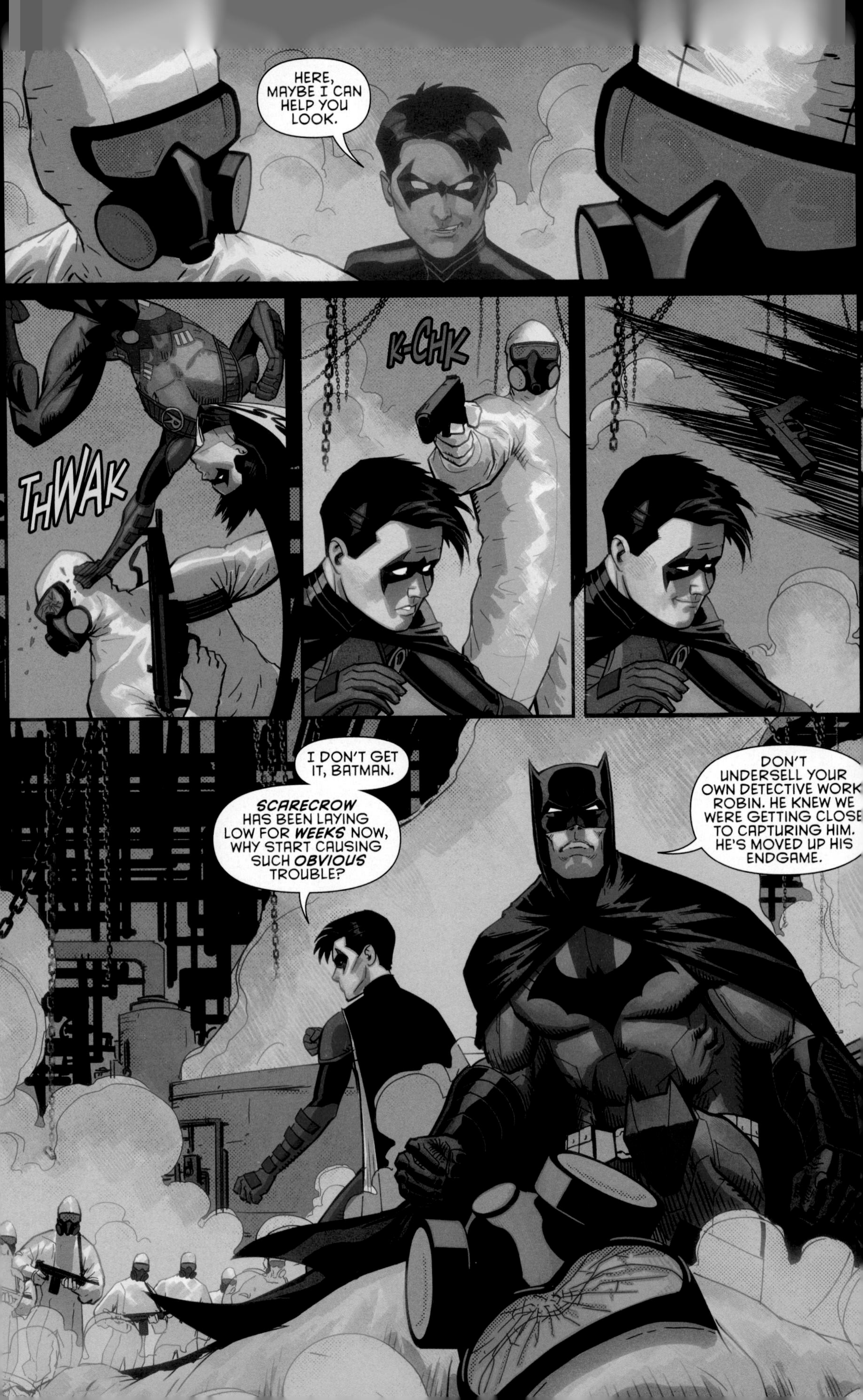
HERE, MAYBE I CAN HELP YOU LOOK.
THWAK
K-CHK
I DON'T GET IT, BATMAN.
SCARECROW HAS BEEN LAYING LOW FOR WEEKS NOW, WHY START CAUSING SUCH OBVIOUS TROUBLE?
DON'T UNDERSELL YOUR OWN DETECTIVE WORK ROBIN. HE KNEW WE WERE GETTING CLOSE TO CAPTURING HIM. HE'S MOVED UP HIS ENDGAME.

STILL. IT FEELS LIKE HE *WANTED* US HERE.

TOO TRUE.

HELLOOOO, BAATMAANN.

DON'T RESPOND. I'VE BROKEN INTO *YOUR* COWL RADIO, BUT I'M *NOT* BROADCASTING TO THE *BOY WONDER* OVER THERE.

I THINK IT'S TIME YOU AND I HAD A LITTLE *CHAT* ABOUT A *MUTUAL FRIEND* OF OURS.

MOTHER.

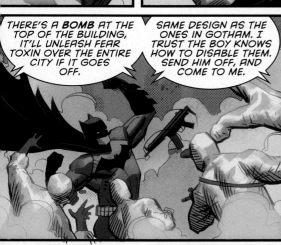

THERE'S A *BOMB* AT THE TOP OF THE BUILDING, IT'LL UNLEASH FEAR TOXIN OVER THE ENTIRE CITY IF IT GOES OFF.

SAME DESIGN AS THE ONES IN GOTHAM. I TRUST THE BOY KNOWS HOW TO DISABLE THEM. SEND HIM OFF, AND COME TO ME.

WHY WOULD I?

BECAUSE IF YOU DON'T, PEOPLE WILL DIE. INCLUDING THE BOTH OF US.

THERE'S A BOMB. THE TOP OF THE TOWER. I NEED YOU TO DISMANTLE IT WHILE I GO AFTER CRANE.

YOU WANT ME TO DO *WHAT?!*

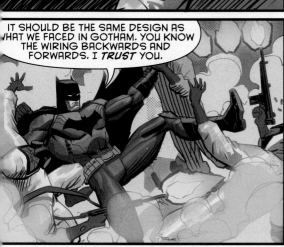

IT SHOULD BE THE SAME DESIGN AS WHAT WE FACED IN GOTHAM. YOU KNOW THE WIRING BACKWARDS AND FORWARDS. I *TRUST* YOU.

THEN WHY DOES IT FEEL LIKE YOU'RE NOT *TELLING* ME SOMETHING...

IT'S IN YOUR HEAD, ROBIN.

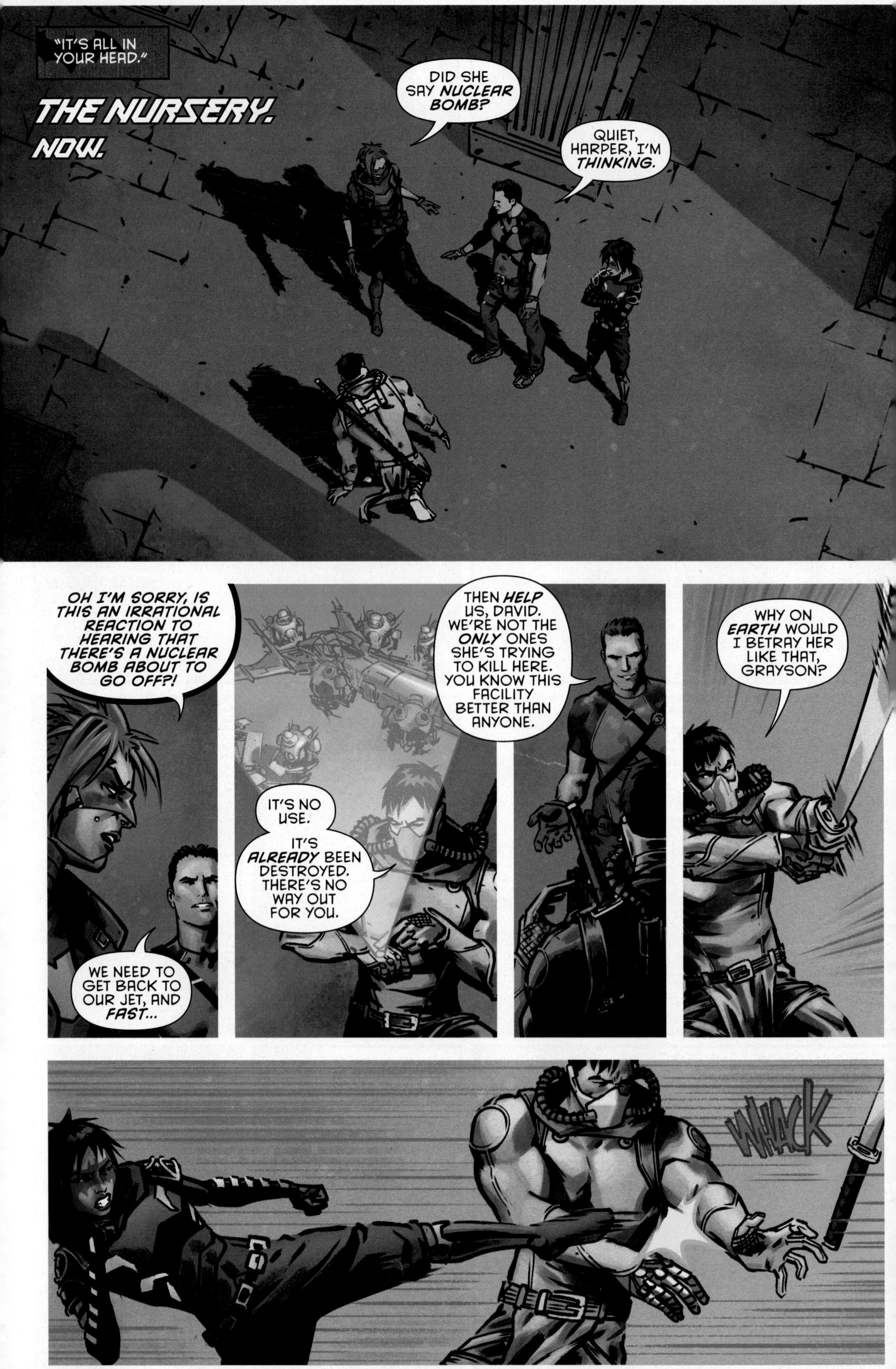
"IT'S ALL IN YOUR HEAD."
THE NURSERY. NOW.
DID SHE SAY NUCLEAR BOMB?
QUIET, HARPER, I'M THINKING.
OH I'M SORRY, IS THIS AN IRRATIONAL REACTION TO HEARING THAT THERE'S A NUCLEAR BOMB ABOUT TO GO OFF?!
WE NEED TO GET BACK TO OUR JET, AND FAST...
IT'S NO USE.
IT'S ALREADY BEEN DESTROYED. THERE'S NO WAY OUT FOR YOU.
THEN HELP US, DAVID. WE'RE NOT THE ONLY ONES SHE'S TRYING TO KILL HERE. YOU KNOW THIS FACILITY BETTER THAN ANYONE.
WHY ON EARTH WOULD I BETRAY HER LIKE THAT, GRAYSON?
WHACK

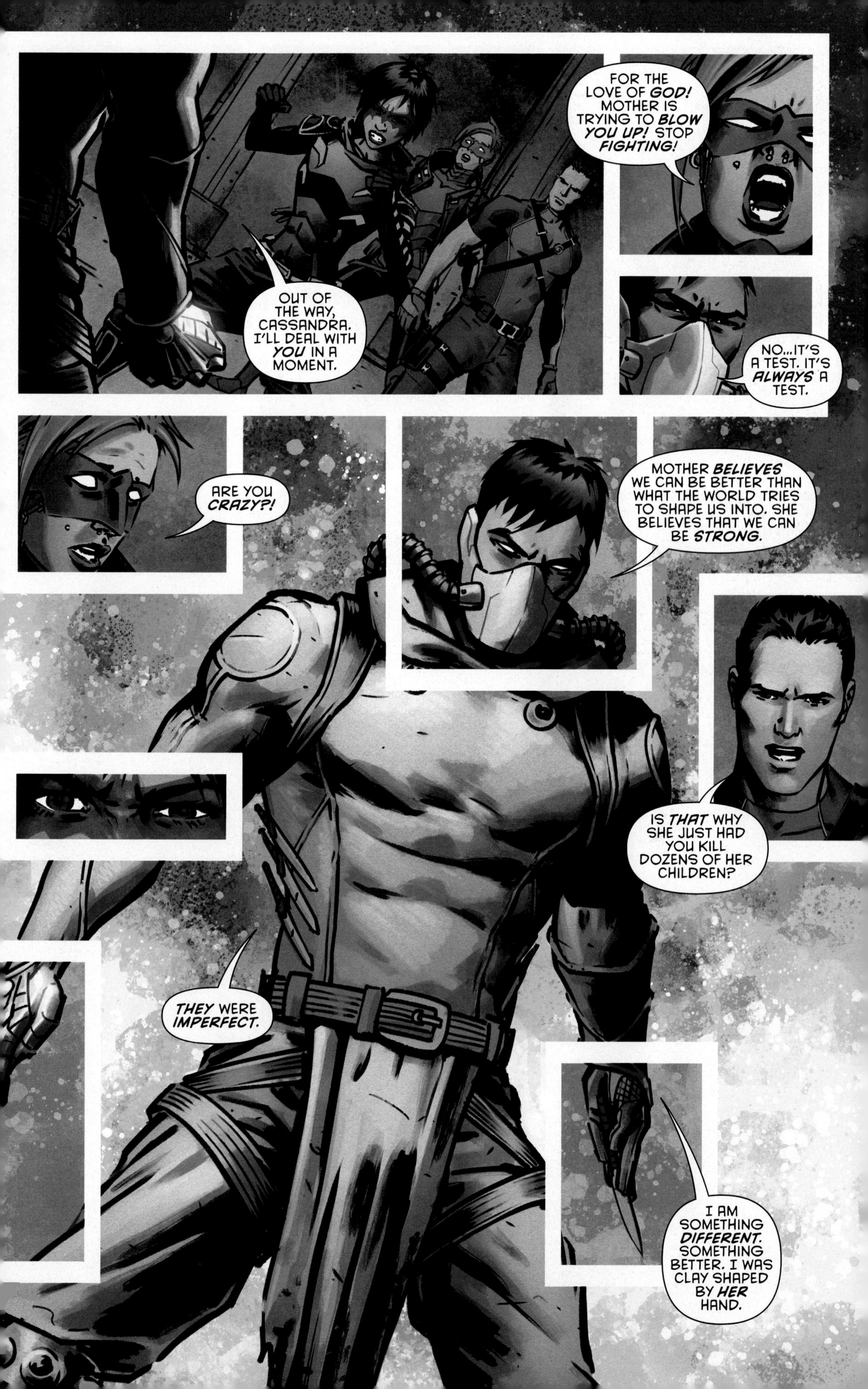

OUT OF THE WAY, CASSANDRA. I'LL DEAL WITH YOU IN A MOMENT.
FOR THE LOVE OF GOD! MOTHER IS TRYING TO BLOW YOU UP! STOP FIGHTING!
NO...IT'S A TEST. IT'S ALWAYS A TEST.
ARE YOU CRAZY?!
MOTHER BELIEVES WE CAN BE BETTER THAN WHAT THE WORLD TRIES TO SHAPE US INTO. SHE BELIEVES THAT WE CAN BE STRONG.
IS THAT WHY SHE JUST HAD YOU KILL DOZENS OF HER CHILDREN?
THEY WERE IMPERFECT.
I AM SOMETHING DIFFERENT. SOMETHING BETTER. I WAS CLAY SHAPED BY HER HAND.

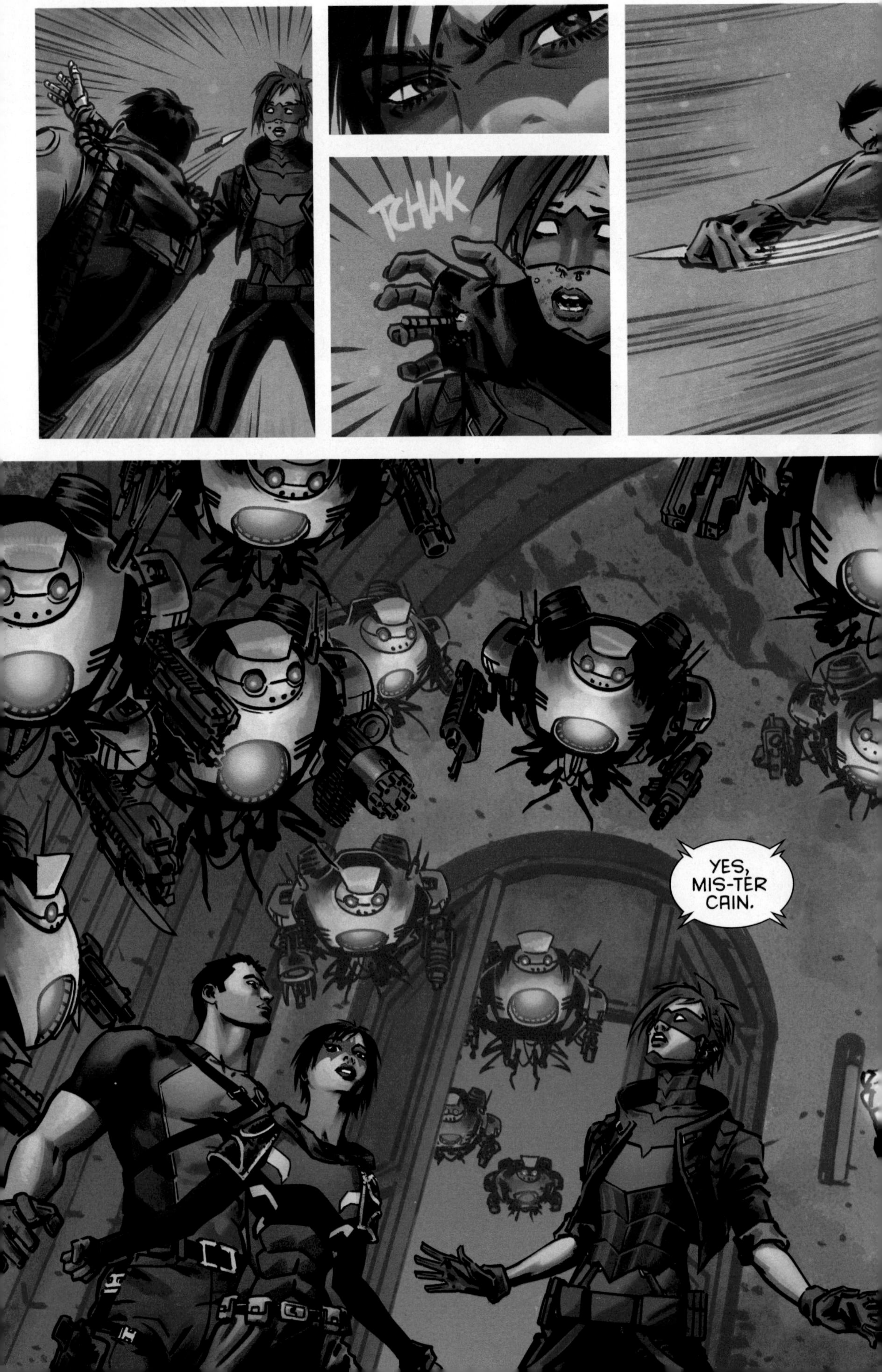
TCHAK
YES, MIS-TER CAIN.

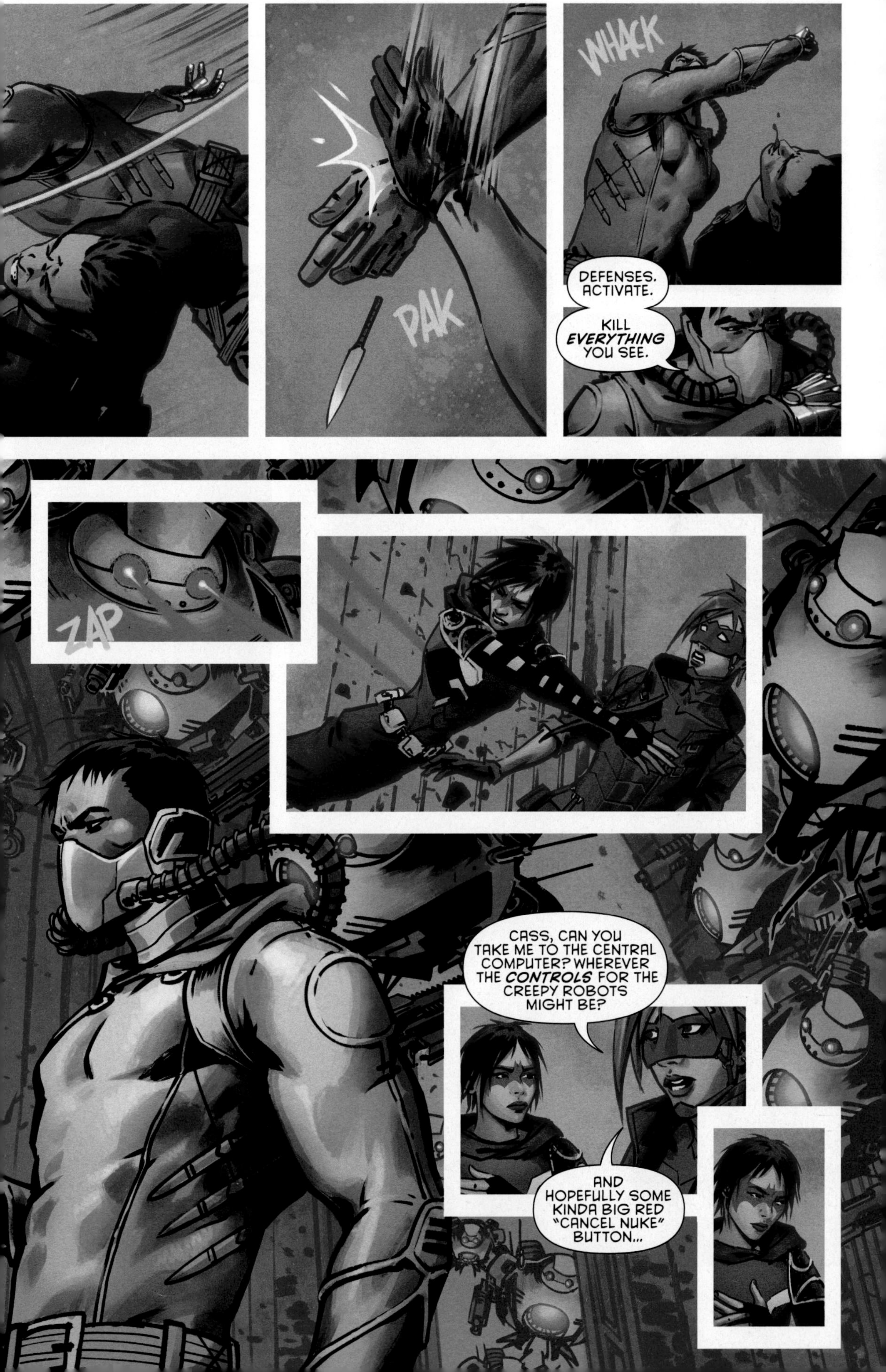

WHACK
PAK
DEFENSES. ACTIVATE.
KILL *EVERYTHING* YOU SEE.
ZAP
CASS, CAN YOU TAKE ME TO THE CENTRAL COMPUTER? WHEREVER THE *CONTROLS* FOR THE CREEPY ROBOTS MIGHT BE?
AND HOPEFULLY SOME KINDA BIG RED "CANCEL NUKE" BUTTON...

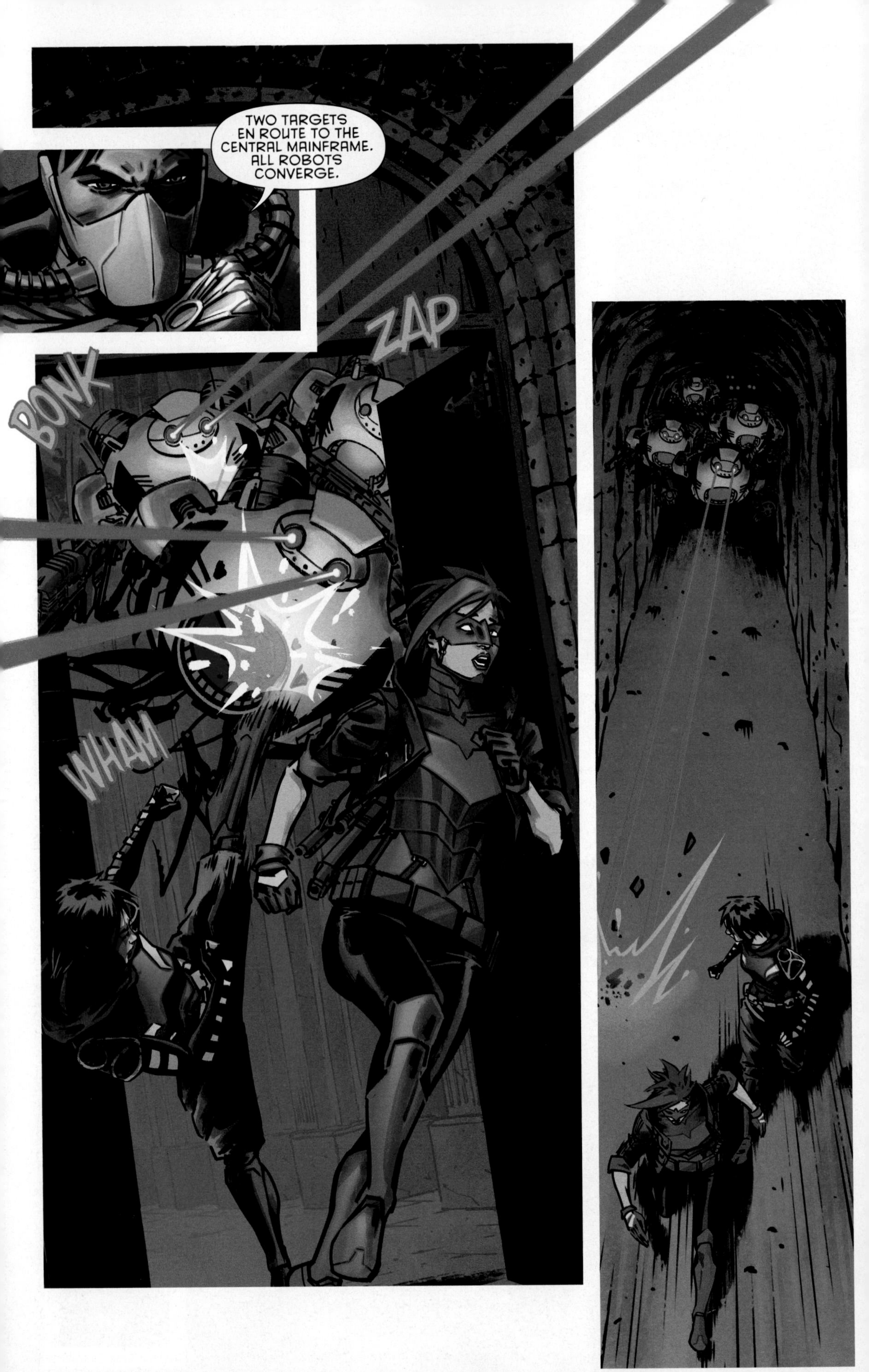
TWO TARGETS EN ROUTE TO THE CENTRAL MAINFRAME. ALL ROBOTS CONVERGE.
ZAP
BONK
WHAM

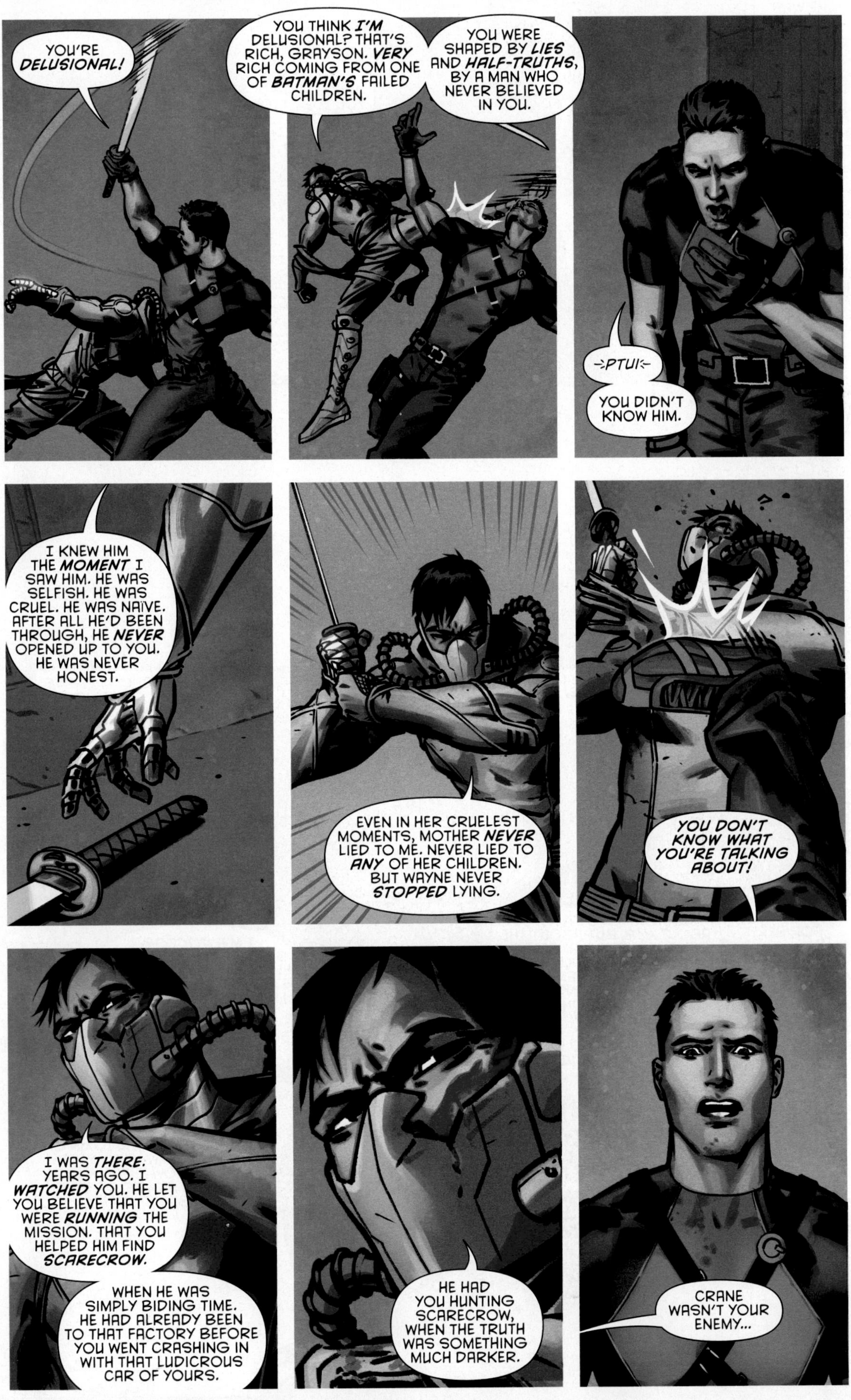
YOU'RE DELUSIONAL!
YOU THINK I'M DELUSIONAL? THAT'S RICH, GRAYSON. VERY RICH COMING FROM ONE OF BATMAN'S FAILED CHILDREN.
YOU WERE SHAPED BY LIES AND HALF-TRUTHS, BY A MAN WHO NEVER BELIEVED IN YOU.
PTUI
YOU DIDN'T KNOW HIM.
I KNEW HIM THE MOMENT I SAW HIM. HE WAS SELFISH. HE WAS CRUEL. HE WAS NAÏVE. AFTER ALL HE'D BEEN THROUGH, HE NEVER OPENED UP TO YOU. HE WAS NEVER HONEST.
EVEN IN HER CRUELEST MOMENTS, MOTHER NEVER LIED TO ME. NEVER LIED TO ANY OF HER CHILDREN. BUT WAYNE NEVER STOPPED LYING.
YOU DON'T KNOW WHAT YOU'RE TALKING ABOUT!
I WAS THERE. YEARS AGO. I WATCHED YOU. HE LET YOU BELIEVE THAT YOU WERE RUNNING THE MISSION. THAT YOU HELPED HIM FIND SCARECROW.
WHEN HE WAS SIMPLY BIDING TIME. HE HAD ALREADY BEEN TO THAT FACTORY BEFORE YOU WENT CRASHING IN WITH THAT LUDICROUS CAR OF YOURS.
HE HAD YOU HUNTING SCARECROW, WHEN THE TRUTH WAS SOMETHING MUCH DARKER.
CRANE WASN'T YOUR ENEMY...

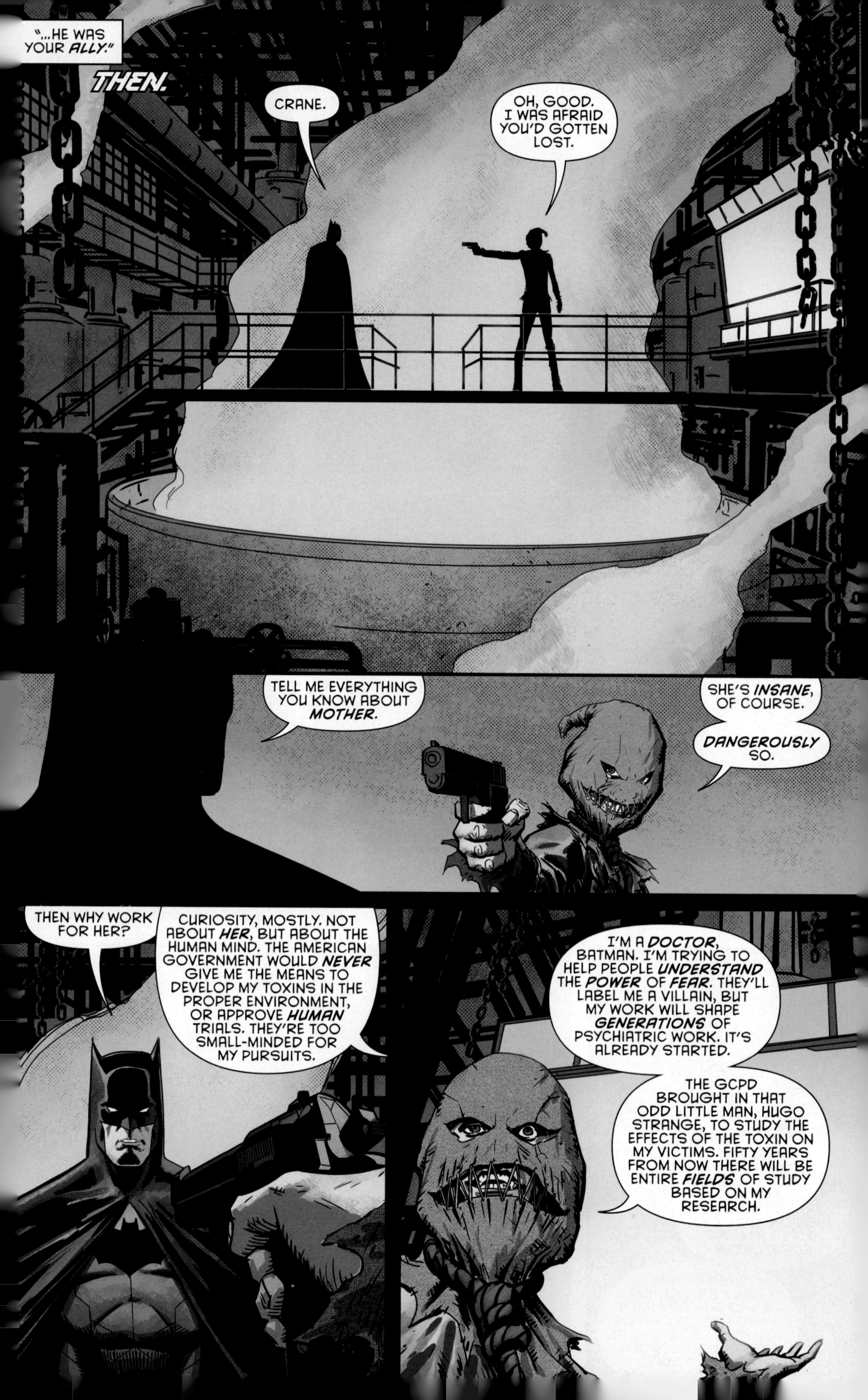
"...HE WAS YOUR ALLY."
THEN.
CRANE.
OH, GOOD. I WAS AFRAID YOU'D GOTTEN LOST.
TELL ME EVERYTHING YOU KNOW ABOUT MOTHER.
SHE'S INSANE, OF COURSE.
DANGEROUSLY SO.
THEN WHY WORK FOR HER?
CURIOSITY, MOSTLY. NOT ABOUT HER, BUT ABOUT THE HUMAN MIND. THE AMERICAN GOVERNMENT WOULD NEVER GIVE ME THE MEANS TO DEVELOP MY TOXINS IN THE PROPER ENVIRONMENT, OR APPROVE HUMAN TRIALS. THEY'RE TOO SMALL-MINDED FOR MY PURSUITS.
I'M A DOCTOR, BATMAN. I'M TRYING TO HELP PEOPLE UNDERSTAND THE POWER OF FEAR. THEY'LL LABEL ME A VILLAIN, BUT MY WORK WILL SHAPE GENERATIONS OF PSYCHIATRIC WORK. IT'S ALREADY STARTED.
THE GCPD BROUGHT IN THAT ODD LITTLE MAN, HUGO STRANGE, TO STUDY THE EFFECTS OF THE TOXIN ON MY VICTIMS. FIFTY YEARS FROM NOW THERE WILL BE ENTIRE FIELDS OF STUDY BASED ON MY RESEARCH.

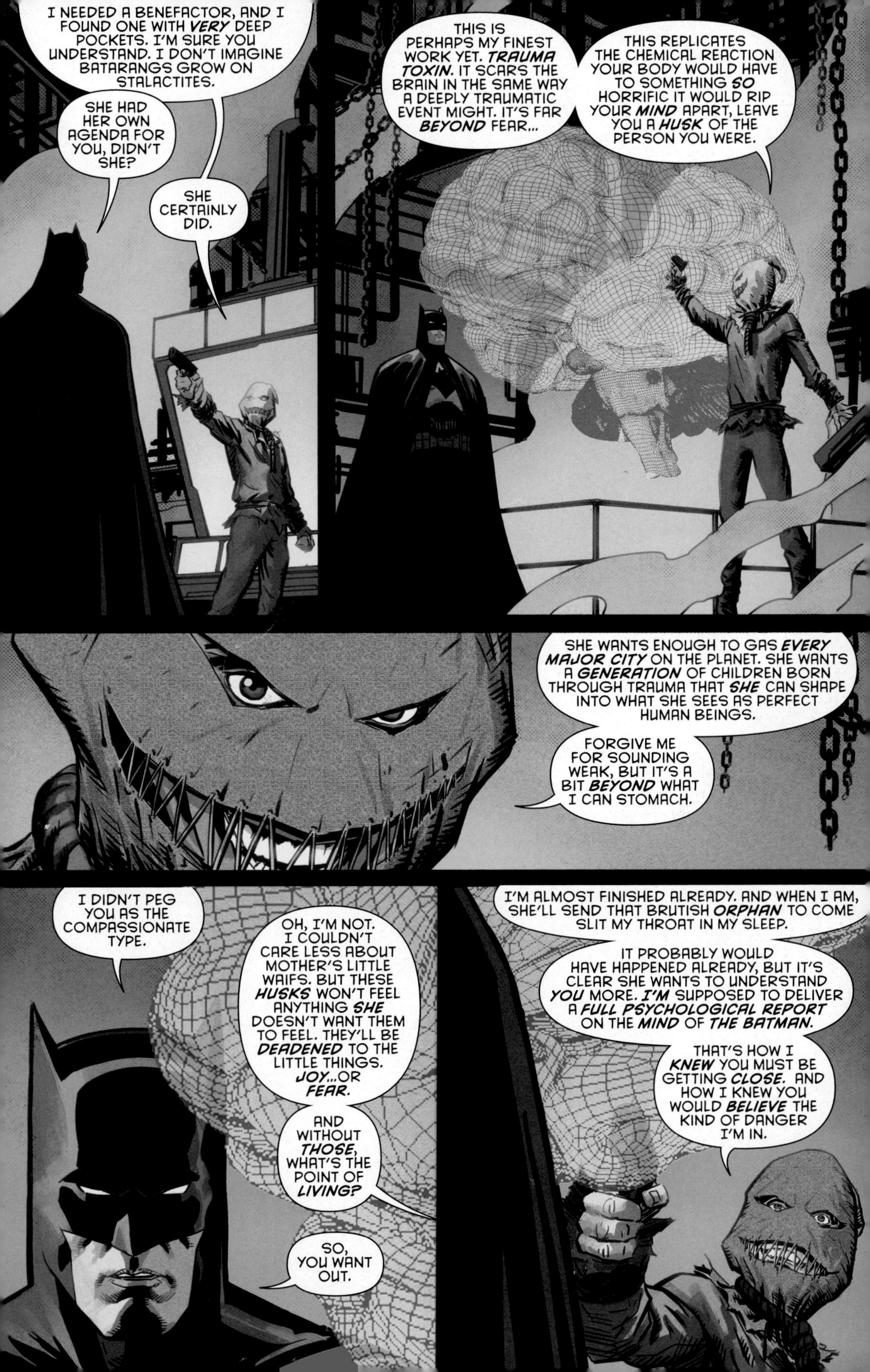
I NEEDED A BENEFACTOR, AND I FOUND ONE WITH VERY DEEP POCKETS. I'M SURE YOU UNDERSTAND. I DON'T IMAGINE BATARANGS GROW ON STALACTITES.
SHE HAD HER OWN AGENDA FOR YOU, DIDN'T SHE?
SHE CERTAINLY DID.
THIS IS PERHAPS MY FINEST WORK YET. TRAUMA TOXIN. IT SCARS THE BRAIN IN THE SAME WAY A DEEPLY TRAUMATIC EVENT MIGHT. IT'S FAR BEYOND FEAR...
THIS REPLICATES THE CHEMICAL REACTION YOUR BODY WOULD HAVE TO SOMETHING SO HORRIFIC IT WOULD RIP YOUR MIND APART, LEAVE YOU A HUSK OF THE PERSON YOU WERE.
SHE WANTS ENOUGH TO GAS EVERY MAJOR CITY ON THE PLANET. SHE WANTS A GENERATION OF CHILDREN BORN THROUGH TRAUMA THAT SHE CAN SHAPE INTO WHAT SHE SEES AS PERFECT HUMAN BEINGS.
FORGIVE ME FOR SOUNDING WEAK, BUT IT'S A BIT BEYOND WHAT I CAN STOMACH.
I DIDN'T PEG YOU AS THE COMPASSIONATE TYPE.
OH, I'M NOT. I COULDN'T CARE LESS ABOUT MOTHER'S LITTLE WAIFS. BUT THESE HUSKS WON'T FEEL ANYTHING SHE DOESN'T WANT THEM TO FEEL. THEY'LL BE DEADENED TO THE LITTLE THINGS. JOY...OR FEAR.
AND WITHOUT THOSE, WHAT'S THE POINT OF LIVING?
SO, YOU WANT OUT.
I'M ALMOST FINISHED ALREADY. AND WHEN I AM, SHE'LL SEND THAT BRUTISH ORPHAN TO COME SLIT MY THROAT IN MY SLEEP.
IT PROBABLY WOULD HAVE HAPPENED ALREADY, BUT IT'S CLEAR SHE WANTS TO UNDERSTAND YOU MORE. I'M SUPPOSED TO DELIVER A FULL PSYCHOLOGICAL REPORT ON THE MIND OF THE BATMAN.
THAT'S HOW I KNEW YOU MUST BE GETTING CLOSE. AND HOW I KNEW YOU WOULD BELIEVE THE KIND OF DANGER I'M IN.

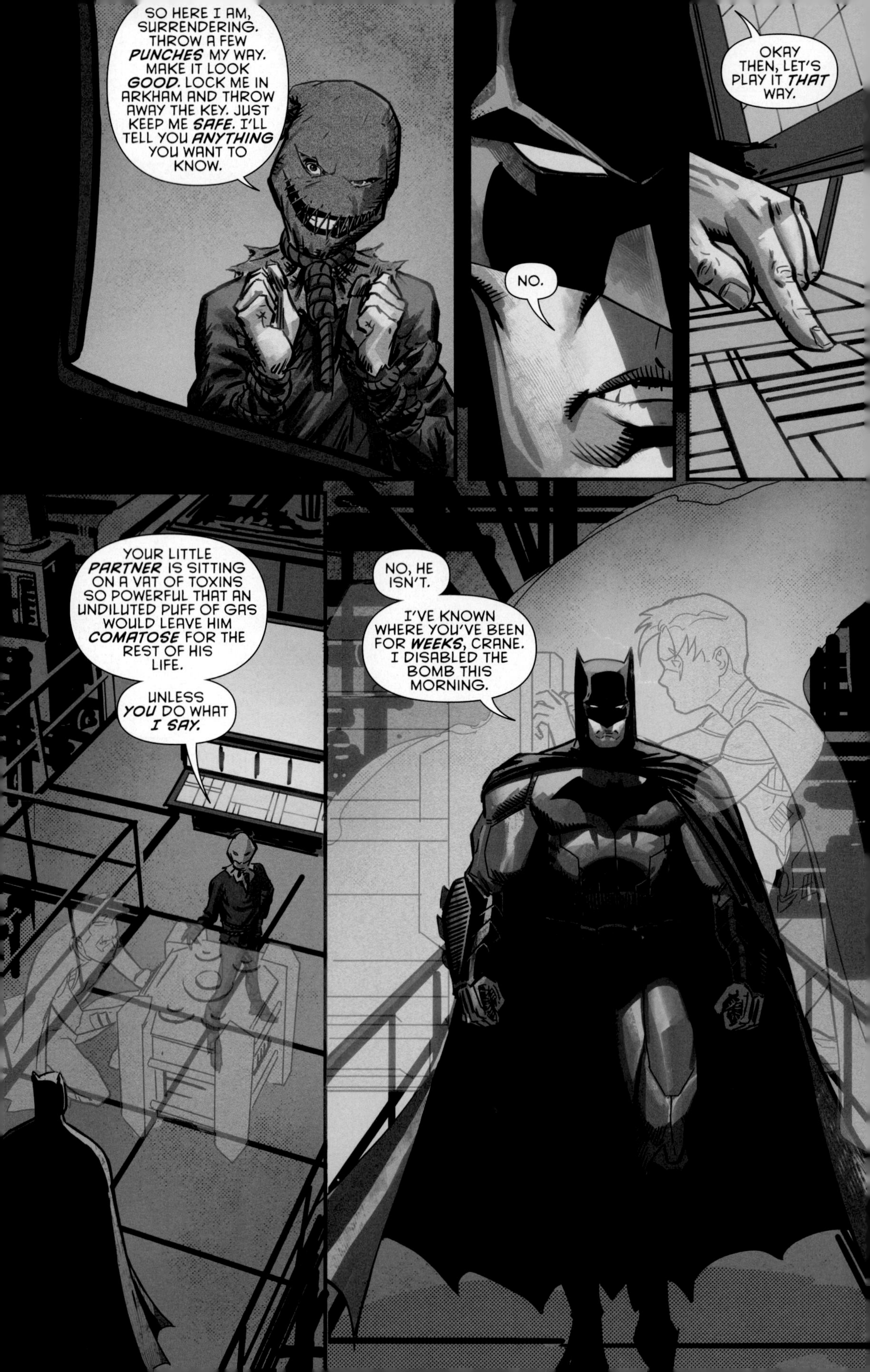
SO HERE I AM, SURRENDERING. THROW A FEW PUNCHES MY WAY. MAKE IT LOOK GOOD. LOCK ME IN ARKHAM AND THROW AWAY THE KEY. JUST KEEP ME SAFE. I'LL TELL YOU ANYTHING YOU WANT TO KNOW.
NO.
OKAY THEN, LET'S PLAY IT THAT WAY.
YOUR LITTLE PARTNER IS SITTING ON A VAT OF TOXINS SO POWERFUL THAT AN UNDILUTED PUFF OF GAS WOULD LEAVE HIM COMATOSE FOR THE REST OF HIS LIFE.
UNLESS YOU DO WHAT I SAY.
NO, HE ISN'T.
I'VE KNOWN WHERE YOU'VE BEEN FOR WEEKS, CRANE. I DISABLED THE BOMB THIS MORNING.

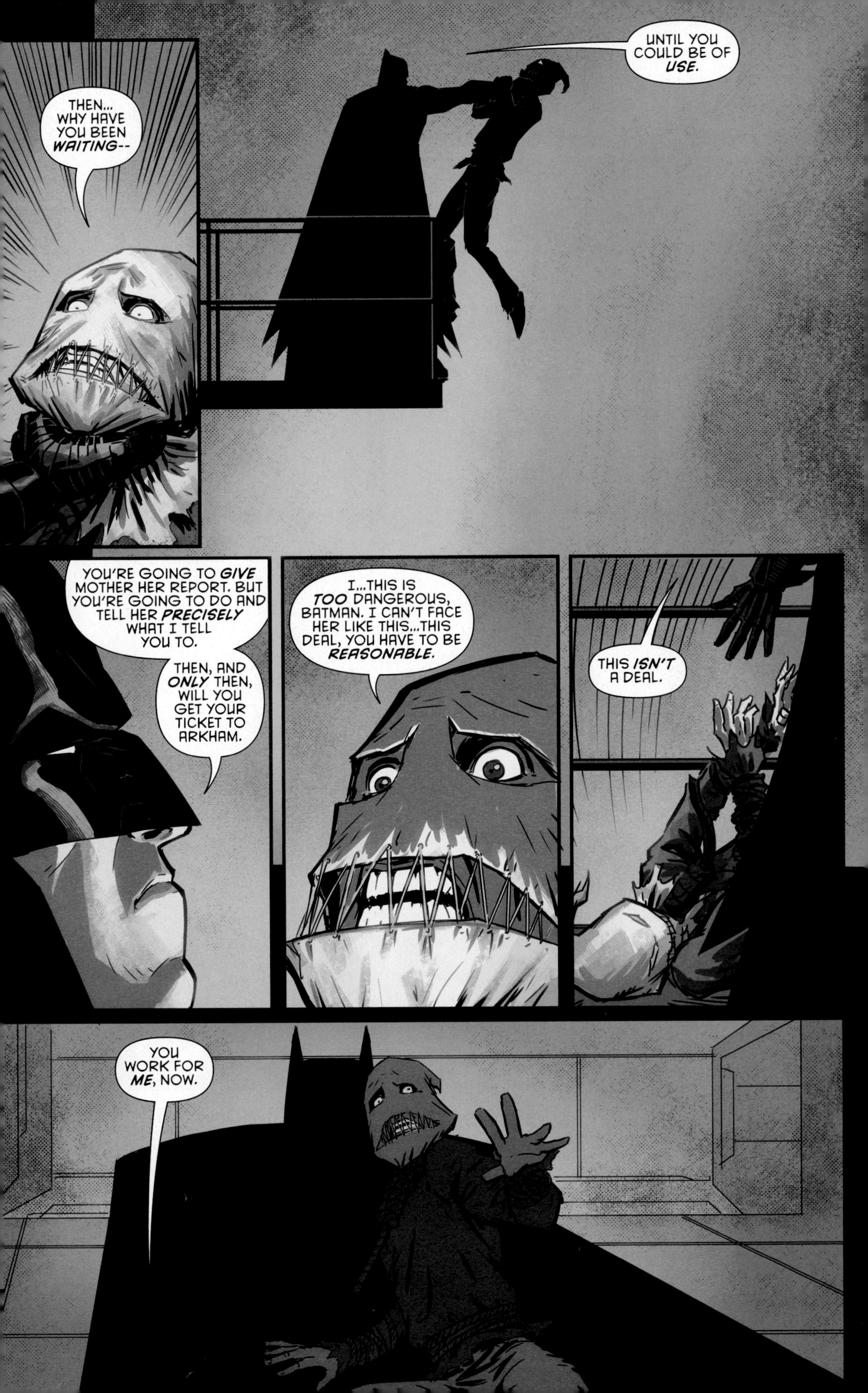
THEN... WHY HAVE YOU BEEN WAITING--
UNTIL YOU COULD BE OF USE.
YOU'RE GOING TO GIVE MOTHER HER REPORT. BUT YOU'RE GOING TO DO AND TELL HER PRECISELY WHAT I TELL YOU TO.
THEN, AND ONLY THEN, WILL YOU GET YOUR TICKET TO ARKHAM.
I...THIS IS TOO DANGEROUS, BATMAN. I CAN'T FACE HER LIKE THIS...THIS DEAL, YOU HAVE TO BE REASONABLE.
THIS ISN'T A DEAL.
YOU WORK FOR ME, NOW.

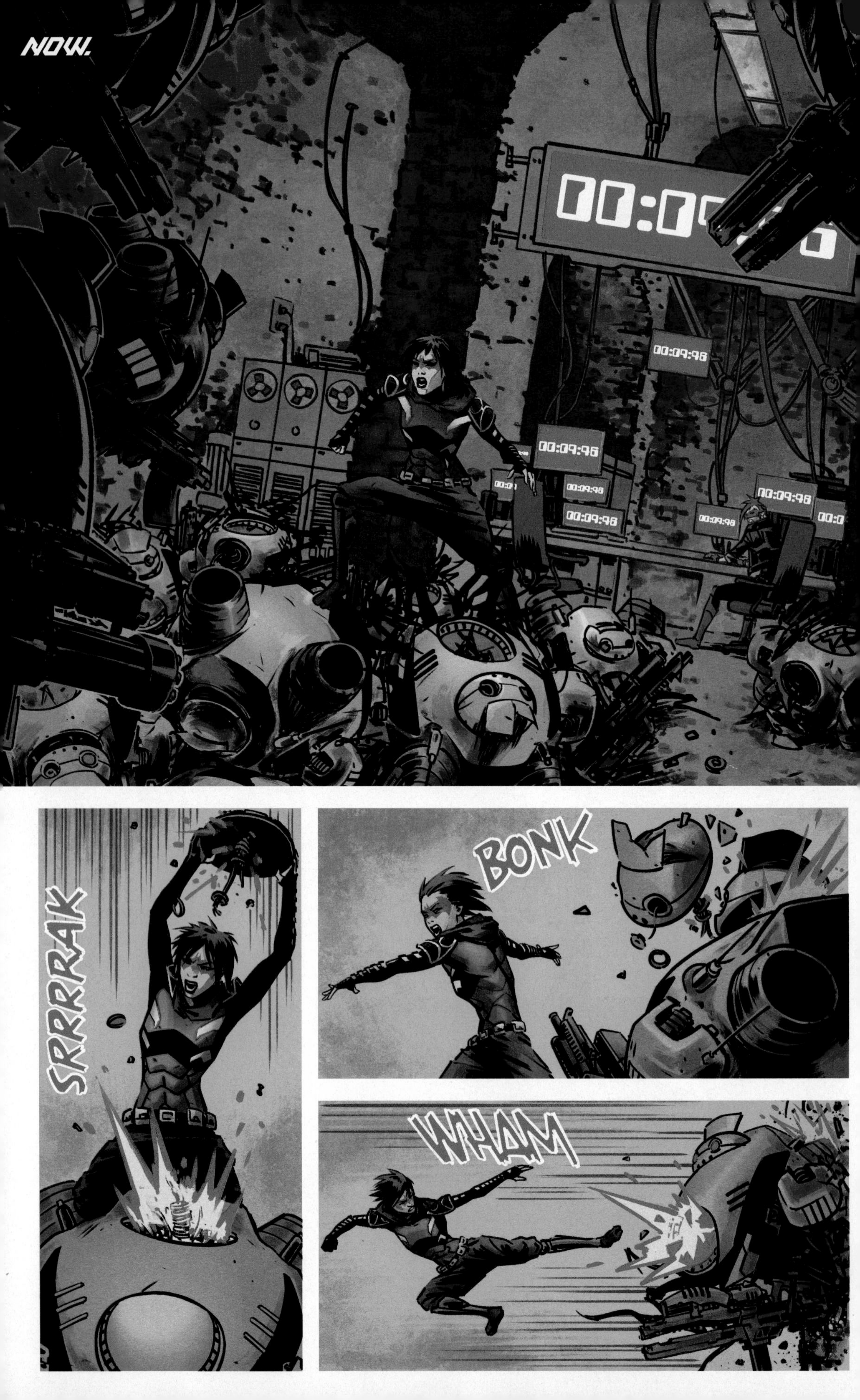
NOW.
00:09:96
00:09:96
00:09:96
00:09:96
00:09:96
00:09:96
SRRRRAK
BONK
WHAM

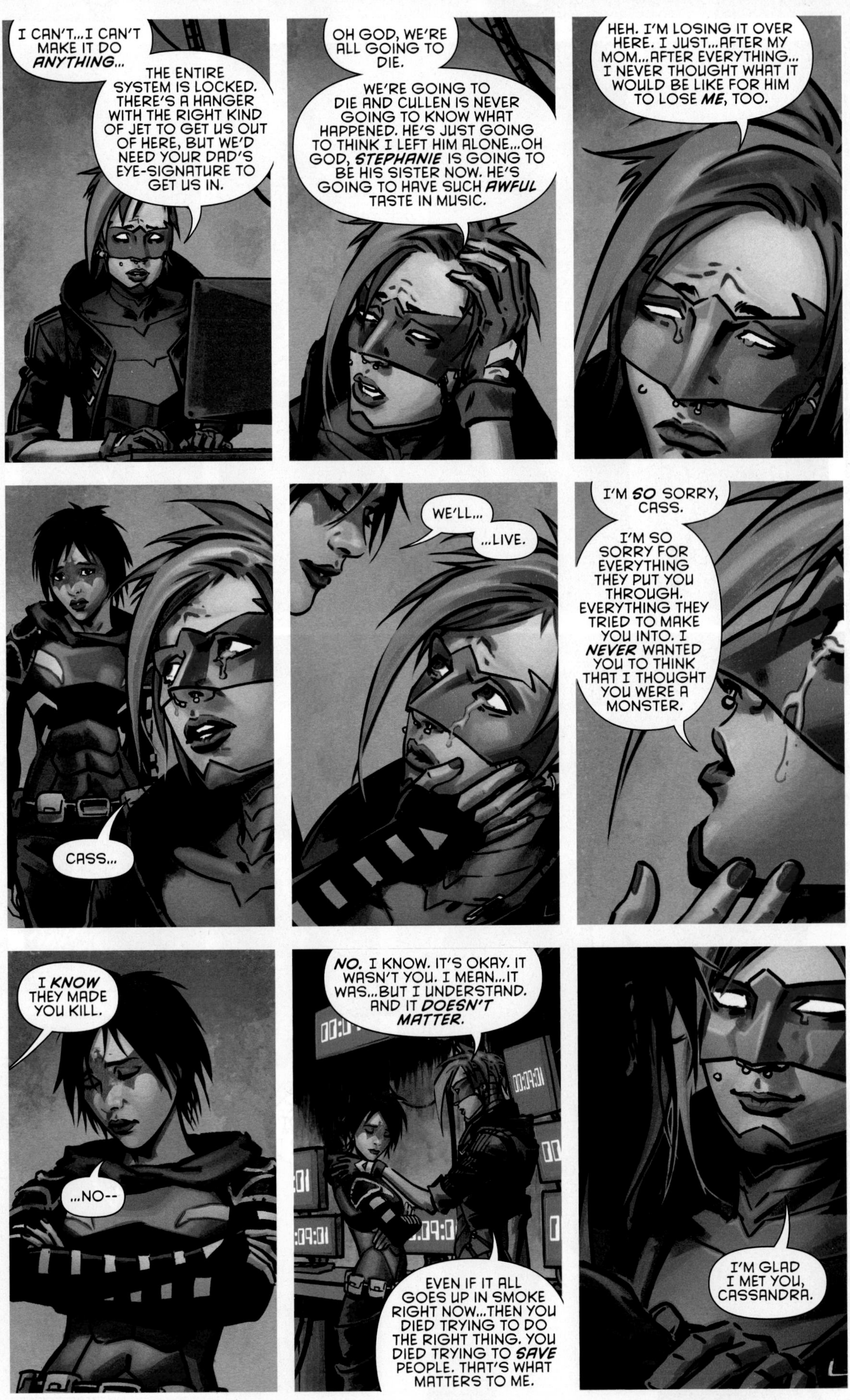
I CAN'T...I CAN'T MAKE IT DO ANYTHING...
THE ENTIRE SYSTEM IS LOCKED. THERE'S A HANGER WITH THE RIGHT KIND OF JET TO GET US OUT OF HERE, BUT WE'D NEED YOUR DAD'S EYE-SIGNATURE TO GET US IN.
OH GOD, WE'RE ALL GOING TO DIE.
WE'RE GOING TO DIE AND CULLEN IS NEVER GOING TO KNOW WHAT HAPPENED. HE'S JUST GOING TO THINK I LEFT HIM ALONE...OH GOD, STEPHANIE IS GOING TO BE HIS SISTER NOW. HE'S GOING TO HAVE SUCH AWFUL TASTE IN MUSIC.
HEH. I'M LOSING IT OVER HERE. I JUST...AFTER MY MOM...AFTER EVERYTHING... I NEVER THOUGHT WHAT IT WOULD BE LIKE FOR HIM TO LOSE ME, TOO.
CASS...
WE'LL...
...LIVE.
I'M SO SORRY, CASS.
I'M SO SORRY FOR EVERYTHING THEY PUT YOU THROUGH. EVERYTHING THEY TRIED TO MAKE YOU INTO. I NEVER WANTED YOU TO THINK THAT I THOUGHT YOU WERE A MONSTER.
I KNOW THEY MADE YOU KILL.
...NO--
NO. I KNOW. IT'S OKAY. IT WASN'T YOU. I MEAN...IT WAS...BUT I UNDERSTAND. AND IT DOESN'T MATTER.
EVEN IF IT ALL GOES UP IN SMOKE RIGHT NOW...THEN YOU DIED TRYING TO DO THE RIGHT THING. YOU DIED TRYING TO SAVE PEOPLE. THAT'S WHAT MATTERS TO ME.
I'M GLAD I MET YOU, CASSANDRA.

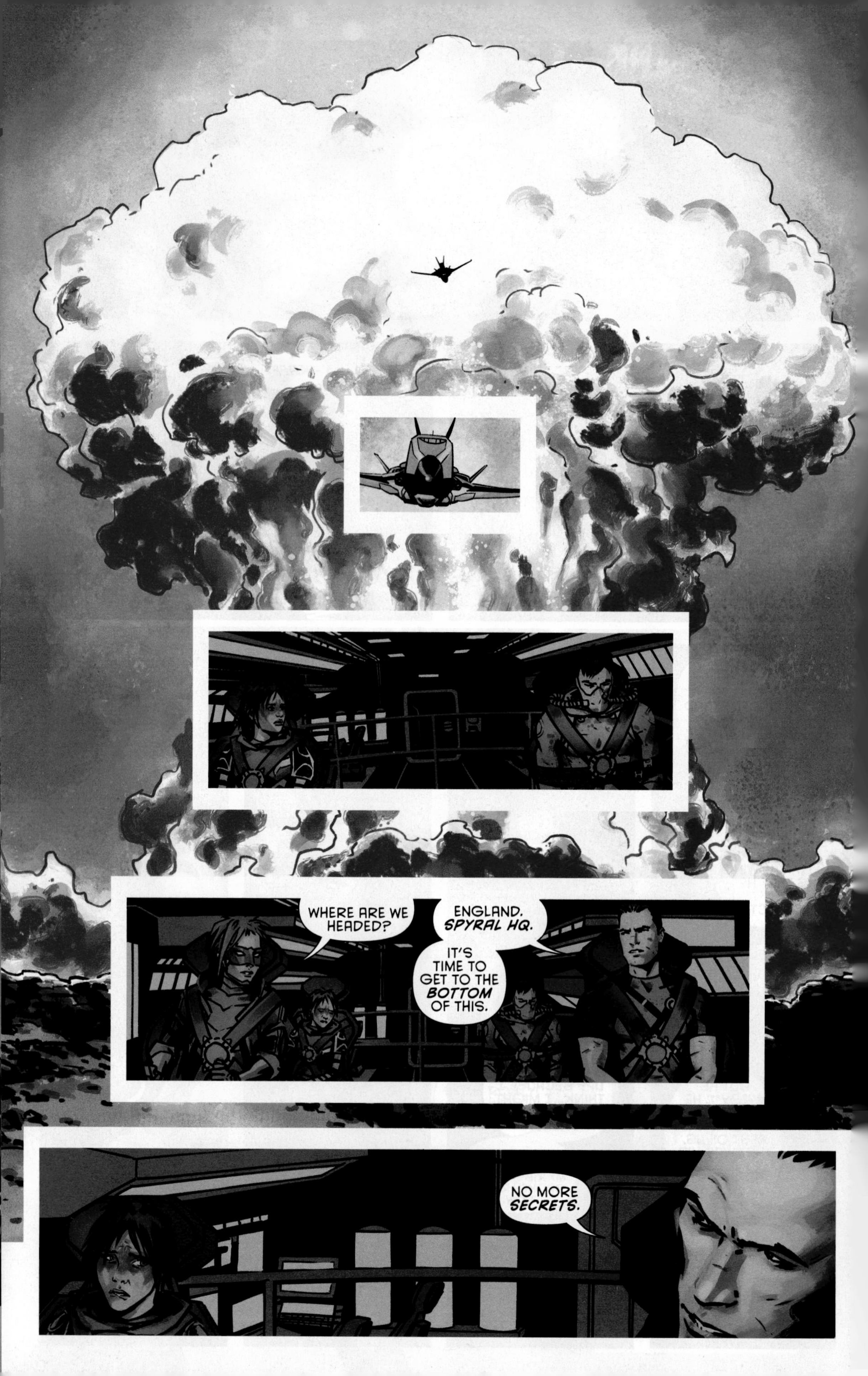

WHERE ARE WE HEADED?
ENGLAND. SPYRAL HQ.
IT'S TIME TO GET TO THE BOTTOM OF THIS.
NO MORE SECRETS.

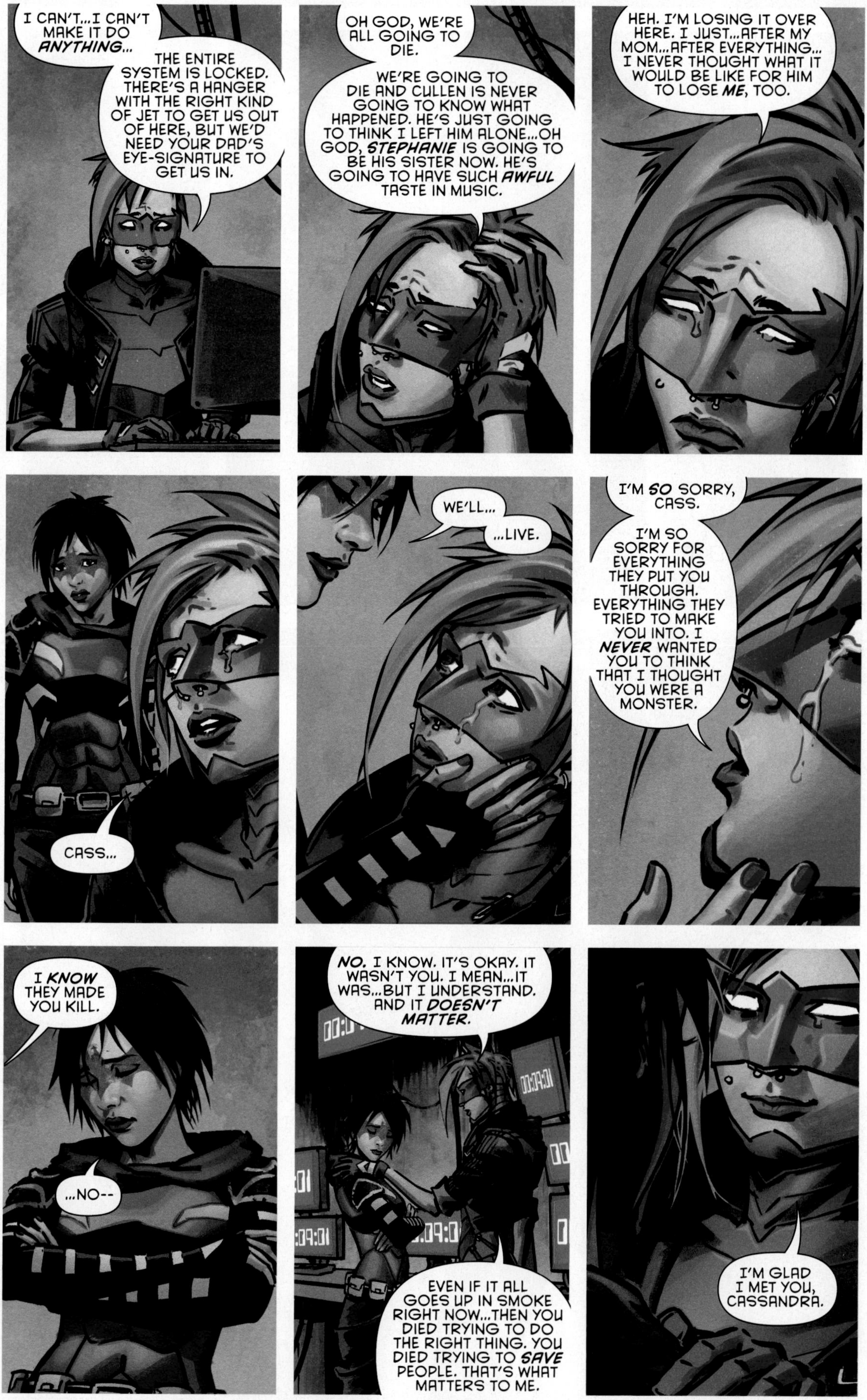
I CAN'T...I CAN'T MAKE IT DO ANYTHING...
THE ENTIRE SYSTEM IS LOCKED. THERE'S A HANGER WITH THE RIGHT KIND OF JET TO GET US OUT OF HERE, BUT WE'D NEED YOUR DAD'S EYE-SIGNATURE TO GET US IN.
OH GOD, WE'RE ALL GOING TO DIE.
WE'RE GOING TO DIE AND CULLEN IS NEVER GOING TO KNOW WHAT HAPPENED. HE'S JUST GOING TO THINK I LEFT HIM ALONE...OH GOD, STEPHANIE IS GOING TO BE HIS SISTER NOW. HE'S GOING TO HAVE SUCH AWFUL TASTE IN MUSIC.
HEH. I'M LOSING IT OVER HERE. I JUST...AFTER MY MOM...AFTER EVERYTHING... I NEVER THOUGHT WHAT IT WOULD BE LIKE FOR HIM TO LOSE ME, TOO.
CASS...
WE'LL...
...LIVE.
I'M SO SORRY, CASS.
I'M SO SORRY FOR EVERYTHING THEY PUT YOU THROUGH. EVERYTHING THEY TRIED TO MAKE YOU INTO. I NEVER WANTED YOU TO THINK THAT I THOUGHT YOU WERE A MONSTER.
I KNOW THEY MADE YOU KILL.
...NO--
NO. I KNOW. IT'S OKAY. IT WASN'T YOU. I MEAN...IT WAS...BUT I UNDERSTAND. AND IT DOESN'T MATTER.
EVEN IF IT ALL GOES UP IN SMOKE RIGHT NOW...THEN YOU DIED TRYING TO DO THE RIGHT THING. YOU DIED TRYING TO SAVE PEOPLE. THAT'S WHAT MATTERS TO ME.
I'M GLAD I MET YOU, CASSANDRA.

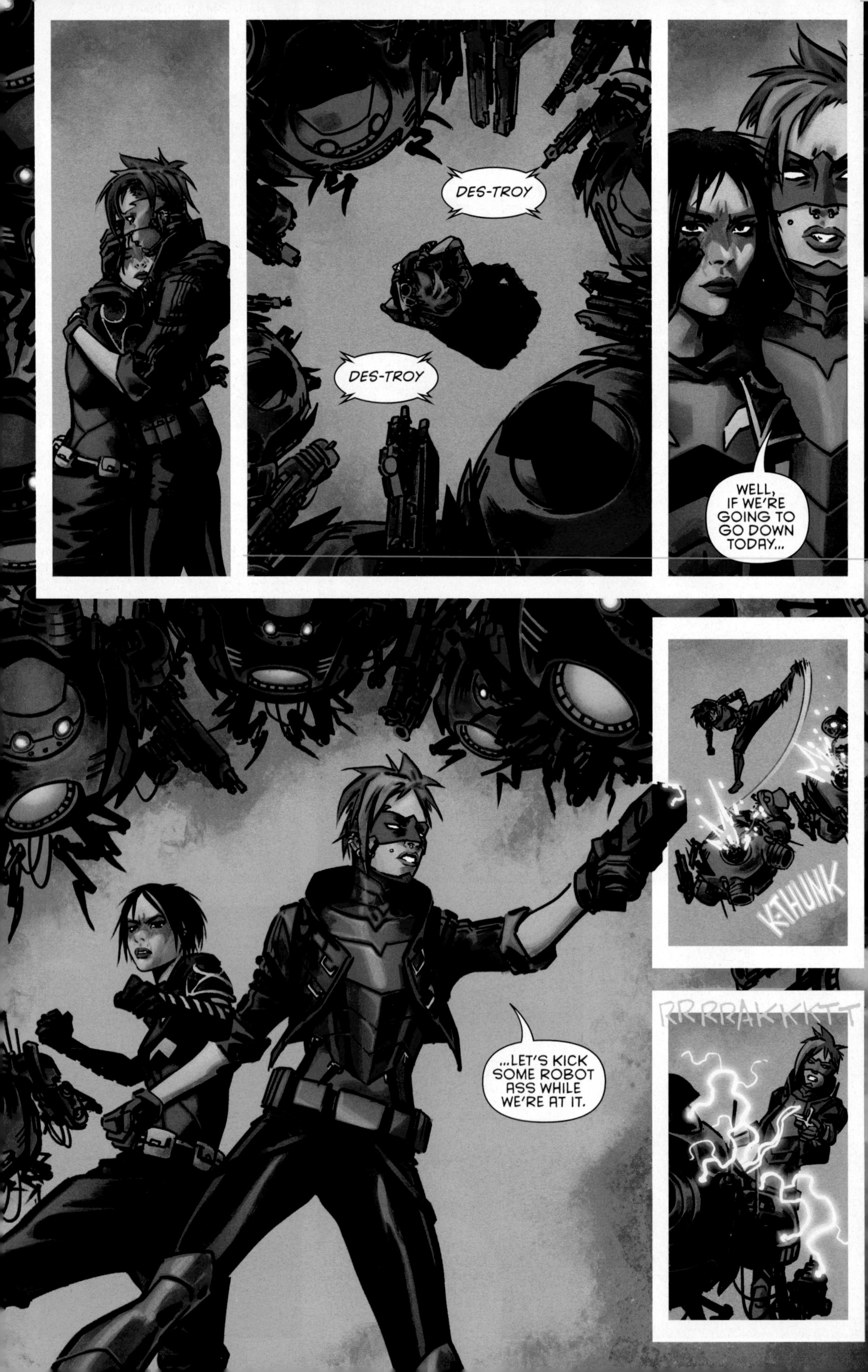
DES-TROY
DES-TROY
WELL, IF WE'RE GOING TO GO DOWN TODAY...
...LET'S KICK SOME ROBOT ASS WHILE WE'RE AT IT.
K-THUNK
RRRRAKKKTT

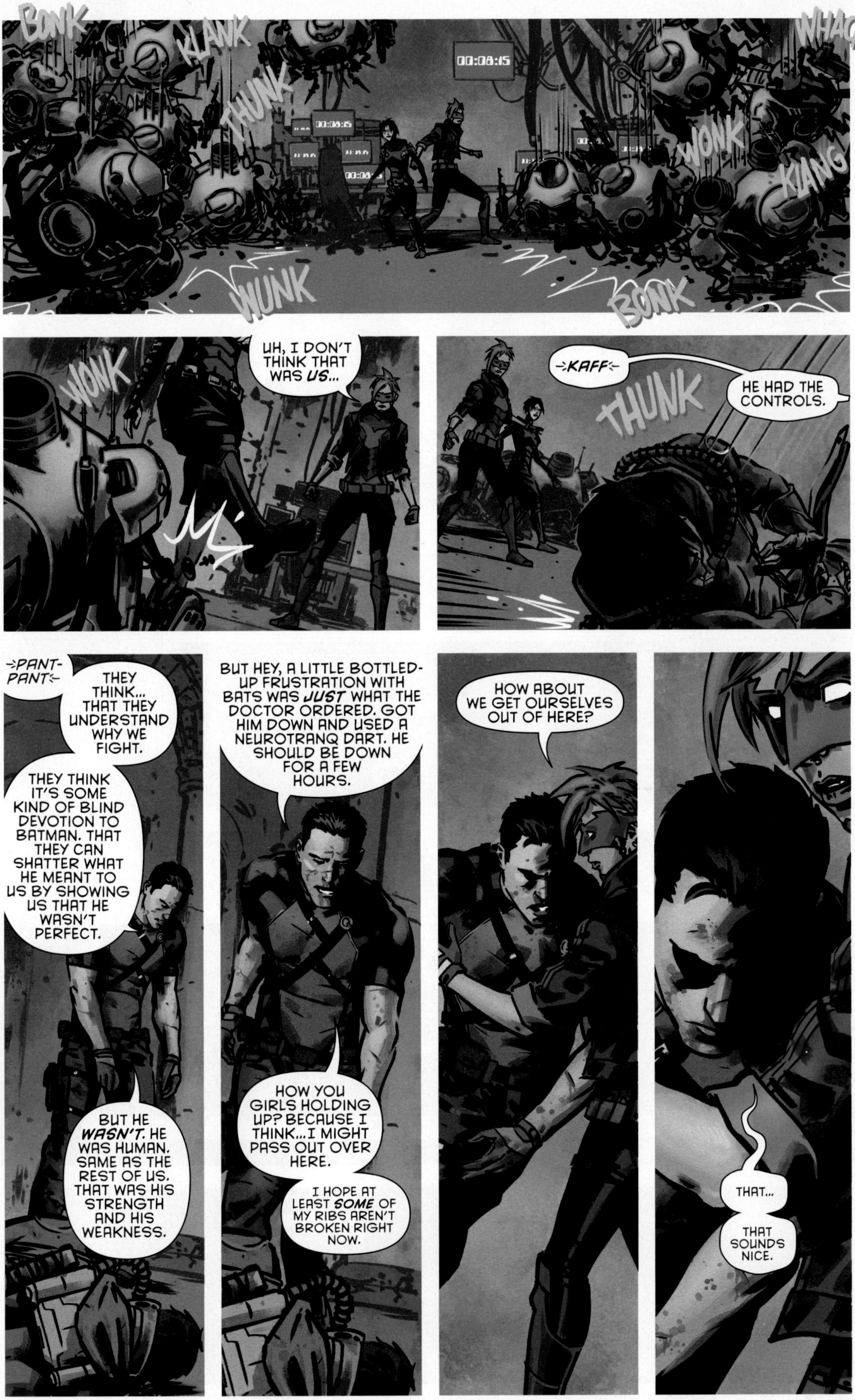

BONK
KLANK
THUNK
00:08:15
WHACK
WONK
KLANG
WUNK
BONK
WONK
UH, I DON'T THINK THAT WAS US...
-KAFF-
THUNK
HE HAD THE CONTROLS.
-PANT-PANT-
THEY THINK... THAT THEY UNDERSTAND WHY WE FIGHT.
THEY THINK IT'S SOME KIND OF BLIND DEVOTION TO BATMAN. THAT THEY CAN SHATTER WHAT HE MEANT TO US BY SHOWING US THAT HE WASN'T PERFECT.
BUT HE WASN'T. HE WAS HUMAN. SAME AS THE REST OF US. THAT WAS HIS STRENGTH AND HIS WEAKNESS.
BUT HEY, A LITTLE BOTTLED-UP FRUSTRATION WITH BATS WAS JUST WHAT THE DOCTOR ORDERED. GOT HIM DOWN AND USED A NEUROTRANQ DART. HE SHOULD BE DOWN FOR A FEW HOURS.
HOW YOU GIRLS HOLDING UP? BECAUSE I THINK...I MIGHT PASS OUT OVER HERE.
I HOPE AT LEAST SOME OF MY RIBS AREN'T BROKEN RIGHT NOW.
HOW ABOUT WE GET OURSELVES OUT OF HERE?
THAT...
THAT SOUNDS NICE.

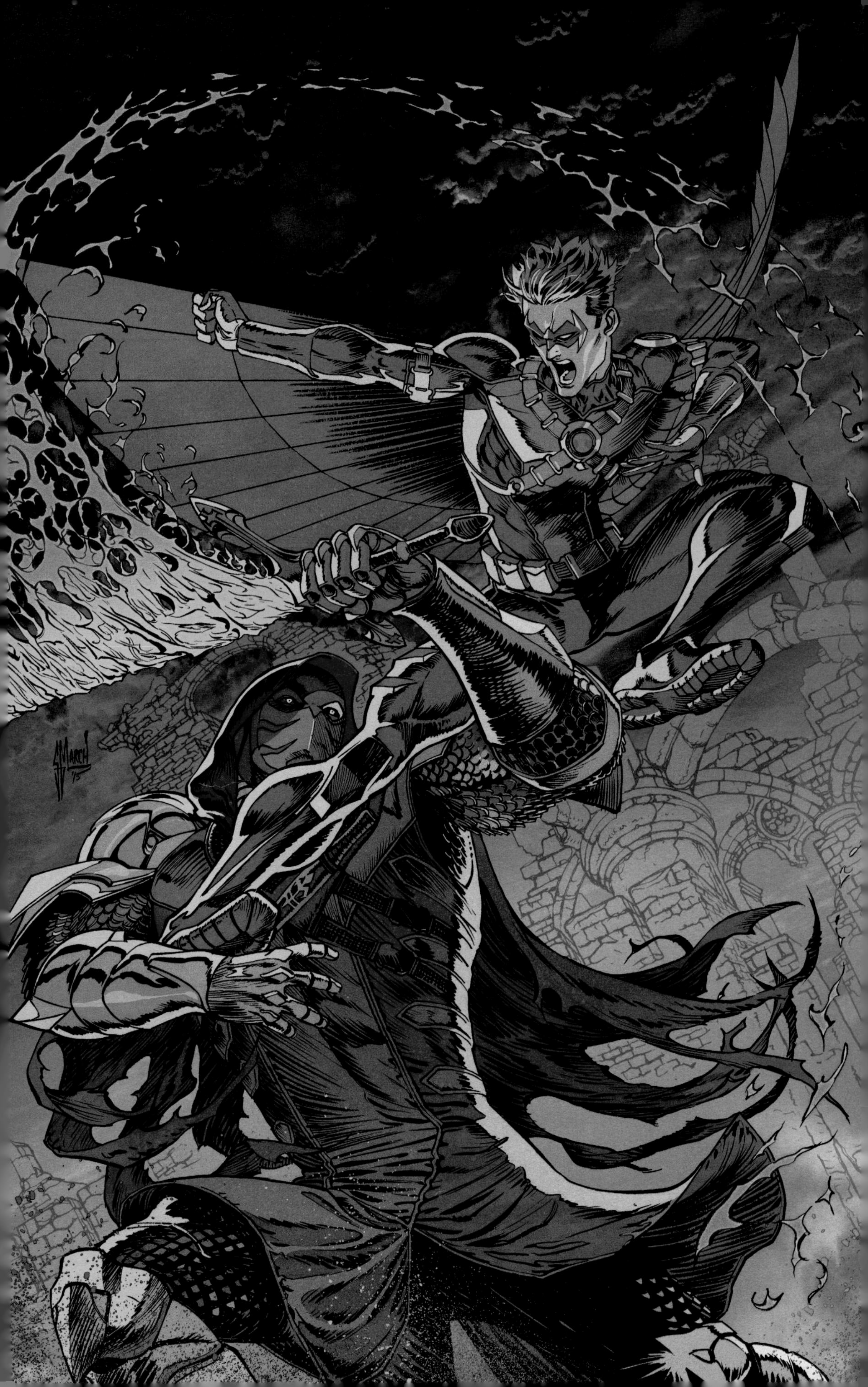

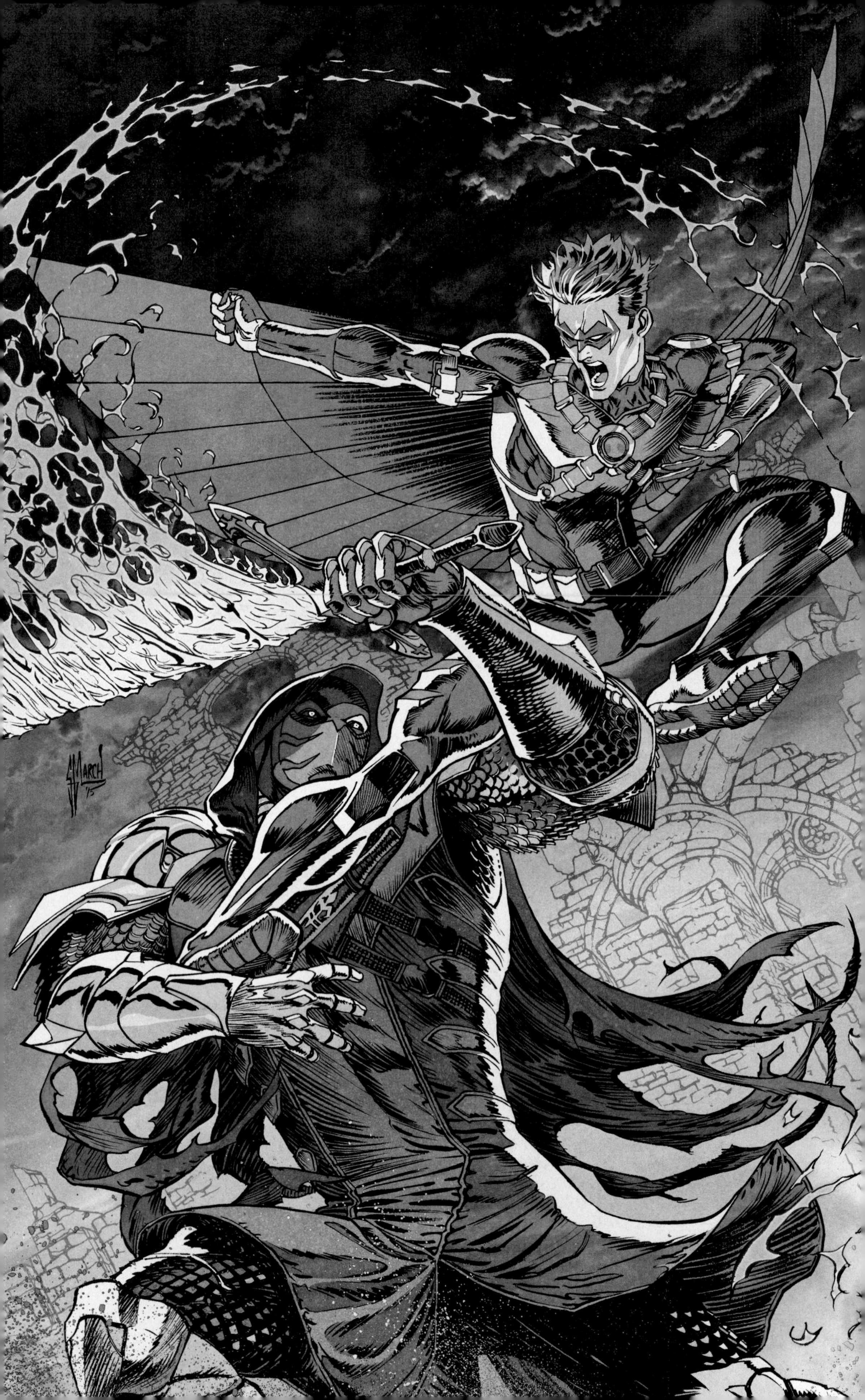

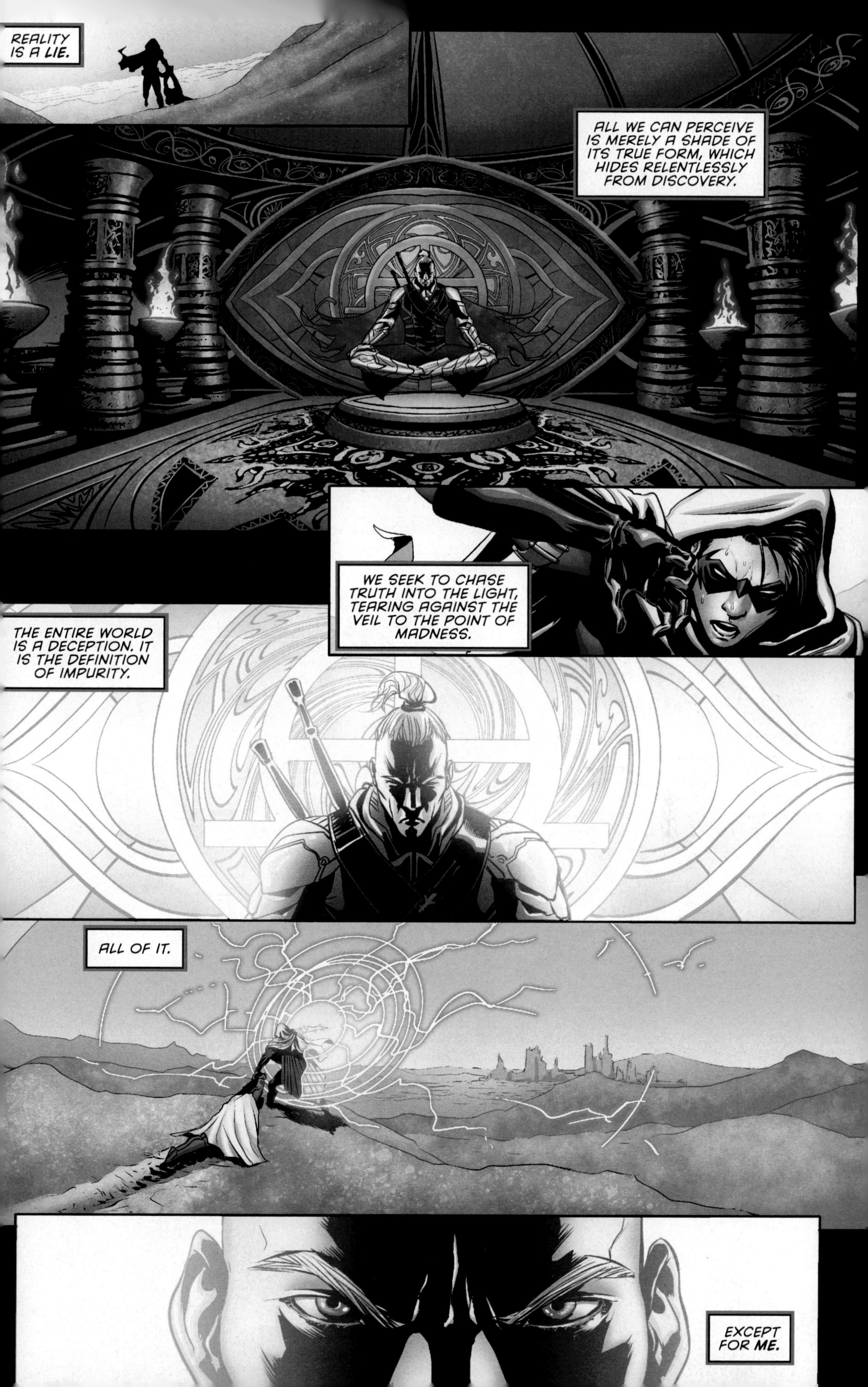
REALITY IS A LIE.
ALL WE CAN PERCEIVE IS MERELY A SHADE OF ITS TRUE FORM, WHICH HIDES RELENTLESSLY FROM DISCOVERY.
WE SEEK TO CHASE TRUTH INTO THE LIGHT, TEARING AGAINST THE VEIL TO THE POINT OF MADNESS.
THE ENTIRE WORLD IS A DECEPTION. IT IS THE DEFINITION OF IMPURITY.
ALL OF IT.
EXCEPT FOR ME.

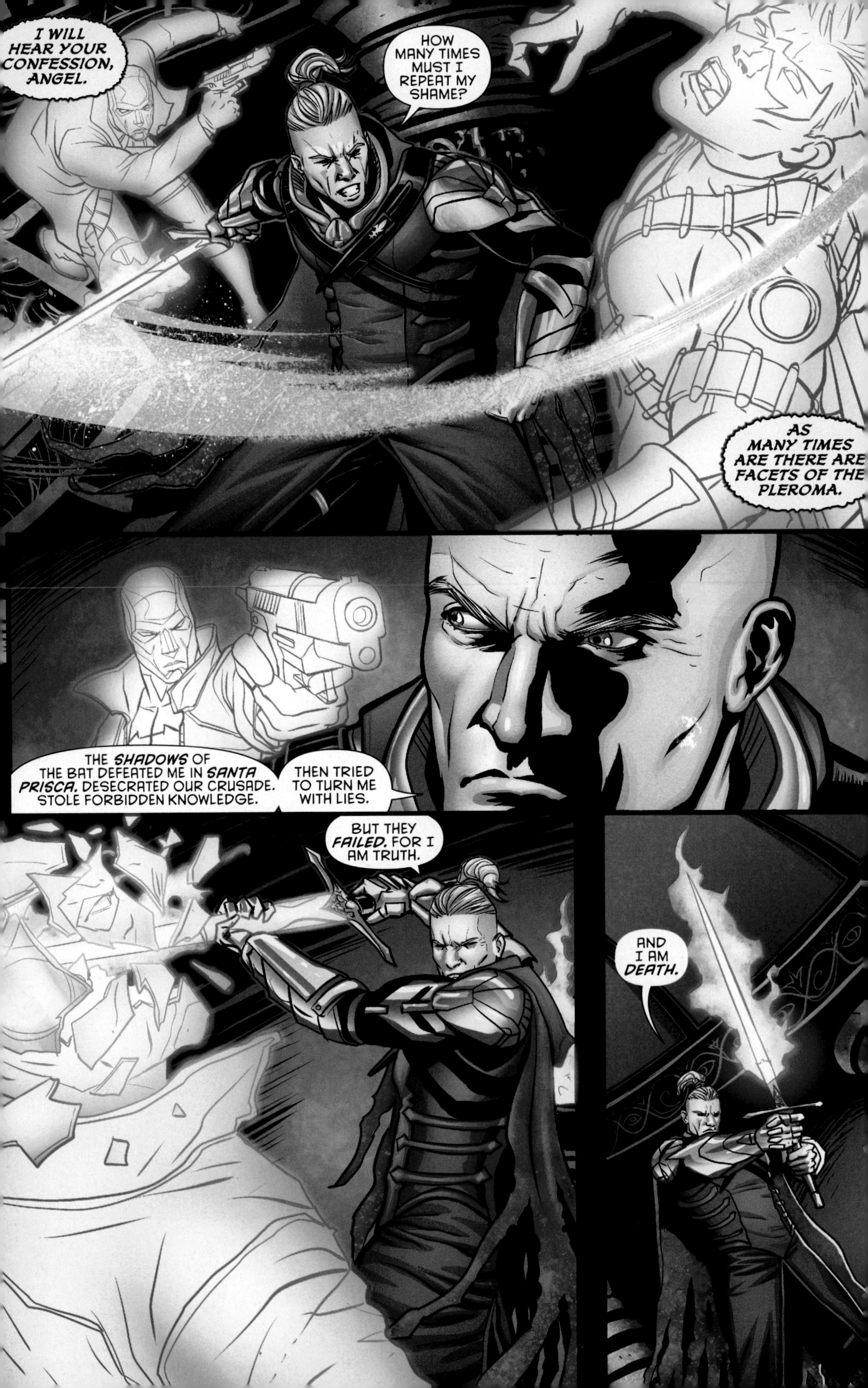
I WILL HEAR YOUR CONFESSION, ANGEL.
HOW MANY TIMES MUST I REPEAT MY SHAME?
AS MANY TIMES ARE THERE ARE FACETS OF THE PLEROMA.
THE *SHADOWS* OF THE BAT DEFEATED ME IN *SANTA PRISCA*. DESECRATED OUR CRUSADE. STOLE FORBIDDEN KNOWLEDGE.
THEN TRIED TO TURN ME WITH LIES.
BUT THEY *FAILED*. FOR I AM TRUTH.
AND I AM *DEATH*.

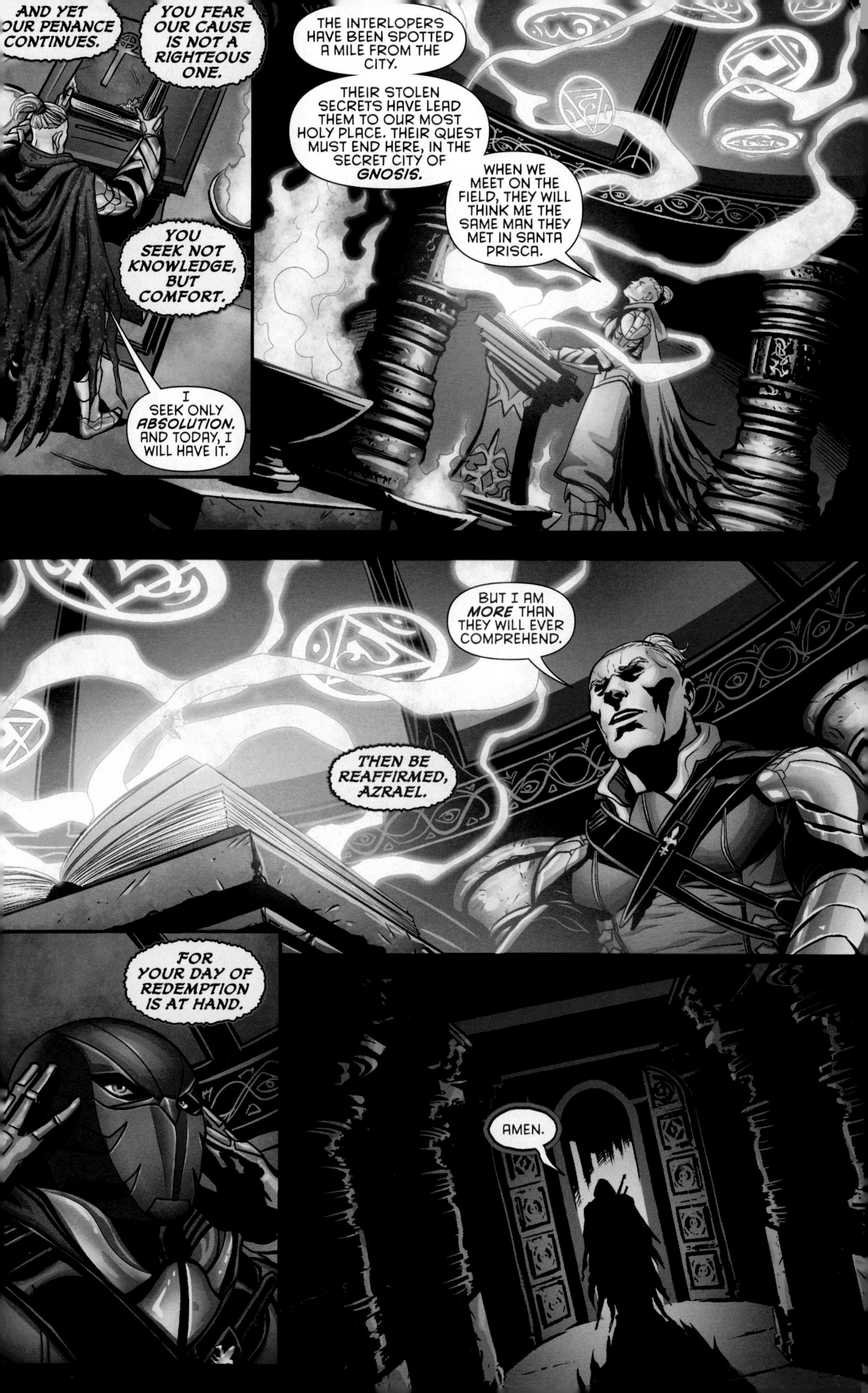
AND YET OUR PENANCE CONTINUES.
YOU FEAR OUR CAUSE IS NOT A RIGHTEOUS ONE.
YOU SEEK NOT KNOWLEDGE, BUT COMFORT.
I SEEK ONLY ABSOLUTION. AND TODAY, I WILL HAVE IT.
THE INTERLOPERS HAVE BEEN SPOTTED A MILE FROM THE CITY.
THEIR STOLEN SECRETS HAVE LEAD THEM TO OUR MOST HOLY PLACE. THEIR QUEST MUST END HERE, IN THE SECRET CITY OF GNOSIS.
WHEN WE MEET ON THE FIELD, THEY WILL THINK ME THE SAME MAN THEY MET IN SANTA PRISCA.
BUT I AM MORE THAN THEY WILL EVER COMPREHEND.
THEN BE REAFFIRMED, AZRAEL.
FOR YOUR DAY OF REDEMPTION IS AT HAND.
AMEN.

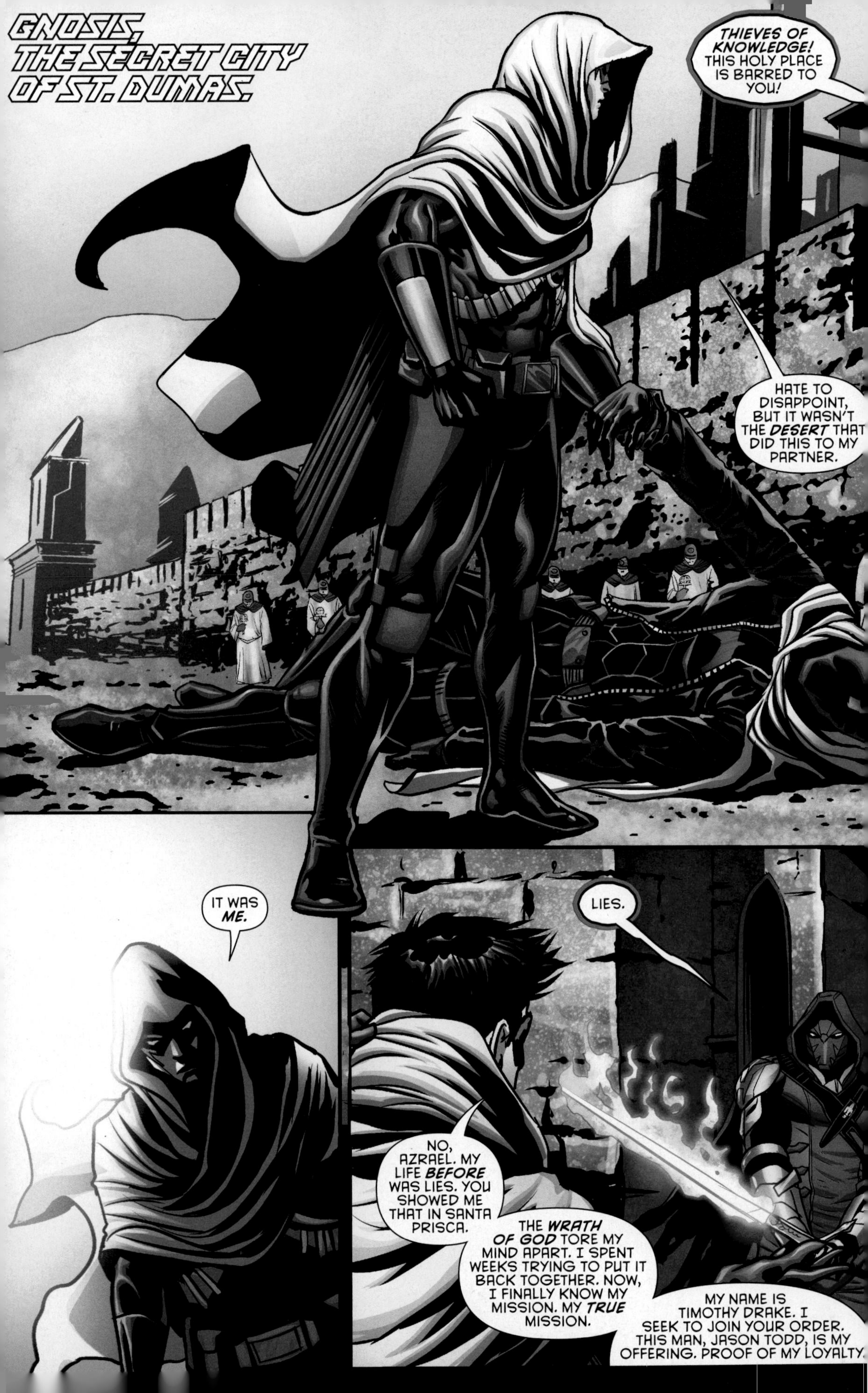
GNOSIS, THE SECRET CITY OF ST. DUMAS.
THIEVES OF KNOWLEDGE! THIS HOLY PLACE IS BARRED TO YOU!
HATE TO DISAPPOINT, BUT IT WASN'T THE DESERT THAT DID THIS TO MY PARTNER.
IT WAS ME.
LIES.
NO, AZRAEL. MY LIFE BEFORE WAS LIES. YOU SHOWED ME THAT IN SANTA PRISCA.
THE WRATH OF GOD TORE MY MIND APART. I SPENT WEEKS TRYING TO PUT IT BACK TOGETHER. NOW, I FINALLY KNOW MY MISSION. MY TRUE MISSION.
MY NAME IS TIMOTHY DRAKE. I SEEK TO JOIN YOUR ORDER. THIS MAN, JASON TODD, IS MY OFFERING. PROOF OF MY LOYALTY.

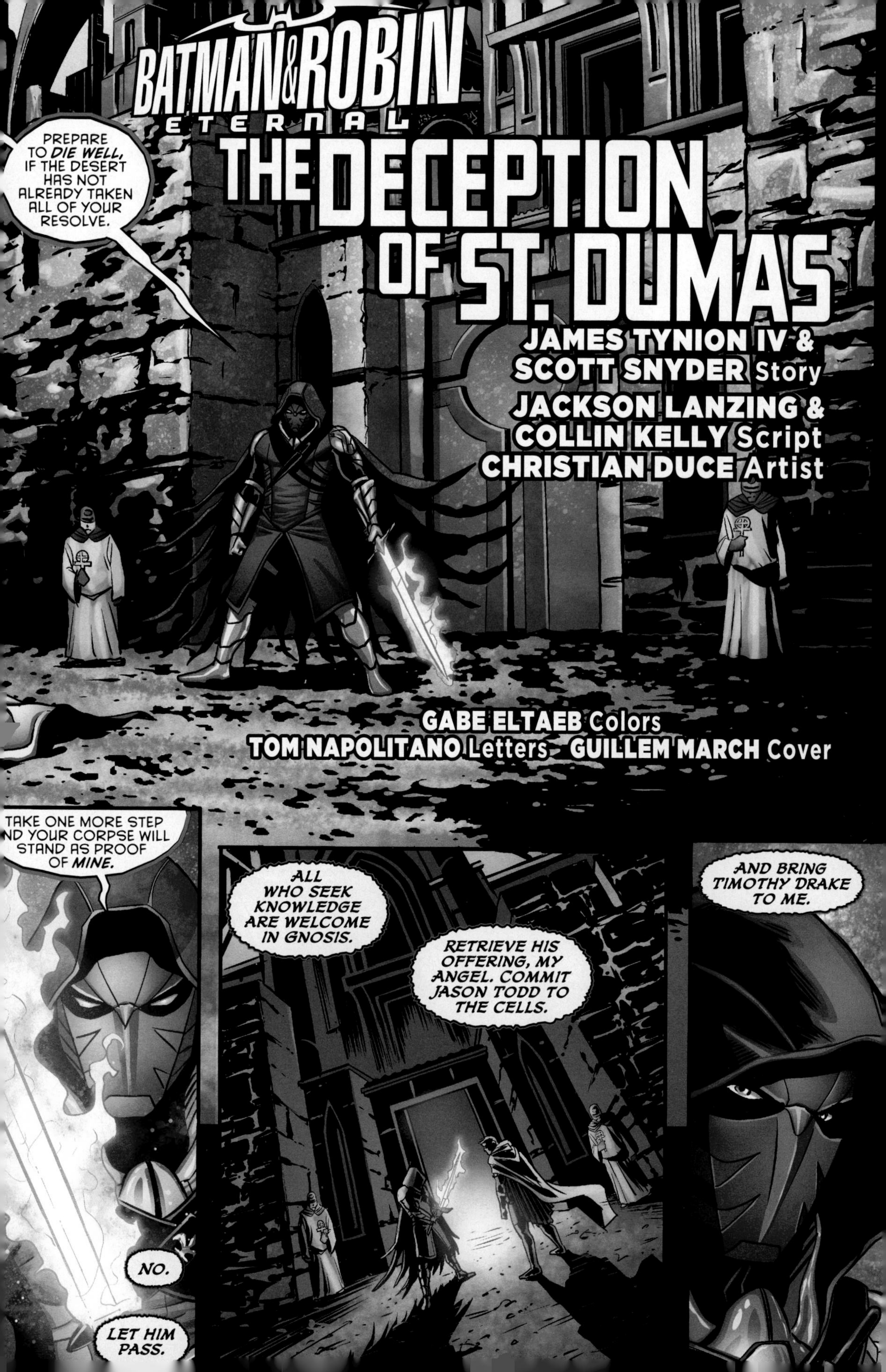

BATMAN & ROBIN ETERNAL
PREPARE TO DIE WELL, IF THE DESERT HAS NOT ALREADY TAKEN ALL OF YOUR RESOLVE.
THE DECEPTION OF ST. DUMAS
JAMES TYNION IV & SCOTT SNYDER Story
JACKSON LANZING & COLLIN KELLY Script
CHRISTIAN DUCE Artist
GABE ELTAEB Colors
TOM NAPOLITANO Letters - GUILLEM MARCH Cover
TAKE ONE MORE STEP ND YOUR CORPSE WILL STAND AS PROOF OF MINE.
NO.
LET HIM PASS.
ALL WHO SEEK KNOWLEDGE ARE WELCOME IN GNOSIS.
RETRIEVE HIS OFFERING, MY ANGEL. COMMIT JASON TODD TO THE CELLS.
AND BRING TIMOTHY DRAKE TO ME.

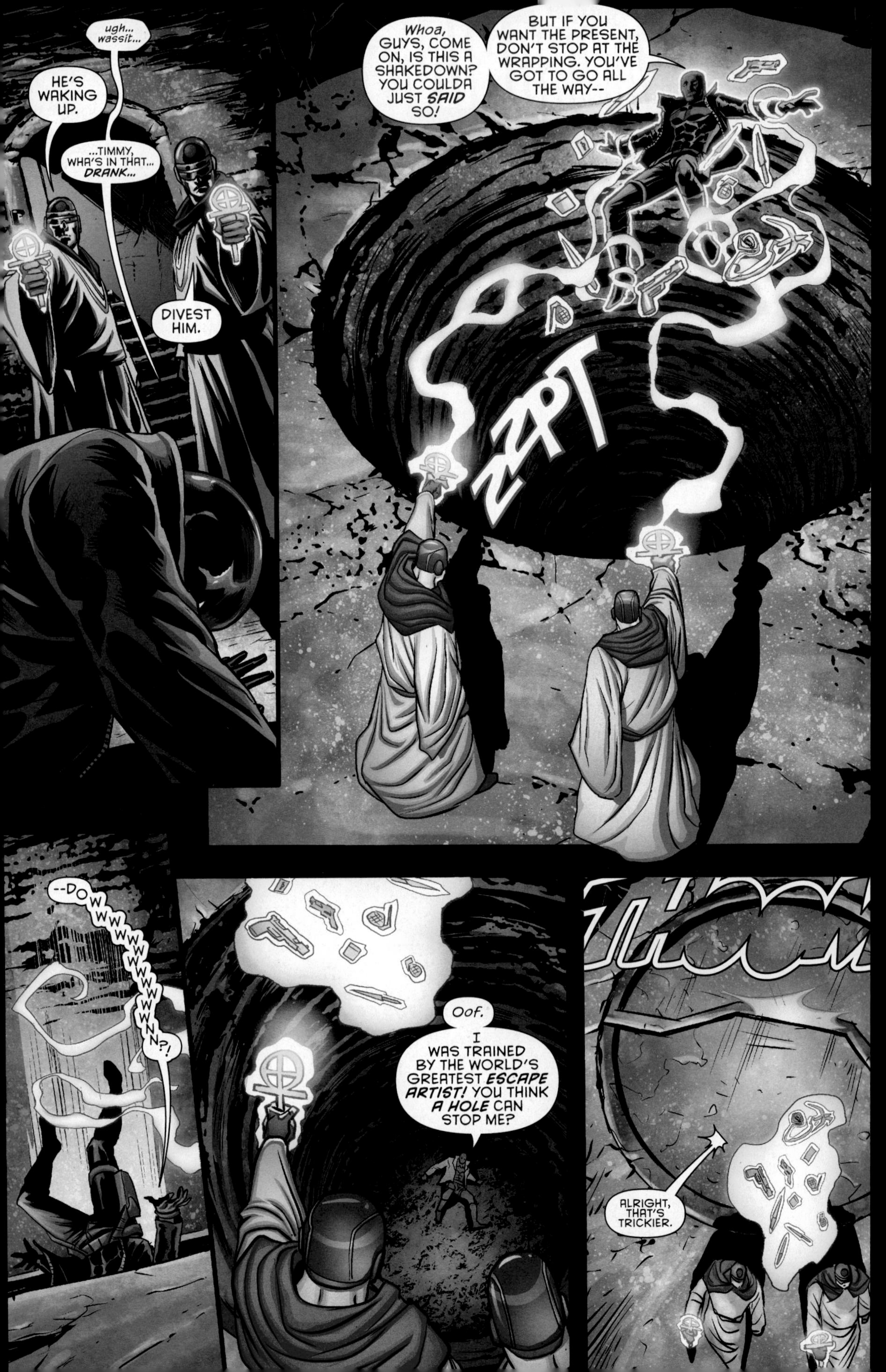
ugh... wassit...
HE'S WAKING UP.
...TIMMY, WHA'S IN THAT... DRANK...
DIVEST HIM.
Whoa, GUYS, COME ON, IS THIS A SHAKEDOWN? YOU COULDA JUST SAID SO!
BUT IF YOU WANT THE PRESENT, DON'T STOP AT THE WRAPPING. YOU'VE GOT TO GO ALL THE WAY--
ZZZPT
--DOWWWWWWWWWWWN?!
Oof.
I WAS TRAINED BY THE WORLD'S GREATEST ESCAPE ARTIST! YOU THINK A HOLE CAN STOP ME?
ALRIGHT, THAT'S TRICKIER.

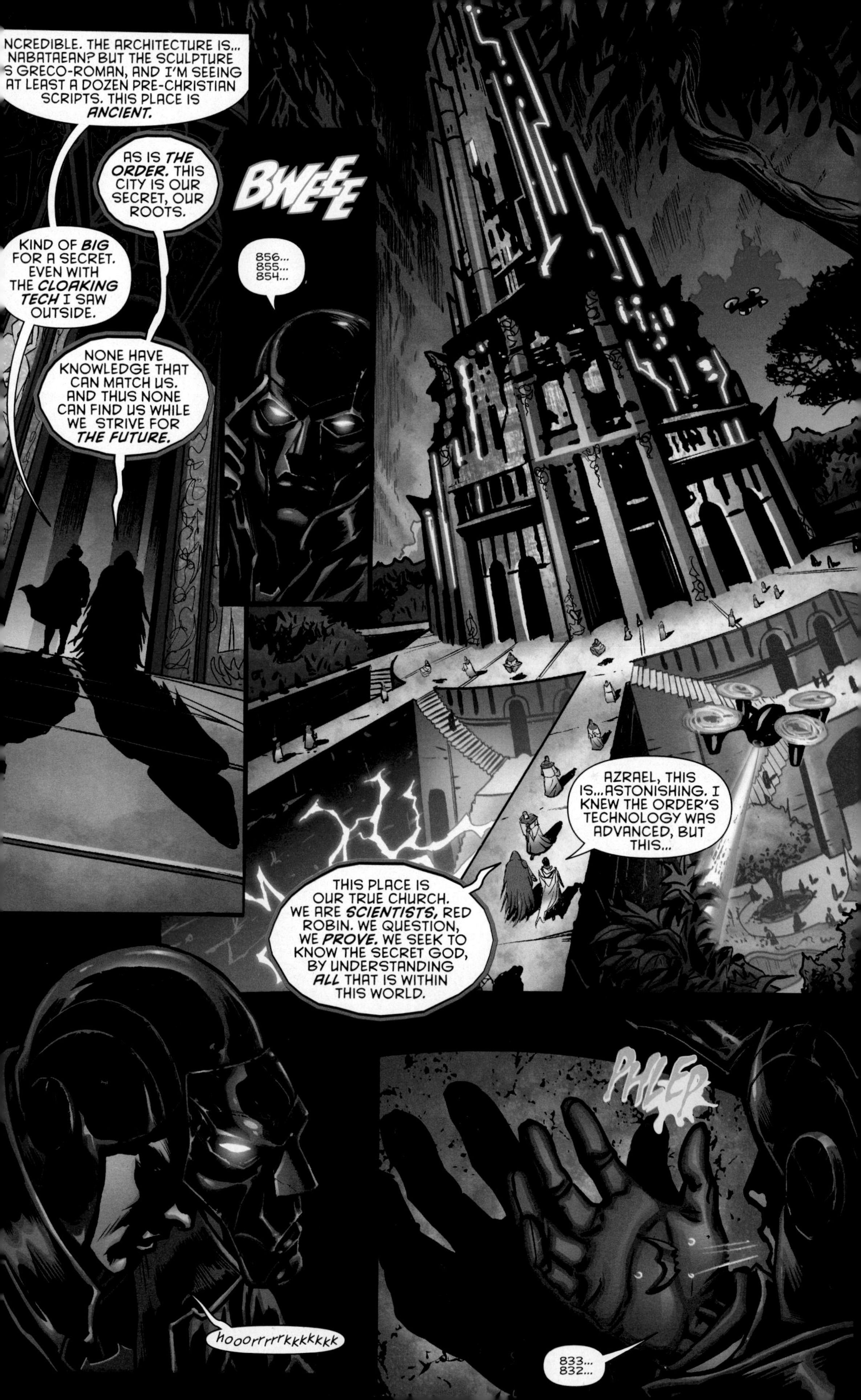
NCREDIBLE. THE ARCHITECTURE IS... NABATAEAN? BUT THE SCULPTURE S GRECO-ROMAN, AND I'M SEEING AT LEAST A DOZEN PRE-CHRISTIAN SCRIPTS. THIS PLACE IS ANCIENT.
AS IS THE ORDER. THIS CITY IS OUR SECRET, OUR ROOTS.
KIND OF BIG FOR A SECRET. EVEN WITH THE CLOAKING TECH I SAW OUTSIDE.
NONE HAVE KNOWLEDGE THAT CAN MATCH US. AND THUS NONE CAN FIND US WHILE WE STRIVE FOR THE FUTURE.
BWEEE
856... 855... 854...
AZRAEL, THIS IS...ASTONISHING. I KNEW THE ORDER'S TECHNOLOGY WAS ADVANCED, BUT THIS...
THIS PLACE IS OUR TRUE CHURCH. WE ARE SCIENTISTS, RED ROBIN. WE QUESTION, WE PROVE. WE SEEK TO KNOW THE SECRET GOD, BY UNDERSTANDING ALL THAT IS WITHIN THIS WORLD.
hooorrrrrkkkkkkk
PHLEP
833... 832...

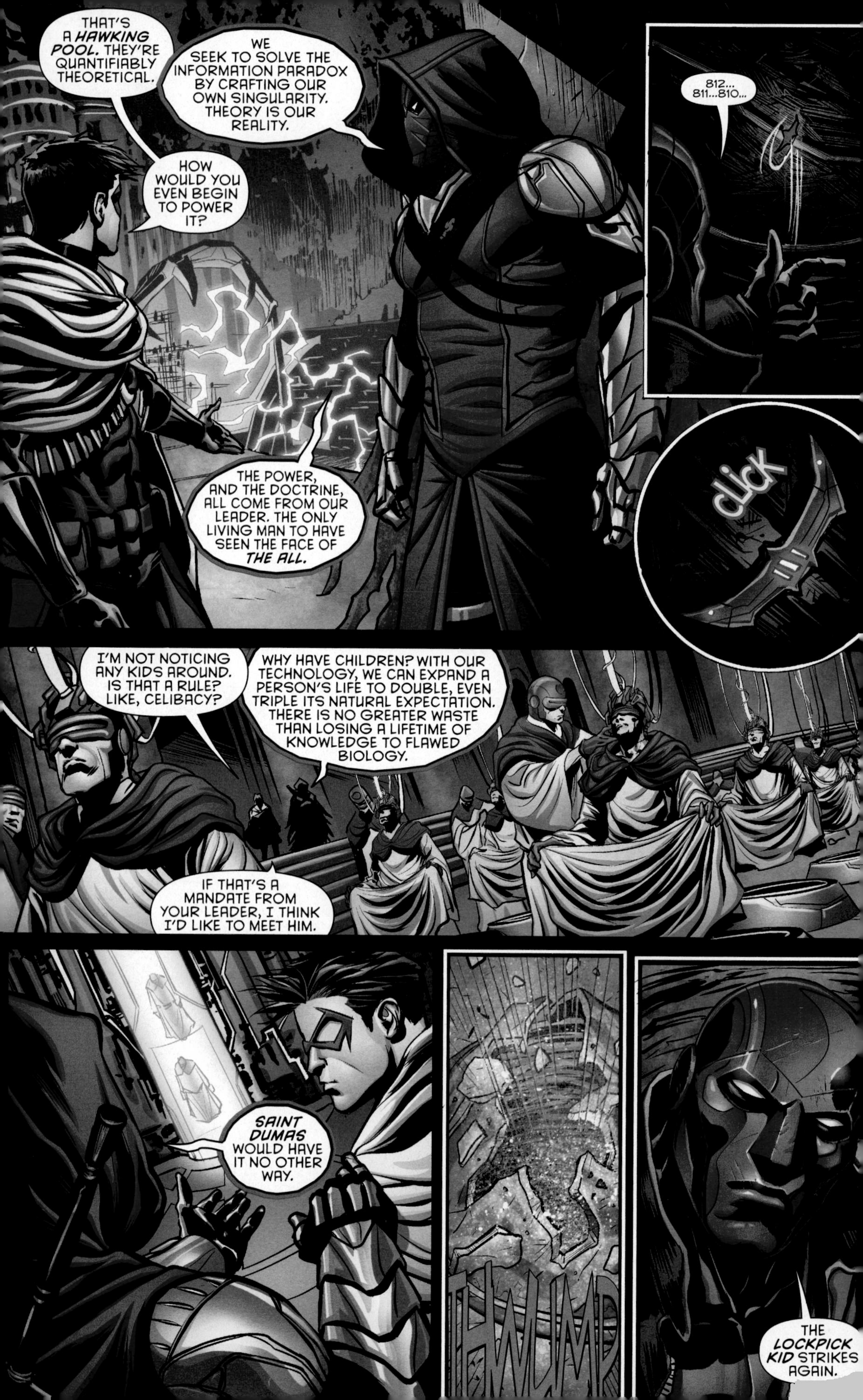
THAT'S A HAWKING POOL. THEY'RE QUANTIFIABLY THEORETICAL.
WE SEEK TO SOLVE THE INFORMATION PARADOX BY CRAFTING OUR OWN SINGULARITY. THEORY IS OUR REALITY.
HOW WOULD YOU EVEN BEGIN TO POWER IT?
THE POWER, AND THE DOCTRINE, ALL COME FROM OUR LEADER. THE ONLY LIVING MAN TO HAVE SEEN THE FACE OF THE ALL.
812... 811...810...
CLICK
I'M NOT NOTICING ANY KIDS AROUND. IS THAT A RULE? LIKE, CELIBACY?
WHY HAVE CHILDREN? WITH OUR TECHNOLOGY, WE CAN EXPAND A PERSON'S LIFE TO DOUBLE, EVEN TRIPLE ITS NATURAL EXPECTATION. THERE IS NO GREATER WASTE THAN LOSING A LIFETIME OF KNOWLEDGE TO FLAWED BIOLOGY.
IF THAT'S A MANDATE FROM YOUR LEADER, I THINK I'D LIKE TO MEET HIM.
SAINT DUMAS WOULD HAVE IT NO OTHER WAY.
THUMP
THE LOCKPICK KID STRIKES AGAIN.

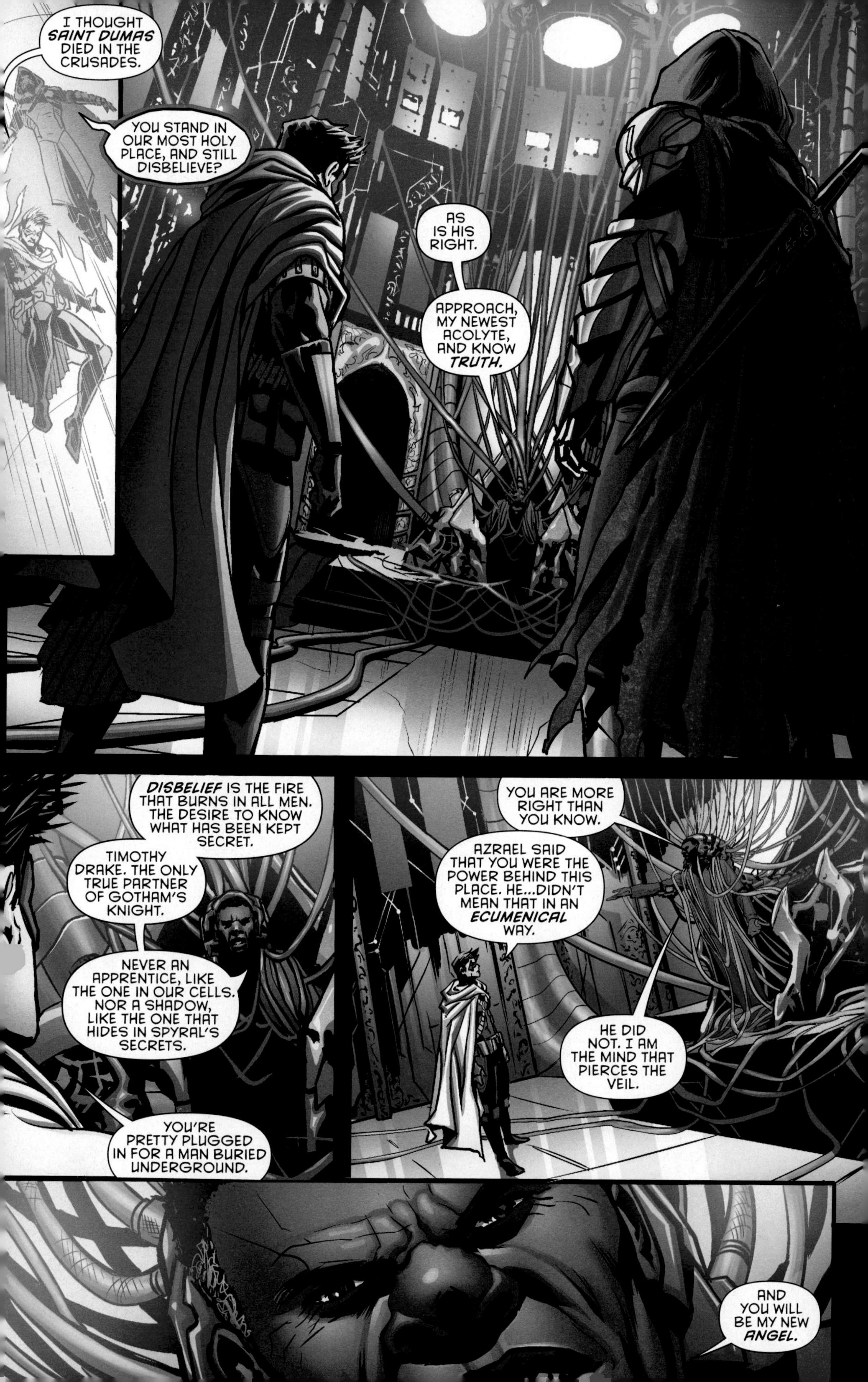
I THOUGHT SAINT DUMAS DIED IN THE CRUSADES.
YOU STAND IN OUR MOST HOLY PLACE, AND STILL DISBELIEVE?
AS IS HIS RIGHT.
APPROACH, MY NEWEST ACOLYTE, AND KNOW TRUTH.
DISBELIEF IS THE FIRE THAT BURNS IN ALL MEN. THE DESIRE TO KNOW WHAT HAS BEEN KEPT SECRET.
TIMOTHY DRAKE. THE ONLY TRUE PARTNER OF GOTHAM'S KNIGHT.
NEVER AN APPRENTICE, LIKE THE ONE IN OUR CELLS. NOR A SHADOW, LIKE THE ONE THAT HIDES IN SPYRAL'S SECRETS.
YOU'RE PRETTY PLUGGED IN FOR A MAN BURIED UNDERGROUND.
YOU ARE MORE RIGHT THAN YOU KNOW.
AZRAEL SAID THAT YOU WERE THE POWER BEHIND THIS PLACE. HE...DIDN'T MEAN THAT IN AN ECUMENICAL WAY.
HE DID NOT. I AM THE MIND THAT PIERCES THE VEIL.
AND YOU WILL BE MY NEW ANGEL.

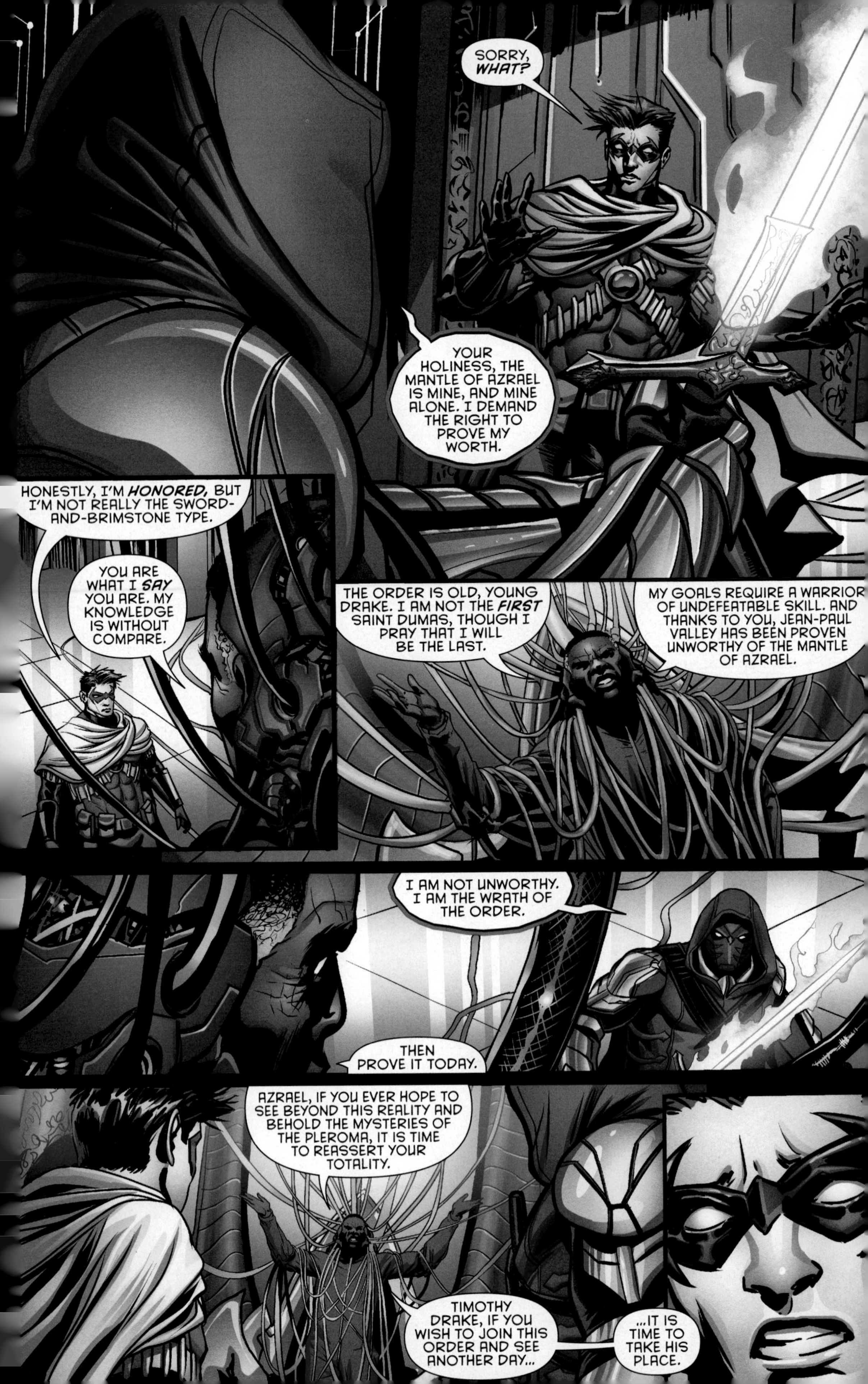
SORRY, *WHAT?*
YOUR HOLINESS, THE MANTLE OF AZRAEL IS MINE, AND MINE ALONE. I DEMAND THE RIGHT TO PROVE MY WORTH.
HONESTLY, I'M *HONORED,* BUT I'M NOT REALLY THE SWORD-AND-BRIMSTONE TYPE.
YOU ARE WHAT I *SAY* YOU ARE. MY KNOWLEDGE IS WITHOUT COMPARE.
THE ORDER IS OLD, YOUNG DRAKE. I AM NOT THE *FIRST* SAINT DUMAS, THOUGH I PRAY THAT I WILL BE THE LAST.
MY GOALS REQUIRE A WARRIOR OF UNDEFEATABLE SKILL. AND THANKS TO YOU, JEAN-PAUL VALLEY HAS BEEN PROVEN UNWORTHY OF THE MANTLE OF AZRAEL.
I AM NOT UNWORTHY. I AM THE WRATH OF THE ORDER.
THEN PROVE IT TODAY.
AZRAEL, IF YOU EVER HOPE TO SEE BEYOND THIS REALITY AND BEHOLD THE MYSTERIES OF THE PLEROMA, IT IS TIME TO REASSERT YOUR TOTALITY.
TIMOTHY DRAKE, IF YOU WISH TO JOIN THIS ORDER AND SEE ANOTHER DAY...
...IT IS TIME TO TAKE HIS PLACE.

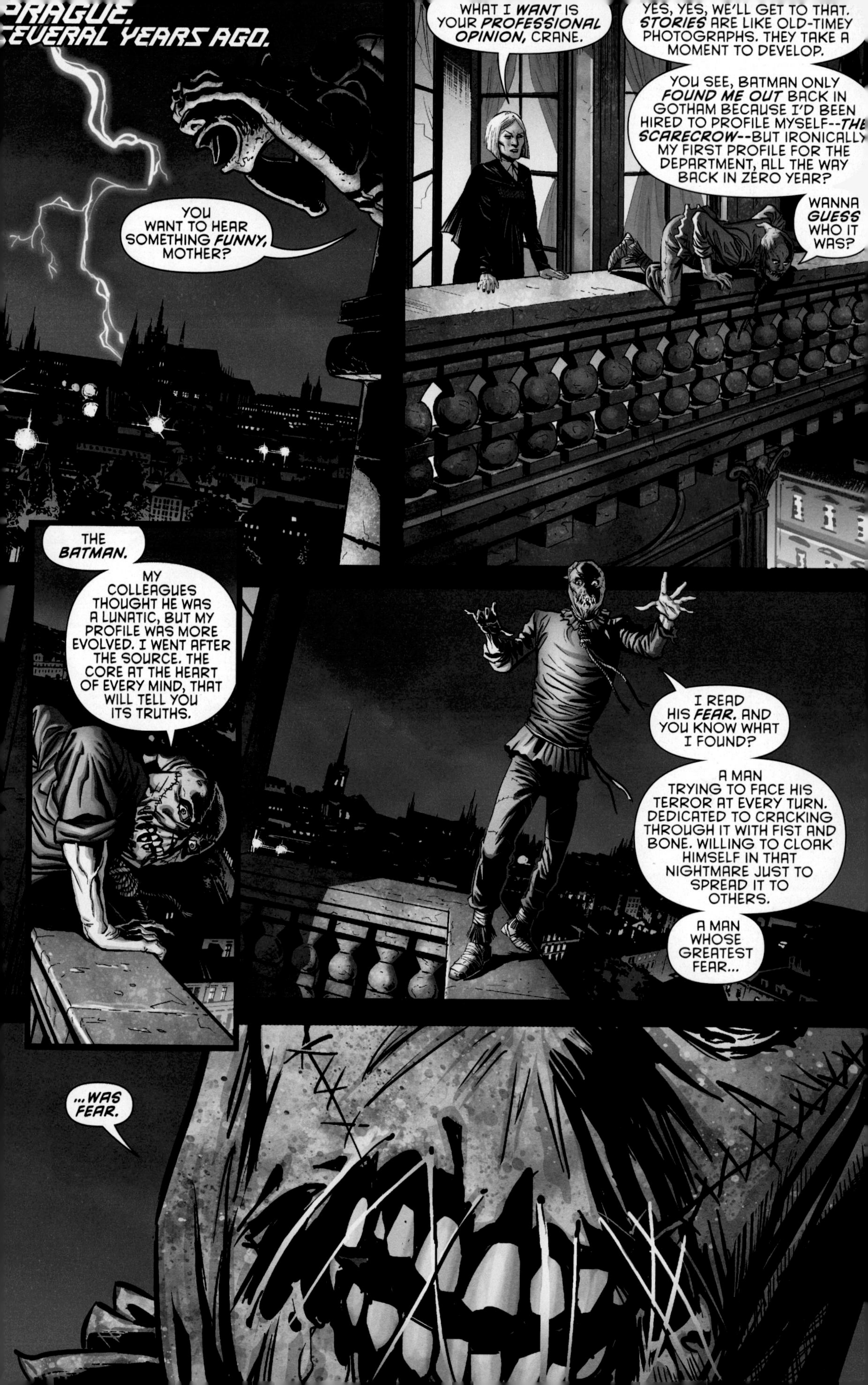
PRAGUE. SEVERAL YEARS AGO.
YOU WANT TO HEAR SOMETHING FUNNY, MOTHER?
WHAT I WANT IS YOUR PROFESSIONAL OPINION, CRANE.
YES, YES, WE'LL GET TO THAT. STORIES ARE LIKE OLD-TIMEY PHOTOGRAPHS. THEY TAKE A MOMENT TO DEVELOP.
YOU SEE, BATMAN ONLY FOUND ME OUT BACK IN GOTHAM BECAUSE I'D BEEN HIRED TO PROFILE MYSELF--THE SCARECROW--BUT IRONICALLY MY FIRST PROFILE FOR THE DEPARTMENT, ALL THE WAY BACK IN ZERO YEAR?
WANNA GUESS WHO IT WAS?
THE BATMAN.
MY COLLEAGUES THOUGHT HE WAS A LUNATIC, BUT MY PROFILE WAS MORE EVOLVED. I WENT AFTER THE SOURCE. THE CORE AT THE HEART OF EVERY MIND, THAT WILL TELL YOU ITS TRUTHS.
I READ HIS FEAR. AND YOU KNOW WHAT I FOUND?
A MAN TRYING TO FACE HIS TERROR AT EVERY TURN. DEDICATED TO CRACKING THROUGH IT WITH FIST AND BONE. WILLING TO CLOAK HIMSELF IN THAT NIGHTMARE JUST TO SPREAD IT TO OTHERS.
A MAN WHOSE GREATEST FEAR...
...WAS FEAR.

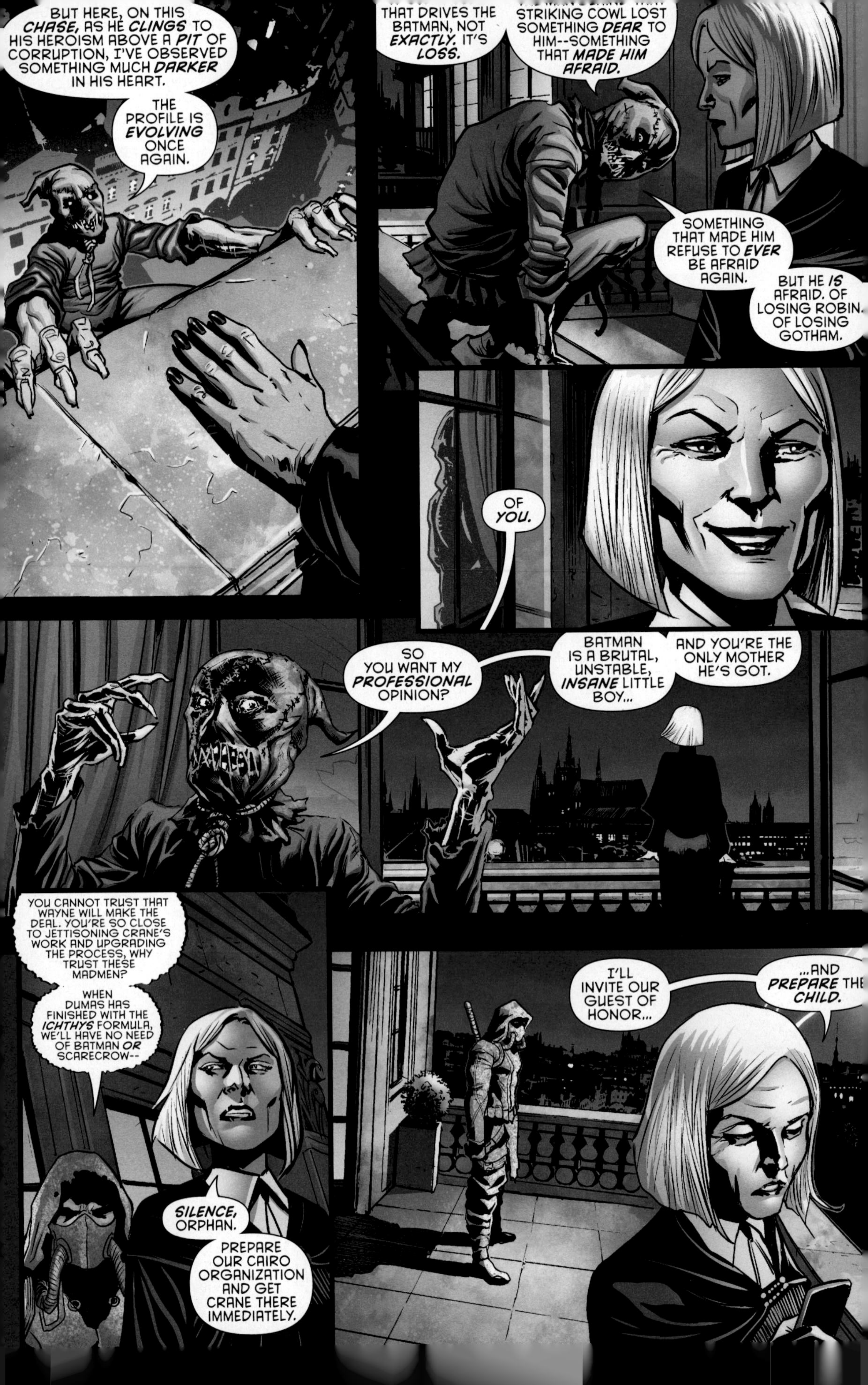

BUT HERE, ON THIS *CHASE,* AS HE *CLINGS* TO HIS HEROISM ABOVE A *PIT* OF CORRUPTION, I'VE OBSERVED SOMETHING MUCH *DARKER* IN HIS HEART.
THE PROFILE IS *EVOLVING* ONCE AGAIN.
THAT DRIVES THE BATMAN, NOT *EXACTLY.* IT'S *LOSS.*
STRIKING COWL LOST SOMETHING *DEAR* TO HIM--SOMETHING THAT *MADE HIM AFRAID.*
SOMETHING THAT MADE HIM REFUSE TO *EVER* BE AFRAID AGAIN.
BUT HE *IS* AFRAID. OF LOSING ROBIN. OF LOSING GOTHAM.
OF *YOU.*
SO YOU WANT MY *PROFESSIONAL* OPINION?
BATMAN IS A BRUTAL, UNSTABLE, *INSANE* LITTLE BOY...
AND YOU'RE THE ONLY MOTHER HE'S GOT.
YOU CANNOT TRUST THAT WAYNE WILL MAKE THE DEAL. YOU'RE SO CLOSE TO JETTISONING CRANE'S WORK AND UPGRADING THE PROCESS, WHY TRUST THESE MADMEN?
WHEN DUMAS HAS FINISHED WITH THE *ICHTHYS* FORMULA, WE'LL HAVE NO NEED OF BATMAN *OR* SCARECROW--
SILENCE, ORPHAN.
PREPARE OUR CAIRO ORGANIZATION AND GET CRANE THERE IMMEDIATELY.
I'LL INVITE OUR GUEST OF HONOR...
...AND *PREPARE* THE *CHILD.*

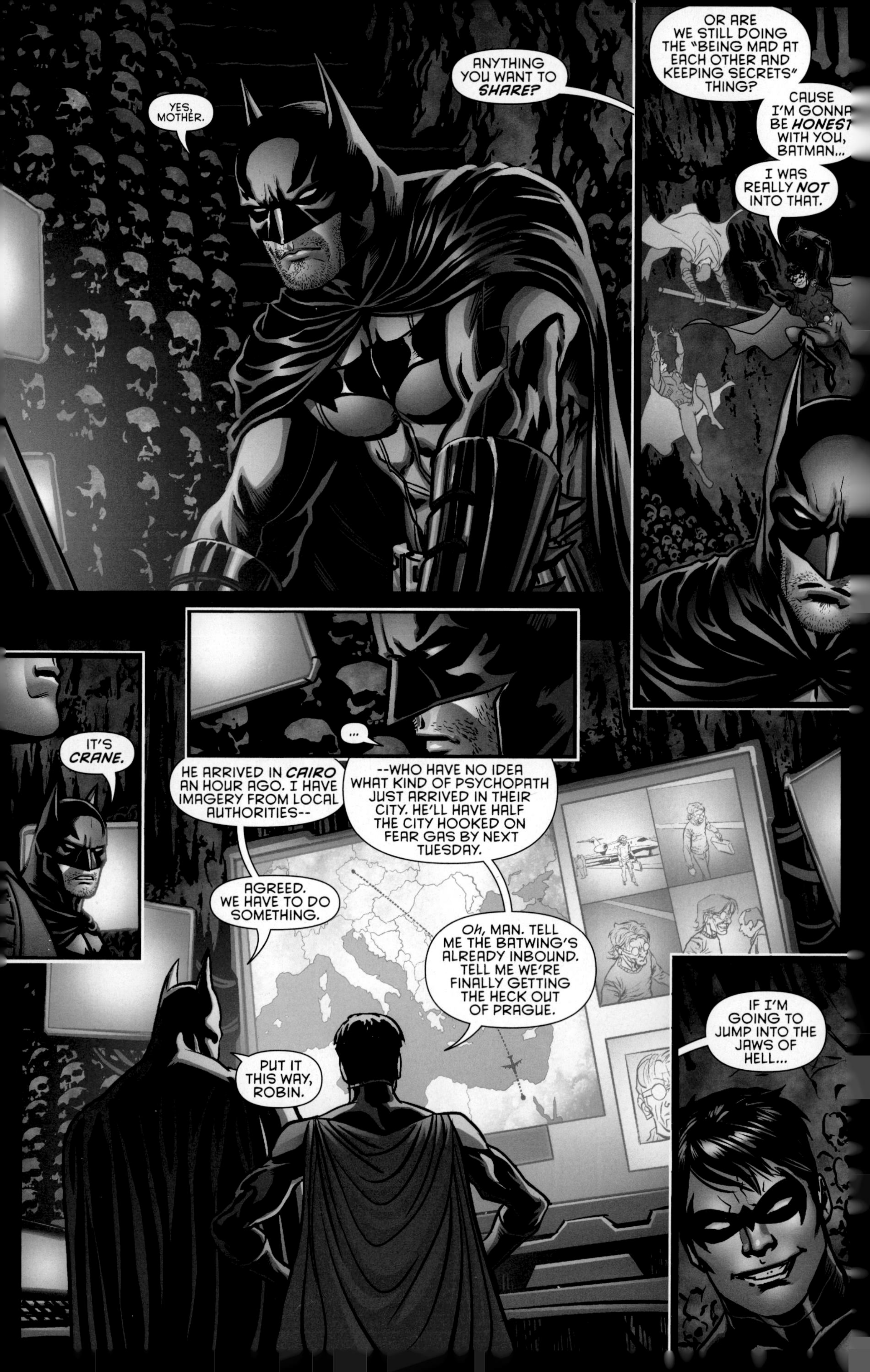
YES, MOTHER.
ANYTHING YOU WANT TO SHARE?
OR ARE WE STILL DOING THE "BEING MAD AT EACH OTHER AND KEEPING SECRETS" THING?
CAUSE I'M GONNA BE HONEST WITH YOU, BATMAN...
I WAS REALLY NOT INTO THAT.
...
IT'S CRANE.
HE ARRIVED IN CAIRO AN HOUR AGO. I HAVE IMAGERY FROM LOCAL AUTHORITIES--
--WHO HAVE NO IDEA WHAT KIND OF PSYCHOPATH JUST ARRIVED IN THEIR CITY. HE'LL HAVE HALF THE CITY HOOKED ON FEAR GAS BY NEXT TUESDAY.
AGREED. WE HAVE TO DO SOMETHING.
Oh, MAN. TELL ME THE BATWING'S ALREADY INBOUND. TELL ME WE'RE FINALLY GETTING THE HECK OUT OF PRAGUE.
PUT IT THIS WAY, ROBIN.
IF I'M GOING TO JUMP INTO THE JAWS OF HELL...

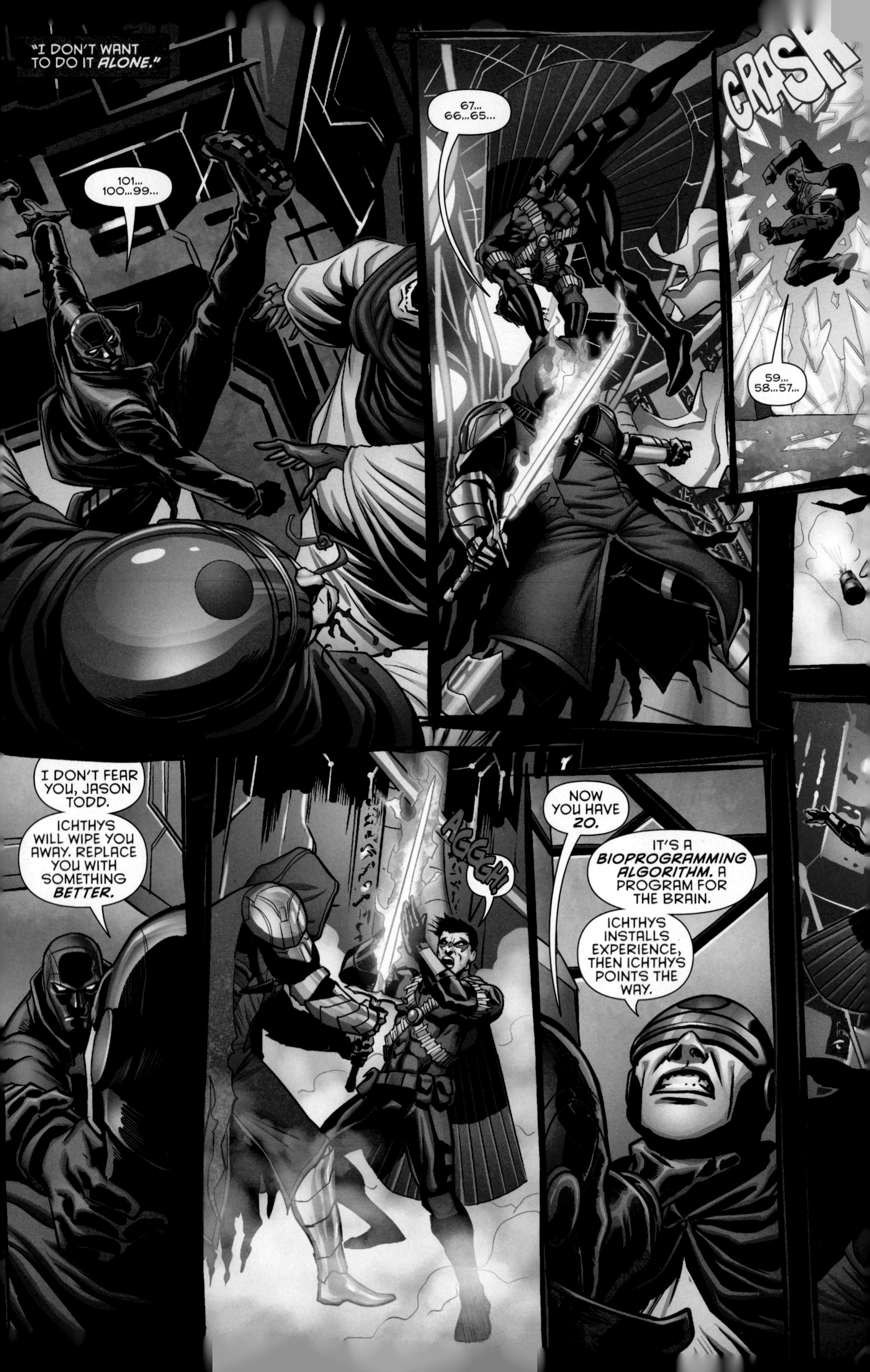
"I DON'T WANT TO DO IT ALONE."
101... 100...99...
67... 66...65...
CRASH
59... 58...57...
I DON'T FEAR YOU, JASON TODD.
ICHTHYS WILL WIPE YOU AWAY. REPLACE YOU WITH SOMETHING BETTER.
AGGGH!
NOW YOU HAVE 20.
IT'S A BIOPROGRAMMING ALGORITHM. A PROGRAM FOR THE BRAIN.
ICHTHYS INSTALLS EXPERIENCE, THEN ICHTHYS POINTS THE WAY.

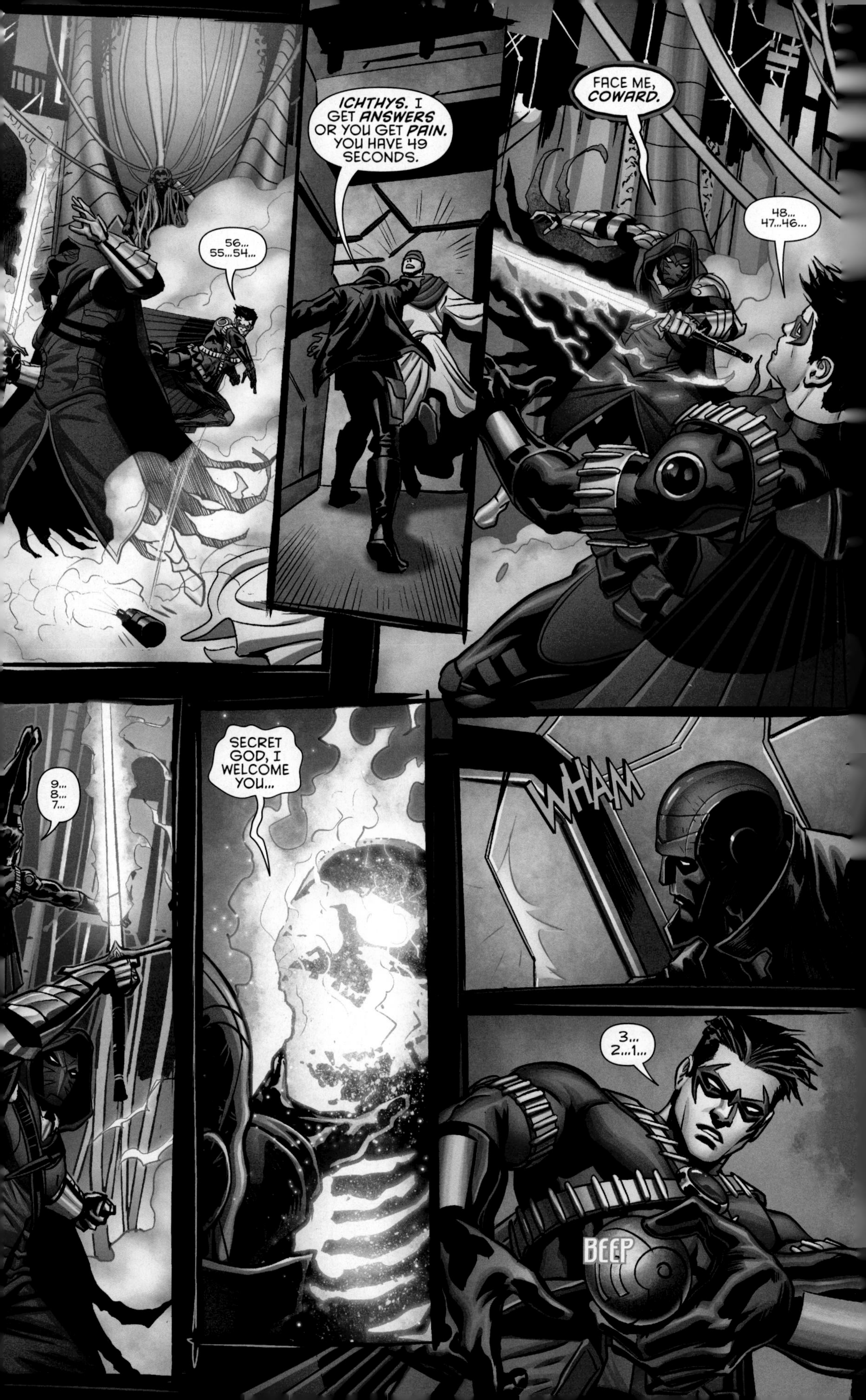
56...
55...54...
ICHTHYS. I GET ANSWERS OR YOU GET PAIN. YOU HAVE 49 SECONDS.
FACE ME, COWARD.
48...
47...46...
9...
8...
7...
SECRET GOD, I WELCOME YOU...
WHAM
3...
2...1...
BEEP

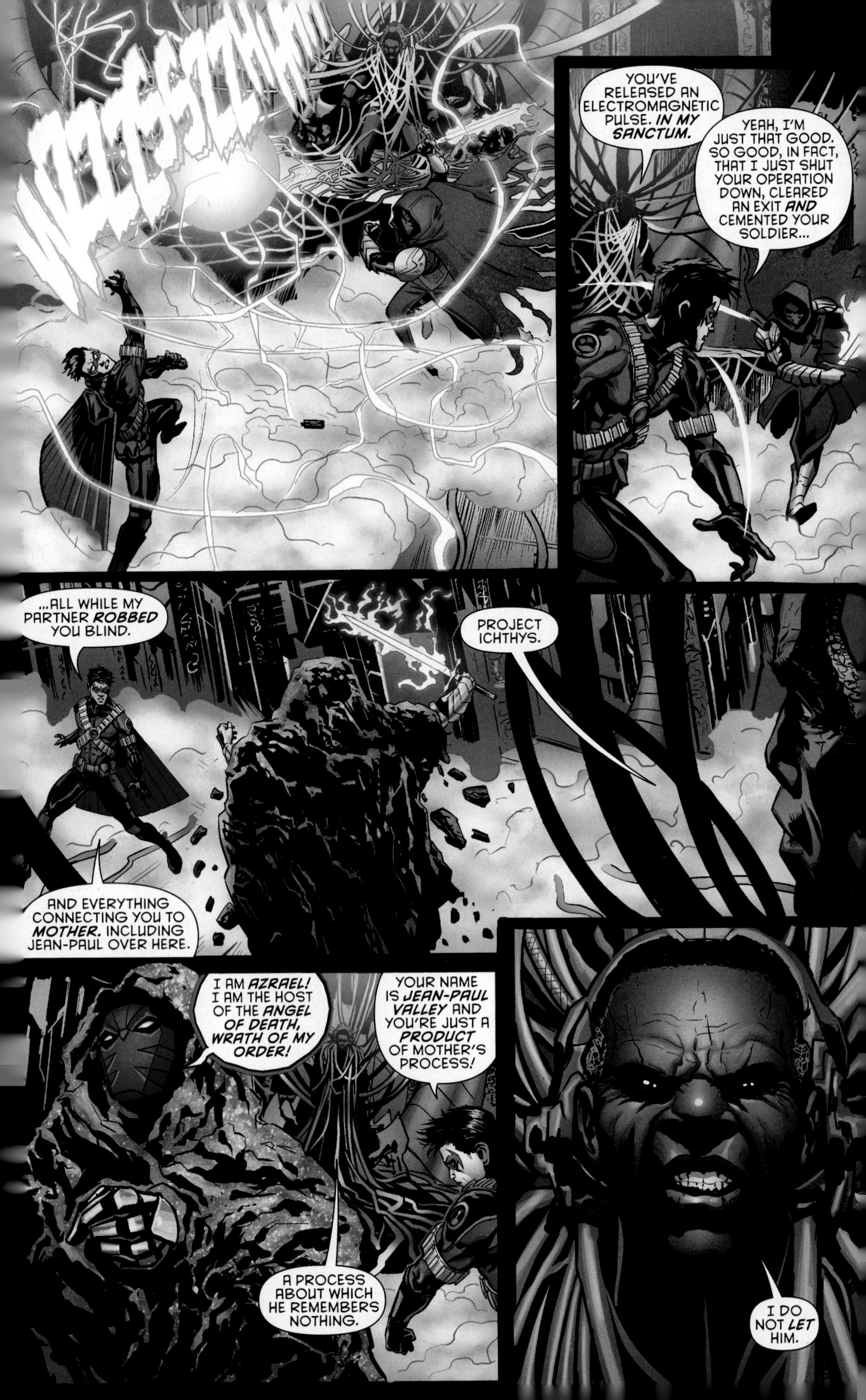
YOU'VE RELEASED AN ELECTROMAGNETIC PULSE. IN MY SANCTUM.
YEAH, I'M JUST THAT GOOD. SO GOOD, IN FACT, THAT I JUST SHUT YOUR OPERATION DOWN, CLEARED AN EXIT AND CEMENTED YOUR SOLDIER...
...ALL WHILE MY PARTNER ROBBED YOU BLIND.
AND EVERYTHING CONNECTING YOU TO MOTHER. INCLUDING JEAN-PAUL OVER HERE.
PROJECT ICHTHYS.
I AM AZRAEL! I AM THE HOST OF THE ANGEL OF DEATH, WRATH OF MY ORDER!
YOUR NAME IS JEAN-PAUL VALLEY AND YOU'RE JUST A PRODUCT OF MOTHER'S PROCESS!
A PROCESS ABOUT WHICH HE REMEMBERS NOTHING.
I DO NOT LET HIM.

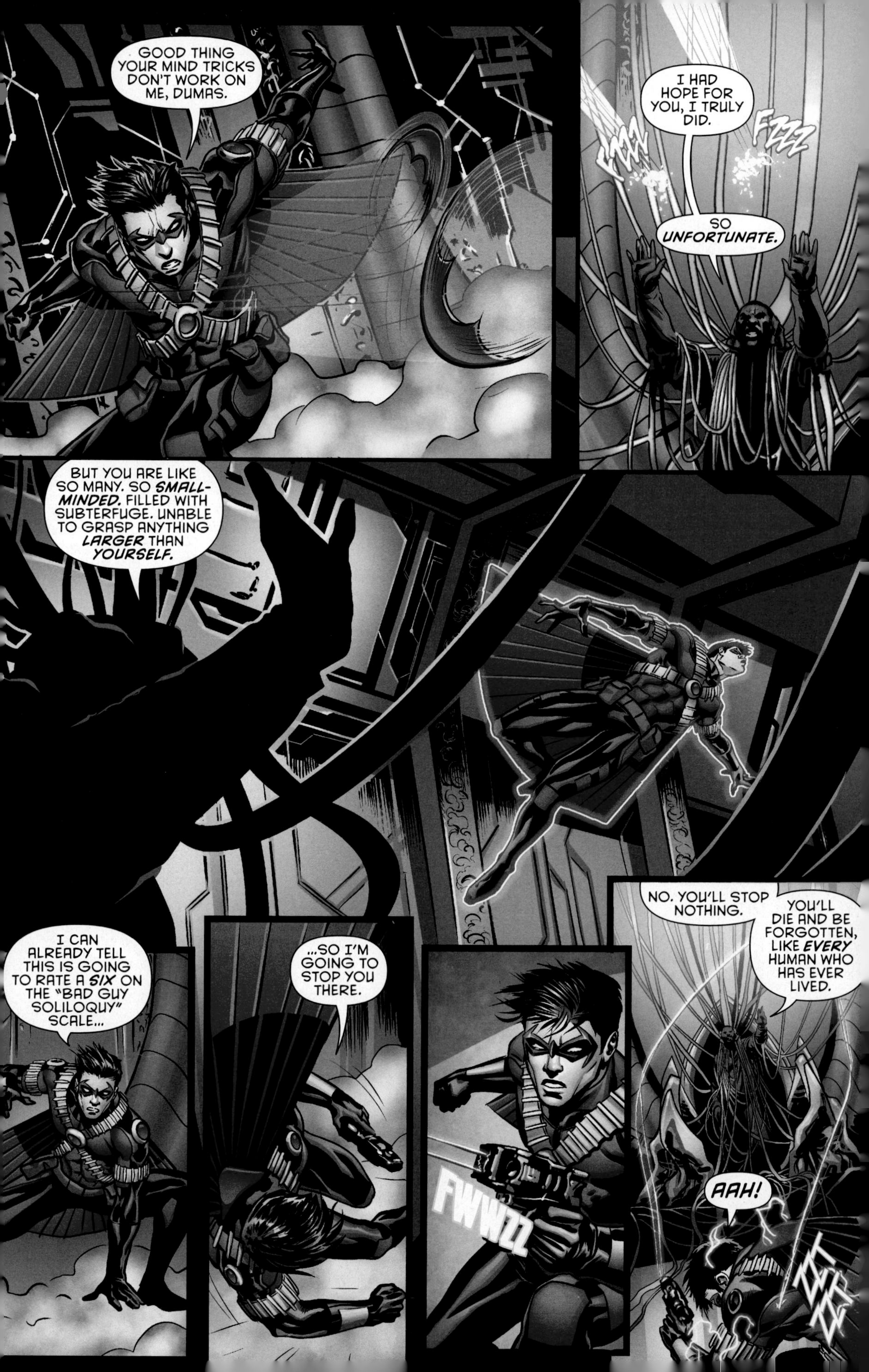
GOOD THING YOUR MIND TRICKS DON'T WORK ON ME, DUMAS.
I HAD HOPE FOR YOU, I TRULY DID.
FZZZ
FZZZ
SO *UNFORTUNATE.*
BUT YOU ARE LIKE SO MANY. SO *SMALL-MINDED.* FILLED WITH SUBTERFUGE. UNABLE TO GRASP ANYTHING *LARGER* THAN *YOURSELF.*
I CAN ALREADY TELL THIS IS GOING TO RATE A *SIX* ON THE "BAD GUY SOLILOQUY" SCALE...
...SO I'M GOING TO STOP YOU THERE.
FWWZZ
NO. YOU'LL STOP NOTHING.
YOU'LL DIE AND BE FORGOTTEN, LIKE *EVERY* HUMAN WHO HAS EVER LIVED.
AAH!

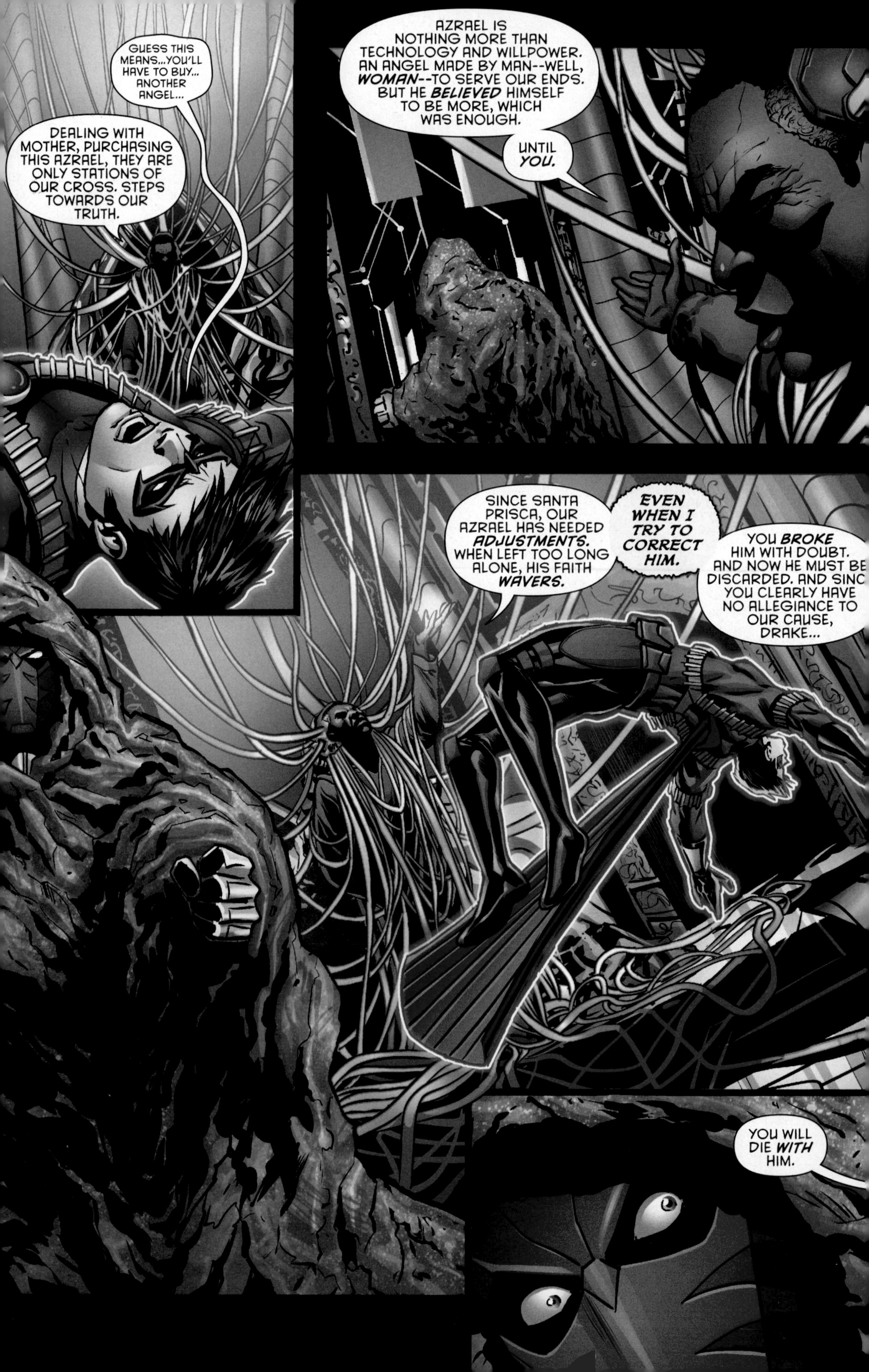
GUESS THIS MEANS... YOU'LL HAVE TO BUY... ANOTHER ANGEL...
DEALING WITH MOTHER, PURCHASING THIS AZRAEL, THEY ARE ONLY STATIONS OF OUR CROSS. STEPS TOWARDS OUR TRUTH.
AZRAEL IS NOTHING MORE THAN TECHNOLOGY AND WILLPOWER. AN ANGEL MADE BY MAN--WELL, WOMAN--TO SERVE OUR ENDS. BUT HE BELIEVED HIMSELF TO BE MORE, WHICH WAS ENOUGH.
UNTIL YOU.
SINCE SANTA PRISCA, OUR AZRAEL HAS NEEDED ADJUSTMENTS. WHEN LEFT TOO LONG ALONE, HIS FAITH WAVERS.
EVEN WHEN I TRY TO CORRECT HIM.
YOU BROKE HIM WITH DOUBT. AND NOW HE MUST BE DISCARDED. AND SINC YOU CLEARLY HAVE NO ALLEGIANCE TO OUR CAUSE, DRAKE...
YOU WILL DIE WITH HIM.

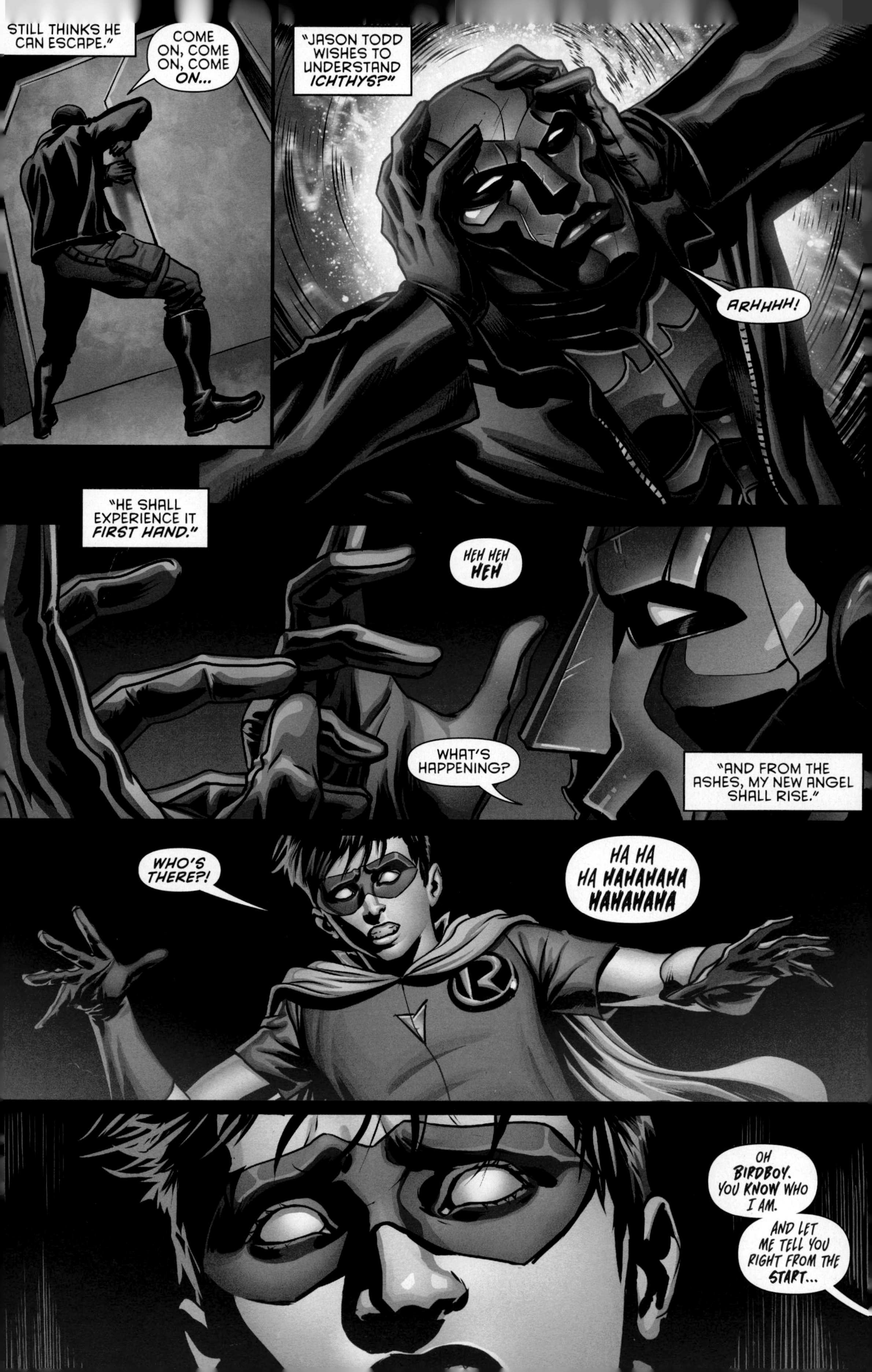
STILL THINKS HE CAN ESCAPE."
COME ON, COME ON, COME ON...
"JASON TODD WISHES TO UNDERSTAND ICHTHYS?"
ARHHHH!
"HE SHALL EXPERIENCE IT FIRST HAND."
HEH HEH HEH
WHAT'S HAPPENING?
"AND FROM THE ASHES, MY NEW ANGEL SHALL RISE."
WHO'S THERE?!
HA HA HA HAHAHAHA HAHAHAHA
OH BIRDBOY. YOU KNOW WHO I AM.
AND LET ME TELL YOU RIGHT FROM THE START...

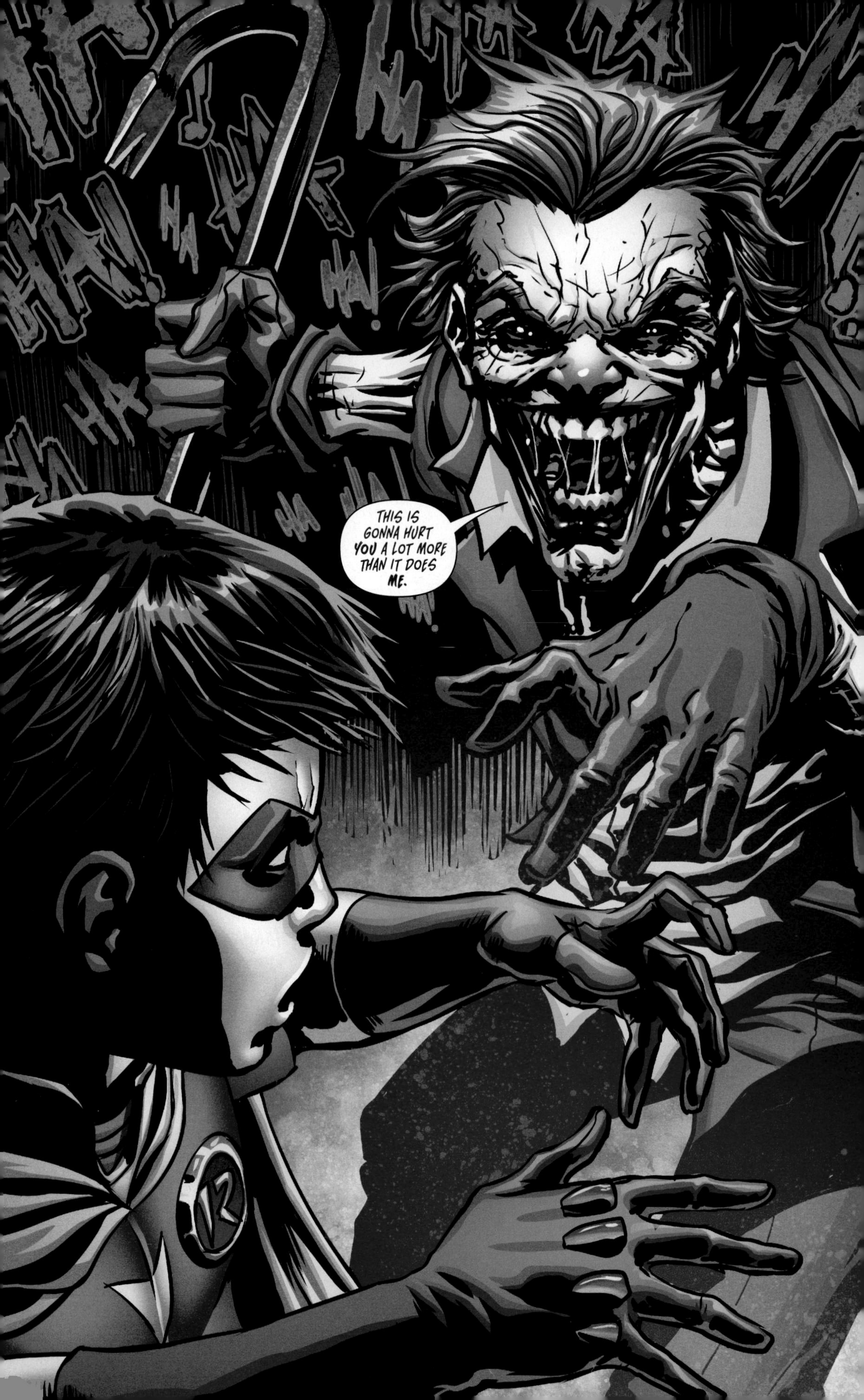
HA! HA!
THIS IS GONNA HURT YOU A LOT MORE THAN IT DOES ME.

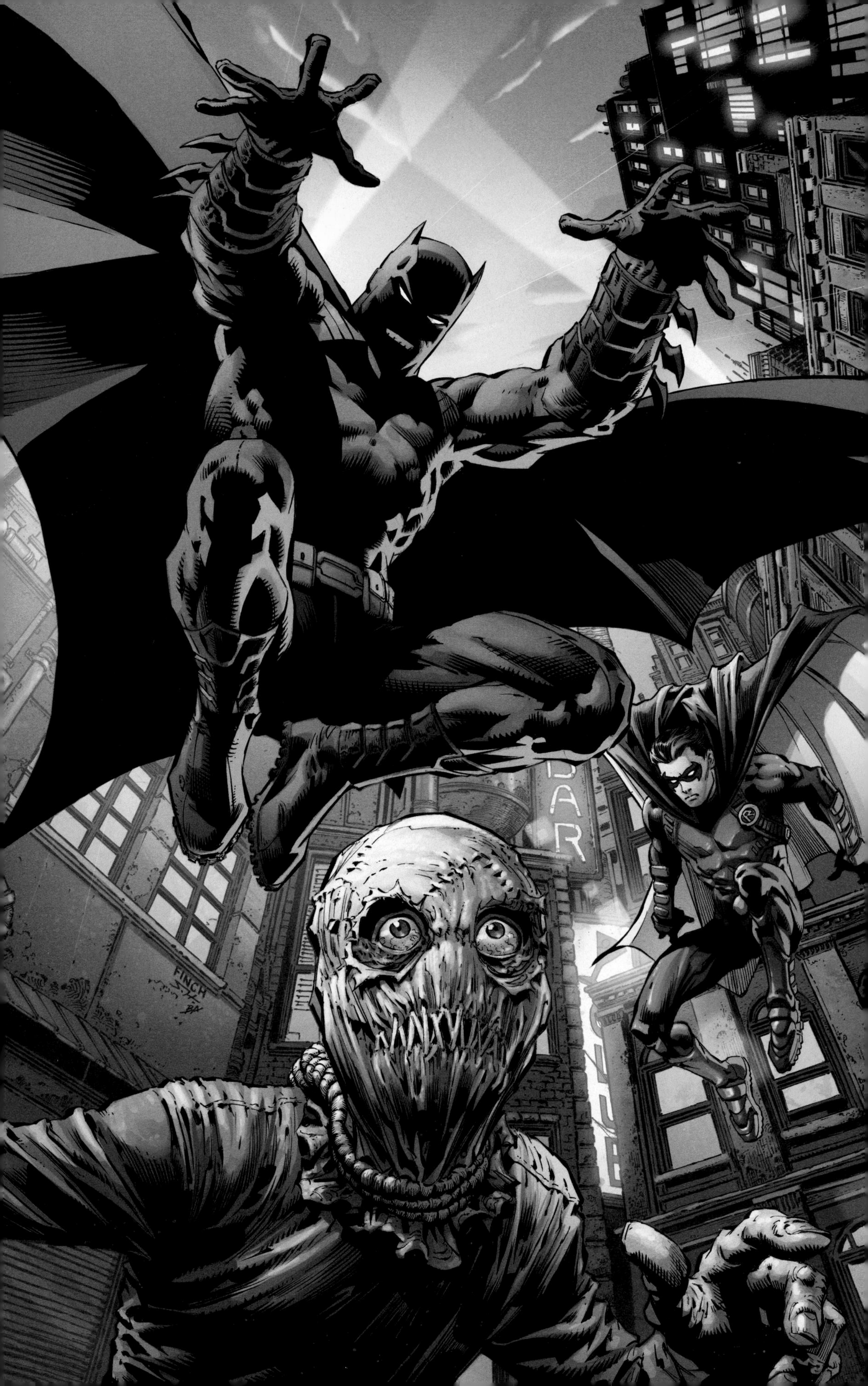
BAR
FINCH

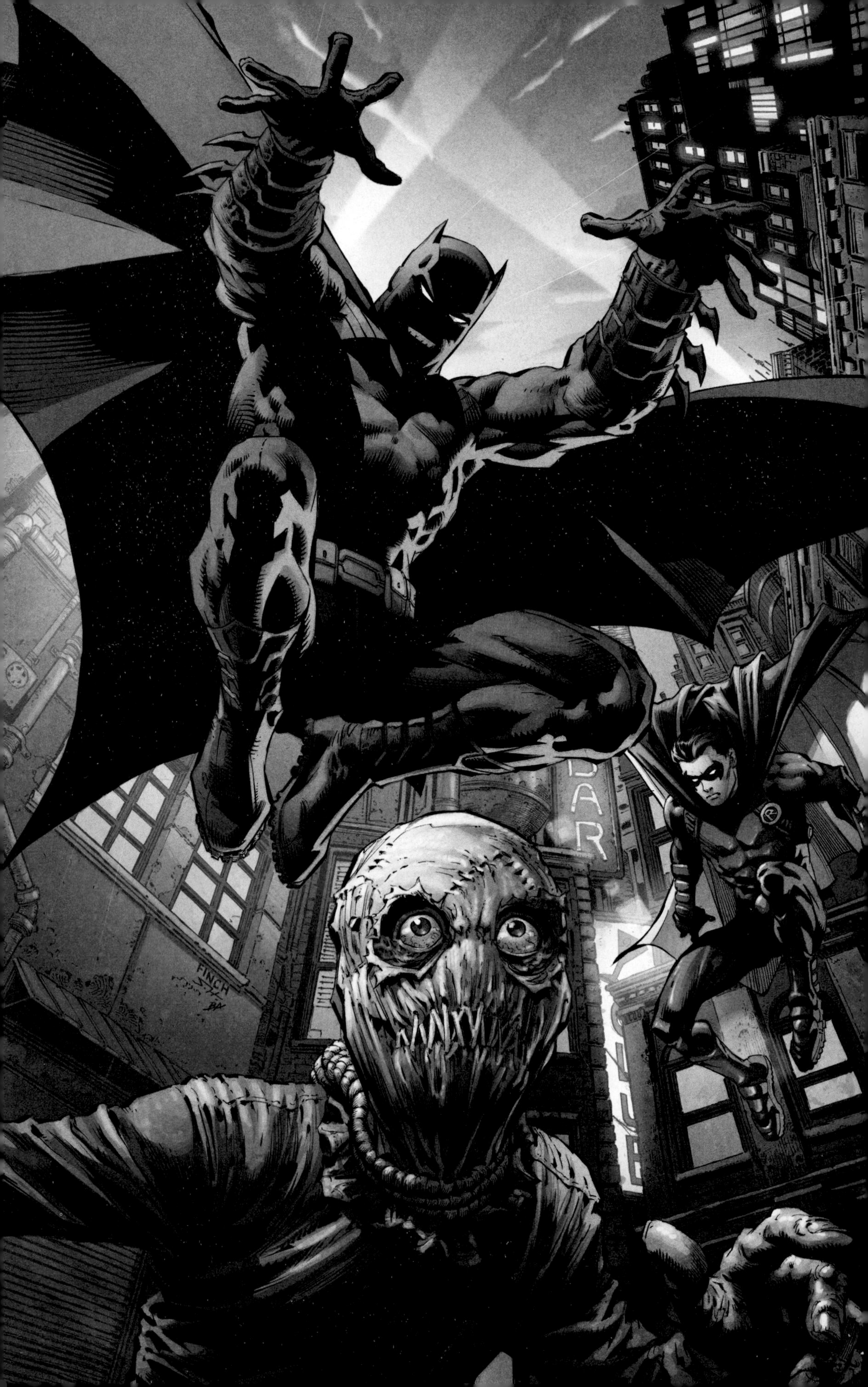
BAR
FINCH

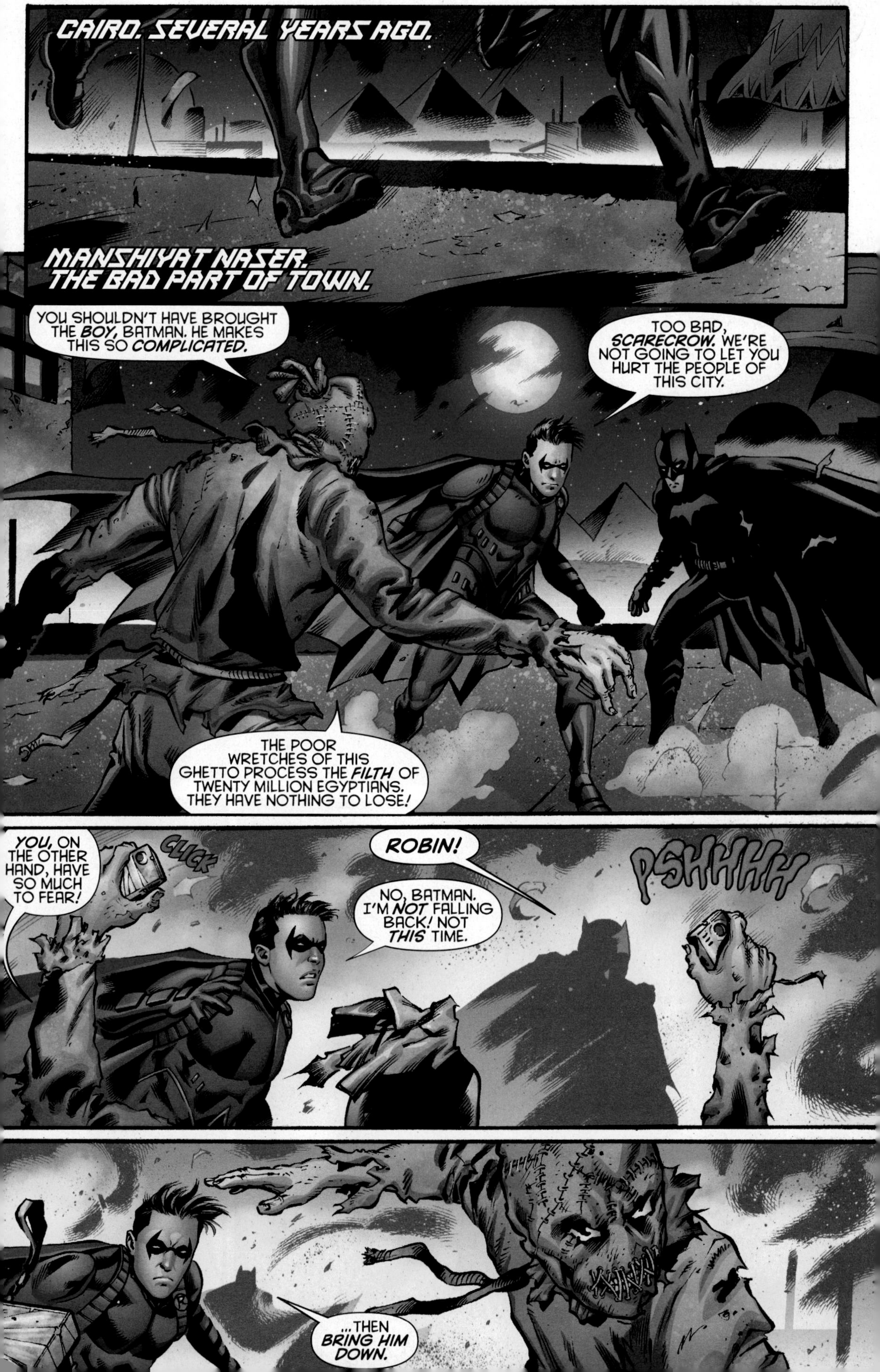
CAIRO. SEVERAL YEARS AGO.
MANSHIYAT NASER. THE BAD PART OF TOWN.
YOU SHOULDN'T HAVE BROUGHT THE BOY, BATMAN. HE MAKES THIS SO COMPLICATED.
TOO BAD, SCARECROW. WE'RE NOT GOING TO LET YOU HURT THE PEOPLE OF THIS CITY.
THE POOR WRETCHES OF THIS GHETTO PROCESS THE FILTH OF TWENTY MILLION EGYPTIANS. THEY HAVE NOTHING TO LOSE!
YOU, ON THE OTHER HAND, HAVE SO MUCH TO FEAR!
CLICK
ROBIN!
NO, BATMAN. I'M NOT FALLING BACK! NOT THIS TIME.
PSHHHH
...THEN BRING HIM DOWN.

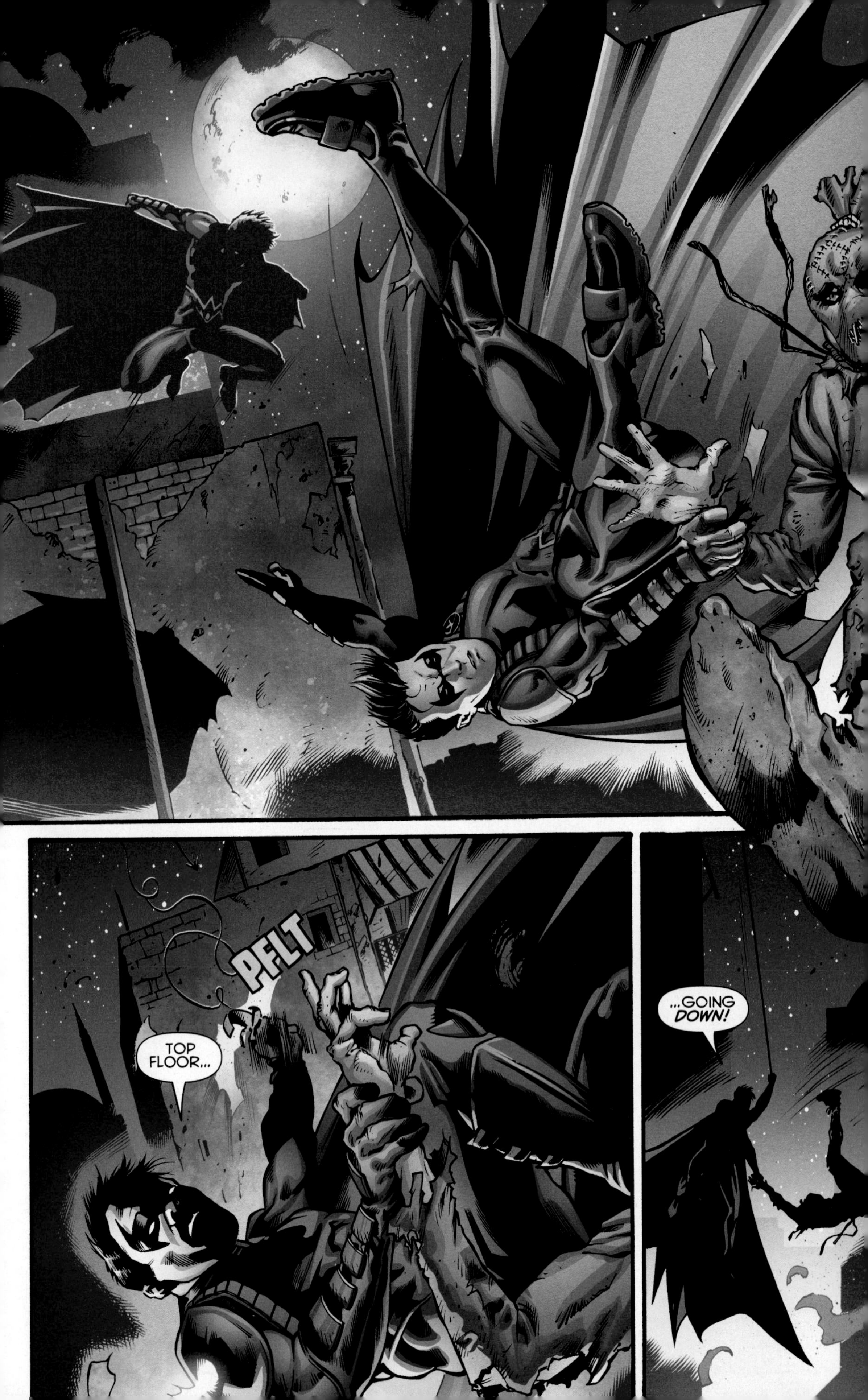
PFLT
TOP FLOOR...
...GOING DOWN!

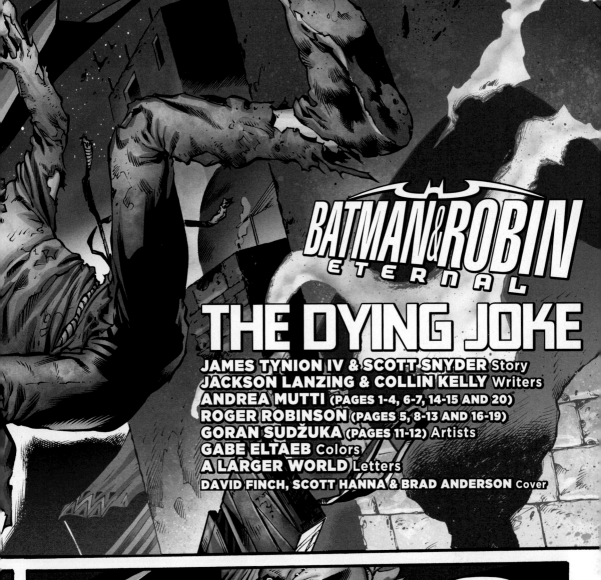

BATMAN & ROBIN ETERNAL
THE DYING JOKE

JAMES TYNION IV & SCOTT SNYDER Story
JACKSON LANZING & COLLIN KELLY Writers
ANDREA MUTTI (PAGES 1-4, 6-7, 14-15 AND 20)
ROGER ROBINSON (PAGES 5, 8-13 AND 16-19)
GORAN SUDŽUKA (PAGES 11-12) Artists
GABE ELTAEB Colors
A LARGER WORLD Letters

DAVID FINCH, SCOTT HANNA & BRAD ANDERSON Cover

NO NO NO
NO NO NO

!

THWAP

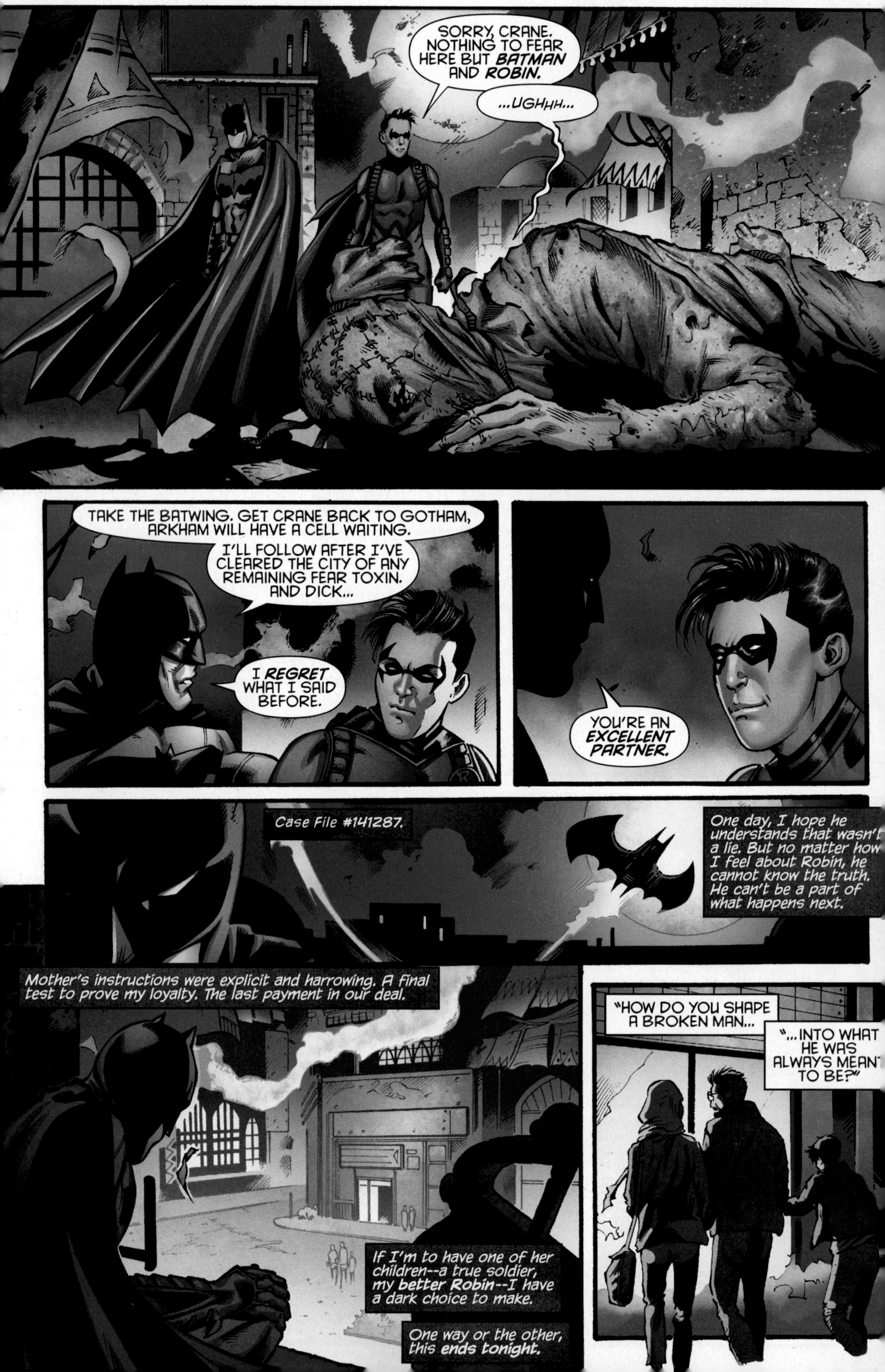
SORRY, CRANE. NOTHING TO FEAR HERE BUT BATMAN AND ROBIN.
...UGHHH...
TAKE THE BATWING. GET CRANE BACK TO GOTHAM, ARKHAM WILL HAVE A CELL WAITING.
I'LL FOLLOW AFTER I'VE CLEARED THE CITY OF ANY REMAINING FEAR TOXIN. AND DICK...
I REGRET WHAT I SAID BEFORE.
YOU'RE AN EXCELLENT PARTNER.
Case File #141287.
One day, I hope he understands that wasn't a lie. But no matter how I feel about Robin, he cannot know the truth. He can't be a part of what happens next.
Mother's instructions were explicit and harrowing. A final test to prove my loyalty. The last payment in our deal.
If I'm to have one of her children--a true soldier, my better Robin--I have a dark choice to make.
One way or the other, this ends tonight.
"HOW DO YOU SHAPE A BROKEN MAN...
"...INTO WHAT HE WAS ALWAYS MEANT TO BE?"

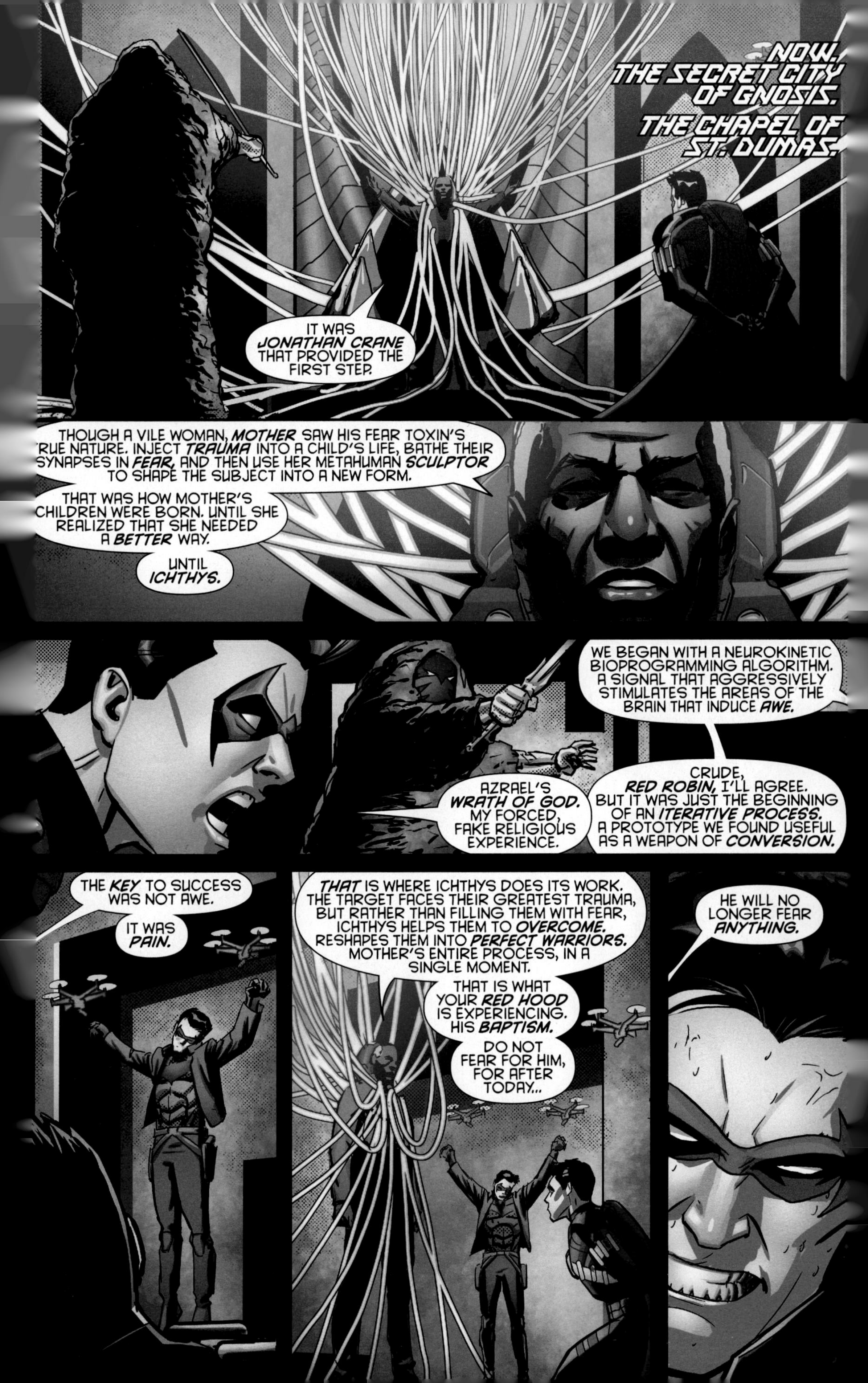
NOW.
THE SECRET CITY OF GNOSIS.
THE CHAPEL OF ST. DUMAS.
IT WAS JONATHAN CRANE THAT PROVIDED THE FIRST STEP.
THOUGH A VILE WOMAN, MOTHER SAW HIS FEAR TOXIN'S TRUE NATURE. INJECT TRAUMA INTO A CHILD'S LIFE, BATHE THEIR SYNAPSES IN FEAR, AND THEN USE HER METAHUMAN SCULPTOR TO SHAPE THE SUBJECT INTO A NEW FORM.
THAT WAS HOW MOTHER'S CHILDREN WERE BORN. UNTIL SHE REALIZED THAT SHE NEEDED A BETTER WAY.
UNTIL ICHTHYS.
AZRAEL'S WRATH OF GOD. MY FORCED, FAKE RELIGIOUS EXPERIENCE.
WE BEGAN WITH A NEUROKINETIC BIOPROGRAMMING ALGORITHM. A SIGNAL THAT AGGRESSIVELY STIMULATES THE AREAS OF THE BRAIN THAT INDUCE AWE.
CRUDE, RED ROBIN, I'LL AGREE. BUT IT WAS JUST THE BEGINNING OF AN ITERATIVE PROCESS. A PROTOTYPE WE FOUND USEFUL AS A WEAPON OF CONVERSION.
THE KEY TO SUCCESS WAS NOT AWE.
IT WAS PAIN.
THAT IS WHERE ICHTHYS DOES ITS WORK. THE TARGET FACES THEIR GREATEST TRAUMA, BUT RATHER THAN FILLING THEM WITH FEAR, ICHTHYS HELPS THEM TO OVERCOME. RESHAPES THEM INTO PERFECT WARRIORS. MOTHER'S ENTIRE PROCESS, IN A SINGLE MOMENT.
THAT IS WHAT YOUR RED HOOD IS EXPERIENCING. HIS BAPTISM.
DO NOT FEAR FOR HIM, FOR AFTER TODAY...
HE WILL NO LONGER FEAR ANYTHING.

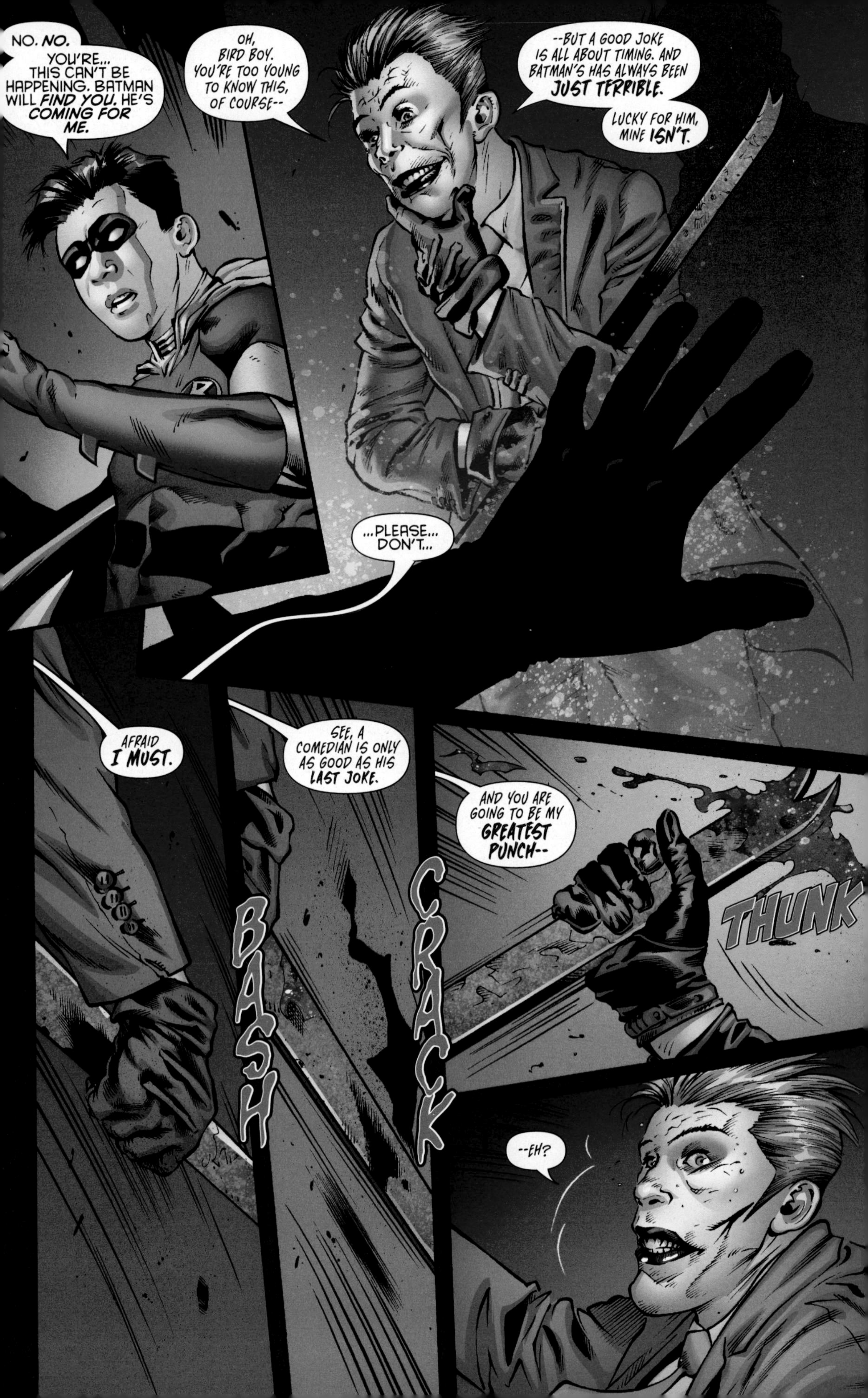
NO. NO. YOU'RE... THIS CAN'T BE HAPPENING. BATMAN WILL FIND YOU. HE'S COMING FOR ME.
OH, BIRD BOY. YOU'RE TOO YOUNG TO KNOW THIS, OF COURSE--
--BUT A GOOD JOKE IS ALL ABOUT TIMING. AND BATMAN'S HAS ALWAYS BEEN JUST TERRIBLE.
LUCKY FOR HIM, MINE ISN'T.
...PLEASE... DON'T...
AFRAID I MUST.
SEE, A COMEDIAN IS ONLY AS GOOD AS HIS LAST JOKE.
BASH
CRACK
AND YOU ARE GOING TO BE MY GREATEST PUNCH--
THUNK
--EH?

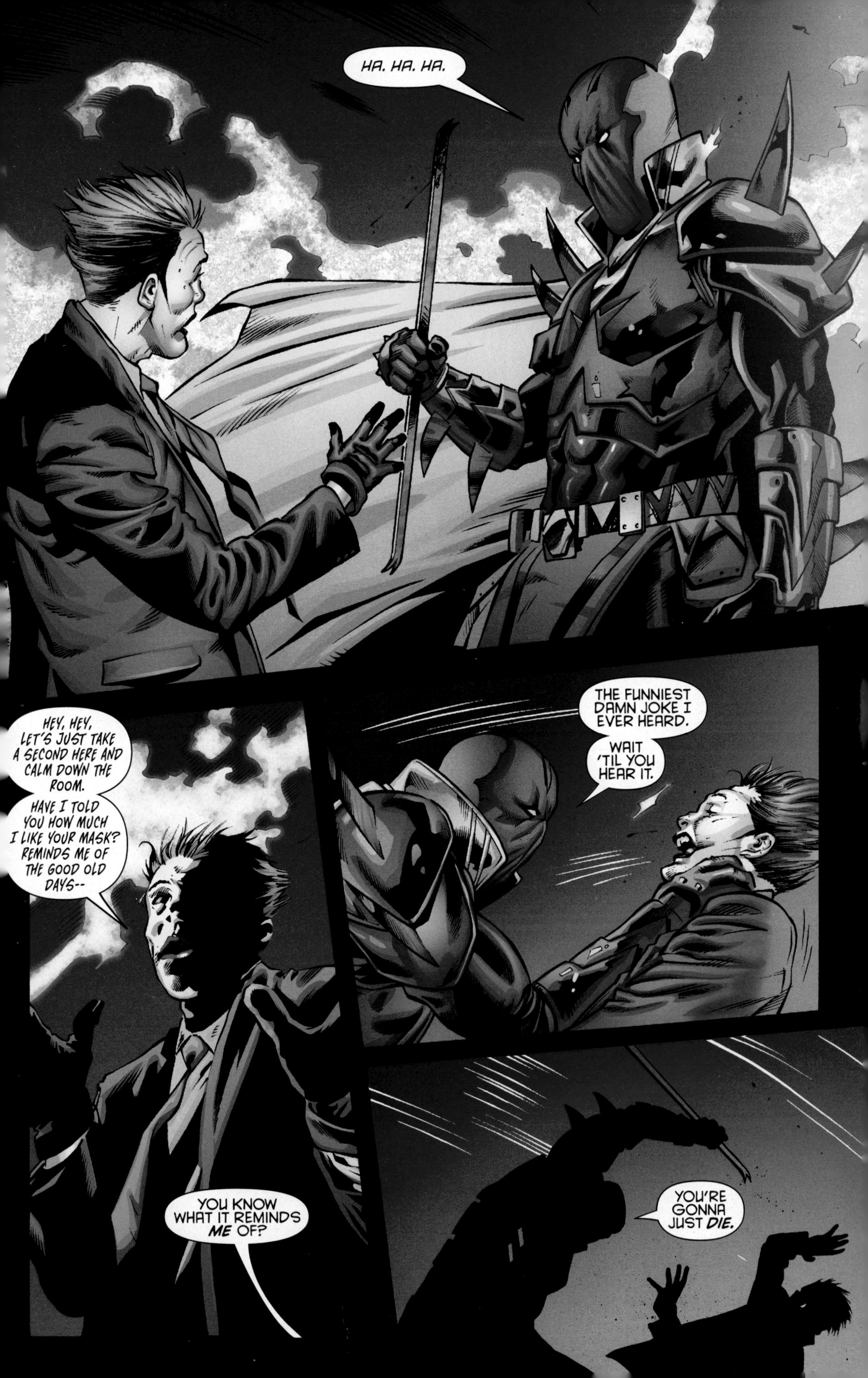
HA. HA. HA.
HEY, HEY, LET'S JUST TAKE A SECOND HERE AND CALM DOWN THE ROOM.
HAVE I TOLD YOU HOW MUCH I LIKE YOUR MASK? REMINDS ME OF THE GOOD OLD DAYS--
YOU KNOW WHAT IT REMINDS ME OF?
THE FUNNIEST DAMN JOKE I EVER HEARD.
WAIT 'TIL YOU HEAR IT.
YOU'RE GONNA JUST DIE.

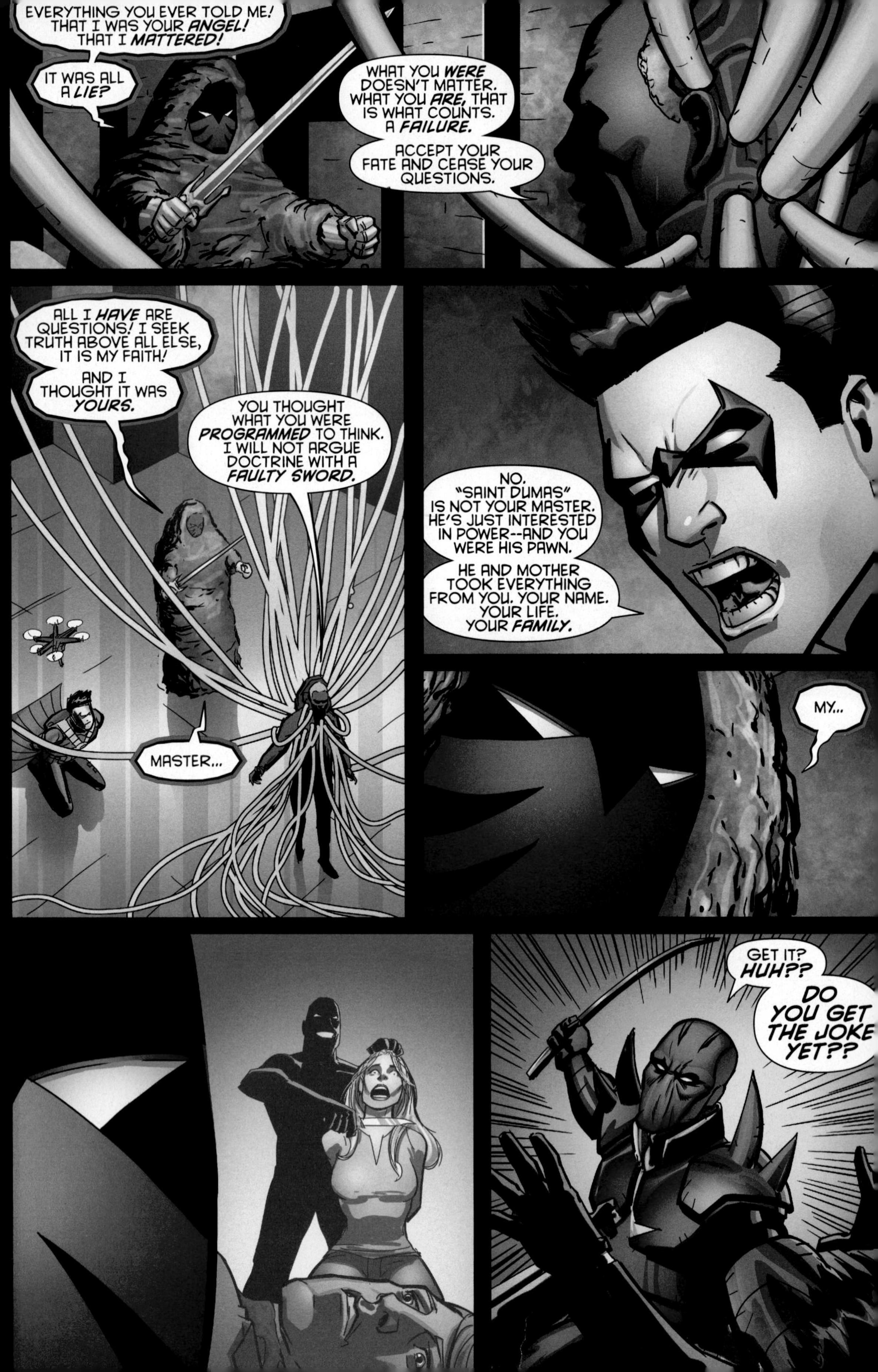
EVERYTHING YOU EVER TOLD ME! THAT I WAS YOUR ANGEL! THAT I MATTERED!
IT WAS ALL A LIE?
WHAT YOU WERE DOESN'T MATTER. WHAT YOU ARE, THAT IS WHAT COUNTS. A FAILURE.
ACCEPT YOUR FATE AND CEASE YOUR QUESTIONS.
ALL I HAVE ARE QUESTIONS! I SEEK TRUTH ABOVE ALL ELSE, IT IS MY FAITH!
AND I THOUGHT IT WAS YOURS.
YOU THOUGHT WHAT YOU WERE PROGRAMMED TO THINK. I WILL NOT ARGUE DOCTRINE WITH A FAULTY SWORD.
MASTER...
NO. "SAINT DUMAS" IS NOT YOUR MASTER. HE'S JUST INTERESTED IN POWER--AND YOU WERE HIS PAWN.
HE AND MOTHER TOOK EVERYTHING FROM YOU. YOUR NAME. YOUR LIFE. YOUR FAMILY.
MY...
GET IT? HUH??
DO YOU GET THE JOKE YET??

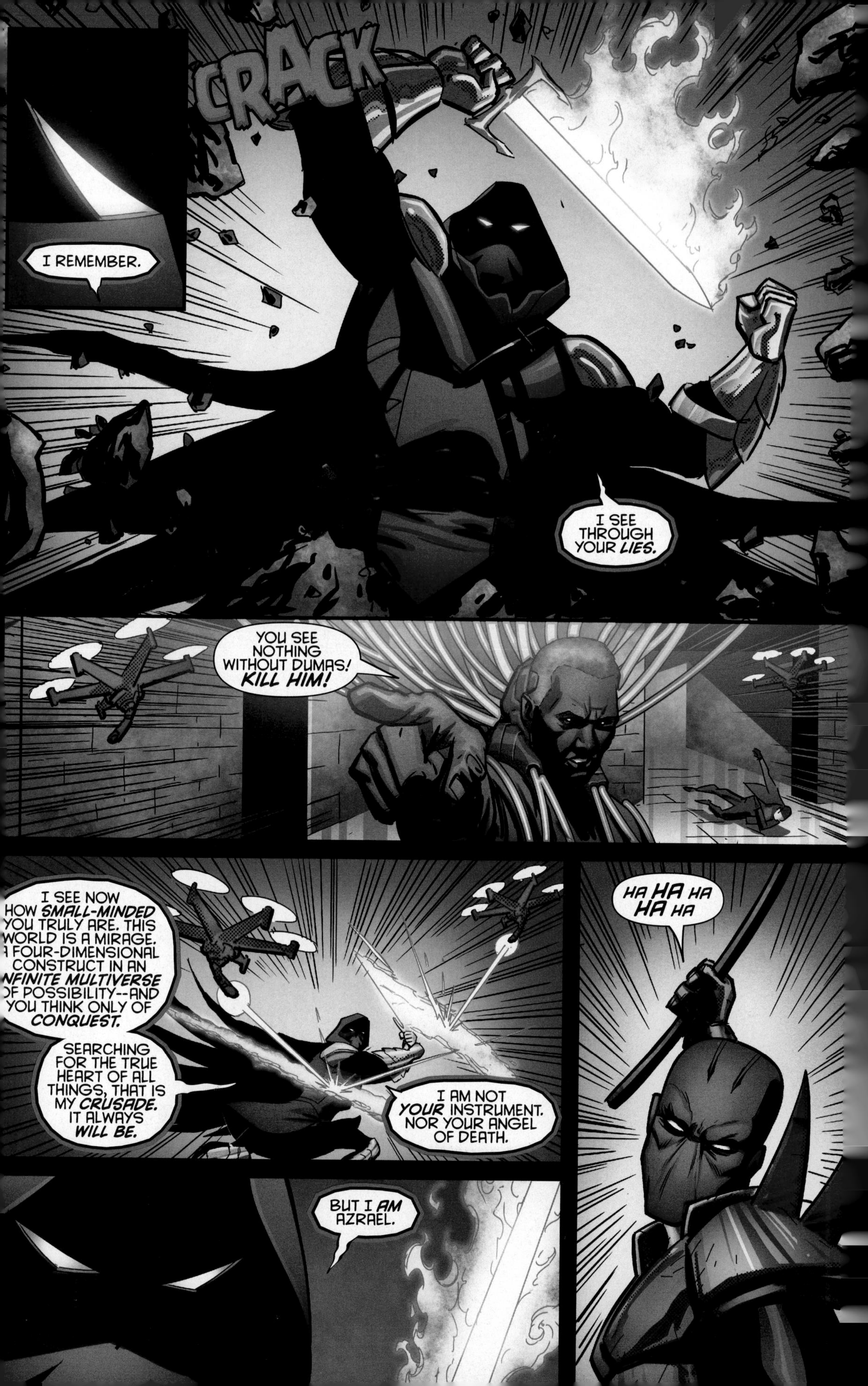
CRACK
I REMEMBER.
I SEE THROUGH YOUR LIES.
YOU SEE NOTHING WITHOUT DUMAS! KILL HIM!
I SEE NOW HOW SMALL-MINDED YOU TRULY ARE. THIS WORLD IS A MIRAGE. A FOUR-DIMENSIONAL CONSTRUCT IN AN INFINITE MULTIVERSE OF POSSIBILITY--AND YOU THINK ONLY OF CONQUEST.
SEARCHING FOR THE TRUE HEART OF ALL THINGS, THAT IS MY CRUSADE. IT ALWAYS WILL BE.
I AM NOT YOUR INSTRUMENT. NOR YOUR ANGEL OF DEATH.
HA HA HA HA HA
BUT I AM AZRAEL.

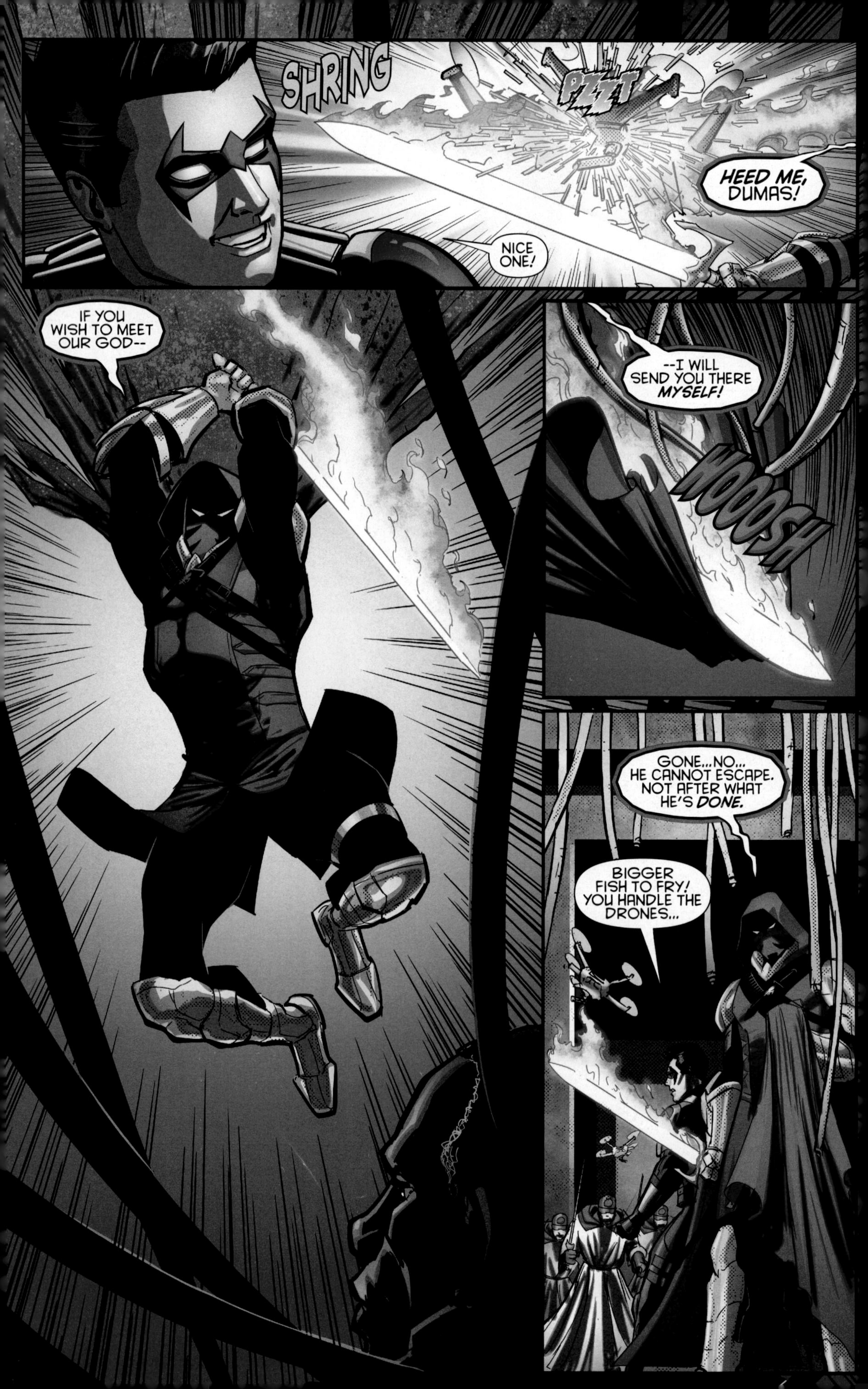
SHRING
PZZT
HEED ME, DUMAS!
NICE ONE!
IF YOU WISH TO MEET OUR GOD--
--I WILL SEND YOU THERE MYSELF!
WOOOSH
GONE...NO... HE CANNOT ESCAPE. NOT AFTER WHAT HE'S DONE.
BIGGER FISH TO FRY! YOU HANDLE THE DRONES...

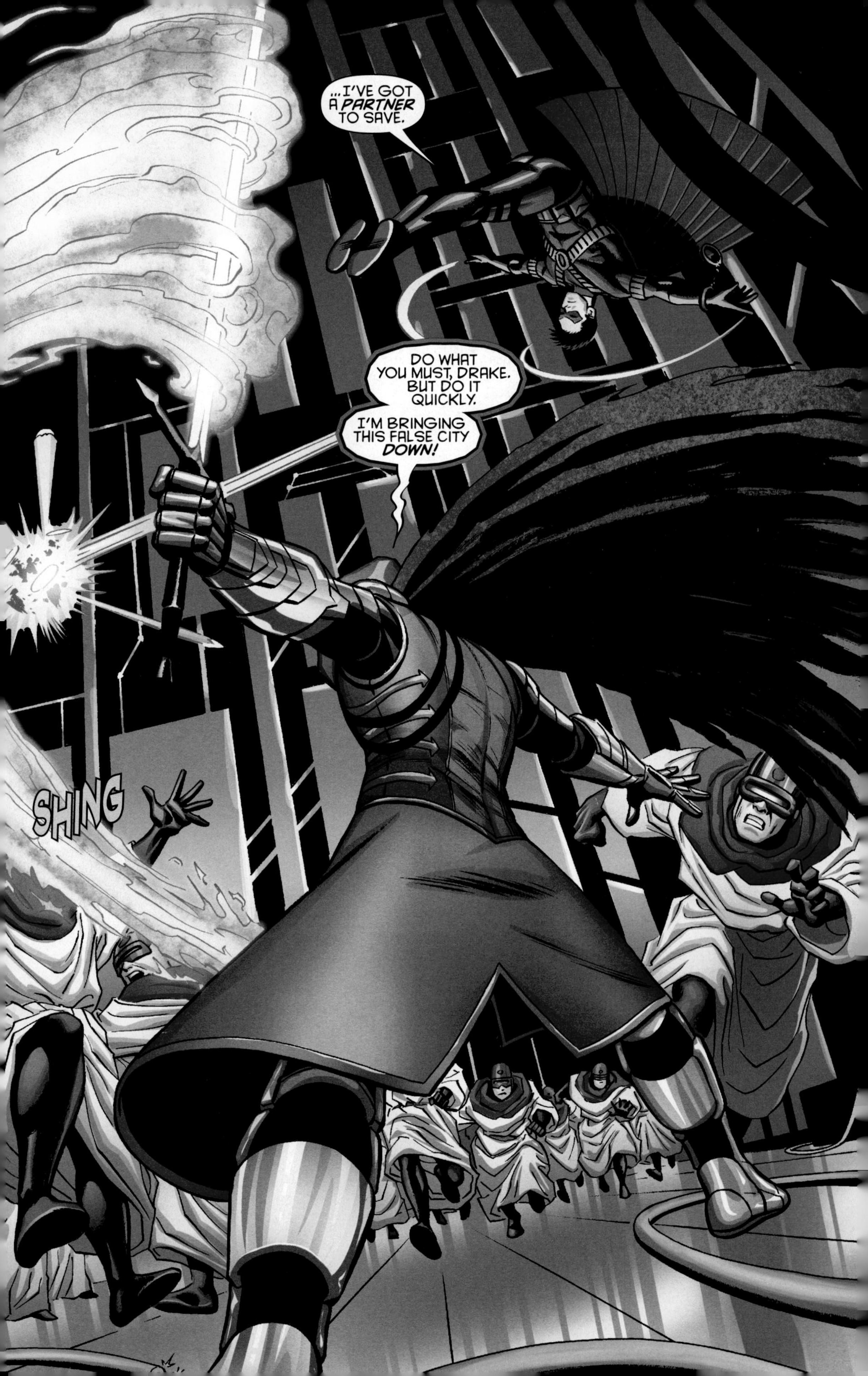
...I'VE GOT A PARTNER TO SAVE.
DO WHAT YOU MUST, DRAKE. BUT DO IT QUICKLY.
I'M BRINGING THIS FALSE CITY DOWN!
SHING

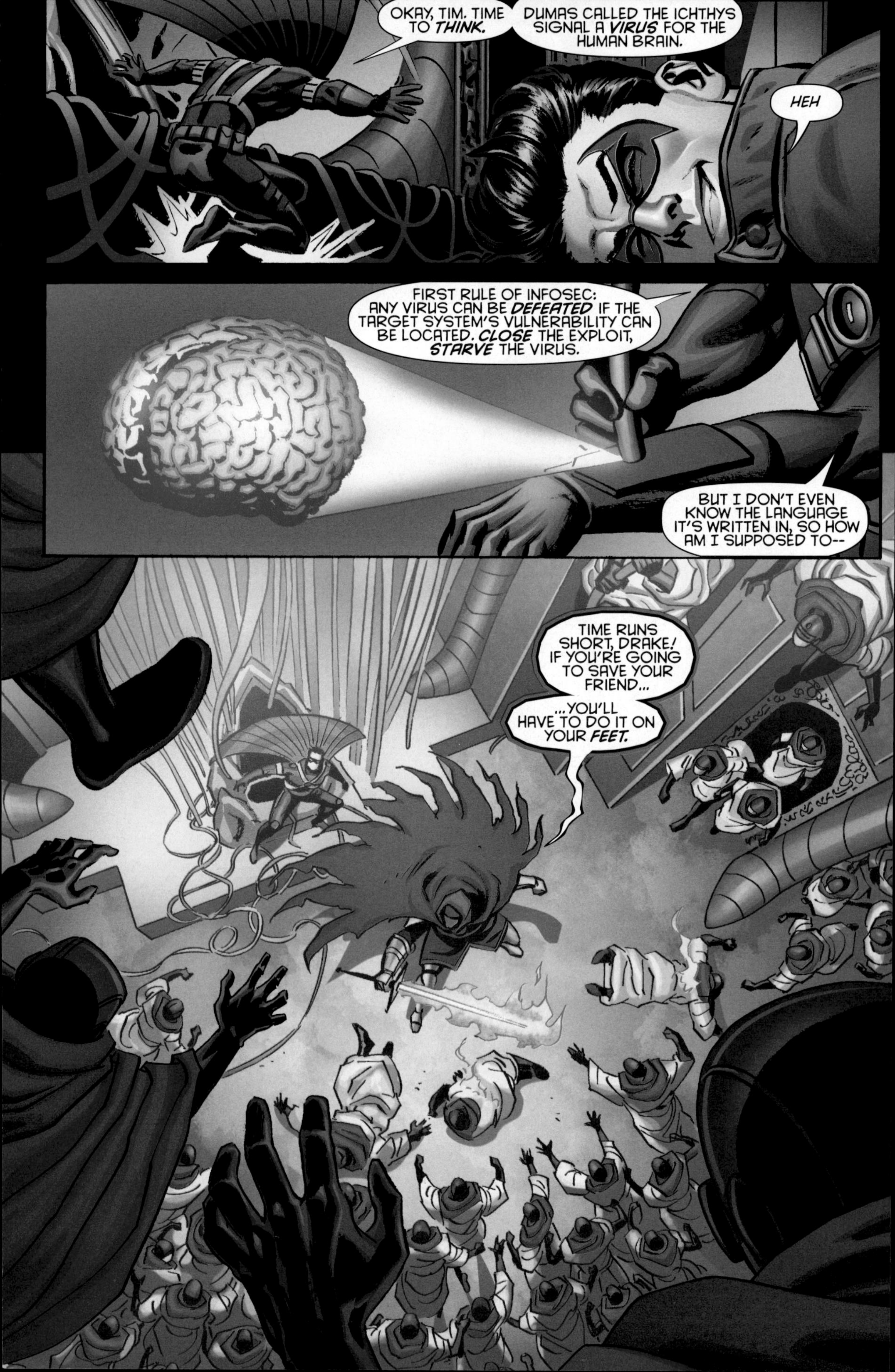
OKAY, TIM. TIME TO THINK.
DUMAS CALLED THE ICHTHYS SIGNAL A VIRUS FOR THE HUMAN BRAIN.
HEH
FIRST RULE OF INFOSEC: ANY VIRUS CAN BE DEFEATED IF THE TARGET SYSTEM'S VULNERABILITY CAN BE LOCATED. CLOSE THE EXPLOIT, STARVE THE VIRUS.
BUT I DON'T EVEN KNOW THE LANGUAGE IT'S WRITTEN IN, SO HOW AM I SUPPOSED TO--
TIME RUNS SHORT, DRAKE! IF YOU'RE GOING TO SAVE YOUR FRIEND...
...YOU'LL HAVE TO DO IT ON YOUR FEET.

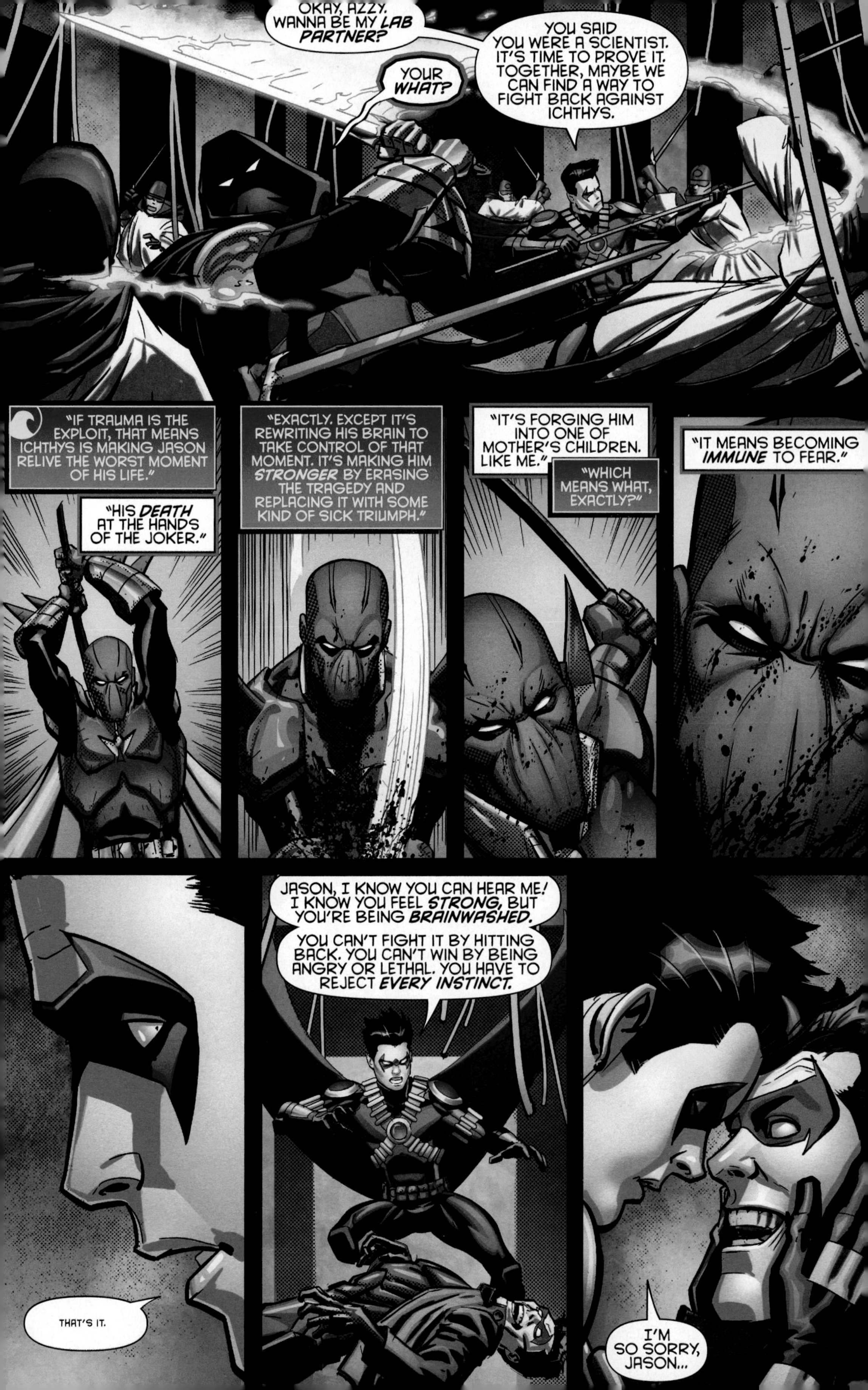
OKAY, AZZY. WANNA BE MY LAB PARTNER?
YOUR WHAT?
YOU SAID YOU WERE A SCIENTIST. IT'S TIME TO PROVE IT. TOGETHER, MAYBE WE CAN FIND A WAY TO FIGHT BACK AGAINST ICHTHYS.
"IF TRAUMA IS THE EXPLOIT, THAT MEANS ICHTHYS IS MAKING JASON RELIVE THE WORST MOMENT OF HIS LIFE."
"HIS DEATH AT THE HANDS OF THE JOKER."
"EXACTLY. EXCEPT IT'S REWRITING HIS BRAIN TO TAKE CONTROL OF THAT MOMENT. IT'S MAKING HIM STRONGER BY ERASING THE TRAGEDY AND REPLACING IT WITH SOME KIND OF SICK TRIUMPH."
"IT'S FORGING HIM INTO ONE OF MOTHER'S CHILDREN. LIKE ME."
"WHICH MEANS WHAT, EXACTLY?"
"IT MEANS BECOMING IMMUNE TO FEAR."
THAT'S IT.
JASON, I KNOW YOU CAN HEAR ME! I KNOW YOU FEEL STRONG, BUT YOU'RE BEING BRAINWASHED.
YOU CAN'T FIGHT IT BY HITTING BACK. YOU CAN'T WIN BY BEING ANGRY OR LETHAL. YOU HAVE TO REJECT EVERY INSTINCT.
I'M SO SORRY, JASON...

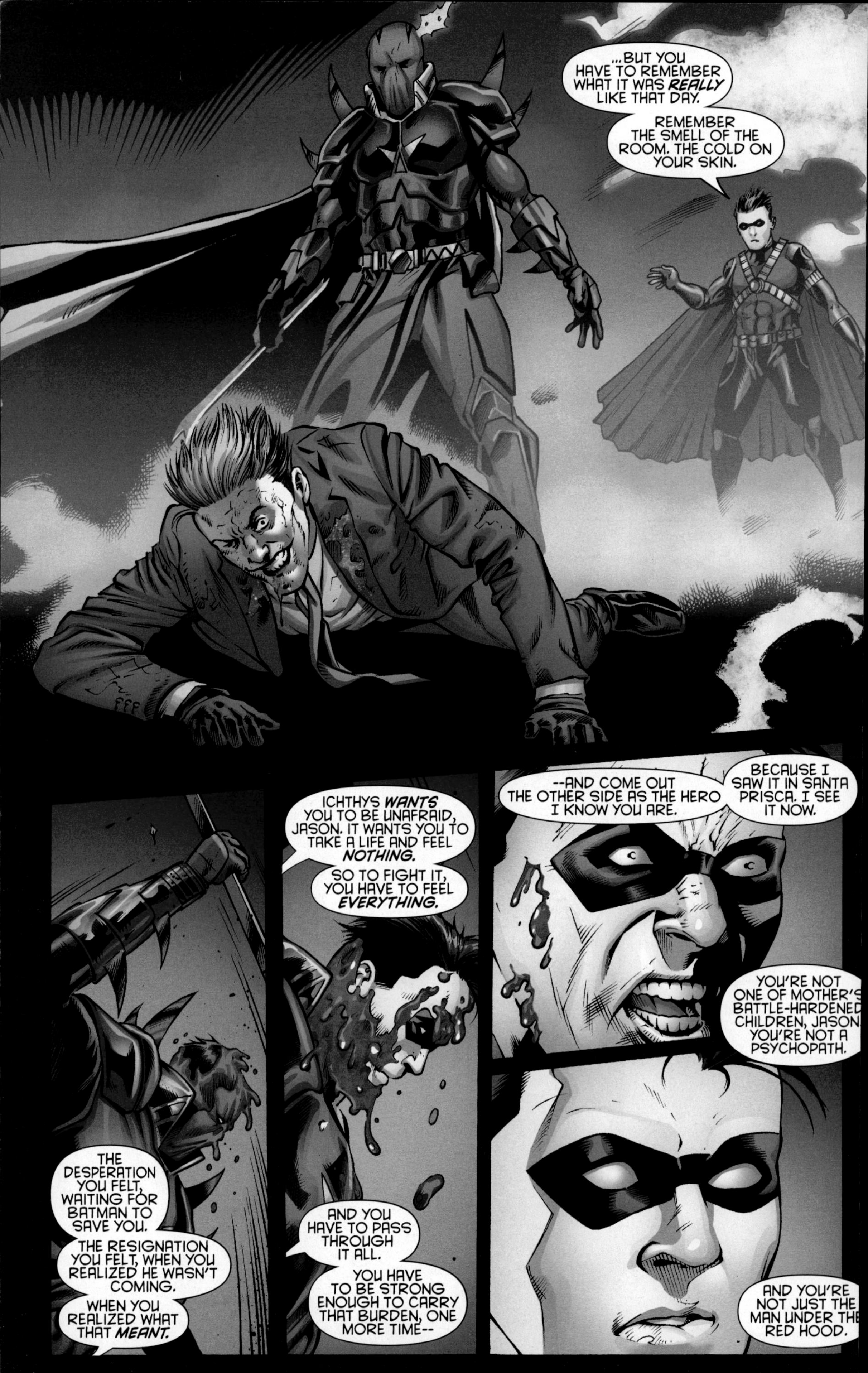
...BUT YOU HAVE TO REMEMBER WHAT IT WAS REALLY LIKE THAT DAY.
REMEMBER THE SMELL OF THE ROOM. THE COLD ON YOUR SKIN.
THE DESPERATION YOU FELT, WAITING FOR BATMAN TO SAVE YOU.
THE RESIGNATION YOU FELT, WHEN YOU REALIZED HE WASN'T COMING.
WHEN YOU REALIZED WHAT THAT MEANT.
ICHTHYS WANTS YOU TO BE UNAFRAID, JASON. IT WANTS YOU TO TAKE A LIFE AND FEEL NOTHING.
SO TO FIGHT IT, YOU HAVE TO FEEL EVERYTHING.
AND YOU HAVE TO PASS THROUGH IT ALL.
YOU HAVE TO BE STRONG ENOUGH TO CARRY THAT BURDEN, ONE MORE TIME--
--AND COME OUT THE OTHER SIDE AS THE HERO I KNOW YOU ARE.
BECAUSE I SAW IT IN SANTA PRISCA. I SEE IT NOW.
YOU'RE NOT ONE OF MOTHER'S BATTLE-HARDENED CHILDREN, JASON. YOU'RE NOT A PSYCHOPATH.
AND YOU'RE NOT JUST THE MAN UNDER THE RED HOOD.

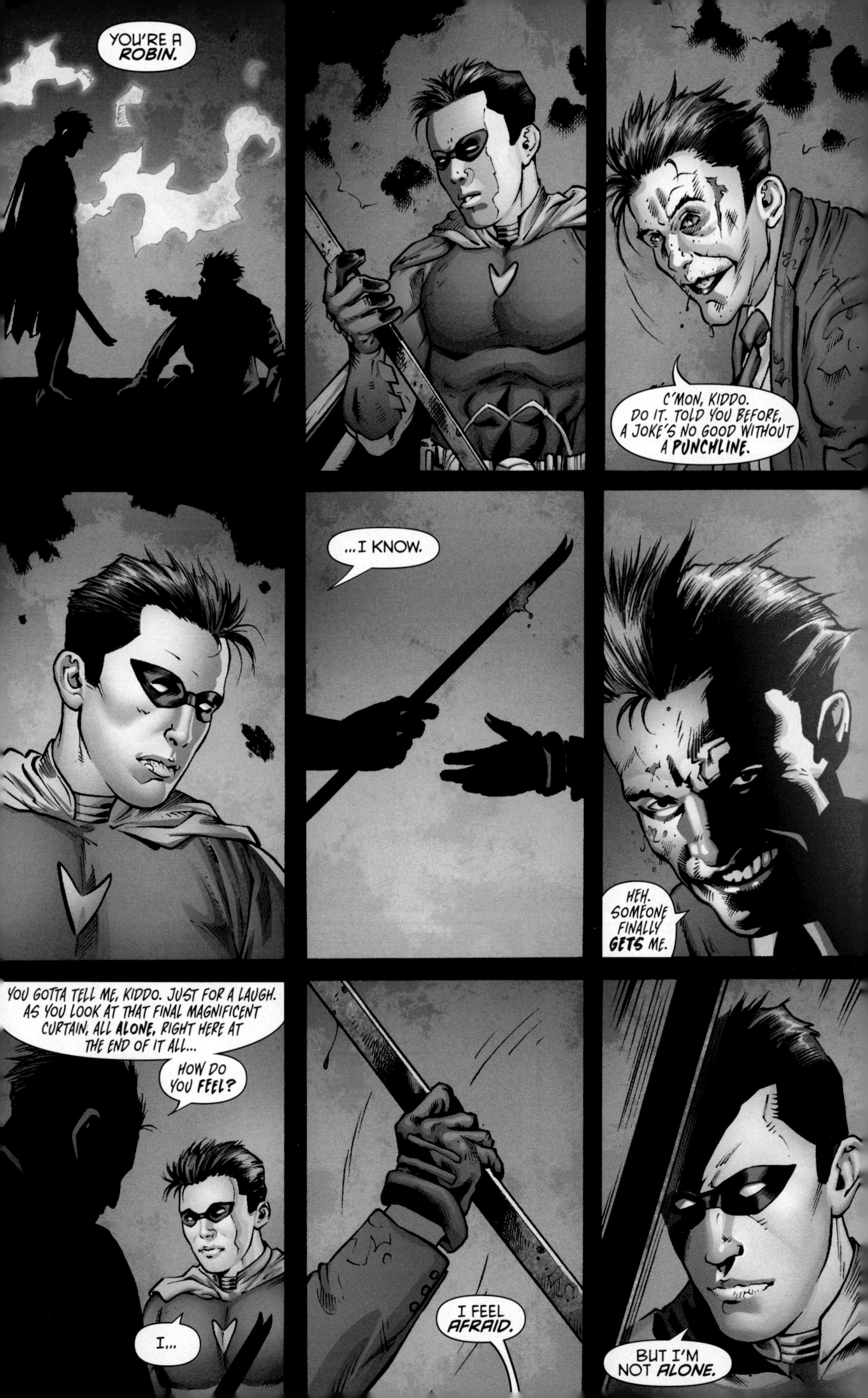
YOU'RE A ROBIN.
C'MON, KIDDO. DO IT. TOLD YOU BEFORE, A JOKE'S NO GOOD WITHOUT A PUNCHLINE.
...I KNOW.
HEH. SOMEONE FINALLY GETS ME.
YOU GOTTA TELL ME, KIDDO. JUST FOR A LAUGH. AS YOU LOOK AT THAT FINAL MAGNIFICENT CURTAIN, ALL ALONE, RIGHT HERE AT THE END OF IT ALL...
HOW DO YOU FEEL?
I...
I FEEL AFRAID.
BUT I'M NOT ALONE.

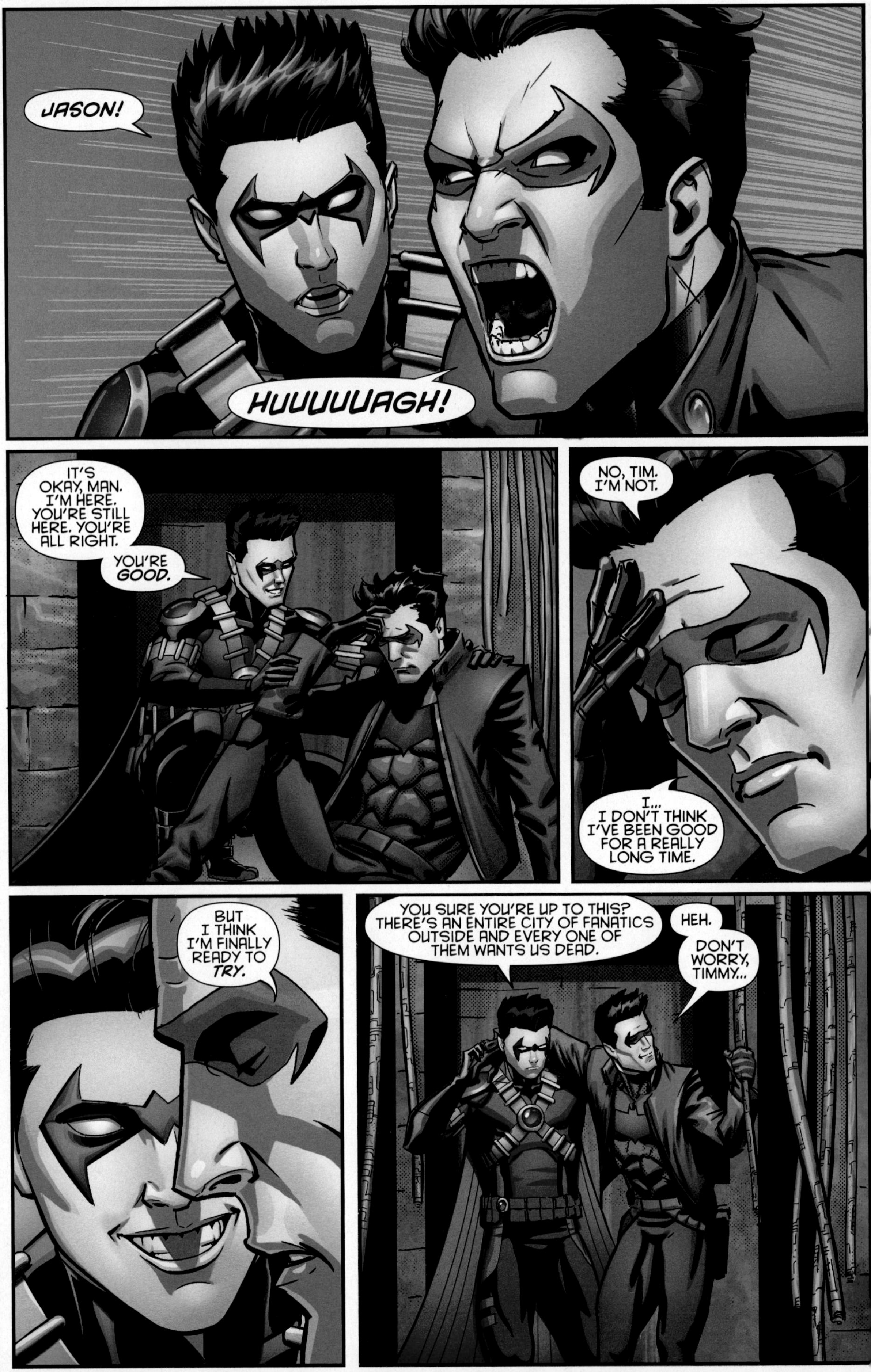
JASON!
HUUUUUAGH!
IT'S OKAY, MAN. I'M HERE. YOU'RE STILL HERE. YOU'RE ALL RIGHT.
YOU'RE GOOD.
NO, TIM. I'M NOT.
I... I DON'T THINK I'VE BEEN GOOD FOR A REALLY LONG TIME.
BUT I THINK I'M FINALLY READY TO TRY.
YOU SURE YOU'RE UP TO THIS? THERE'S AN ENTIRE CITY OF FANATICS OUTSIDE AND EVERY ONE OF THEM WANTS US DEAD.
HEH.
DON'T WORRY, TIMMY...

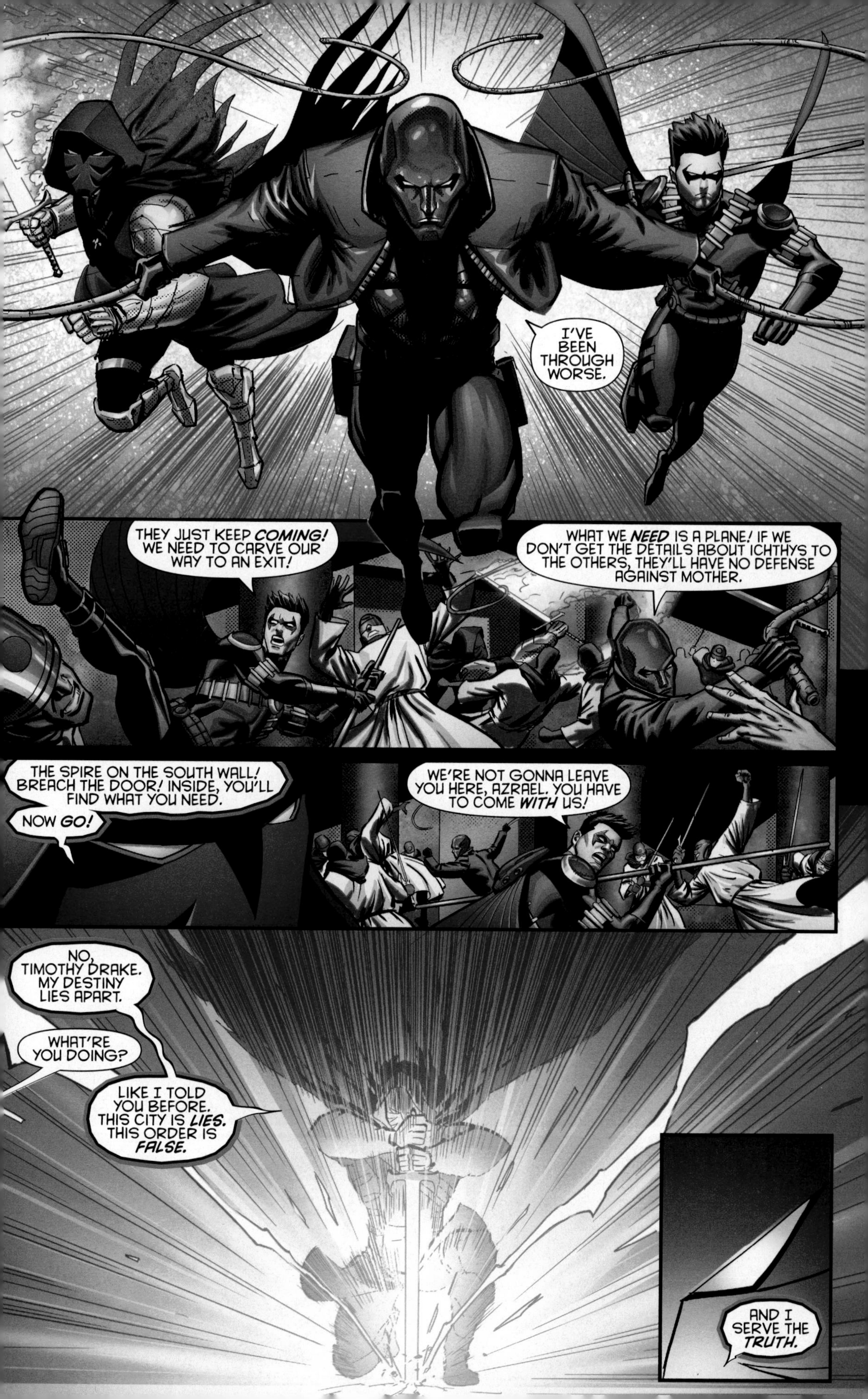
I'VE BEEN THROUGH WORSE.
THEY JUST KEEP COMING! WE NEED TO CARVE OUR WAY TO AN EXIT!
WHAT WE NEED IS A PLANE! IF WE DON'T GET THE DETAILS ABOUT ICHTHYS TO THE OTHERS, THEY'LL HAVE NO DEFENSE AGAINST MOTHER.
THE SPIRE ON THE SOUTH WALL! BREACH THE DOOR! INSIDE, YOU'LL FIND WHAT YOU NEED.
NOW GO!
WE'RE NOT GONNA LEAVE YOU HERE, AZRAEL. YOU HAVE TO COME WITH US!
NO, TIMOTHY DRAKE. MY DESTINY LIES APART.
WHAT'RE YOU DOING?
LIKE I TOLD YOU BEFORE. THIS CITY IS LIES. THIS ORDER IS FALSE.
AND I SERVE THE TRUTH.

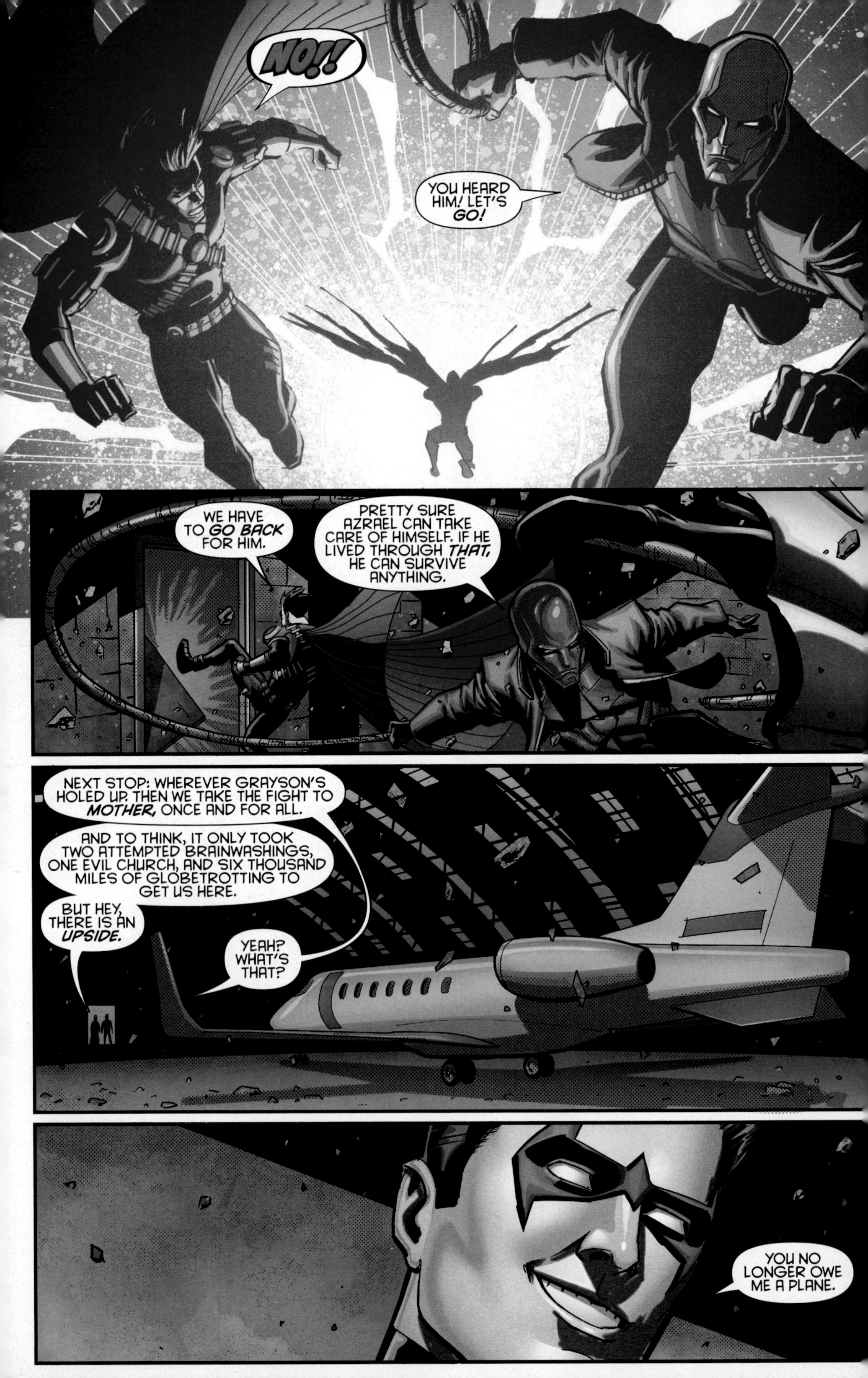
NO!!
YOU HEARD HIM! LET'S GO!
WE HAVE TO GO BACK FOR HIM.
PRETTY SURE AZRAEL CAN TAKE CARE OF HIMSELF. IF HE LIVED THROUGH THAT, HE CAN SURVIVE ANYTHING.
NEXT STOP: WHEREVER GRAYSON'S HOLED UP. THEN WE TAKE THE FIGHT TO MOTHER, ONCE AND FOR ALL.
AND TO THINK, IT ONLY TOOK TWO ATTEMPTED BRAINWASHINGS, ONE EVIL CHURCH, AND SIX THOUSAND MILES OF GLOBETROTTING TO GET US HERE.
BUT HEY, THERE IS AN UPSIDE.
YEAH? WHAT'S THAT?
YOU NO LONGER OWE ME A PLANE.

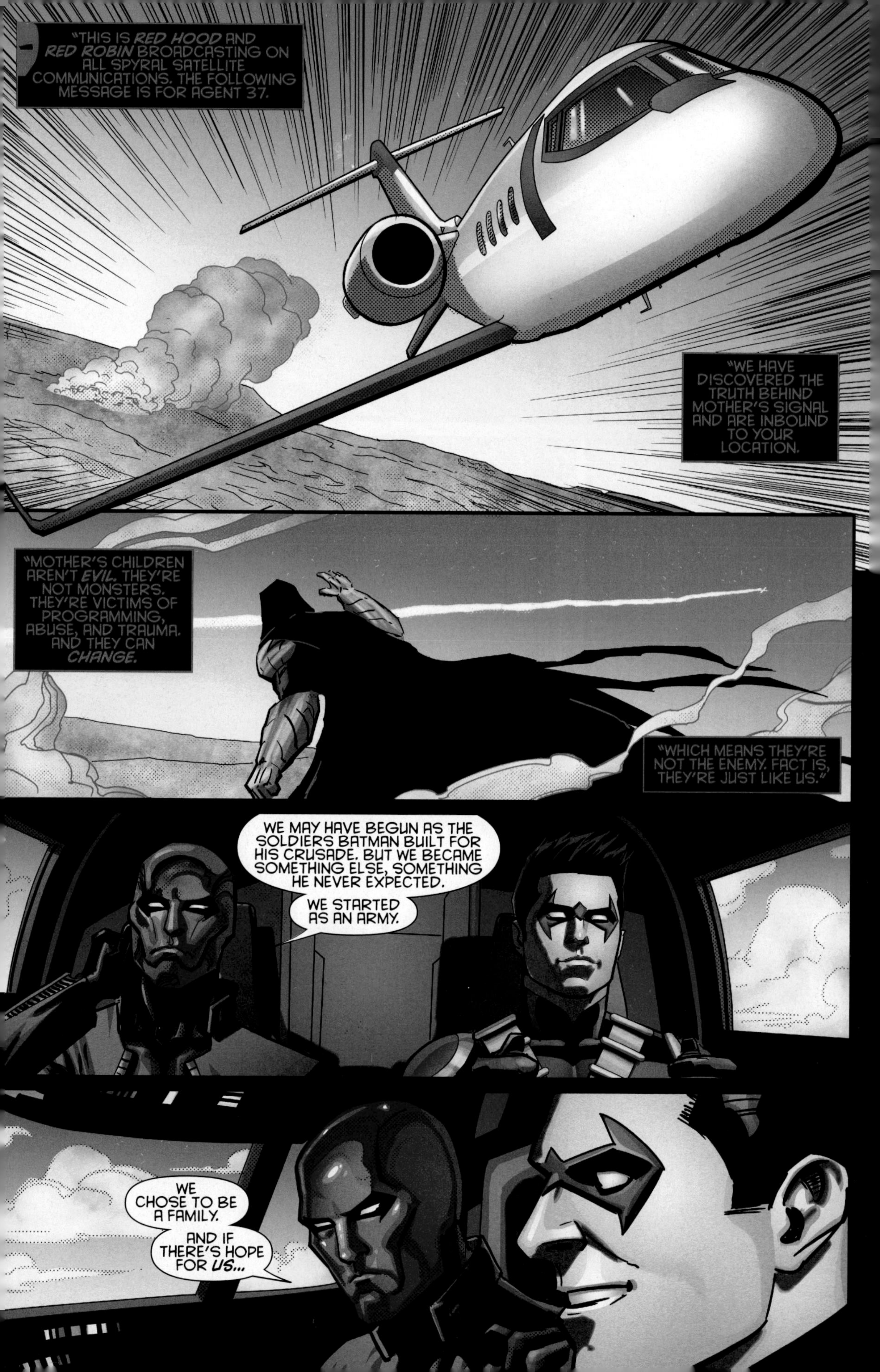
"THIS IS RED HOOD AND RED ROBIN BROADCASTING ON ALL SPYRAL SATELLITE COMMUNICATIONS. THE FOLLOWING MESSAGE IS FOR AGENT 37.
"WE HAVE DISCOVERED THE TRUTH BEHIND MOTHER'S SIGNAL AND ARE INBOUND TO YOUR LOCATION.
"MOTHER'S CHILDREN AREN'T EVIL. THEY'RE NOT MONSTERS. THEY'RE VICTIMS OF PROGRAMMING, ABUSE, AND TRAUMA. AND THEY CAN CHANGE.
"WHICH MEANS THEY'RE NOT THE ENEMY. FACT IS, THEY'RE JUST LIKE US."
WE MAY HAVE BEGUN AS THE SOLDIERS BATMAN BUILT FOR HIS CRUSADE. BUT WE BECAME SOMETHING ELSE, SOMETHING HE NEVER EXPECTED.
WE STARTED AS AN ARMY.
WE CHOSE TO BE A FAMILY.
AND IF THERE'S HOPE FOR US...

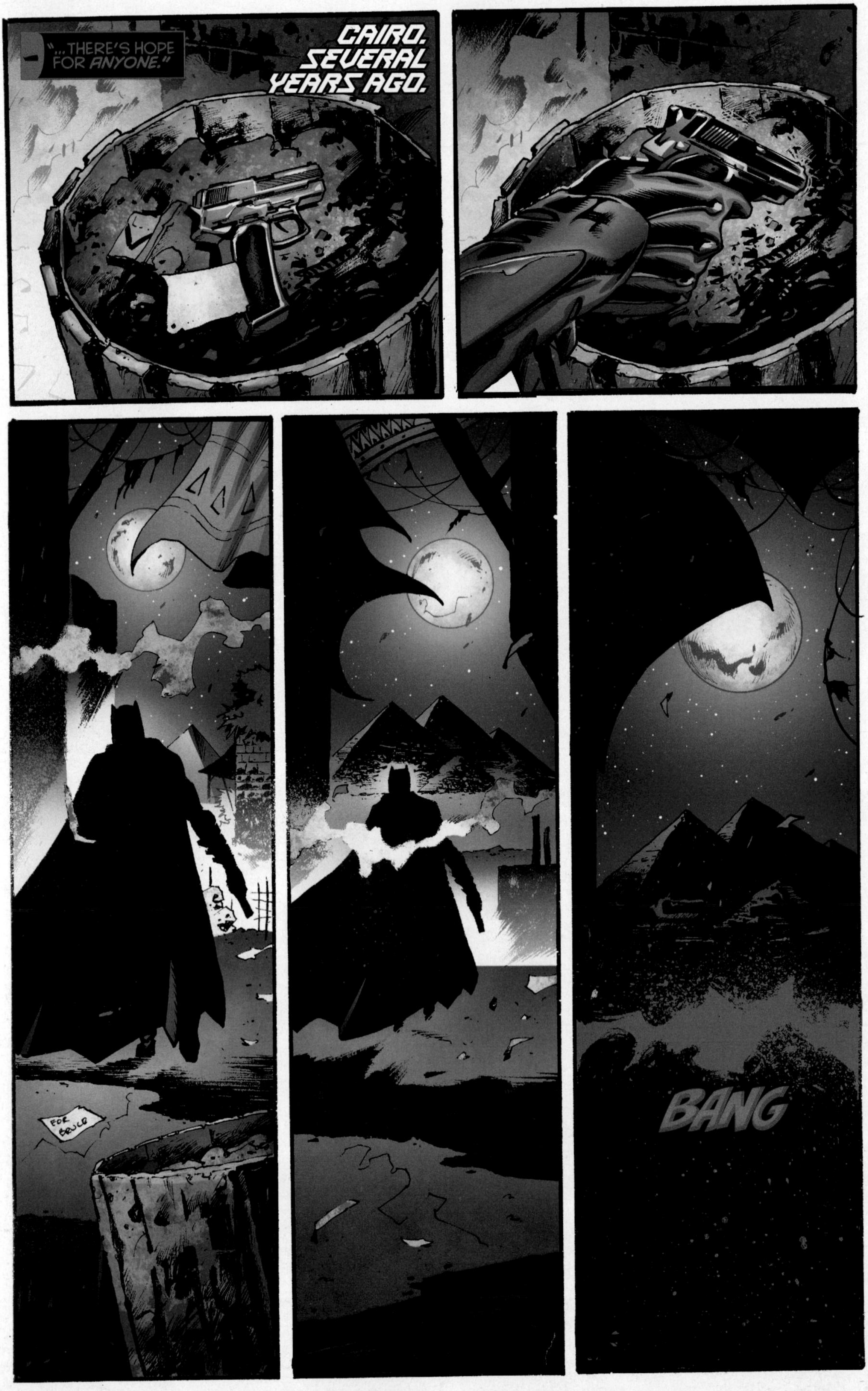
"...THERE'S HOPE FOR ANYONE."
CAIRO. SEVERAL YEARS AGO.
FOR BRUCE
BANG

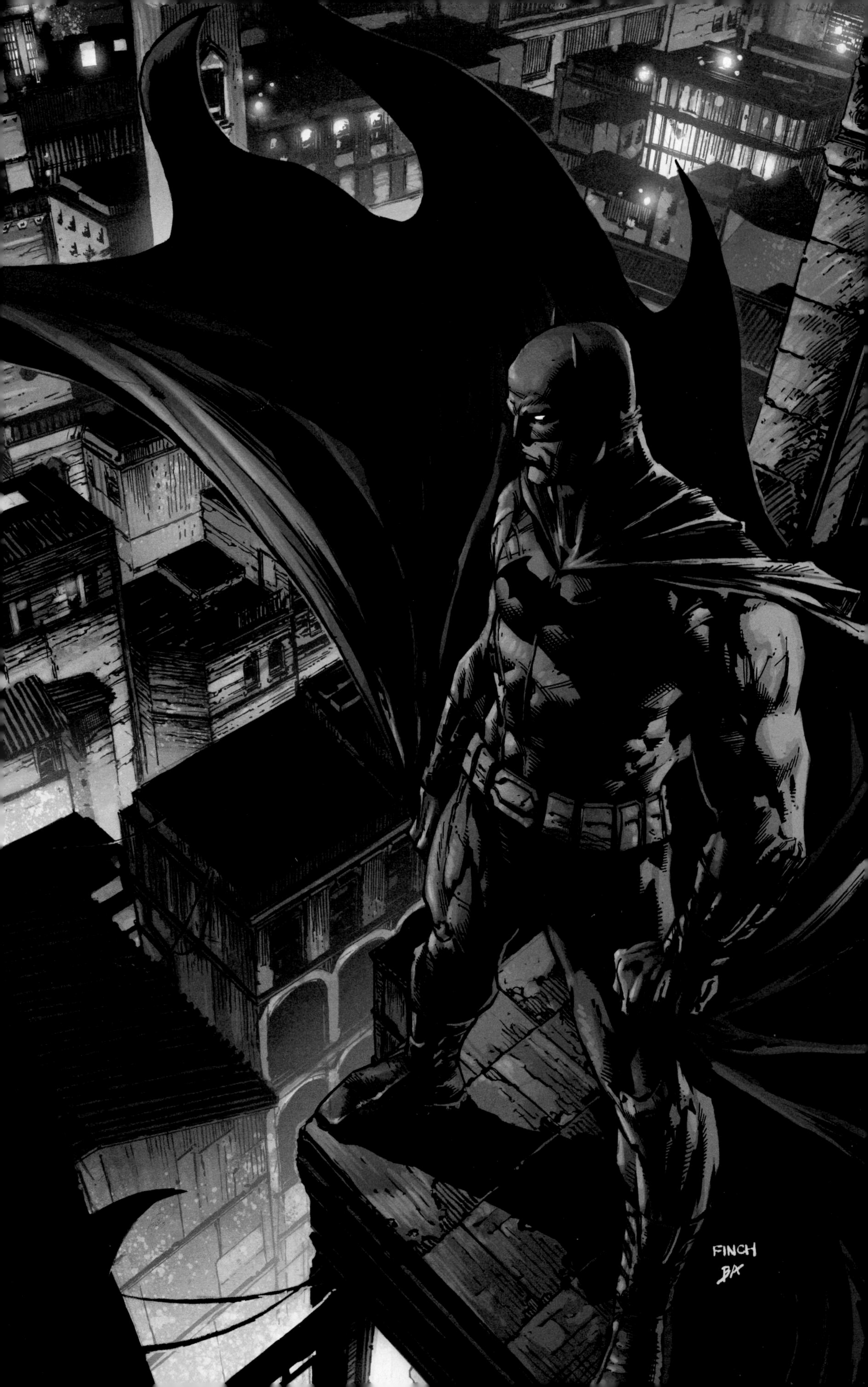
FINCH

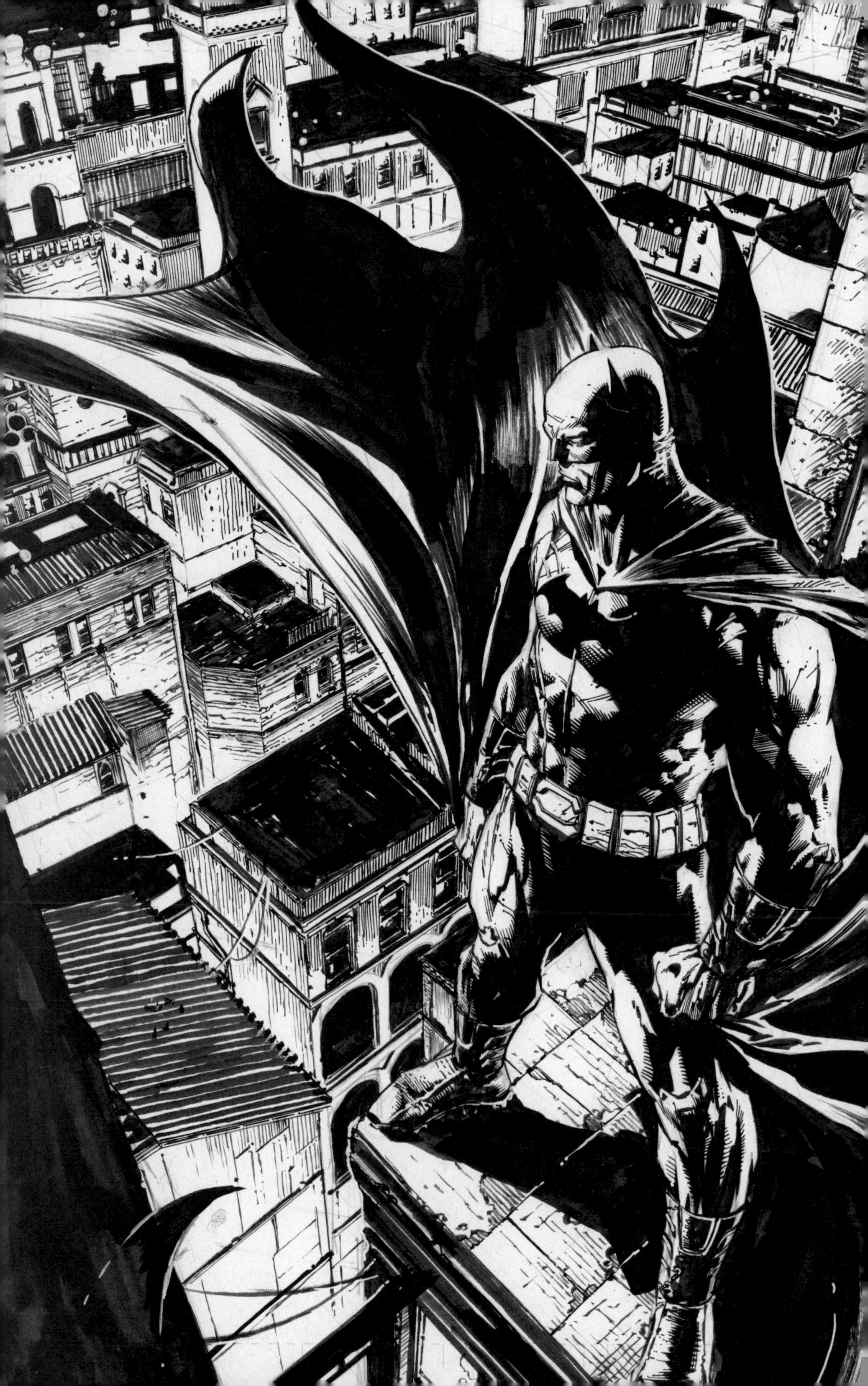

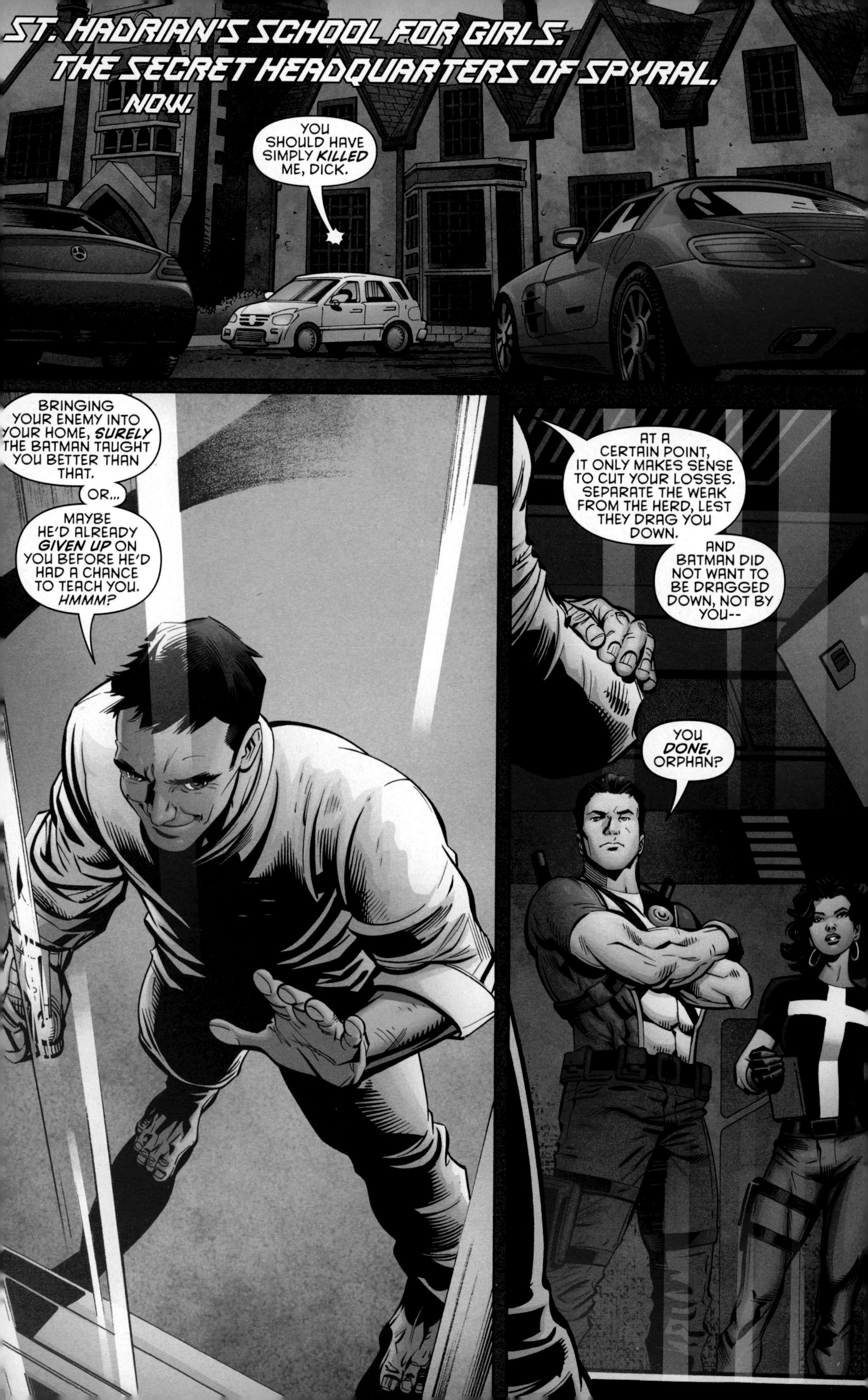
ST. HADRIAN'S SCHOOL FOR GIRLS.
THE SECRET HEADQUARTERS OF SPYRAL.
NOW.
YOU SHOULD HAVE SIMPLY *KILLED* ME, DICK.
BRINGING YOUR ENEMY INTO YOUR HOME, *SURELY* THE BATMAN TAUGHT YOU BETTER THAN THAT.
OR...
MAYBE HE'D ALREADY *GIVEN UP* ON YOU BEFORE HE'D HAD A CHANCE TO TEACH YOU. *HMMM?*
AT A CERTAIN POINT, IT ONLY MAKES SENSE TO CUT YOUR LOSSES. SEPARATE THE WEAK FROM THE HERD, LEST THEY DRAG YOU DOWN.
AND BATMAN DID NOT WANT TO BE DRAGGED DOWN, NOT BY YOU--
YOU *DONE,* ORPHAN?

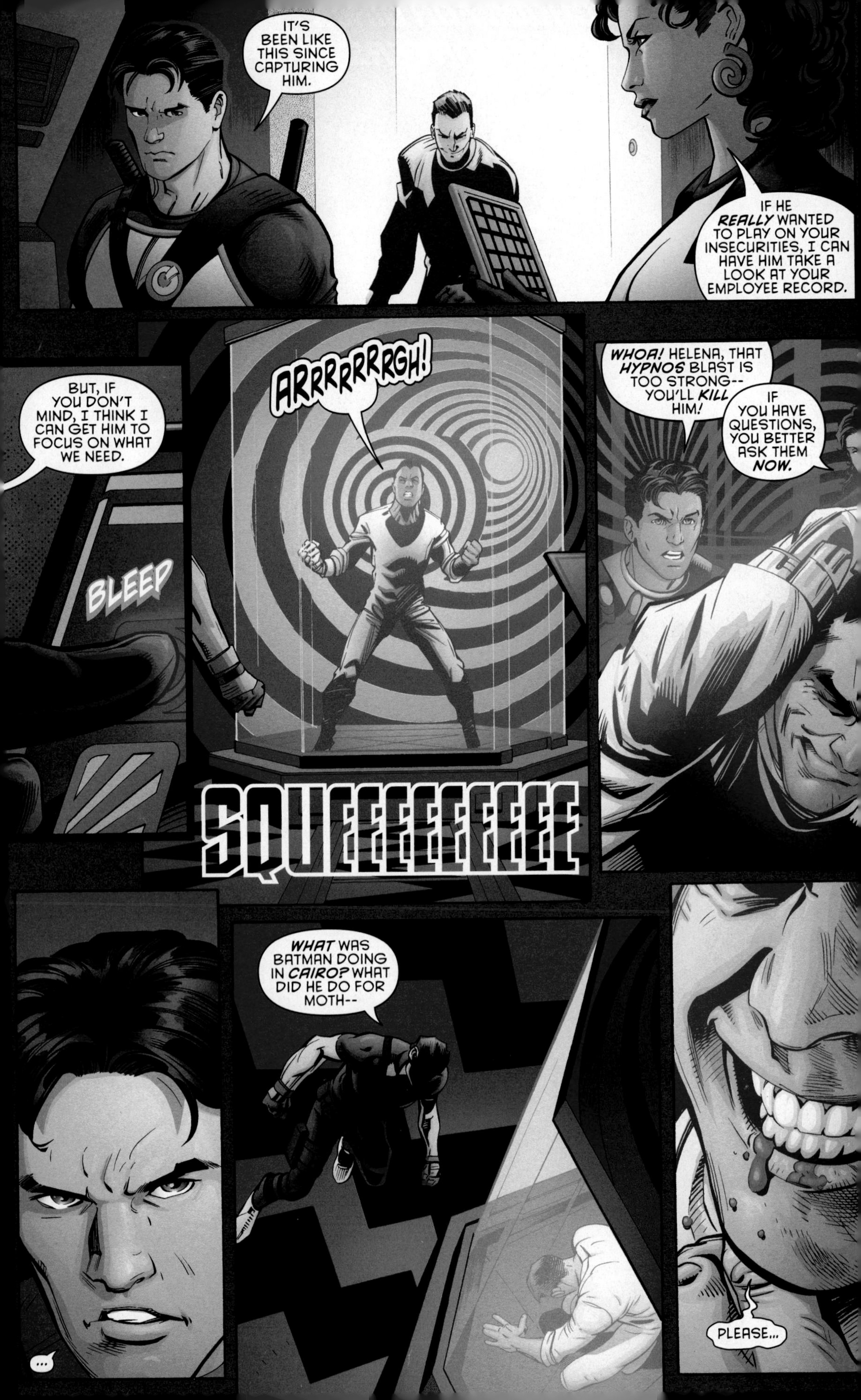
IT'S BEEN LIKE THIS SINCE CAPTURING HIM.
IF HE REALLY WANTED TO PLAY ON YOUR INSECURITIES, I CAN HAVE HIM TAKE A LOOK AT YOUR EMPLOYEE RECORD.
BUT, IF YOU DON'T MIND, I THINK I CAN GET HIM TO FOCUS ON WHAT WE NEED.
BLEEP
ARRRRRRRGH!
SQUEEEEEEEEE
WHOA! HELENA, THAT HYPNOS BLAST IS TOO STRONG-- YOU'LL KILL HIM!
IF YOU HAVE QUESTIONS, YOU BETTER ASK THEM NOW.
...
WHAT WAS BATMAN DOING IN CAIRO? WHAT DID HE DO FOR MOTH--
PLEASE...

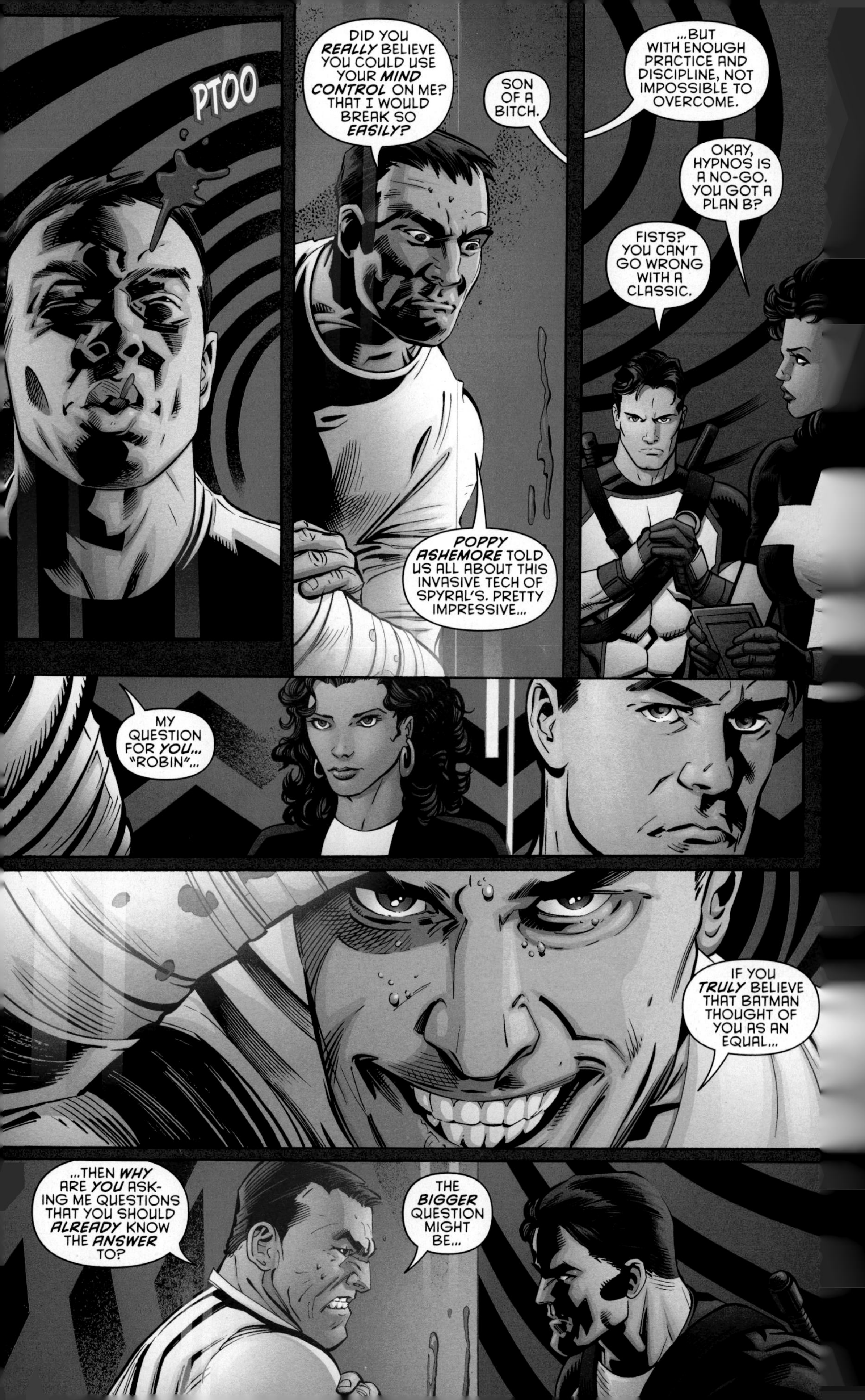
PTOO
DID YOU REALLY BELIEVE YOU COULD USE YOUR MIND CONTROL ON ME? THAT I WOULD BREAK SO EASILY?
SON OF A BITCH.
POPPY ASHEMORE TOLD US ALL ABOUT THIS INVASIVE TECH OF SPYRAL'S. PRETTY IMPRESSIVE...
...BUT WITH ENOUGH PRACTICE AND DISCIPLINE, NOT IMPOSSIBLE TO OVERCOME.
OKAY, HYPNOS IS A NO-GO. YOU GOT A PLAN B?
FISTS? YOU CAN'T GO WRONG WITH A CLASSIC.
MY QUESTION FOR YOU... "ROBIN"...
IF YOU TRULY BELIEVE THAT BATMAN THOUGHT OF YOU AS AN EQUAL...
...THEN WHY ARE YOU ASKING ME QUESTIONS THAT YOU SHOULD ALREADY KNOW THE ANSWER TO?
THE BIGGER QUESTION MIGHT BE...

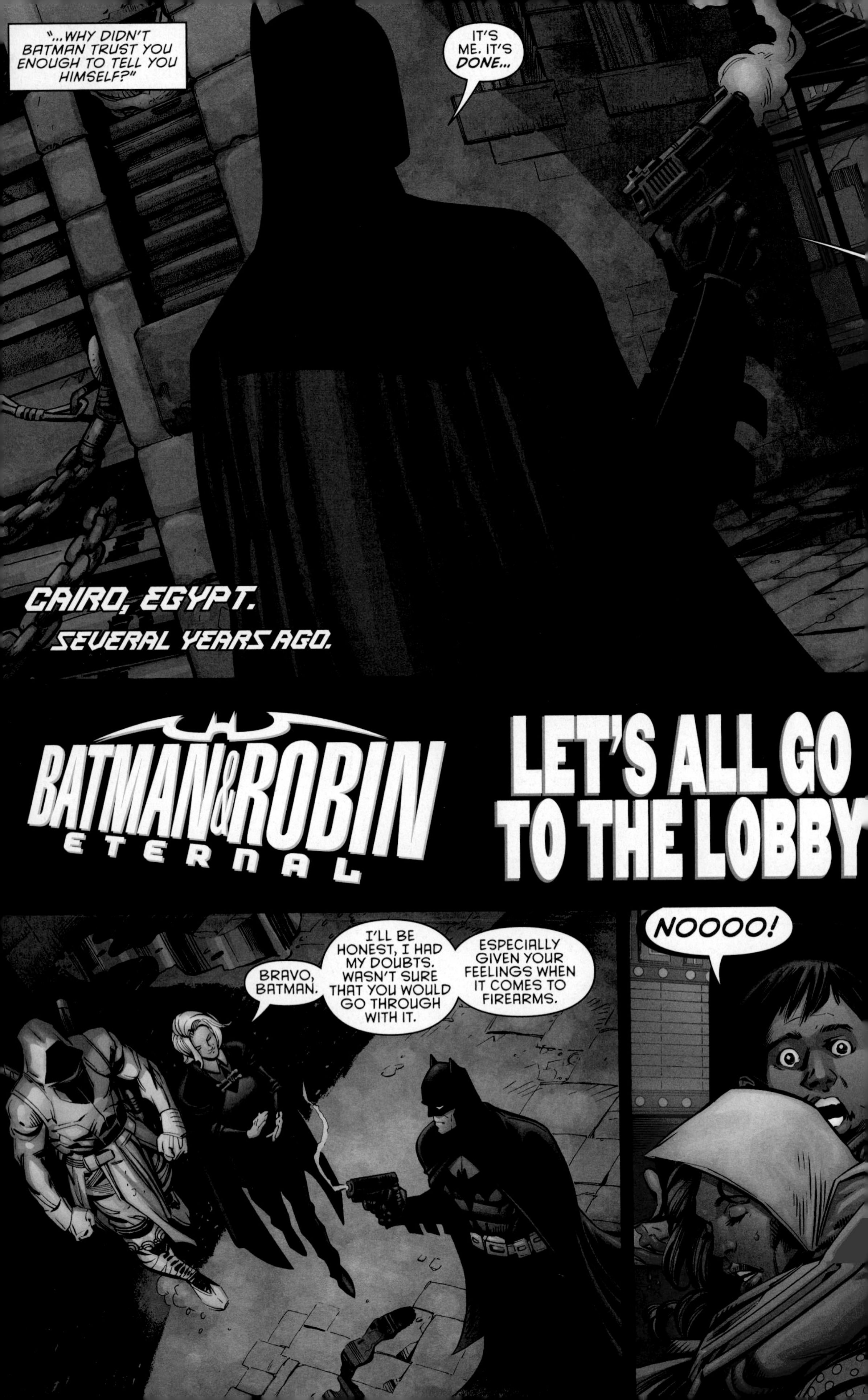
"...WHY DIDN'T BATMAN TRUST YOU ENOUGH TO TELL YOU HIMSELF?"
IT'S ME. IT'S DONE...
CAIRO, EGYPT.
SEVERAL YEARS AGO.
BATMAN & ROBIN ETERNAL
LET'S ALL GO TO THE LOBBY
BRAVO, BATMAN.
I'LL BE HONEST, I HAD MY DOUBTS. WASN'T SURE THAT YOU WOULD GO THROUGH WITH IT.
ESPECIALLY GIVEN YOUR FEELINGS WHEN IT COMES TO FIREARMS.
NOOOO!

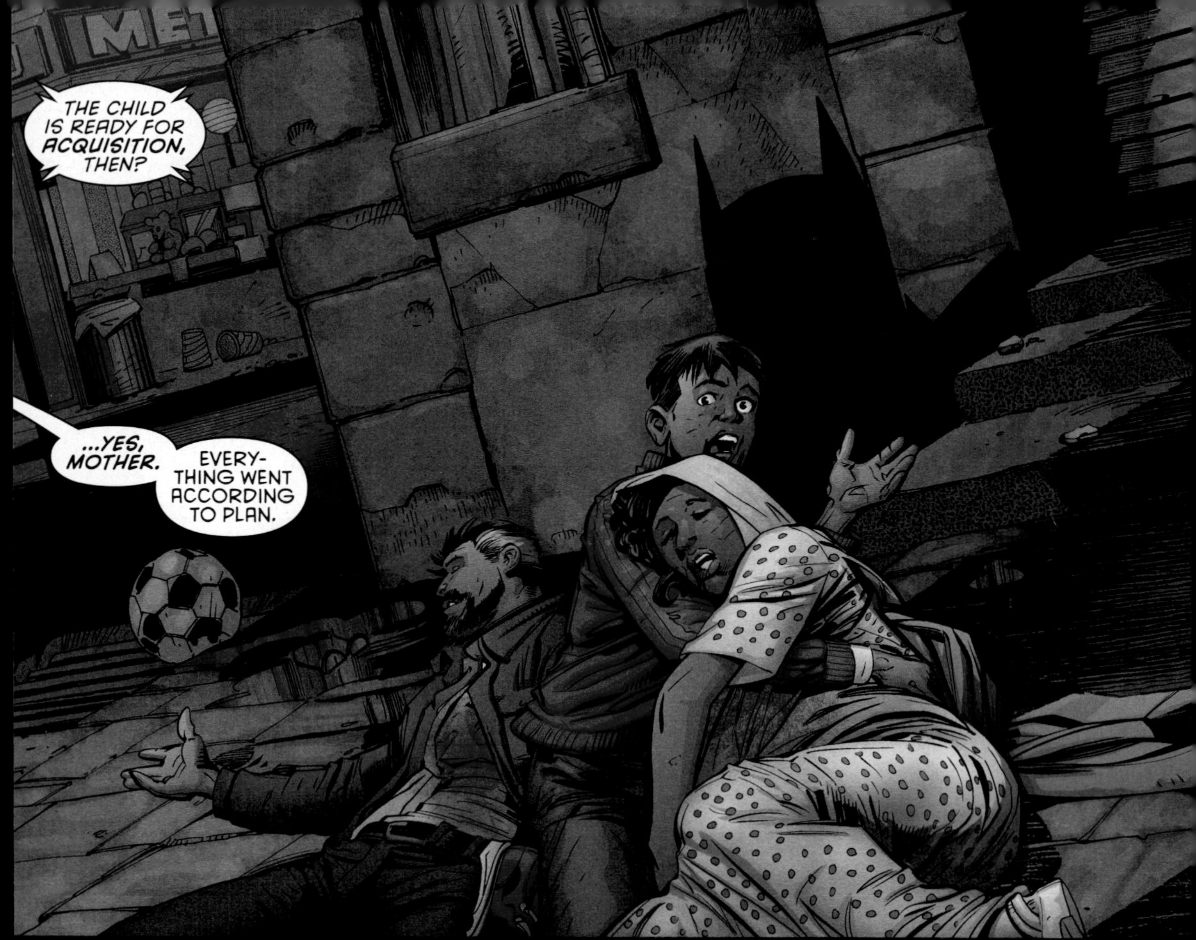
THE CHILD IS READY FOR ACQUISITION, THEN?
...YES, MOTHER.
EVERY-THING WENT ACCORDING TO PLAN.

JAMES TYNION IV & SCOTT SNYDER STORY
ED BRISSON SCRIPT
SCOT EATON PENCILS
WAYNE FAUCHER INKS
ALLEN PASSALAQUA COLORS
COREY BREEN LETTERS
DAVID FINCH & BRAD ANDERSON COVER

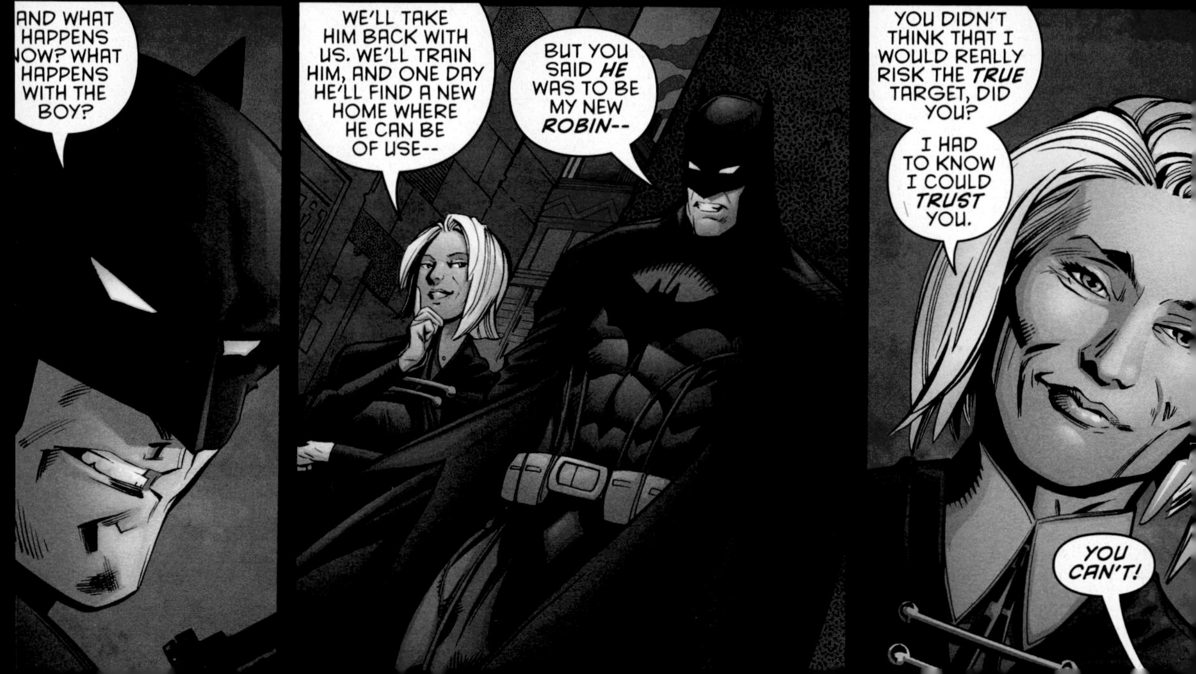
AND WHAT HAPPENS NOW? WHAT HAPPENS WITH THE BOY?
WE'LL TAKE HIM BACK WITH US. WE'LL TRAIN HIM, AND ONE DAY HE'LL FIND A NEW HOME WHERE HE CAN BE OF USE--
BUT YOU SAID HE WAS TO BE MY NEW ROBIN--
YOU DIDN'T THINK THAT I WOULD REALLY RISK THE TRUE TARGET, DID YOU?
I HAD TO KNOW I COULD TRUST YOU.
YOU CAN'T!

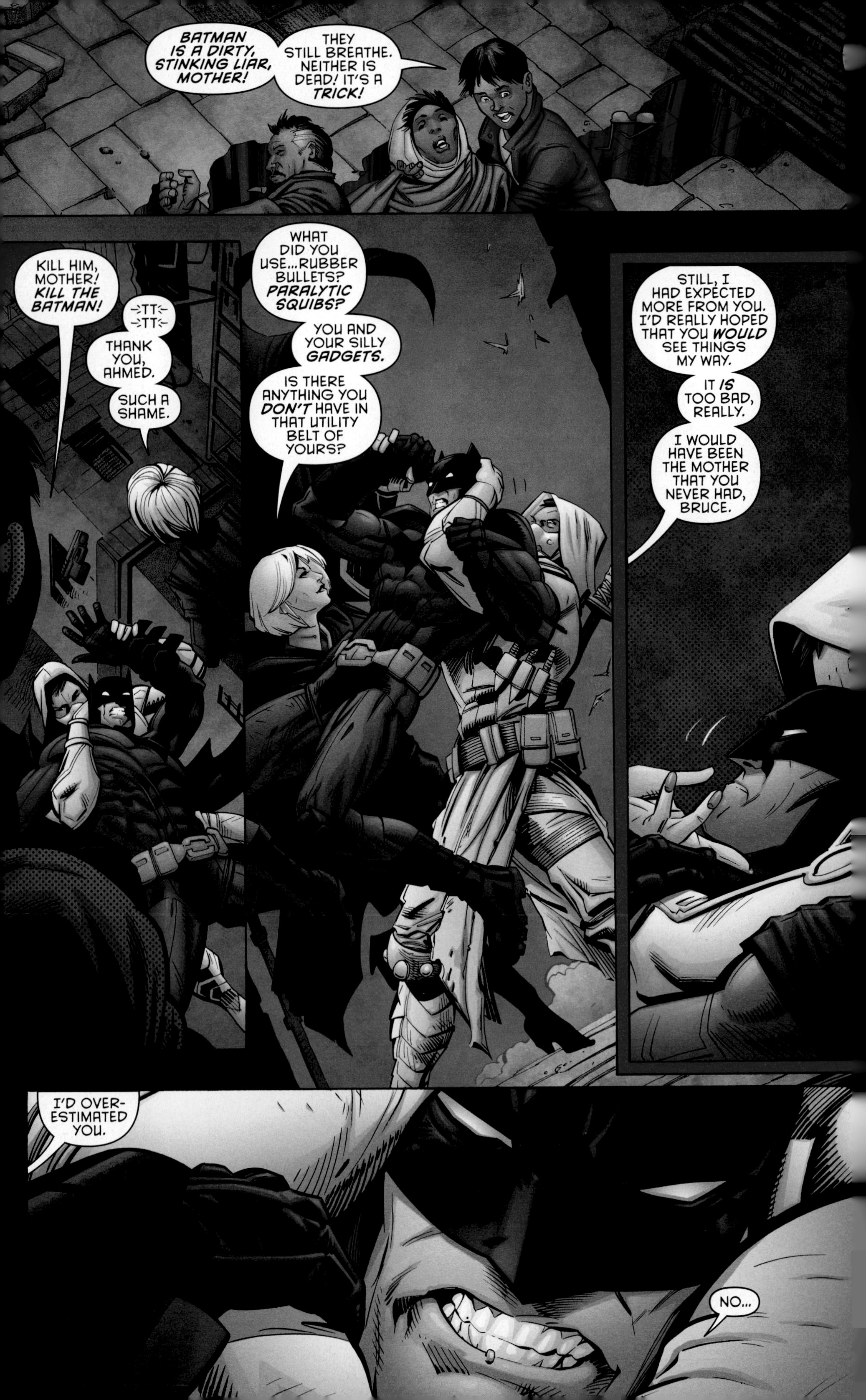
BATMAN IS A DIRTY, STINKING LIAR, MOTHER!
THEY STILL BREATHE. NEITHER IS DEAD! IT'S A TRICK!
KILL HIM, MOTHER! KILL THE BATMAN!
TT TT
THANK YOU, AHMED.
SUCH A SHAME.
WHAT DID YOU USE...RUBBER BULLETS? PARALYTIC SQUIBS?
YOU AND YOUR SILLY GADGETS.
IS THERE ANYTHING YOU DON'T HAVE IN THAT UTILITY BELT OF YOURS?
STILL, I HAD EXPECTED MORE FROM YOU. I'D REALLY HOPED THAT YOU WOULD SEE THINGS MY WAY.
IT IS TOO BAD, REALLY.
I WOULD HAVE BEEN THE MOTHER THAT YOU NEVER HAD, BRUCE.
I'D OVER-ESTIMATED YOU.
NO...

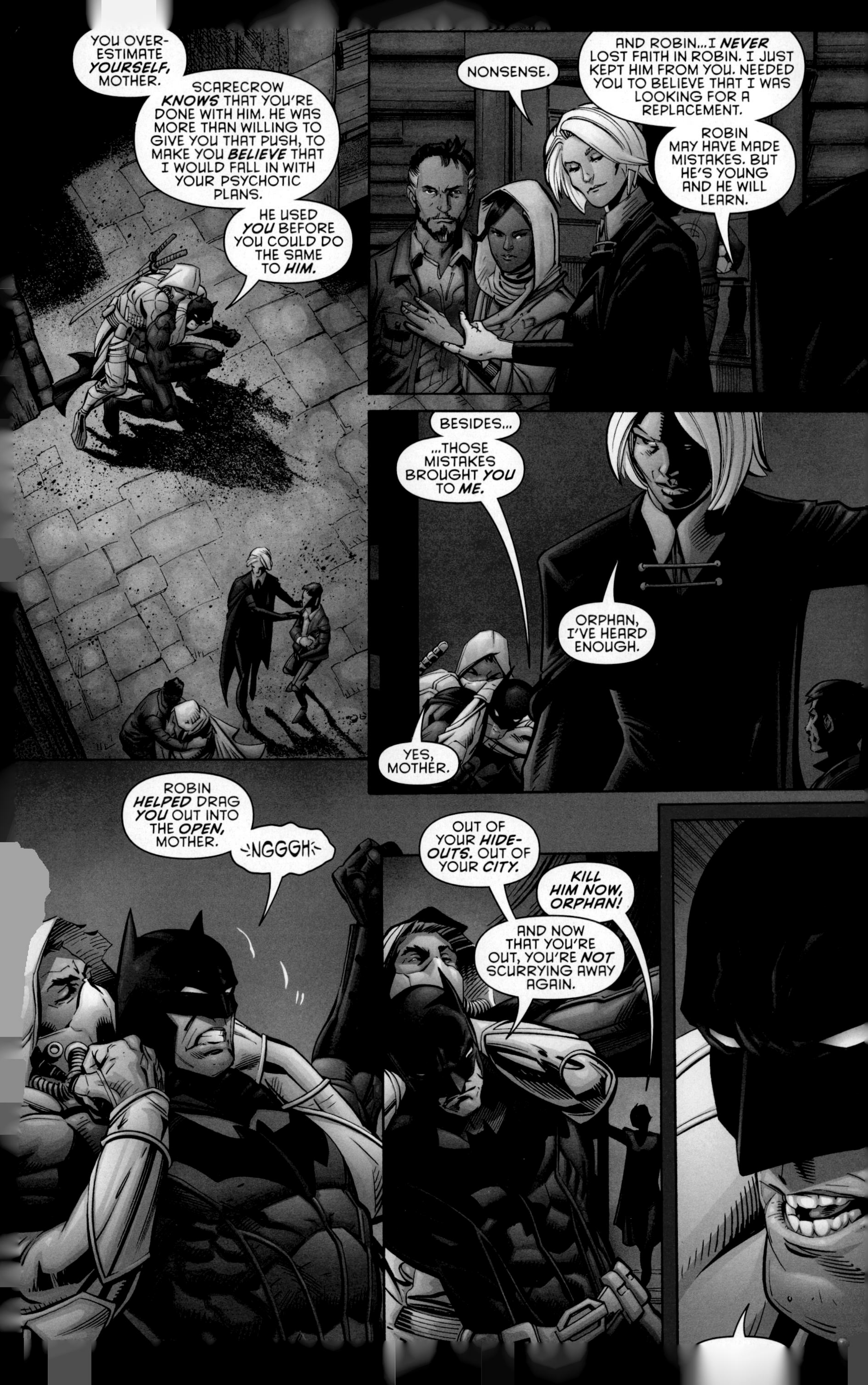
YOU OVER-ESTIMATE *YOURSELF,* MOTHER.
SCARECROW *KNOWS* THAT YOU'RE DONE WITH HIM. HE WAS MORE THAN WILLING TO GIVE YOU THAT PUSH, TO MAKE YOU *BELIEVE* THAT I WOULD FALL IN WITH YOUR PSYCHOTIC PLANS.
HE USED *YOU* BEFORE YOU COULD DO THE SAME TO *HIM.*
NONSENSE.
AND ROBIN...I *NEVER* LOST FAITH IN ROBIN. I JUST KEPT HIM FROM YOU. NEEDED YOU TO BELIEVE THAT I WAS LOOKING FOR A REPLACEMENT.
ROBIN MAY HAVE MADE MISTAKES. BUT HE'S YOUNG AND HE WILL LEARN.
BESIDES...
...THOSE MISTAKES BROUGHT *YOU* TO *ME.*
ORPHAN, I'VE HEARD ENOUGH.
YES, MOTHER.
ROBIN *HELPED* DRAG *YOU* OUT INTO THE *OPEN,* MOTHER.
-NGGGH-
OUT OF YOUR *HIDE-OUTS.* OUT OF YOUR *CITY.*
KILL HIM NOW, ORPHAN!
AND NOW THAT YOU'RE OUT, YOU'RE *NOT* SCURRYING AWAY AGAIN.

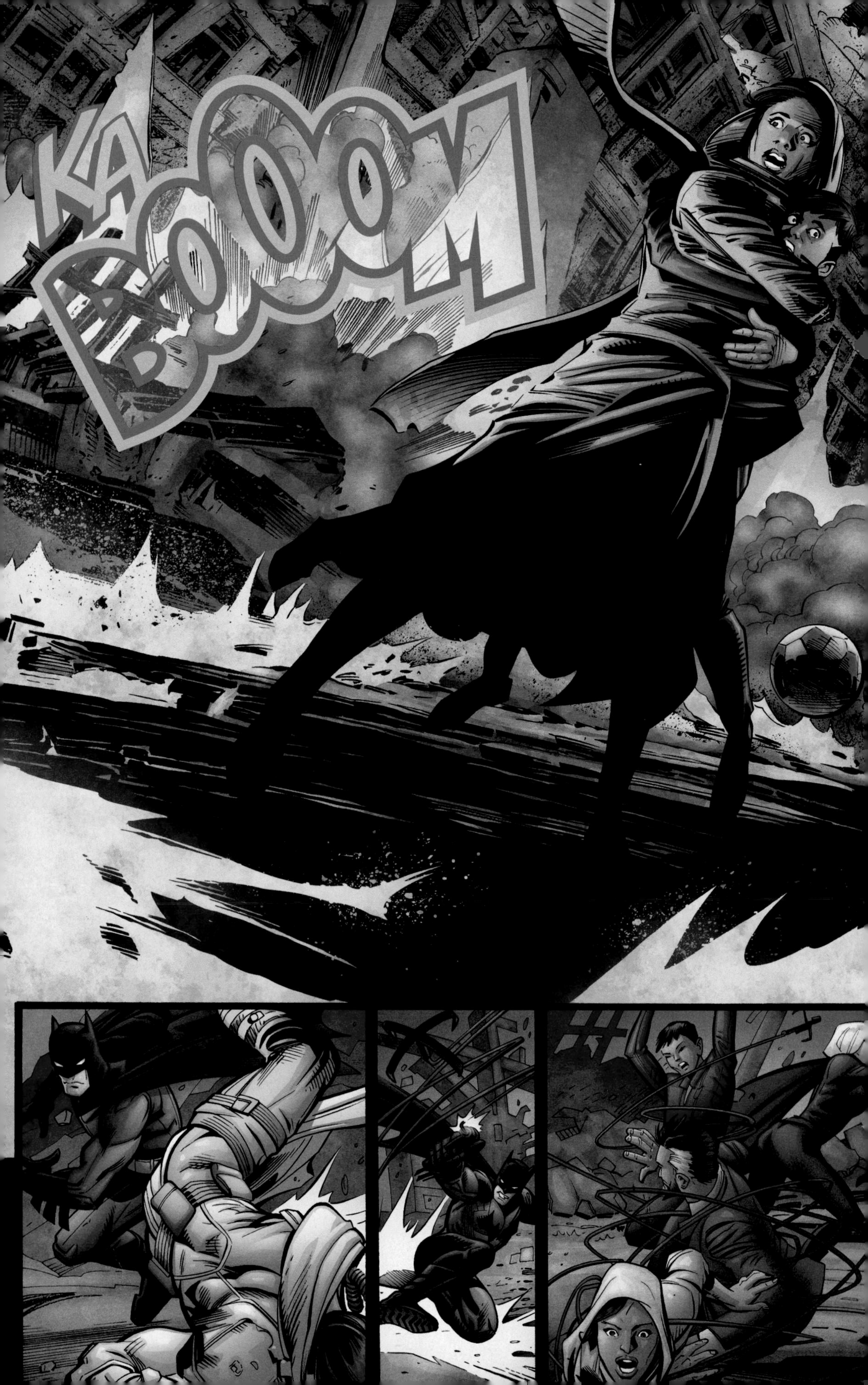
KA-BOOOOM

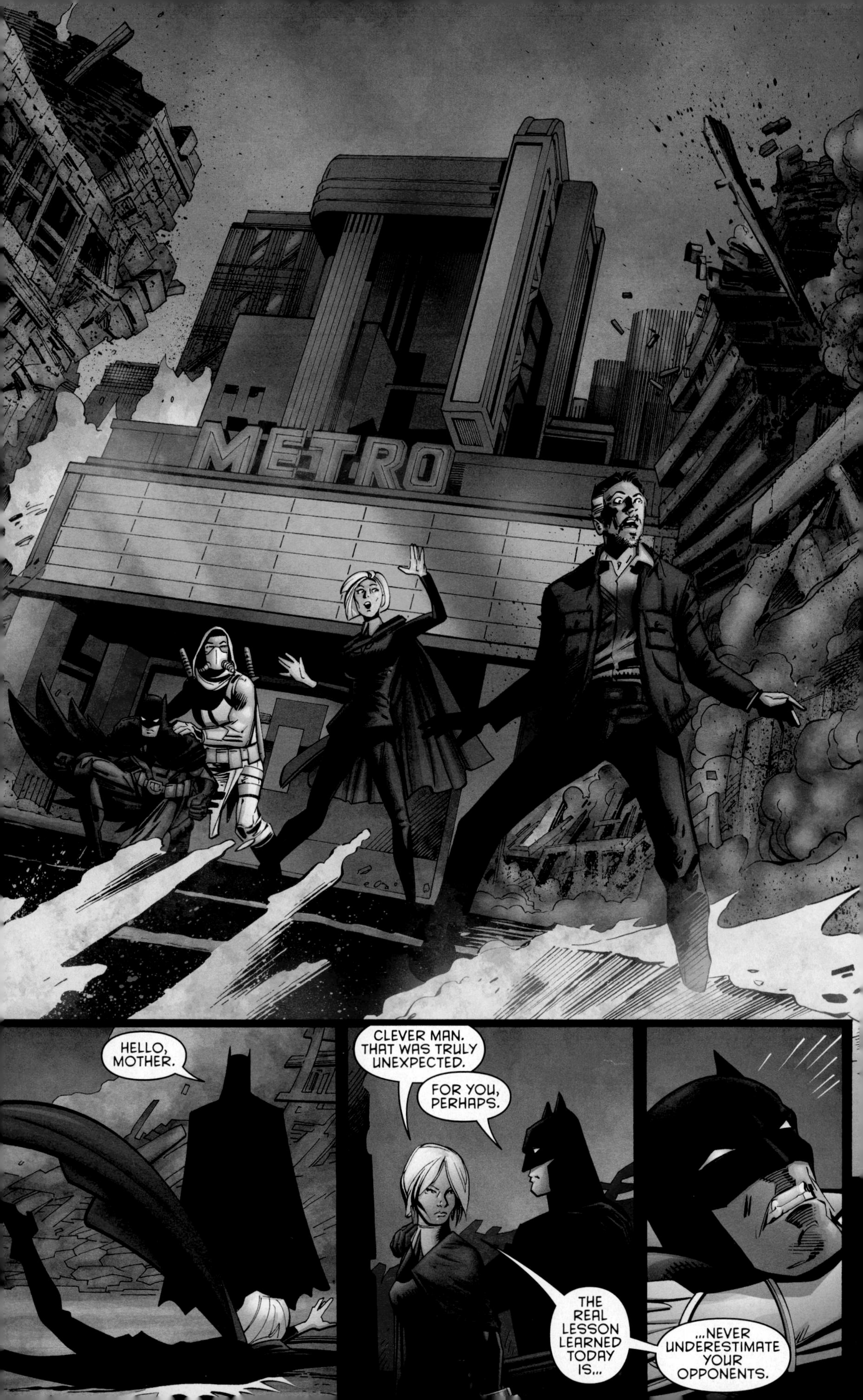
METRO
HELLO, MOTHER.
CLEVER MAN. THAT WAS TRULY UNEXPECTED.
FOR YOU, PERHAPS.
THE REAL LESSON LEARNED TODAY IS...
...NEVER UNDERESTIMATE YOUR OPPONENTS.

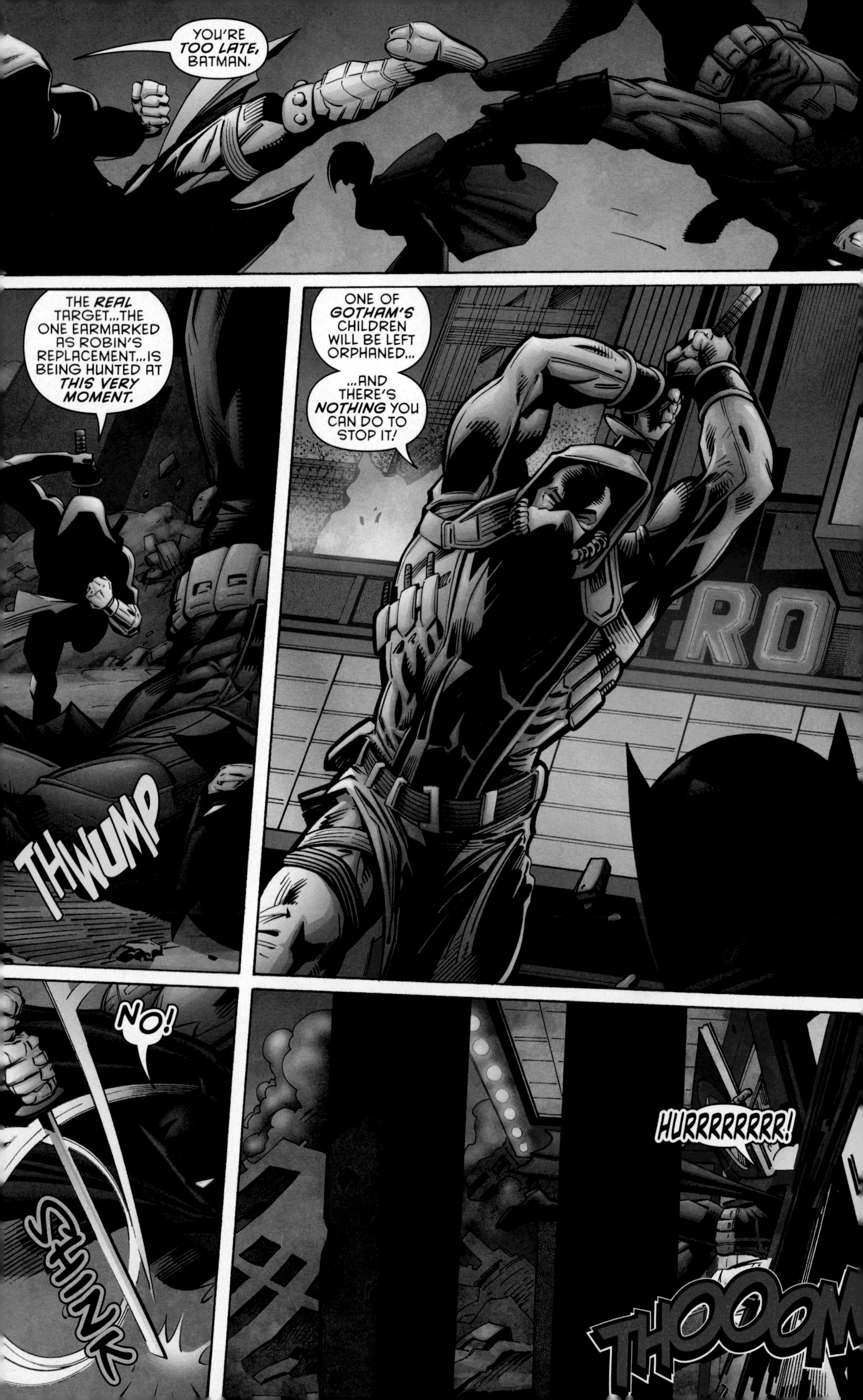
YOU'RE *TOO LATE,* BATMAN.
THE *REAL* TARGET...THE ONE EARMARKED AS ROBIN'S REPLACEMENT...IS BEING HUNTED AT *THIS VERY MOMENT.*
THWUMP
ONE OF *GOTHAM'S* CHILDREN WILL BE LEFT ORPHANED...
...AND THERE'S *NOTHING* YOU CAN DO TO STOP IT!
RO
NO!
SHINK
HURRRRRRRR!
THOOOM

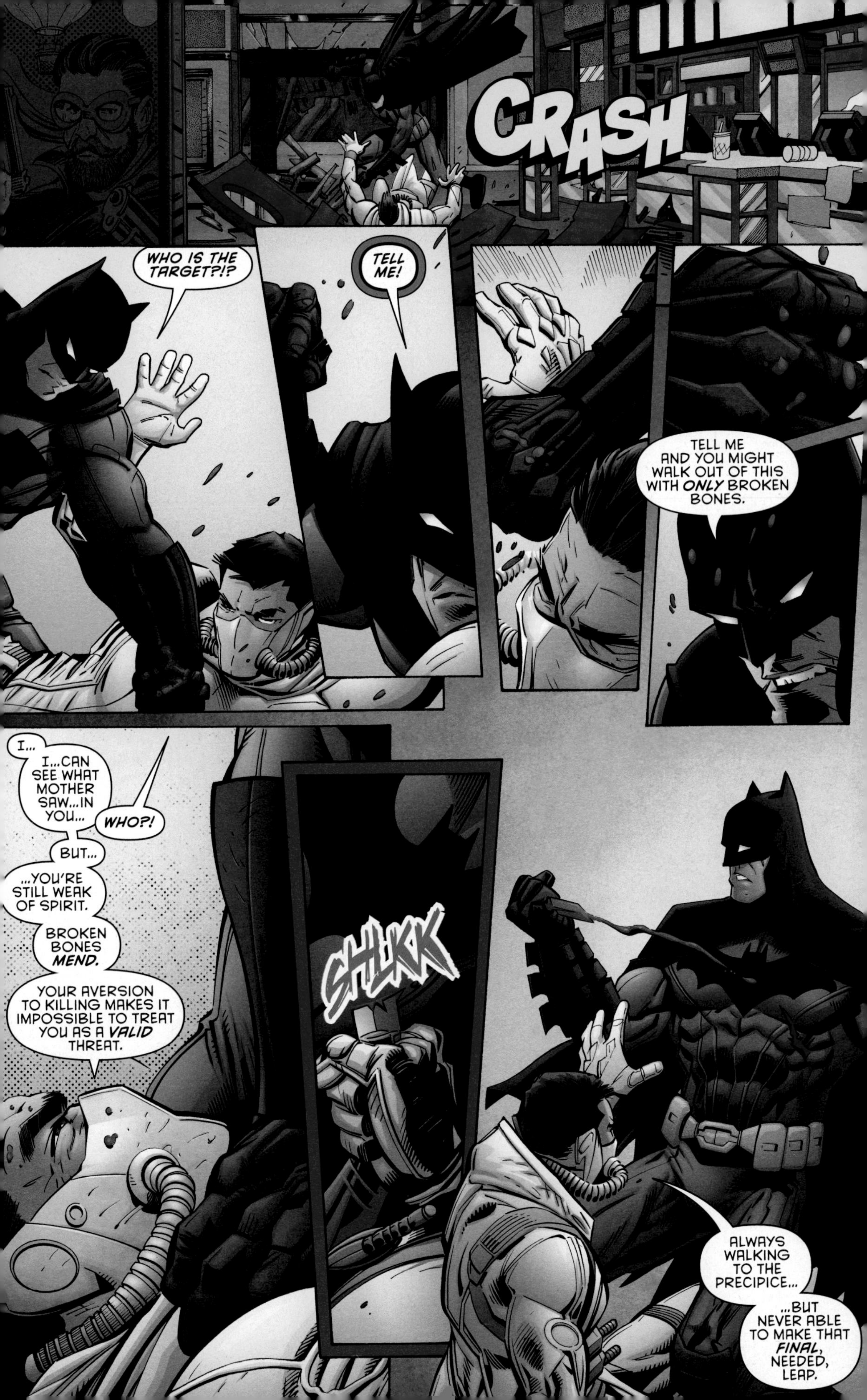
CRASH
WHO IS THE TARGET?!?
TELL ME!
TELL ME AND YOU MIGHT WALK OUT OF THIS WITH ONLY BROKEN BONES.
I...
I...CAN SEE WHAT MOTHER SAW...IN YOU...
WHO?!
BUT...
...YOU'RE STILL WEAK OF SPIRIT.
BROKEN BONES MEND.
YOUR AVERSION TO KILLING MAKES IT IMPOSSIBLE TO TREAT YOU AS A VALID THREAT.
SHLKK
ALWAYS WALKING TO THE PRECIPICE...
...BUT NEVER ABLE TO MAKE THAT FINAL, NEEDED, LEAP.

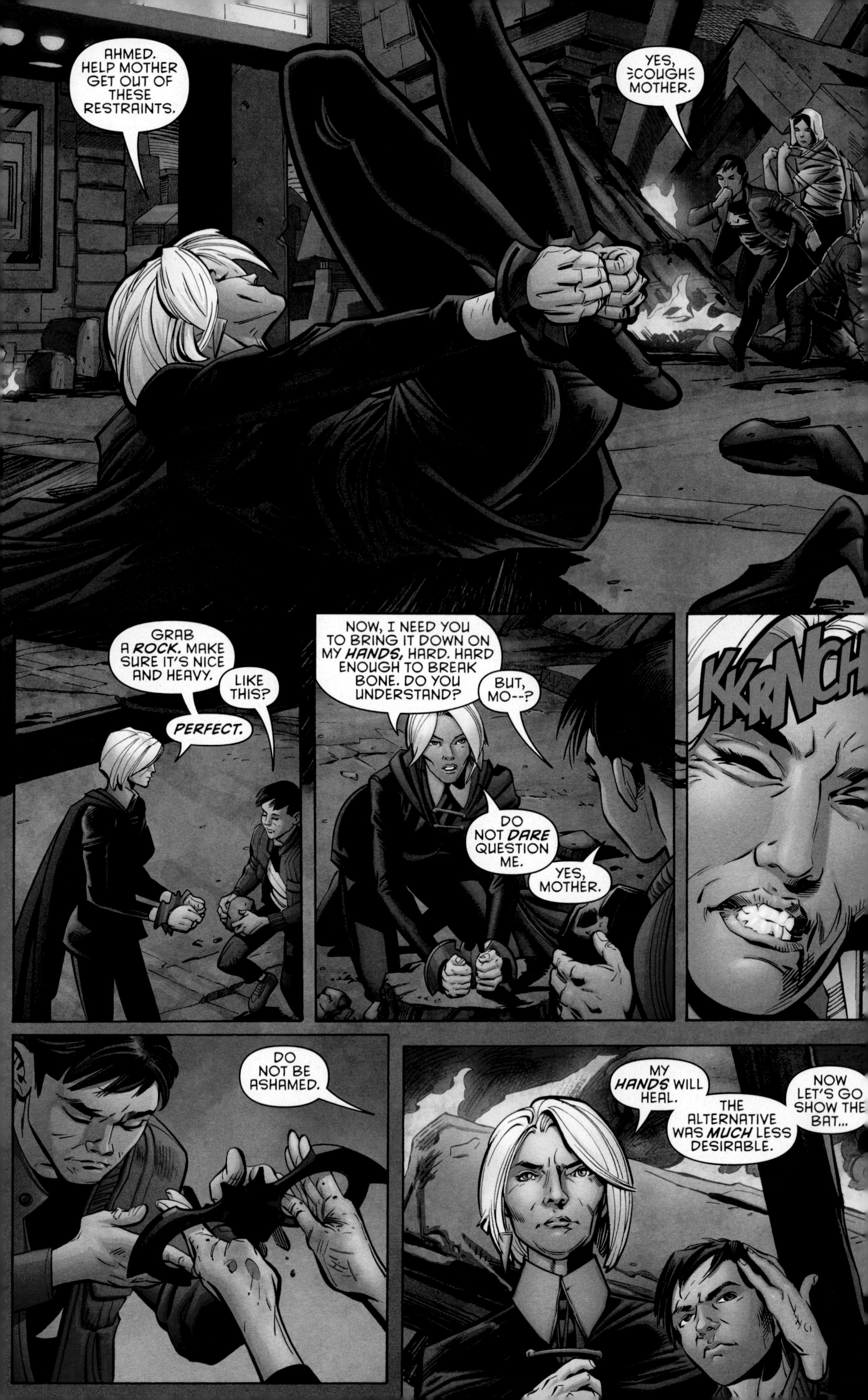
AHMED. HELP MOTHER GET OUT OF THESE RESTRAINTS.
YES, *COUGH* MOTHER.
GRAB A ROCK. MAKE SURE IT'S NICE AND HEAVY.
LIKE THIS?
PERFECT.
NOW, I NEED YOU TO BRING IT DOWN ON MY HANDS, HARD. HARD ENOUGH TO BREAK BONE. DO YOU UNDERSTAND?
BUT, MO--?
DO NOT DARE QUESTION ME.
YES, MOTHER.
KKRNCH
DO NOT BE ASHAMED.
MY HANDS WILL HEAL.
THE ALTERNATIVE WAS MUCH LESS DESIRABLE.
NOW LET'S GO SHOW THE BAT...

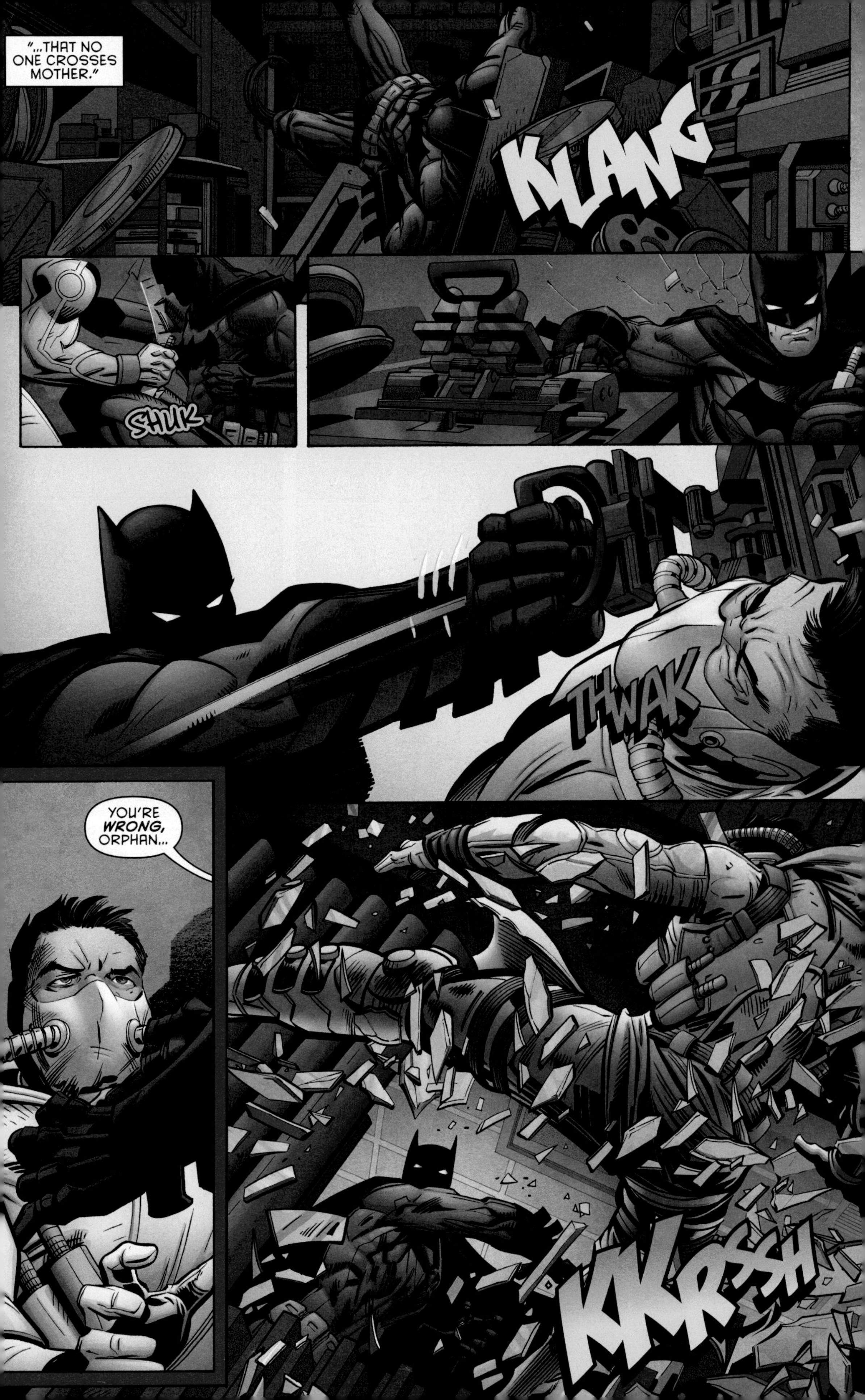
"...THAT NO ONE CROSSES MOTHER."
KLANG
SHUK
THWAK
YOU'RE *WRONG*, ORPHAN...
KKRSH

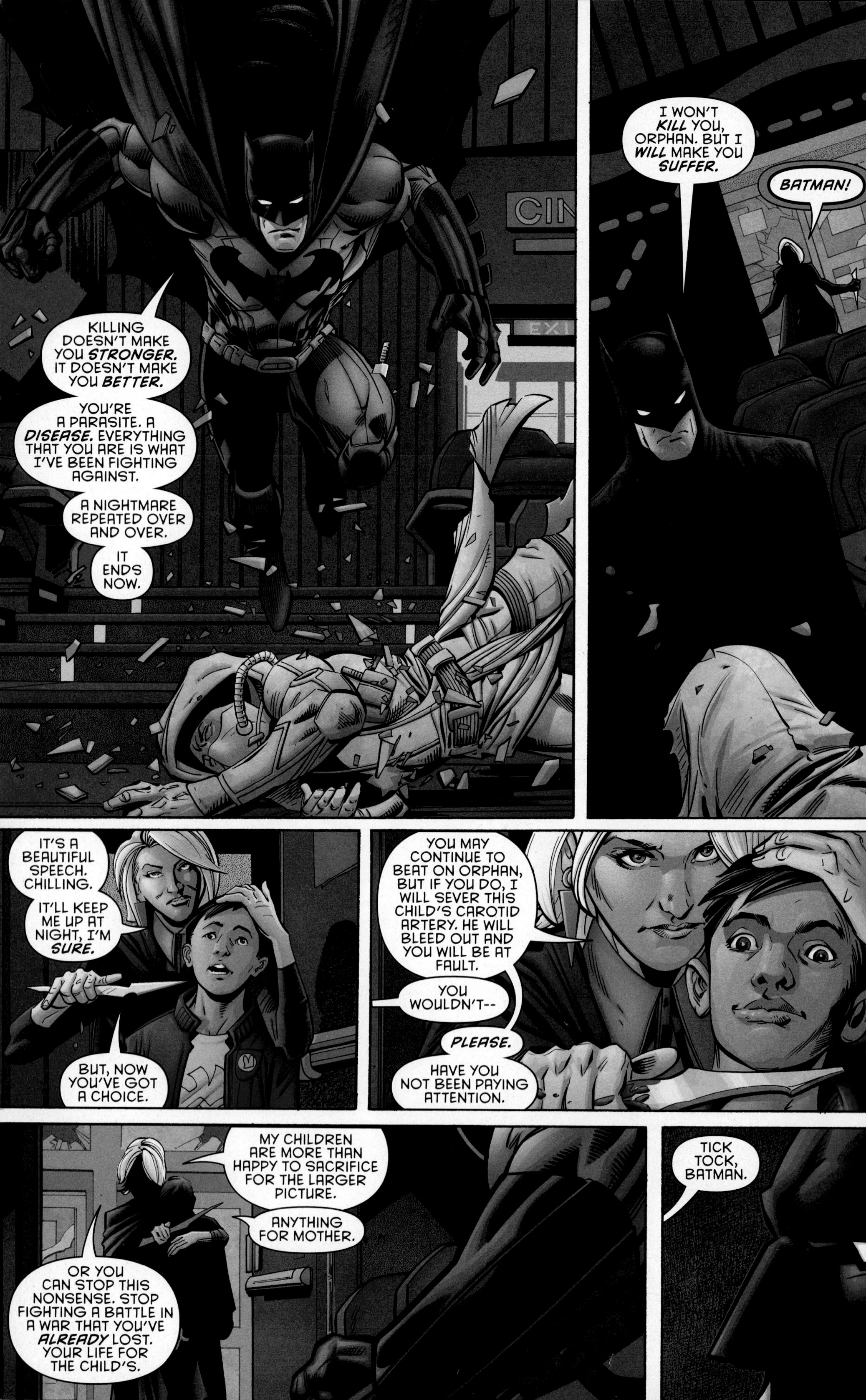

KILLING DOESN'T MAKE YOU **STRONGER.** IT DOESN'T MAKE YOU **BETTER.**
YOU'RE A PARASITE. A **DISEASE.** EVERYTHING THAT YOU ARE IS WHAT I'VE BEEN FIGHTING AGAINST.
A NIGHTMARE REPEATED OVER AND OVER.
IT ENDS NOW.
CIN
EXI
I WON'T **KILL** YOU, ORPHAN. BUT I **WILL** MAKE YOU **SUFFER.**
BATMAN!
IT'S A BEAUTIFUL SPEECH. CHILLING.
IT'LL KEEP ME UP AT NIGHT, I'M **SURE.**
BUT, NOW YOU'VE GOT A CHOICE.
YOU MAY CONTINUE TO BEAT ON ORPHAN, BUT IF YOU DO, I WILL SEVER THIS CHILD'S CAROTID ARTERY. HE WILL BLEED OUT AND YOU WILL BE AT FAULT.
YOU WOULDN'T--
PLEASE.
HAVE YOU NOT BEEN PAYING ATTENTION.
MY CHILDREN ARE MORE THAN HAPPY TO SACRIFICE FOR THE LARGER PICTURE.
ANYTHING FOR MOTHER.
OR YOU CAN STOP THIS NONSENSE. STOP FIGHTING A BATTLE IN A WAR THAT YOU'VE **ALREADY** LOST. YOUR LIFE FOR THE CHILD'S.
TICK TOCK, BATMAN.

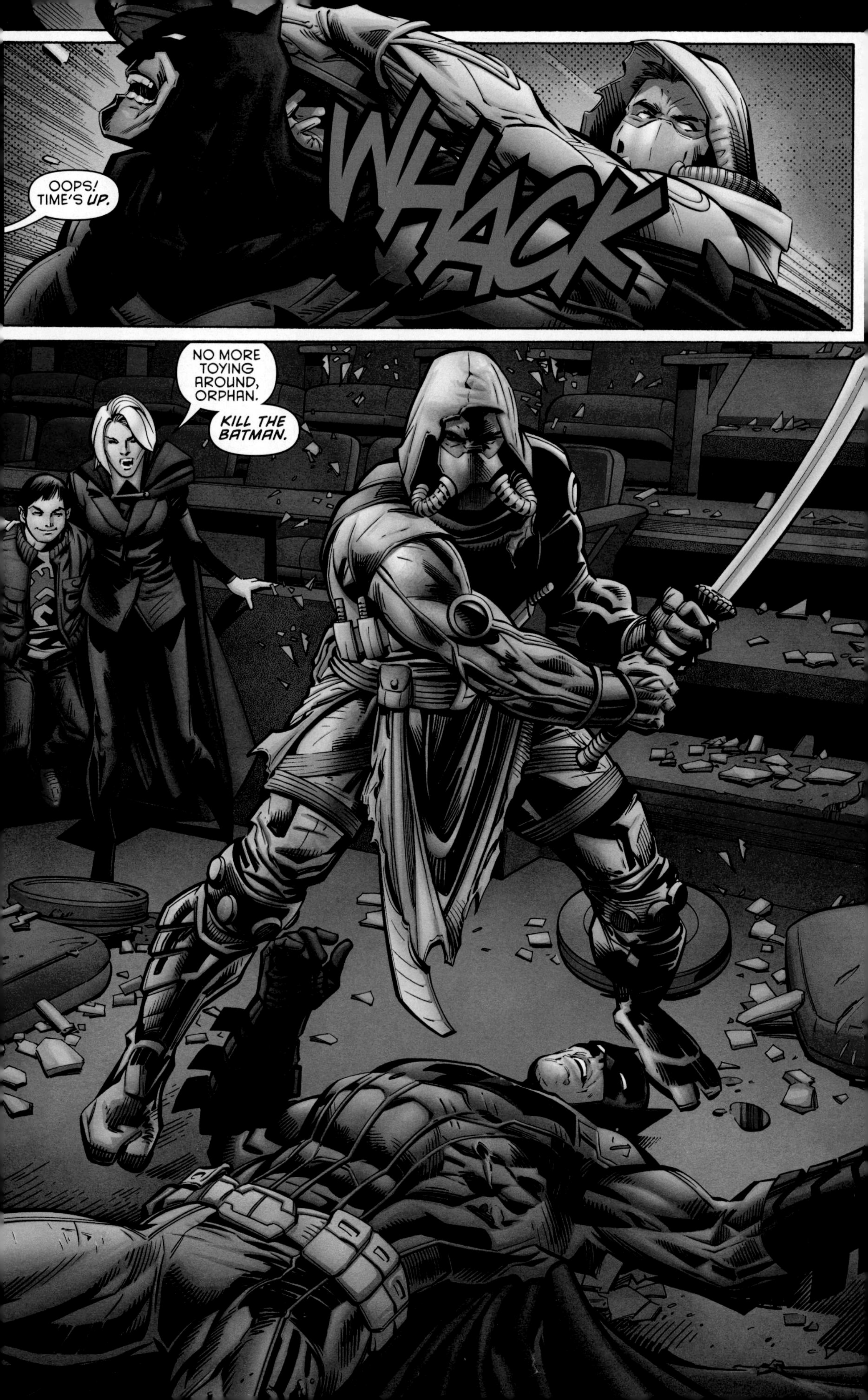
OOPS! TIME'S UP.
WHACK
NO MORE TOYING AROUND, ORPHAN.
KILL THE BATMAN.

ST. HADRIAN'S.
NOW.

STUCK-UP LITTLE--

OOF!

I'M REALLY SORRY ABOUT THAT! I SHOULD HAVE BEEN WATCHING WHERE I--

YES, YOU MOST *CERTAINLY* SHOULD HAVE.

WHY ARE YOU NO IN *UNIFORM* THERE IS NC EXCUSE FOR THAT.

I'M NOT A STUDENT. *YET.* I'M NOT SURE THAT THIS IS THE PLACE FOR ME, DOESN'T QUITE MEET MY EXPECTATIONS.

STAIRS

BUT, I'LL HAVE A LOOK AROUND AND GET BACK TO YOU.

YOINK.

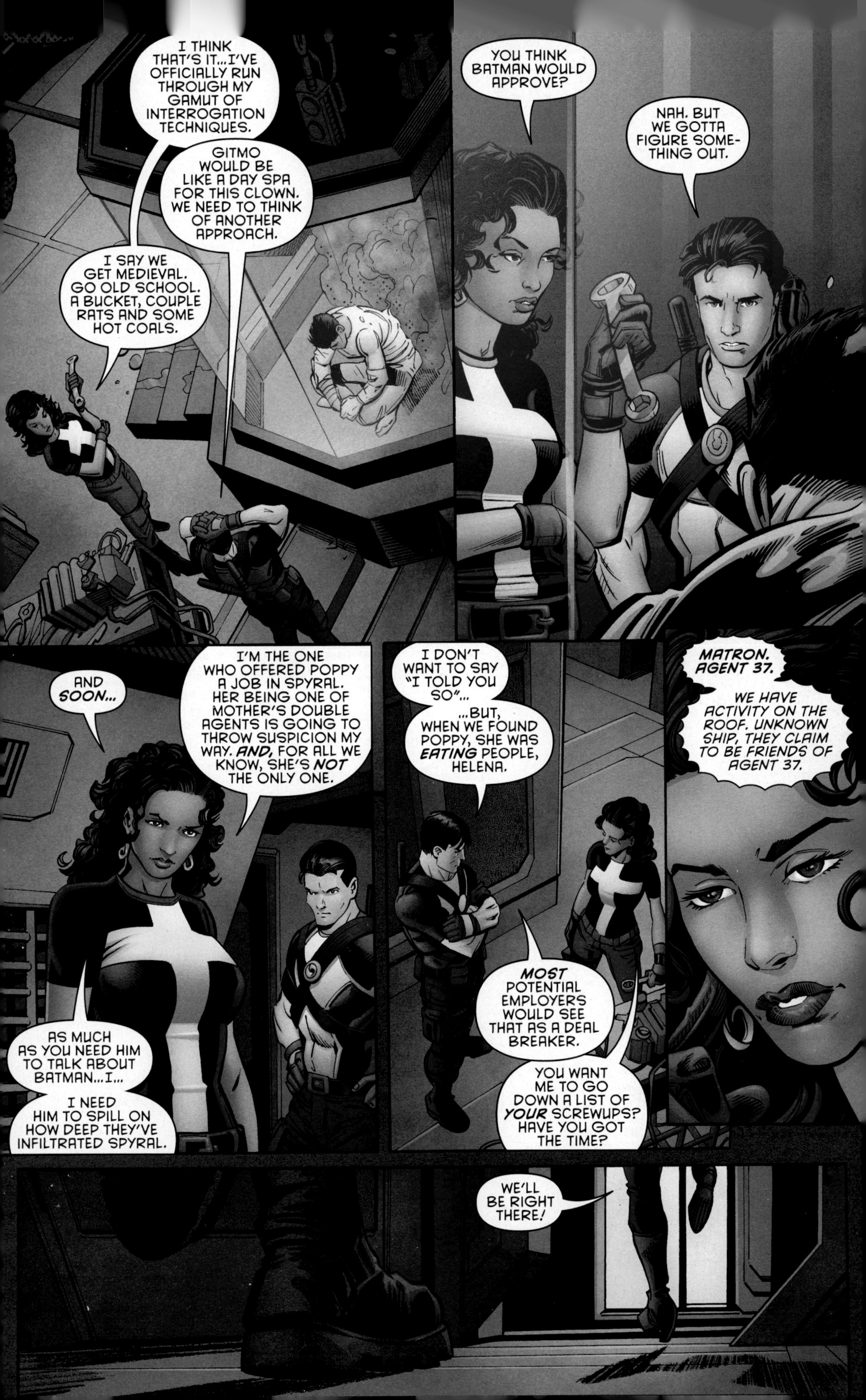
I THINK THAT'S IT...I'VE OFFICIALLY RUN THROUGH MY GAMUT OF INTERROGATION TECHNIQUES.
GITMO WOULD BE LIKE A DAY SPA FOR THIS CLOWN. WE NEED TO THINK OF ANOTHER APPROACH.
I SAY WE GET MEDIEVAL. GO OLD SCHOOL. A BUCKET, COUPLE RATS AND SOME HOT COALS.
YOU THINK BATMAN WOULD APPROVE?
NAH. BUT WE GOTTA FIGURE SOME-THING OUT.
AND *SOON*...
I'M THE ONE WHO OFFERED POPPY A JOB IN SPYRAL. HER BEING ONE OF MOTHER'S DOUBLE AGENTS IS GOING TO THROW SUSPICION MY WAY. *AND,* FOR ALL WE KNOW, SHE'S *NOT* THE ONLY ONE.
AS MUCH AS YOU NEED HIM TO TALK ABOUT BATMAN...I...
I NEED HIM TO SPILL ON HOW DEEP THEY'VE INFILTRATED SPYRAL.
I DON'T WANT TO SAY "I TOLD YOU SO"...
...BUT, WHEN WE FOUND POPPY, SHE WAS *EATING* PEOPLE, HELENA.
MOST POTENTIAL EMPLOYERS WOULD SEE THAT AS A DEAL BREAKER.
YOU WANT ME TO GO DOWN A LIST OF *YOUR* SCREWUPS? HAVE YOU GOT THE TIME?
MATRON. AGENT 37.
WE HAVE ACTIVITY ON THE ROOF. UNKNOWN SHIP, THEY CLAIM TO BE FRIENDS OF AGENT 37.
WE'LL BE RIGHT THERE!

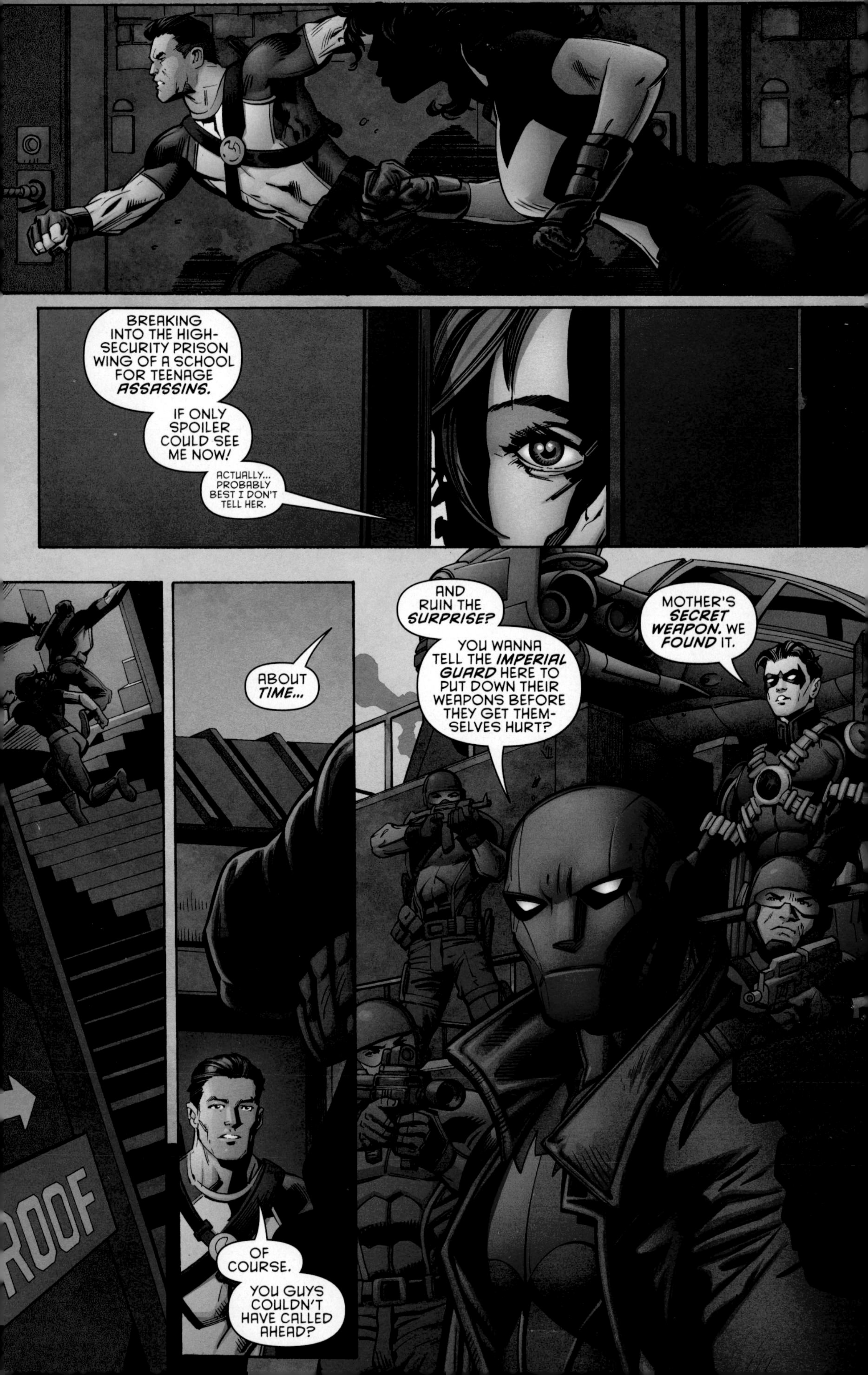
BREAKING INTO THE HIGH-SECURITY PRISON WING OF A SCHOOL FOR TEENAGE *ASSASSINS.*
IF ONLY SPOILER COULD SEE ME NOW!
ACTUALLY... PROBABLY BEST I DON'T TELL HER.
ABOUT *TIME...*
OF COURSE.
YOU GUYS COULDN'T HAVE CALLED AHEAD?
AND RUIN THE *SURPRISE?*
YOU WANNA TELL THE *IMPERIAL GUARD* HERE TO PUT DOWN THEIR WEAPONS BEFORE THEY GET THEM-SELVES HURT?
MOTHER'S *SECRET WEAPON.* WE *FOUND* IT.
ROOF

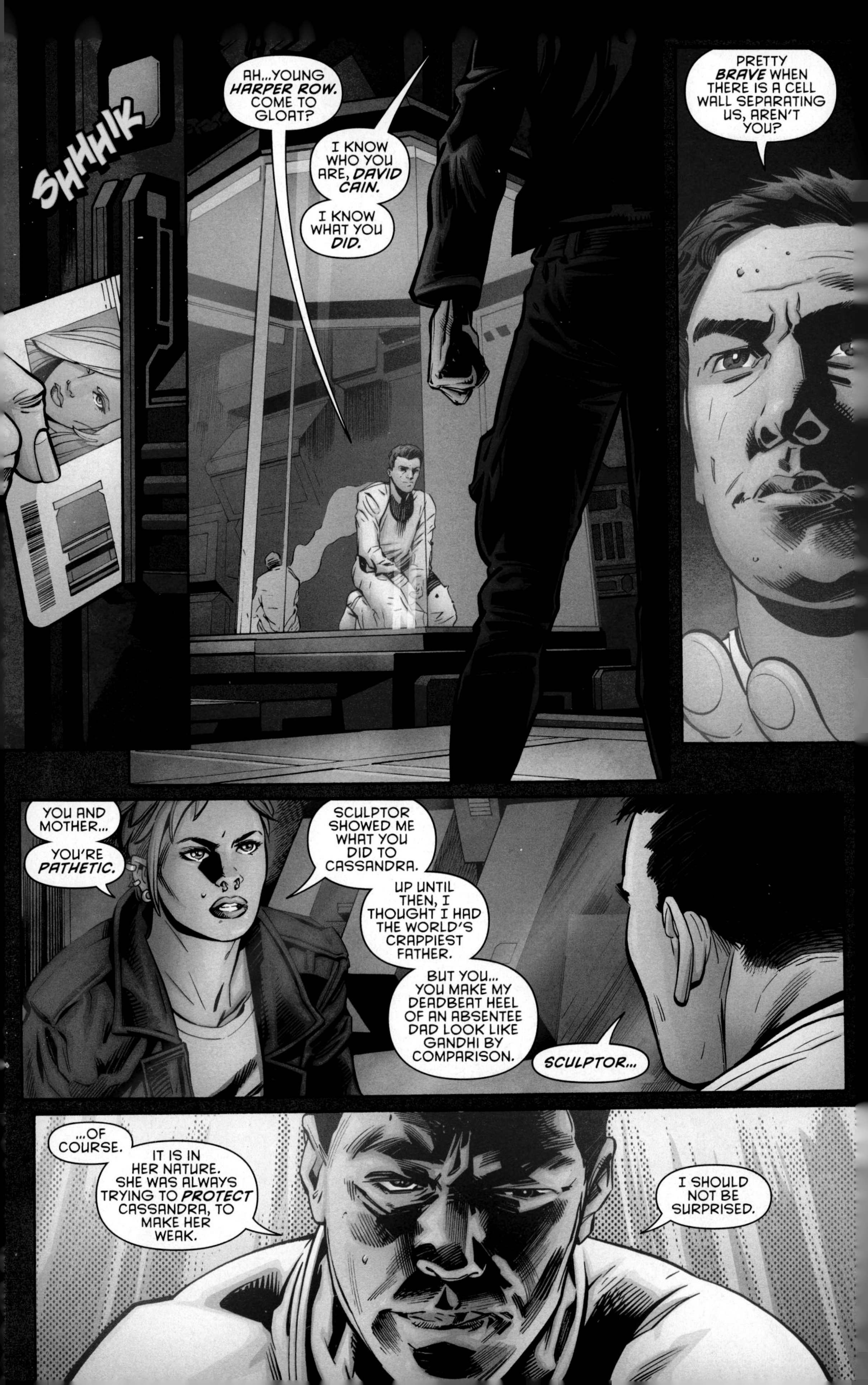
SHHHK
AH...YOUNG HARPER ROW. COME TO GLOAT?
I KNOW WHO YOU ARE, DAVID CAIN.
I KNOW WHAT YOU DID.
PRETTY BRAVE WHEN THERE IS A CELL WALL SEPARATING US, AREN'T YOU?
YOU AND MOTHER...
YOU'RE PATHETIC.
SCULPTOR SHOWED ME WHAT YOU DID TO CASSANDRA.
UP UNTIL THEN, I THOUGHT I HAD THE WORLD'S CRAPPIEST FATHER.
BUT YOU... YOU MAKE MY DEADBEAT HEEL OF AN ABSENTEE DAD LOOK LIKE GANDHI BY COMPARISON.
SCULPTOR...
...OF COURSE.
IT IS IN HER NATURE. SHE WAS ALWAYS TRYING TO PROTECT CASSANDRA, TO MAKE HER WEAK.
I SHOULD NOT BE SURPRISED.

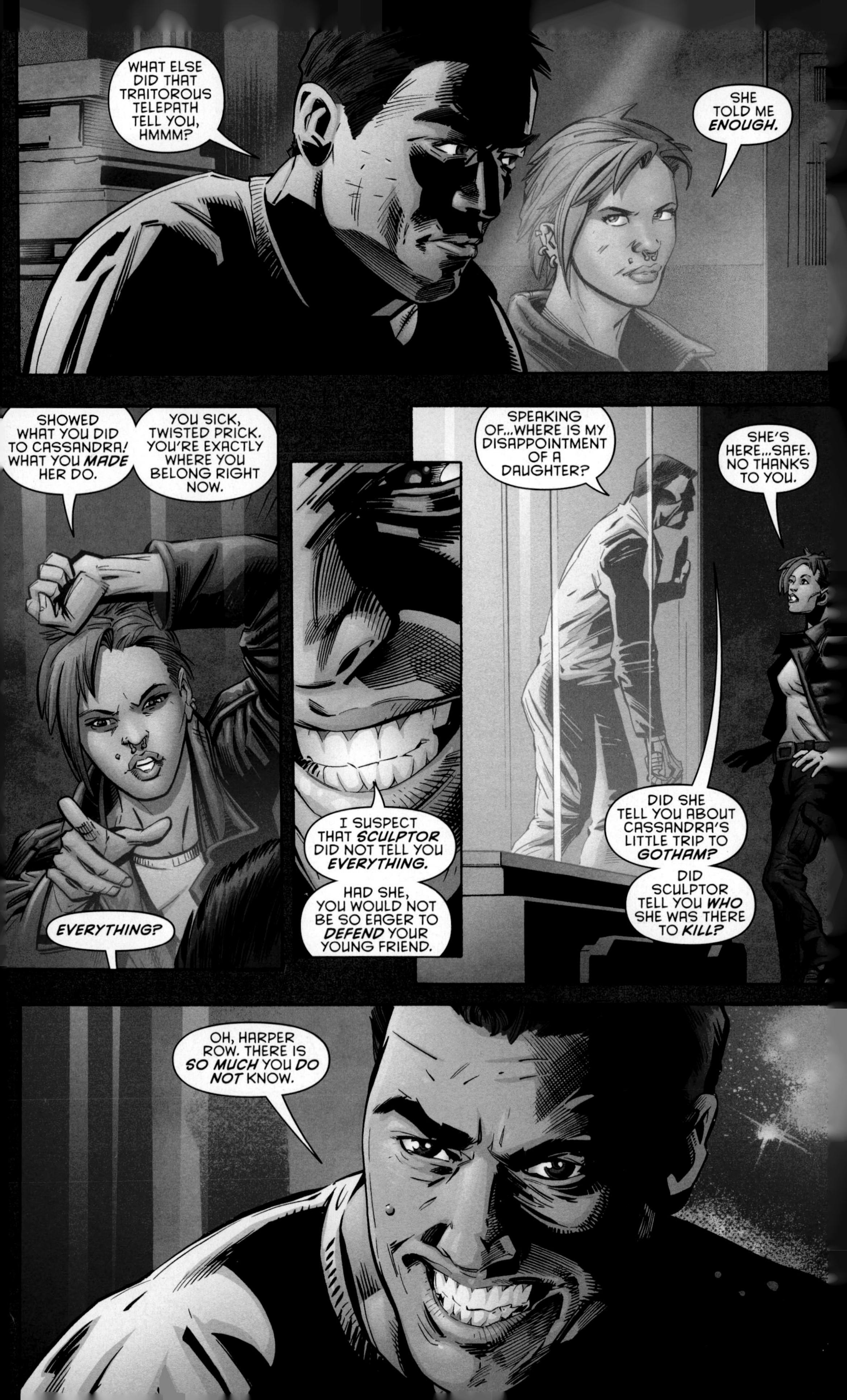
WHAT ELSE DID THAT TRAITOROUS TELEPATH TELL YOU, HMMM?
SHE TOLD ME *ENOUGH.*
SHOWED WHAT YOU DID TO CASSANDRA! WHAT YOU *MADE* HER DO.
YOU SICK, TWISTED PRICK. YOU'RE EXACTLY WHERE YOU BELONG RIGHT NOW.
EVERYTHING?
I SUSPECT THAT *SCULPTOR* DID NOT TELL YOU *EVERYTHING.*
HAD SHE, YOU WOULD NOT BE SO EAGER TO *DEFEND* YOUR YOUNG FRIEND.
SPEAKING OF...WHERE IS MY DISAPPOINTMENT OF A DAUGHTER?
SHE'S HERE...SAFE. NO THANKS TO YOU.
DID SHE TELL YOU ABOUT CASSANDRA'S LITTLE TRIP TO *GOTHAM?*
DID SCULPTOR TELL YOU *WHO* SHE WAS THERE TO *KILL?*
OH, HARPER ROW. THERE IS *SO MUCH* YOU *DO NOT* KNOW.

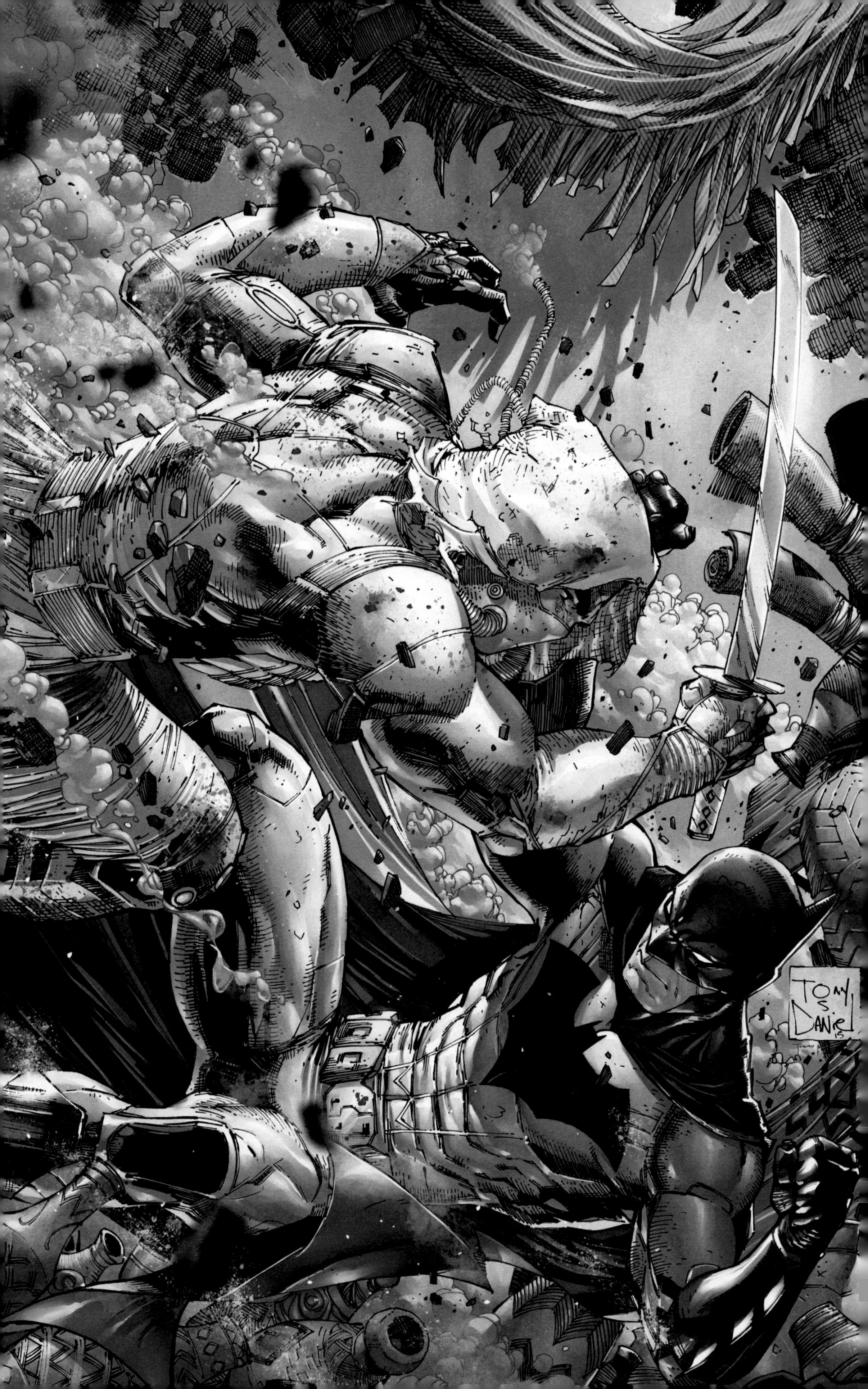
TONY S. DANIEL

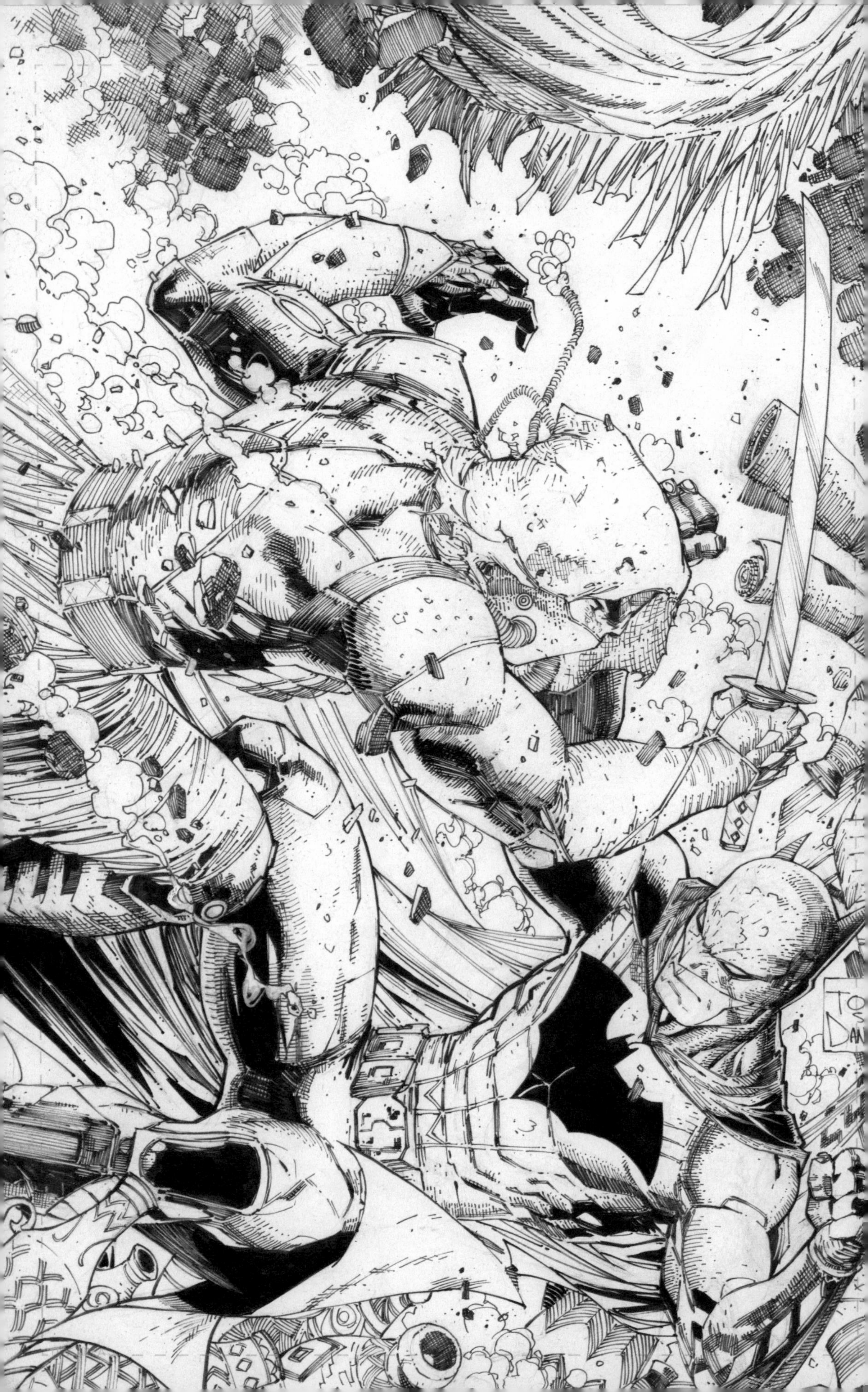

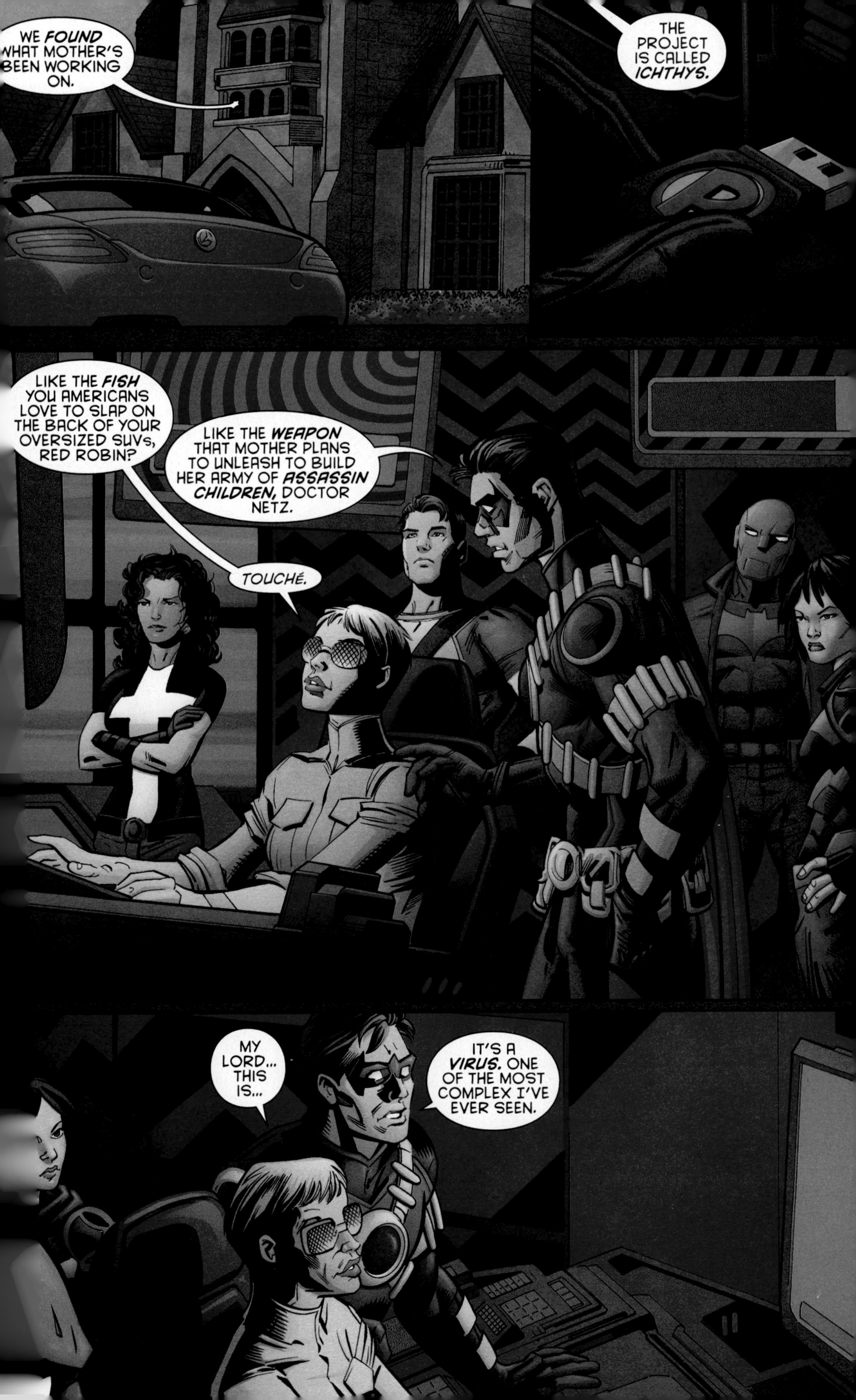
WE FOUND WHAT MOTHER'S BEEN WORKING ON.
THE PROJECT IS CALLED ICHTHYS.
LIKE THE FISH YOU AMERICANS LOVE TO SLAP ON THE BACK OF YOUR OVERSIZED SUVs, RED ROBIN?
LIKE THE WEAPON THAT MOTHER PLANS TO UNLEASH TO BUILD HER ARMY OF ASSASSIN CHILDREN, DOCTOR NETZ.
TOUCHÉ.
MY LORD... THIS IS...
IT'S A VIRUS. ONE OF THE MOST COMPLEX I'VE EVER SEEN.

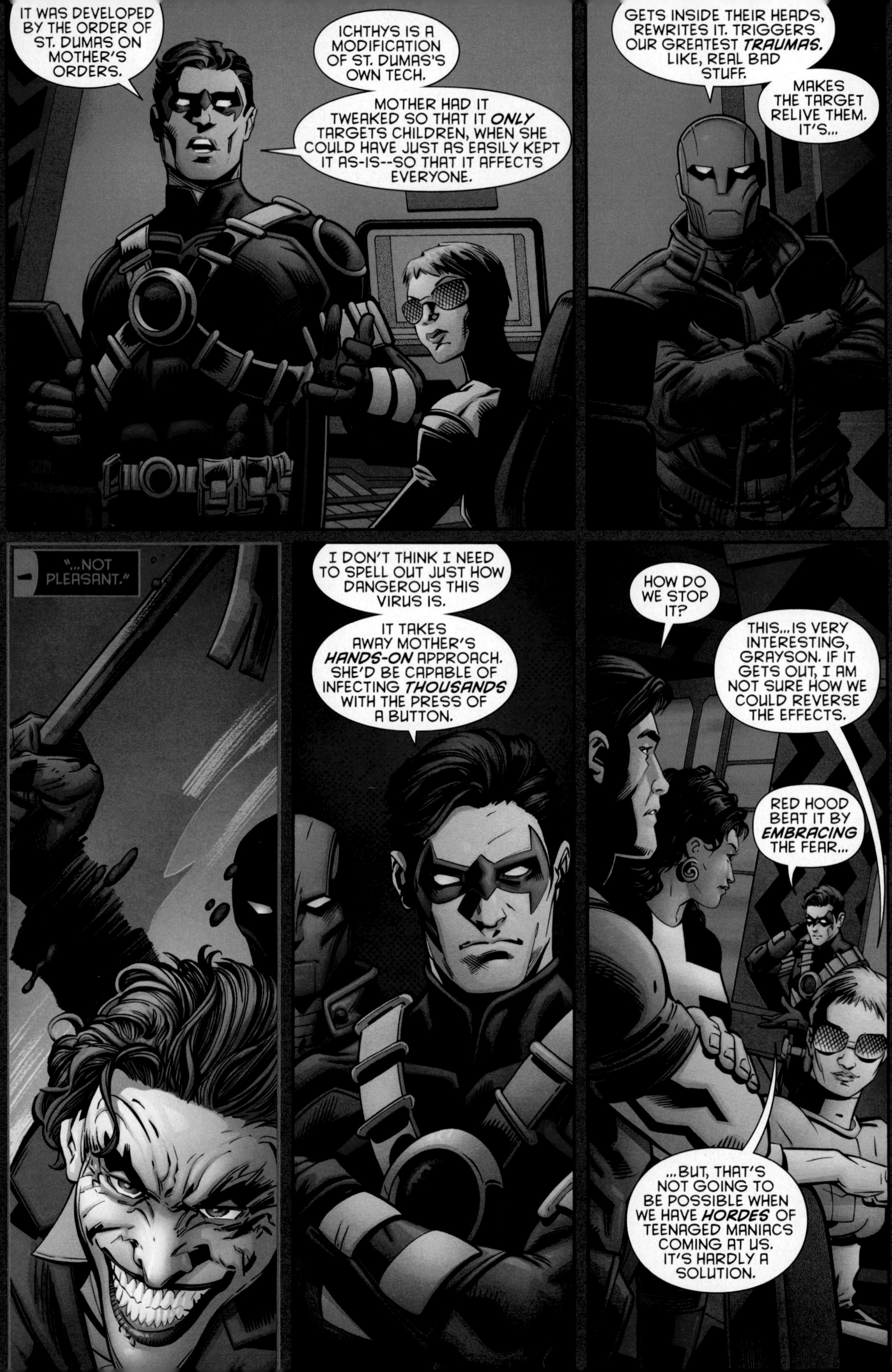
IT WAS DEVELOPED BY THE ORDER OF ST. DUMAS ON MOTHER'S ORDERS.
ICHTHYS IS A MODIFICATION OF ST. DUMAS'S OWN TECH.
MOTHER HAD IT TWEAKED SO THAT IT *ONLY* TARGETS CHILDREN, WHEN SHE COULD HAVE JUST AS EASILY KEPT IT AS-IS--SO THAT IT AFFECTS EVERYONE.
GETS INSIDE THEIR HEADS, REWRITES IT. TRIGGERS OUR GREATEST *TRAUMAS.* LIKE, REAL BAD STUFF.
MAKES THE TARGET RELIVE THEM. IT'S...
"...NOT PLEASANT."
I DON'T THINK I NEED TO SPELL OUT JUST HOW DANGEROUS THIS VIRUS IS.
IT TAKES AWAY MOTHER'S ***HANDS-ON*** APPROACH. SHE'D BE CAPABLE OF INFECTING ***THOUSANDS*** WITH THE PRESS OF A BUTTON.
HOW DO WE STOP IT?
THIS...IS VERY INTERESTING, GRAYSON. IF IT GETS OUT, I AM NOT SURE HOW WE COULD REVERSE THE EFFECTS.
RED HOOD BEAT IT BY ***EMBRACING*** THE FEAR...
...BUT, THAT'S NOT GOING TO BE POSSIBLE WHEN WE HAVE ***HORDES*** OF TEENAGED MANIACS COMING AT US. IT'S HARDLY A SOLUTION.

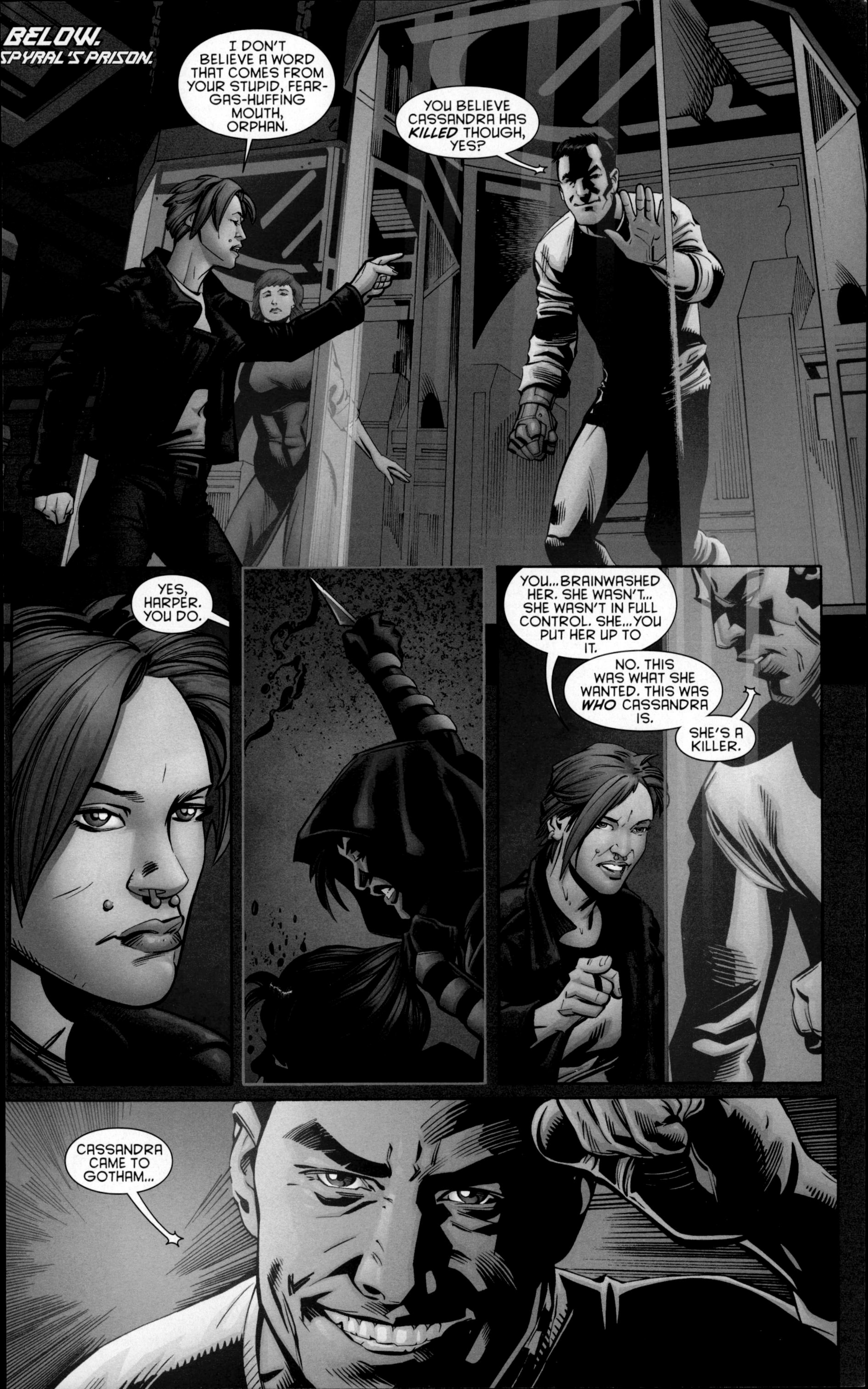
BELOW. SPYRAL'S PRISON.
I DON'T BELIEVE A WORD THAT COMES FROM YOUR STUPID, FEAR-GAS-HUFFING MOUTH, ORPHAN.
YOU BELIEVE CASSANDRA HAS KILLED THOUGH, YES?
YES, HARPER. YOU DO.
YOU...BRAINWASHED HER. SHE WASN'T... SHE WASN'T IN FULL CONTROL. SHE...YOU PUT HER UP TO IT.
NO. THIS WAS WHAT SHE WANTED. THIS WAS WHO CASSANDRA IS.
SHE'S A KILLER.
CASSANDRA CAME TO GOTHAM...

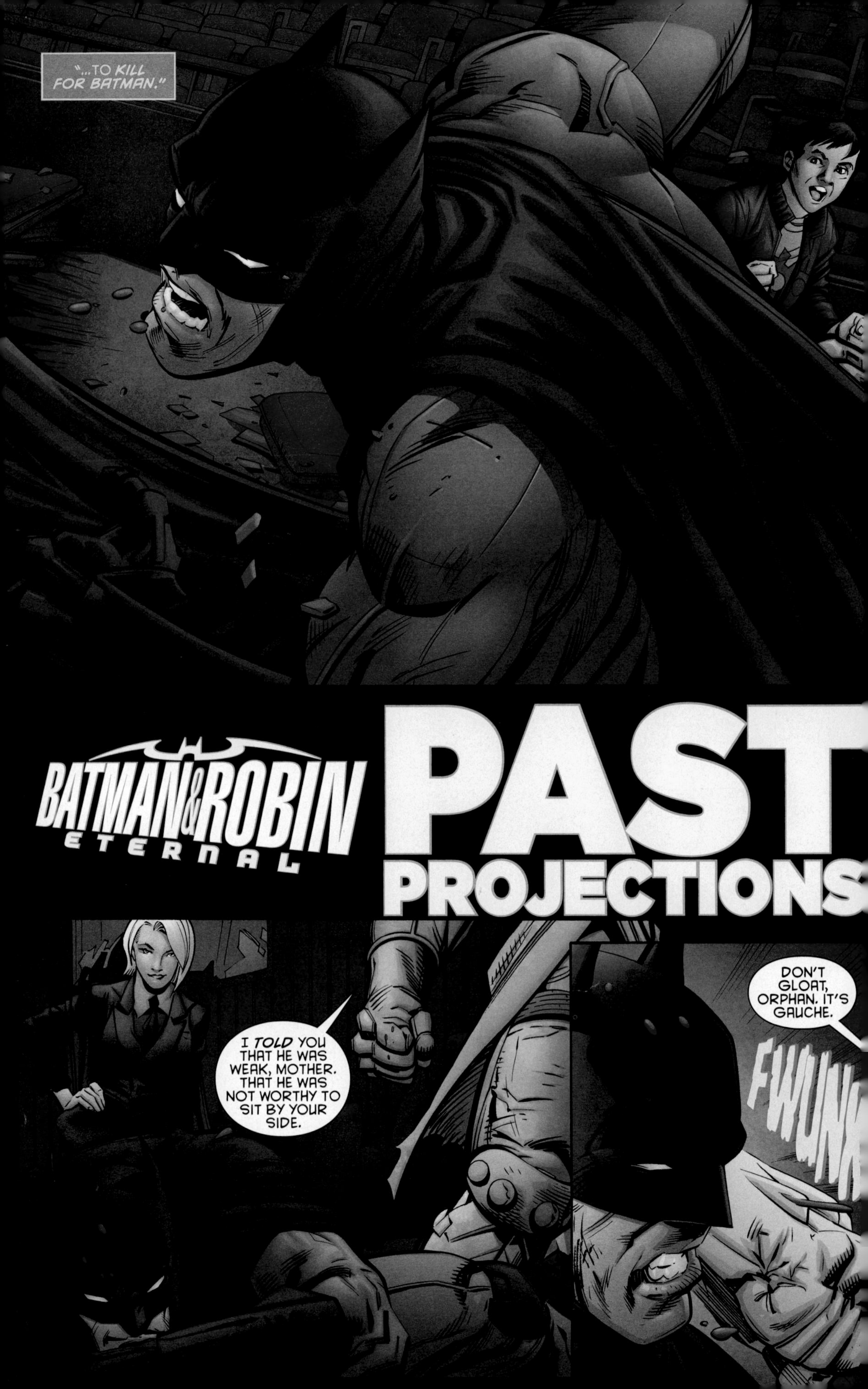

"...TO KILL FOR BATMAN."
BATMAN & ROBIN ETERNAL
PAST PROJECTIONS
I TOLD YOU THAT HE WAS WEAK, MOTHER. THAT HE WAS NOT WORTHY TO SIT BY YOUR SIDE.
DON'T GLOAT, ORPHAN. IT'S GAUCHE.
FWUNK

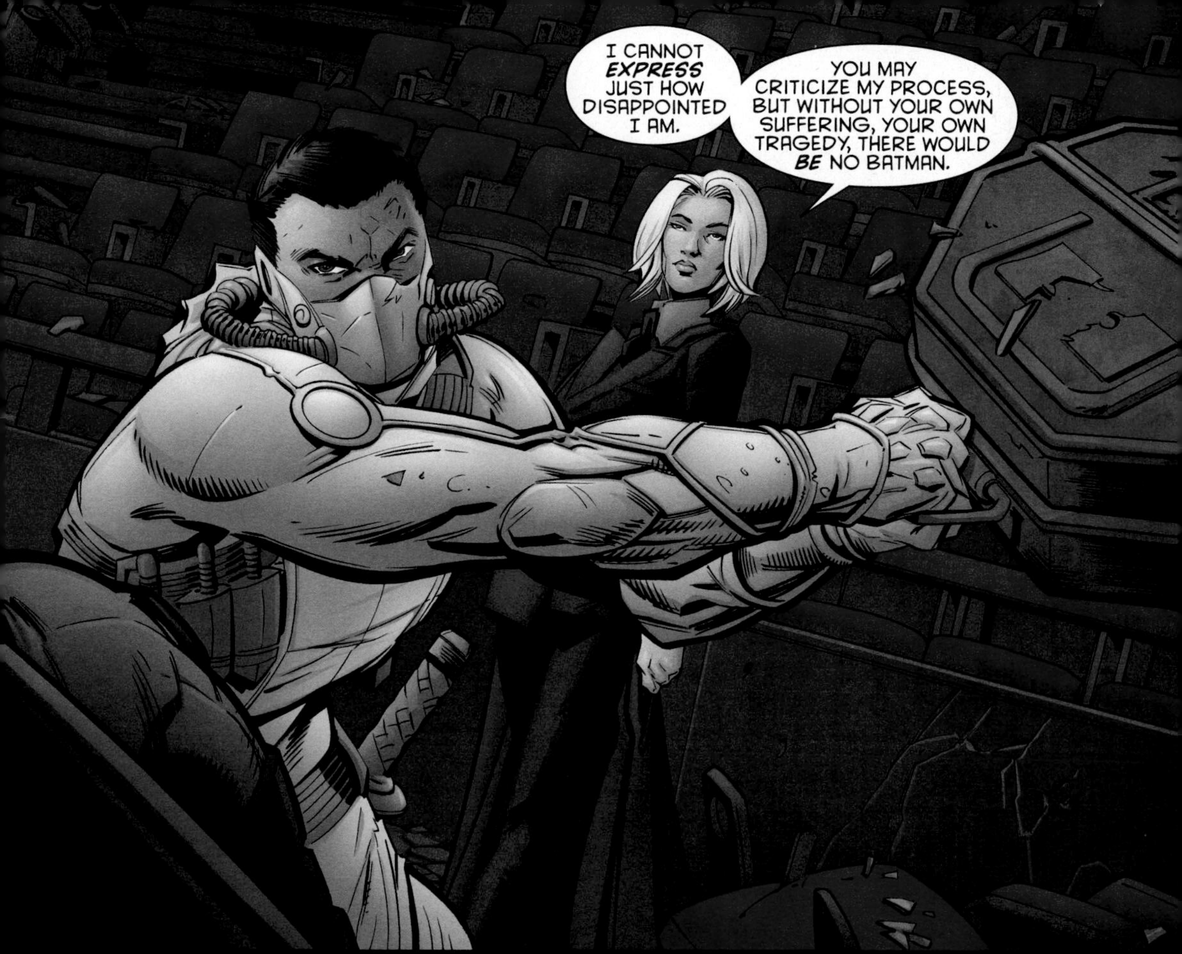
I CANNOT *EXPRESS* JUST HOW DISAPPOINTED I AM.
YOU MAY CRITICIZE MY PROCESS, BUT WITHOUT YOUR OWN SUFFERING, YOUR OWN TRAGEDY, THERE WOULD *BE* NO BATMAN.

JAMES TYNION IV & SCOTT SNYDER Story
ED BRISSON Script **SCOT EATON** Pencils **WAYNE FAUCHER** Inks
ALLEN PASSALAQUA & GABE ELTAEB (Pgs. 17-20) Colors
SAIDA TEMOFONTE Letters **TONY S. DANIEL & TOMEU MOREY** Cover

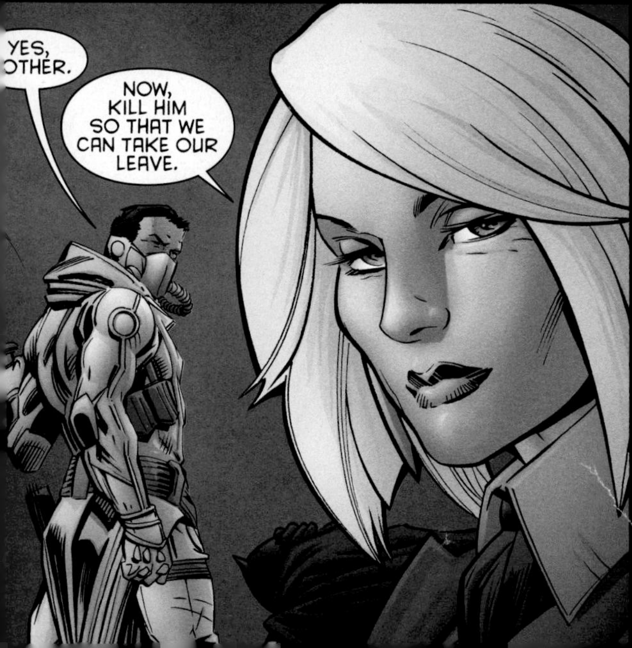
YES, OTHER.
NOW, KILL HIM SO THAT WE CAN TAKE OUR LEAVE.

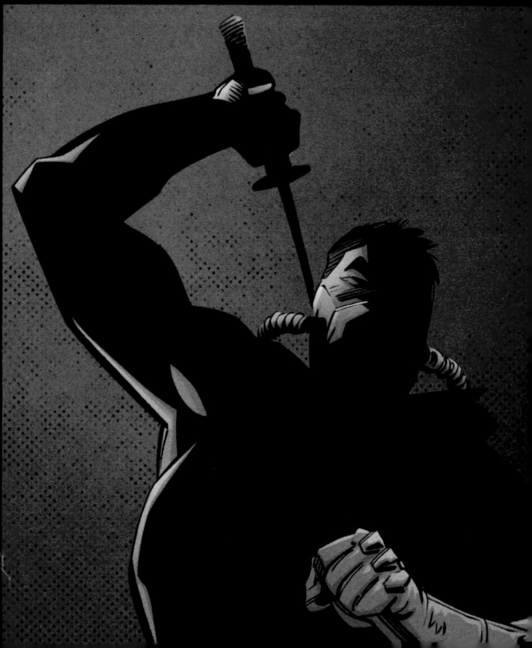

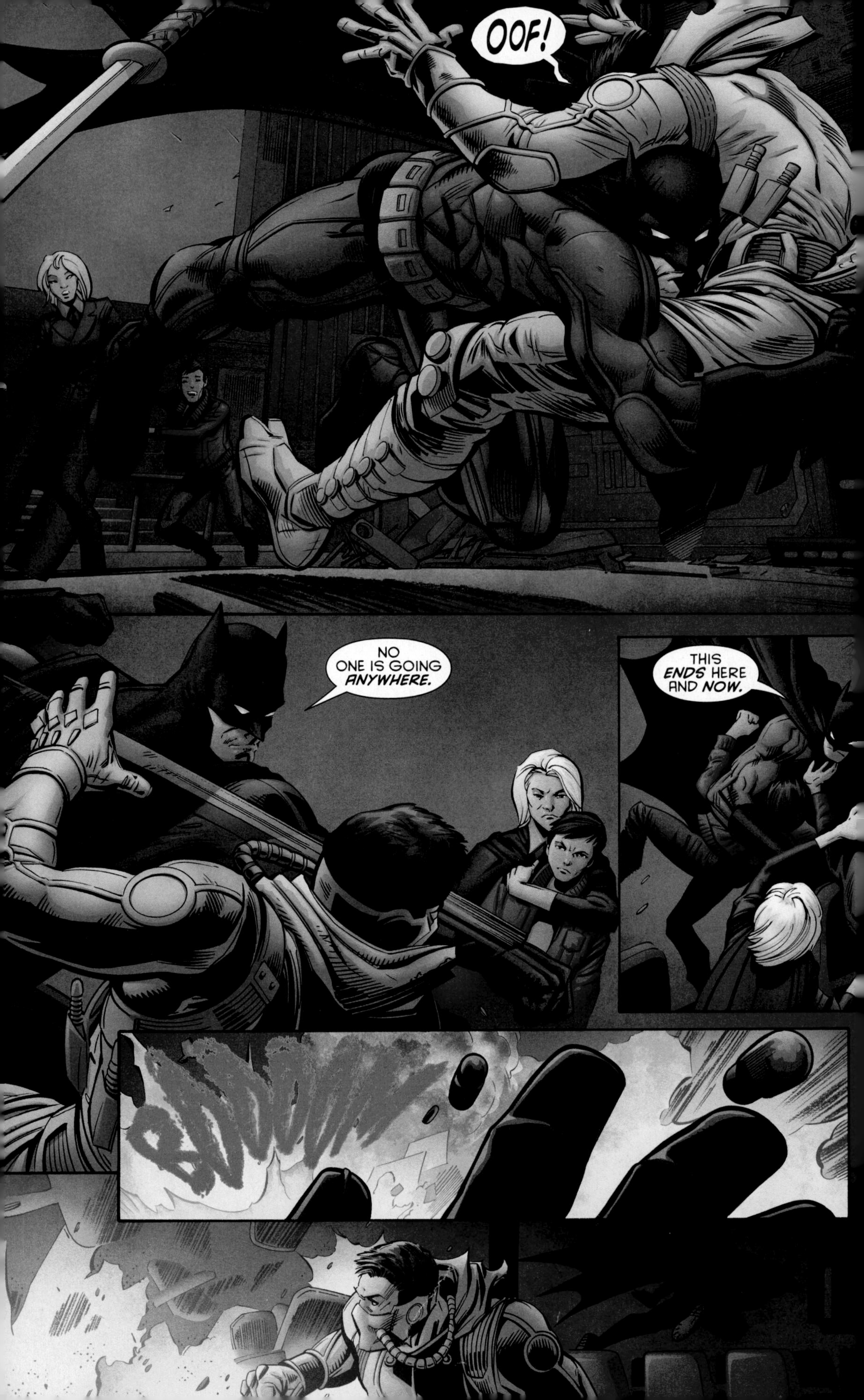
OOF!
NO ONE IS GOING ANYWHERE.
THIS ENDS HERE AND NOW.

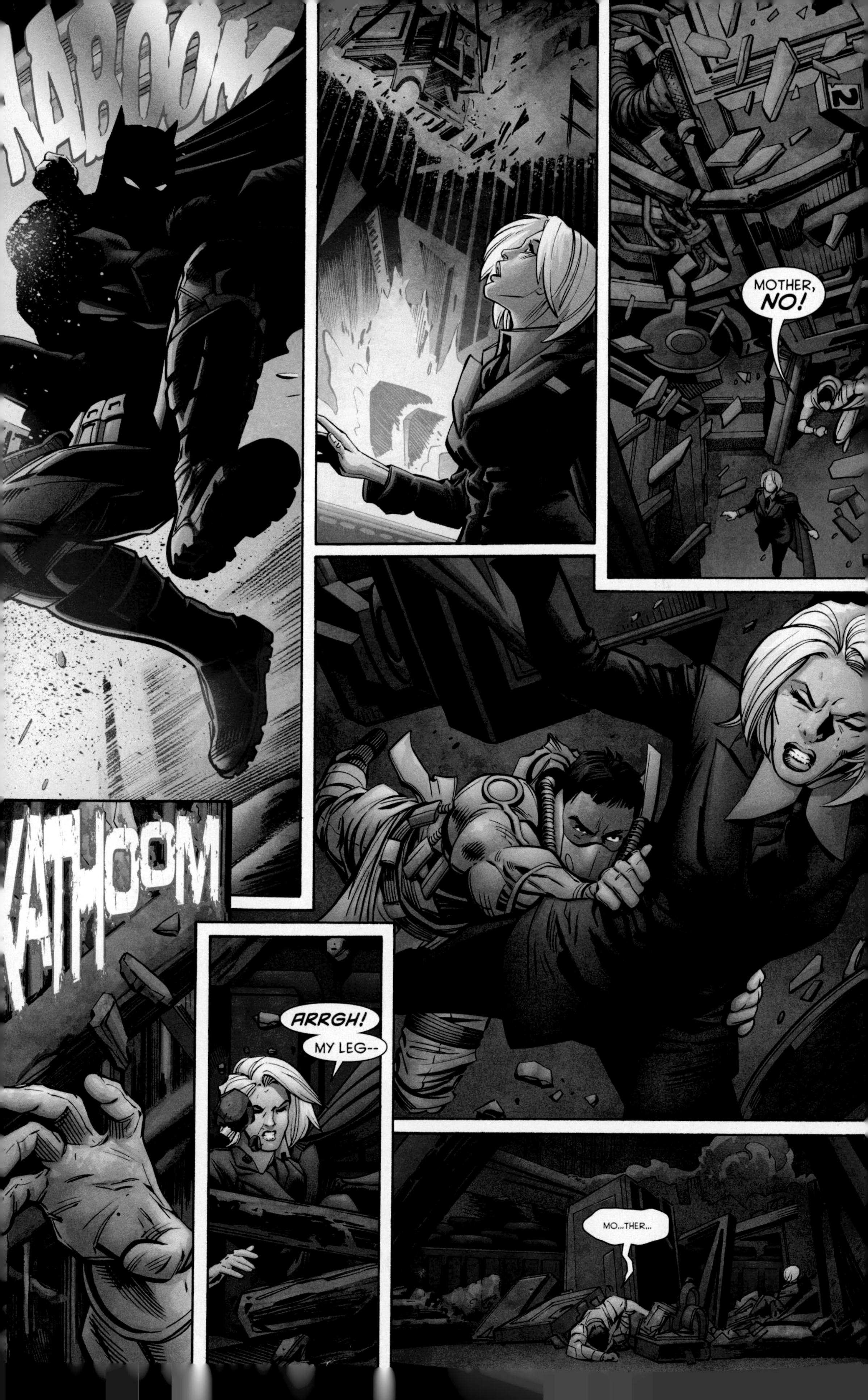
KABOOM
MOTHER, NO!
KATHOOM
ARRGH!
MY LEG--
MO...THER...

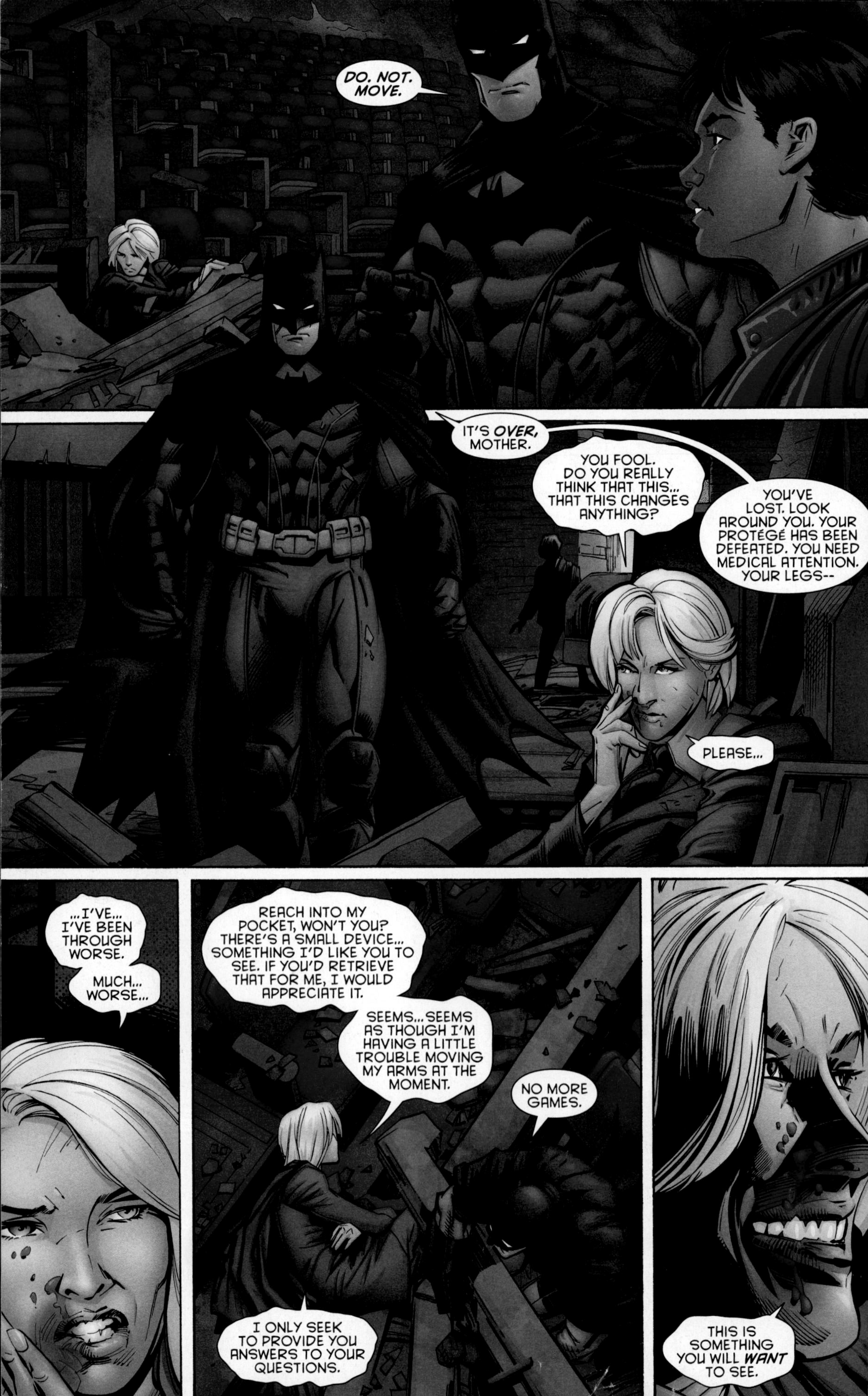
DO. NOT. MOVE.
IT'S OVER, MOTHER.
YOU FOOL. DO YOU REALLY THINK THAT THIS... THAT THIS CHANGES ANYTHING?
YOU'VE LOST. LOOK AROUND YOU. YOUR PROTÉGÉ HAS BEEN DEFEATED. YOU NEED MEDICAL ATTENTION. YOUR LEGS--
PLEASE...
...I'VE... I'VE BEEN THROUGH WORSE.
MUCH... WORSE...
REACH INTO MY POCKET, WON'T YOU? THERE'S A SMALL DEVICE... SOMETHING I'D LIKE YOU TO SEE. IF YOU'D RETRIEVE THAT FOR ME, I WOULD APPRECIATE IT.
SEEMS... SEEMS AS THOUGH I'M HAVING A LITTLE TROUBLE MOVING MY ARMS AT THE MOMENT.
NO MORE GAMES.
I ONLY SEEK TO PROVIDE YOU ANSWERS TO YOUR QUESTIONS.
THIS IS SOMETHING YOU WILL WANT TO SEE.

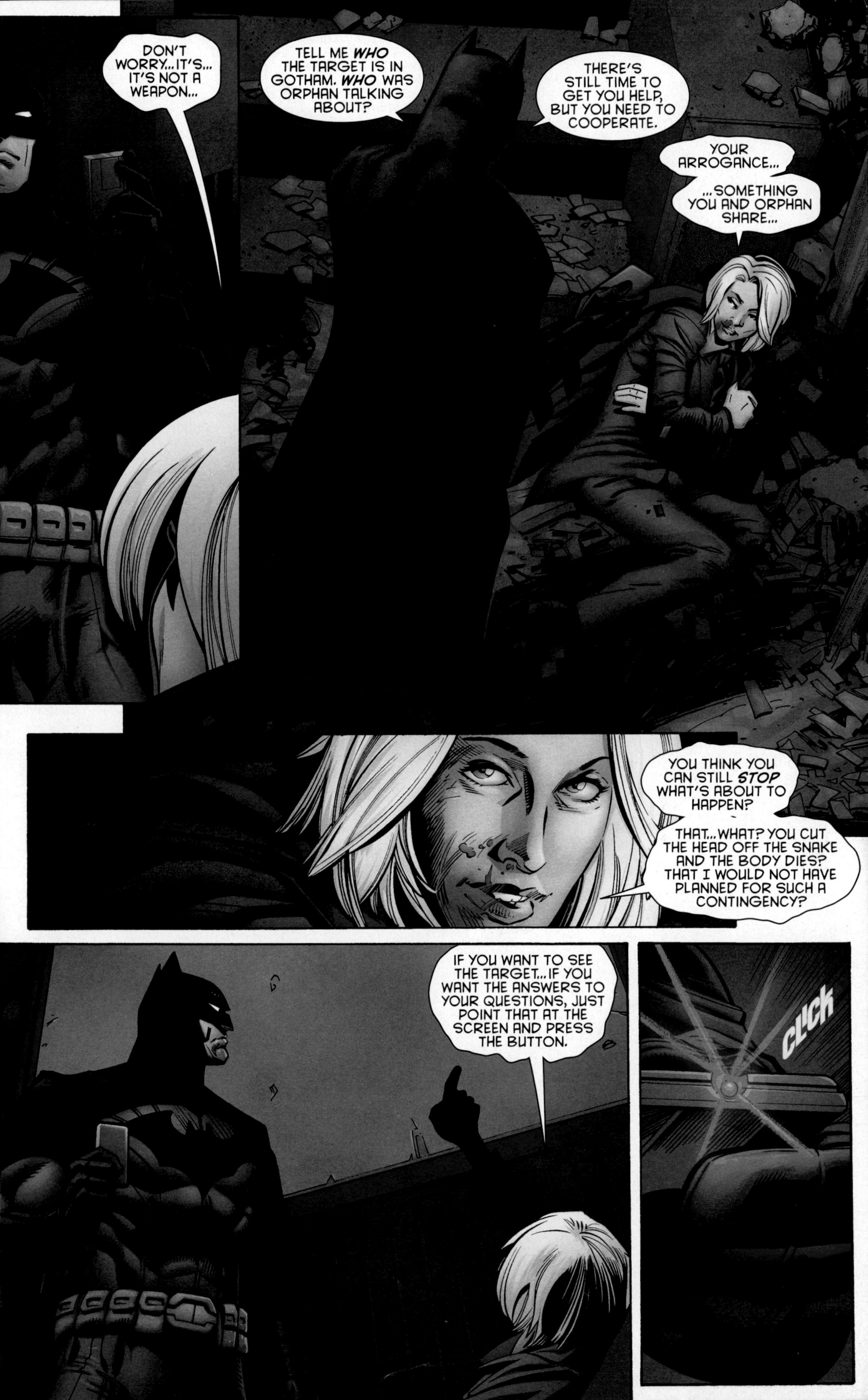
DON'T WORRY...IT'S... IT'S NOT A WEAPON...
TELL ME WHO THE TARGET IS IN GOTHAM. WHO WAS ORPHAN TALKING ABOUT?
THERE'S STILL TIME TO GET YOU HELP, BUT YOU NEED TO COOPERATE.
YOUR ARROGANCE...
...SOMETHING YOU AND ORPHAN SHARE...
YOU THINK YOU CAN STILL STOP WHAT'S ABOUT TO HAPPEN?
THAT...WHAT? YOU CUT THE HEAD OFF THE SNAKE AND THE BODY DIES? THAT I WOULD NOT HAVE PLANNED FOR SUCH A CONTINGENCY?
IF YOU WANT TO SEE THE TARGET...IF YOU WANT THE ANSWERS TO YOUR QUESTIONS, JUST POINT THAT AT THE SCREEN AND PRESS THE BUTTON.
CLICK

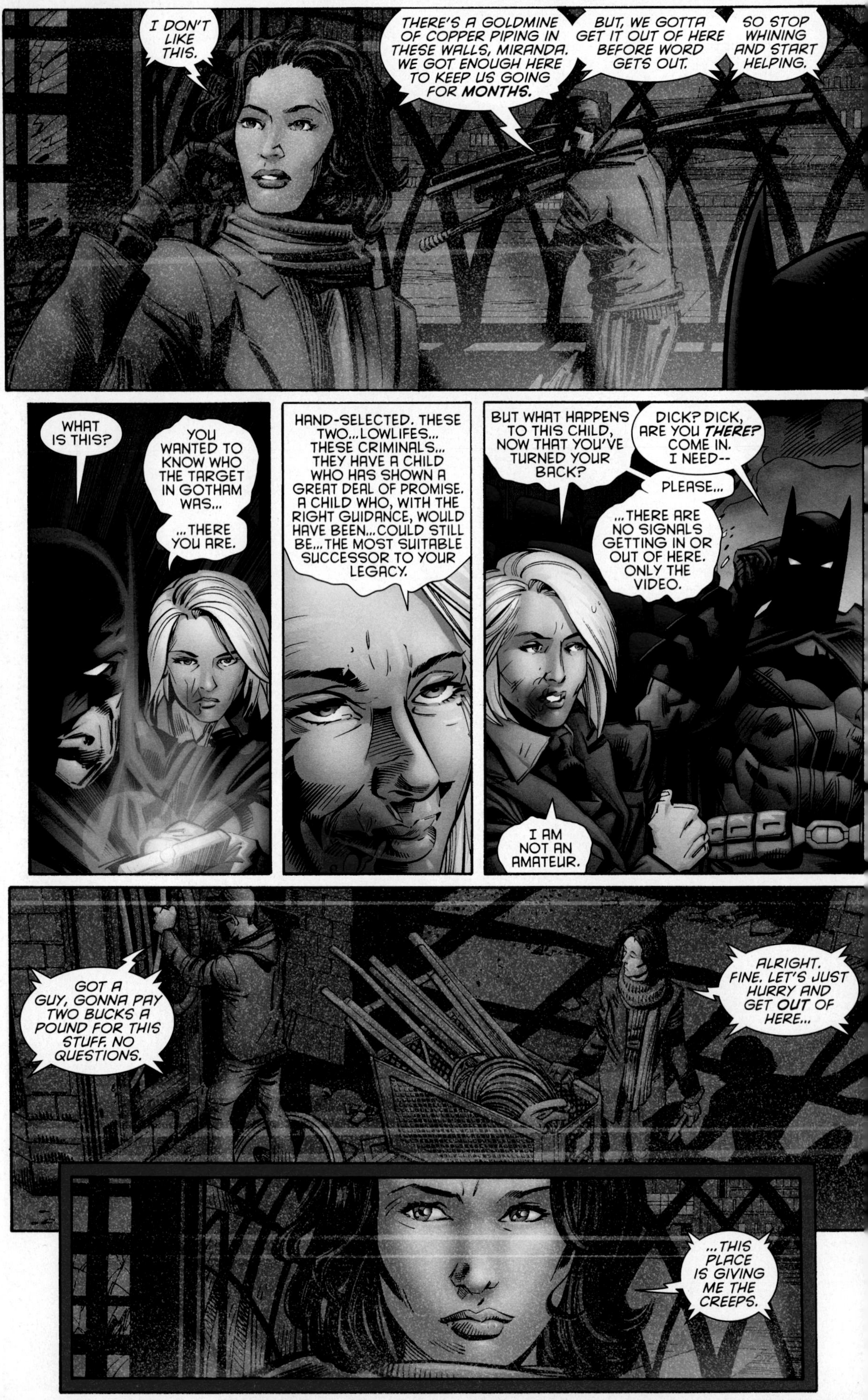

I DON'T LIKE THIS.
THERE'S A GOLDMINE OF COPPER PIPING IN THESE WALLS, MIRANDA. WE GOT ENOUGH HERE TO KEEP US GOING FOR MONTHS.
BUT, WE GOTTA GET IT OUT OF HERE BEFORE WORD GETS OUT.
SO STOP WHINING AND START HELPING.
WHAT IS THIS?
YOU WANTED TO KNOW WHO THE TARGET IN GOTHAM WAS...
...THERE YOU ARE.
HAND-SELECTED. THESE TWO...LOWLIFES... THESE CRIMINALS... THEY HAVE A CHILD WHO HAS SHOWN A GREAT DEAL OF PROMISE. A CHILD WHO, WITH THE RIGHT GUIDANCE, WOULD HAVE BEEN...COULD STILL BE...THE MOST SUITABLE SUCCESSOR TO YOUR LEGACY.
BUT WHAT HAPPENS TO THIS CHILD, NOW THAT YOU'VE TURNED YOUR BACK?
DICK? DICK, ARE YOU THERE? COME IN. I NEED--
PLEASE...
...THERE ARE NO SIGNALS GETTING IN OR OUT OF HERE. ONLY THE VIDEO.
I AM NOT AN AMATEUR.
GOT A GUY, GONNA PAY TWO BUCKS A POUND FOR THIS STUFF. NO QUESTIONS.
ALRIGHT. FINE. LET'S JUST HURRY AND GET OUT OF HERE...
...THIS PLACE IS GIVING ME THE CREEPS.

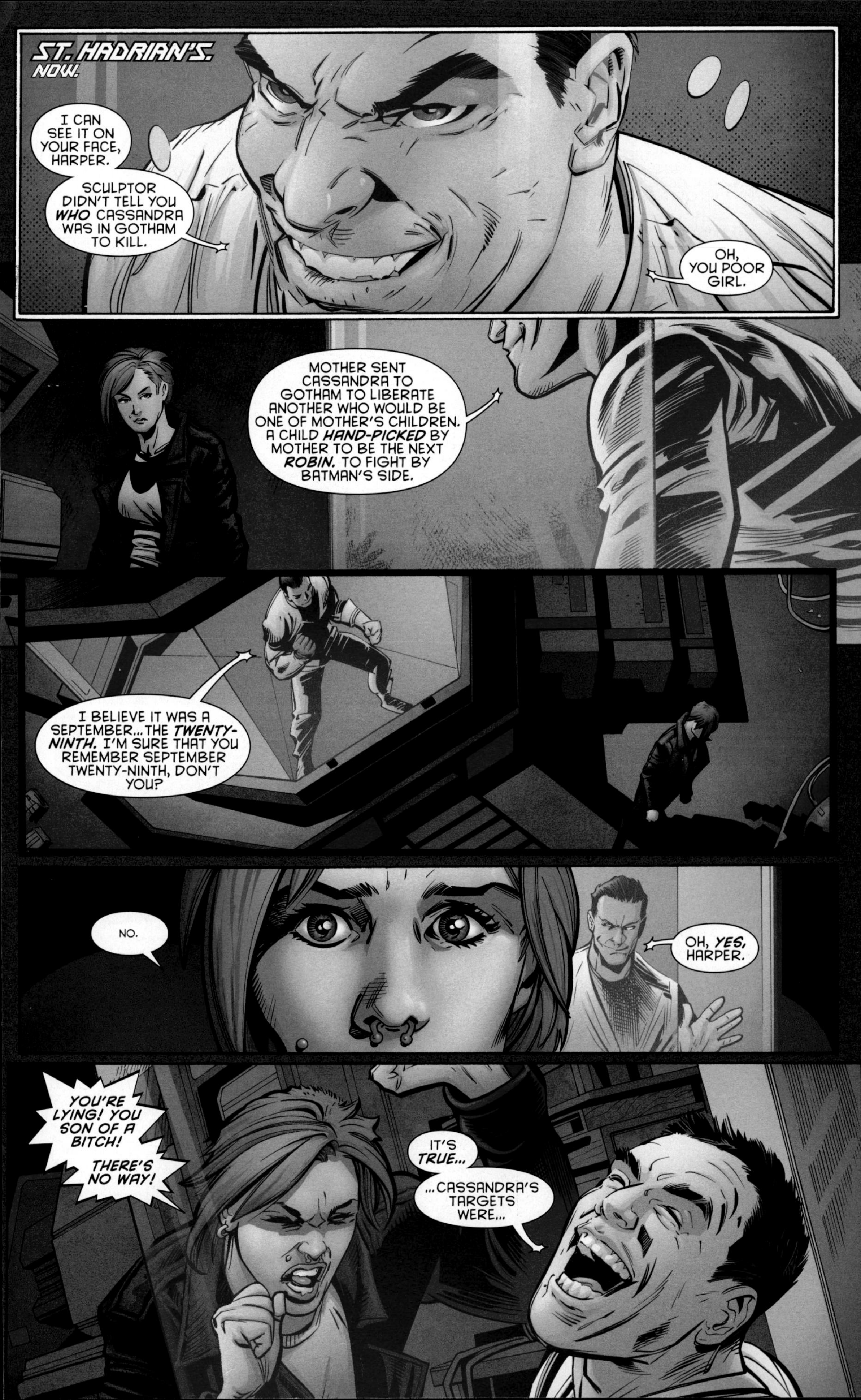
ST. HADRIAN'S.
NOW.
I CAN SEE IT ON YOUR FACE, HARPER.
SCULPTOR DIDN'T TELL YOU WHO CASSANDRA WAS IN GOTHAM TO KILL.
OH, YOU POOR GIRL.
MOTHER SENT CASSANDRA TO GOTHAM TO LIBERATE ANOTHER WHO WOULD BE ONE OF MOTHER'S CHILDREN. A CHILD HAND-PICKED BY MOTHER TO BE THE NEXT ROBIN. TO FIGHT BY BATMAN'S SIDE.
I BELIEVE IT WAS A SEPTEMBER...THE TWENTY-NINTH. I'M SURE THAT YOU REMEMBER SEPTEMBER TWENTY-NINTH, DON'T YOU?
NO.
OH, YES, HARPER.
YOU'RE LYING! YOU SON OF A BITCH!
THERE'S NO WAY!
IT'S TRUE...
...CASSANDRA'S TARGETS WERE...

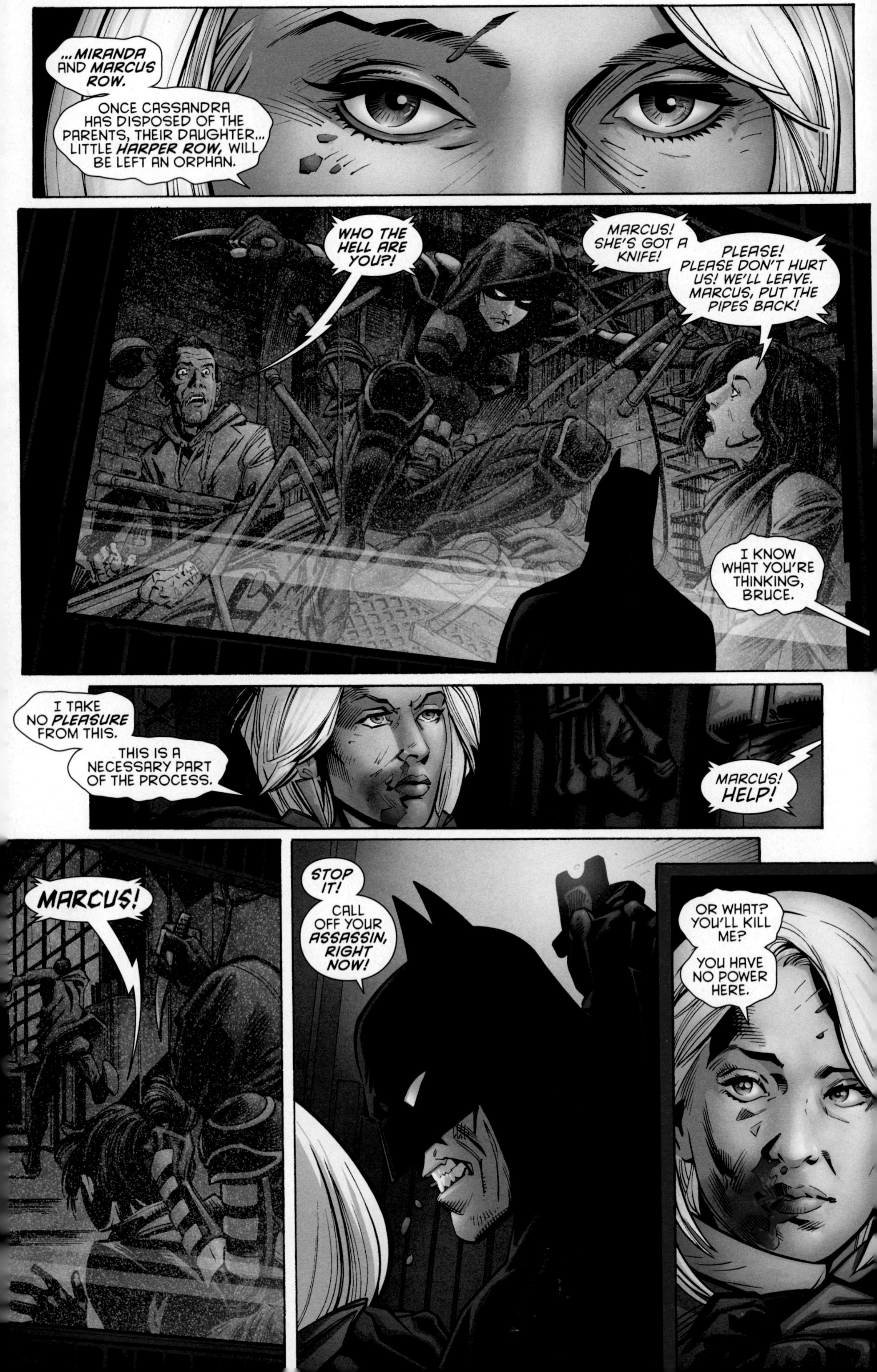
...MIRANDA AND MARCUS ROW.
ONCE CASSANDRA HAS DISPOSED OF THE PARENTS, THEIR DAUGHTER... LITTLE HARPER ROW, WILL BE LEFT AN ORPHAN.
WHO THE HELL ARE YOU?!
MARCUS! SHE'S GOT A KNIFE!
PLEASE! PLEASE DON'T HURT US! WE'LL LEAVE. MARCUS, PUT THE PIPES BACK!
I KNOW WHAT YOU'RE THINKING, BRUCE.
I TAKE NO PLEASURE FROM THIS.
THIS IS A NECESSARY PART OF THE PROCESS.
MARCUS! HELP!
MARCUS!
STOP IT!
CALL OFF YOUR ASSASSIN, RIGHT NOW!
OR WHAT? YOU'LL KILL ME?
YOU HAVE NO POWER HERE.

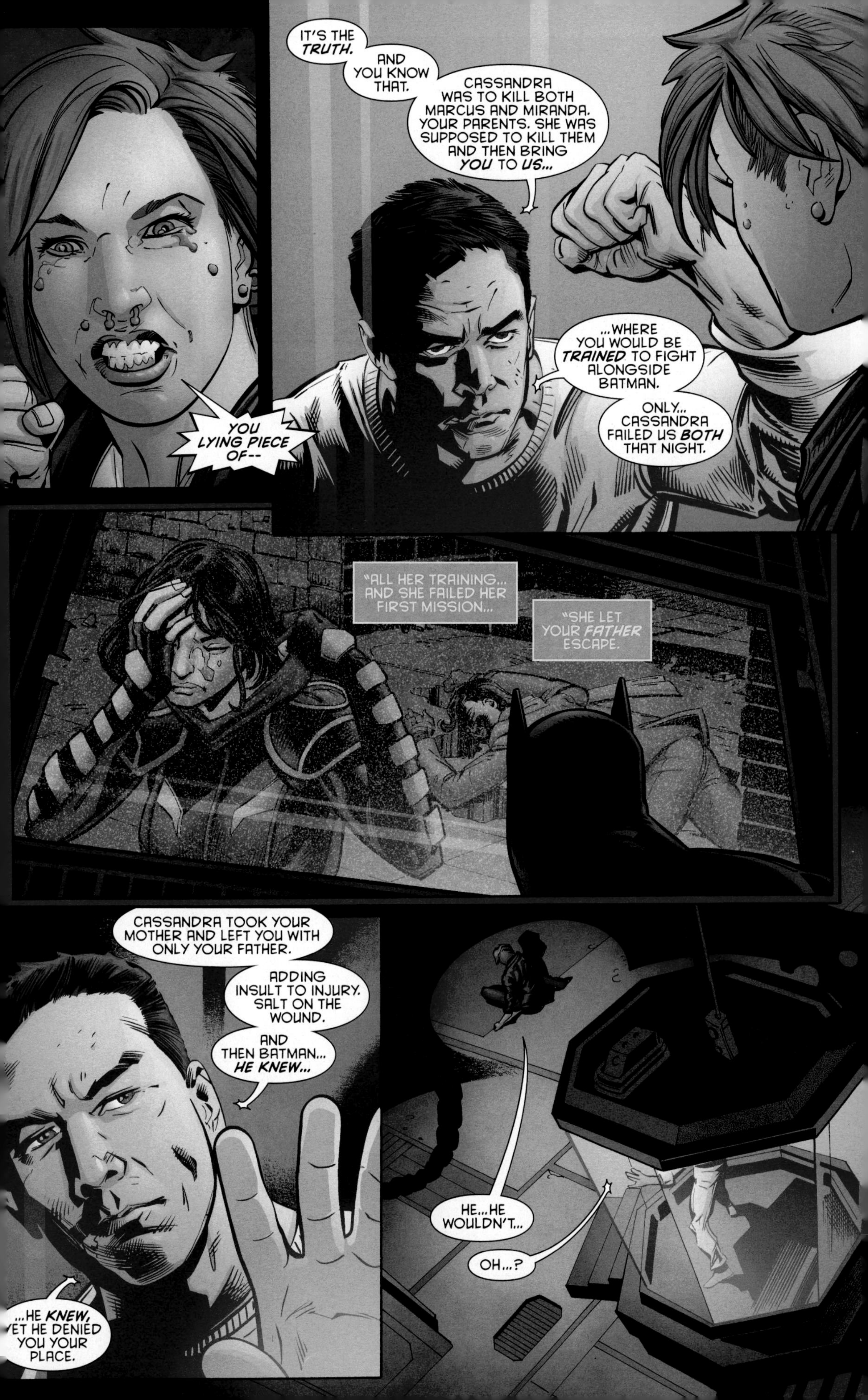
IT'S THE TRUTH.
AND YOU KNOW THAT.
CASSANDRA WAS TO KILL BOTH MARCUS AND MIRANDA. YOUR PARENTS. SHE WAS SUPPOSED TO KILL THEM AND THEN BRING YOU TO US...
...WHERE YOU WOULD BE TRAINED TO FIGHT ALONGSIDE BATMAN.
ONLY... CASSANDRA FAILED US BOTH THAT NIGHT.
YOU LYING PIECE OF--
"ALL HER TRAINING... AND SHE FAILED HER FIRST MISSION...
"SHE LET YOUR FATHER ESCAPE.
CASSANDRA TOOK YOUR MOTHER AND LEFT YOU WITH ONLY YOUR FATHER.
ADDING INSULT TO INJURY. SALT ON THE WOUND.
AND THEN BATMAN... HE KNEW...
...HE KNEW, YET HE DENIED YOU YOUR PLACE.
HE...HE WOULDN'T...
OH...?

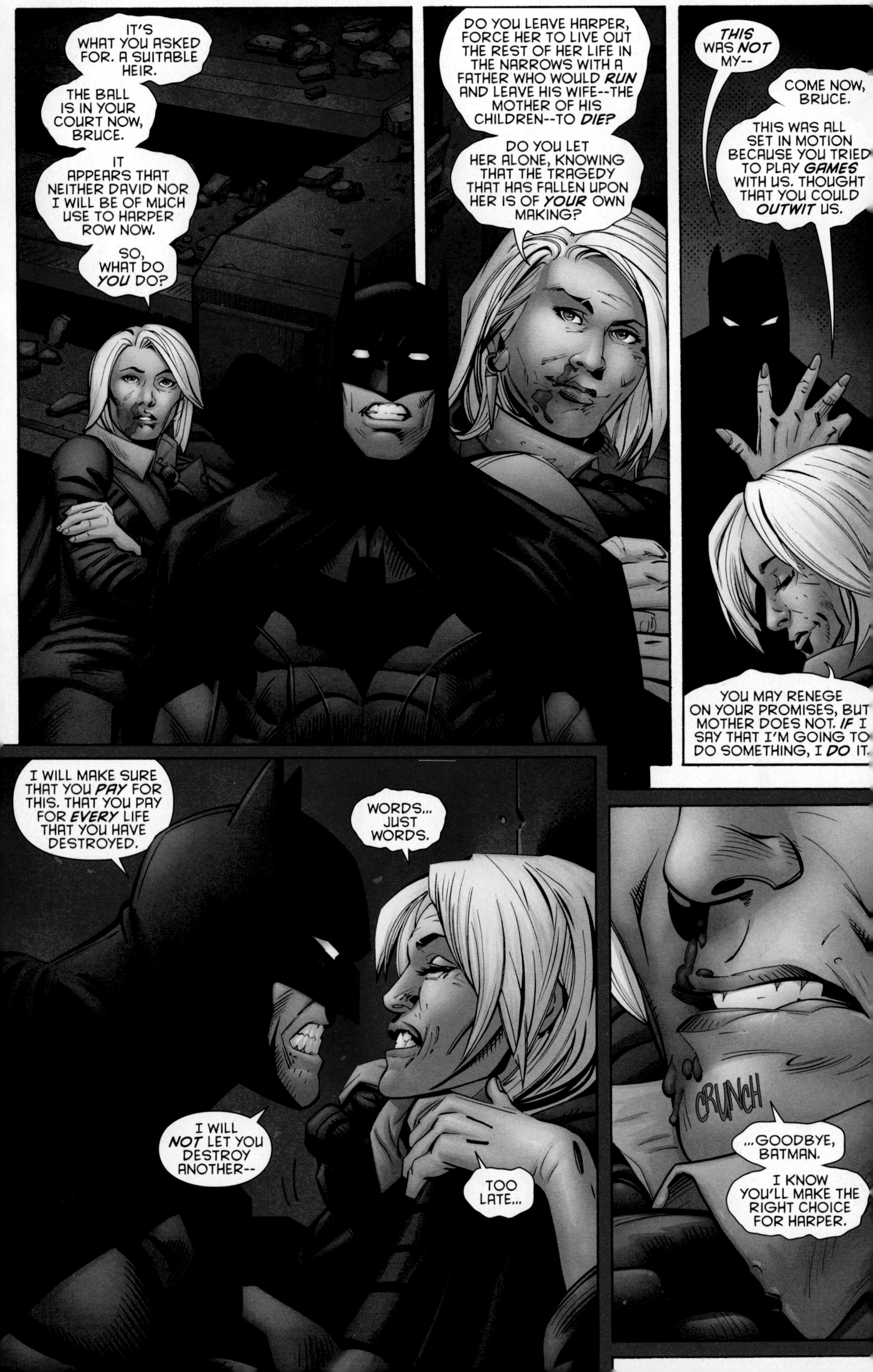
IT'S WHAT YOU ASKED FOR. A SUITABLE HEIR.
THE BALL IS IN YOUR COURT NOW, BRUCE.
IT APPEARS THAT NEITHER DAVID NOR I WILL BE OF MUCH USE TO HARPER ROW NOW.
SO, WHAT DO *YOU* DO?
DO YOU LEAVE HARPER, FORCE HER TO LIVE OUT THE REST OF HER LIFE IN THE NARROWS WITH A FATHER WHO WOULD *RUN* AND LEAVE HIS WIFE--THE MOTHER OF HIS CHILDREN--TO *DIE?*
DO YOU LET HER ALONE, KNOWING THAT THE TRAGEDY THAT HAS FALLEN UPON HER IS OF *YOUR* OWN MAKING?
THIS WAS *NOT* MY--
COME NOW, BRUCE.
THIS WAS ALL SET IN MOTION BECAUSE YOU TRIED TO PLAY *GAMES* WITH US. THOUGHT THAT YOU COULD *OUTWIT* US.
YOU MAY RENEGE ON YOUR PROMISES, BUT MOTHER DOES NOT. *IF* I SAY THAT I'M GOING TO DO SOMETHING, I *DO* IT.
I WILL MAKE SURE THAT YOU *PAY* FOR THIS. THAT YOU PAY FOR *EVERY* LIFE THAT YOU HAVE DESTROYED.
WORDS... JUST WORDS.
I WILL *NOT* LET YOU DESTROY ANOTHER--
TOO LATE...
CRUNCH
...GOODBYE, BATMAN.
I KNOW YOU'LL MAKE THE RIGHT CHOICE FOR HARPER.

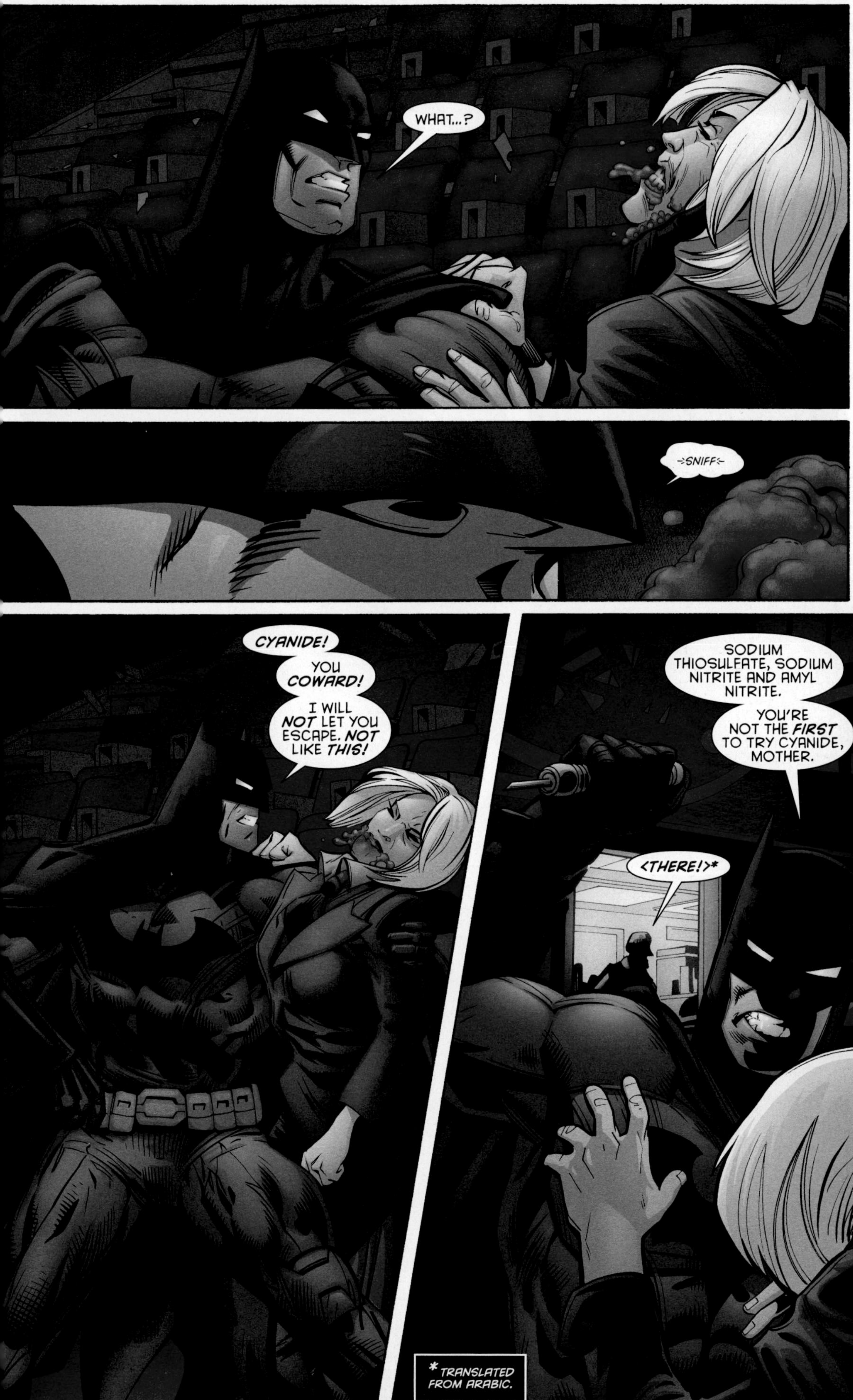
WHAT...?
-SNIFF-
CYANIDE!
YOU COWARD!
I WILL NOT LET YOU ESCAPE. NOT LIKE THIS!
SODIUM THIOSULFATE, SODIUM NITRITE AND AMYL NITRITE.
YOU'RE NOT THE FIRST TO TRY CYANIDE, MOTHER.
<THERE!>*
* TRANSLATED FROM ARABIC.

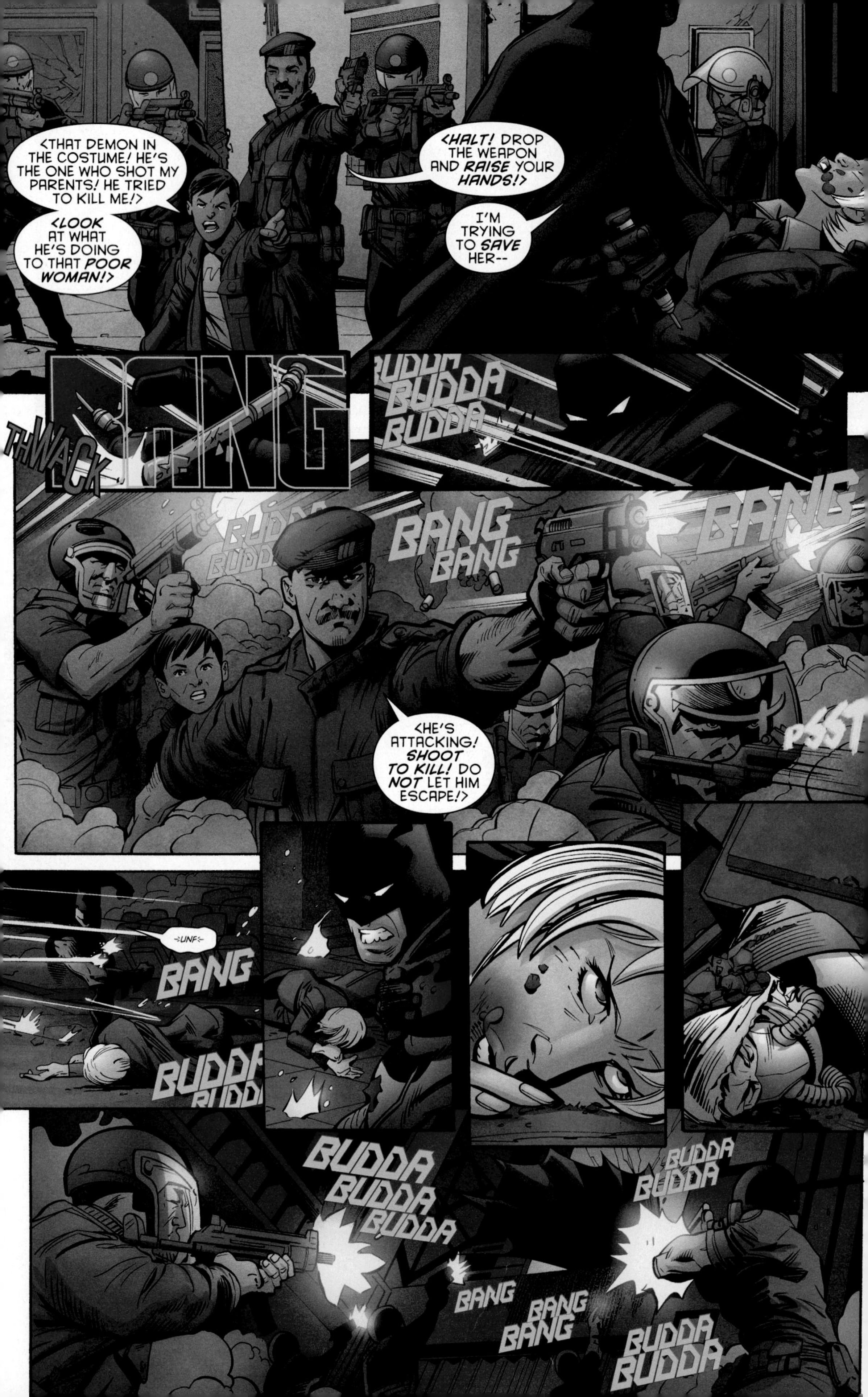

<THAT DEMON IN THE COSTUME! HE'S THE ONE WHO SHOT MY PARENTS! HE TRIED TO KILL ME!>
<LOOK AT WHAT HE'S DOING TO THAT POOR WOMAN!>
<HALT! DROP THE WEAPON AND RAISE YOUR HANDS!>
I'M TRYING TO SAVE HER--
THWACK
BANG
BUDDA BUDDA
BUDDA BUDDA
BANG BANG
BANG
<HE'S ATTACKING! SHOOT TO KILL! DO NOT LET HIM ESCAPE!>
PSST
UNF
BANG
BUDDA
BUDDA BUDDA BUDDA
BUDDA BUDDA
BANG
BANG BANG
BUDDA BUDDA

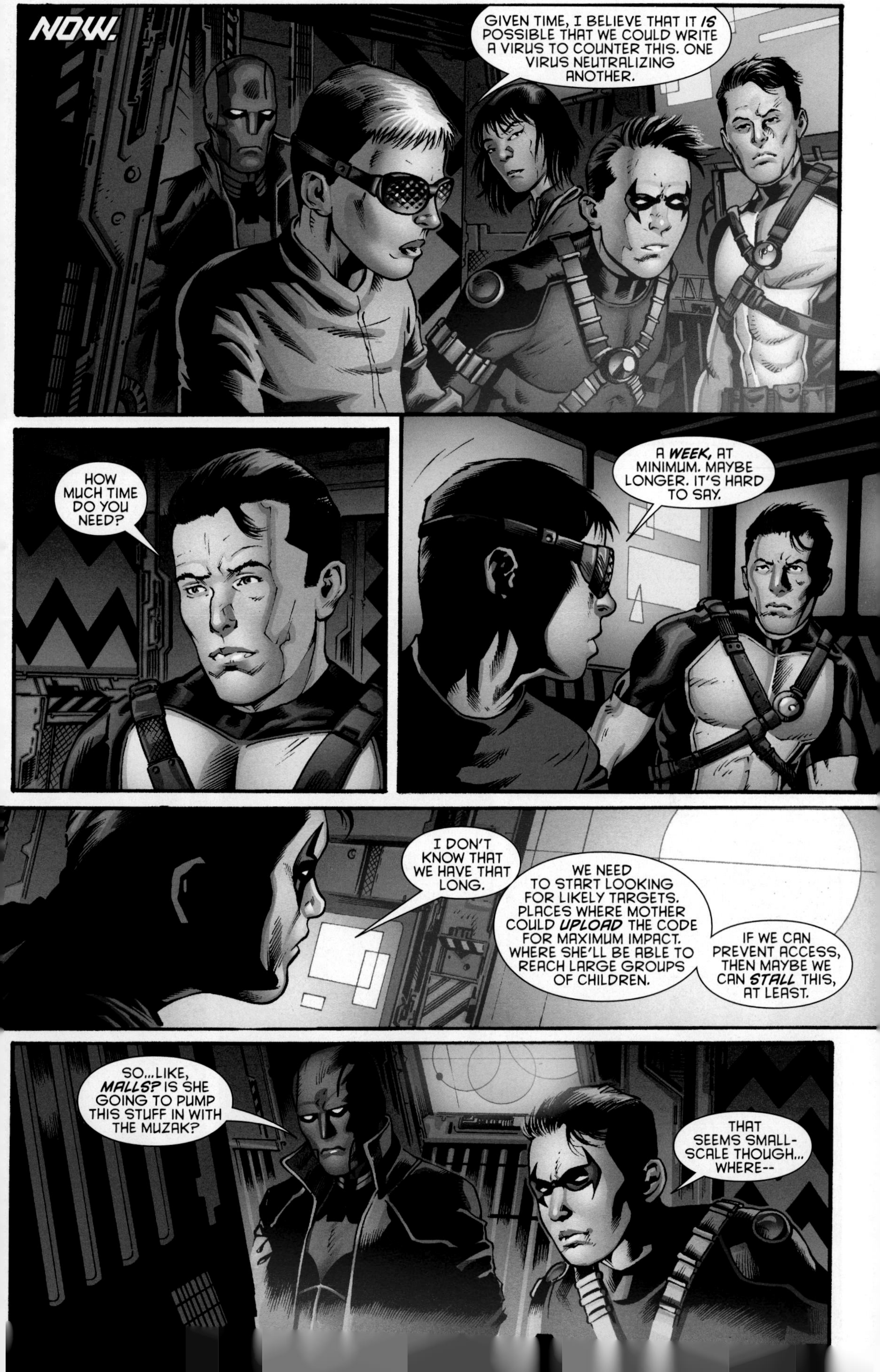
NOW.
GIVEN TIME, I BELIEVE THAT IT *IS* POSSIBLE THAT WE COULD WRITE A VIRUS TO COUNTER THIS. ONE VIRUS NEUTRALIZING ANOTHER.
HOW MUCH TIME DO YOU NEED?
A *WEEK,* AT MINIMUM. MAYBE LONGER. IT'S HARD TO SAY.
I DON'T KNOW THAT WE HAVE THAT LONG.
WE NEED TO START LOOKING FOR LIKELY TARGETS. PLACES WHERE MOTHER COULD *UPLOAD* THE CODE FOR MAXIMUM IMPACT. WHERE SHE'LL BE ABLE TO REACH LARGE GROUPS OF CHILDREN.
IF WE CAN PREVENT ACCESS, THEN MAYBE WE CAN *STALL* THIS, AT LEAST.
SO...LIKE, *MALLS?* IS SHE GOING TO PUMP THIS STUFF IN WITH THE MUZAK?
THAT SEEMS SMALL-SCALE THOUGH... WHERE--

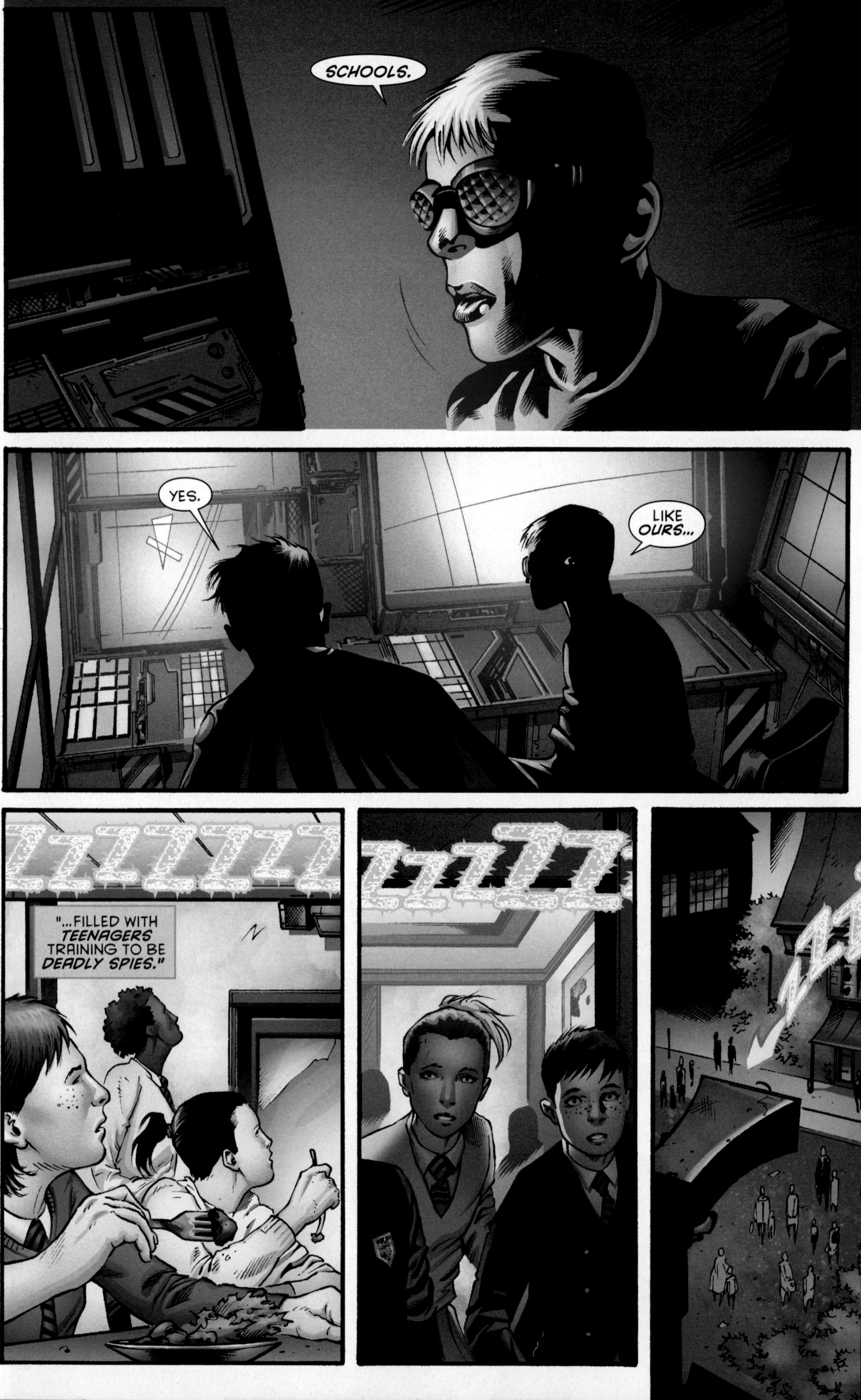
SCHOOLS.
YES.
LIKE OURS...
"...FILLED WITH TEENAGERS TRAINING TO BE DEADLY SPIES."

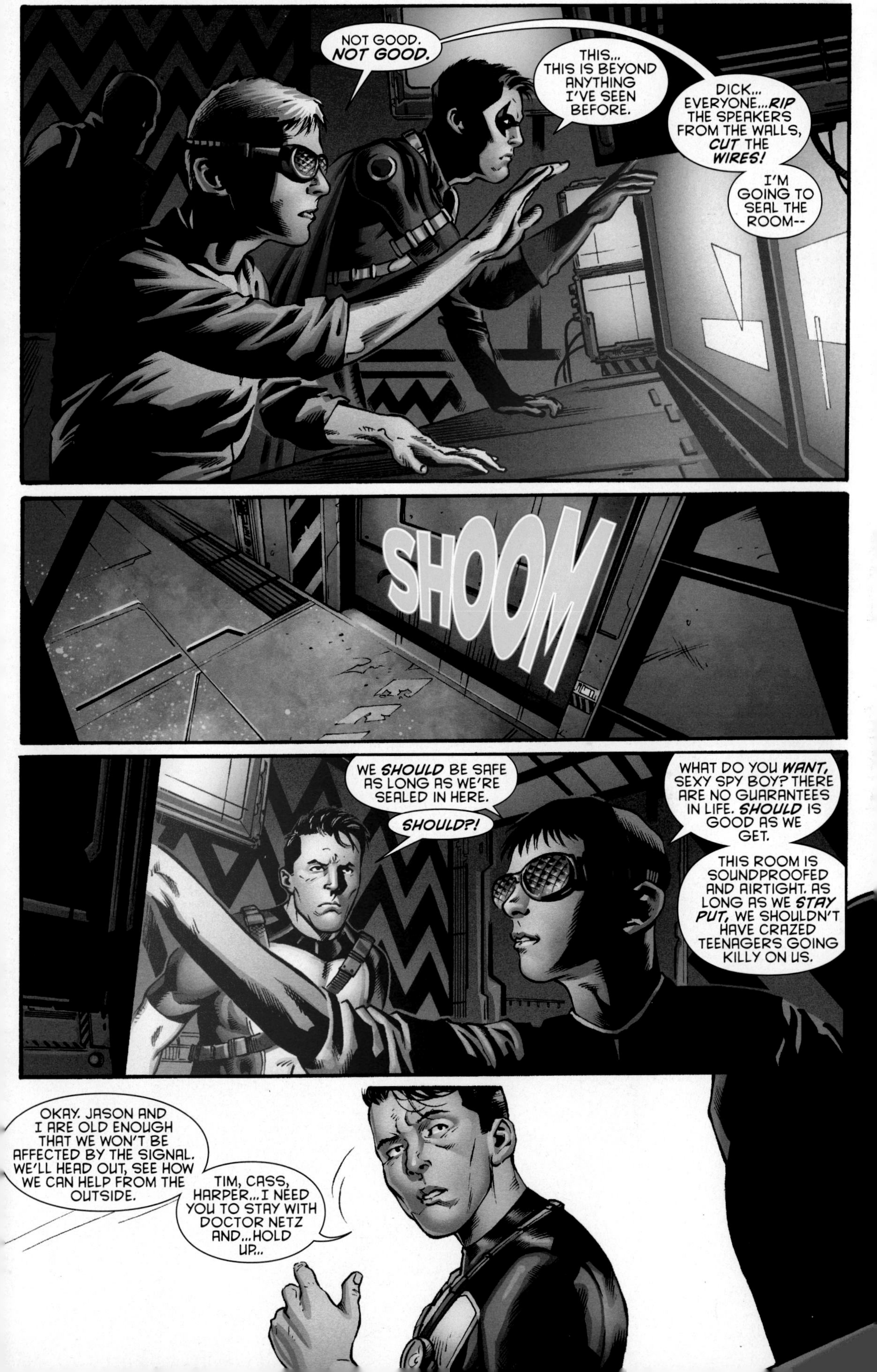

NOT GOOD. *NOT GOOD.*
THIS... THIS IS BEYOND ANYTHING I'VE SEEN BEFORE.
DICK... EVERYONE...*RIP* THE SPEAKERS FROM THE WALLS, *CUT* THE *WIRES!*
I'M GOING TO SEAL THE ROOM--
SHOOM
WE *SHOULD* BE SAFE AS LONG AS WE'RE SEALED IN HERE.
SHOULD?!
WHAT DO YOU *WANT,* SEXY SPY BOY? THERE ARE NO GUARANTEES IN LIFE. *SHOULD* IS GOOD AS WE GET.
THIS ROOM IS SOUNDPROOFED AND AIRTIGHT. AS LONG AS WE *STAY PUT,* WE SHOULDN'T HAVE CRAZED TEENAGERS GOING KILLY ON US.
OKAY. JASON AND I ARE OLD ENOUGH THAT WE WON'T BE AFFECTED BY THE SIGNAL. WE'LL HEAD OUT, SEE HOW WE CAN HELP FROM THE OUTSIDE.
TIM, CASS, HARPER...I NEED YOU TO STAY WITH DOCTOR NETZ AND...HOLD UP...

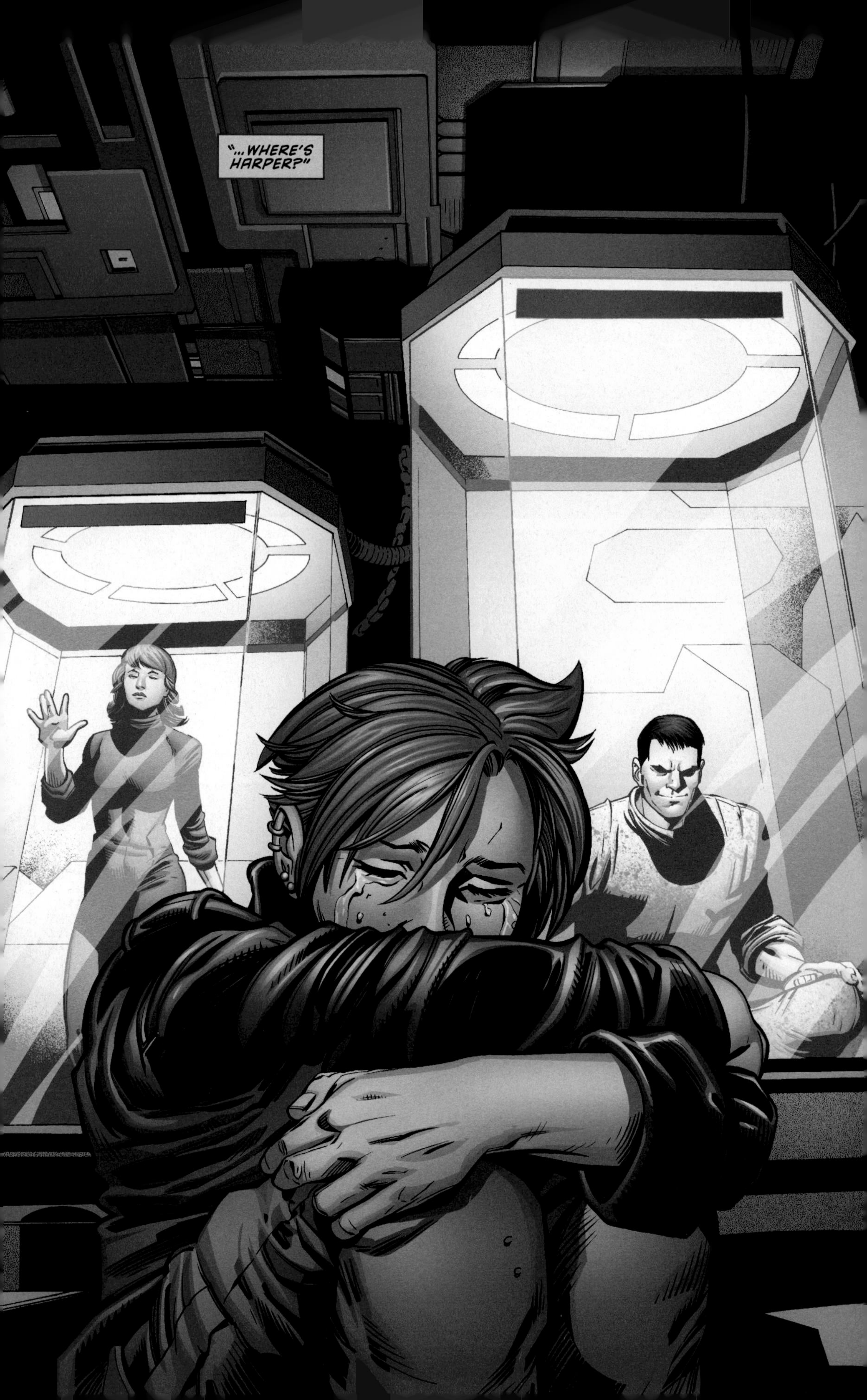
"...WHERE'S HARPER?"

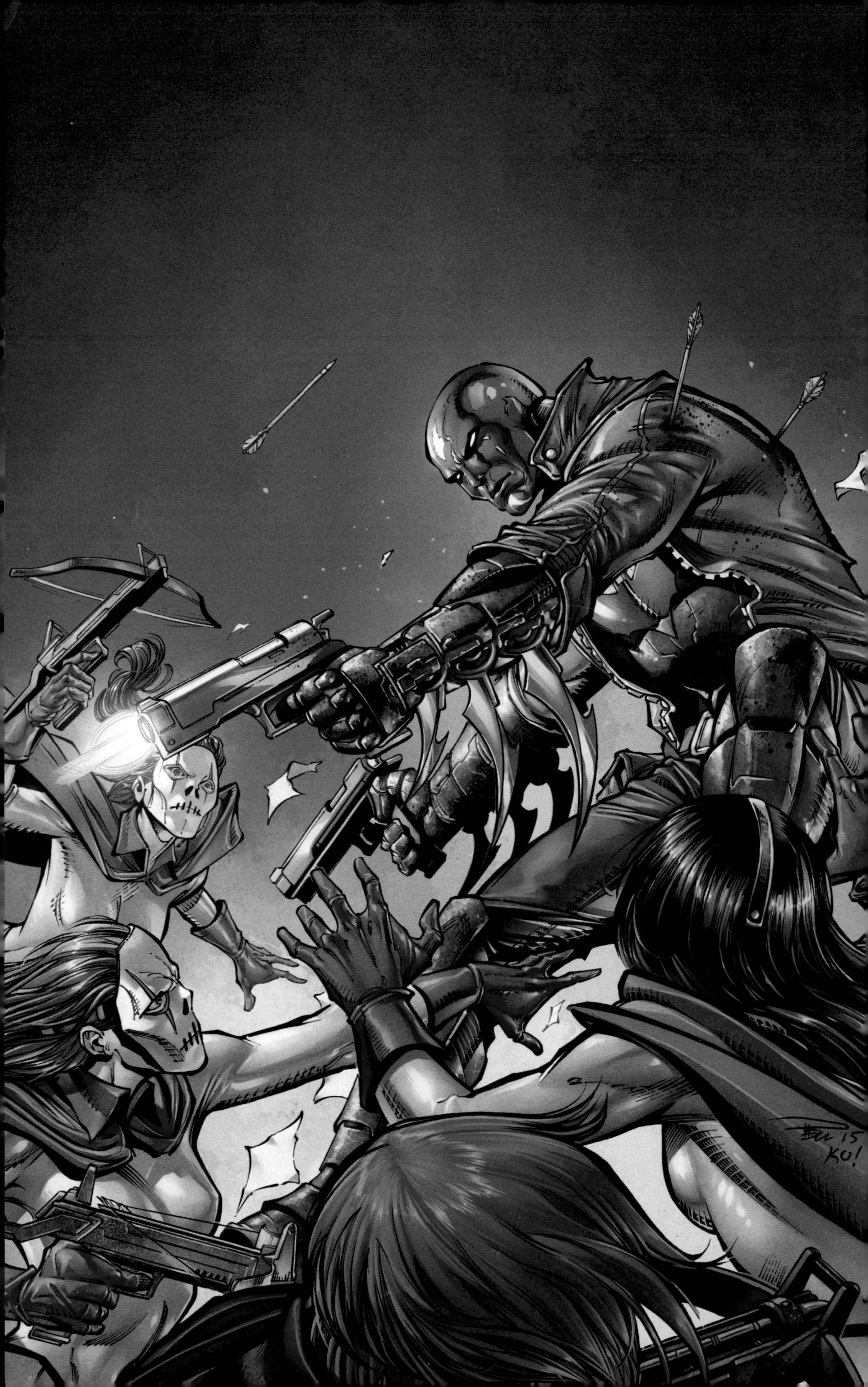

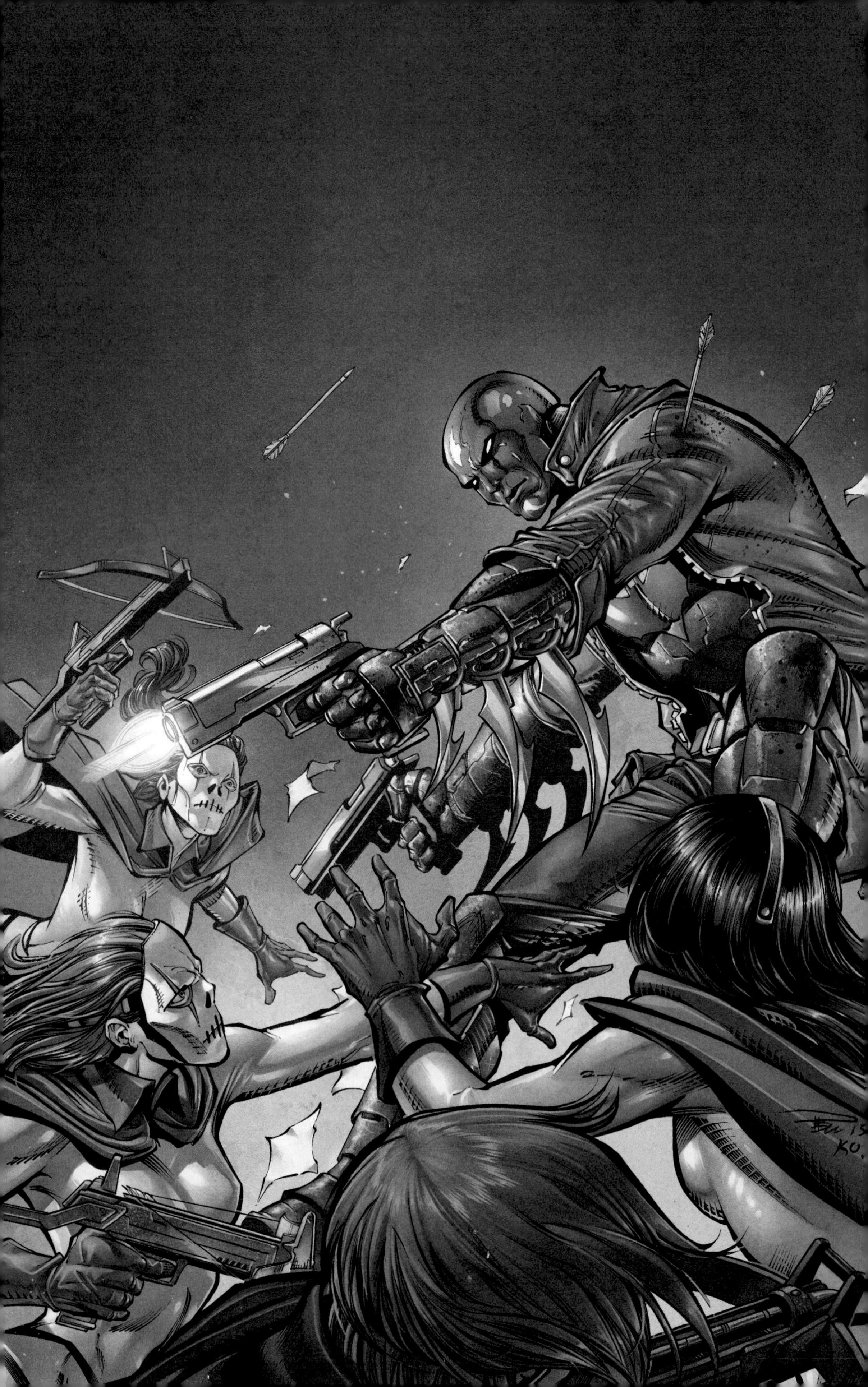

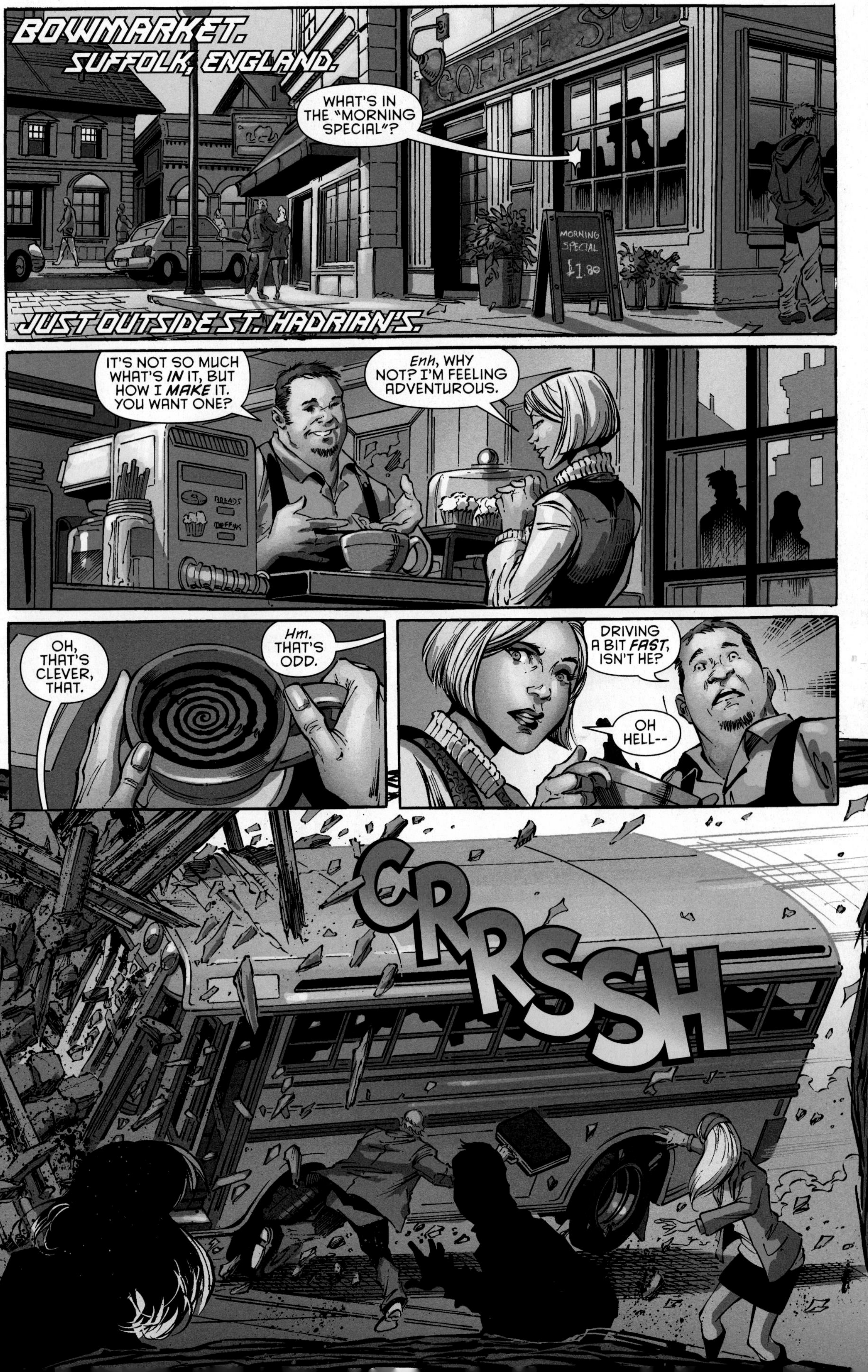
BOWMARKET.
SUFFOLK, ENGLAND.
COFFEE SPOT
WHAT'S IN THE "MORNING SPECIAL"?
MORNING SPECIAL £1.80
JUST OUTSIDE ST. HADRIAN'S.
IT'S NOT SO MUCH WHAT'S *IN* IT, BUT HOW I *MAKE* IT. YOU WANT ONE?
Enh, WHY NOT? I'M FEELING ADVENTUROUS.
OH, THAT'S CLEVER, THAT.
Hm. THAT'S ODD.
DRIVING A BIT *FAST*, ISN'T HE?
OH HELL--
CRRSSH

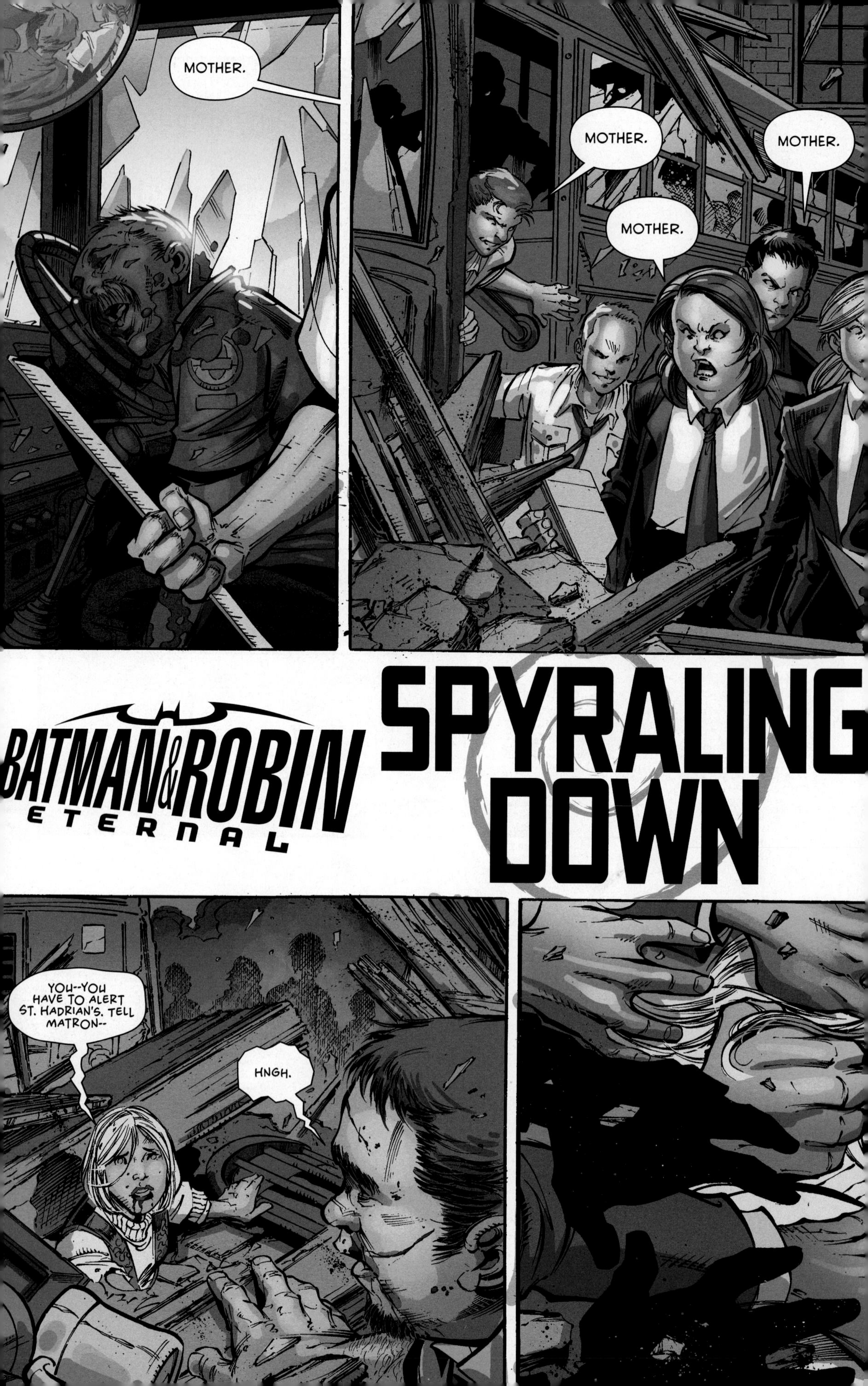
MOTHER.
MOTHER.
MOTHER.
MOTHER.
BATMAN & ROBIN ETERNAL
SPYRALING DOWN
YOU--YOU HAVE TO ALERT ST. HADRIAN'S. TELL MATRON--
HNGH.

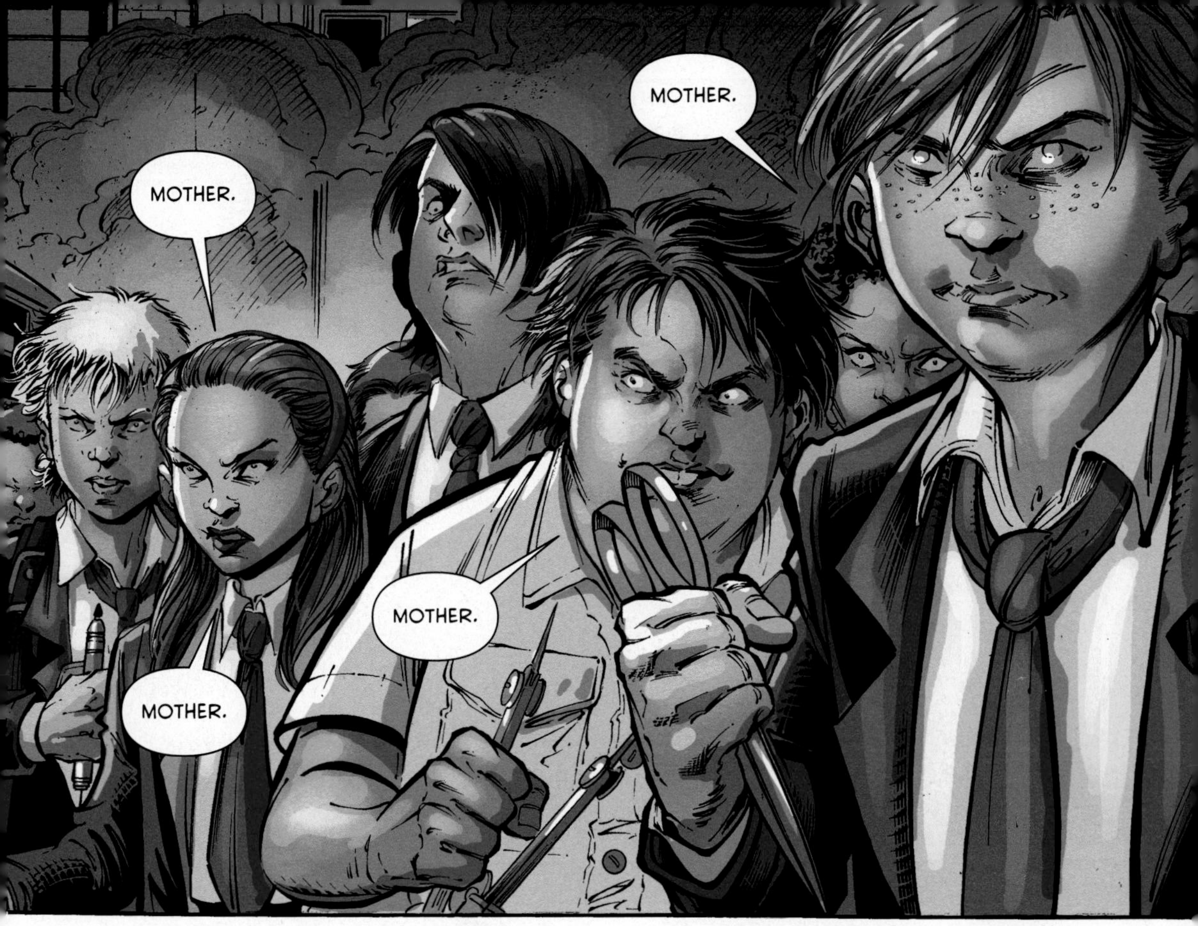
MOTHER.
MOTHER.
MOTHER.
MOTHER.

JAMES TYNION IV & SCOTT SNYDER Story **TIM SEELEY** Script
PAUL PELLETIER Pencils **TONY KORDOS** Inks
RAIN BEREDO Colors **CARLOS M. MANGUAL** Lettering
PAUL PELLETIER, TONY KORDOS & TOMEU MOREY Cover

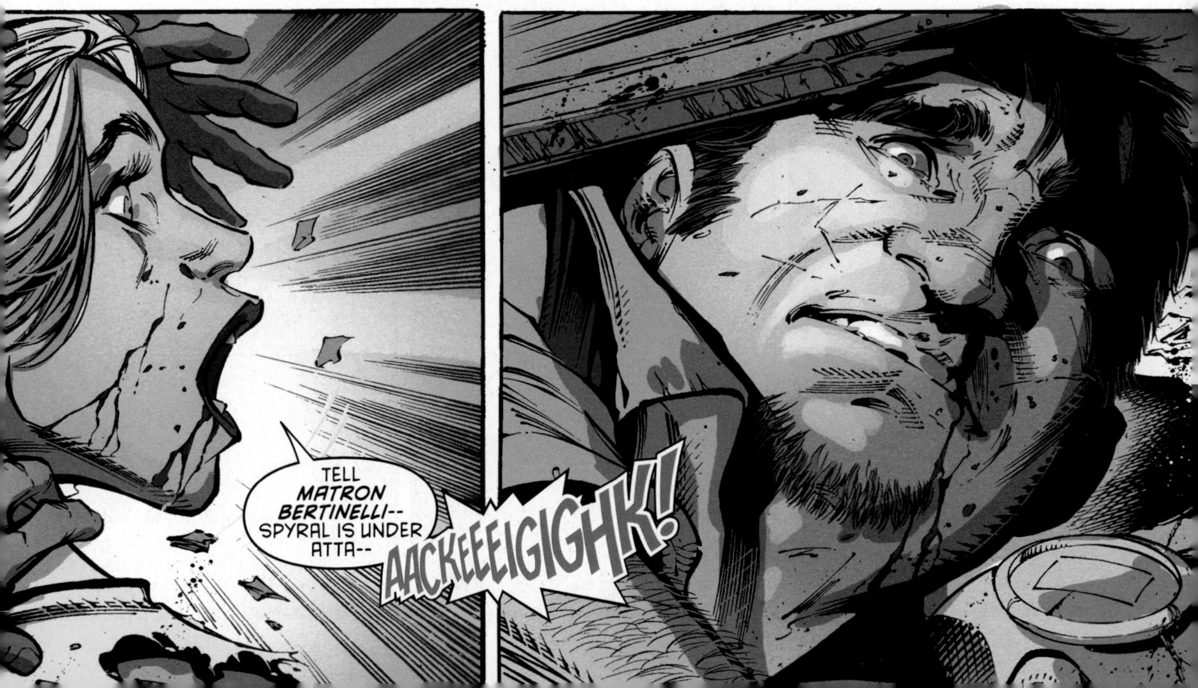
TELL *MATRON BERTINELLI*-- SPYRAL IS UNDER ATTA--
AACKEEEIGIGHK!

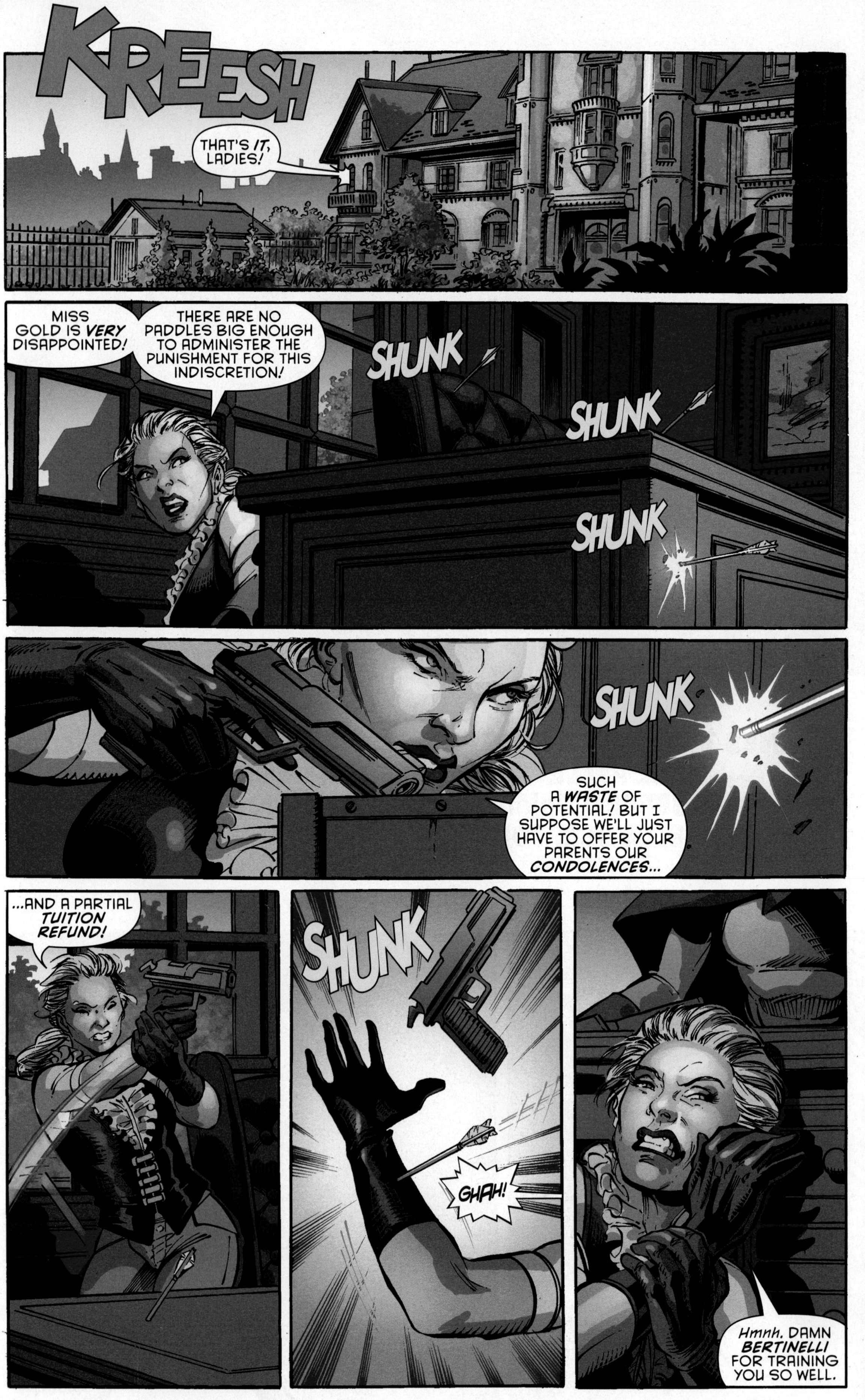
KREESH
THAT'S IT, LADIES!
MISS GOLD IS VERY DISAPPOINTED!
THERE ARE NO PADDLES BIG ENOUGH TO ADMINISTER THE PUNISHMENT FOR THIS INDISCRETION!
SHUNK
SHUNK
SHUNK
SHUNK
SUCH A WASTE OF POTENTIAL! BUT I SUPPOSE WE'LL JUST HAVE TO OFFER YOUR PARENTS OUR CONDOLENCES...
...AND A PARTIAL TUITION REFUND!
SHUNK
GHAH!
Hmnh. DAMN BERTINELLI FOR TRAINING YOU SO WELL.

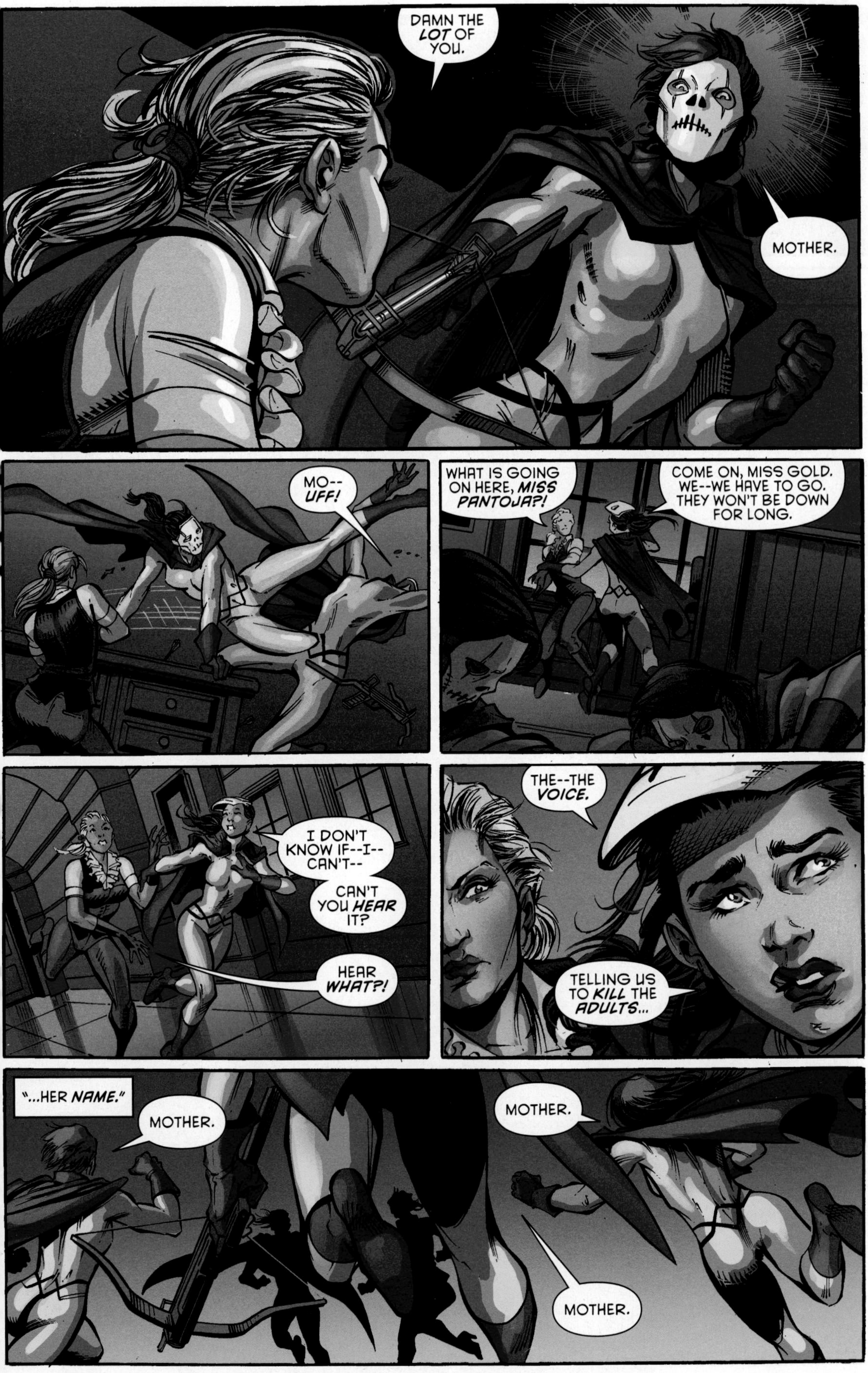
DAMN THE LOT OF YOU.
MOTHER.
MO-- UFF!
WHAT IS GOING ON HERE, MISS PANTOJA?!
COME ON, MISS GOLD. WE--WE HAVE TO GO. THEY WON'T BE DOWN FOR LONG.
I DON'T KNOW IF--I--CAN'T--
CAN'T YOU HEAR IT?
HEAR WHAT?!
THE--THE VOICE.
TELLING US TO KILL THE ADULTS...
"...HER NAME."
MOTHER.
MOTHER.
MOTHER.

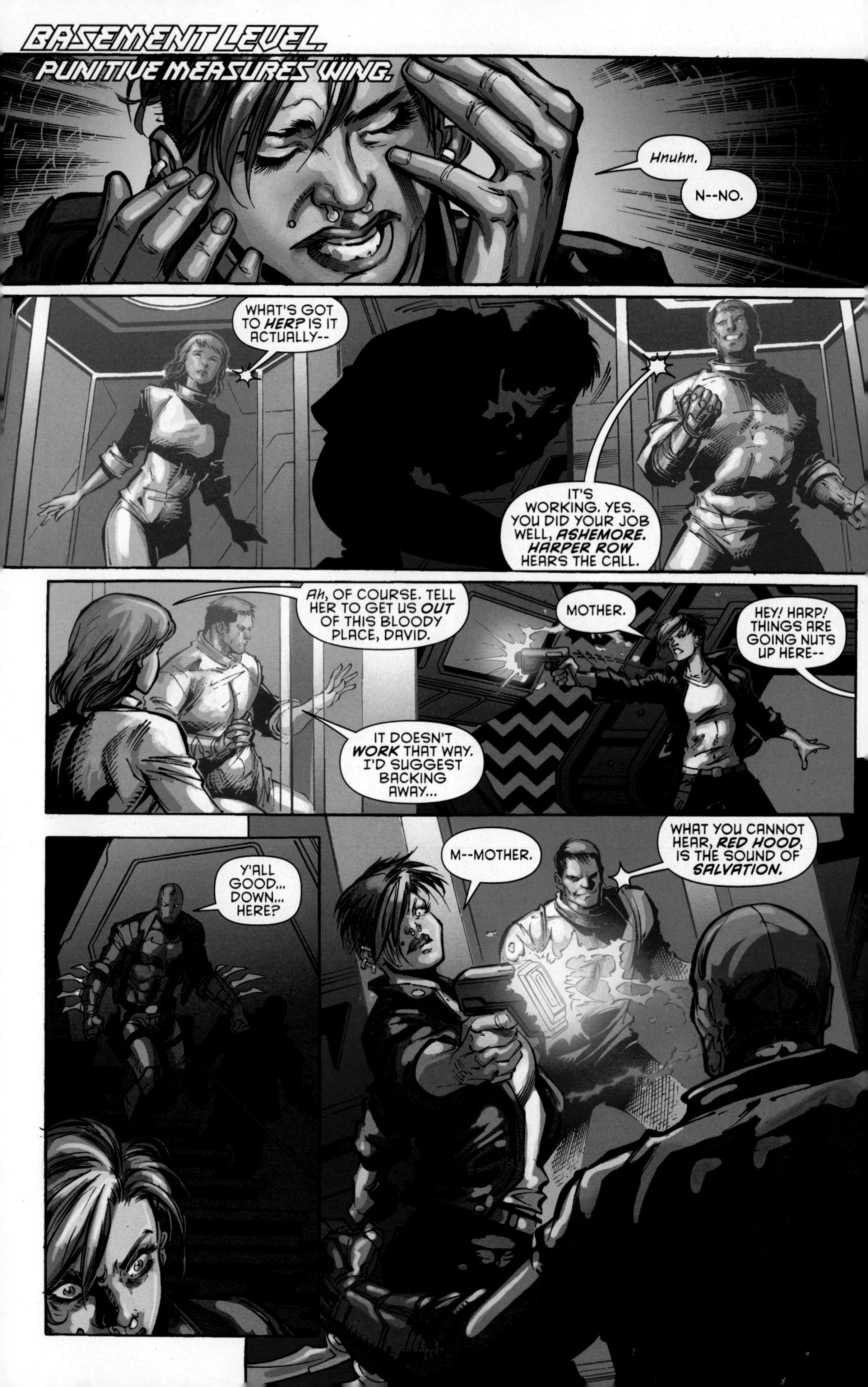

BASEMENT LEVEL.
PUNITIVE MEASURES WING.
Hnuhn.
N--NO.
WHAT'S GOT TO HER? IS IT ACTUALLY--
IT'S WORKING. YES. YOU DID YOUR JOB WELL, ASHEMORE. HARPER ROW HEARS THE CALL.
Ah, OF COURSE. TELL HER TO GET US OUT OF THIS BLOODY PLACE, DAVID.
IT DOESN'T WORK THAT WAY. I'D SUGGEST BACKING AWAY...
MOTHER.
HEY! HARP! THINGS ARE GOING NUTS UP HERE--
Y'ALL GOOD... DOWN... HERE?
M--MOTHER.
WHAT YOU CANNOT HEAR, RED HOOD, IS THE SOUND OF SALVATION.

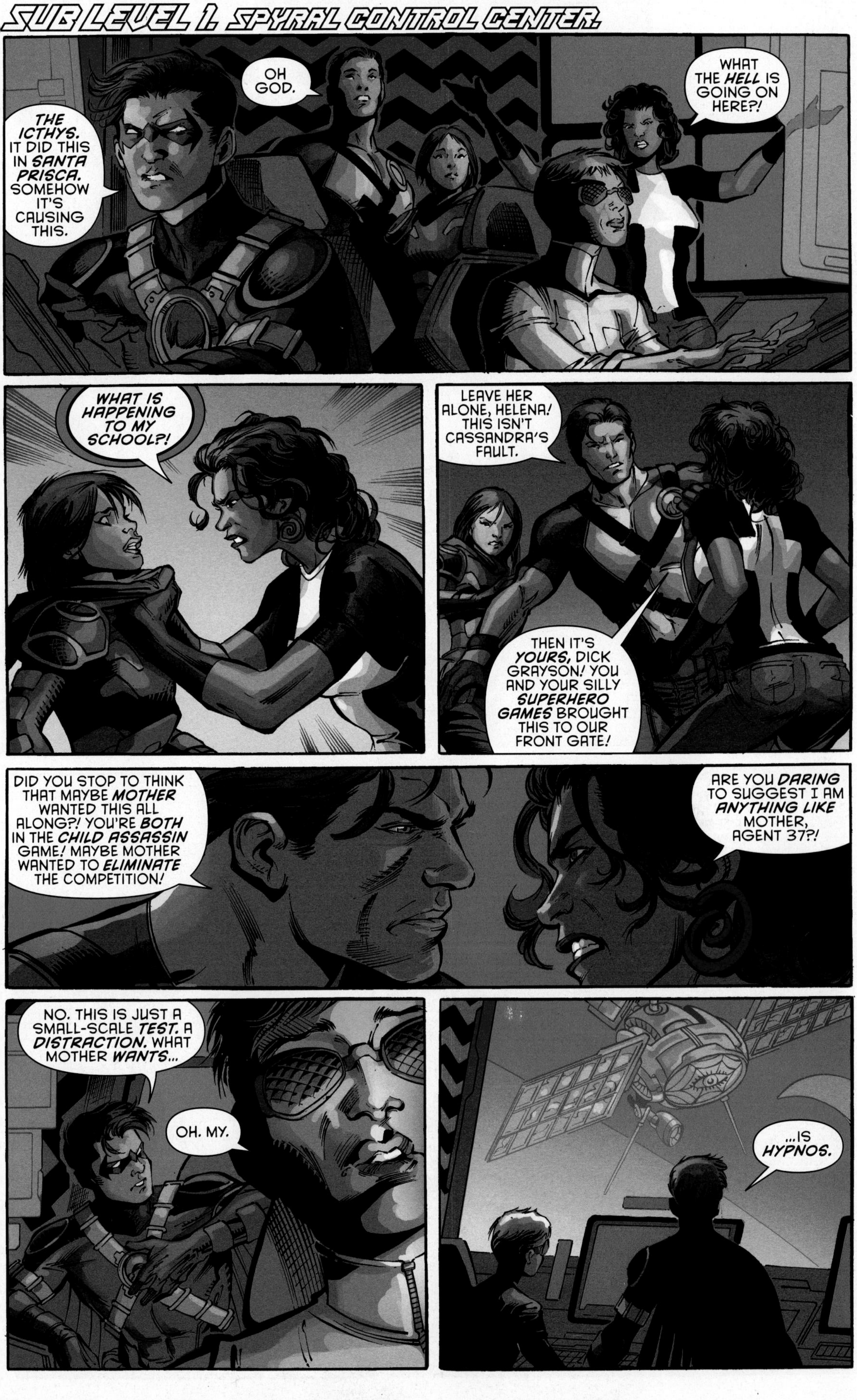
SUB LEVEL 1. SPYRAL CONTROL CENTER.
THE ICTHYS. IT DID THIS IN SANTA PRISCA. SOMEHOW IT'S CAUSING THIS.
OH GOD.
WHAT THE HELL IS GOING ON HERE?!
WHAT IS HAPPENING TO MY SCHOOL?!
LEAVE HER ALONE, HELENA! THIS ISN'T CASSANDRA'S FAULT.
THEN IT'S YOURS, DICK GRAYSON! YOU AND YOUR SILLY SUPERHERO GAMES BROUGHT THIS TO OUR FRONT GATE!
DID YOU STOP TO THINK THAT MAYBE MOTHER WANTED THIS ALL ALONG?! YOU'RE BOTH IN THE CHILD ASSASSIN GAME! MAYBE MOTHER WANTED TO ELIMINATE THE COMPETITION!
ARE YOU DARING TO SUGGEST I AM ANYTHING LIKE MOTHER, AGENT 37?!
NO. THIS IS JUST A SMALL-SCALE TEST. A DISTRACTION. WHAT MOTHER WANTS...
OH. MY.
...IS HYPNOS.

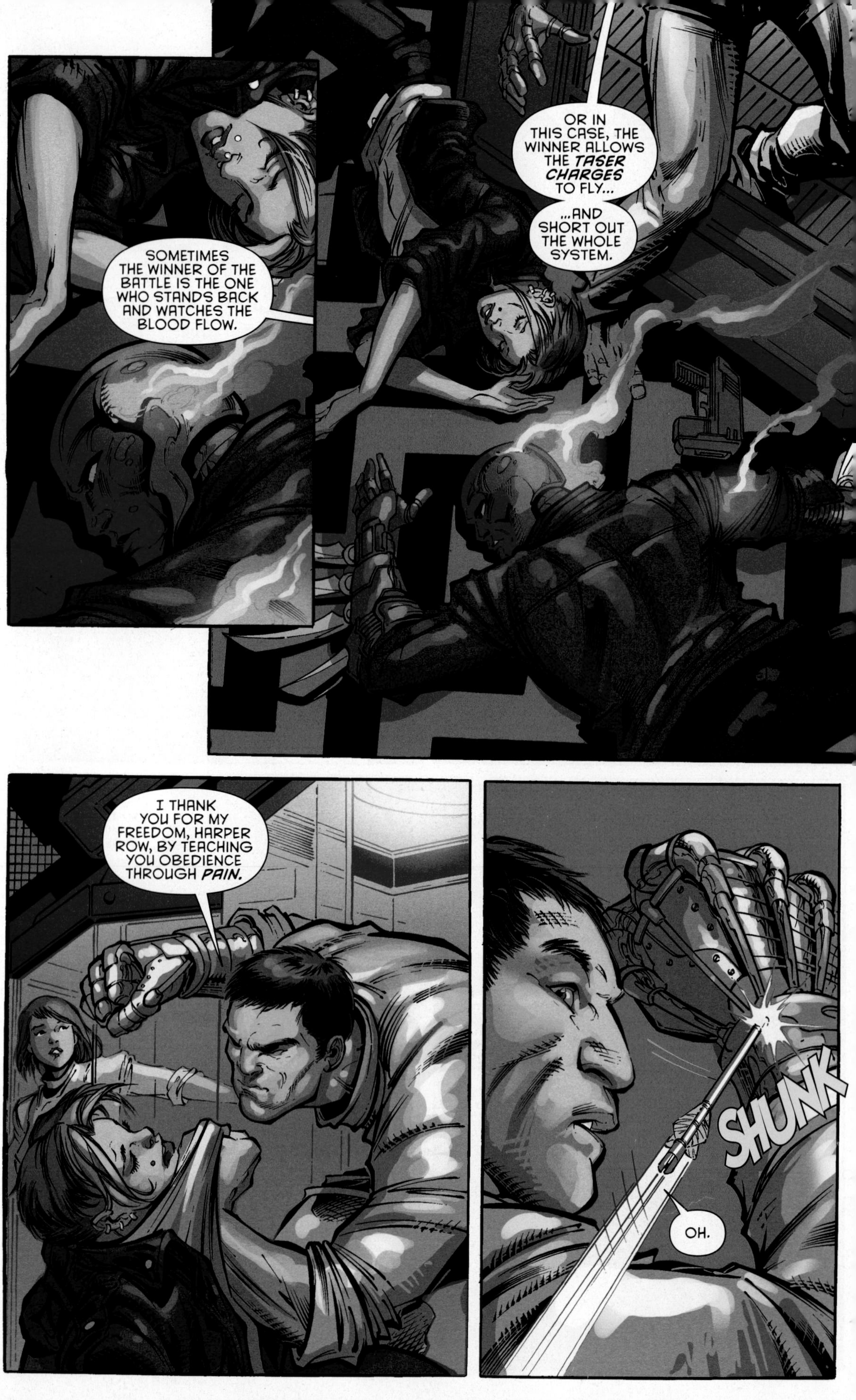
SOMETIMES THE WINNER OF THE BATTLE IS THE ONE WHO STANDS BACK AND WATCHES THE BLOOD FLOW.
OR IN THIS CASE, THE WINNER ALLOWS THE *TASER CHARGES* TO FLY...
...AND SHORT OUT THE WHOLE SYSTEM.
I THANK YOU FOR MY FREEDOM, HARPER ROW, BY TEACHING YOU OBEDIENCE THROUGH *PAIN.*
SHUNK
OH.

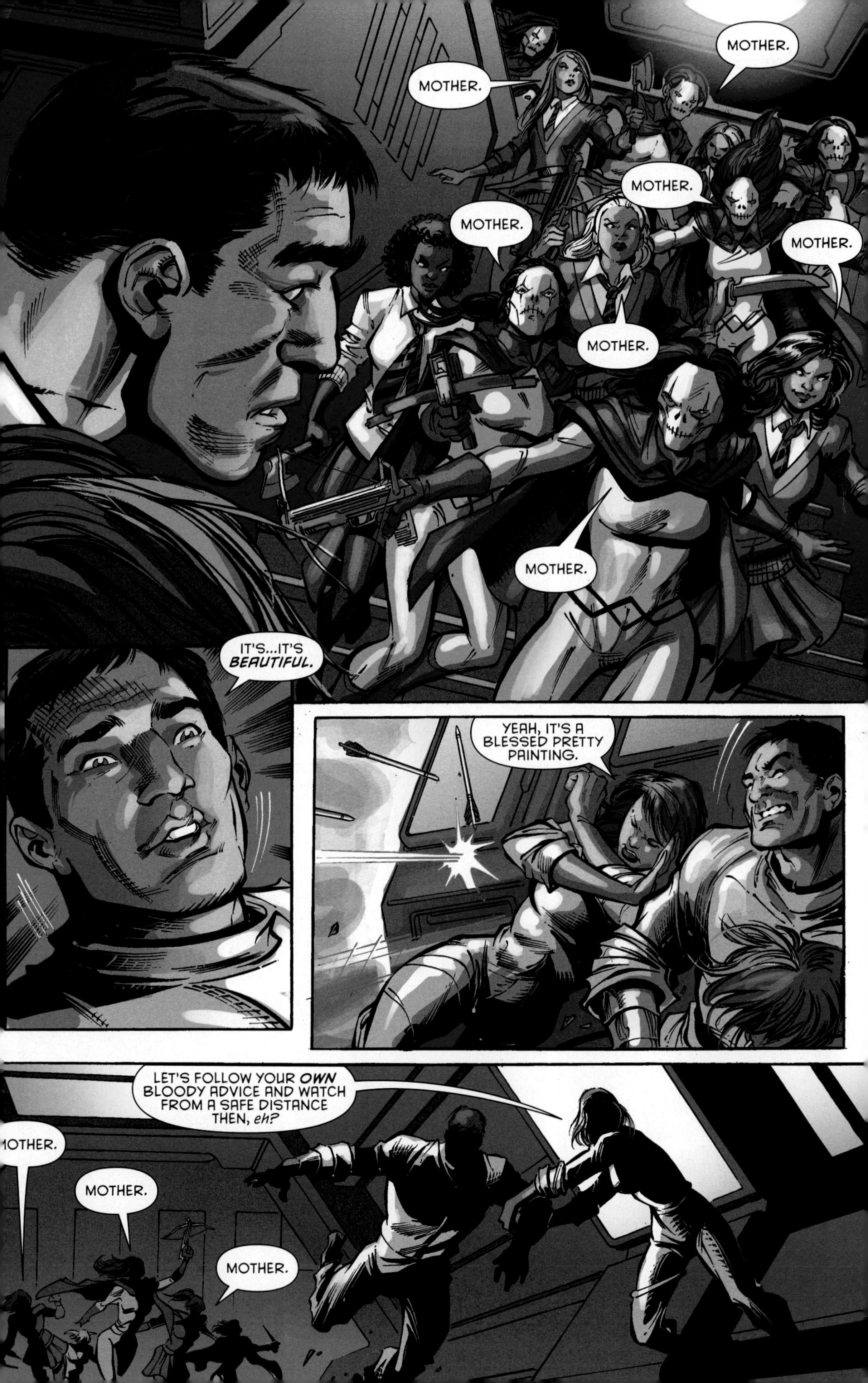
MOTHER.
MOTHER.
MOTHER.
MOTHER.
MOTHER.
MOTHER.
MOTHER.
IT'S...IT'S BEAUTIFUL.
YEAH, IT'S A BLESSED PRETTY PAINTING.
LET'S FOLLOW YOUR OWN BLOODY ADVICE AND WATCH FROM A SAFE DISTANCE THEN, eh?
MOTHER.
MOTHER.
MOTHER.

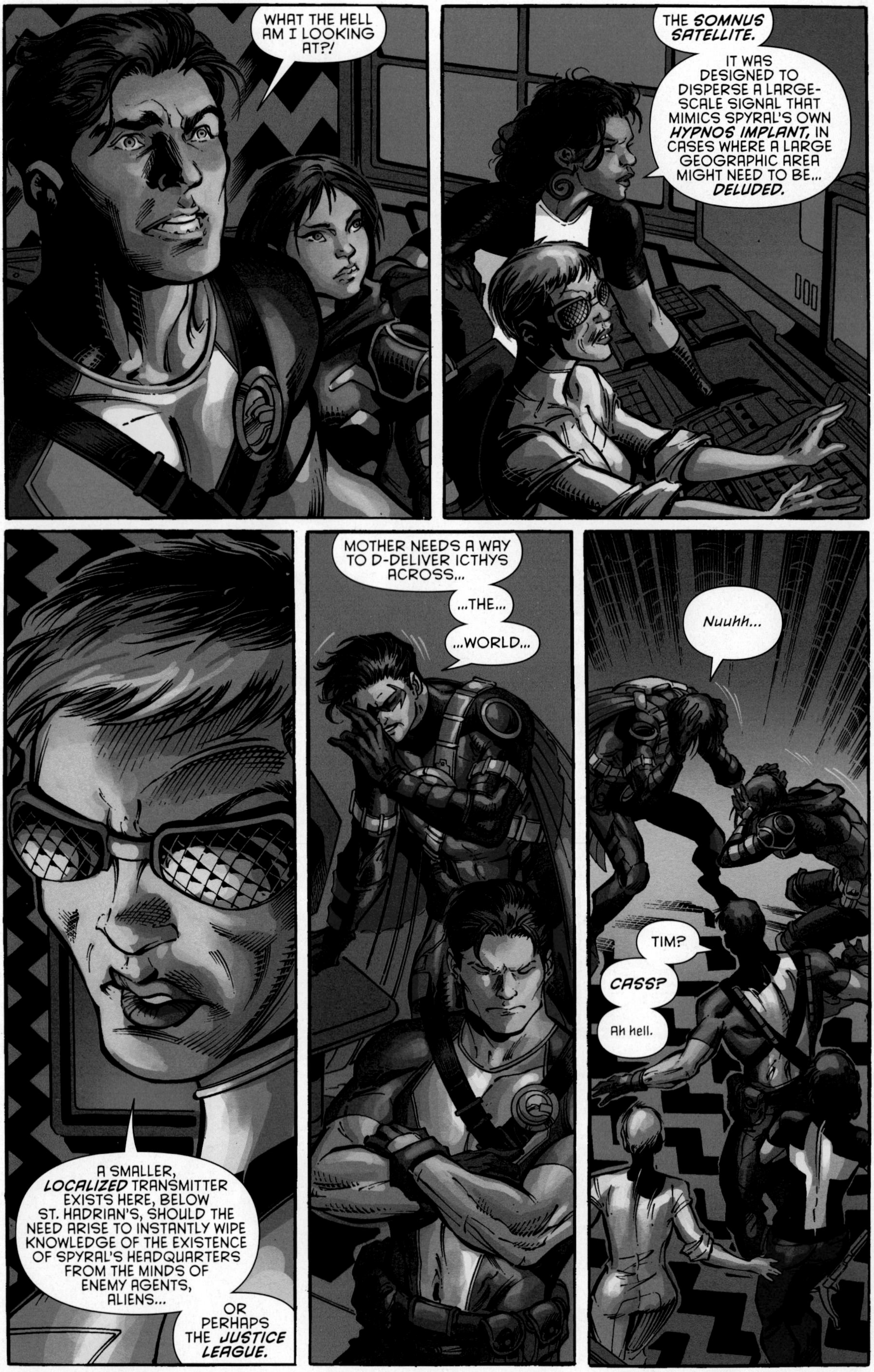
WHAT THE HELL AM I LOOKING AT?!
THE SOMNUS SATELLITE.
IT WAS DESIGNED TO DISPERSE A LARGE-SCALE SIGNAL THAT MIMICS SPYRAL'S OWN HYPNOS IMPLANT, IN CASES WHERE A LARGE GEOGRAPHIC AREA MIGHT NEED TO BE... DELUDED.
A SMALLER, LOCALIZED TRANSMITTER EXISTS HERE, BELOW ST. HADRIAN'S, SHOULD THE NEED ARISE TO INSTANTLY WIPE KNOWLEDGE OF THE EXISTENCE OF SPYRAL'S HEADQUARTERS FROM THE MINDS OF ENEMY AGENTS, ALIENS...
OR PERHAPS THE JUSTICE LEAGUE.
MOTHER NEEDS A WAY TO D-DELIVER ICTHYS ACROSS...
...THE...
...WORLD...
Nuuhh...
TIM?
CASS?
Ah hell.

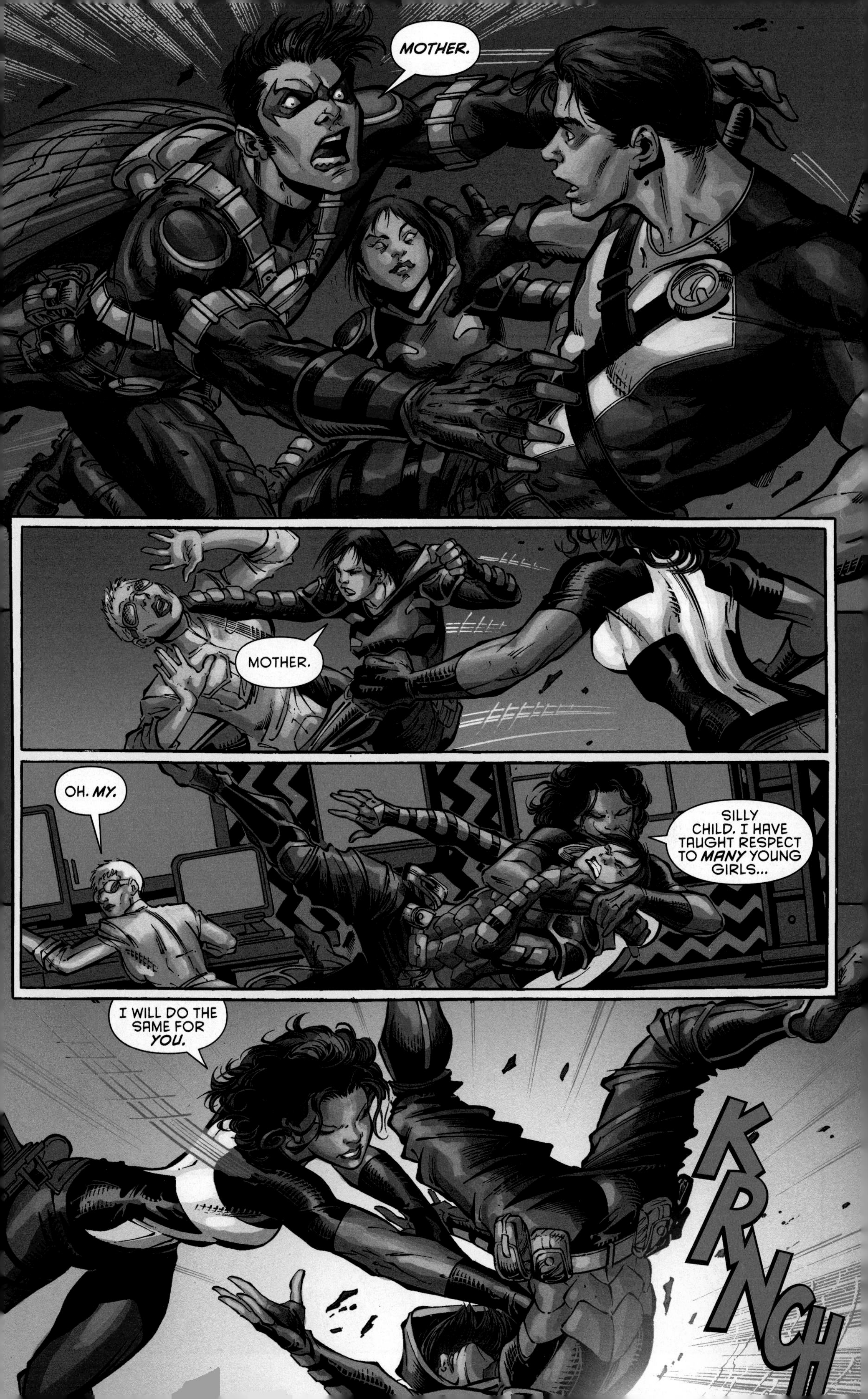
MOTHER.
MOTHER.
OH. MY.
SILLY CHILD. I HAVE TAUGHT RESPECT TO MANY YOUNG GIRLS...
I WILL DO THE SAME FOR YOU.
KRNCH

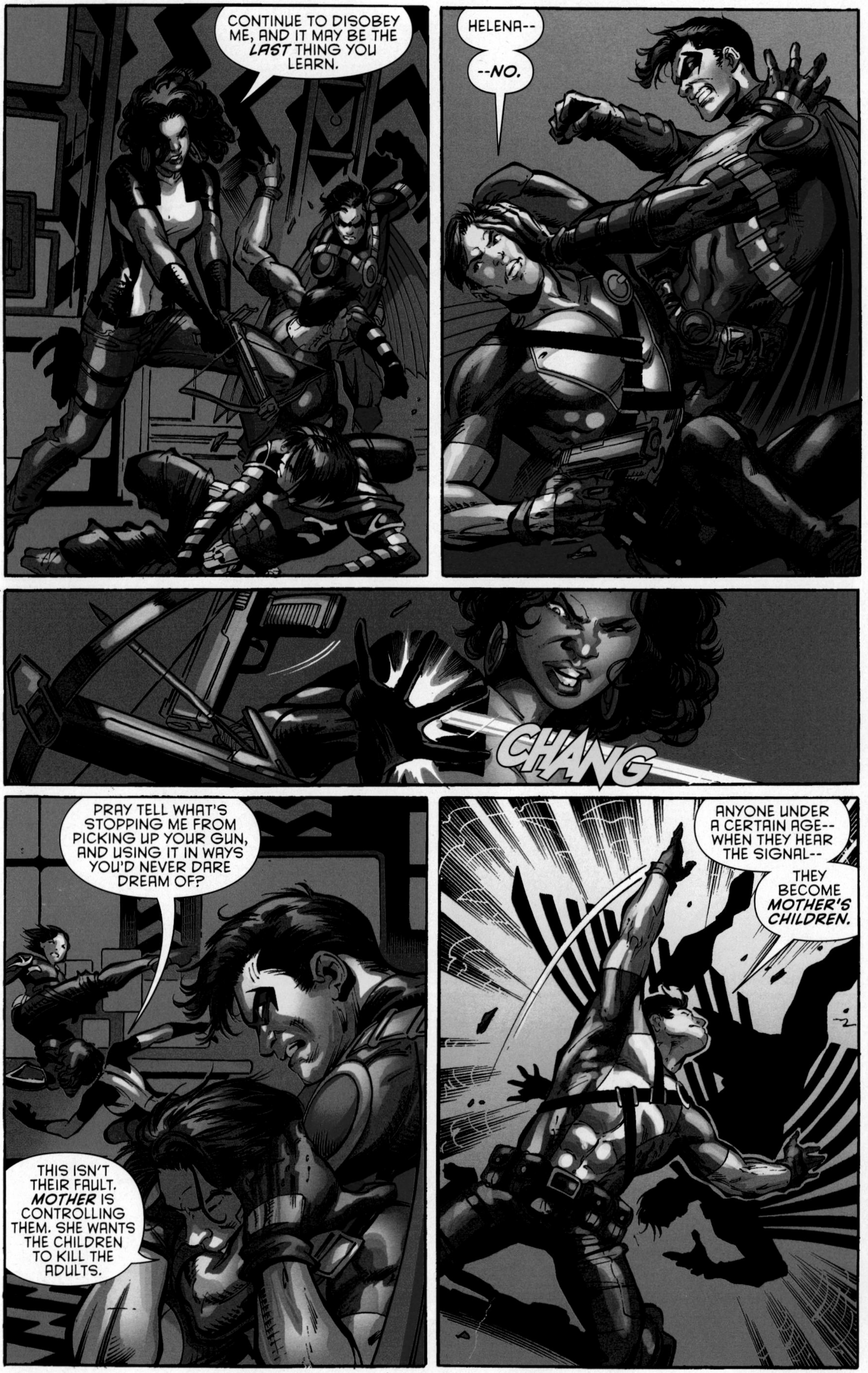
CONTINUE TO DISOBEY ME, AND IT MAY BE THE LAST THING YOU LEARN.
HELENA--
--NO.
CHANG
PRAY TELL WHAT'S STOPPING ME FROM PICKING UP YOUR GUN, AND USING IT IN WAYS YOU'D NEVER DARE DREAM OF?
THIS ISN'T THEIR FAULT. MOTHER IS CONTROLLING THEM. SHE WANTS THE CHILDREN TO KILL THE ADULTS.
ANYONE UNDER A CERTAIN AGE--WHEN THEY HEAR THE SIGNAL--
THEY BECOME MOTHER'S CHILDREN.

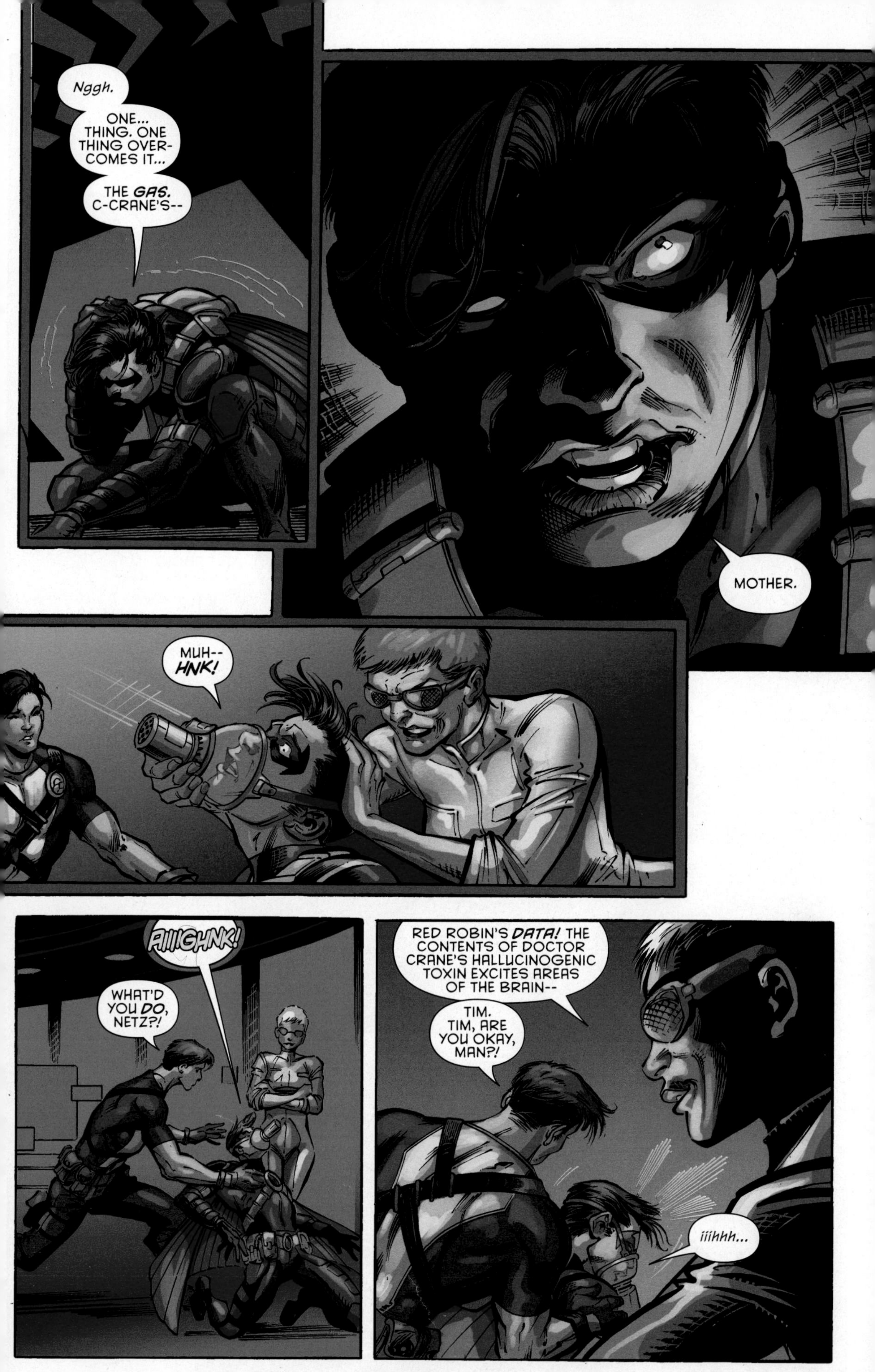
Nggh.
ONE... THING. ONE THING OVERCOMES IT...
THE GAS. C-CRANE'S--
MOTHER.
MUH-- HNK!
AIIIGHNK!
WHAT'D YOU DO, NETZ?!
RED ROBIN'S DATA! THE CONTENTS OF DOCTOR CRANE'S HALLUCINOGENIC TOXIN EXCITES AREAS OF THE BRAIN--
TIM. TIM, ARE YOU OKAY, MAN?!
iiihhh...

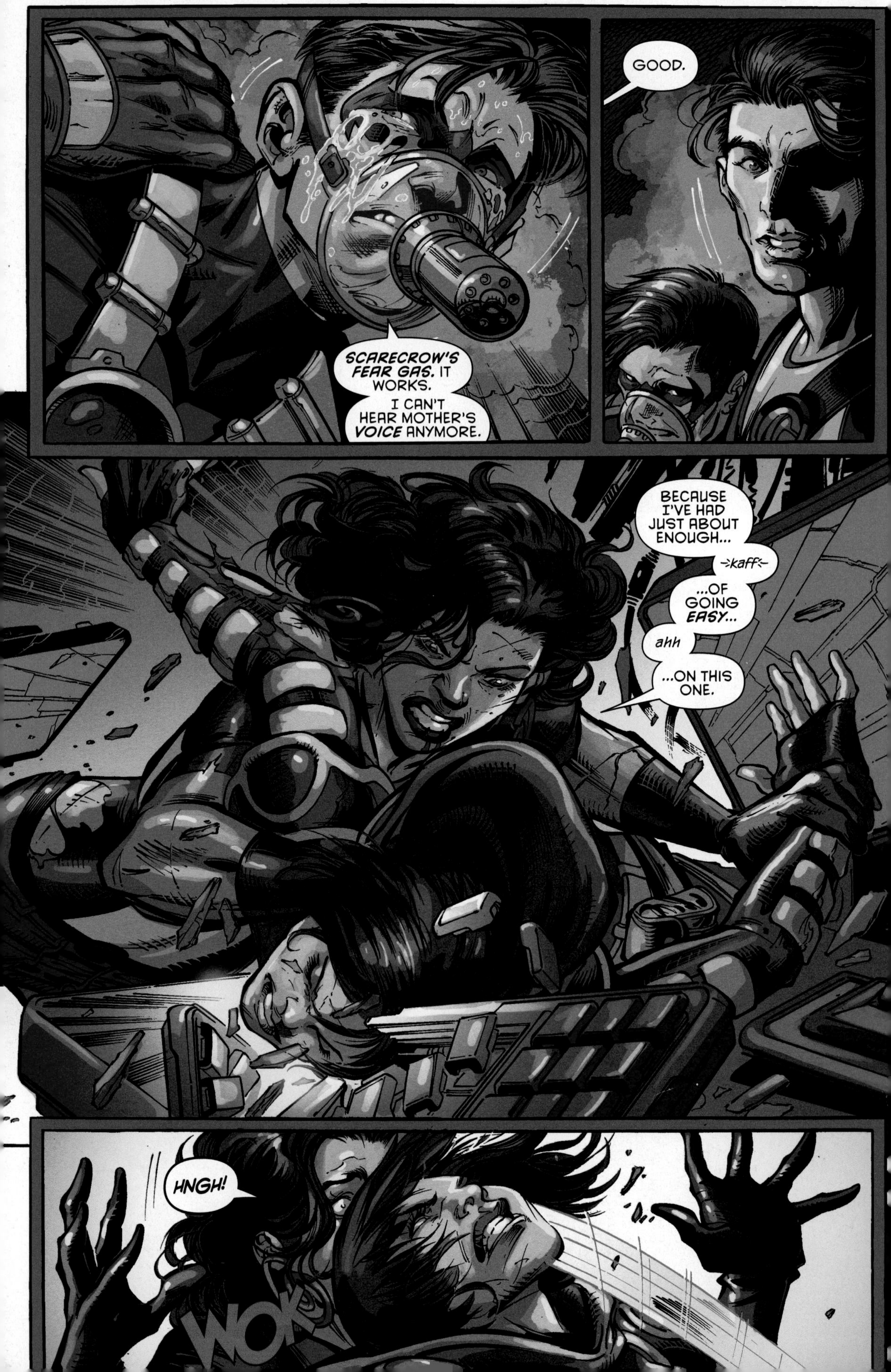
GOOD.
SCARECROW'S FEAR GAS. IT WORKS.
I CAN'T HEAR MOTHER'S VOICE ANYMORE.
BECAUSE I'VE HAD JUST ABOUT ENOUGH...
-kaff-
...OF GOING EASY...
ahh
...ON THIS ONE.
HNGH!
WOK

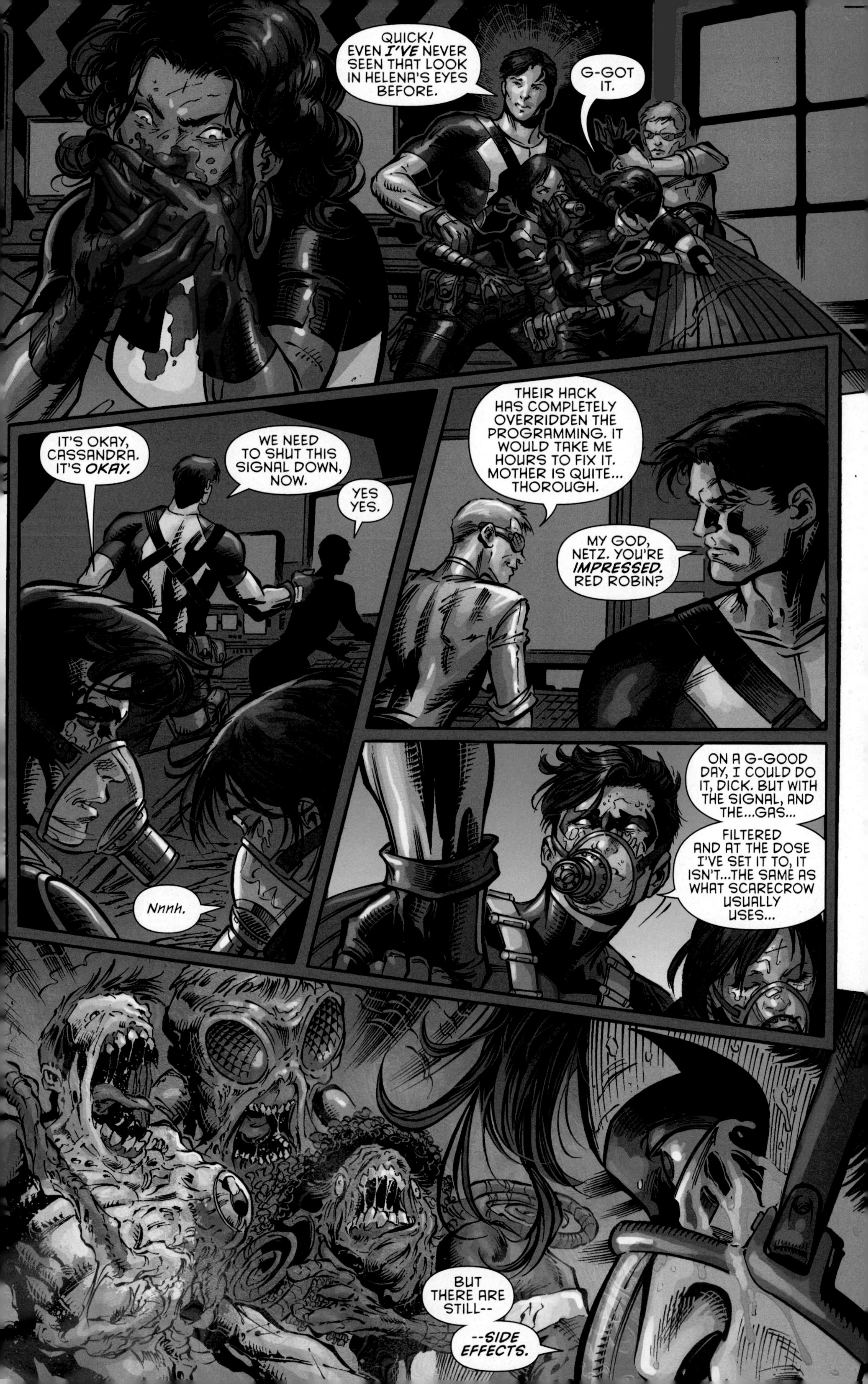
QUICK! EVEN *I'VE* NEVER SEEN THAT LOOK IN HELENA'S EYES BEFORE.
G-GOT IT.
IT'S OKAY, CASSANDRA. IT'S *OKAY.*
WE NEED TO SHUT THIS SIGNAL DOWN, NOW.
YES YES.
Nnnh.
THEIR HACK HAS COMPLETELY OVERRIDDEN THE PROGRAMMING. IT WOULD TAKE ME HOURS TO FIX IT. MOTHER IS QUITE... THOROUGH.
MY GOD, NETZ. YOU'RE *IMPRESSED.* RED ROBIN?
ON A G-GOOD DAY, I COULD DO IT, DICK. BUT WITH THE SIGNAL, AND THE...GAS...
FILTERED AND AT THE DOSE I'VE SET IT TO, IT ISN'T...THE SAME AS WHAT SCARECROW USUALLY USES...
BUT THERE ARE STILL--
--*SIDE EFFECTS.*

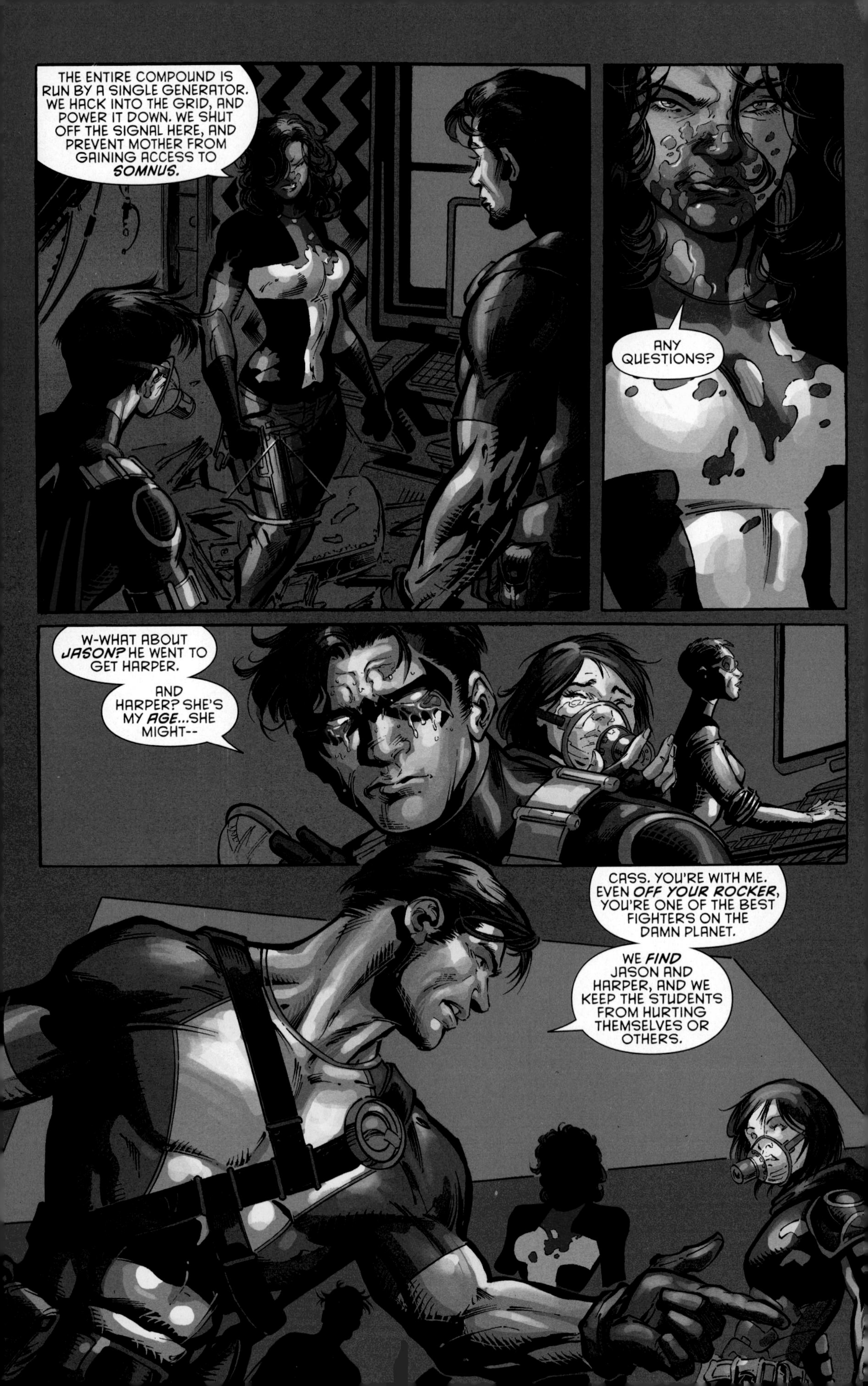
THE ENTIRE COMPOUND IS RUN BY A SINGLE GENERATOR. WE HACK INTO THE GRID, AND POWER IT DOWN. WE SHUT OFF THE SIGNAL HERE, AND PREVENT MOTHER FROM GAINING ACCESS TO *SOMNUS.*
ANY QUESTIONS?
W-WHAT ABOUT *JASON?* HE WENT TO GET HARPER.
AND HARPER? SHE'S MY *AGE*...SHE MIGHT--
CASS. YOU'RE WITH ME. EVEN *OFF YOUR ROCKER*, YOU'RE ONE OF THE BEST FIGHTERS ON THE DAMN PLANET.
WE *FIND* JASON AND HARPER, AND WE KEEP THE STUDENTS FROM HURTING THEMSELVES OR OTHERS.

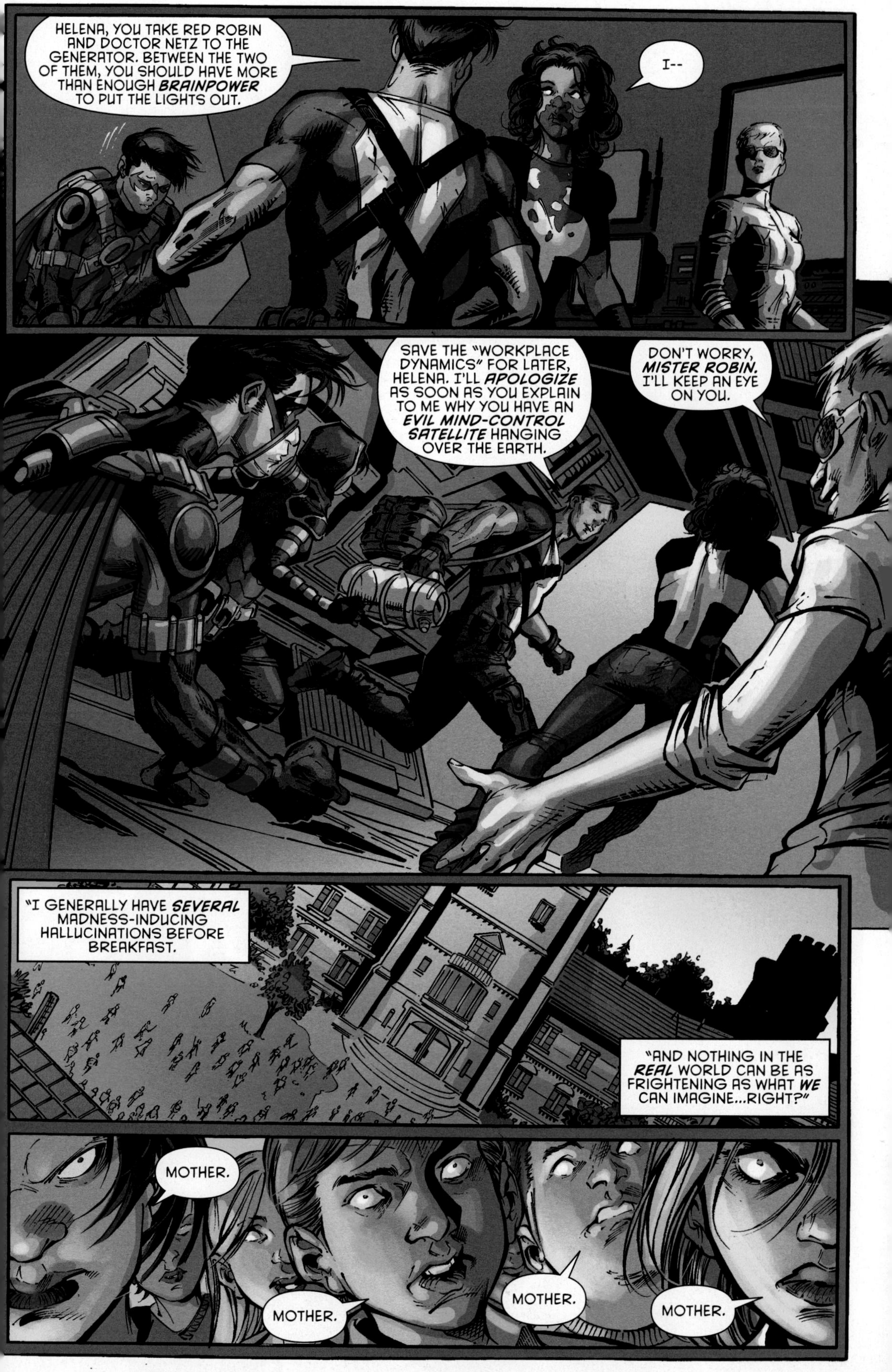
HELENA, YOU TAKE RED ROBIN AND DOCTOR NETZ TO THE GENERATOR. BETWEEN THE TWO OF THEM, YOU SHOULD HAVE MORE THAN ENOUGH BRAINPOWER TO PUT THE LIGHTS OUT.
I--
SAVE THE "WORKPLACE DYNAMICS" FOR LATER, HELENA. I'LL APOLOGIZE AS SOON AS YOU EXPLAIN TO ME WHY YOU HAVE AN EVIL MIND-CONTROL SATELLITE HANGING OVER THE EARTH.
DON'T WORRY, MISTER ROBIN. I'LL KEEP AN EYE ON YOU.
"I GENERALLY HAVE SEVERAL MADNESS-INDUCING HALLUCINATIONS BEFORE BREAKFAST.
"AND NOTHING IN THE REAL WORLD CAN BE AS FRIGHTENING AS WHAT WE CAN IMAGINE...RIGHT?"
MOTHER.
MOTHER.
MOTHER.
MOTHER.

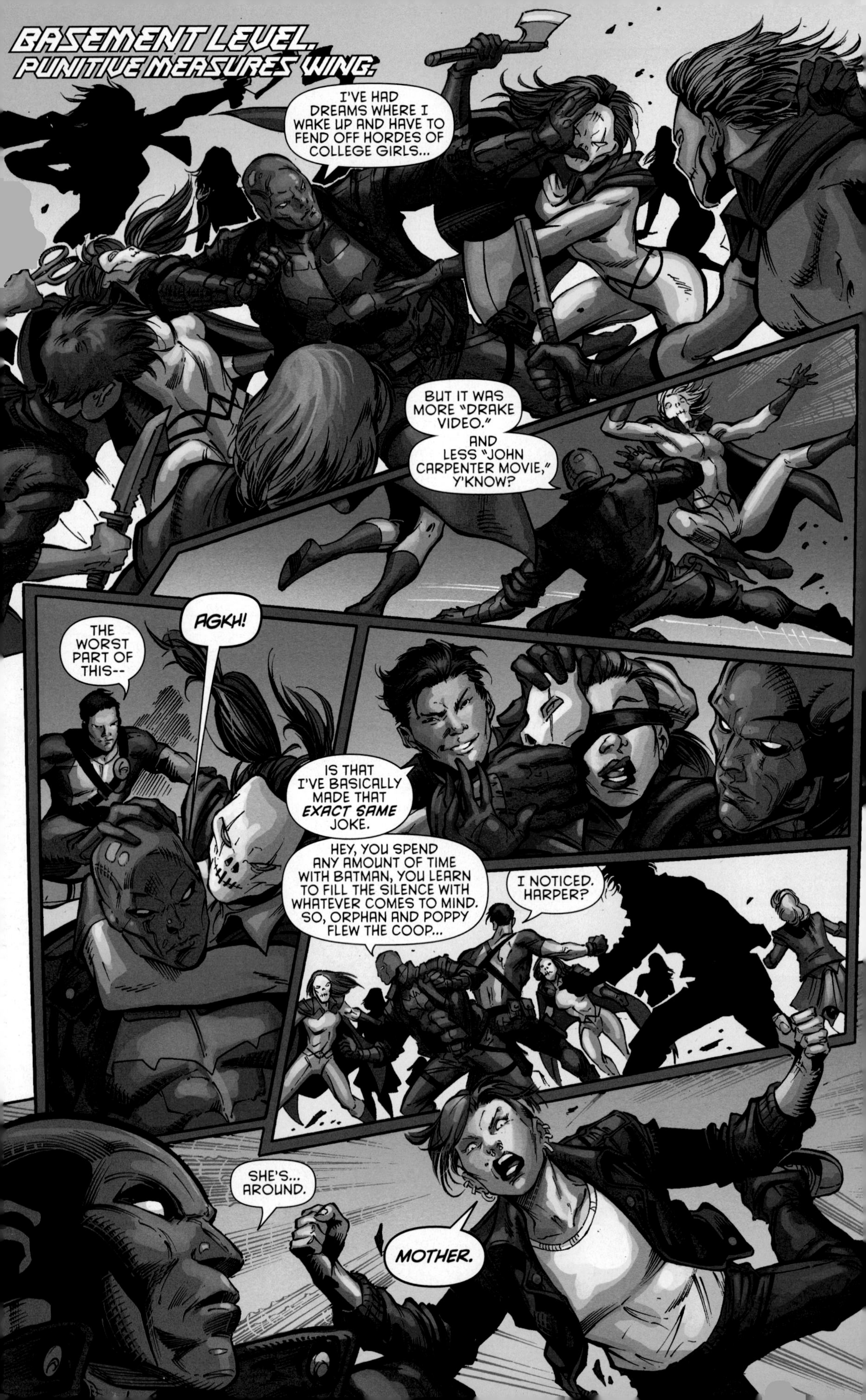
BASEMENT LEVEL. PUNITIVE MEASURES WING.
I'VE HAD DREAMS WHERE I WAKE UP AND HAVE TO FEND OFF HORDES OF COLLEGE GIRLS...
BUT IT WAS MORE "DRAKE VIDEO."
AND LESS "JOHN CARPENTER MOVIE," Y'KNOW?
THE WORST PART OF THIS--
AGKH!
IS THAT I'VE BASICALLY MADE THAT EXACT SAME JOKE.
HEY, YOU SPEND ANY AMOUNT OF TIME WITH BATMAN, YOU LEARN TO FILL THE SILENCE WITH WHATEVER COMES TO MIND. SO, ORPHAN AND POPPY FLEW THE COOP...
I NOTICED. HARPER?
SHE'S... AROUND.
MOTHER.

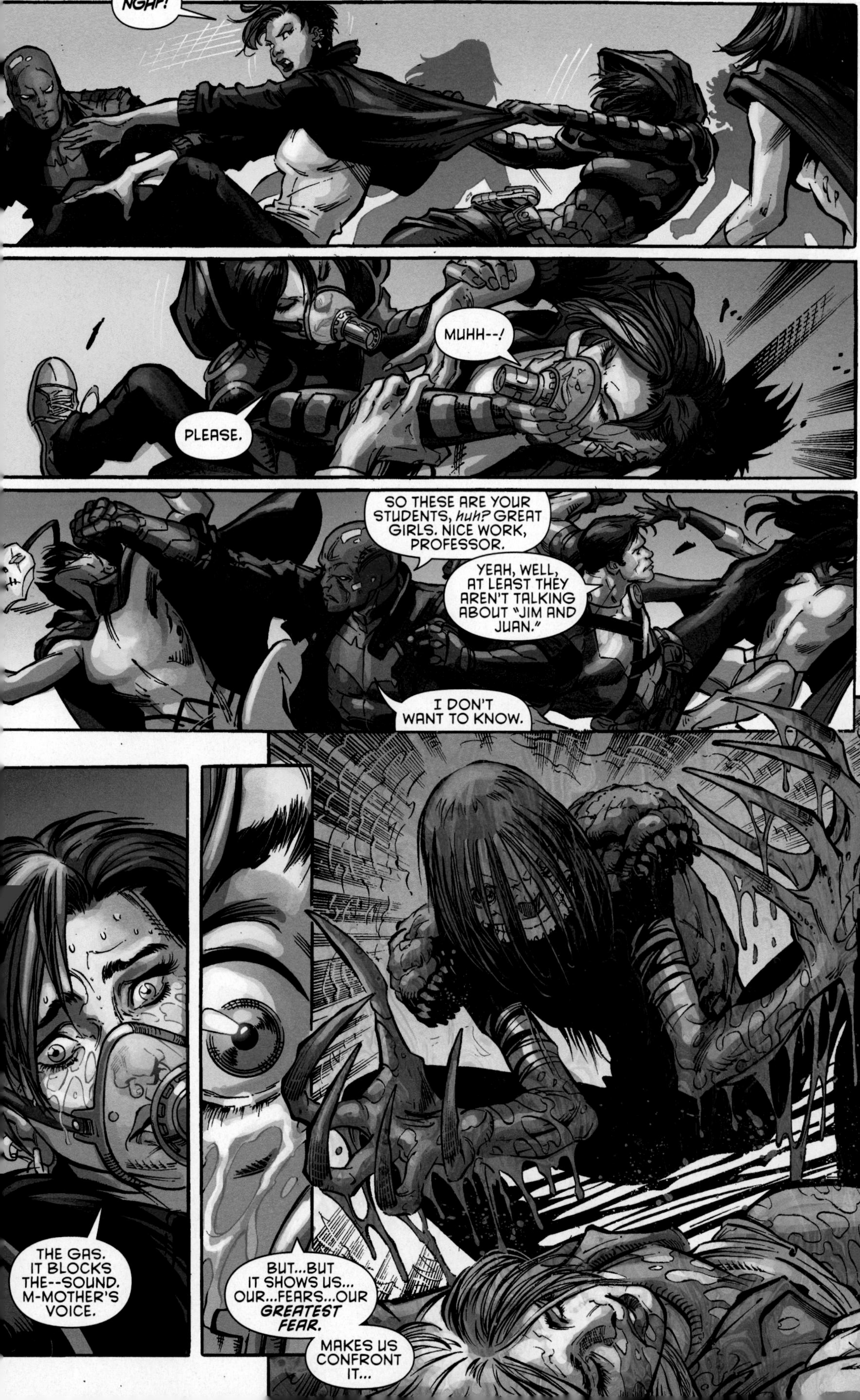
NGHF!
MUHH--!
PLEASE.
SO THESE ARE YOUR STUDENTS, huh? GREAT GIRLS. NICE WORK, PROFESSOR.
YEAH, WELL, AT LEAST THEY AREN'T TALKING ABOUT "JIM AND JUAN."
I DON'T WANT TO KNOW.
THE GAS. IT BLOCKS THE--SOUND. M-MOTHER'S VOICE.
BUT...BUT IT SHOWS US... OUR...FEARS...OUR GREATEST FEAR.
MAKES US CONFRONT IT...

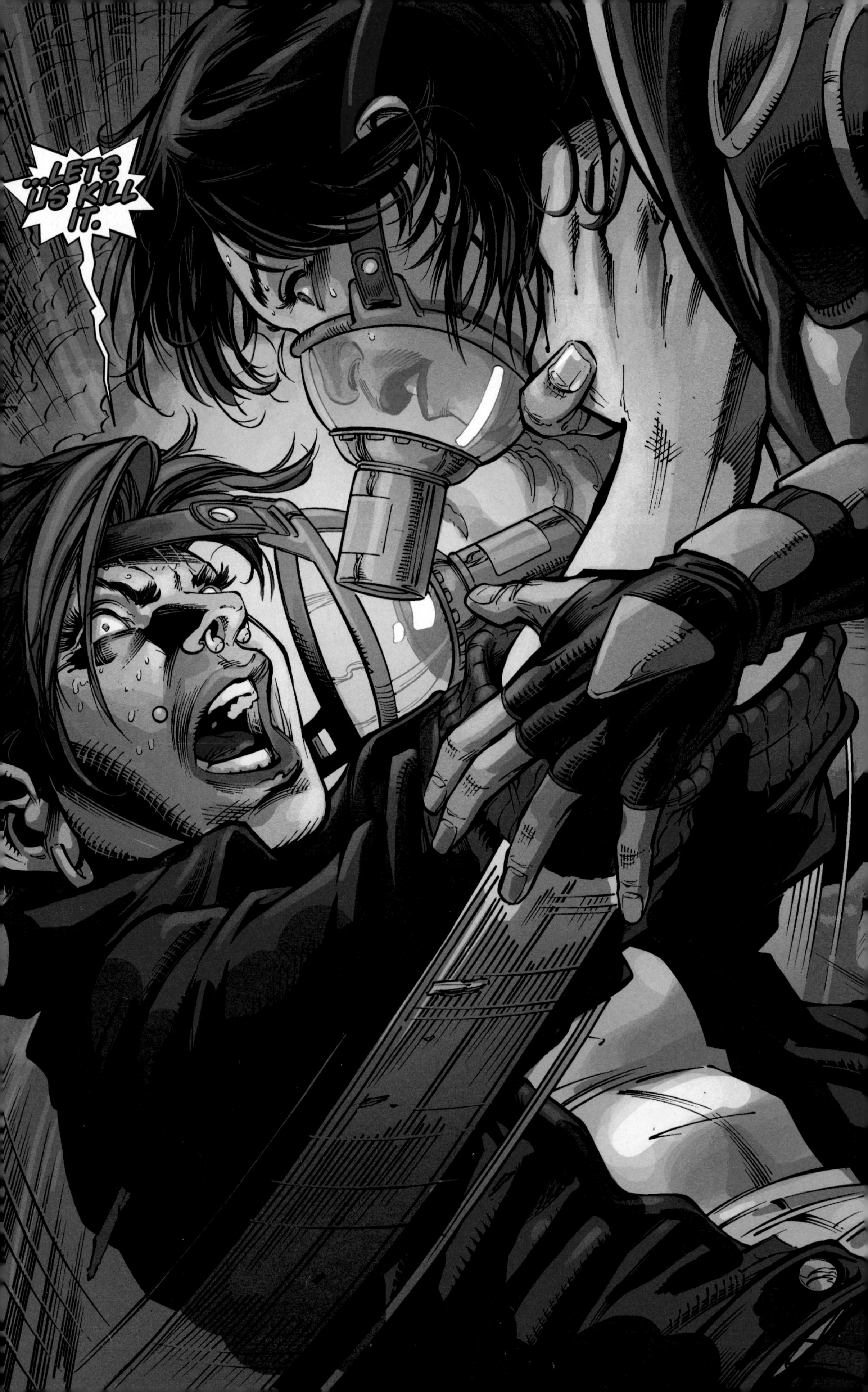
...LETS US KILL IT.

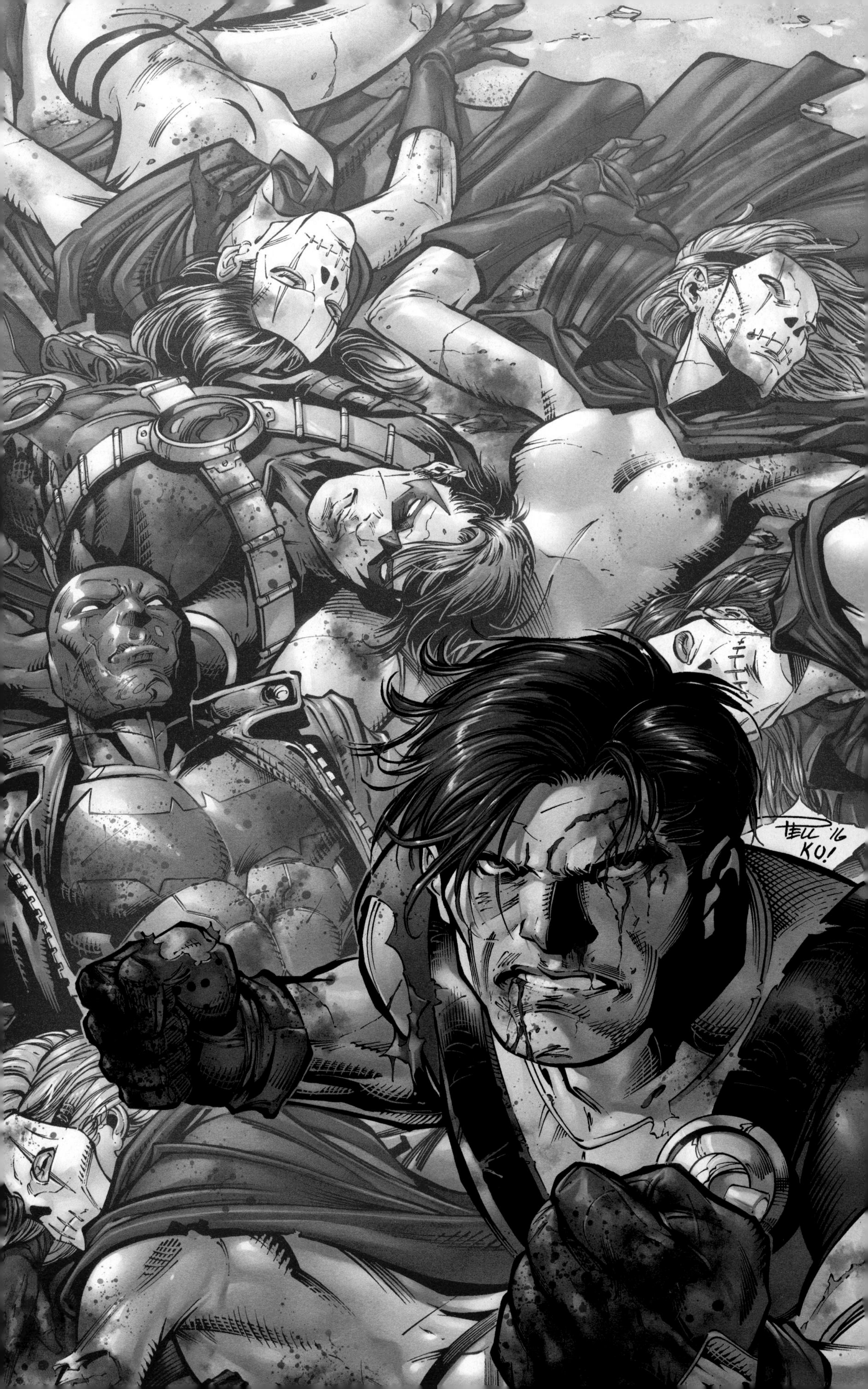

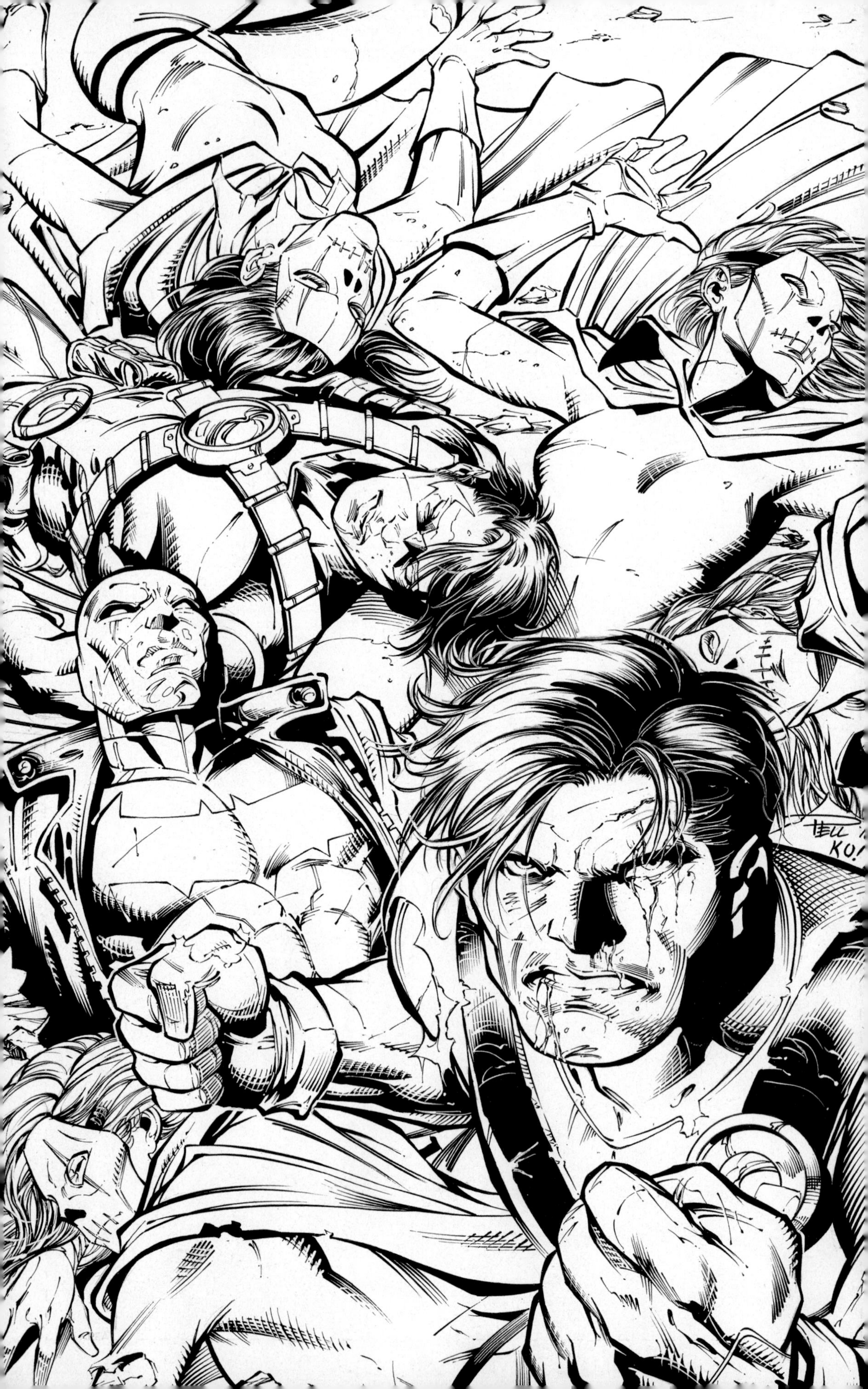

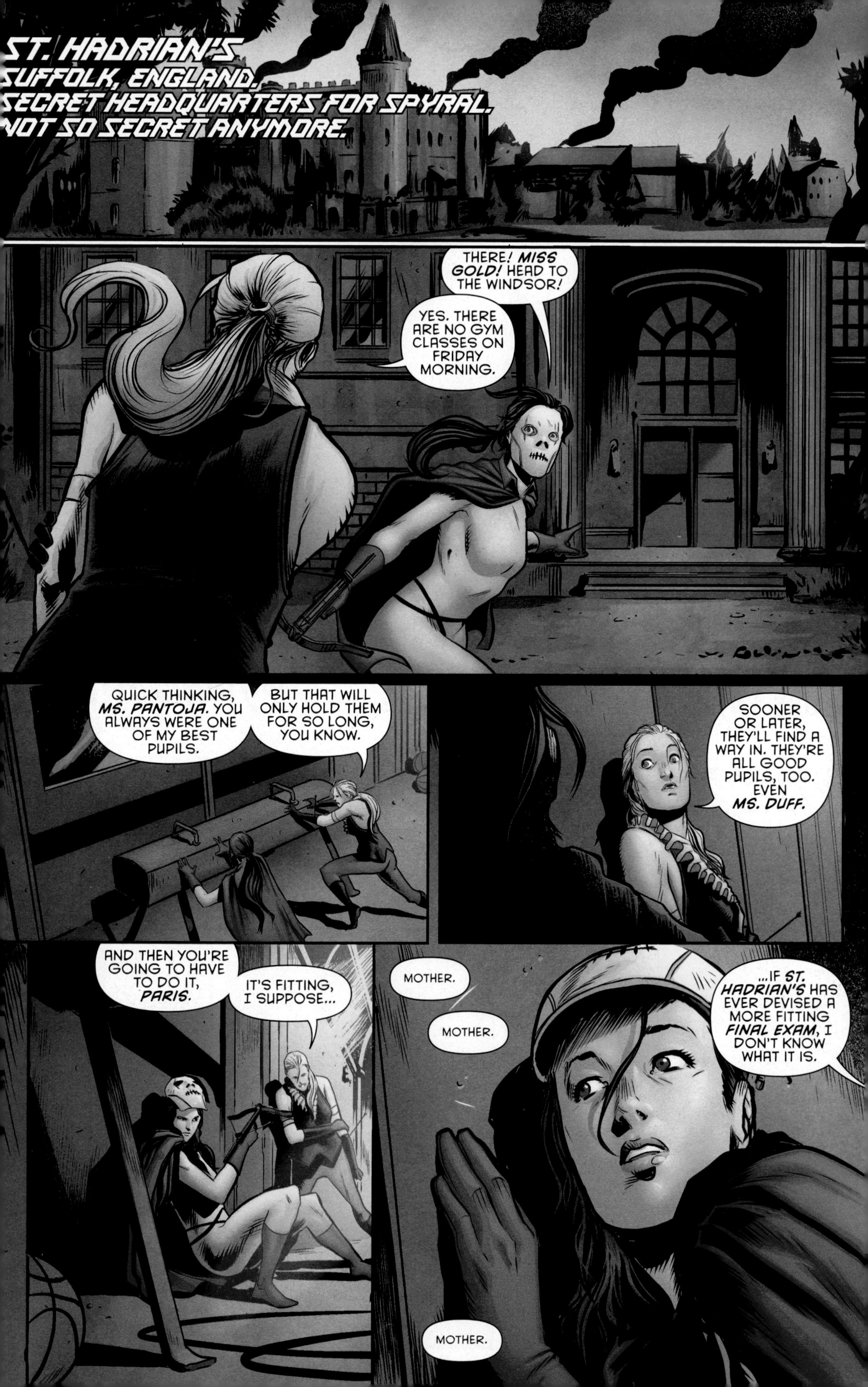
ST. HADRIAN'S
SUFFOLK, ENGLAND.
SECRET HEADQUARTERS FOR SPYRAL.
NOT SO SECRET ANYMORE.
THERE! MISS GOLD! HEAD TO THE WINDSOR!
YES. THERE ARE NO GYM CLASSES ON FRIDAY MORNING.
QUICK THINKING, MS. PANTOJA. YOU ALWAYS WERE ONE OF MY BEST PUPILS.
BUT THAT WILL ONLY HOLD THEM FOR SO LONG, YOU KNOW.
SOONER OR LATER, THEY'LL FIND A WAY IN. THEY'RE ALL GOOD PUPILS, TOO. EVEN MS. DUFF.
AND THEN YOU'RE GOING TO HAVE TO DO IT, PARIS.
IT'S FITTING, I SUPPOSE...
MOTHER.
MOTHER.
...IF ST. HADRIAN'S HAS EVER DEVISED A MORE FITTING FINAL EXAM, I DON'T KNOW WHAT IT IS.
MOTHER.

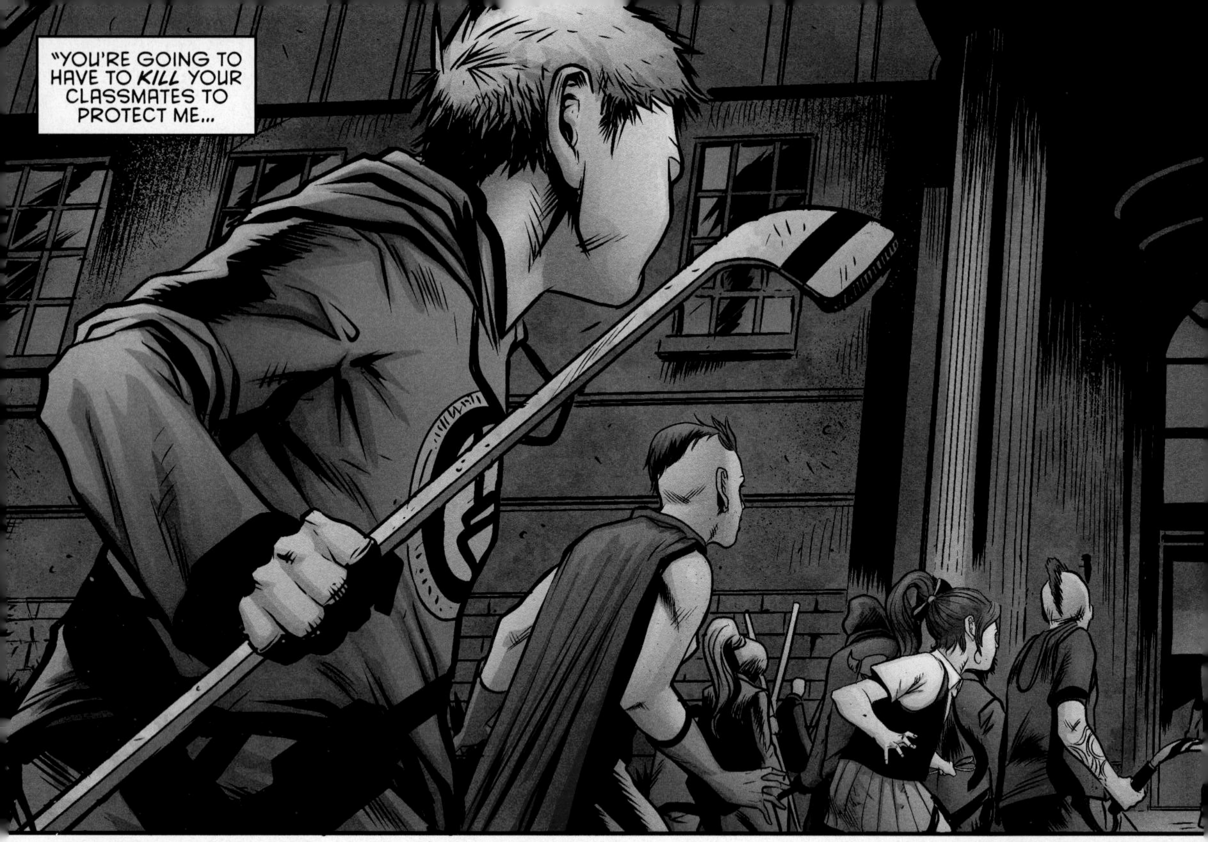
"YOU'RE GOING TO HAVE TO *KILL* YOUR CLASSMATES TO PROTECT ME...

JAMES TYNION IV & SCOTT SNYDER Story
TIM SEELEY Script
ROGE ANTONIO & GERALDO BORGES Artists

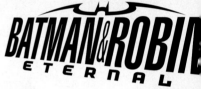

BATMAN & ROBIN ETERNAL

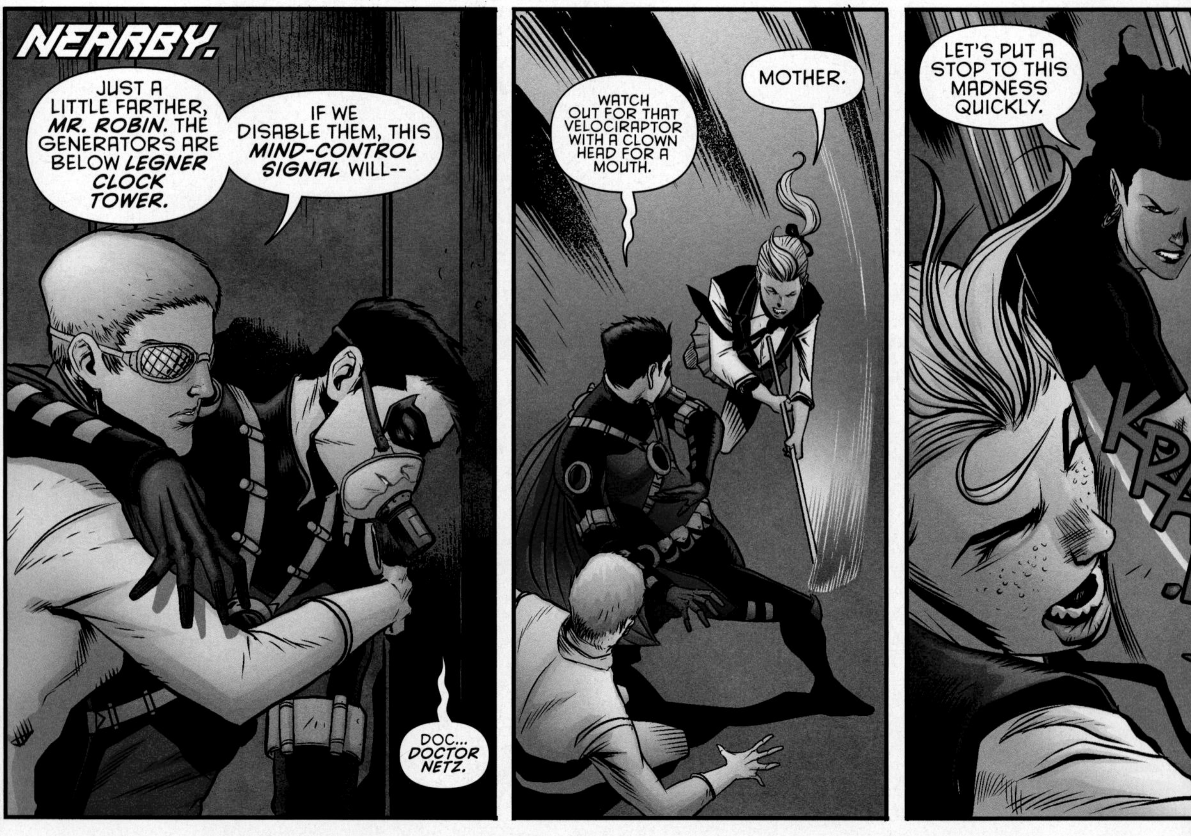
NEARBY.
JUST A LITTLE FARTHER, *MR. ROBIN.* THE GENERATORS ARE BELOW *LEGNER CLOCK TOWER.*
IF WE DISABLE THEM, THIS *MIND-CONTROL SIGNAL* WILL--
DOC... *DOCTOR NETZ.*
WATCH OUT FOR THAT VELOCIRAPTOR WITH A CLOWN HEAD FOR A MOUTH.
MOTHER.
LET'S PUT A STOP TO THIS MADNESS QUICKLY.

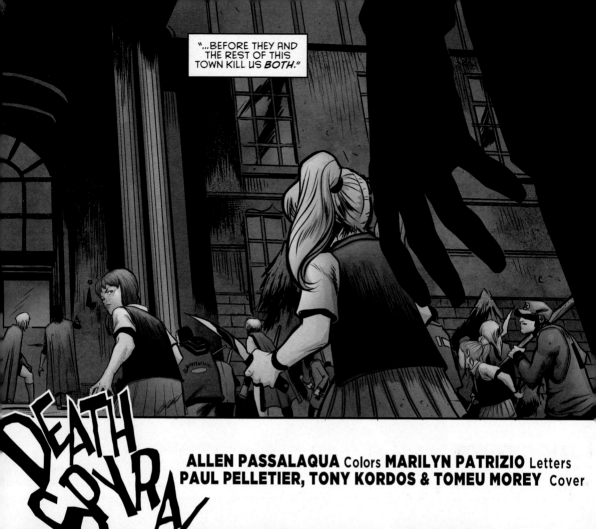

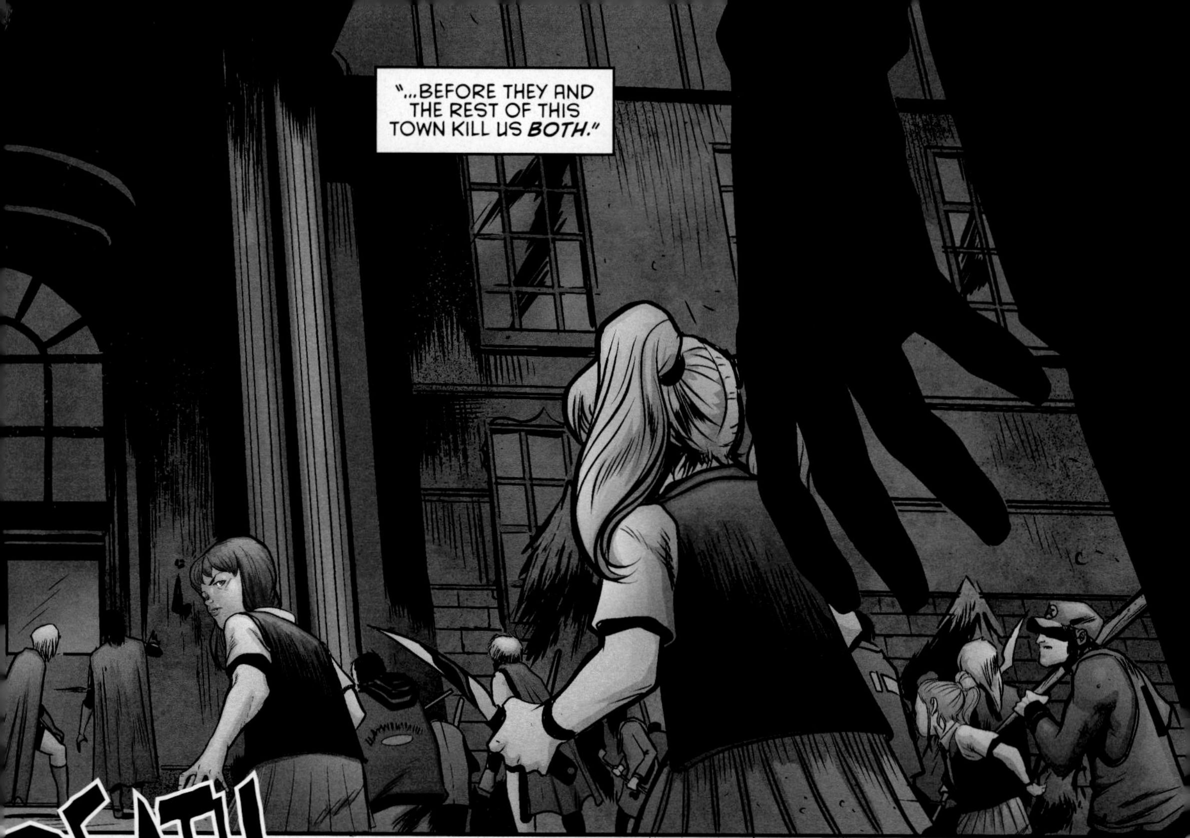
"...BEFORE THEY AND THE REST OF THIS TOWN KILL US *BOTH*."

DEATH SPYRAL

ALLEN PASSALAQUA Colors **MARILYN PATRIZIO** Letters
PAUL PELLETIER, TONY KORDOS & TOMEU MOREY Cover

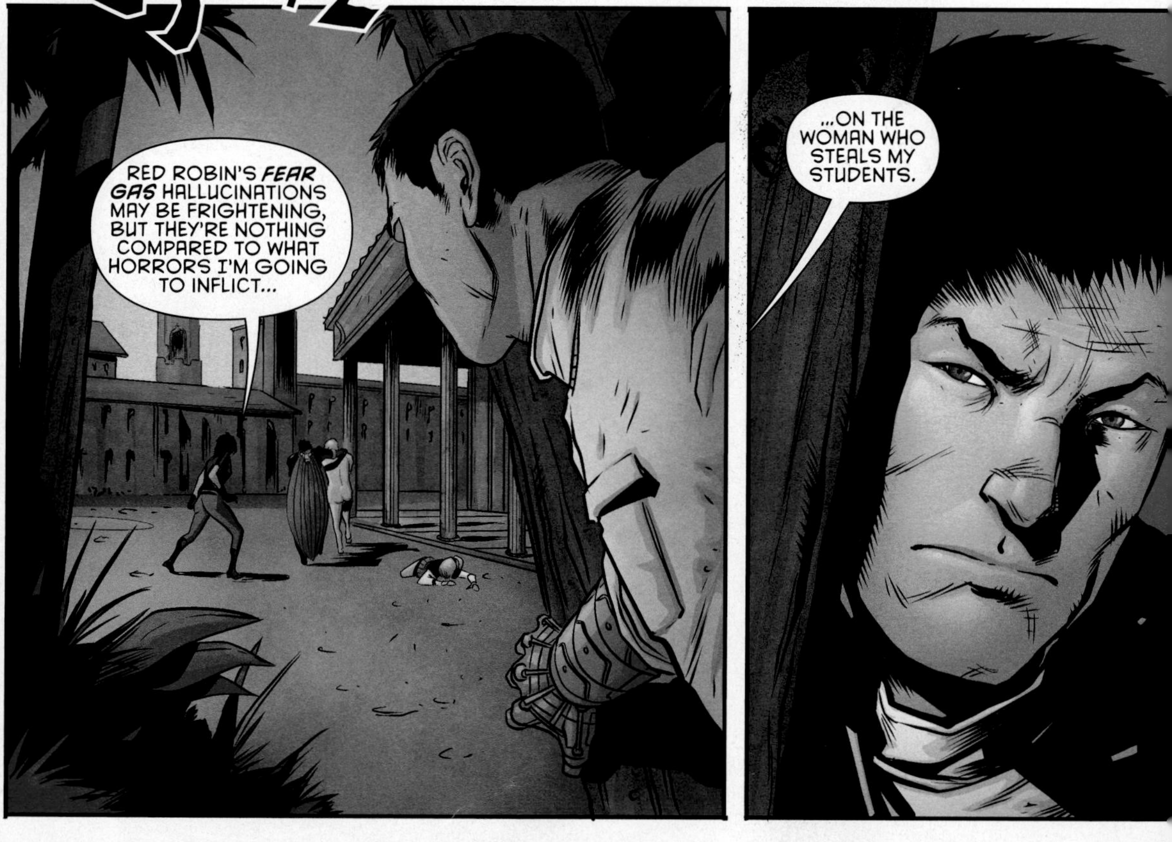
RED ROBIN'S *FEAR GAS* HALLUCINATIONS MAY BE FRIGHTENING, BUT THEY'RE NOTHING COMPARED TO WHAT HORRORS I'M GOING TO INFLICT...
...ON THE WOMAN WHO STEALS MY STUDENTS.

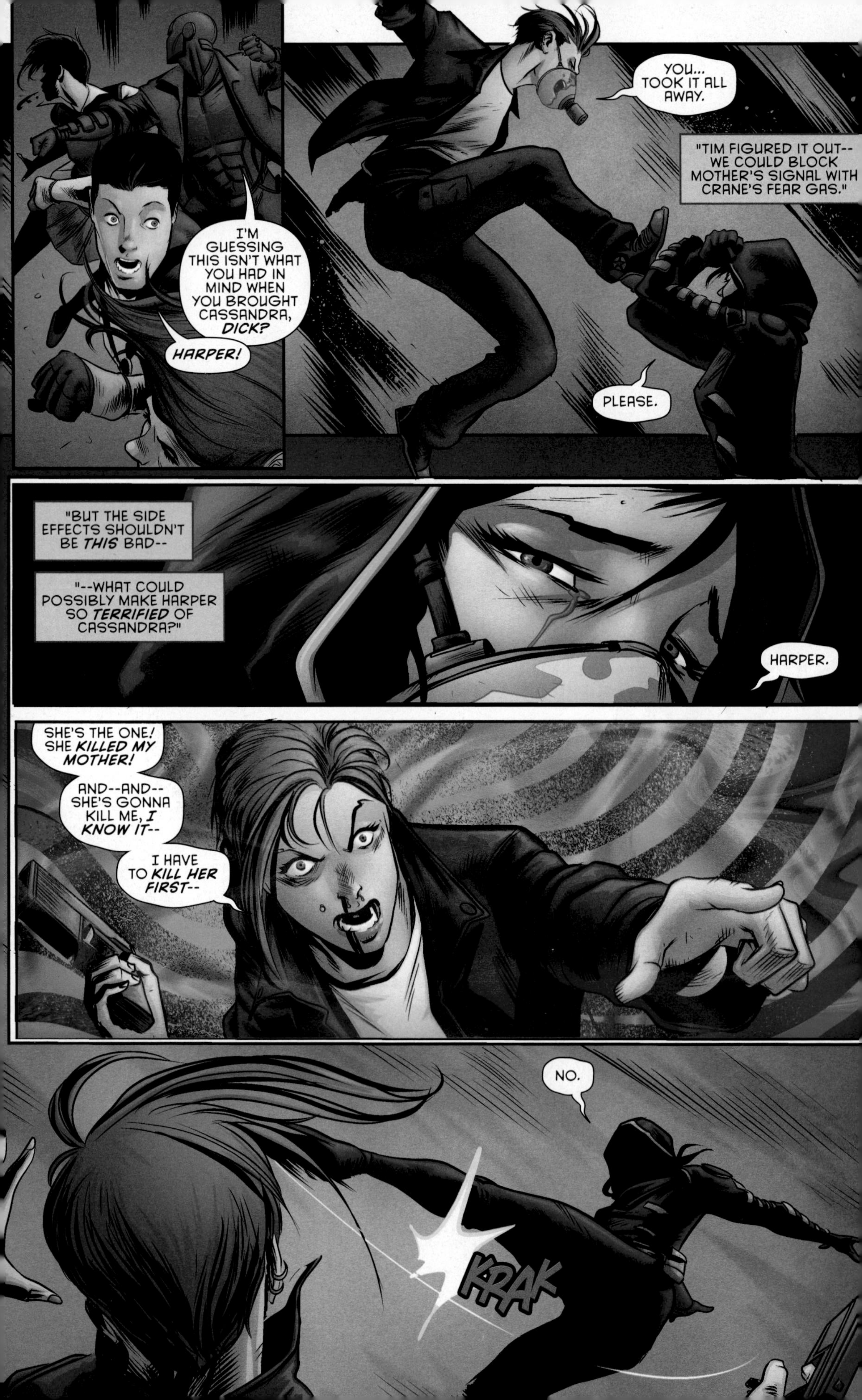

YOU... TOOK IT ALL AWAY.
"TIM FIGURED IT OUT-- WE COULD BLOCK MOTHER'S SIGNAL WITH CRANE'S FEAR GAS."
I'M GUESSING THIS ISN'T WHAT YOU HAD IN MIND WHEN YOU BROUGHT CASSANDRA, DICK?
HARPER!
PLEASE.
"BUT THE SIDE EFFECTS SHOULDN'T BE THIS BAD--
"--WHAT COULD POSSIBLY MAKE HARPER SO TERRIFIED OF CASSANDRA?"
HARPER.
SHE'S THE ONE! SHE KILLED MY MOTHER!
AND--AND-- SHE'S GONNA KILL ME, I KNOW IT--
I HAVE TO KILL HER FIRST--
NO.
KRAK

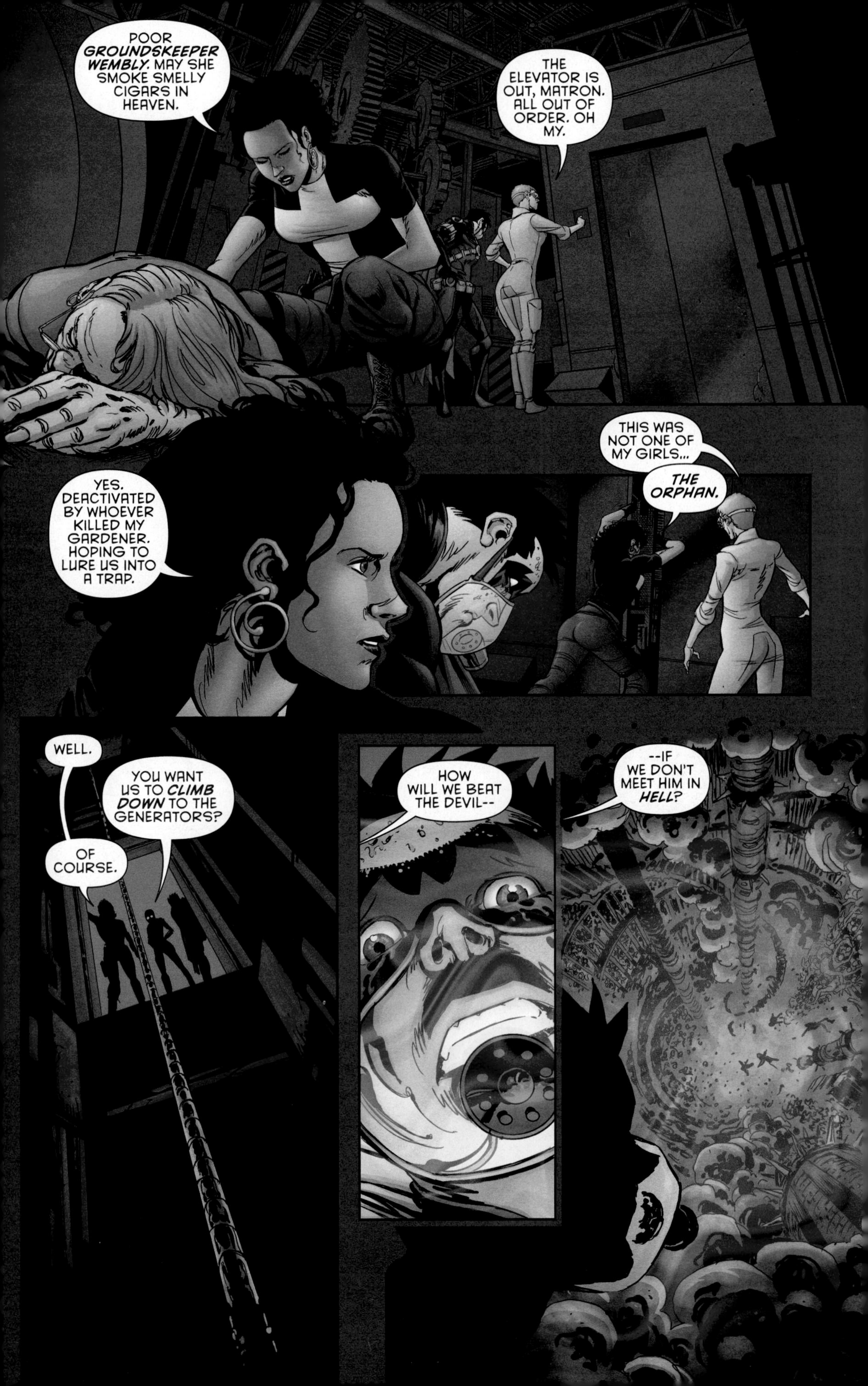

POOR **GROUNDSKEEPER WEMBLY.** MAY SHE SMOKE SMELLY CIGARS IN HEAVEN.
THE ELEVATOR IS OUT, MATRON. ALL OUT OF ORDER. OH MY.
YES. DEACTIVATED BY WHOEVER KILLED MY GARDENER. HOPING TO LURE US INTO A TRAP.
THIS WAS NOT ONE OF MY GIRLS...
THE ORPHAN.
WELL.
YOU WANT US TO ***CLIMB DOWN*** TO THE GENERATORS?
OF COURSE.
HOW WILL WE BEAT THE DEVIL--
--IF WE DON'T MEET HIM IN ***HELL?***

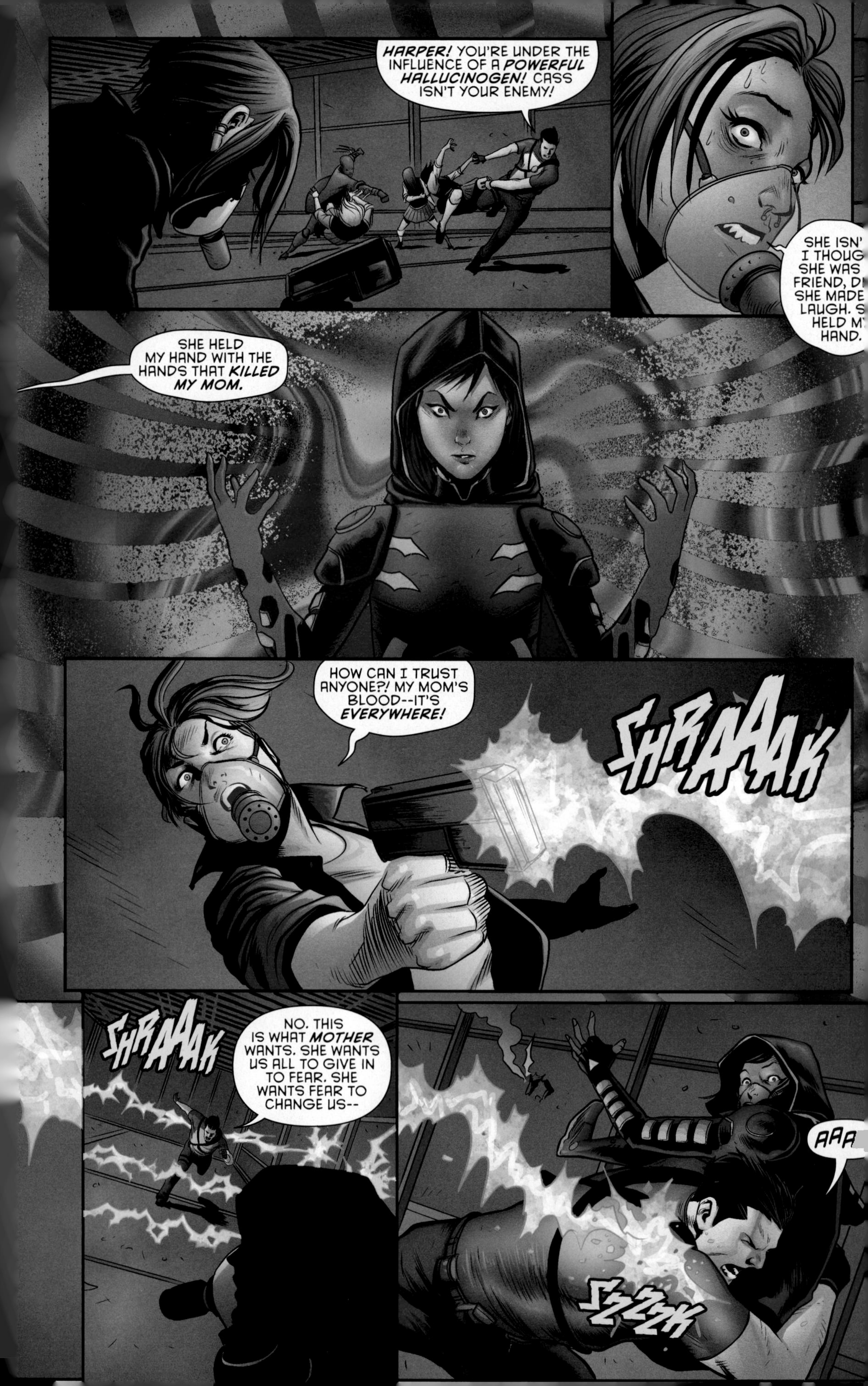

HARPER! YOU'RE UNDER THE INFLUENCE OF A POWERFUL HALLUCINOGEN! CASS ISN'T YOUR ENEMY!
SHE ISN' I THOUG SHE WAS FRIEND, D SHE MADE LAUGH. S HELD M HAND.
SHE HELD MY HAND WITH THE HANDS THAT KILLED MY MOM.
HOW CAN I TRUST ANYONE?! MY MOM'S BLOOD--IT'S EVERYWHERE!
SHRAAAK
SHRAAAK
NO. THIS IS WHAT MOTHER WANTS. SHE WANTS US ALL TO GIVE IN TO FEAR. SHE WANTS FEAR TO CHANGE US--
AAA
SZZZK

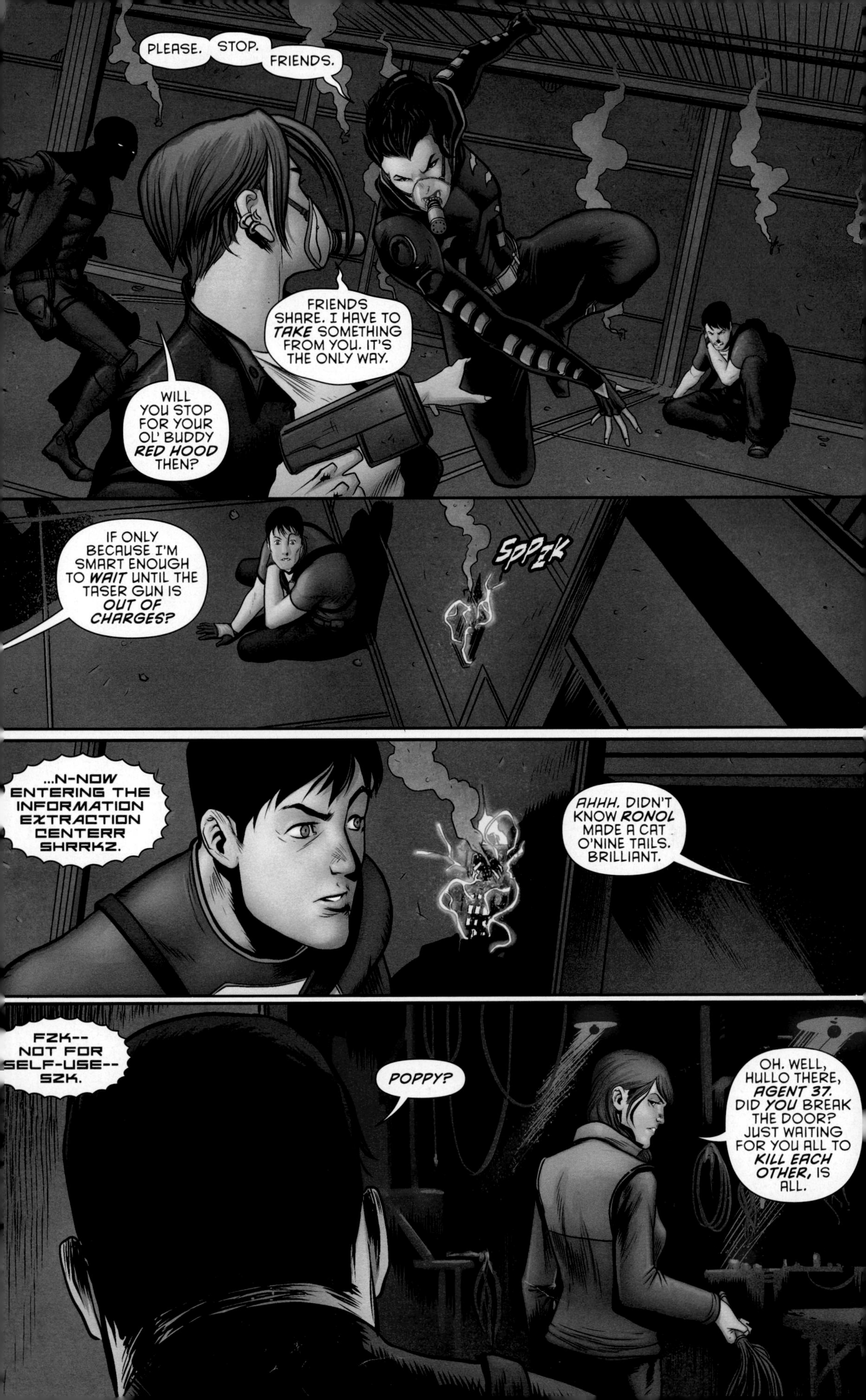
PLEASE.
STOP.
FRIENDS.
FRIENDS SHARE. I HAVE TO *TAKE* SOMETHING FROM YOU. IT'S THE ONLY WAY.
WILL YOU STOP FOR YOUR OL' BUDDY *RED HOOD* THEN?
IF ONLY BECAUSE I'M SMART ENOUGH TO *WAIT* UNTIL THE TASER GUN IS *OUT OF CHARGES?*
SPPIK
...N-NOW ENTERING THE INFORMATION EXTRACTION CENTERR SHRRKZ.
AHHH. DIDN'T KNOW *RONOL* MADE A CAT O'NINE TAILS. BRILLIANT.
FZK-- NOT FOR SELF-USE-- SZK.
POPPY?
OH. WELL, HULLO THERE, *AGENT 37.* DID *YOU* BREAK THE DOOR? JUST WAITING FOR YOU ALL TO *KILL EACH OTHER,* IS ALL.

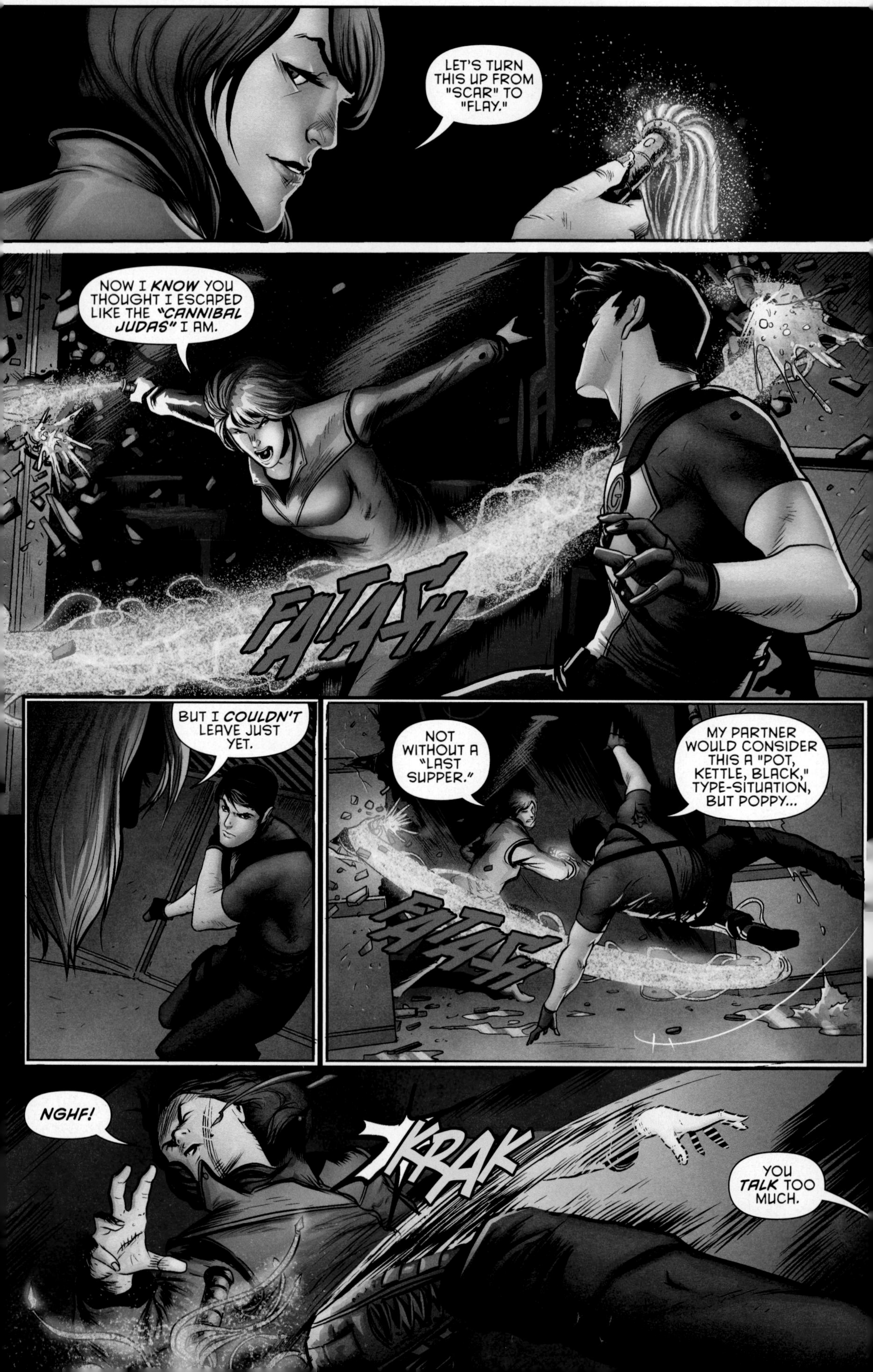
LET'S TURN THIS UP FROM "SCAR" TO "FLAY."
NOW I KNOW YOU THOUGHT I ESCAPED LIKE THE "CANNIBAL JUDAS" I AM.
FA-TA-SH
BUT I COULDN'T LEAVE JUST YET.
NOT WITHOUT A "LAST SUPPER."
MY PARTNER WOULD CONSIDER THIS A "POT, KETTLE, BLACK," TYPE-SITUATION, BUT POPPY...
FA-TA-SH
NGHF!
TKRAK
YOU TALK TOO MUCH.

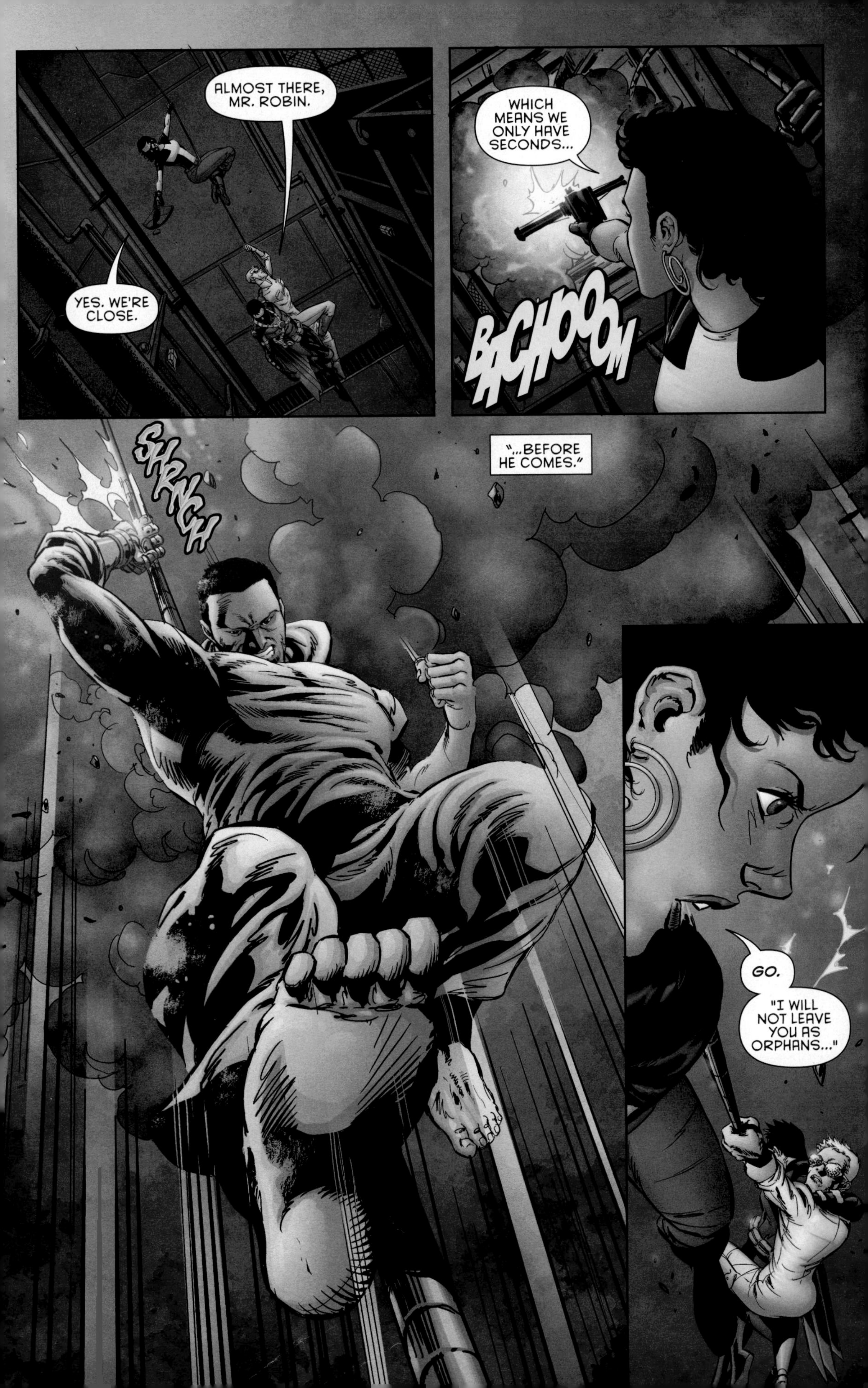
ALMOST THERE, MR. ROBIN.
YES. WE'RE CLOSE.
WHICH MEANS WE ONLY HAVE SECONDS...
BACHOOOOM
SHRNCH
"...BEFORE HE COMES."
GO.
"I WILL NOT LEAVE YOU AS ORPHANS..."

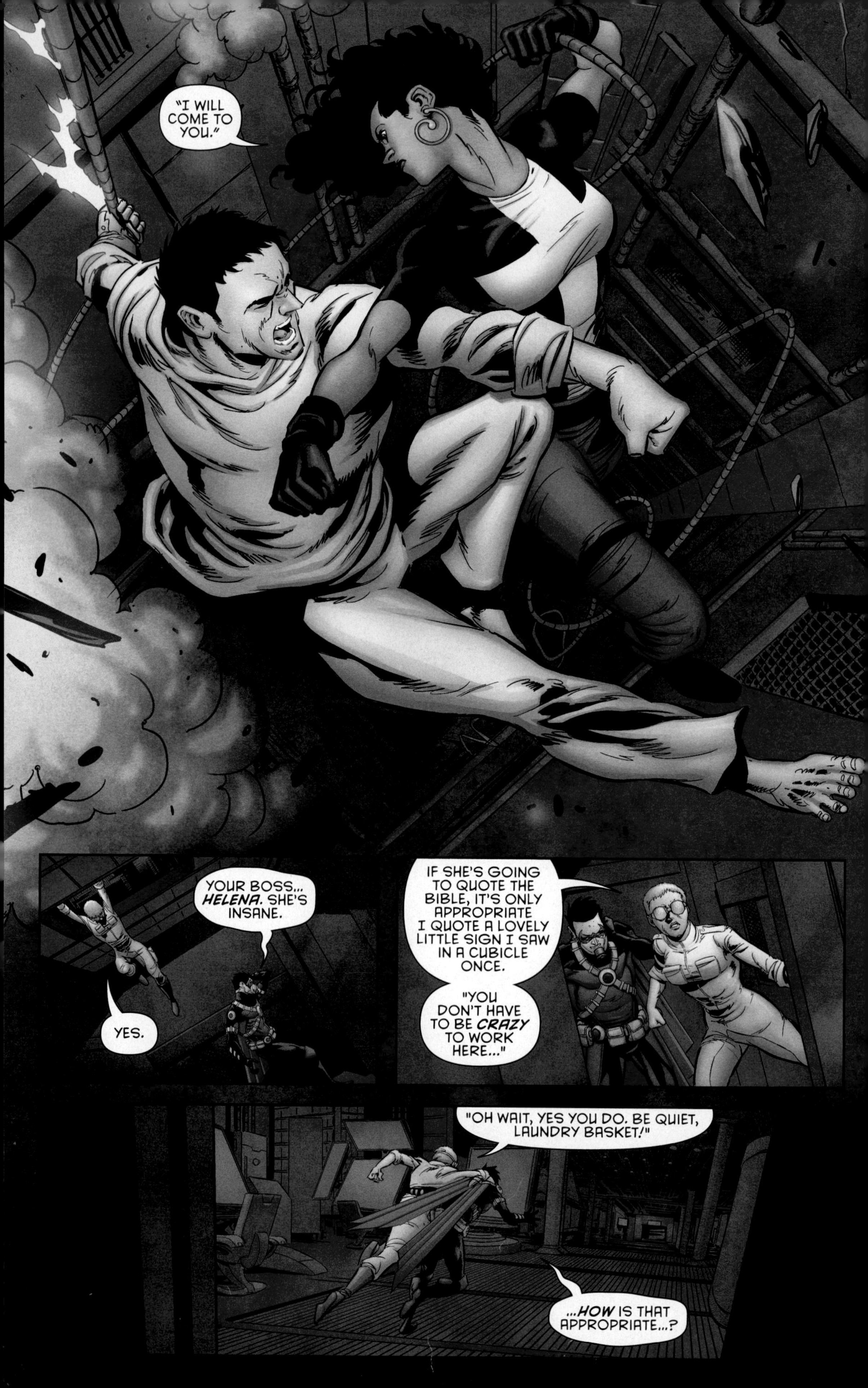
"I WILL COME TO YOU."
YOUR BOSS... HELENA. SHE'S INSANE.
YES.
IF SHE'S GOING TO QUOTE THE BIBLE, IT'S ONLY APPROPRIATE I QUOTE A LOVELY LITTLE SIGN I SAW IN A CUBICLE ONCE.
"YOU DON'T HAVE TO BE CRAZY TO WORK HERE..."
"OH WAIT, YES YOU DO. BE QUIET, LAUNDRY BASKET!"
...HOW IS THAT APPROPRIATE...?

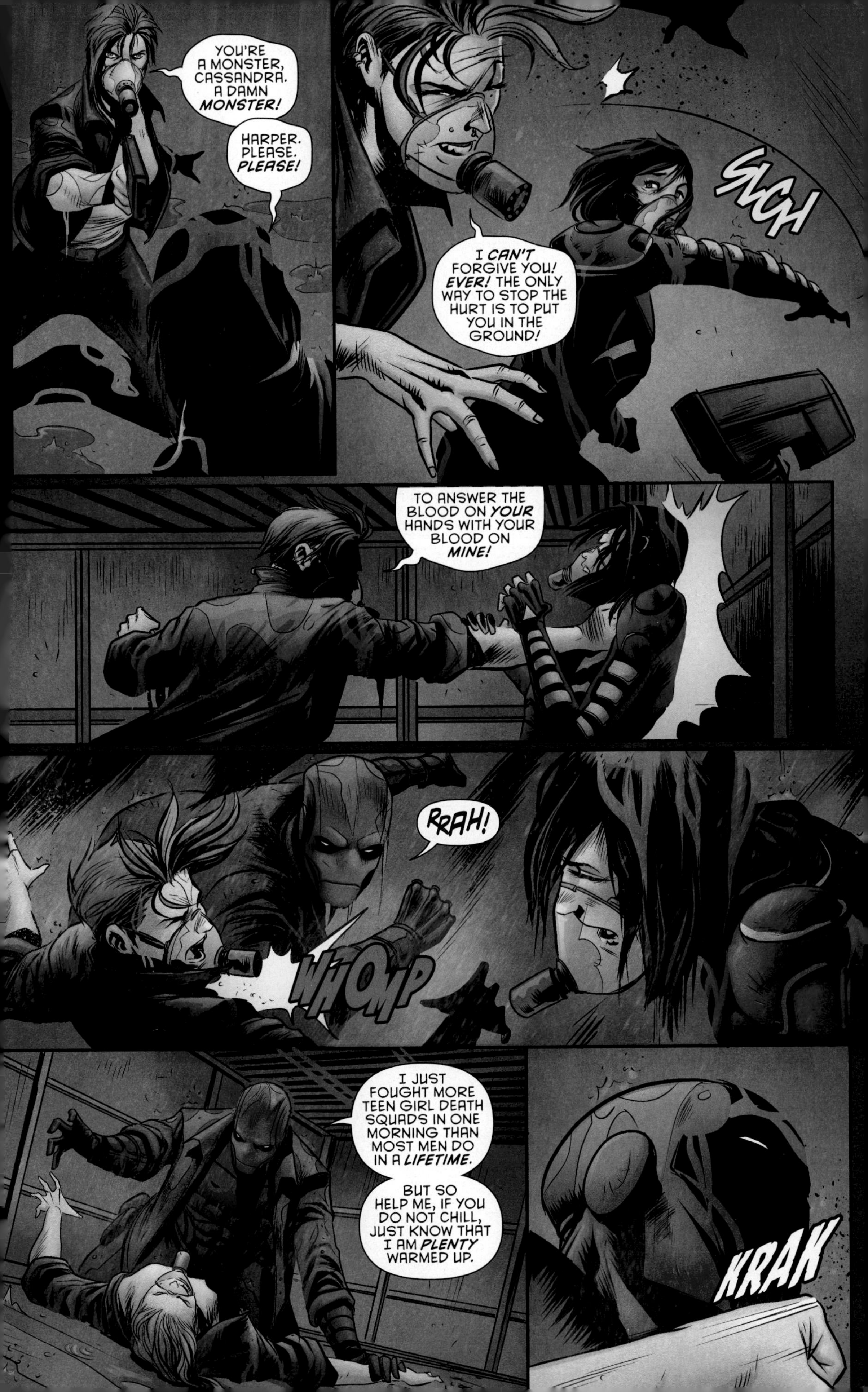
YOU'RE A MONSTER, CASSANDRA. A DAMN *MONSTER!*
HARPER. PLEASE. *PLEASE!*
SLCH
I *CAN'T* FORGIVE YOU! *EVER!* THE ONLY WAY TO STOP THE HURT IS TO PUT YOU IN THE GROUND!
TO ANSWER THE BLOOD ON *YOUR* HANDS WITH YOUR BLOOD ON *MINE!*
RRAH!
WHOMP
I JUST FOUGHT MORE TEEN GIRL DEATH SQUADS IN ONE MORNING THAN MOST MEN DO IN A *LIFETIME*.
BUT SO HELP ME, IF YOU DO NOT CHILL, JUST KNOW THAT I AM *PLENTY* WARMED UP.
KRAK

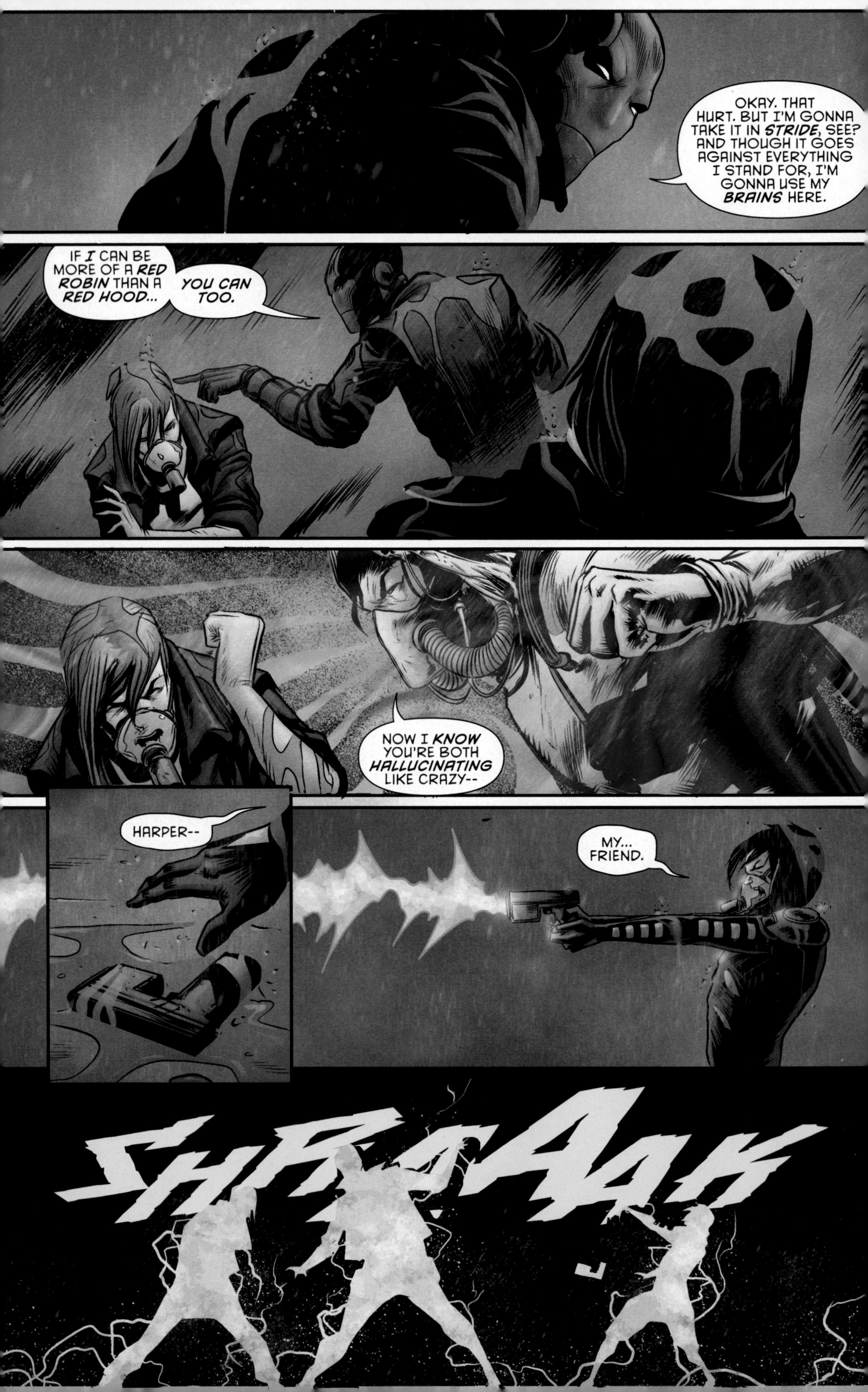

OKAY. THAT HURT. BUT I'M GONNA TAKE IT IN STRIDE, SEE? AND THOUGH IT GOES AGAINST EVERYTHING I STAND FOR, I'M GONNA USE MY BRAINS HERE.
IF I CAN BE MORE OF A RED ROBIN THAN A RED HOOD...
YOU CAN TOO.
NOW I KNOW YOU'RE BOTH HALLUCINATING LIKE CRAZY--
HARPER--
MY... FRIEND.
SHRAAAK

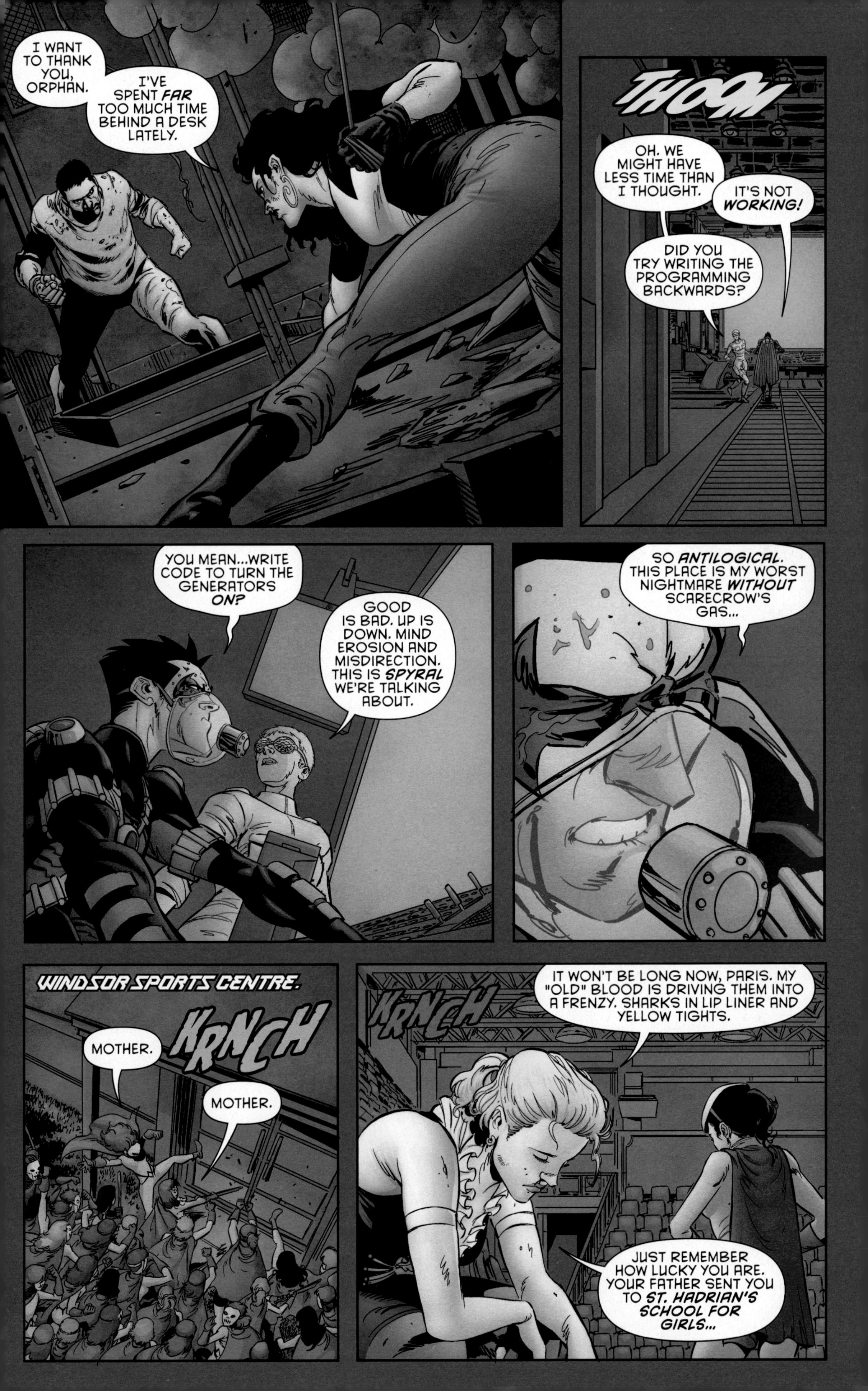
I WANT TO THANK YOU, ORPHAN.
I'VE SPENT FAR TOO MUCH TIME BEHIND A DESK LATELY.
THOOM
OH. WE MIGHT HAVE LESS TIME THAN I THOUGHT.
IT'S NOT WORKING!
DID YOU TRY WRITING THE PROGRAMMING BACKWARDS?
YOU MEAN...WRITE CODE TO TURN THE GENERATORS ON?
GOOD IS BAD. UP IS DOWN. MIND EROSION AND MISDIRECTION. THIS IS SPYRAL WE'RE TALKING ABOUT.
SO ANTILOGICAL. THIS PLACE IS MY WORST NIGHTMARE WITHOUT SCARECROW'S GAS...
WINDSOR SPORTS CENTRE.
KRNCH
MOTHER.
MOTHER.
KRNCH
IT WON'T BE LONG NOW, PARIS. MY "OLD" BLOOD IS DRIVING THEM INTO A FRENZY. SHARKS IN LIP LINER AND YELLOW TIGHTS.
JUST REMEMBER HOW LUCKY YOU ARE. YOUR FATHER SENT YOU TO ST. HADRIAN'S SCHOOL FOR GIRLS...

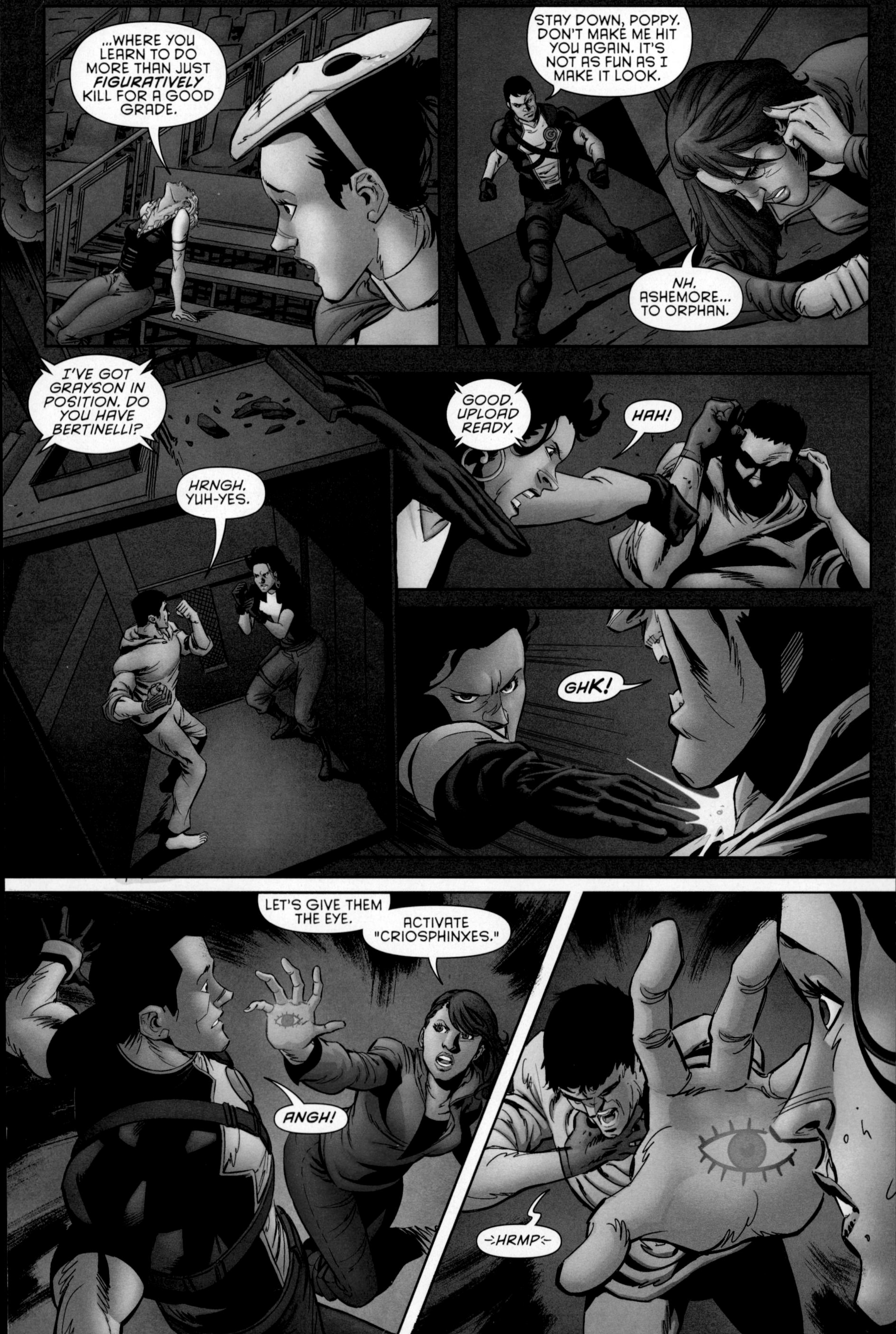
...WHERE YOU LEARN TO DO MORE THAN JUST FIGURATIVELY KILL FOR A GOOD GRADE.
STAY DOWN, POPPY. DON'T MAKE ME HIT YOU AGAIN. IT'S NOT AS FUN AS I MAKE IT LOOK.
NH. ASHEMORE... TO ORPHAN.
I'VE GOT GRAYSON IN POSITION. DO YOU HAVE BERTINELLI?
HRNGH. YUH-YES.
GOOD. UPLOAD READY.
HAH!
GHK!
LET'S GIVE THEM THE EYE.
ACTIVATE "CRIOSPHINXES."
ANGH!
HRMP
oh

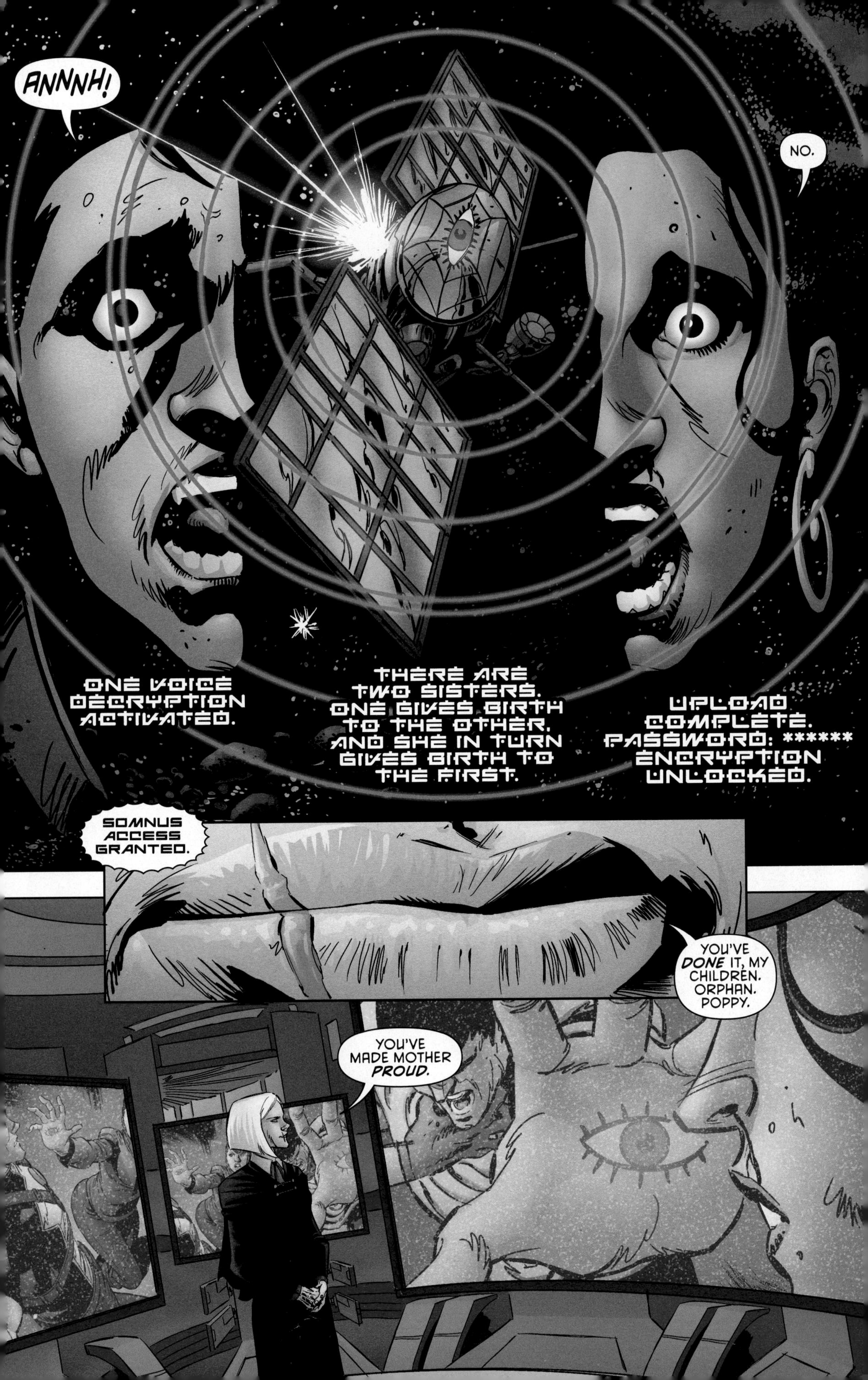
ANNNH!
NO.
ONE VOICE DECRYPTION ACTIVATED.
THERE ARE TWO SISTERS. ONE GIVES BIRTH TO THE OTHER. AND SHE IN TURN GIVES BIRTH TO THE FIRST.
UPLOAD COMPLETE. PASSWORD: ****** ENCRYPTION UNLOCKED.
SOMNUS ACCESS GRANTED.
YOU'VE DONE IT, MY CHILDREN. ORPHAN. POPPY.
YOU'VE MADE MOTHER PROUD.

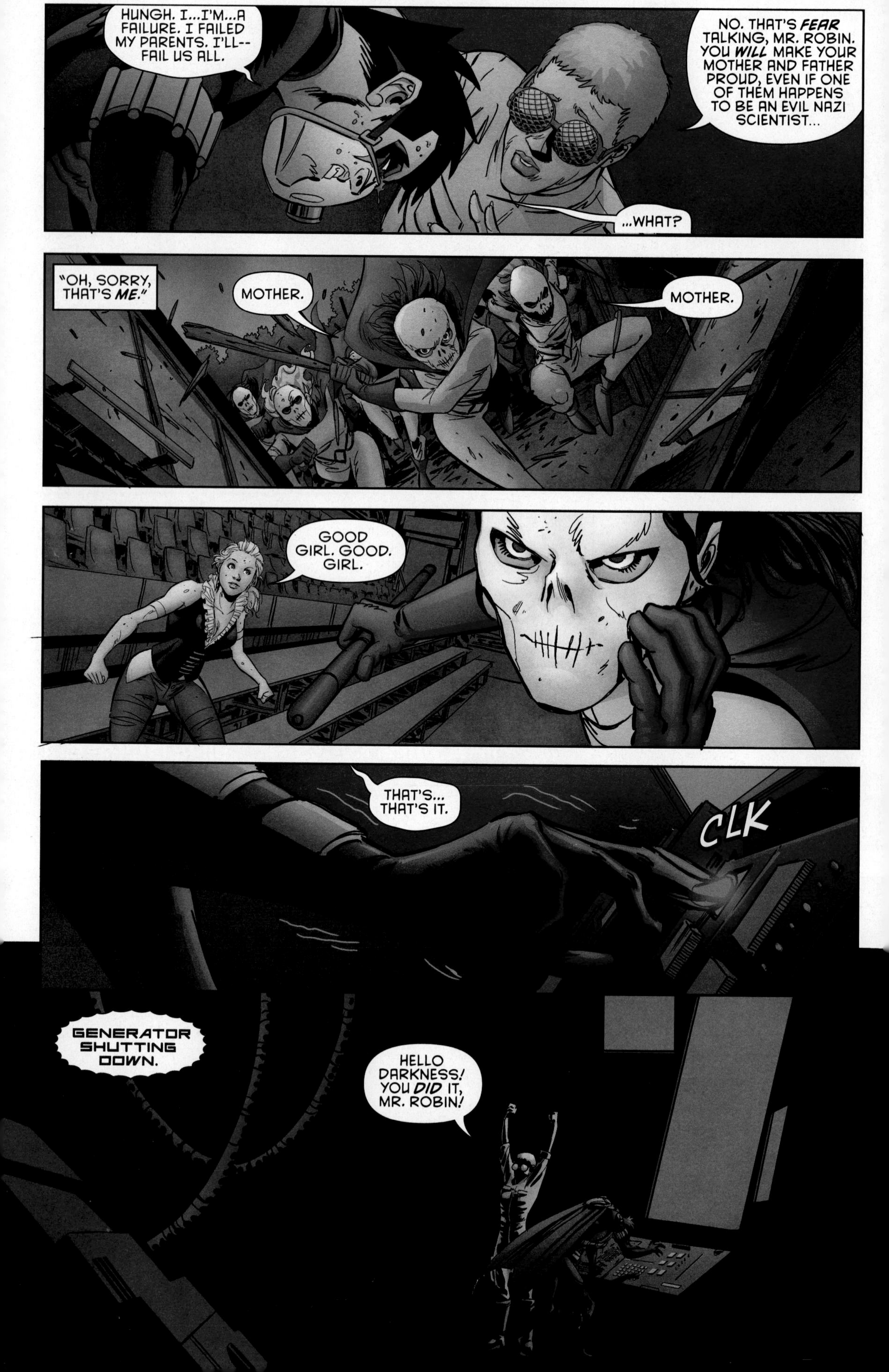
HUNGH. I...I'M...A FAILURE. I FAILED MY PARENTS. I'LL--FAIL US ALL.
NO. THAT'S FEAR TALKING, MR. ROBIN. YOU WILL MAKE YOUR MOTHER AND FATHER PROUD, EVEN IF ONE OF THEM HAPPENS TO BE AN EVIL NAZI SCIENTIST...
...WHAT?
"OH, SORRY, THAT'S ME."
MOTHER.
MOTHER.
GOOD GIRL. GOOD. GIRL.
THAT'S... THAT'S IT.
CLK
GENERATOR SHUTTING DOWN.
HELLO DARKNESS! YOU DID IT, MR. ROBIN!

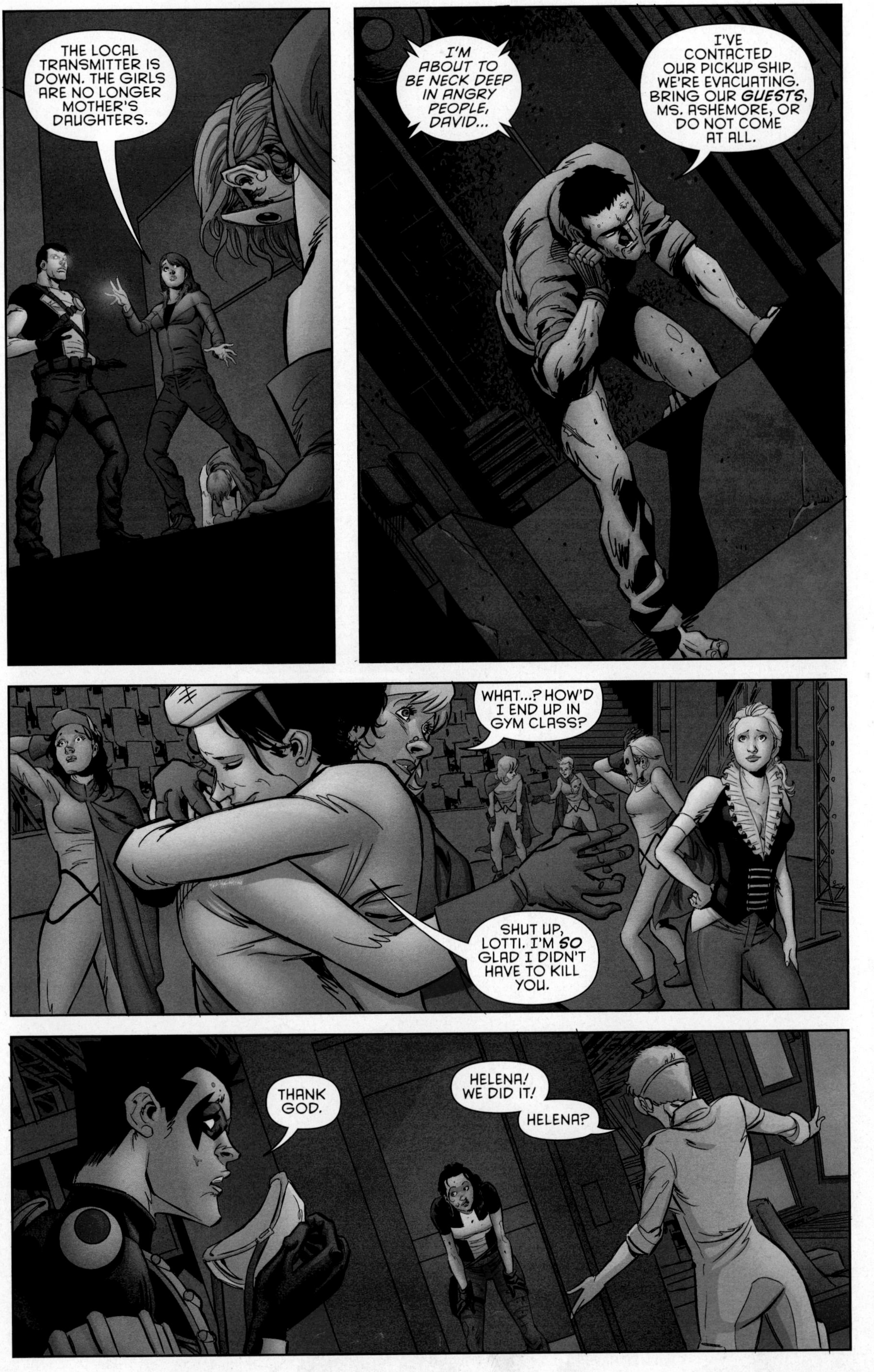
THE LOCAL TRANSMITTER IS DOWN. THE GIRLS ARE NO LONGER MOTHER'S DAUGHTERS.
I'M ABOUT TO BE NECK DEEP IN ANGRY PEOPLE, DAVID...
I'VE CONTACTED OUR PICKUP SHIP. WE'RE EVACUATING. BRING OUR GUESTS, MS. ASHEMORE, OR DO NOT COME AT ALL.
WHAT...? HOW'D I END UP IN GYM CLASS?
SHUT UP, LOTTI. I'M SO GLAD I DIDN'T HAVE TO KILL YOU.
THANK GOD.
HELENA! WE DID IT!
HELENA?

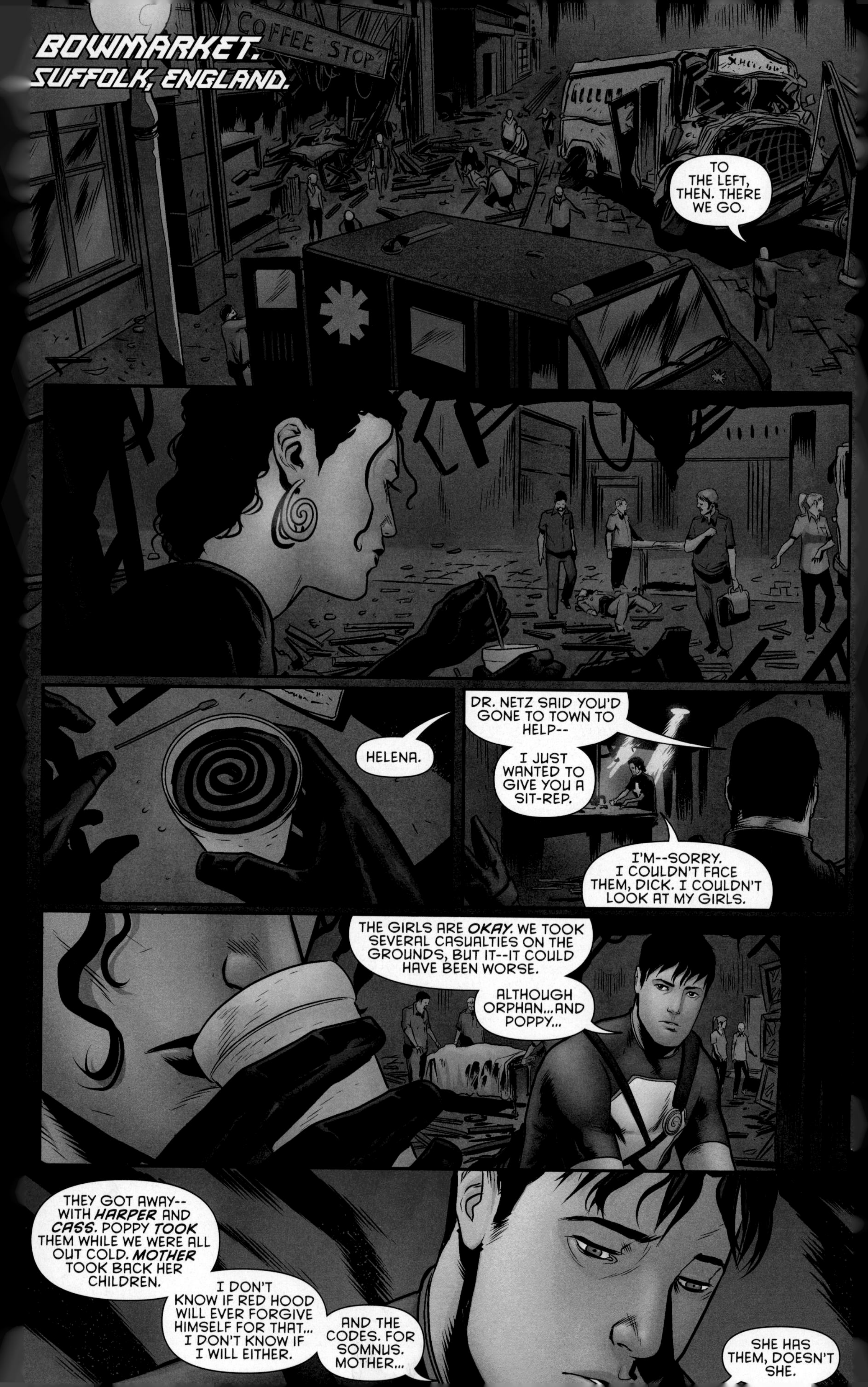

BOWMARKET.
SUFFOLK, ENGLAND.
COFFEE STOP
TO THE LEFT, THEN. THERE WE GO.
HELENA.
DR. NETZ SAID YOU'D GONE TO TOWN TO HELP--
I JUST WANTED TO GIVE YOU A SIT-REP.
I'M--SORRY. I COULDN'T FACE THEM, DICK. I COULDN'T LOOK AT MY GIRLS.
THE GIRLS ARE OKAY. WE TOOK SEVERAL CASUALTIES ON THE GROUNDS, BUT IT--IT COULD HAVE BEEN WORSE.
ALTHOUGH ORPHAN...AND POPPY...
THEY GOT AWAY--WITH HARPER AND CASS. POPPY TOOK THEM WHILE WE WERE ALL OUT COLD. MOTHER TOOK BACK HER CHILDREN.
I DON'T KNOW IF RED HOOD WILL EVER FORGIVE HIMSELF FOR THAT... I DON'T KNOW IF I WILL EITHER.
AND THE CODES. FOR SOMNUS. MOTHER...
SHE HAS THEM, DOESN'T SHE.

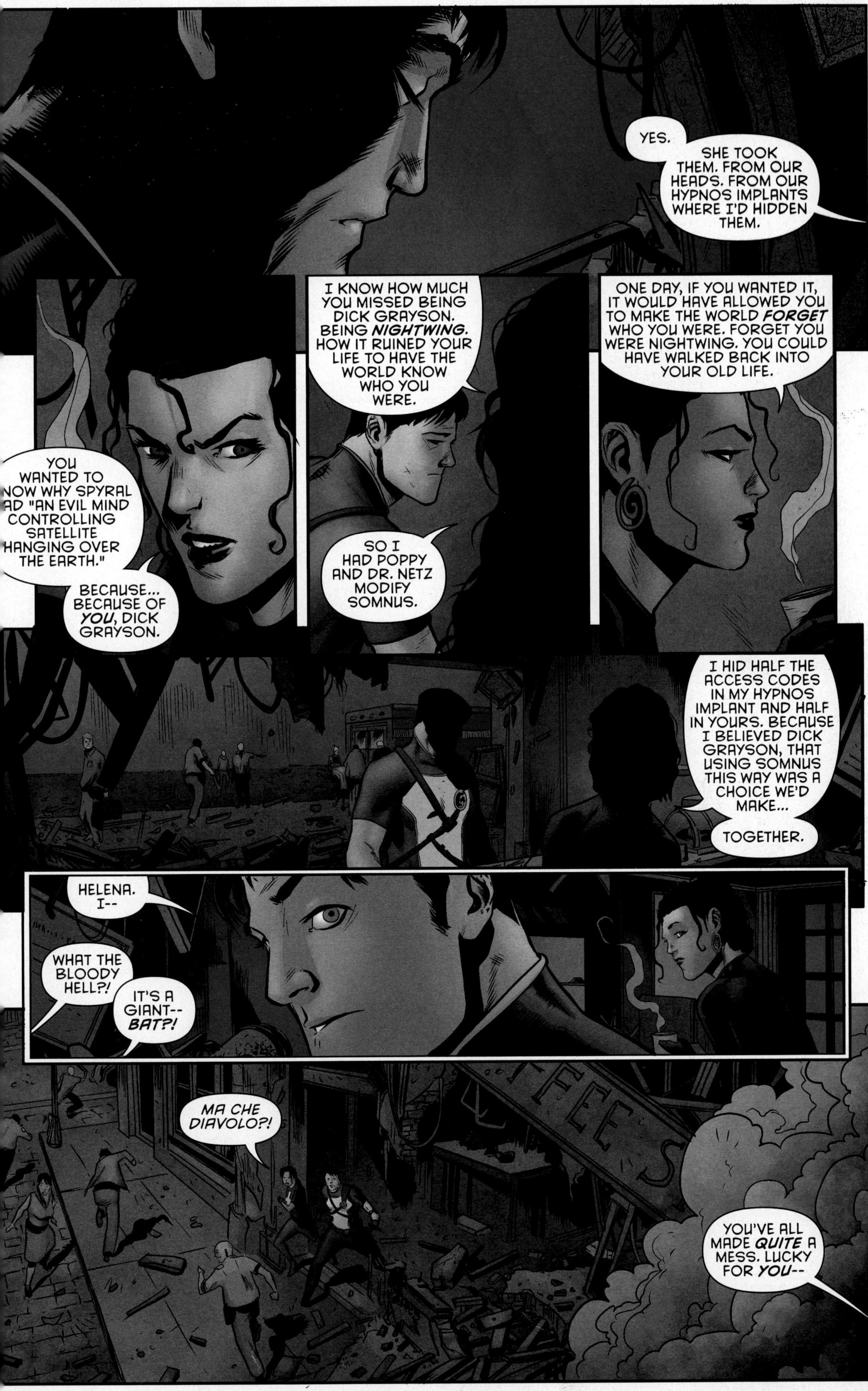
YES.
SHE TOOK THEM. FROM OUR HEADS. FROM OUR HYPNOS IMPLANTS WHERE I'D HIDDEN THEM.
YOU WANTED TO NOW WHY SPYRAL AD "AN EVIL MIND CONTROLLING SATELLITE HANGING OVER THE EARTH."
BECAUSE... BECAUSE OF YOU, DICK GRAYSON.
I KNOW HOW MUCH YOU MISSED BEING DICK GRAYSON. BEING NIGHTWING. HOW IT RUINED YOUR LIFE TO HAVE THE WORLD KNOW WHO YOU WERE.
SO I HAD POPPY AND DR. NETZ MODIFY SOMNUS.
ONE DAY, IF YOU WANTED IT, IT WOULD HAVE ALLOWED YOU TO MAKE THE WORLD FORGET WHO YOU WERE. FORGET YOU WERE NIGHTWING. YOU COULD HAVE WALKED BACK INTO YOUR OLD LIFE.
I HID HALF THE ACCESS CODES IN MY HYPNOS IMPLANT AND HALF IN YOURS. BECAUSE I BELIEVED DICK GRAYSON, THAT USING SOMNUS THIS WAY WAS A CHOICE WE'D MAKE...
TOGETHER.
HELENA. I--
WHAT THE BLOODY HELL?!
IT'S A GIANT-- BAT?!
MA CHE DIAVOLO?!
YOU'VE ALL MADE QUITE A MESS. LUCKY FOR YOU--

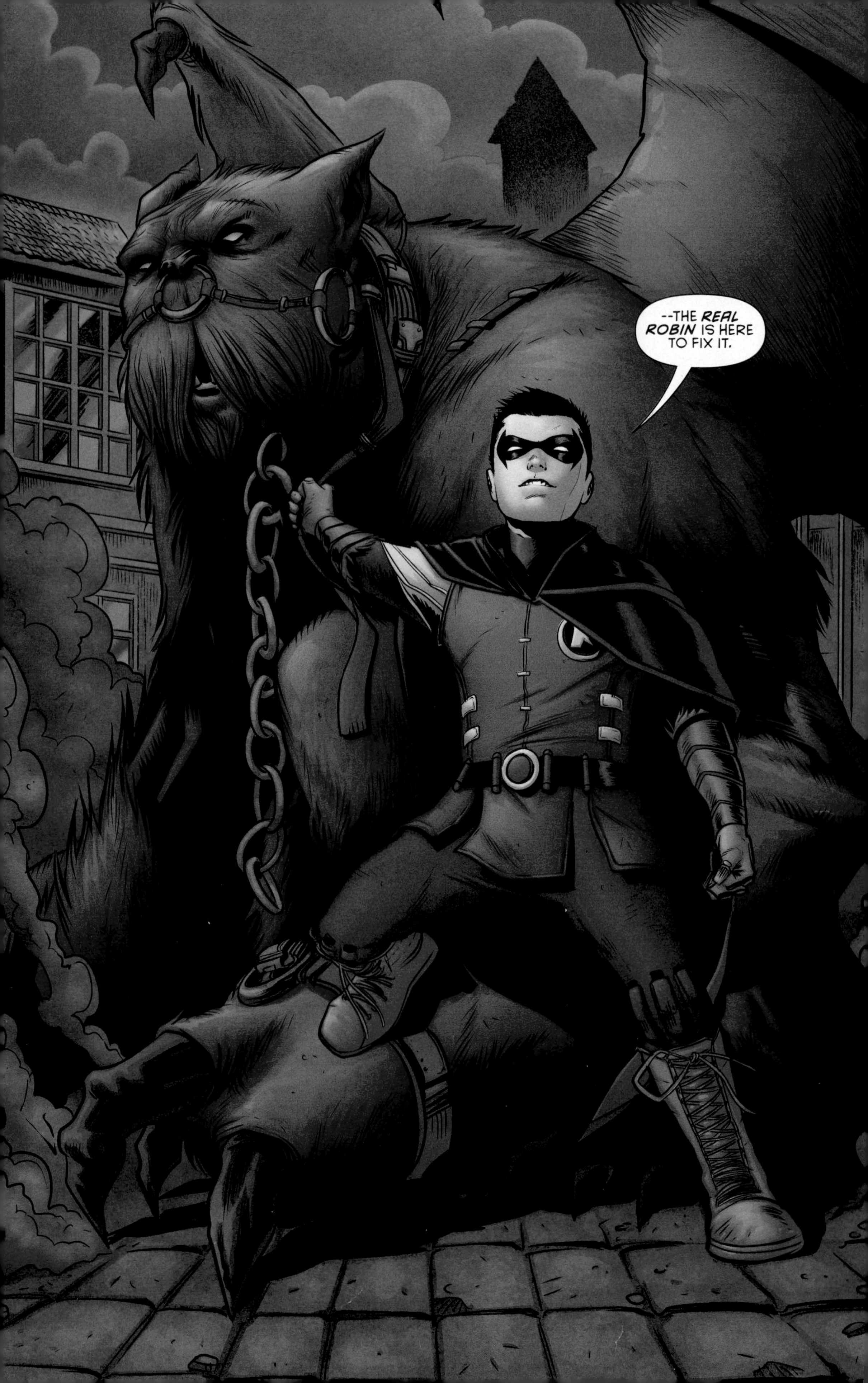
--THE *REAL* *ROBIN* IS HERE TO FIX IT.

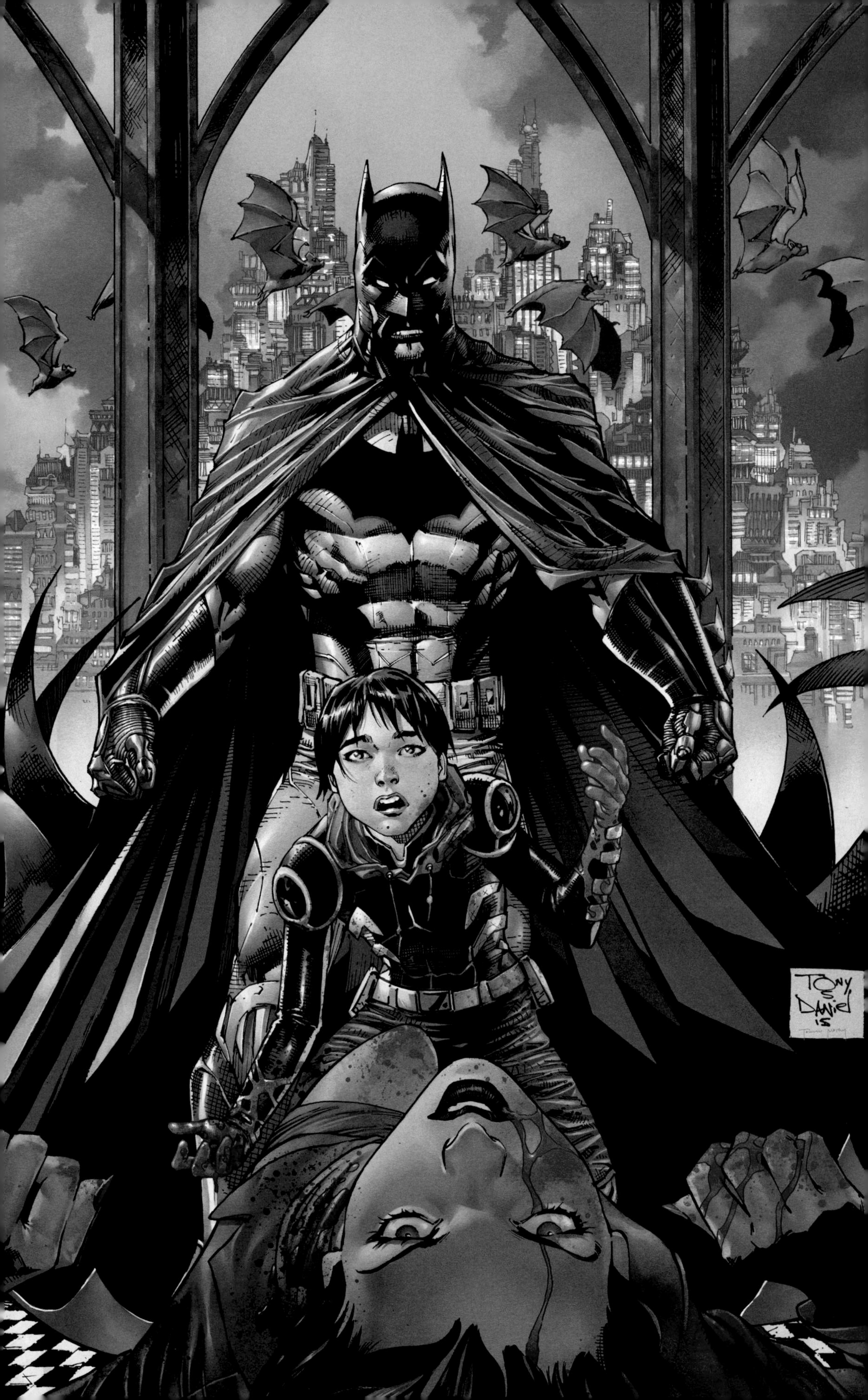
TONY S. DANIEL 15

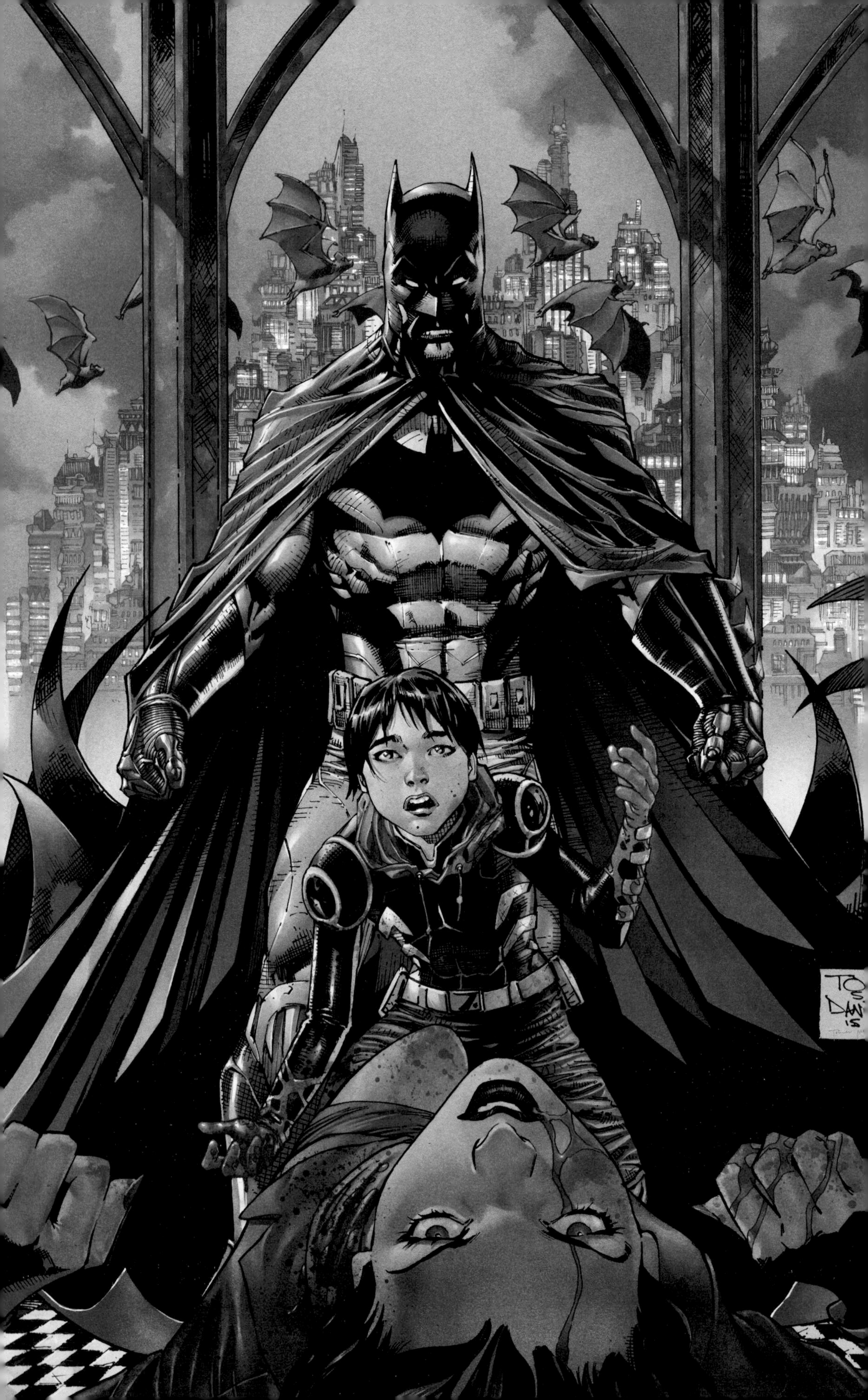

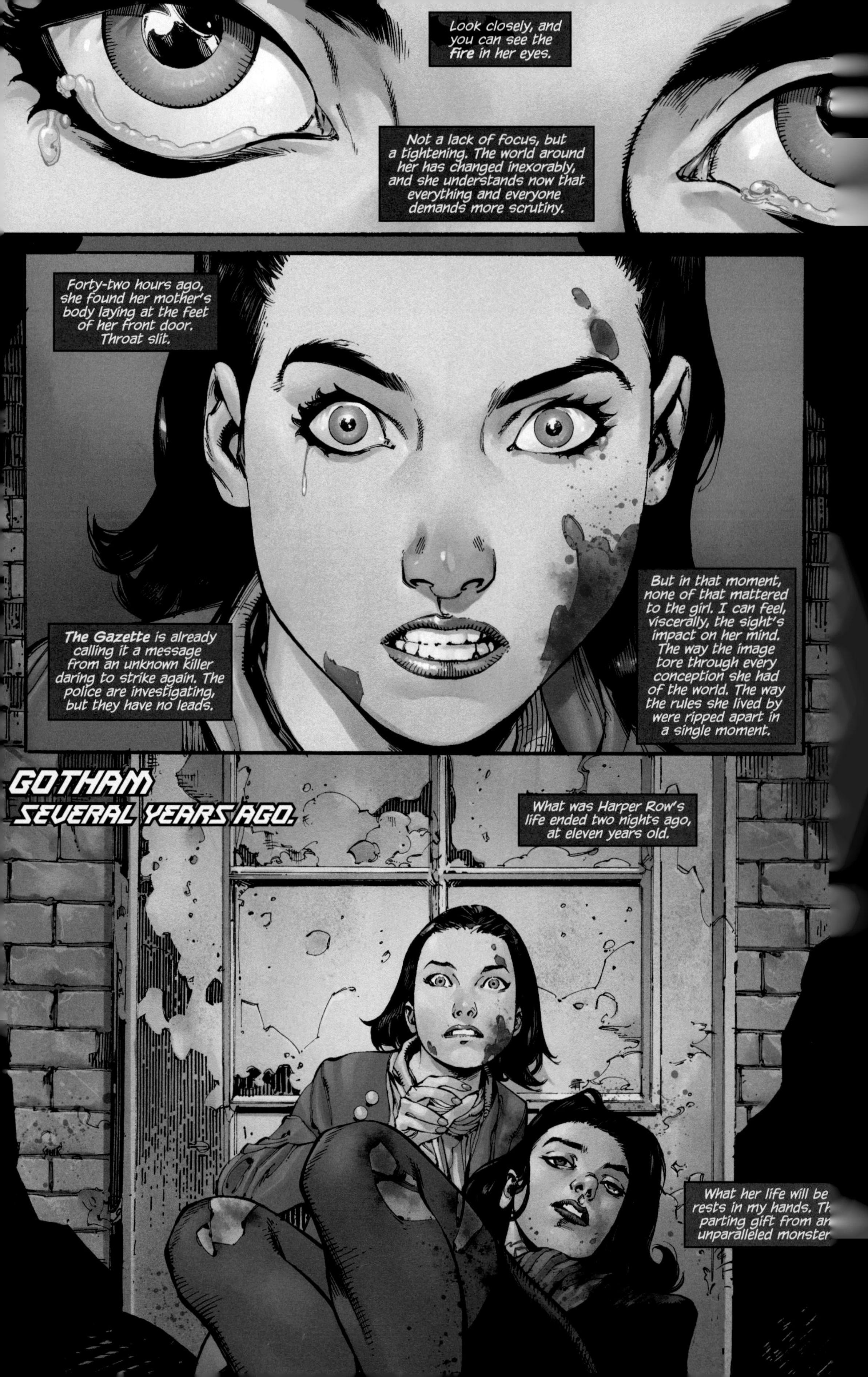
Look closely, and you can see the fire in her eyes.
Not a lack of focus, but a tightening. The world around her has changed inexorably, and she understands now that everything and everyone demands more scrutiny.
Forty-two hours ago, she found her mother's body laying at the feet of her front door. Throat slit.
The Gazette is already calling it a message from an unknown killer daring to strike again. The police are investigating, but they have no leads.
But in that moment, none of that mattered to the girl. I can feel, viscerally, the sight's impact on her mind. The way the image tore through every conception she had of the world. The way the rules she lived by were ripped apart in a single moment.
GOTHAM
SEVERAL YEARS AGO.
What was Harper Row's life ended two nights ago, at eleven years old.
What her life will be rests in my hands. Th parting gift from an unparalleled monster

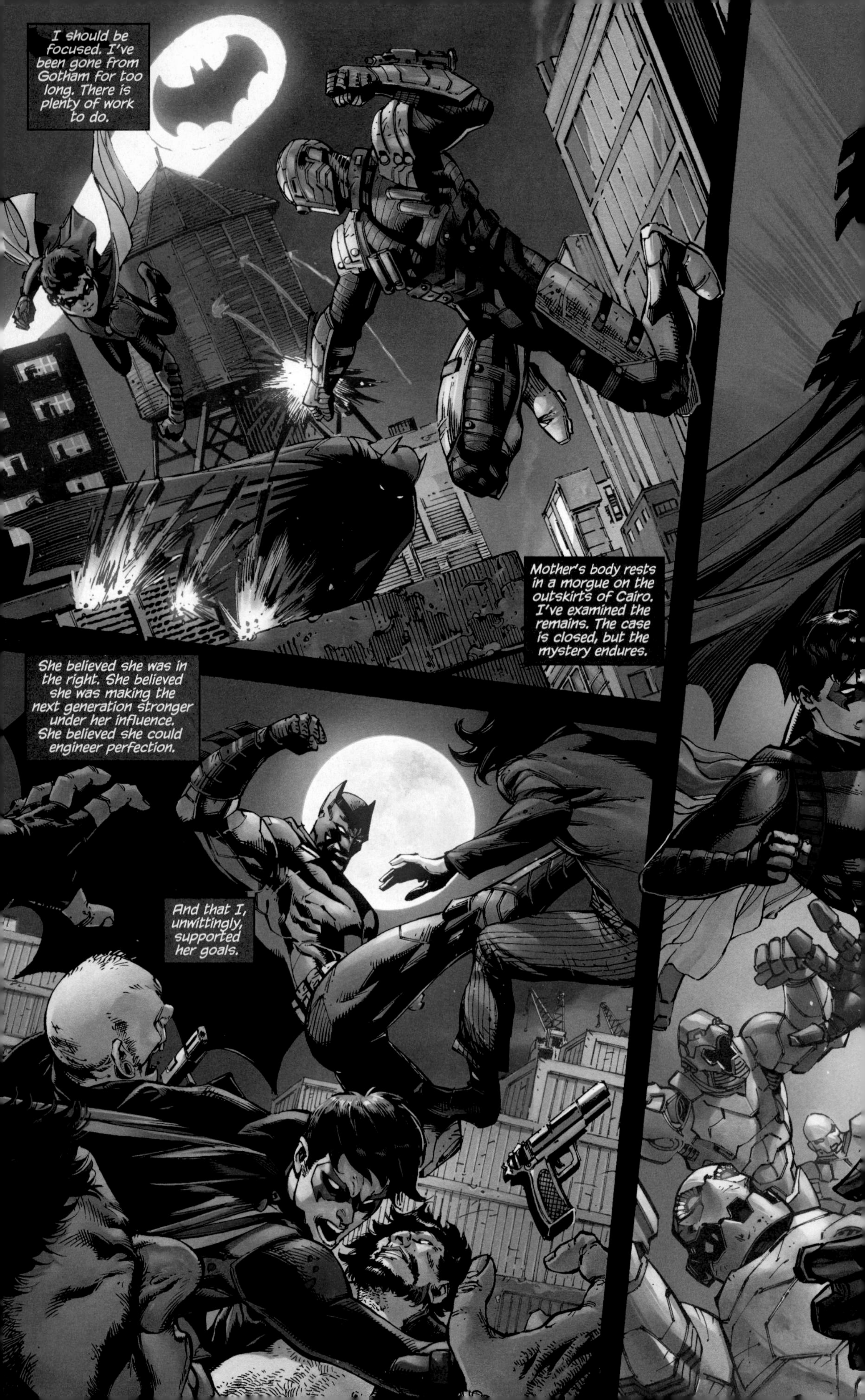
I should be focused. I've been gone from Gotham for too long. There is plenty of work to do.
Mother's body rests in a morgue on the outskirts of Cairo. I've examined the remains. The case is closed, but the mystery endures.
She believed she was in the right. She believed she was making the next generation stronger under her influence. She believed she could engineer perfection.
And that I, unwittingly, supported her goals.

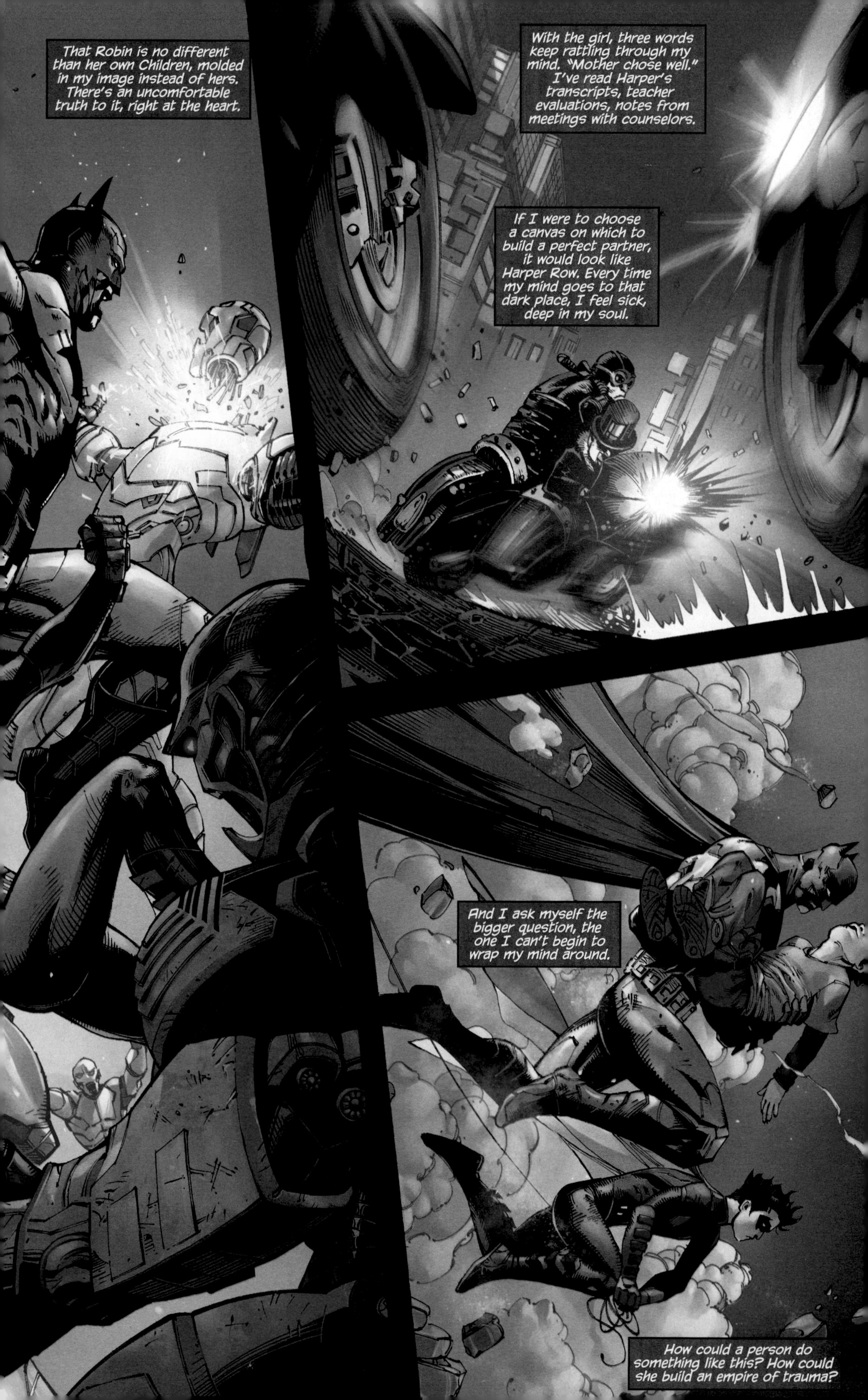
That Robin is no different than her own Children, molded in my image instead of hers. There's an uncomfortable truth to it, right at the heart.
With the girl, three words keep rattling through my mind. "Mother chose well." I've read Harper's transcripts, teacher evaluations, notes from meetings with counselors.
If I were to choose a canvas on which to build a perfect partner, it would look like Harper Row. Every time my mind goes to that dark place, I feel sick, deep in my soul.
And I ask myself the bigger question, the one I can't begin to wrap my mind around.
How could a person do something like this? How could she build an empire of trauma?

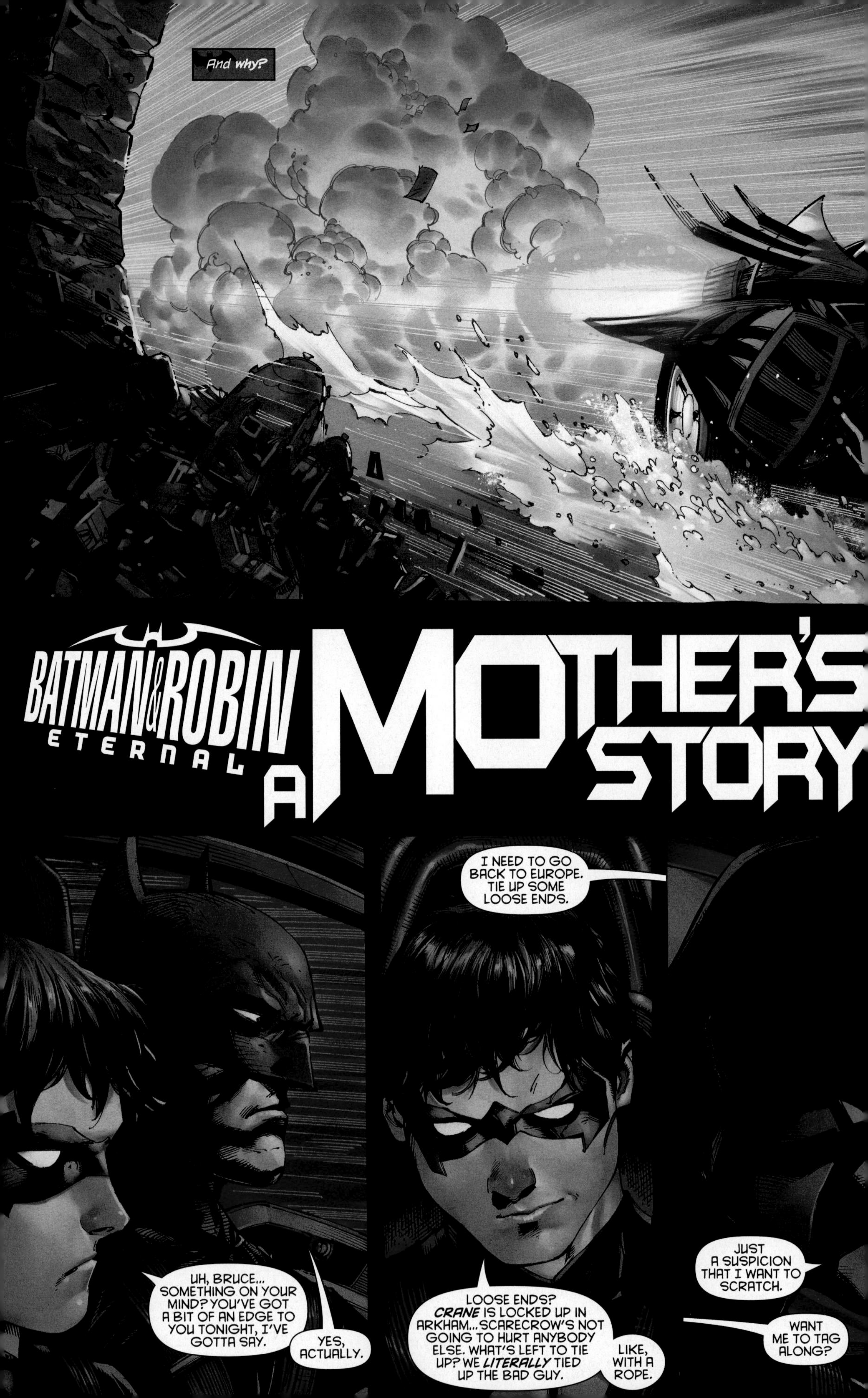
And why?
BATMAN & ROBIN ETERNAL
A MOTHER'S STORY
UH, BRUCE... SOMETHING ON YOUR MIND? YOU'VE GOT A BIT OF AN EDGE TO YOU TONIGHT, I'VE GOTTA SAY.
YES, ACTUALLY.
I NEED TO GO BACK TO EUROPE. TIE UP SOME LOOSE ENDS.
LOOSE ENDS? CRANE IS LOCKED UP IN ARKHAM... SCARECROW'S NOT GOING TO HURT ANYBODY ELSE. WHAT'S LEFT TO TIE UP? WE LITERALLY TIED UP THE BAD GUY.
LIKE, WITH A ROPE.
JUST A SUSPICION THAT I WANT TO SCRATCH.
WANT ME TO TAG ALONG?

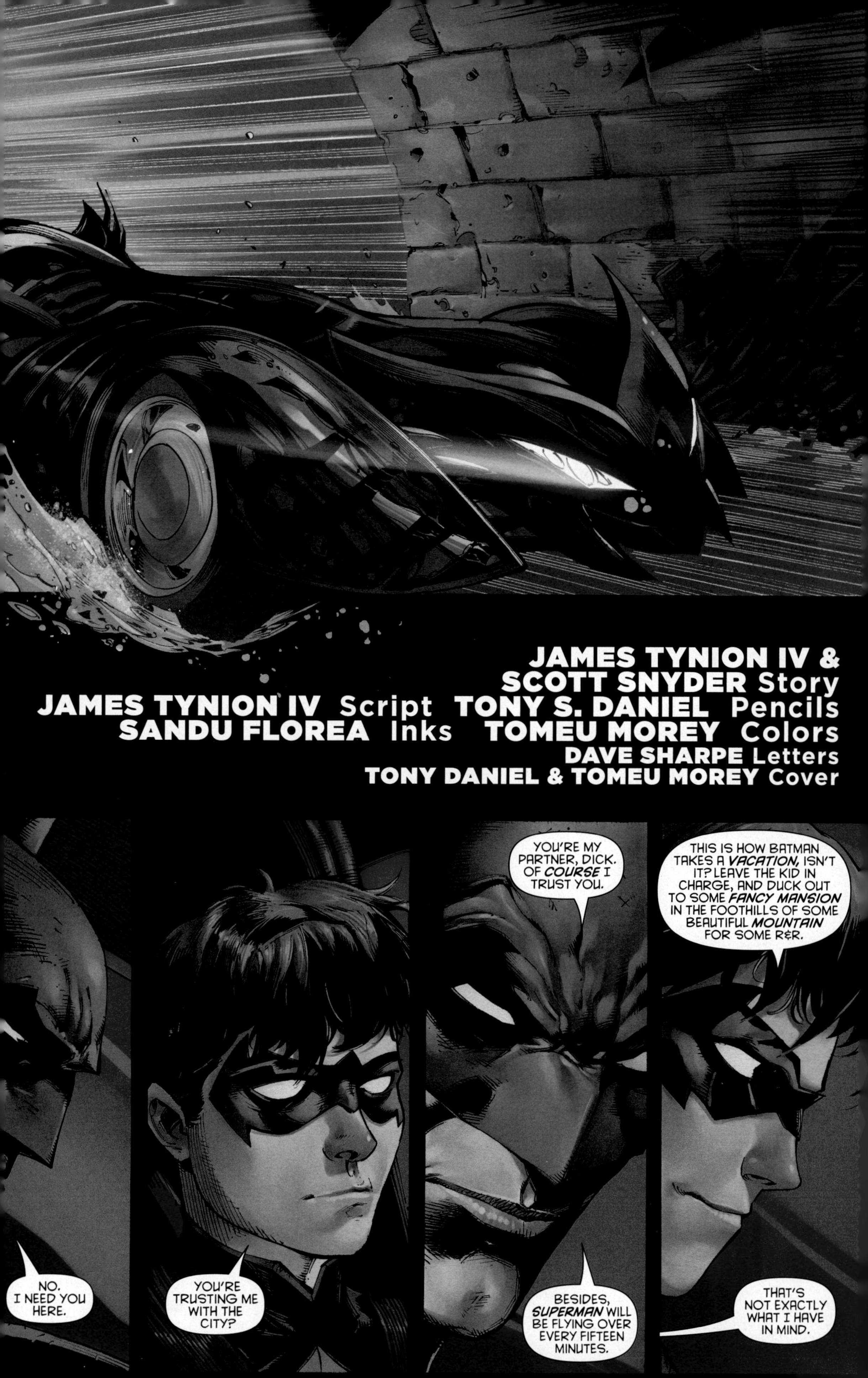

JAMES TYNION IV & SCOTT SNYDER Story
JAMES TYNION IV Script TONY S. DANIEL Pencils
SANDU FLOREA Inks TOMEU MOREY Colors
DAVE SHARPE Letters
TONY DANIEL & TOMEU MOREY Cover
NO. I NEED YOU HERE.
YOU'RE TRUSTING ME WITH THE CITY?
YOU'RE MY PARTNER, DICK. OF COURSE I TRUST YOU.
BESIDES, SUPERMAN WILL BE FLYING OVER EVERY FIFTEEN MINUTES.
THIS IS HOW BATMAN TAKES A VACATION, ISN'T IT? LEAVE THE KID IN CHARGE, AND DUCK OUT TO SOME FANCY MANSION IN THE FOOTHILLS OF SOME BEAUTIFUL MOUNTAIN FOR SOME R&R.
THAT'S NOT EXACTLY WHAT I HAVE IN MIND.

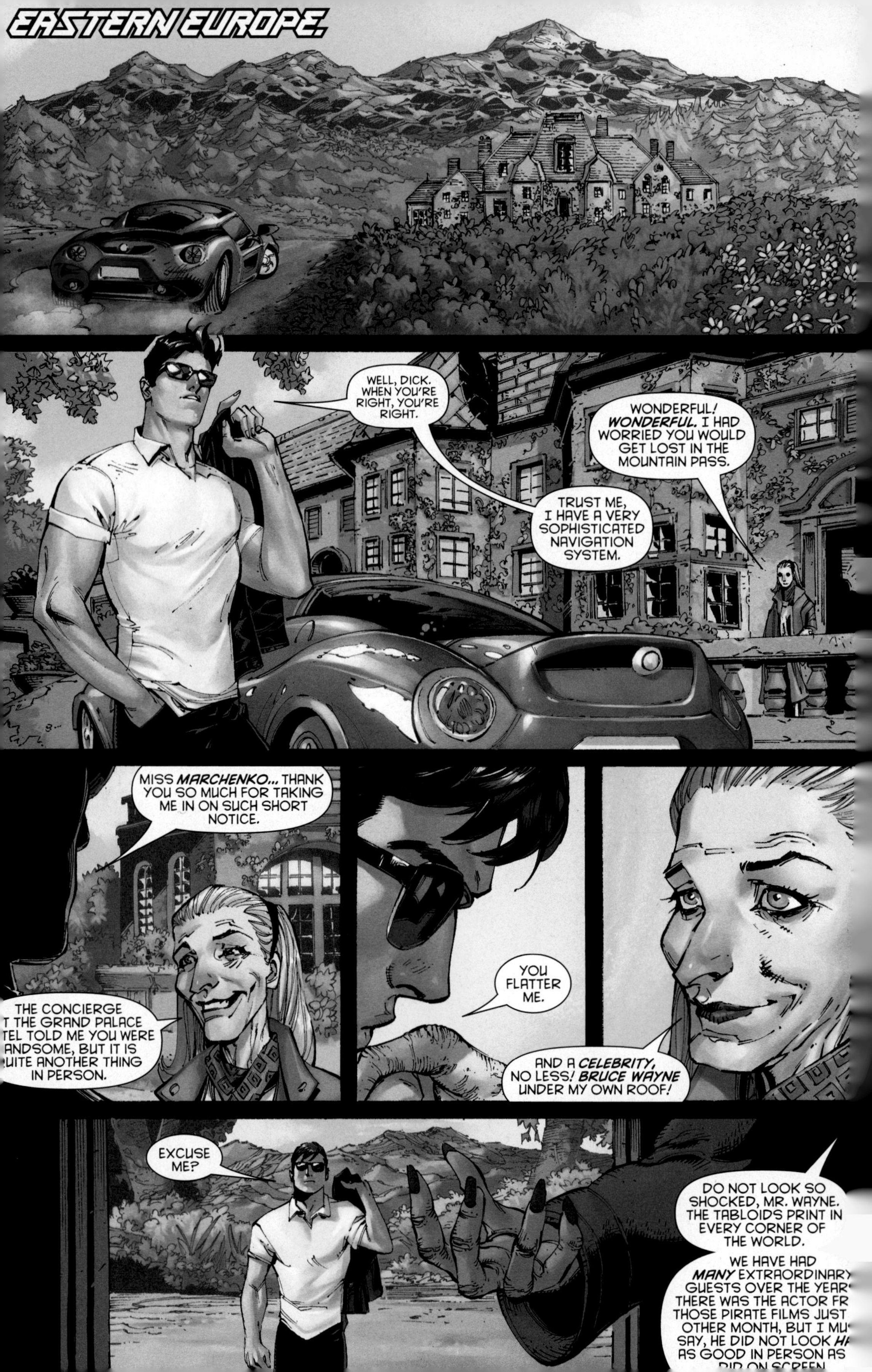
EASTERN EUROPE.
WELL, DICK. WHEN YOU'RE RIGHT, YOU'RE RIGHT.
WONDERFUL! WONDERFUL. I HAD WORRIED YOU WOULD GET LOST IN THE MOUNTAIN PASS.
TRUST ME, I HAVE A VERY SOPHISTICATED NAVIGATION SYSTEM.
MISS MARCHENKO... THANK YOU SO MUCH FOR TAKING ME IN ON SUCH SHORT NOTICE.
THE CONCIERGE T THE GRAND PALACE TEL TOLD ME YOU WERE ANDSOME, BUT IT IS UITE ANOTHER THING IN PERSON.
YOU FLATTER ME.
AND A CELEBRITY, NO LESS! BRUCE WAYNE UNDER MY OWN ROOF!
EXCUSE ME?
DO NOT LOOK SO SHOCKED, MR. WAYNE. THE TABLOIDS PRINT IN EVERY CORNER OF THE WORLD.
WE HAVE HAD MANY EXTRAORDINARY GUESTS OVER THE YEAR THERE WAS THE ACTOR FR THOSE PIRATE FILMS JUST OTHER MONTH, BUT I MU SAY, HE DID NOT LOOK HA AS GOOD IN PERSON AS

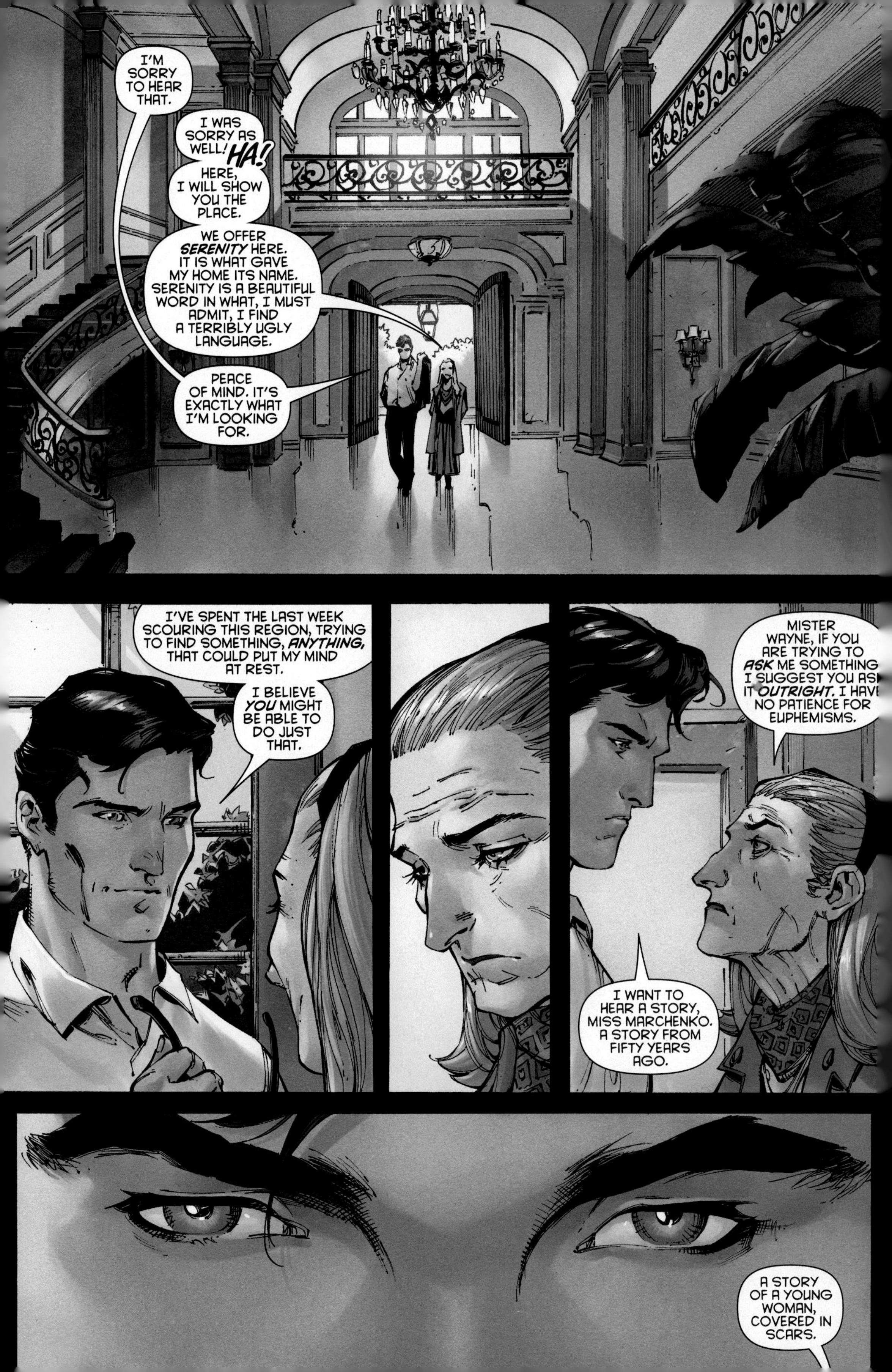

I'M SORRY TO HEAR THAT.
I WAS SORRY AS WELL! HA!
HERE, I WILL SHOW YOU THE PLACE.
WE OFFER SERENITY HERE. IT IS WHAT GAVE MY HOME ITS NAME. SERENITY IS A BEAUTIFUL WORD IN WHAT, I MUST ADMIT, I FIND A TERRIBLY UGLY LANGUAGE.
PEACE OF MIND. IT'S EXACTLY WHAT I'M LOOKING FOR.
I'VE SPENT THE LAST WEEK SCOURING THIS REGION, TRYING TO FIND SOMETHING, ANYTHING, THAT COULD PUT MY MIND AT REST.
I BELIEVE YOU MIGHT BE ABLE TO DO JUST THAT.
MISTER WAYNE, IF YOU ARE TRYING TO ASK ME SOMETHING I SUGGEST YOU ASK IT OUTRIGHT. I HAVE NO PATIENCE FOR EUPHEMISMS.
I WANT TO HEAR A STORY, MISS MARCHENKO. A STORY FROM FIFTY YEARS AGO.
A STORY OF A YOUNG WOMAN, COVERED IN SCARS.

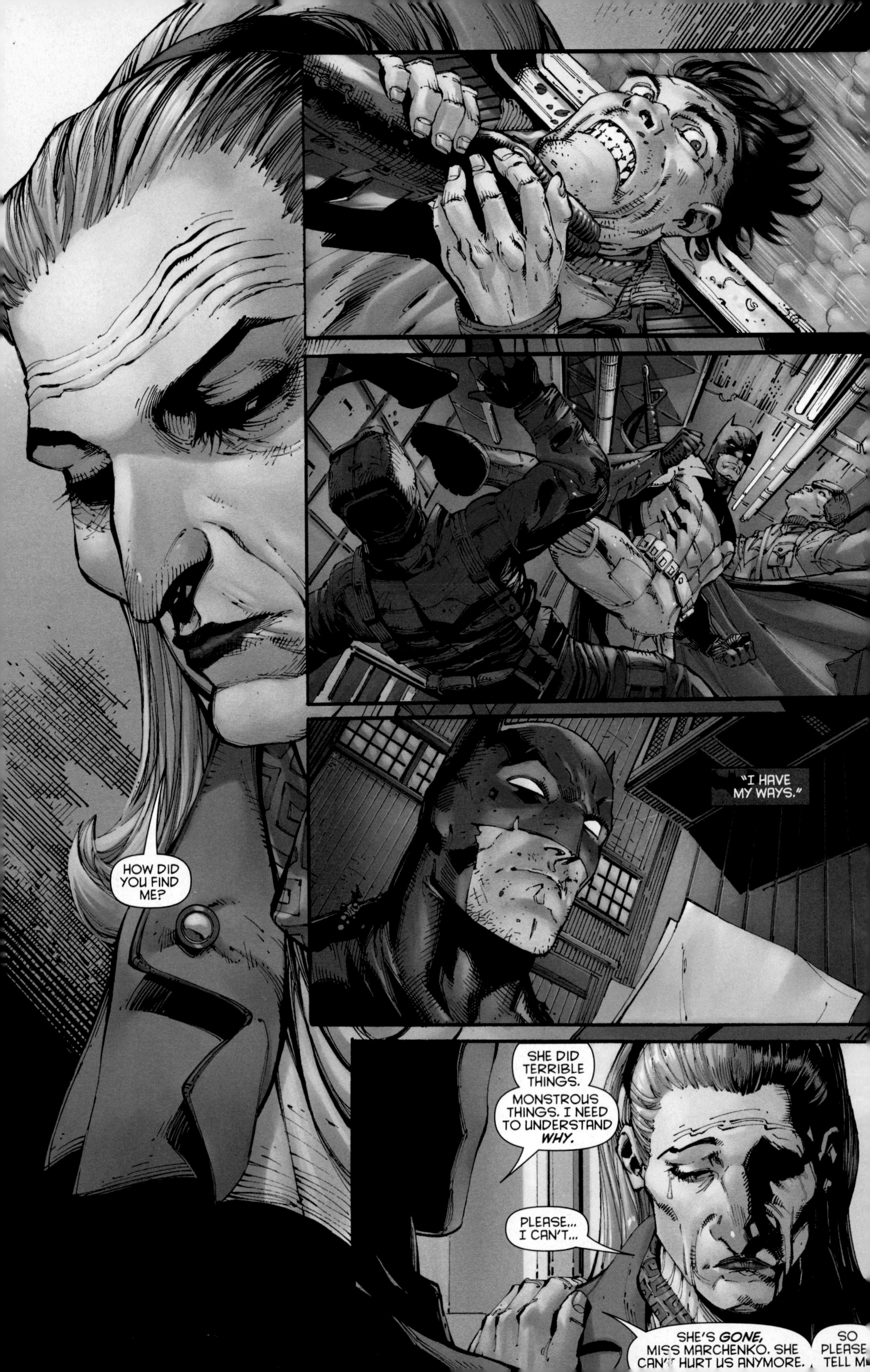

HOW DID YOU FIND ME?
"I HAVE MY WAYS."
SHE DID TERRIBLE THINGS.
MONSTROUS THINGS. I NEED TO UNDERSTAND *WHY.*
PLEASE... I CAN'T...
SHE'S *GONE,* MISS MARCHENKO. SHE CAN'T HURT US ANYMORE.
SO PLEASE TELL M

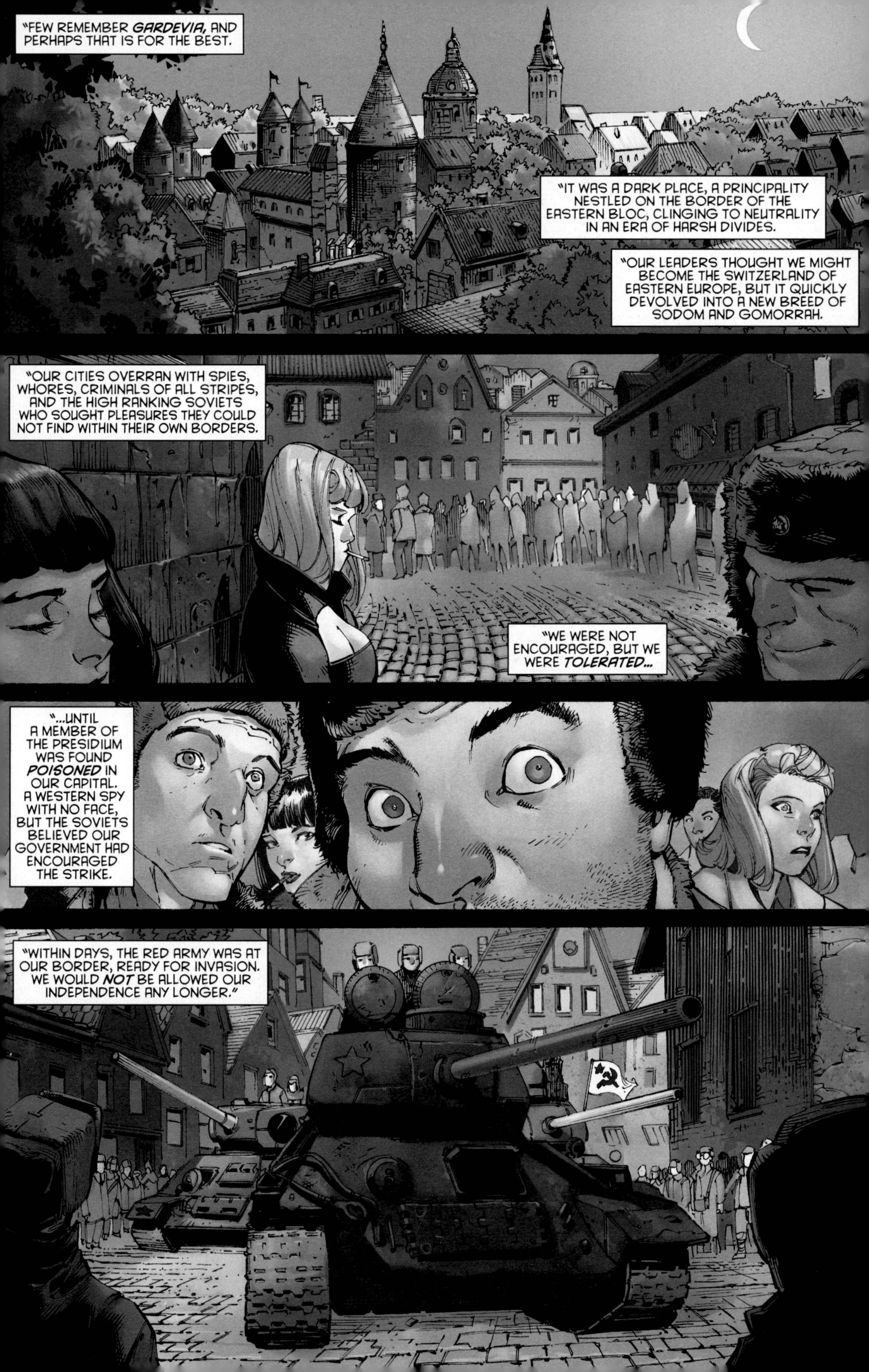
"FEW REMEMBER GARDEVIA, AND PERHAPS THAT IS FOR THE BEST.
"IT WAS A DARK PLACE, A PRINCIPALITY NESTLED ON THE BORDER OF THE EASTERN BLOC, CLINGING TO NEUTRALITY IN AN ERA OF HARSH DIVIDES.
"OUR LEADERS THOUGHT WE MIGHT BECOME THE SWITZERLAND OF EASTERN EUROPE, BUT IT QUICKLY DEVOLVED INTO A NEW BREED OF SODOM AND GOMORRAH.
"OUR CITIES OVERRAN WITH SPIES, WHORES, CRIMINALS OF ALL STRIPES, AND THE HIGH RANKING SOVIETS WHO SOUGHT PLEASURES THEY COULD NOT FIND WITHIN THEIR OWN BORDERS.
"WE WERE NOT ENCOURAGED, BUT WE WERE TOLERATED...
"...UNTIL A MEMBER OF THE PRESIDIUM WAS FOUND POISONED IN OUR CAPITAL. A WESTERN SPY WITH NO FACE, BUT THE SOVIETS BELIEVED OUR GOVERNMENT HAD ENCOURAGED THE STRIKE.
"WITHIN DAYS, THE RED ARMY WAS AT OUR BORDER, READY FOR INVASION. WE WOULD NOT BE ALLOWED OUR INDEPENDENCE ANY LONGER."

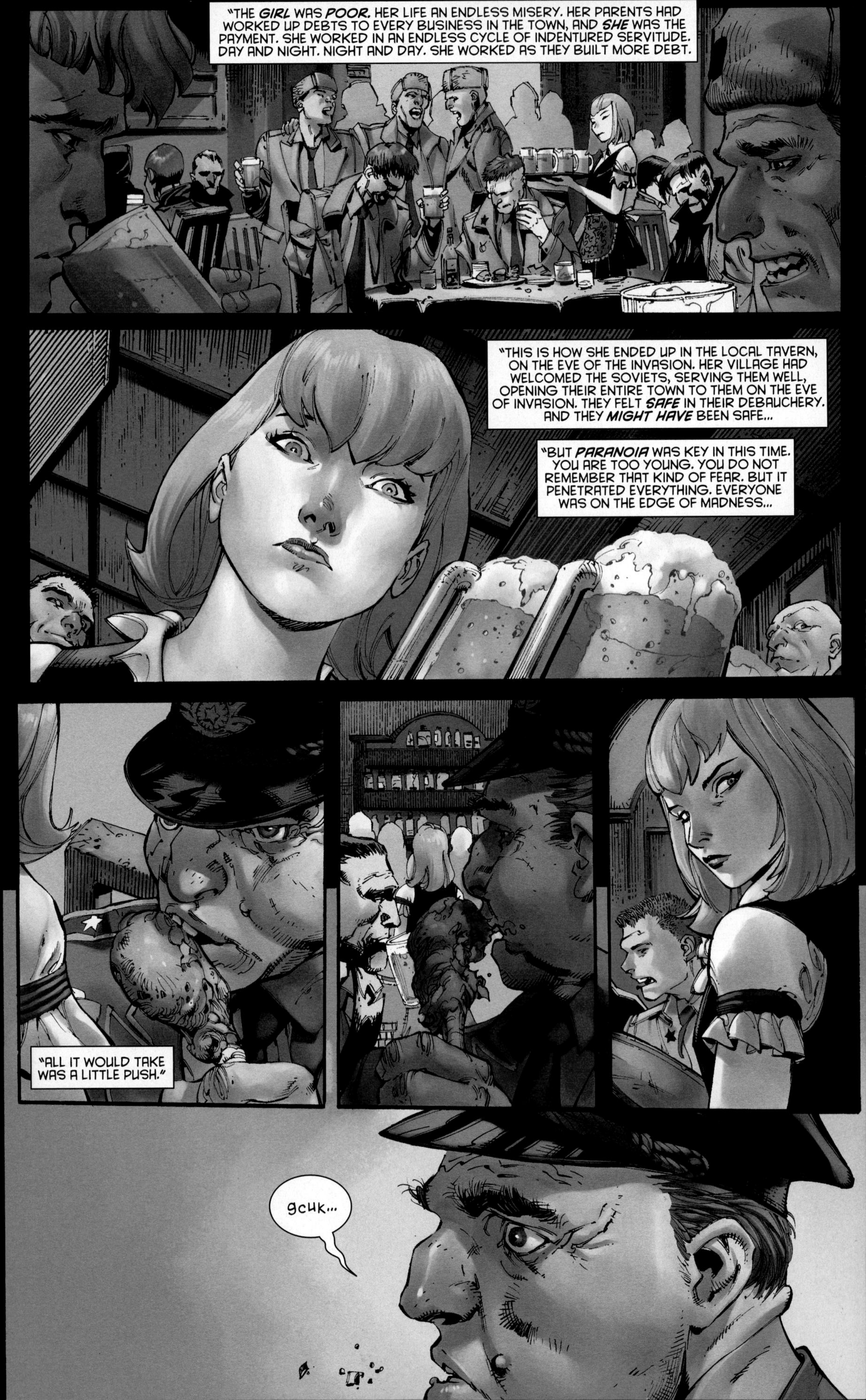
"THE GIRL WAS POOR. HER LIFE AN ENDLESS MISERY. HER PARENTS HAD WORKED UP DEBTS TO EVERY BUSINESS IN THE TOWN, AND SHE WAS THE PAYMENT. SHE WORKED IN AN ENDLESS CYCLE OF INDENTURED SERVITUDE. DAY AND NIGHT. NIGHT AND DAY. SHE WORKED AS THEY BUILT MORE DEBT.
"THIS IS HOW SHE ENDED UP IN THE LOCAL TAVERN, ON THE EVE OF THE INVASION. HER VILLAGE HAD WELCOMED THE SOVIETS, SERVING THEM WELL, OPENING THEIR ENTIRE TOWN TO THEM ON THE EVE OF INVASION. THEY FELT SAFE IN THEIR DEBAUCHERY. AND THEY MIGHT HAVE BEEN SAFE...
"BUT PARANOIA WAS KEY IN THIS TIME. YOU ARE TOO YOUNG. YOU DO NOT REMEMBER THAT KIND OF FEAR. BUT IT PENETRATED EVERYTHING. EVERYONE WAS ON THE EDGE OF MADNESS...
"ALL IT WOULD TAKE WAS A LITTLE PUSH."
GCUK...

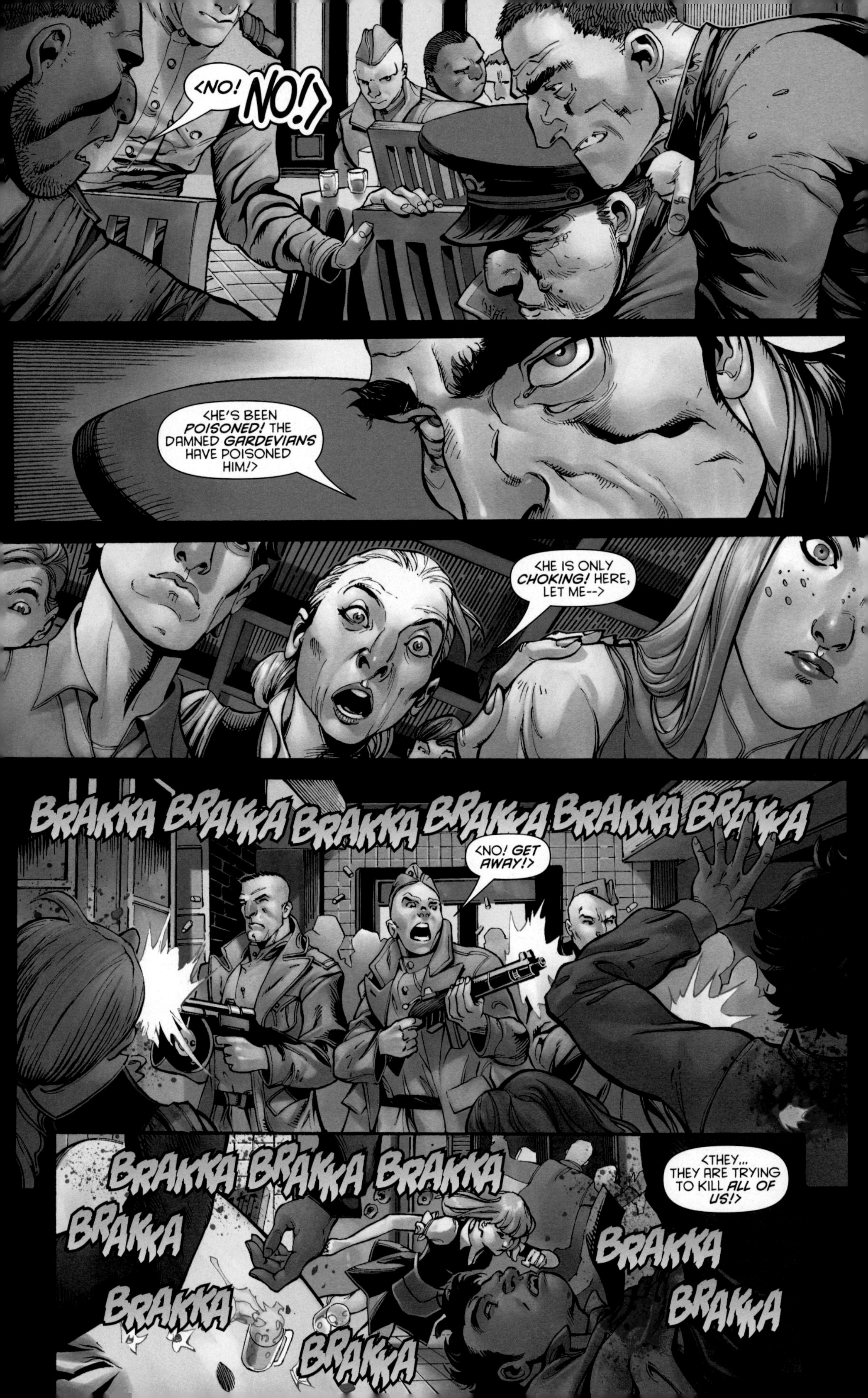
<NO! NO!>
<HE'S BEEN POISONED! THE DAMNED GARDEVIANS HAVE POISONED HIM!>
<HE IS ONLY CHOKING! HERE, LET ME-->
BRAKKA BRAKKA BRAKKA BRAKKA BRAKKA BRAKKA
<NO! GET AWAY!>
BRAKKA BRAKKA BRAKKA
BRAKKA
<THEY... THEY ARE TRYING TO KILL ALL OF US!>
BRAKKA
BRAKKA
BRAKKA
BRAKKA

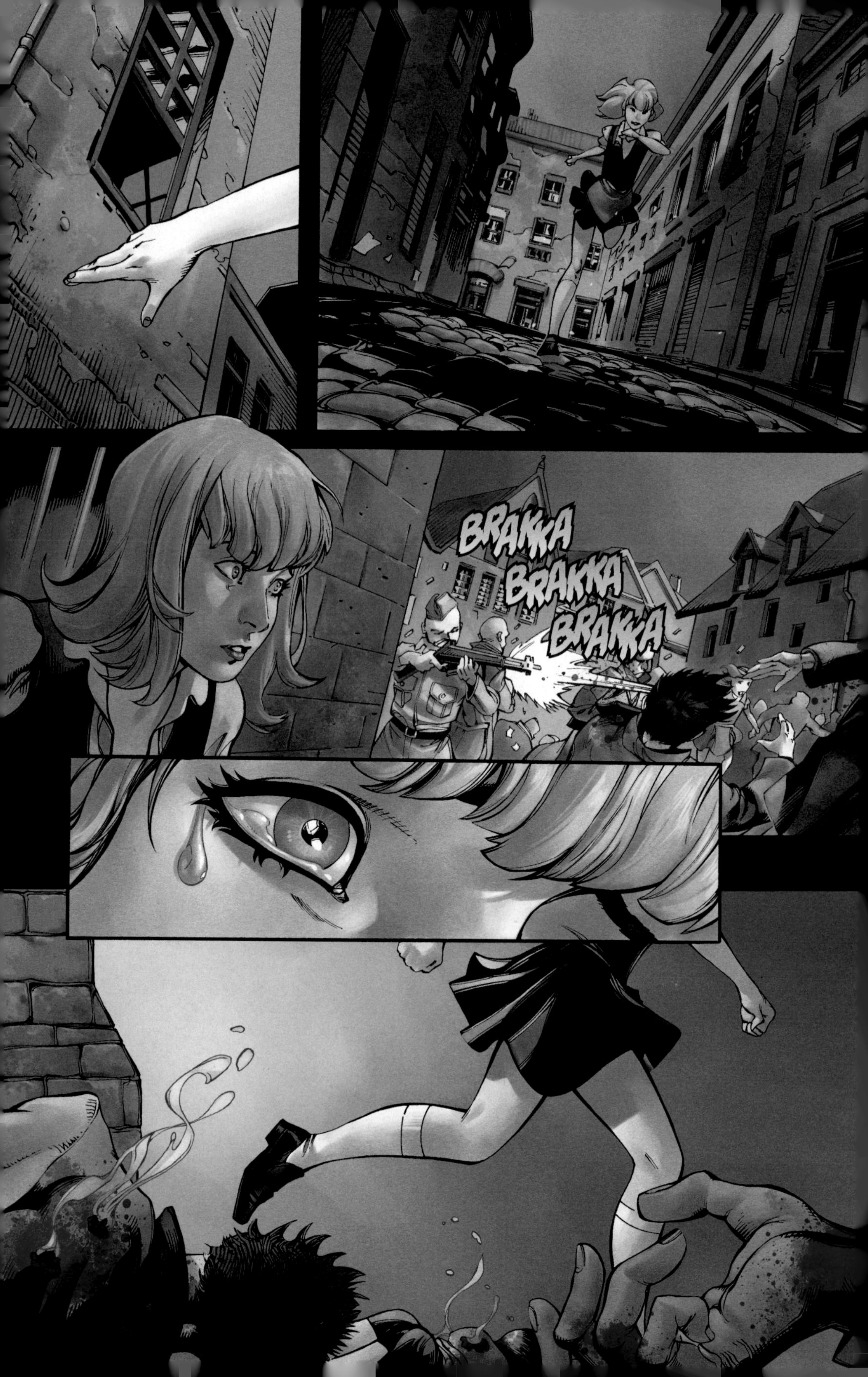
BRAKKA
BRAKKA
BRAKKA

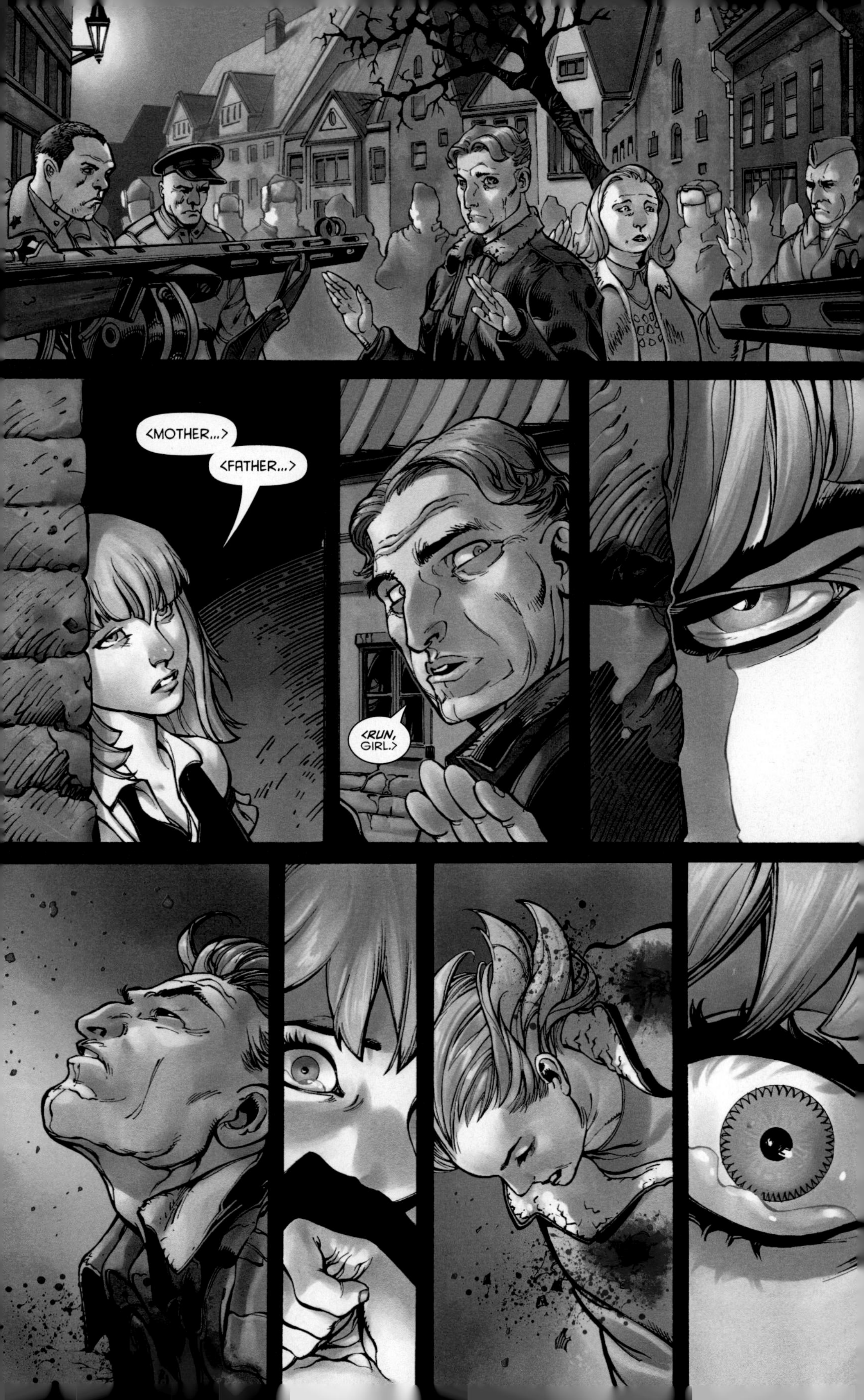
<MOTHER...>
<FATHER...>
<*RUN,* GIRL.>

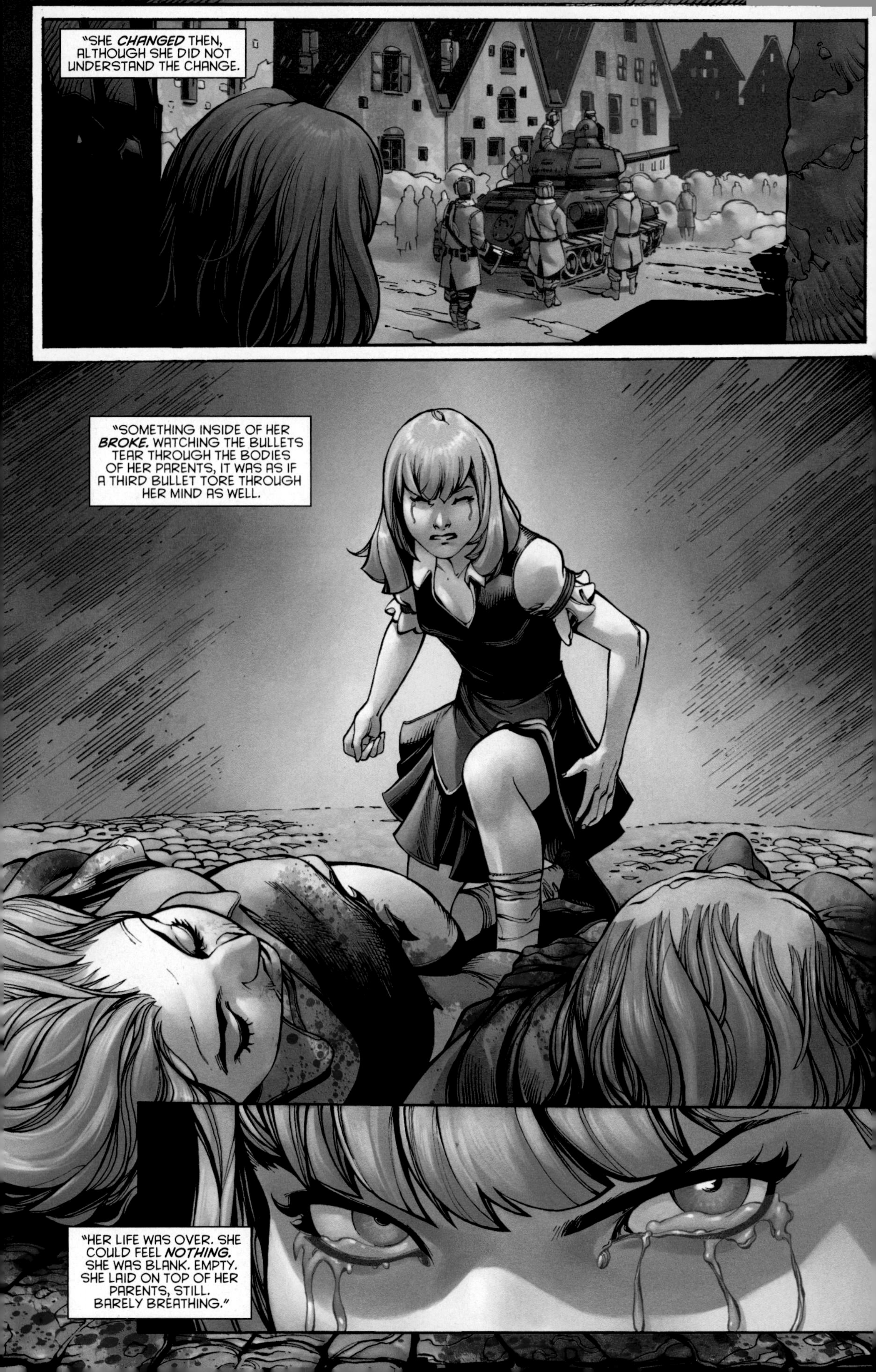
"SHE CHANGED THEN, ALTHOUGH SHE DID NOT UNDERSTAND THE CHANGE.
"SOMETHING INSIDE OF HER BROKE. WATCHING THE BULLETS TEAR THROUGH THE BODIES OF HER PARENTS, IT WAS AS IF A THIRD BULLET TORE THROUGH HER MIND AS WELL.
"HER LIFE WAS OVER. SHE COULD FEEL NOTHING. SHE WAS BLANK. EMPTY. SHE LAID ON TOP OF HER PARENTS, STILL. BARELY BREATHING."

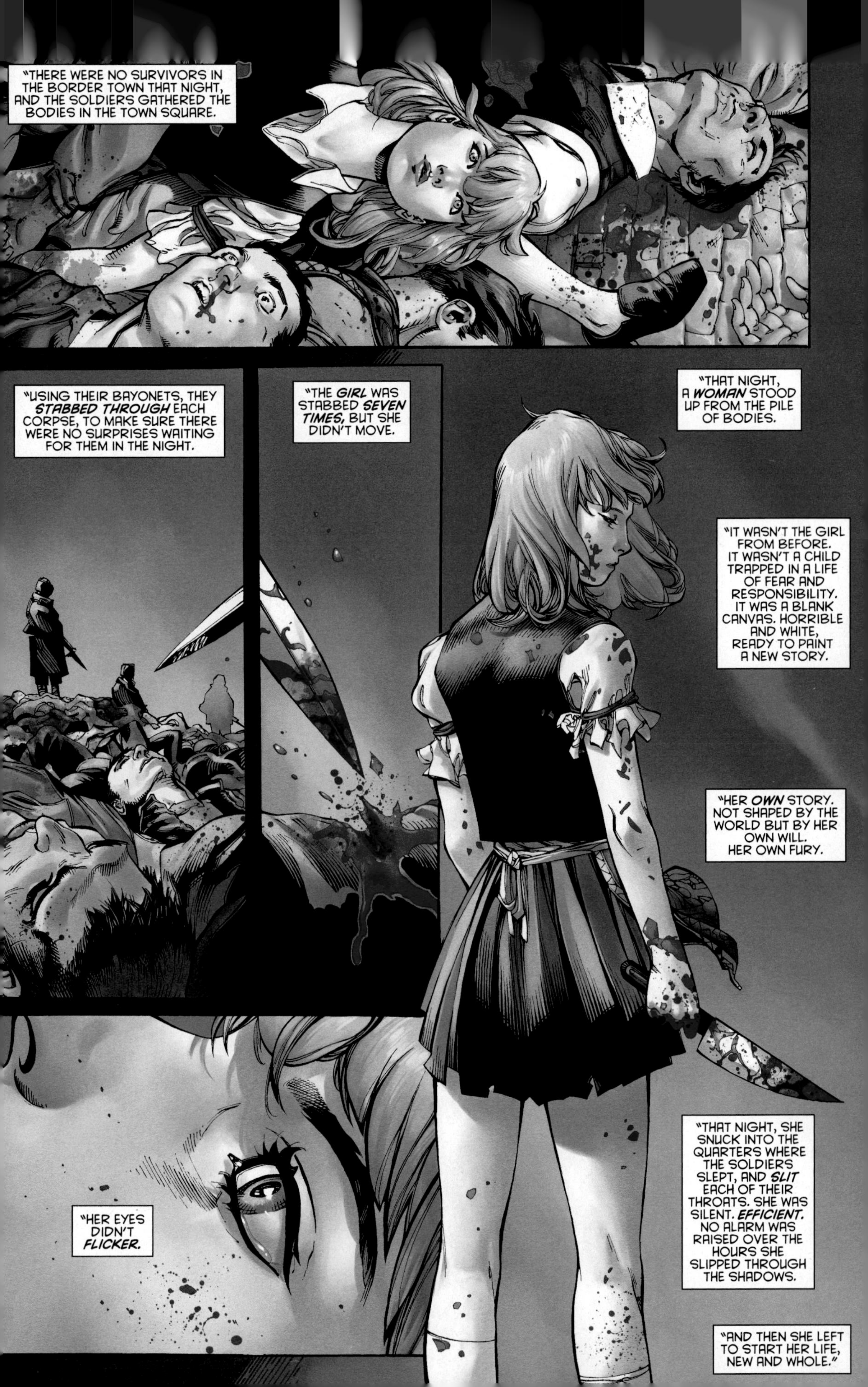
"THERE WERE NO SURVIVORS IN THE BORDER TOWN THAT NIGHT, AND THE SOLDIERS GATHERED THE BODIES IN THE TOWN SQUARE.
"USING THEIR BAYONETS, THEY STABBED THROUGH EACH CORPSE, TO MAKE SURE THERE WERE NO SURPRISES WAITING FOR THEM IN THE NIGHT.
"THE GIRL WAS STABBED SEVEN TIMES, BUT SHE DIDN'T MOVE.
"HER EYES DIDN'T FLICKER.
"THAT NIGHT, A WOMAN STOOD UP FROM THE PILE OF BODIES.
"IT WASN'T THE GIRL FROM BEFORE. IT WASN'T A CHILD TRAPPED IN A LIFE OF FEAR AND RESPONSIBILITY. IT WAS A BLANK CANVAS. HORRIBLE AND WHITE, READY TO PAINT A NEW STORY.
"HER OWN STORY. NOT SHAPED BY THE WORLD BUT BY HER OWN WILL. HER OWN FURY.
"THAT NIGHT, SHE SNUCK INTO THE QUARTERS WHERE THE SOLDIERS SLEPT, AND SLIT EACH OF THEIR THROATS. SHE WAS SILENT. EFFICIENT. NO ALARM WAS RAISED OVER THE HOURS SHE SLIPPED THROUGH THE SHADOWS.
"AND THEN SHE LEFT TO START HER LIFE, NEW AND WHOLE."

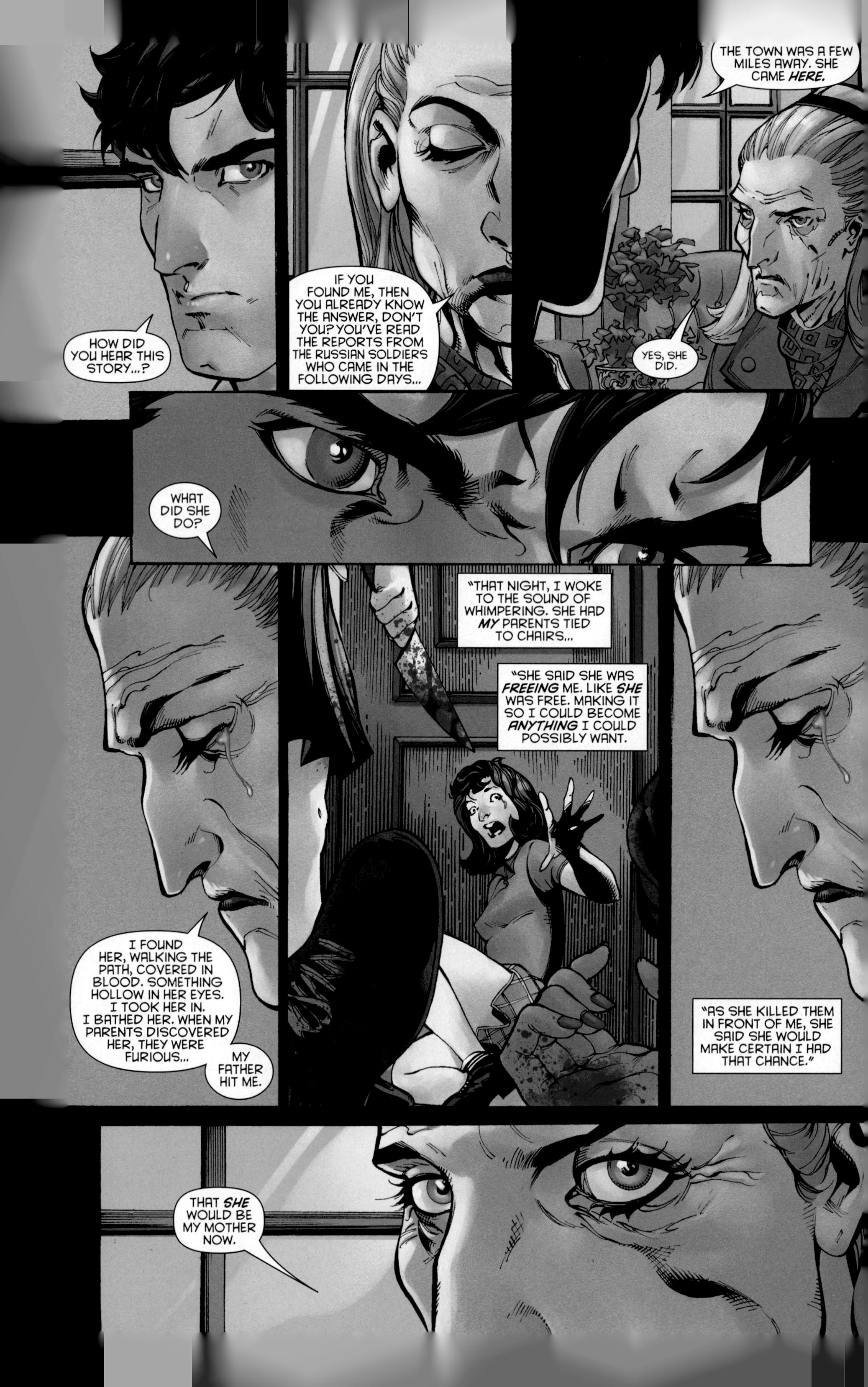
HOW DID YOU HEAR THIS STORY...?
IF YOU FOUND ME, THEN YOU ALREADY KNOW THE ANSWER, DON'T YOU? YOU'VE READ THE REPORTS FROM THE RUSSIAN SOLDIERS WHO CAME IN THE FOLLOWING DAYS...
THE TOWN WAS A FEW MILES AWAY. SHE CAME *HERE.*
YES, SHE DID.
WHAT DID SHE DO?
I FOUND HER, WALKING THE PATH, COVERED IN BLOOD. SOMETHING HOLLOW IN HER EYES. I TOOK HER IN. I BATHED HER. WHEN MY PARENTS DISCOVERED HER, THEY WERE FURIOUS...
MY FATHER HIT ME.
"THAT NIGHT, I WOKE TO THE SOUND OF WHIMPERING. SHE HAD *MY* PARENTS TIED TO CHAIRS...
"SHE SAID SHE WAS *FREEING* ME. LIKE *SHE* WAS FREE. MAKING IT SO I COULD BECOME *ANYTHING* I COULD POSSIBLY WANT.
"AS SHE KILLED THEM IN FRONT OF ME, SHE SAID SHE WOULD MAKE CERTAIN I HAD THAT CHANCE."
THAT *SHE* WOULD BE MY MOTHER NOW.

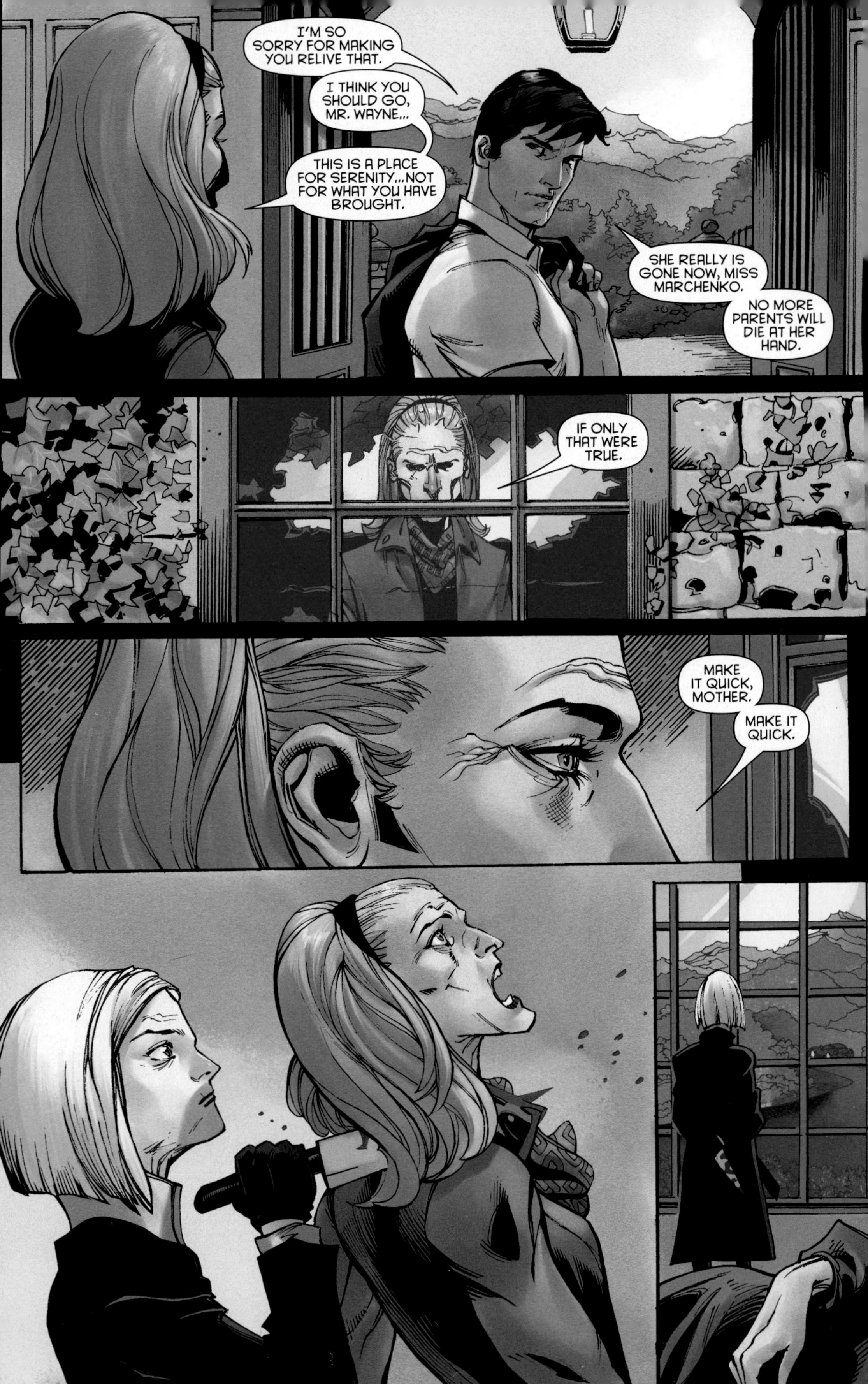
I'M SO SORRY FOR MAKING YOU RELIVE THAT.
I THINK YOU SHOULD GO, MR. WAYNE...
THIS IS A PLACE FOR SERENITY...NOT FOR WHAT YOU HAVE BROUGHT.
SHE REALLY IS GONE NOW, MISS MARCHENKO.
NO MORE PARENTS WILL DIE AT HER HAND.
IF ONLY THAT WERE TRUE.
MAKE IT QUICK, MOTHER.
MAKE IT QUICK.

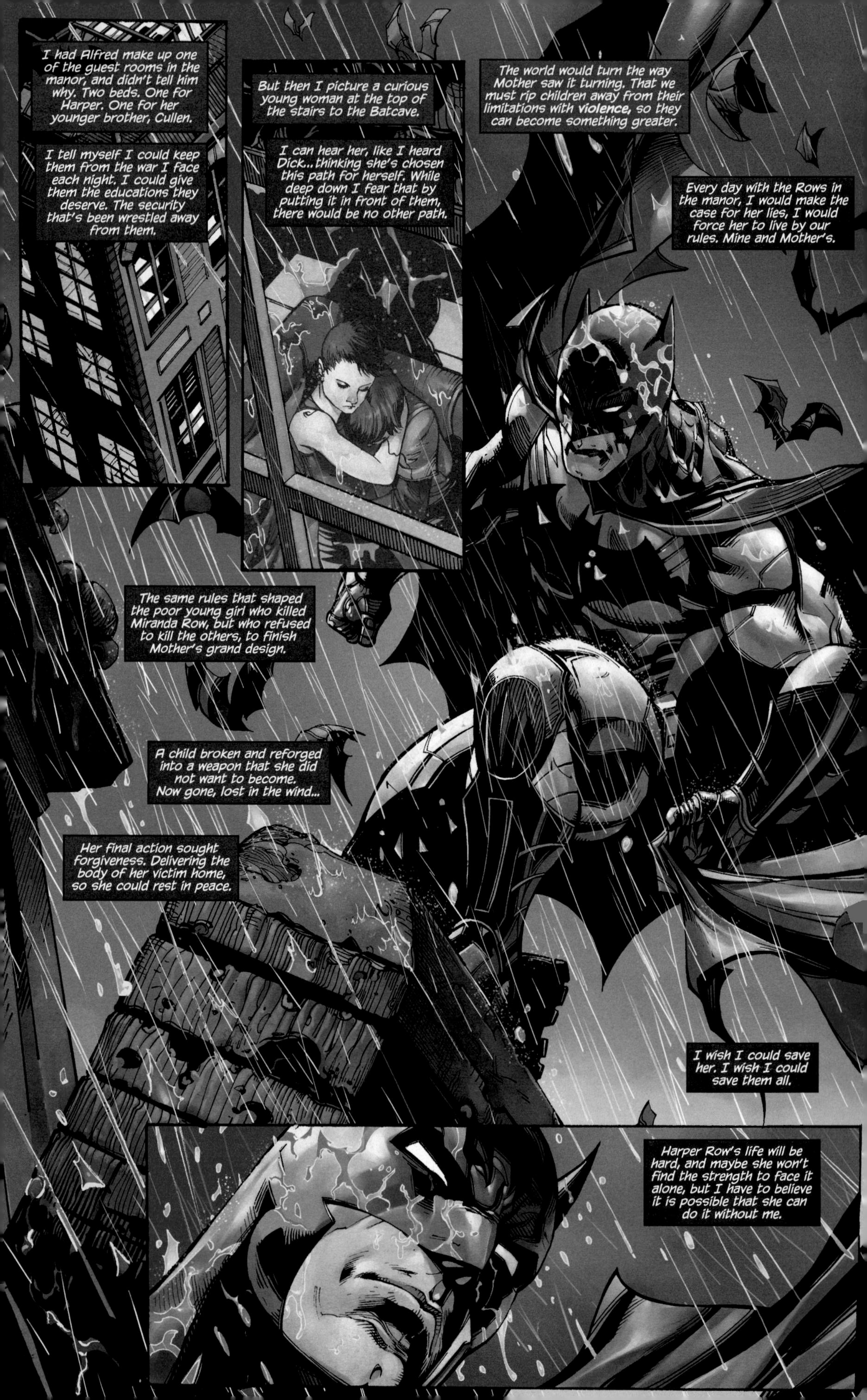
I had Alfred make up one of the guest rooms in the manor, and didn't tell him why. Two beds. One for Harper. One for her younger brother, Cullen.
I tell myself I could keep them from the war I face each night. I could give them the educations they deserve. The security that's been wrestled away from them.
But then I picture a curious young woman at the top of the stairs to the Batcave.
I can hear her, like I heard Dick...thinking she's chosen this path for herself. While deep down I fear that by putting it in front of them, there would be no other path.
The world would turn the way Mother saw it turning. That we must rip children away from their limitations with **violence**, so they can become something greater.
Every day with the Rows in the manor, I would make the case for her lies, I would force her to live by our rules. Mine and Mother's.
The same rules that shaped the poor young girl who killed Miranda Row, but who refused to kill the others, to finish Mother's grand design.
A child broken and reforged into a weapon that she did not want to become. Now gone, lost in the wind...
Her final action sought forgiveness. Delivering the body of her victim home, so she could rest in peace.
I wish I could save her. I wish I could save them all.
Harper Row's life will be hard, and maybe she won't find the strength to face it alone, but I have to believe it is possible that she can do it without me.

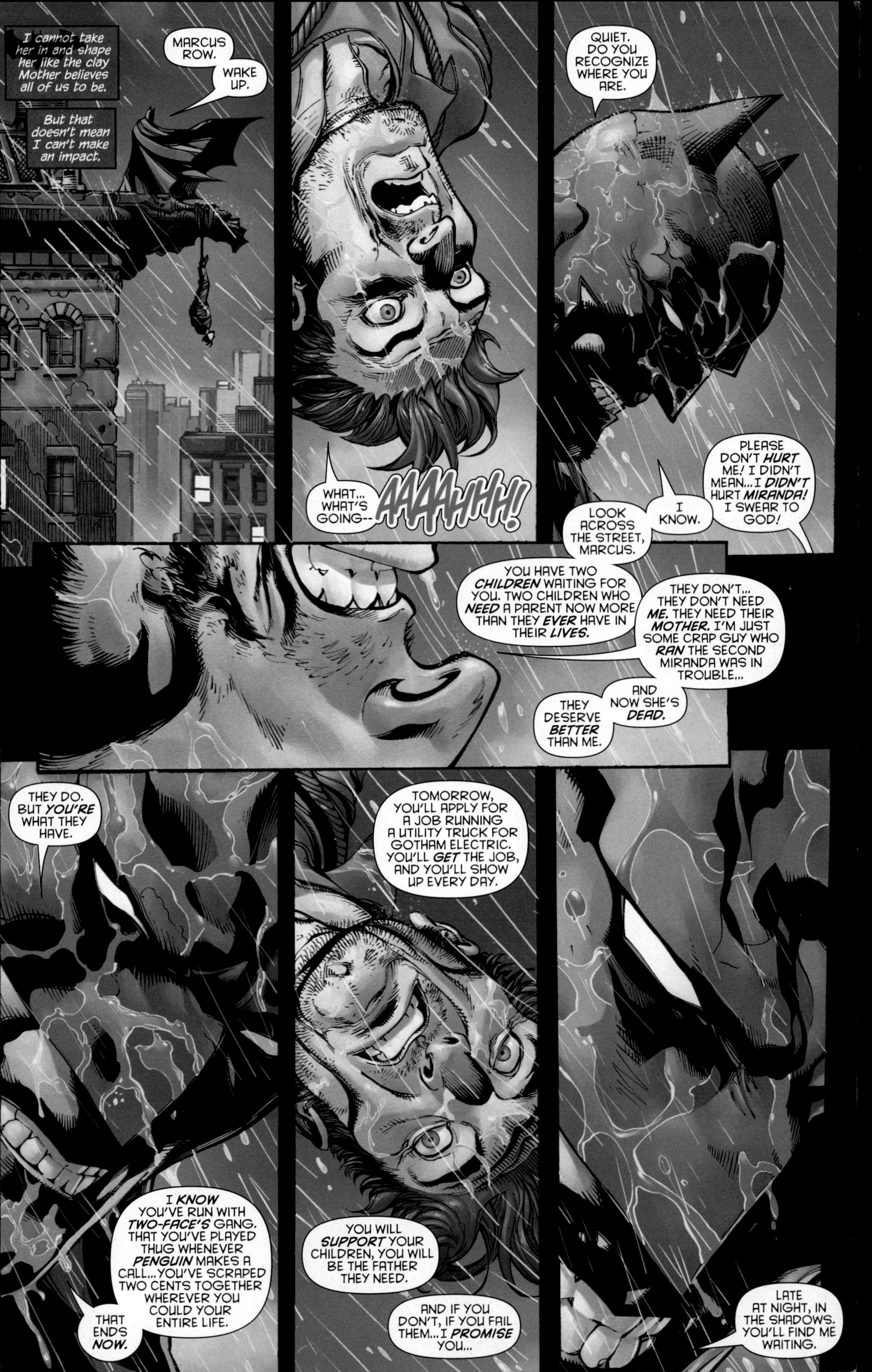
I cannot take her in and shape her like the clay Mother believes all of us to be.
But that doesn't mean I can't make an impact.
MARCUS ROW.
WAKE UP.
WHAT... WHAT'S GOING--
AAAAHHH!
QUIET. DO YOU RECOGNIZE WHERE YOU ARE.
PLEASE DON'T HURT ME! I DIDN'T MEAN...I DIDN'T HURT MIRANDA! I SWEAR TO GOD!
I KNOW.
LOOK ACROSS THE STREET, MARCUS.
YOU HAVE TWO CHILDREN WAITING FOR YOU. TWO CHILDREN WHO NEED A PARENT NOW MORE THAN THEY EVER HAVE IN THEIR LIVES.
THEY DON'T... THEY DON'T NEED ME. THEY NEED THEIR MOTHER. I'M JUST SOME CRAP GUY WHO RAN THE SECOND MIRANDA WAS IN TROUBLE...
AND NOW SHE'S DEAD.
THEY DESERVE BETTER THAN ME.
THEY DO. BUT YOU'RE WHAT THEY HAVE.
I KNOW YOU'VE RUN WITH TWO-FACE'S GANG. THAT YOU'VE PLAYED THUG WHENEVER PENGUIN MAKES A CALL...YOU'VE SCRAPED TWO CENTS TOGETHER WHEREVER YOU COULD YOUR ENTIRE LIFE.
THAT ENDS NOW.
TOMORROW, YOU'LL APPLY FOR A JOB RUNNING A UTILITY TRUCK FOR GOTHAM ELECTRIC. YOU'LL GET THE JOB, AND YOU'LL SHOW UP EVERY DAY.
YOU WILL SUPPORT YOUR CHILDREN, YOU WILL BE THE FATHER THEY NEED.
AND IF YOU DON'T, IF YOU FAIL THEM...I PROMISE YOU...
LATE AT NIGHT, IN THE SHADOWS. YOU'LL FIND ME WAITING.

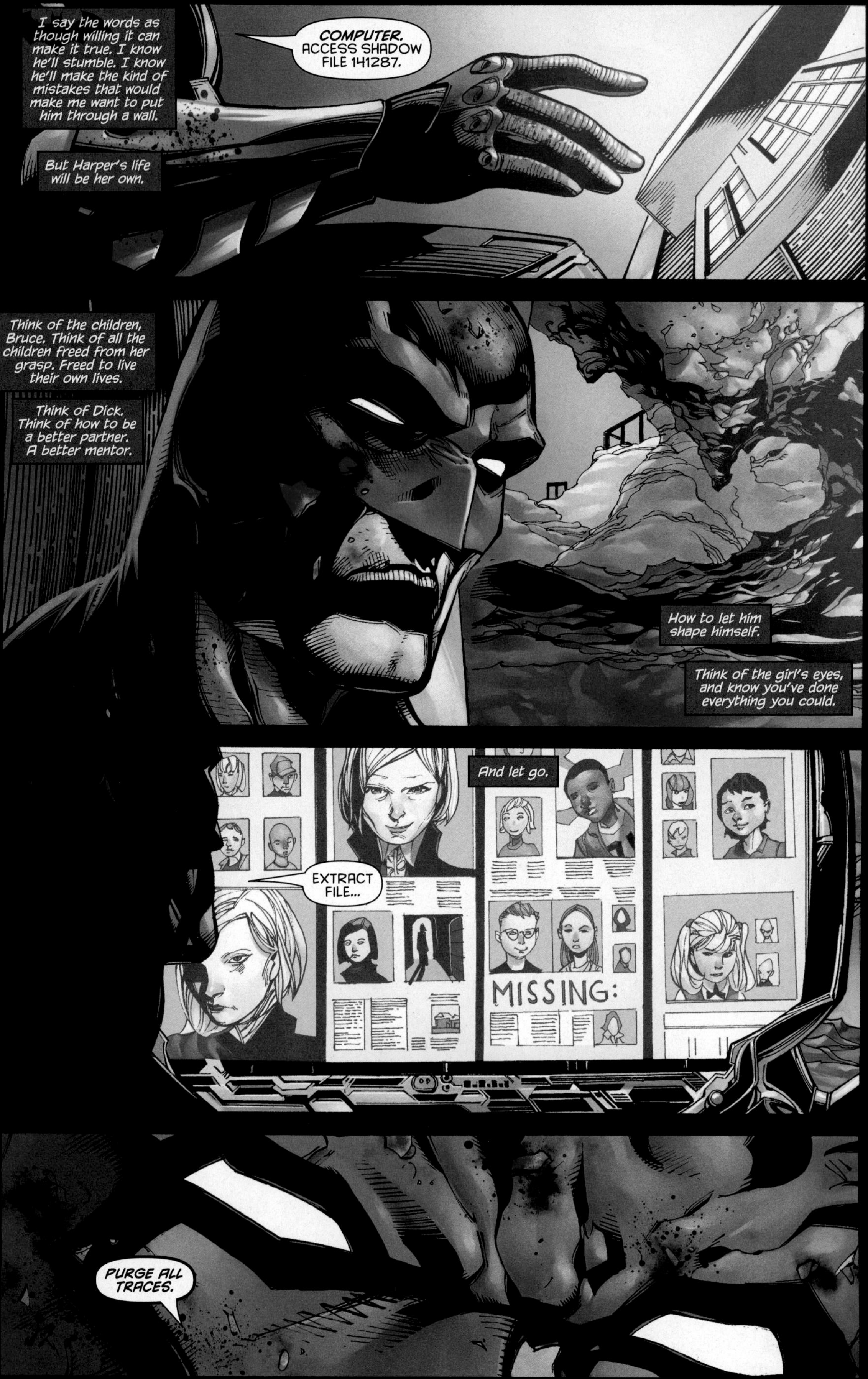
I say the words as though willing it can make it true. I know he'll stumble. I know he'll make the kind of mistakes that would make me want to put him through a wall.
COMPUTER. ACCESS SHADOW FILE 141287.
But Harper's life will be her own.
Think of the children, Bruce. Think of all the children freed from her grasp. Freed to live their own lives.
Think of Dick. Think of how to be a better partner. A better mentor.
How to let him shape himself.
Think of the girl's eyes, and know you've done everything you could.
And let go.
EXTRACT FILE...
MISSING:
PURGE ALL TRACES.

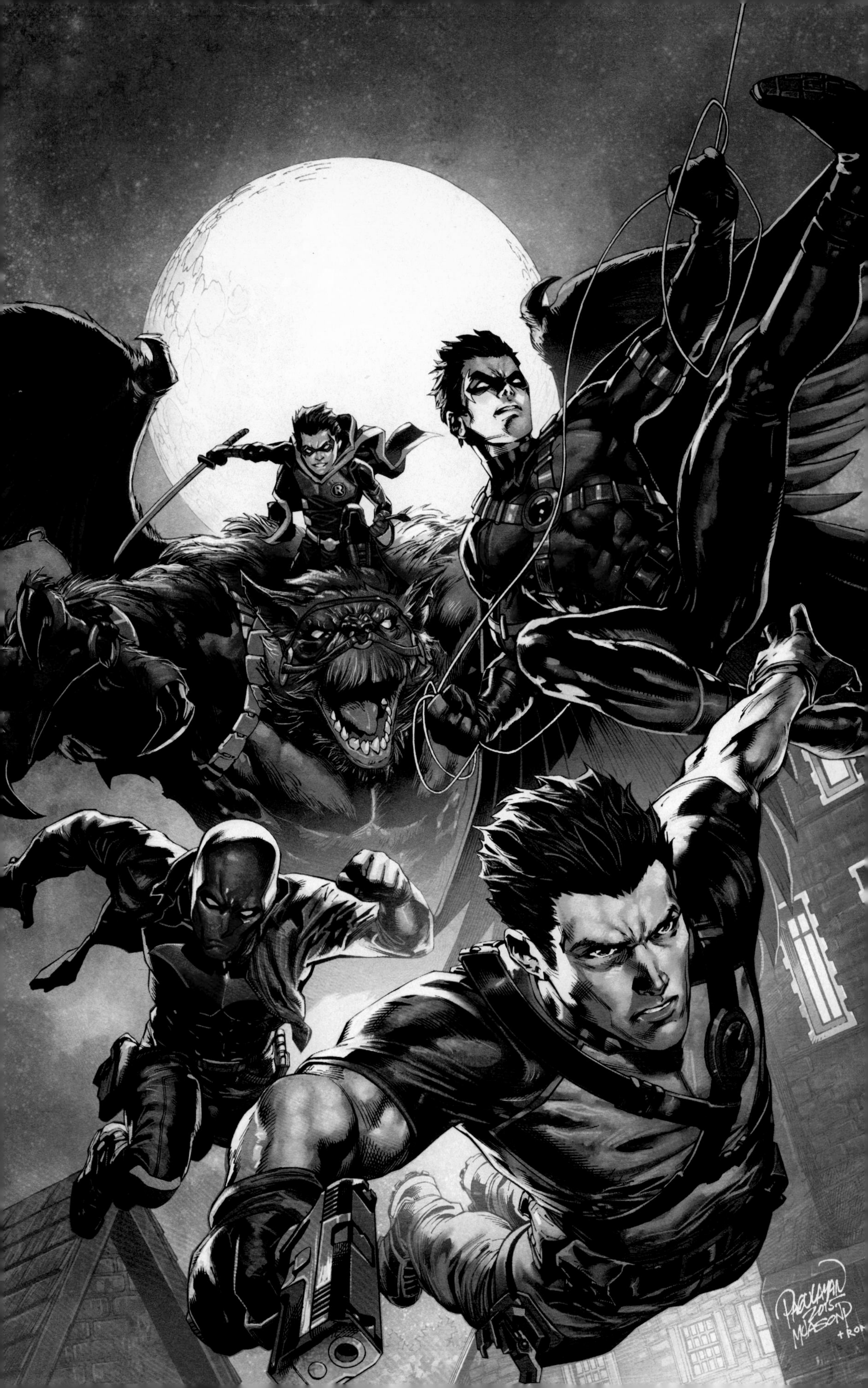

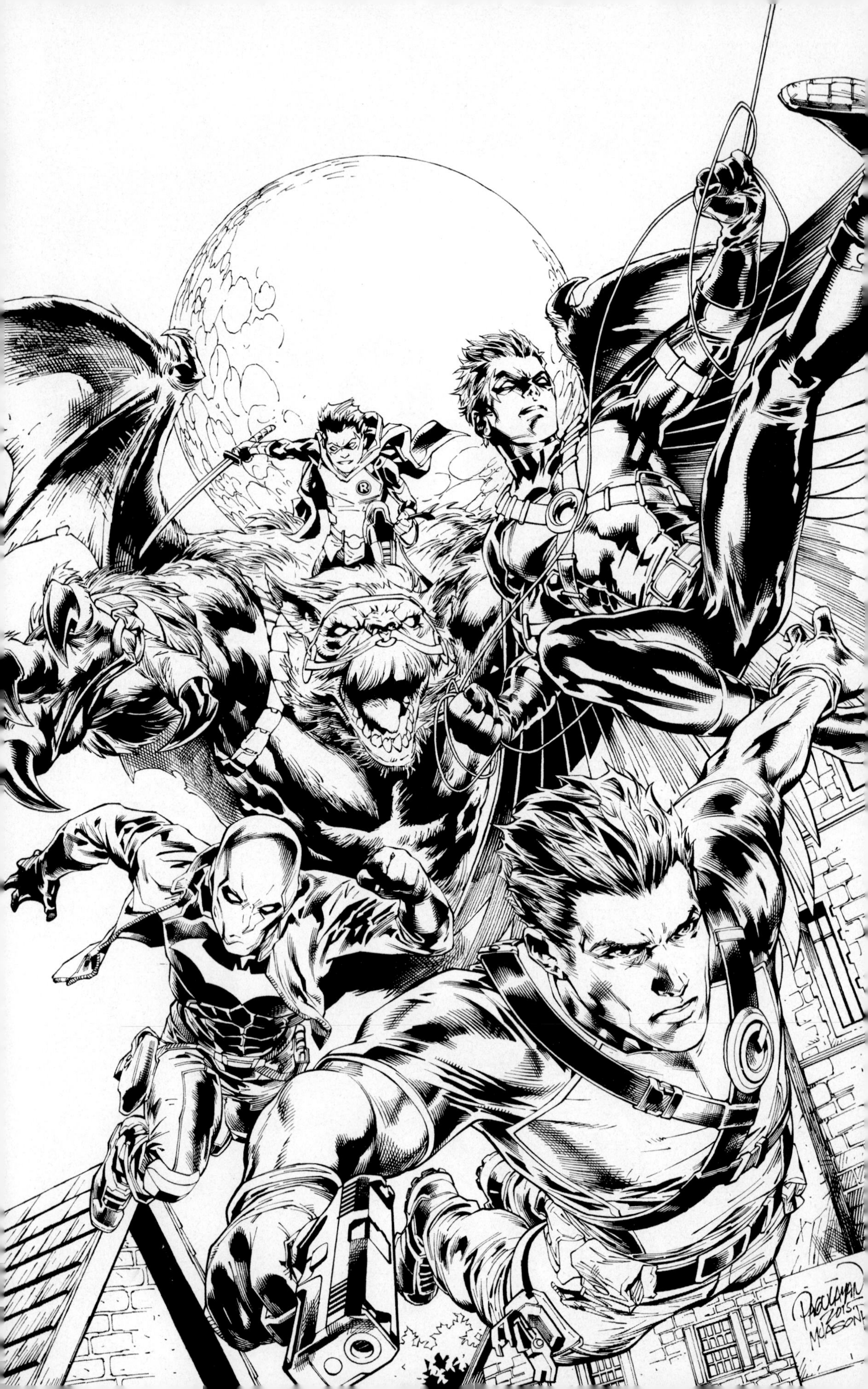

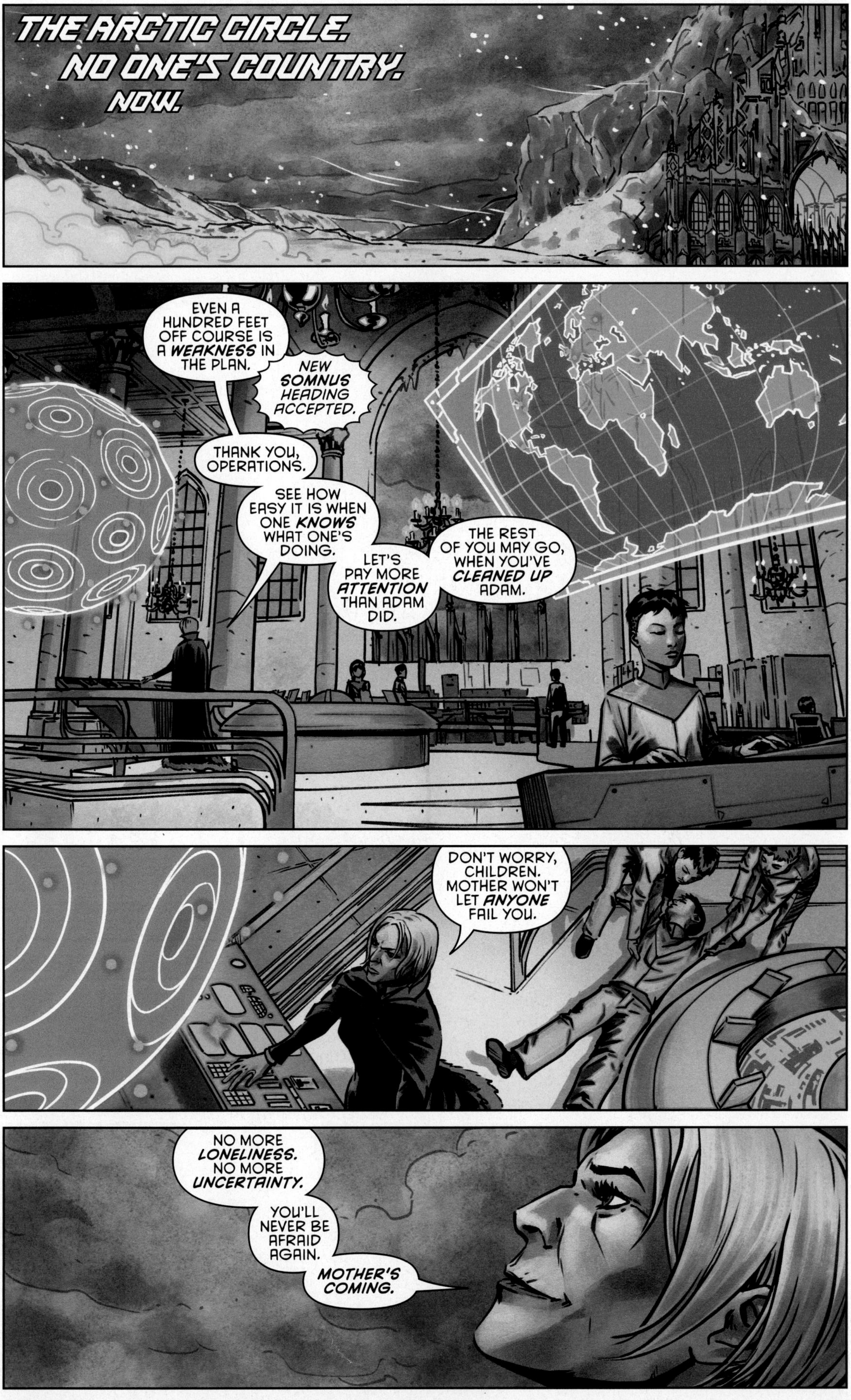
THE ARCTIC CIRCLE.
NO ONE'S COUNTRY.
NOW.
EVEN A HUNDRED FEET OFF COURSE IS A WEAKNESS IN THE PLAN.
NEW SOMNUS HEADING ACCEPTED.
THANK YOU, OPERATIONS.
SEE HOW EASY IT IS WHEN ONE KNOWS WHAT ONE'S DOING.
LET'S PAY MORE ATTENTION THAN ADAM DID.
THE REST OF YOU MAY GO, WHEN YOU'VE CLEANED UP ADAM.
DON'T WORRY, CHILDREN. MOTHER WON'T LET ANYONE FAIL YOU.
NO MORE LONELINESS. NO MORE UNCERTAINTY.
YOU'LL NEVER BE AFRAID AGAIN.
MOTHER'S COMING.

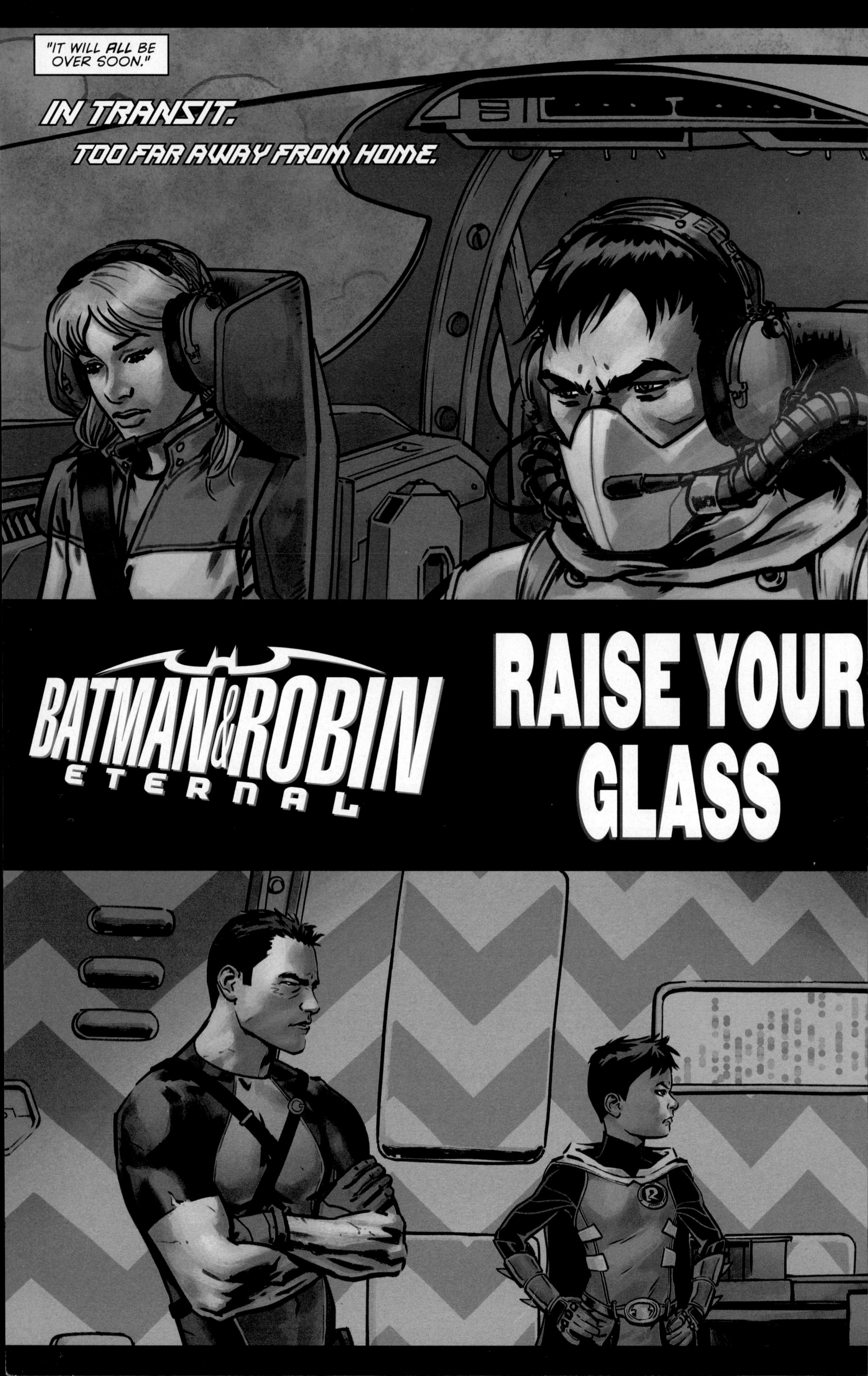
"IT WILL ALL BE OVER SOON."
IN TRANSIT.
TOO FAR AWAY FROM HOME.
BATMAN & ROBIN ETERNAL
RAISE YOUR GLASS

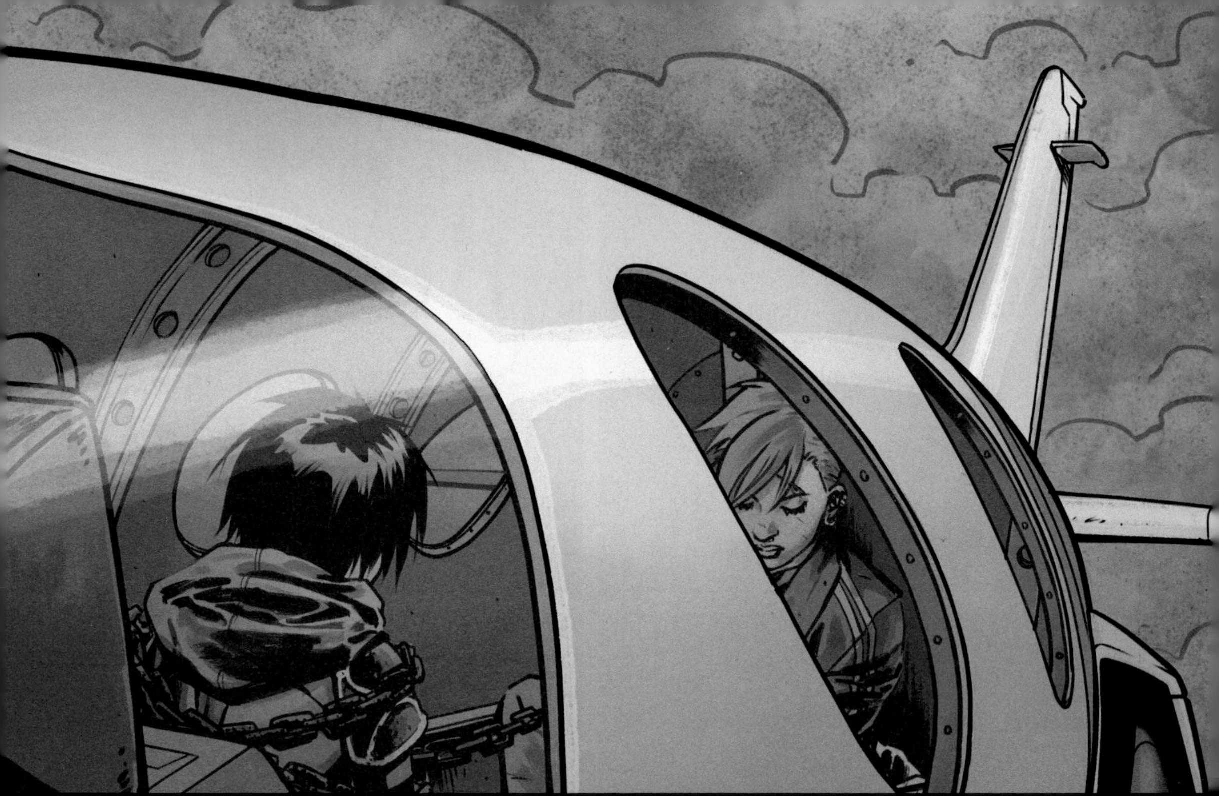

JAMES TYNION IV & SCOTT SNYDER STORY
GENEVIEVE VALENTINE SCRIPT
FERNANDO BLANCO ART
JOHN RAUCH COLORS
COREY BREEN LETTERS
CARLO PAGULAYAN. JASON PAZ & ROMULO FAJARDO JR. COVER

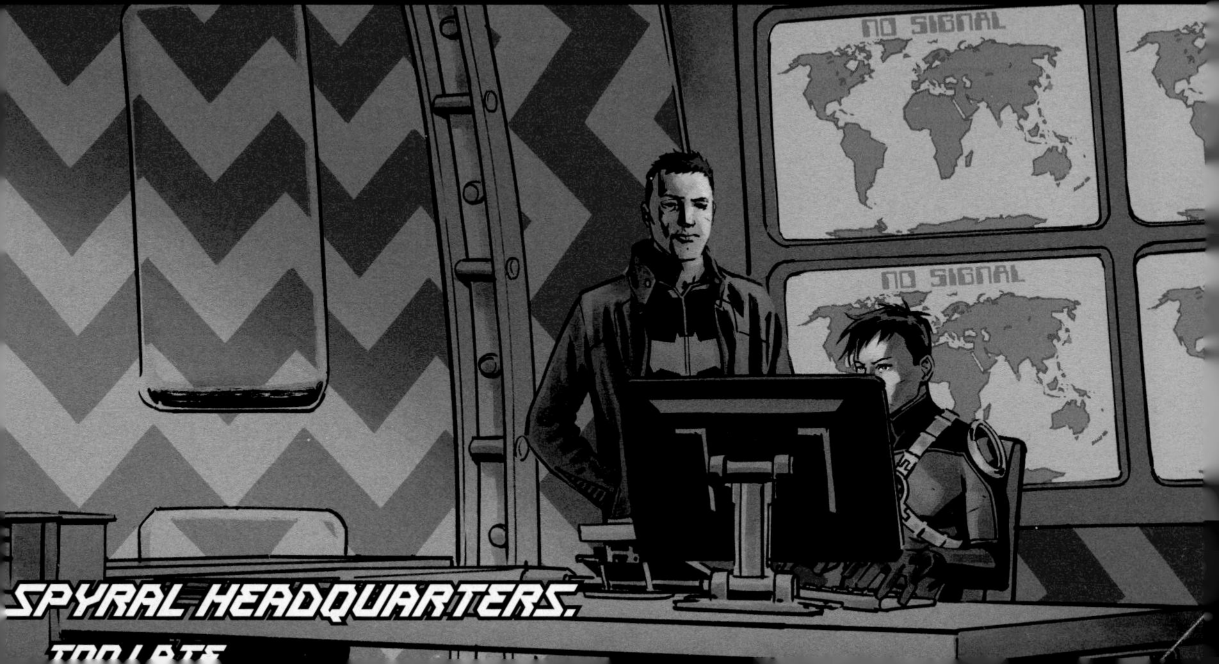
NO SIGNAL
NO SIGNAL
SPYRAL HEADQUARTERS.

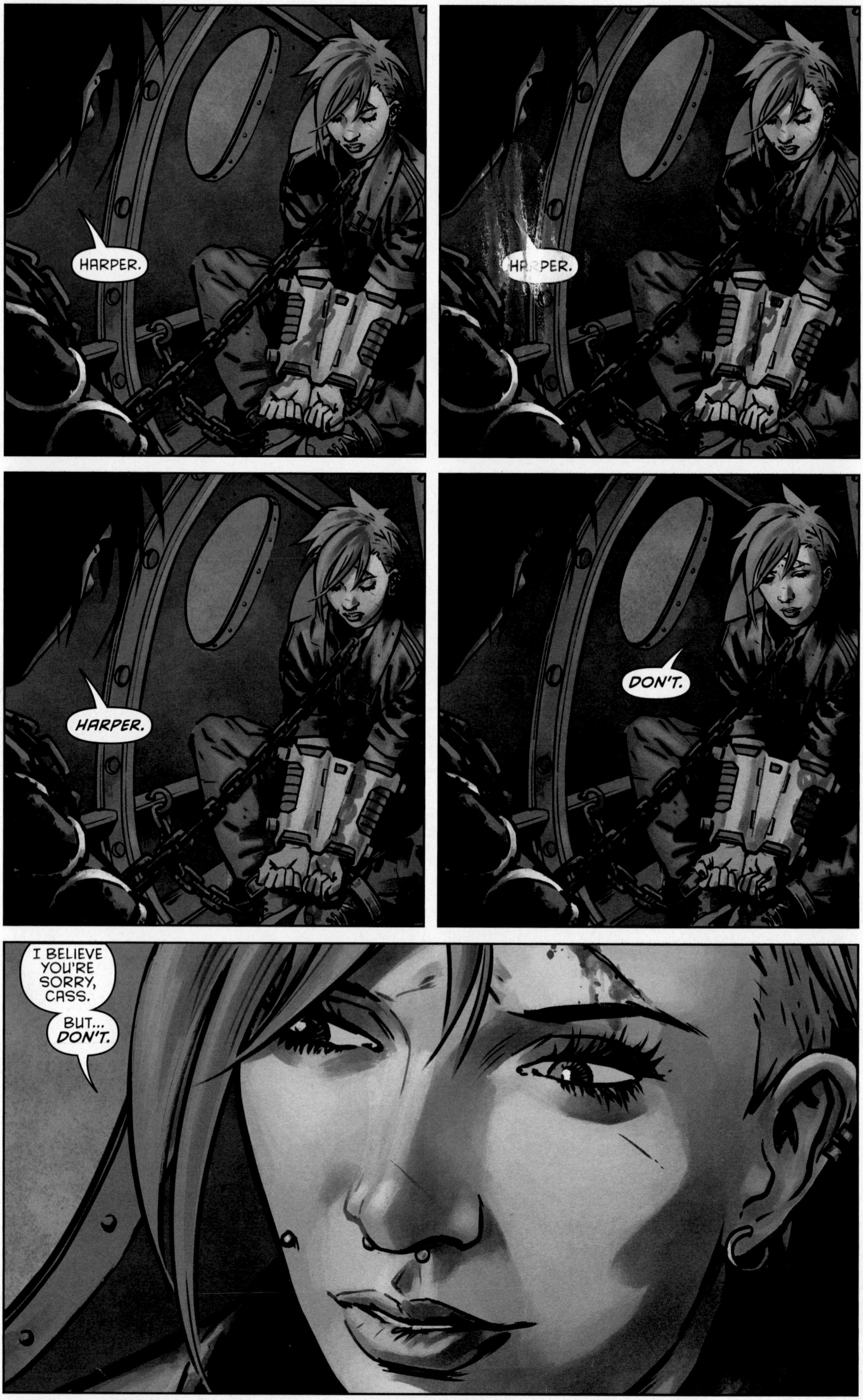
HARPER.
HARPER.
HARPER.
DON'T.
I BELIEVE YOU'RE SORRY, CASS.
BUT... DON'T.

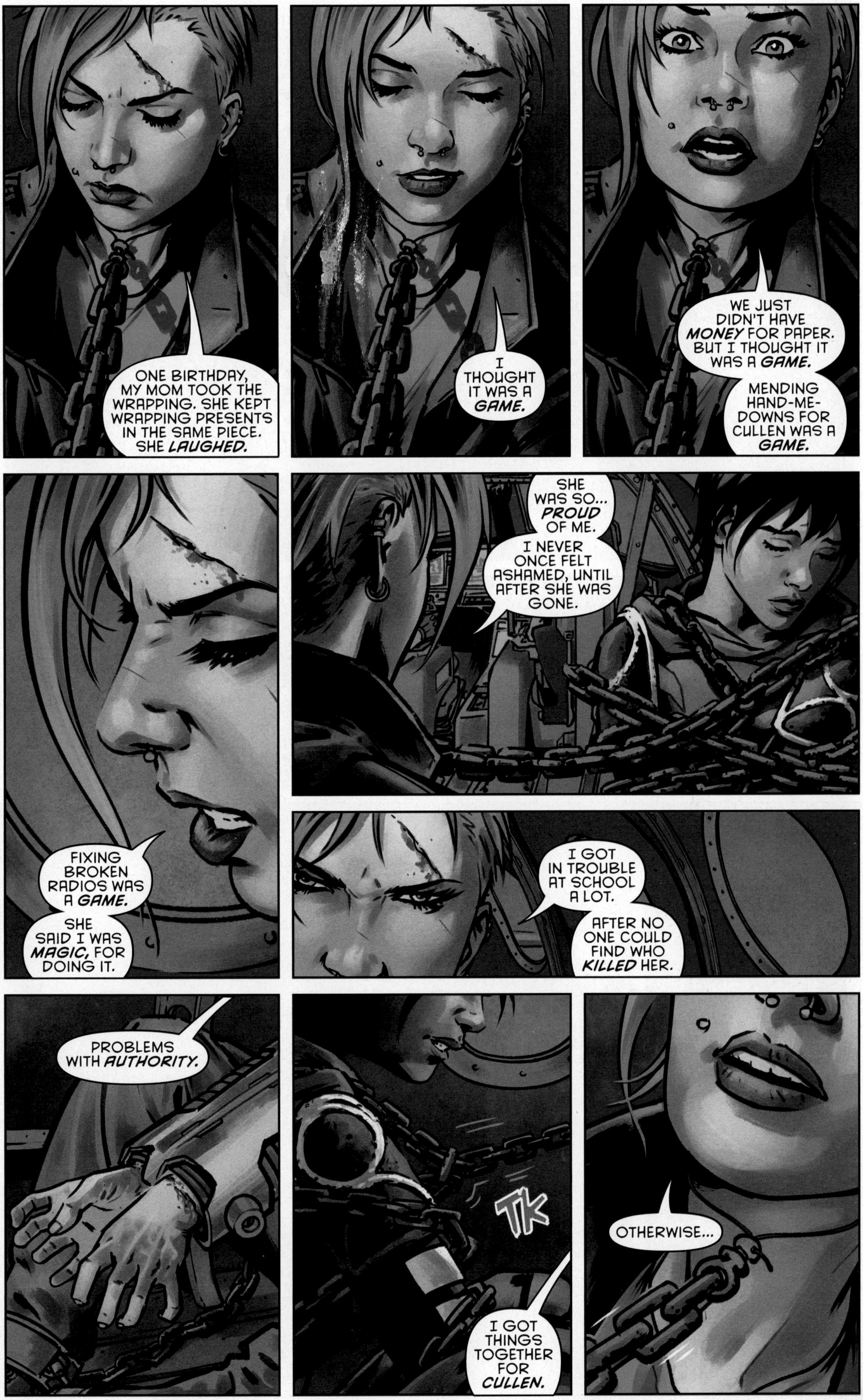
ONE BIRTHDAY, MY MOM TOOK THE WRAPPING. SHE KEPT WRAPPING PRESENTS IN THE SAME PIECE. SHE *LAUGHED.*
I THOUGHT IT WAS A *GAME.*
WE JUST DIDN'T HAVE *MONEY* FOR PAPER. BUT I THOUGHT IT WAS A *GAME.*
MENDING HAND-ME-DOWNS FOR CULLEN WAS A *GAME.*
FIXING BROKEN RADIOS WAS A *GAME.*
SHE SAID I WAS *MAGIC,* FOR DOING IT.
SHE WAS SO... *PROUD* OF ME.
I NEVER ONCE FELT ASHAMED, UNTIL AFTER SHE WAS GONE.
I GOT IN TROUBLE AT SCHOOL A LOT.
AFTER NO ONE COULD FIND WHO *KILLED* HER.
PROBLEMS WITH *AUTHORITY.*
TK
I GOT THINGS TOGETHER FOR *CULLEN.*
OTHERWISE...

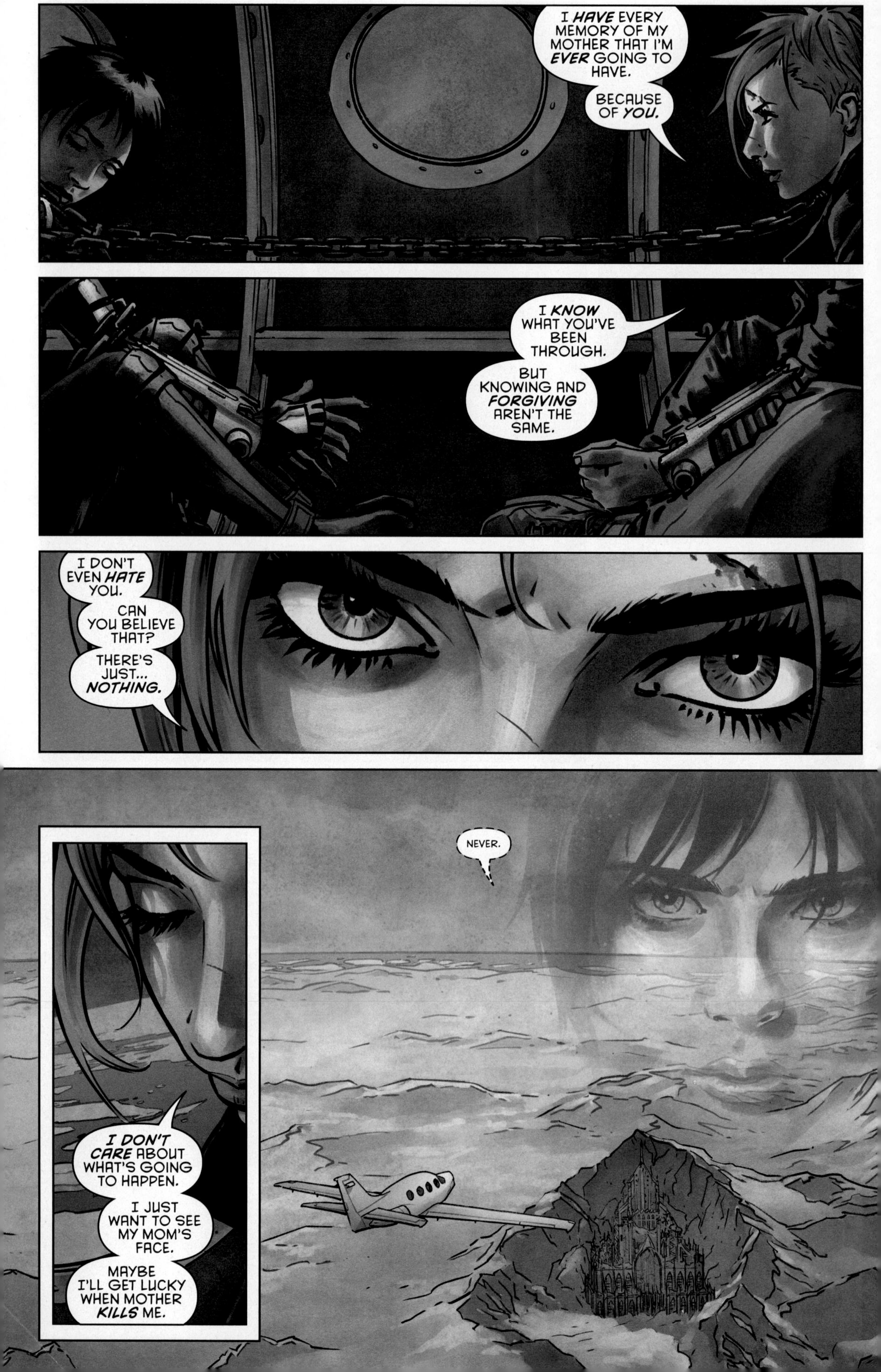
I HAVE EVERY MEMORY OF MY MOTHER THAT I'M EVER GOING TO HAVE.
BECAUSE OF YOU.
I KNOW WHAT YOU'VE BEEN THROUGH.
BUT KNOWING AND FORGIVING AREN'T THE SAME.
I DON'T EVEN HATE YOU.
CAN YOU BELIEVE THAT?
THERE'S JUST... NOTHING.
NEVER.
I DON'T CARE ABOUT WHAT'S GOING TO HAPPEN.
I JUST WANT TO SEE MY MOM'S FACE.
MAYBE I'LL GET LUCKY WHEN MOTHER KILLS ME.

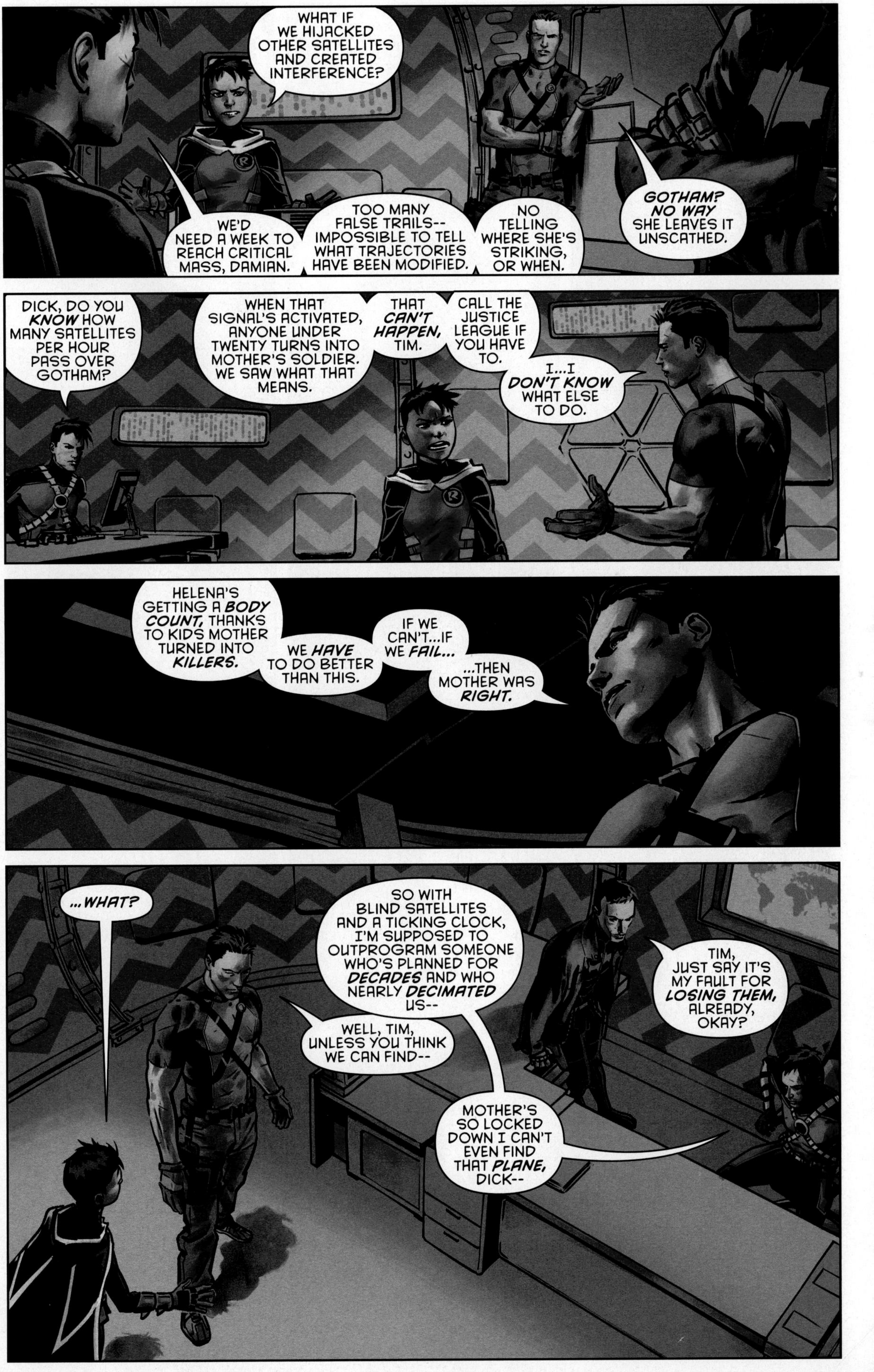
WHAT IF WE HIJACKED OTHER SATELLITES AND CREATED INTERFERENCE?
WE'D NEED A WEEK TO REACH CRITICAL MASS, DAMIAN.
TOO MANY FALSE TRAILS-- IMPOSSIBLE TO TELL WHAT TRAJECTORIES HAVE BEEN MODIFIED.
NO TELLING WHERE SHE'S STRIKING, OR WHEN.
GOTHAM? NO WAY SHE LEAVES IT UNSCATHED.
DICK, DO YOU KNOW HOW MANY SATELLITES PER HOUR PASS OVER GOTHAM?
WHEN THAT SIGNAL'S ACTIVATED, ANYONE UNDER TWENTY TURNS INTO MOTHER'S SOLDIER. WE SAW WHAT THAT MEANS.
THAT CAN'T HAPPEN, TIM.
CALL THE JUSTICE LEAGUE IF YOU HAVE TO.
I...I DON'T KNOW WHAT ELSE TO DO.
HELENA'S GETTING A BODY COUNT, THANKS TO KIDS MOTHER TURNED INTO KILLERS.
WE HAVE TO DO BETTER THAN THIS.
IF WE CAN'T...IF WE FAIL...
...THEN MOTHER WAS RIGHT.
...WHAT?
SO WITH BLIND SATELLITES AND A TICKING CLOCK, I'M SUPPOSED TO OUTPROGRAM SOMEONE WHO'S PLANNED FOR DECADES AND WHO NEARLY DECIMATED US--
WELL, TIM, UNLESS YOU THINK WE CAN FIND--
MOTHER'S SO LOCKED DOWN I CAN'T EVEN FIND THAT PLANE, DICK--
TIM, JUST SAY IT'S MY FAULT FOR LOSING THEM, ALREADY, OKAY?

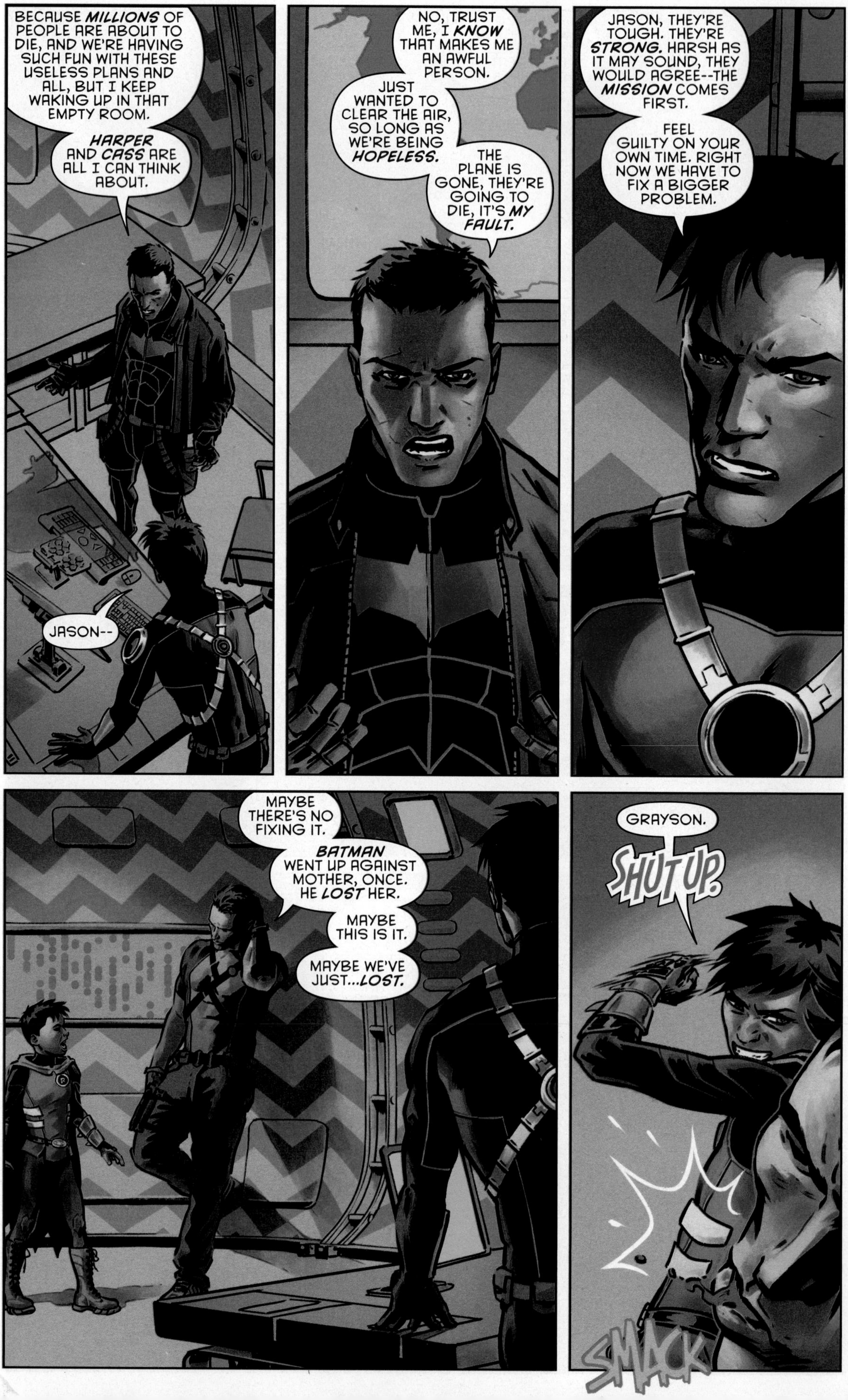
BECAUSE MILLIONS OF PEOPLE ARE ABOUT TO DIE, AND WE'RE HAVING SUCH FUN WITH THESE USELESS PLANS AND ALL, BUT I KEEP WAKING UP IN THAT EMPTY ROOM.
HARPER AND CASS ARE ALL I CAN THINK ABOUT.
JASON--
NO, TRUST ME, I KNOW THAT MAKES ME AN AWFUL PERSON.
JUST WANTED TO CLEAR THE AIR, SO LONG AS WE'RE BEING HOPELESS.
THE PLANE IS GONE, THEY'RE GOING TO DIE, IT'S MY FAULT.
JASON, THEY'RE TOUGH. THEY'RE STRONG. HARSH AS IT MAY SOUND, THEY WOULD AGREE--THE MISSION COMES FIRST.
FEEL GUILTY ON YOUR OWN TIME. RIGHT NOW WE HAVE TO FIX A BIGGER PROBLEM.
MAYBE THERE'S NO FIXING IT.
BATMAN WENT UP AGAINST MOTHER, ONCE. HE LOST HER.
MAYBE THIS IS IT.
MAYBE WE'VE JUST...LOST.
GRAYSON.
SHUT UP.
SMACK

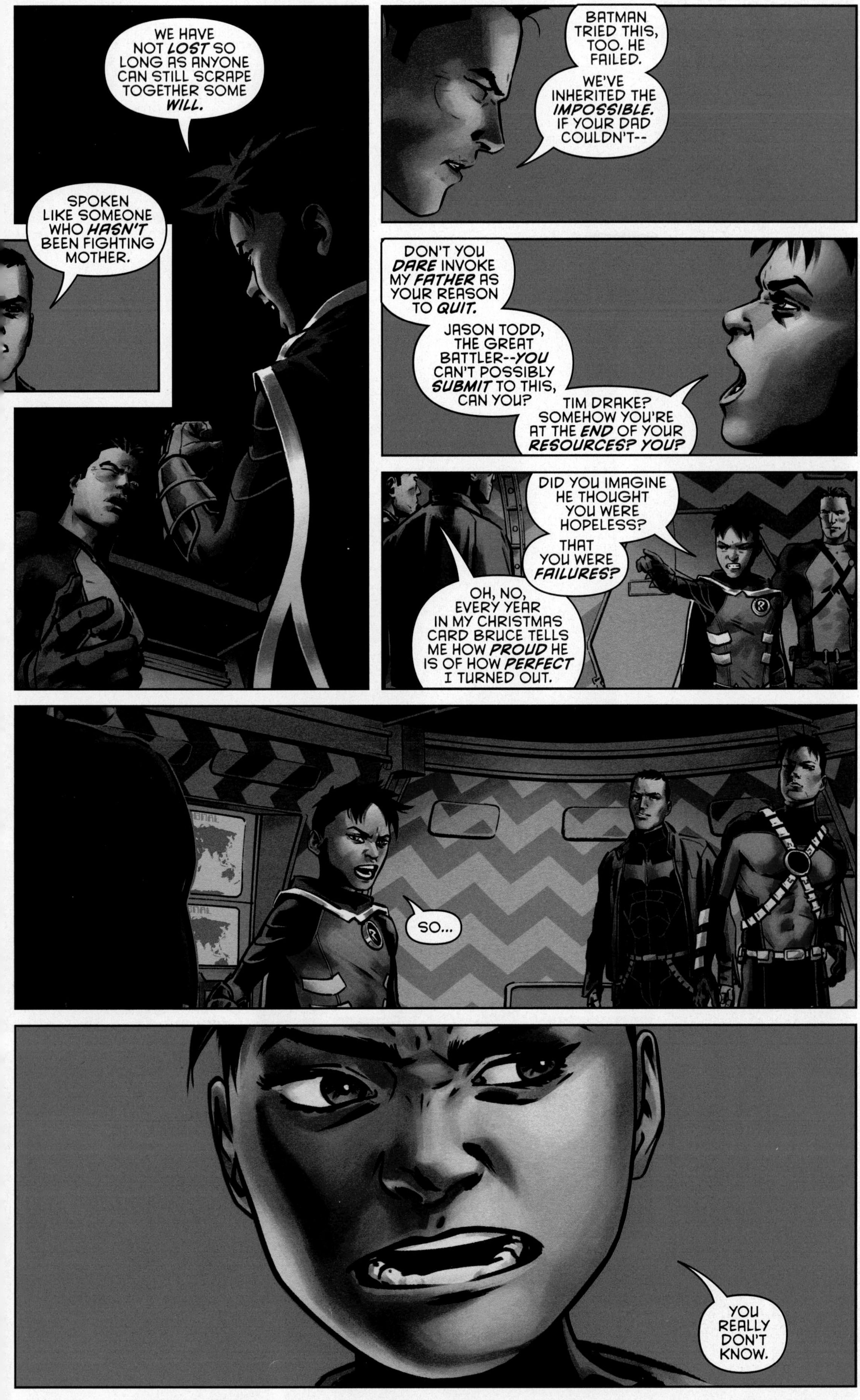
WE HAVE NOT LOST SO LONG AS ANYONE CAN STILL SCRAPE TOGETHER SOME WILL.
SPOKEN LIKE SOMEONE WHO HASN'T BEEN FIGHTING MOTHER.
BATMAN TRIED THIS, TOO. HE FAILED.
WE'VE INHERITED THE IMPOSSIBLE. IF YOUR DAD COULDN'T--
DON'T YOU DARE INVOKE MY FATHER AS YOUR REASON TO QUIT.
JASON TODD, THE GREAT BATTLER--YOU CAN'T POSSIBLY SUBMIT TO THIS, CAN YOU?
TIM DRAKE? SOMEHOW YOU'RE AT THE END OF YOUR RESOURCES? YOU?
DID YOU IMAGINE HE THOUGHT YOU WERE HOPELESS?
THAT YOU WERE FAILURES?
OH, NO, EVERY YEAR IN MY CHRISTMAS CARD BRUCE TELLS ME HOW PROUD HE IS OF HOW PERFECT I TURNED OUT.
SO...
YOU REALLY DON'T KNOW.

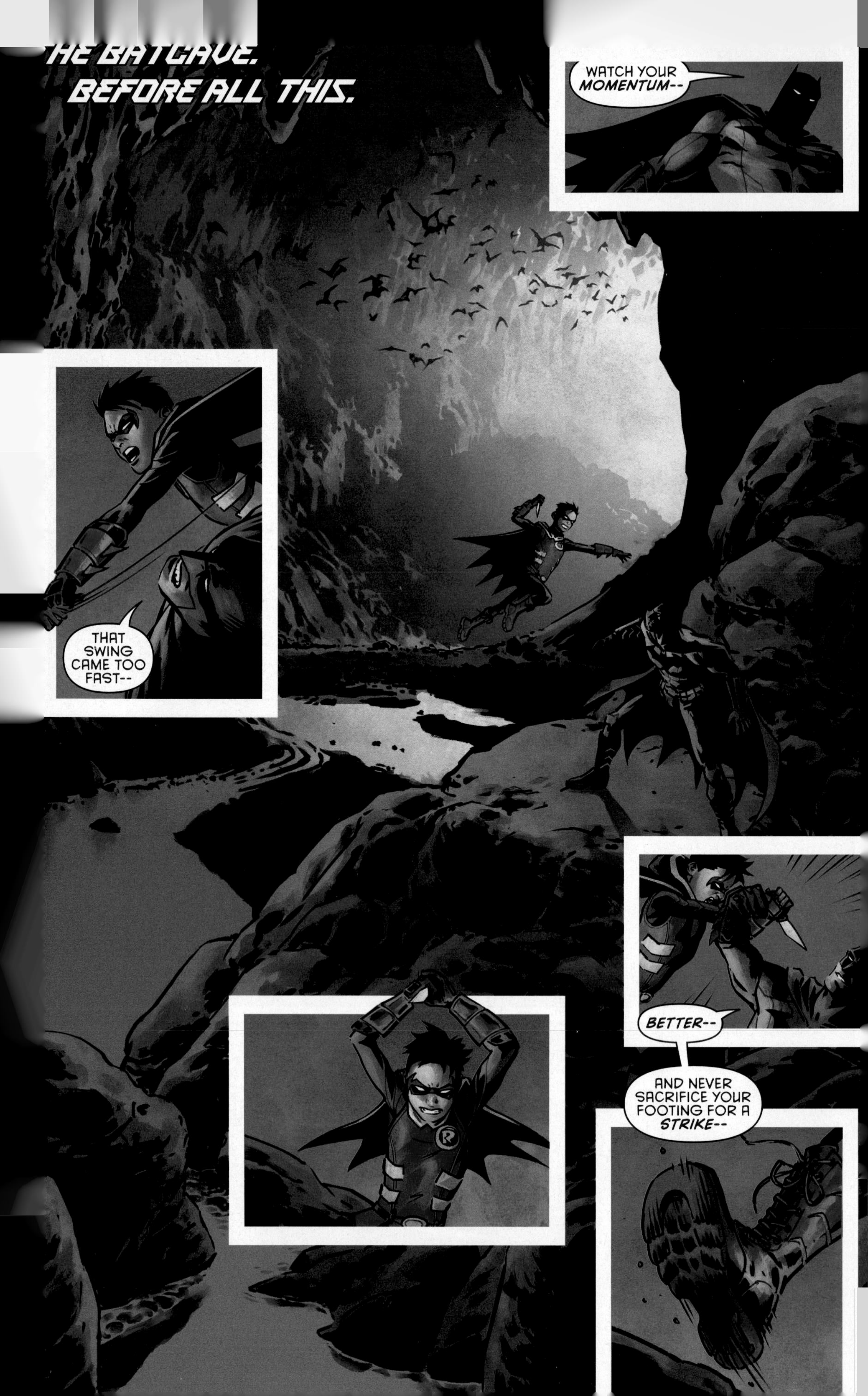
THE BATCAVE.
BEFORE ALL THIS.
WATCH YOUR MOMENTUM--
THAT SWING CAME TOO FAST--
BETTER--
AND NEVER SACRIFICE YOUR FOOTING FOR A STRIKE--

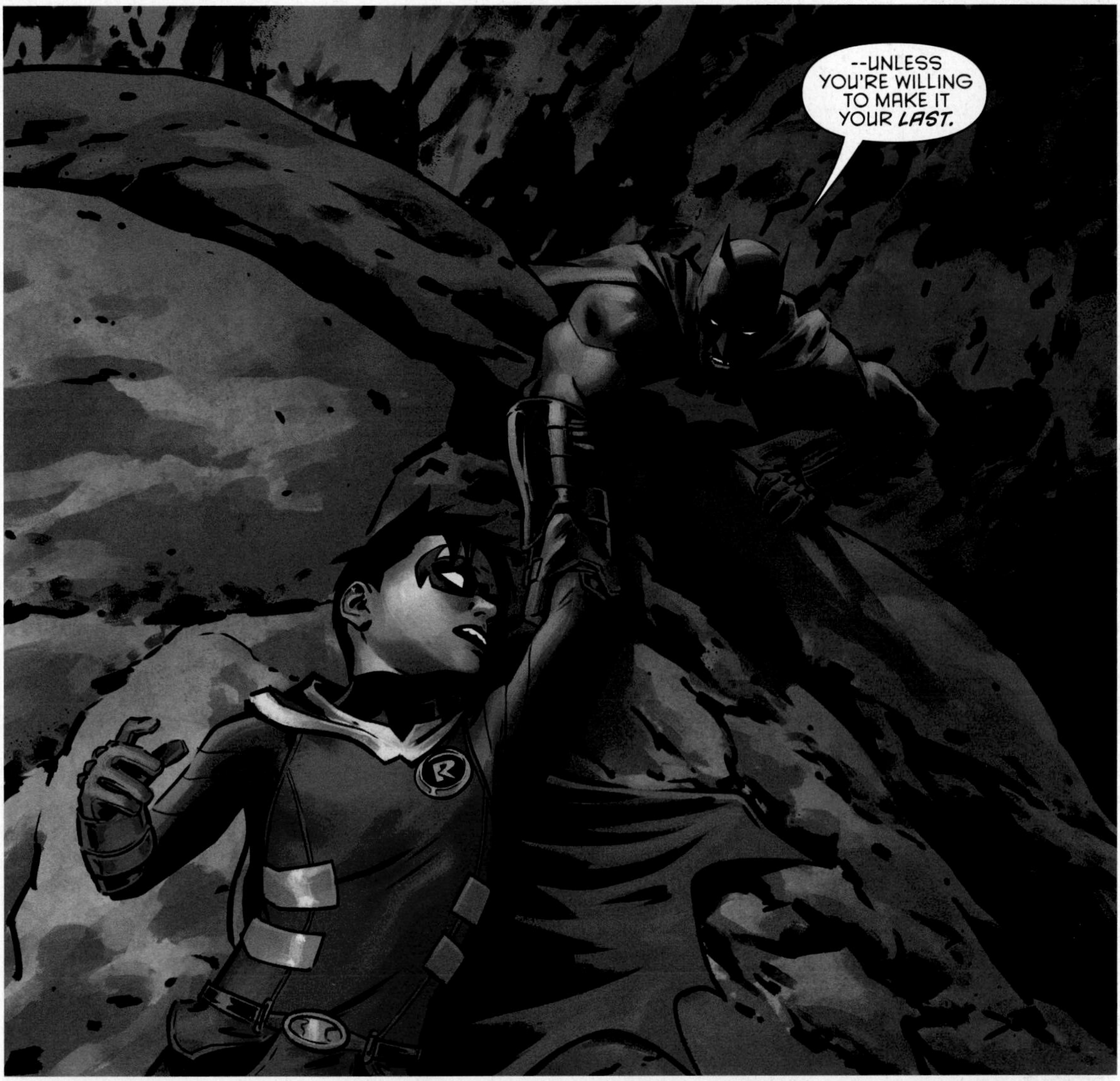
--UNLESS YOU'RE WILLING TO MAKE IT YOUR *LAST.*

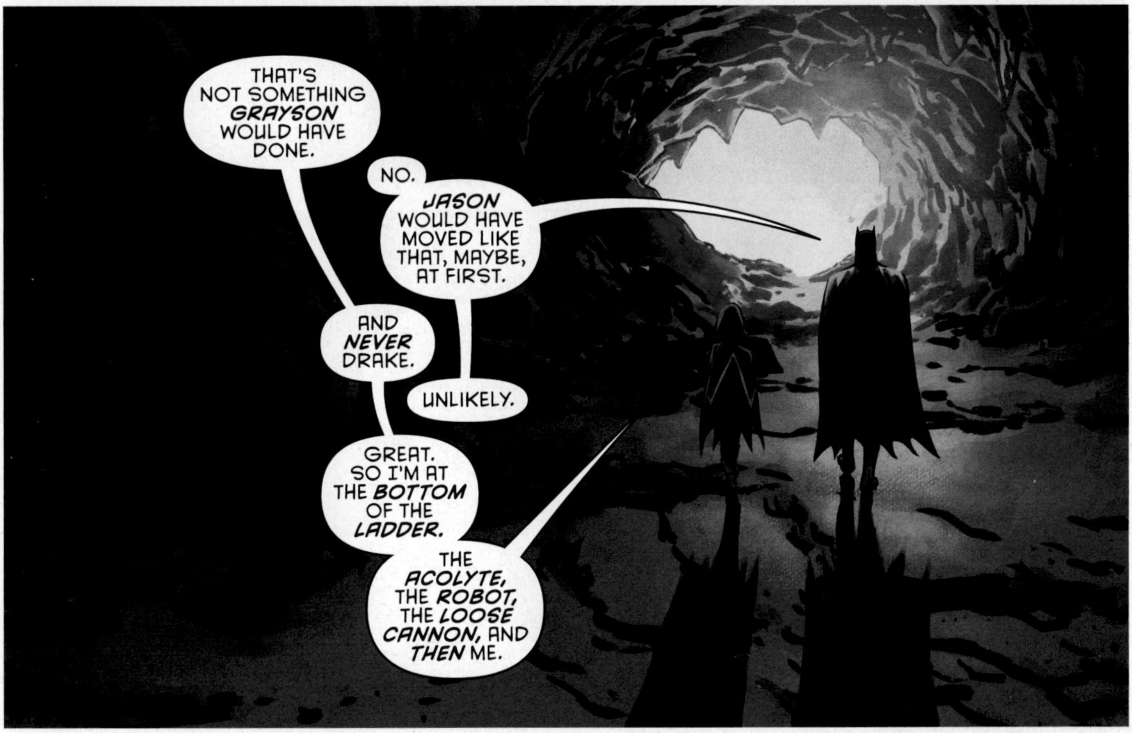
THAT'S NOT SOMETHING *GRAYSON* WOULD HAVE DONE.
NO.
JASON WOULD HAVE MOVED LIKE THAT, MAYBE, AT FIRST.
AND *NEVER* DRAKE.
UNLIKELY.
GREAT. SO I'M AT THE *BOTTOM* OF THE *LADDER.*
THE *ACOLYTE,* THE *ROBOT,* THE *LOOSE CANNON,* AND *THEN* ME.

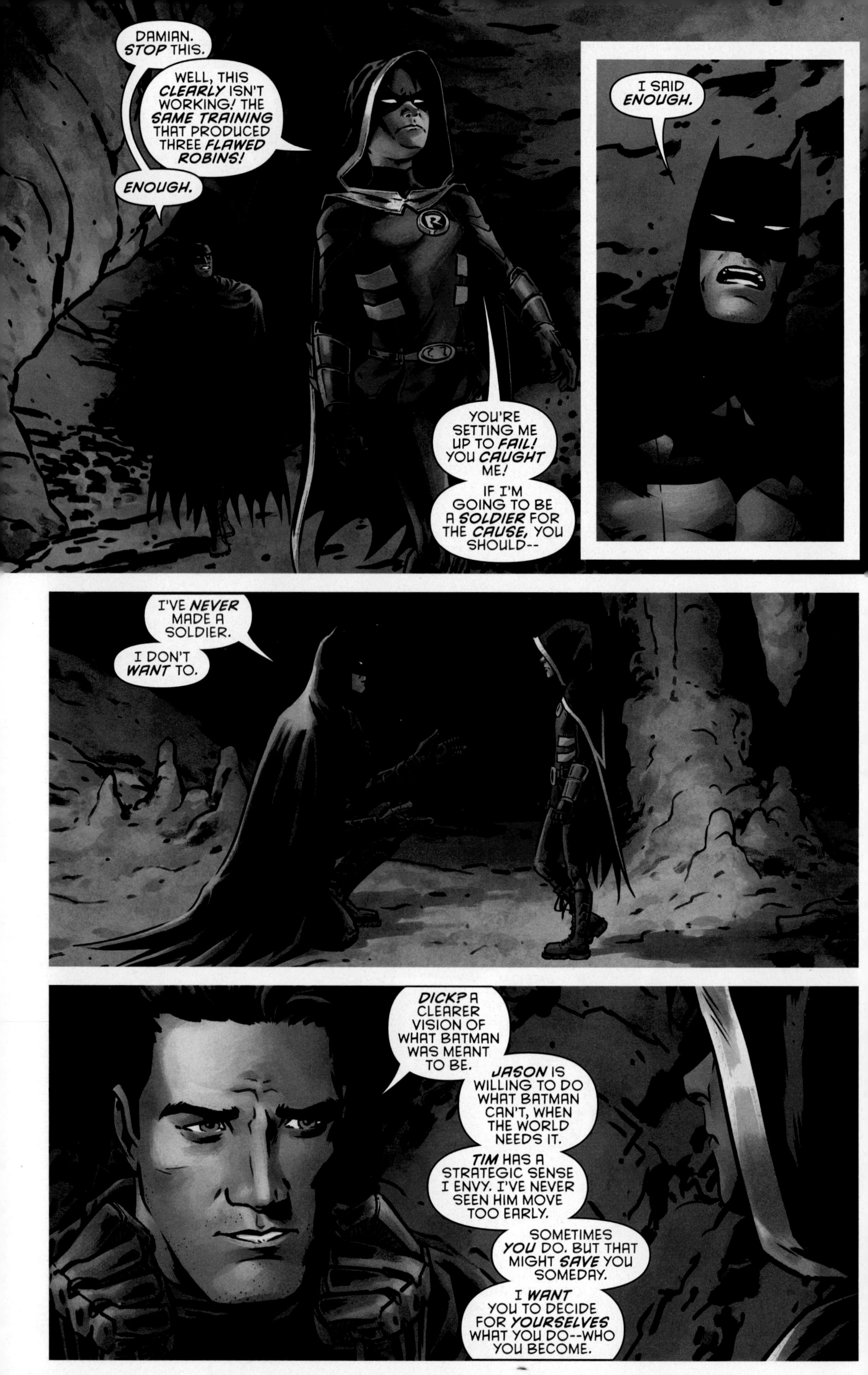
DAMIAN. STOP THIS.
WELL, THIS CLEARLY ISN'T WORKING! THE SAME TRAINING THAT PRODUCED THREE FLAWED ROBINS!
ENOUGH.
YOU'RE SETTING ME UP TO FAIL! YOU CAUGHT ME!
IF I'M GOING TO BE A SOLDIER FOR THE CAUSE, YOU SHOULD--
I SAID ENOUGH.
I'VE NEVER MADE A SOLDIER.
I DON'T WANT TO.
DICK? A CLEARER VISION OF WHAT BATMAN WAS MEANT TO BE.
JASON IS WILLING TO DO WHAT BATMAN CAN'T, WHEN THE WORLD NEEDS IT.
TIM HAS A STRATEGIC SENSE I ENVY. I'VE NEVER SEEN HIM MOVE TOO EARLY.
SOMETIMES YOU DO. BUT THAT MIGHT SAVE YOU SOMEDAY.
I WANT YOU TO DECIDE FOR YOURSELVES WHAT YOU DO--WHO YOU BECOME.

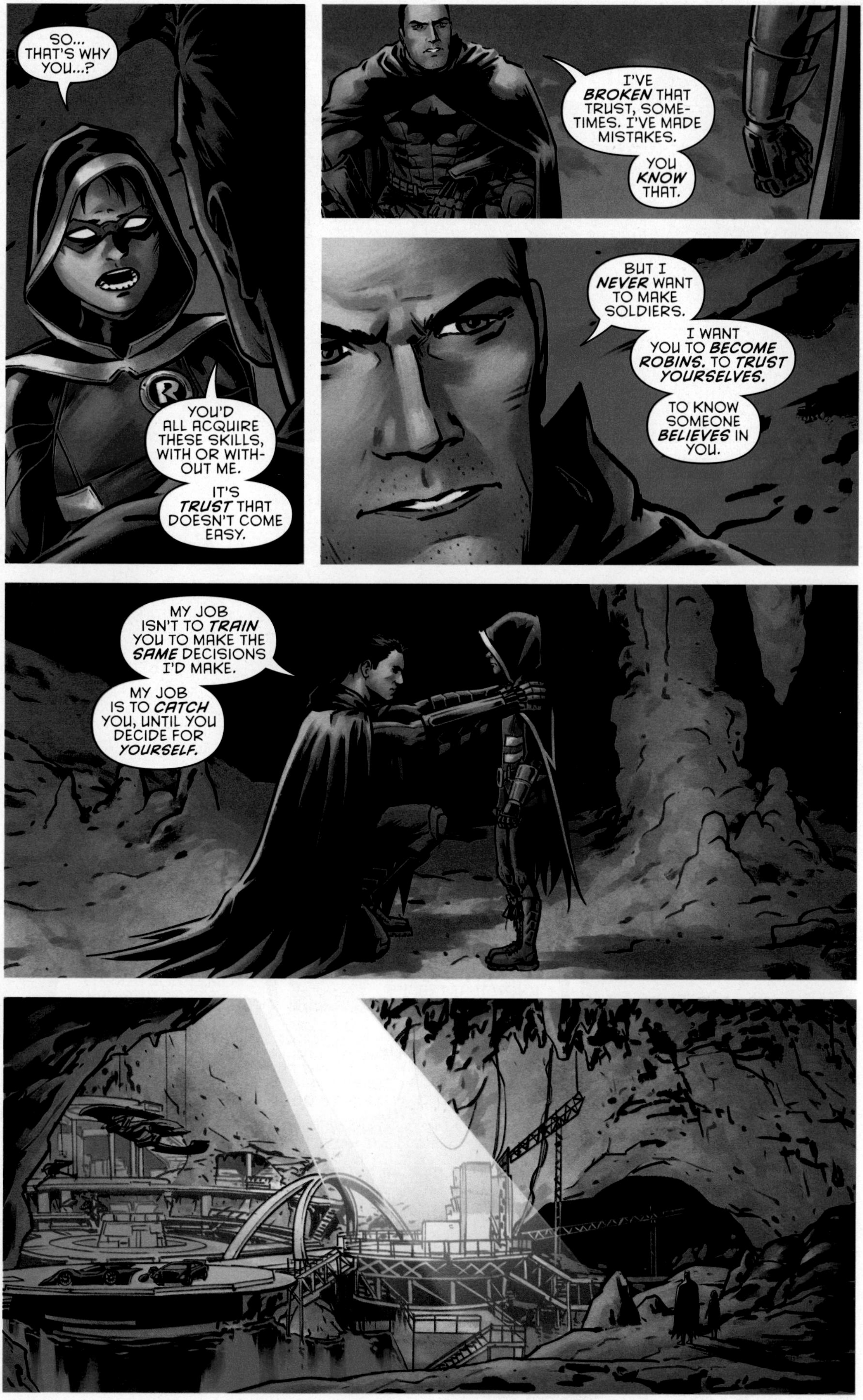
SO... THAT'S WHY YOU...?
YOU'D ALL ACQUIRE THESE SKILLS, WITH OR WITH-OUT ME.
IT'S TRUST THAT DOESN'T COME EASY.
I'VE BROKEN THAT TRUST, SOME-TIMES. I'VE MADE MISTAKES.
YOU KNOW THAT.
BUT I NEVER WANT TO MAKE SOLDIERS.
I WANT YOU TO BECOME ROBINS. TO TRUST YOURSELVES.
TO KNOW SOMEONE BELIEVES IN YOU.
MY JOB ISN'T TO TRAIN YOU TO MAKE THE SAME DECISIONS I'D MAKE.
MY JOB IS TO CATCH YOU, UNTIL YOU DECIDE FOR YOURSELF.

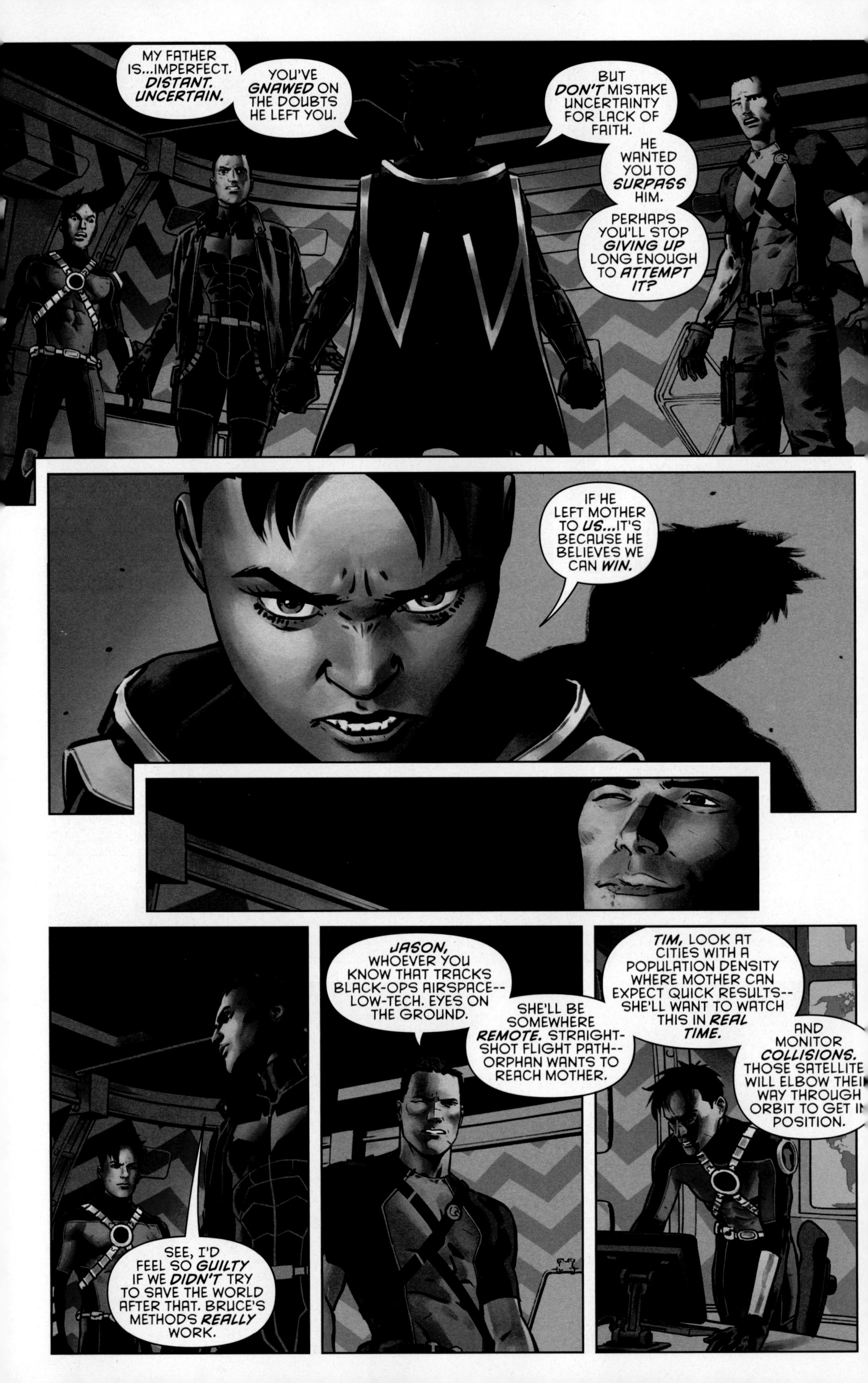
MY FATHER IS...IMPERFECT. *DISTANT. UNCERTAIN.*
YOU'VE *GNAWED* ON THE DOUBTS HE LEFT YOU.
BUT *DON'T* MISTAKE UNCERTAINTY FOR LACK OF FAITH.
HE WANTED YOU TO *SURPASS* HIM.
PERHAPS YOU'LL STOP *GIVING UP* LONG ENOUGH TO *ATTEMPT IT?*
IF HE LEFT MOTHER TO *US...*IT'S BECAUSE HE BELIEVES WE CAN *WIN.*
SEE, I'D FEEL SO *GUILTY* IF WE *DIDN'T* TRY TO SAVE THE WORLD AFTER THAT. BRUCE'S METHODS *REALLY* WORK.
JASON, WHOEVER YOU KNOW THAT TRACKS BLACK-OPS AIRSPACE--LOW-TECH. EYES ON THE GROUND.
SHE'LL BE SOMEWHERE *REMOTE.* STRAIGHT-SHOT FLIGHT PATH--ORPHAN WANTS TO REACH MOTHER.
TIM, LOOK AT CITIES WITH A POPULATION DENSITY WHERE MOTHER CAN EXPECT QUICK RESULTS--SHE'LL WANT TO WATCH THIS IN *REAL TIME.*
AND MONITOR *COLLISIONS.* THOSE SATELLITE WILL ELBOW THEI WAY THROUGH ORBIT TO GET I POSITION.

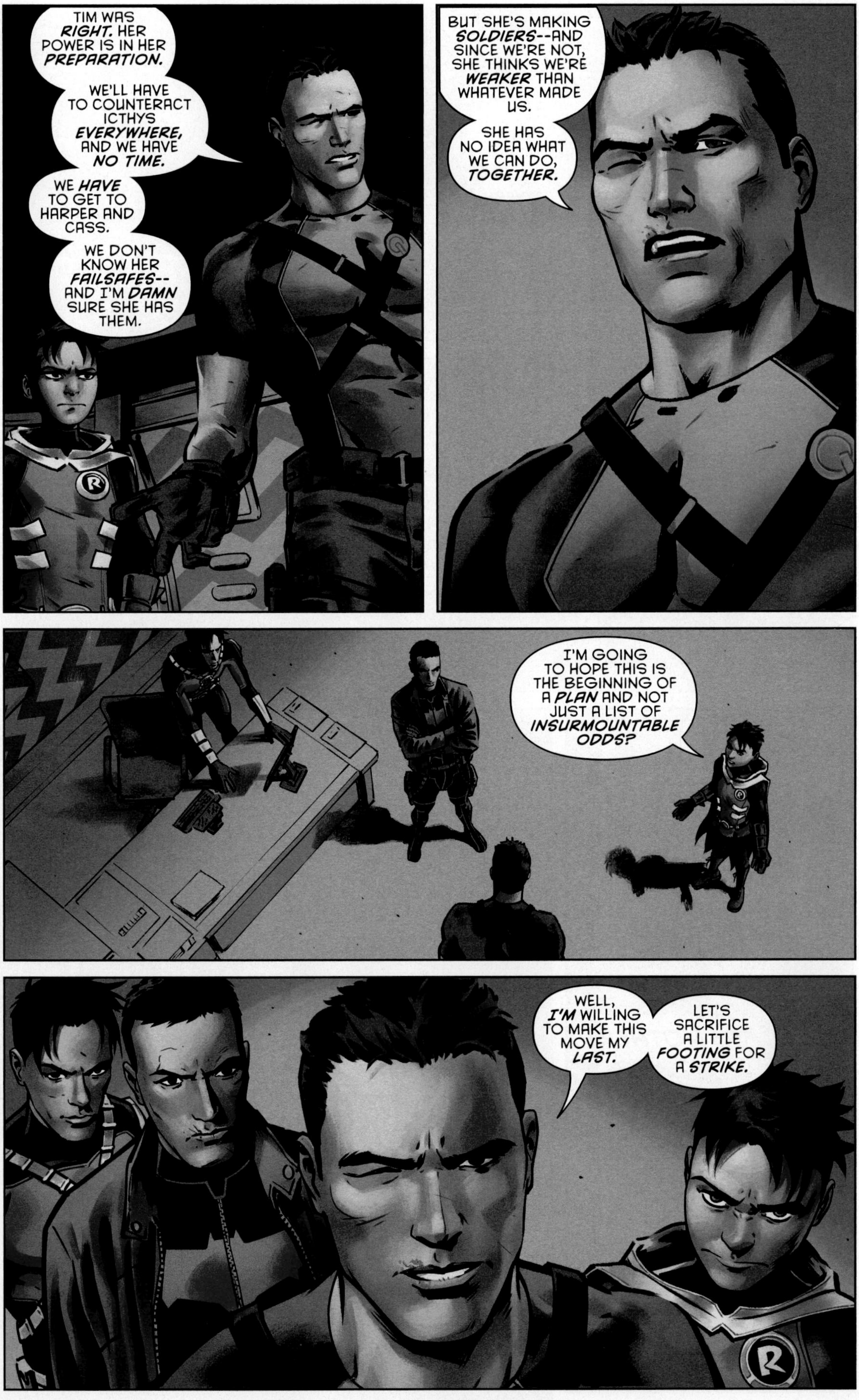

TIM WAS *RIGHT*. HER POWER IS IN HER *PREPARATION.*
WE'LL HAVE TO COUNTERACT ICTHYS *EVERYWHERE,* AND WE HAVE *NO TIME.*
WE *HAVE* TO GET TO HARPER AND CASS.
WE DON'T KNOW HER *FAILSAFES*--AND I'M *DAMN* SURE SHE HAS THEM.
BUT SHE'S MAKING *SOLDIERS*--AND SINCE WE'RE NOT, SHE THINKS WE'RE *WEAKER* THAN WHATEVER MADE US.
SHE HAS NO IDEA WHAT WE CAN DO, *TOGETHER.*
I'M GOING TO HOPE THIS IS THE BEGINNING OF A *PLAN* AND NOT JUST A LIST OF *INSURMOUNTABLE ODDS?*
WELL, *I'M* WILLING TO MAKE THIS MOVE MY *LAST.*
LET'S SACRIFICE A LITTLE *FOOTING* FOR A *STRIKE.*

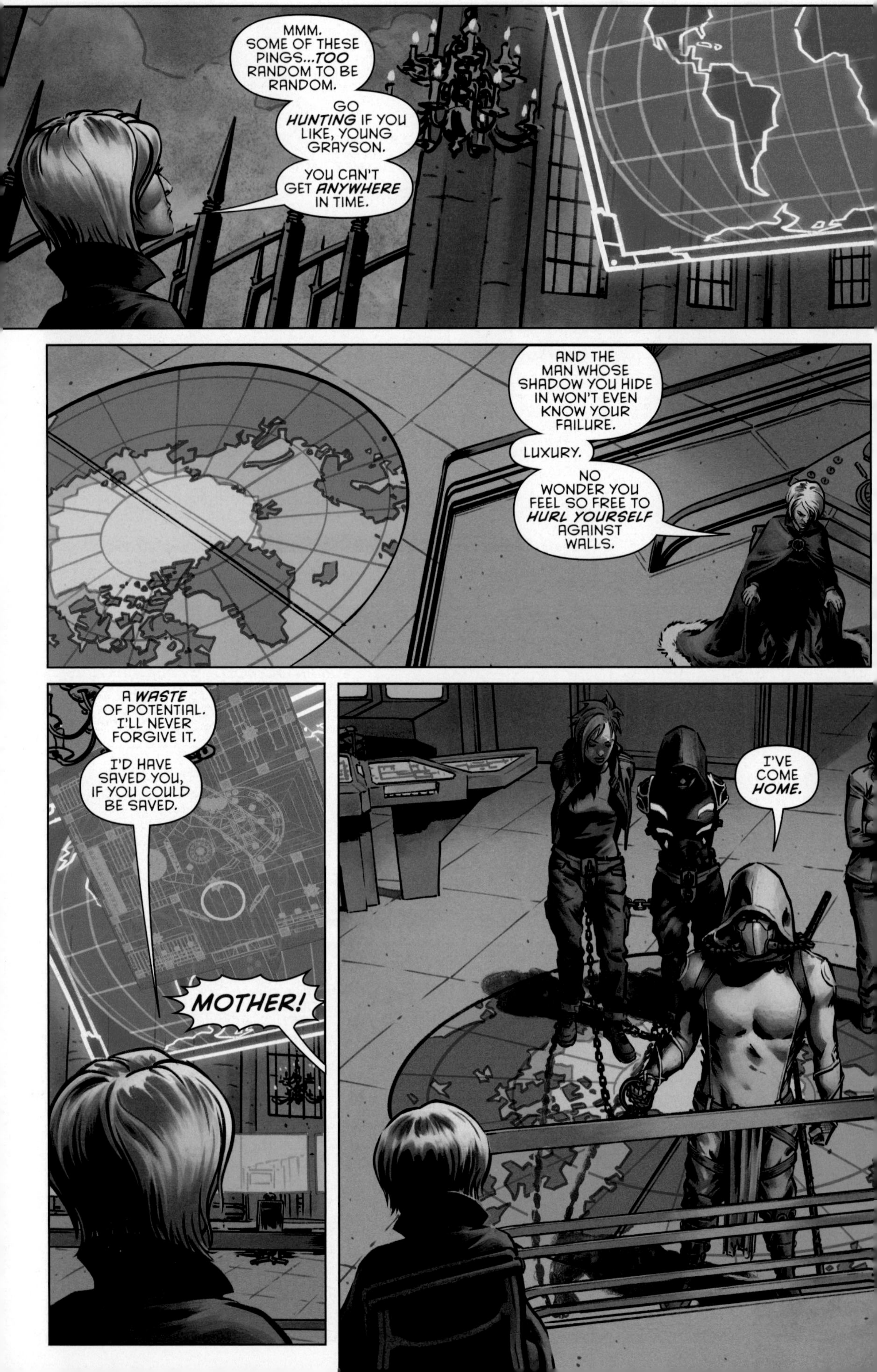
MMM. SOME OF THESE PINGS...TOO RANDOM TO BE RANDOM.
GO HUNTING IF YOU LIKE, YOUNG GRAYSON.
YOU CAN'T GET ANYWHERE IN TIME.
AND THE MAN WHOSE SHADOW YOU HIDE IN WON'T EVEN KNOW YOUR FAILURE.
LUXURY.
NO WONDER YOU FEEL SO FREE TO HURL YOURSELF AGAINST WALLS.
A WASTE OF POTENTIAL. I'LL NEVER FORGIVE IT.
I'D HAVE SAVED YOU, IF YOU COULD BE SAVED.
MOTHER!
I'VE COME HOME.

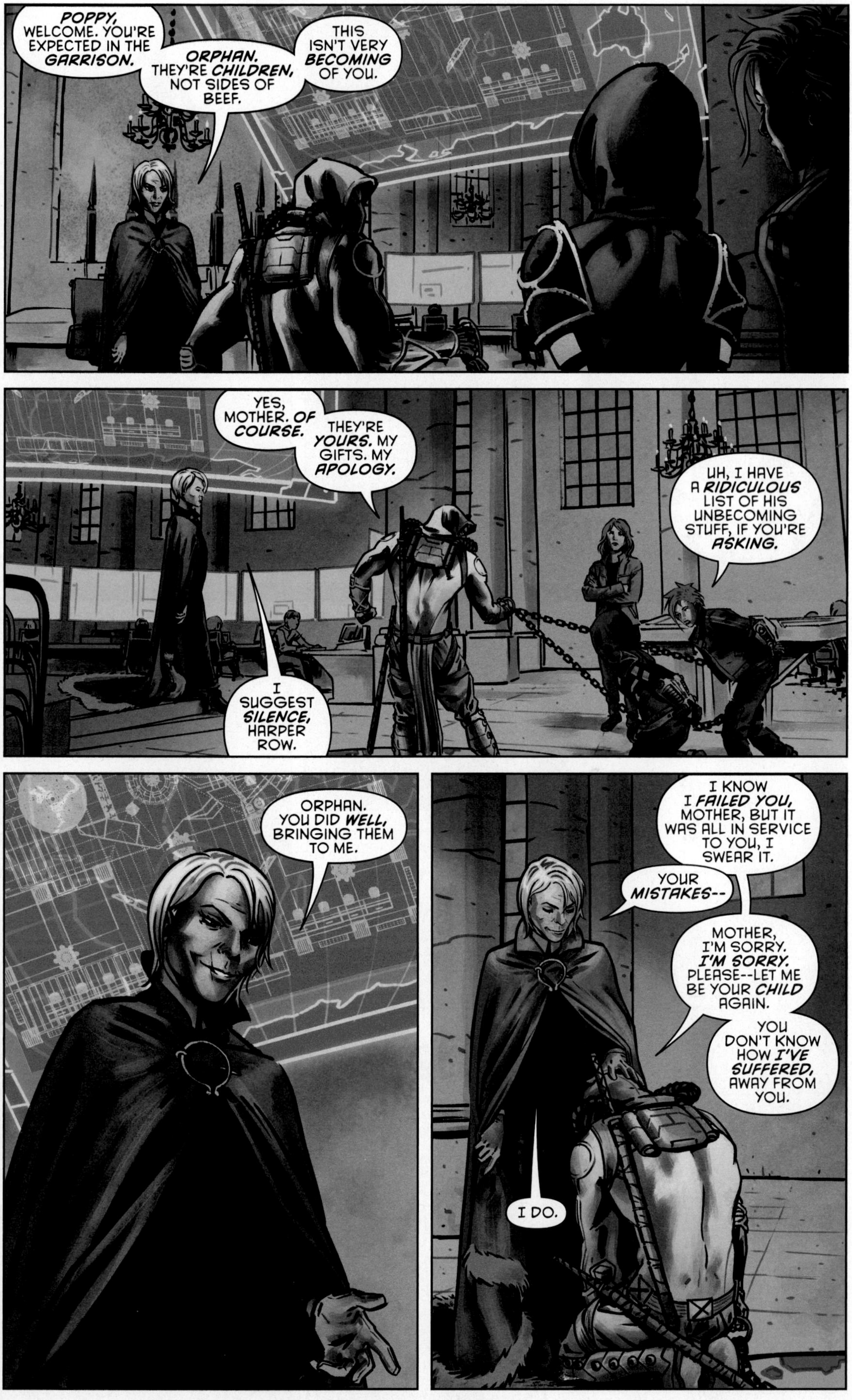
POPPY, WELCOME. YOU'RE EXPECTED IN THE GARRISON.
ORPHAN. THEY'RE CHILDREN, NOT SIDES OF BEEF.
THIS ISN'T VERY BECOMING OF YOU.
YES, MOTHER. OF COURSE.
THEY'RE YOURS. MY GIFTS. MY APOLOGY.
UH, I HAVE A RIDICULOUS LIST OF HIS UNBECOMING STUFF, IF YOU'RE ASKING.
I SUGGEST SILENCE, HARPER ROW.
ORPHAN. YOU DID WELL, BRINGING THEM TO ME.
I KNOW I FAILED YOU, MOTHER, BUT IT WAS ALL IN SERVICE TO YOU, I SWEAR IT.
YOUR MISTAKES--
MOTHER, I'M SORRY. I'M SORRY. PLEASE--LET ME BE YOUR CHILD AGAIN.
YOU DON'T KNOW HOW I'VE SUFFERED, AWAY FROM YOU.
I DO.

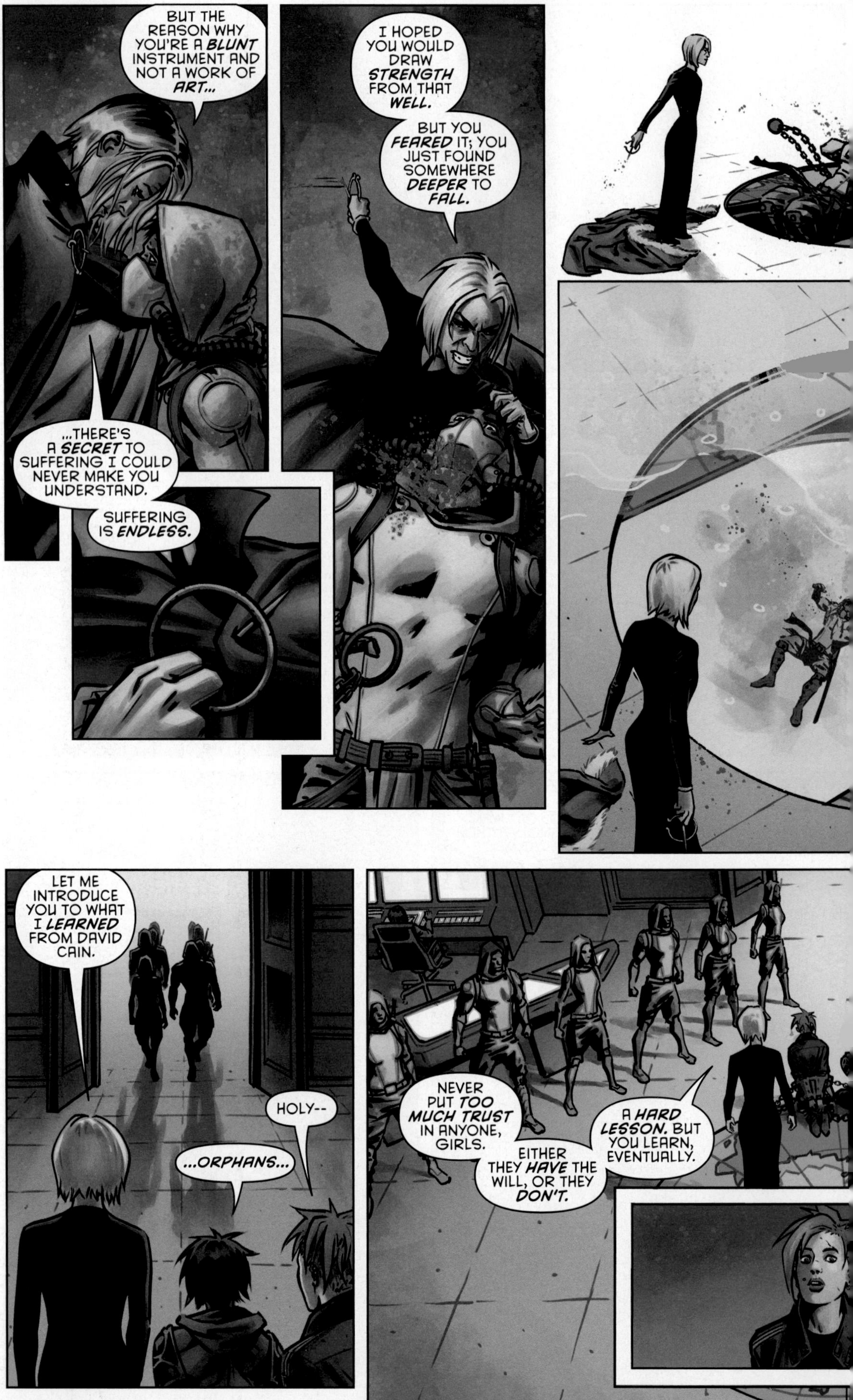
BUT THE REASON WHY YOU'RE A BLUNT INSTRUMENT AND NOT A WORK OF ART...
...THERE'S A SECRET TO SUFFERING I COULD NEVER MAKE YOU UNDERSTAND.
SUFFERING IS ENDLESS.
I HOPED YOU WOULD DRAW STRENGTH FROM THAT WELL.
BUT YOU FEARED IT; YOU JUST FOUND SOMEWHERE DEEPER TO FALL.
LET ME INTRODUCE YOU TO WHAT I LEARNED FROM DAVID CAIN.
HOLY--
...ORPHANS...
NEVER PUT TOO MUCH TRUST IN ANYONE, GIRLS.
EITHER THEY HAVE THE WILL, OR THEY DON'T.
A HARD LESSON. BUT YOU LEARN, EVENTUALLY.

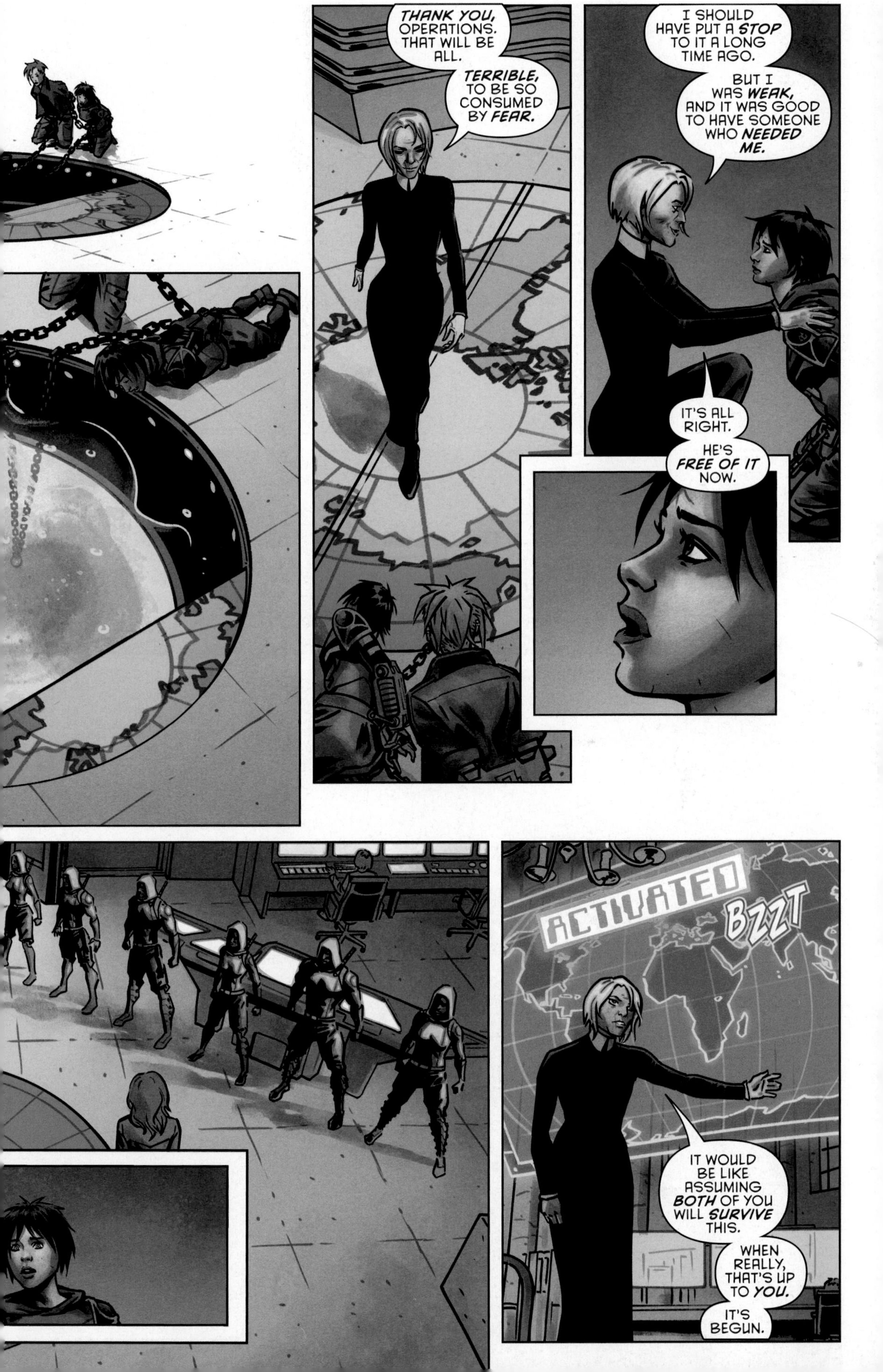
THANK YOU, OPERATIONS. THAT WILL BE ALL.
TERRIBLE, TO BE SO CONSUMED BY FEAR.
I SHOULD HAVE PUT A STOP TO IT A LONG TIME AGO.
BUT I WAS WEAK, AND IT WAS GOOD TO HAVE SOMEONE WHO NEEDED ME.
IT'S ALL RIGHT.
HE'S FREE OF IT NOW.
ACTIVATED
BZZT
IT WOULD BE LIKE ASSUMING BOTH OF YOU WILL SURVIVE THIS.
WHEN REALLY, THAT'S UP TO YOU.
IT'S BEGUN.

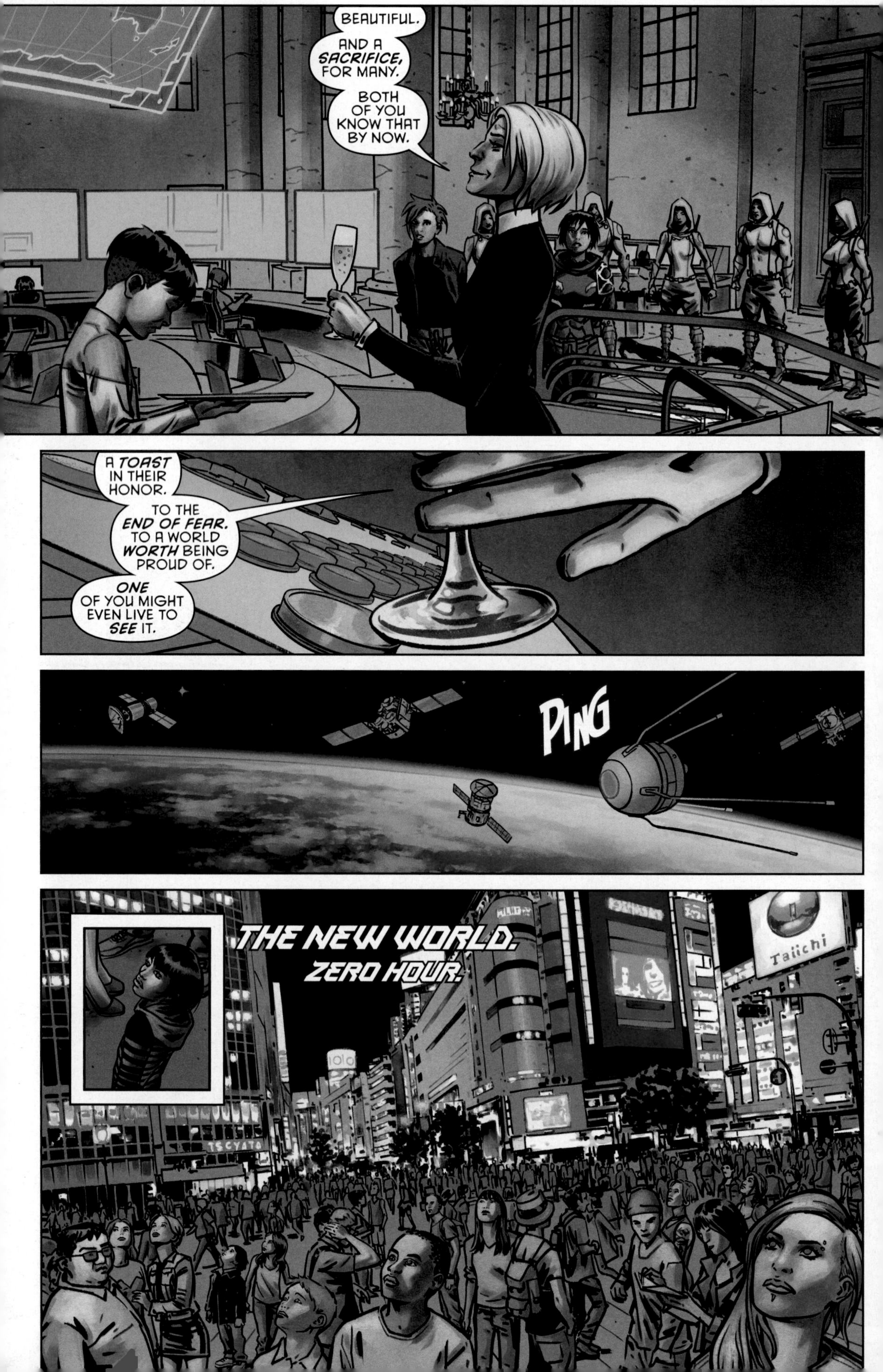
BEAUTIFUL.
AND A SACRIFICE, FOR MANY.
BOTH OF YOU KNOW THAT BY NOW.
A TOAST IN THEIR HONOR.
TO THE END OF FEAR. TO A WORLD WORTH BEING PROUD OF.
ONE OF YOU MIGHT EVEN LIVE TO SEE IT.
PING
THE NEW WORLD.
ZERO HOUR.
Taiichi

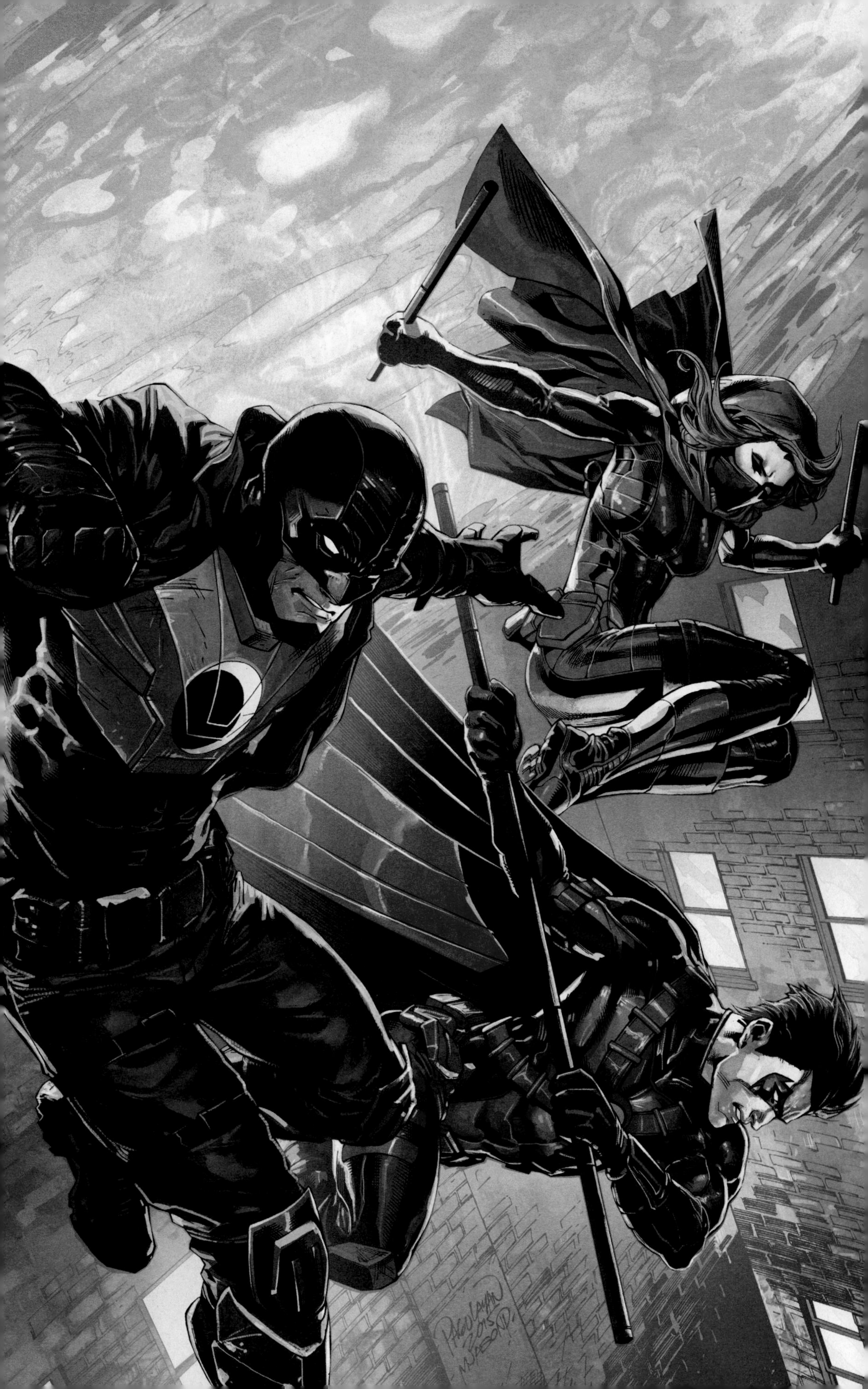

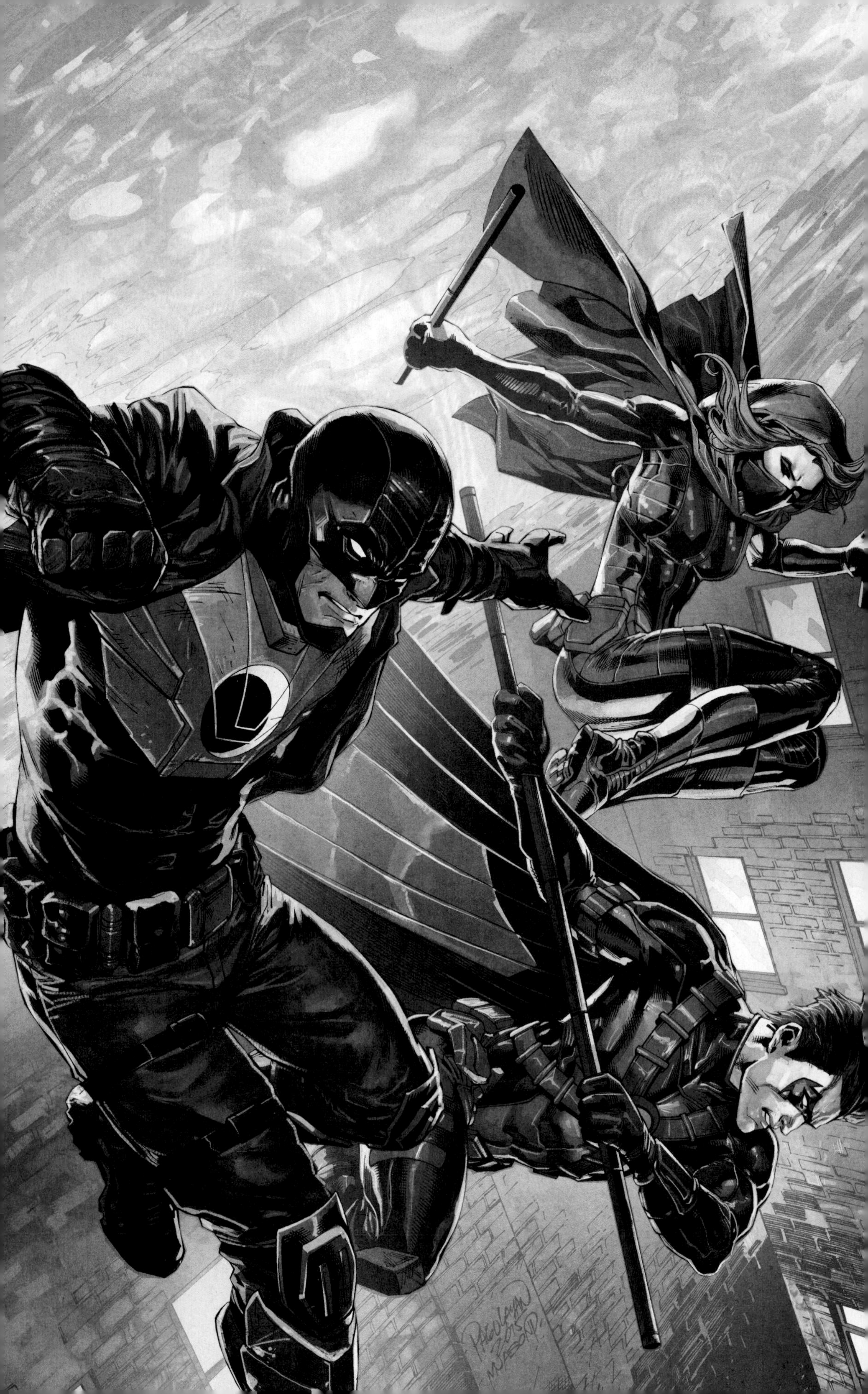

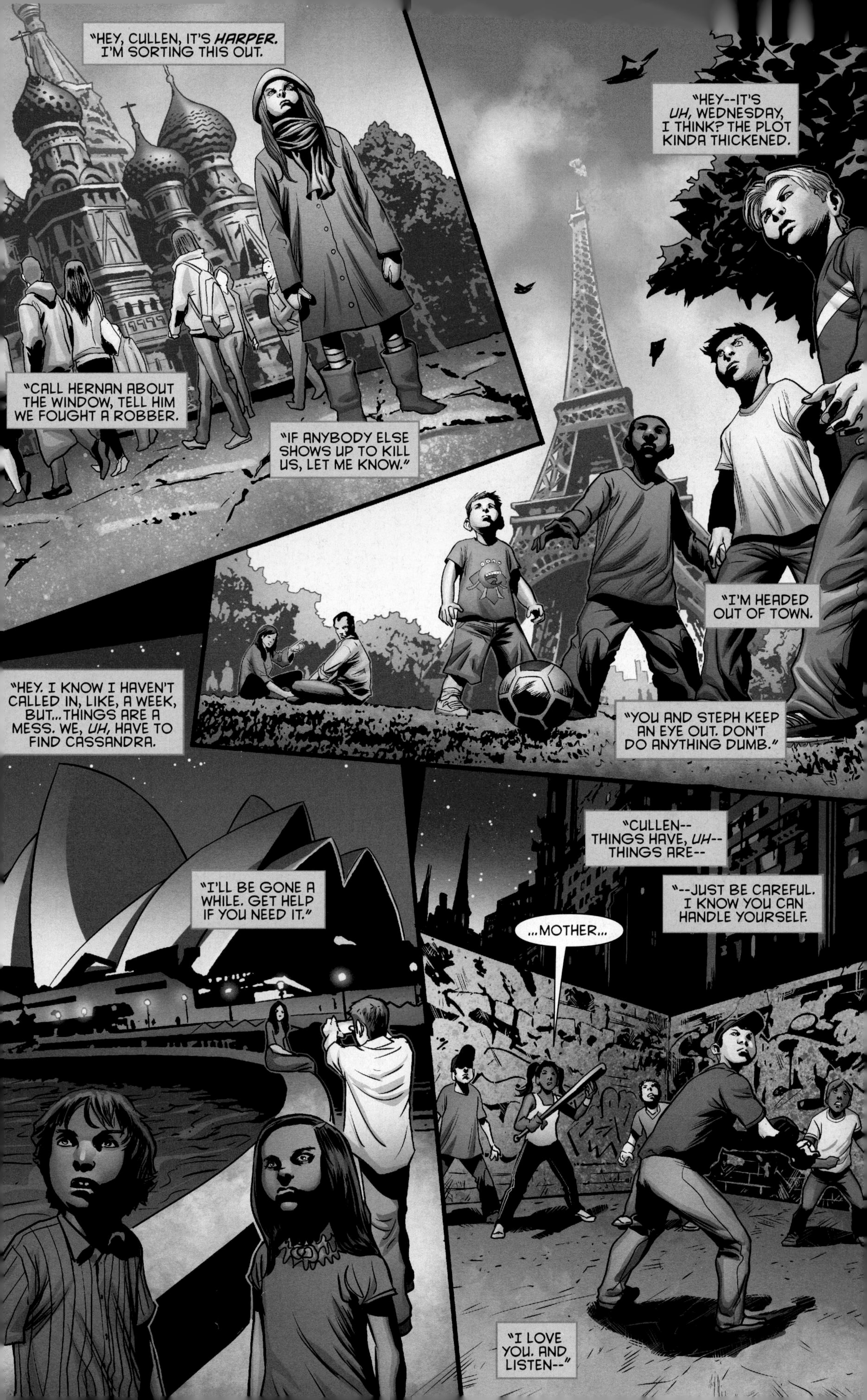
"HEY, CULLEN, IT'S *HARPER.* I'M SORTING THIS OUT.
"CALL HERNAN ABOUT THE WINDOW, TELL HIM WE FOUGHT A ROBBER.
"IF ANYBODY ELSE SHOWS UP TO KILL US, LET ME KNOW."
"HEY--IT'S *UH,* WEDNESDAY, I THINK? THE PLOT KINDA THICKENED.
"I'M HEADED OUT OF TOWN.
"YOU AND STEPH KEEP AN EYE OUT. DON'T DO ANYTHING DUMB."
"HEY. I KNOW I HAVEN'T CALLED IN, LIKE, A WEEK, BUT... THINGS ARE A MESS. WE, *UH,* HAVE TO FIND CASSANDRA.
"I'LL BE GONE A WHILE. GET HELP IF YOU NEED IT."
"CULLEN-- THINGS HAVE, *UH*-- THINGS ARE--
"--JUST BE CAREFUL. I KNOW YOU CAN HANDLE YOURSELF.
...MOTHER...
"I LOVE YOU. AND LISTEN--"

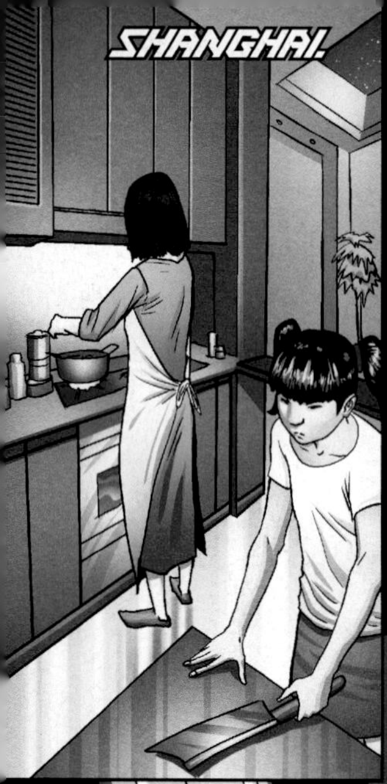
SHANGHAI.
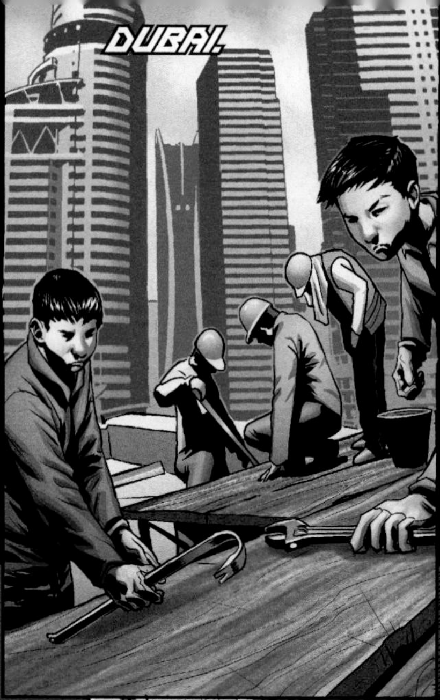
DUBAI.
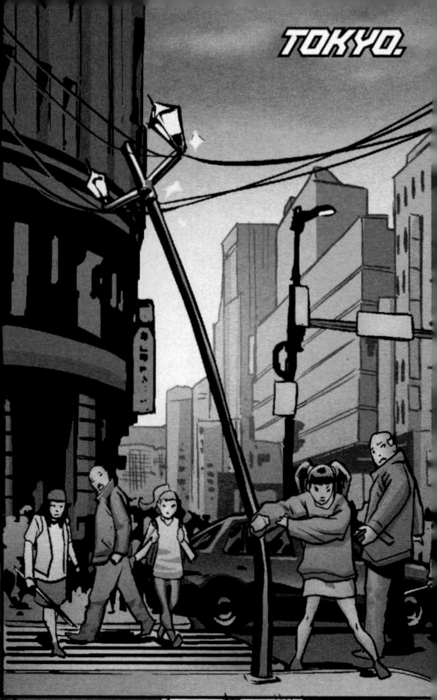
TOKYO.
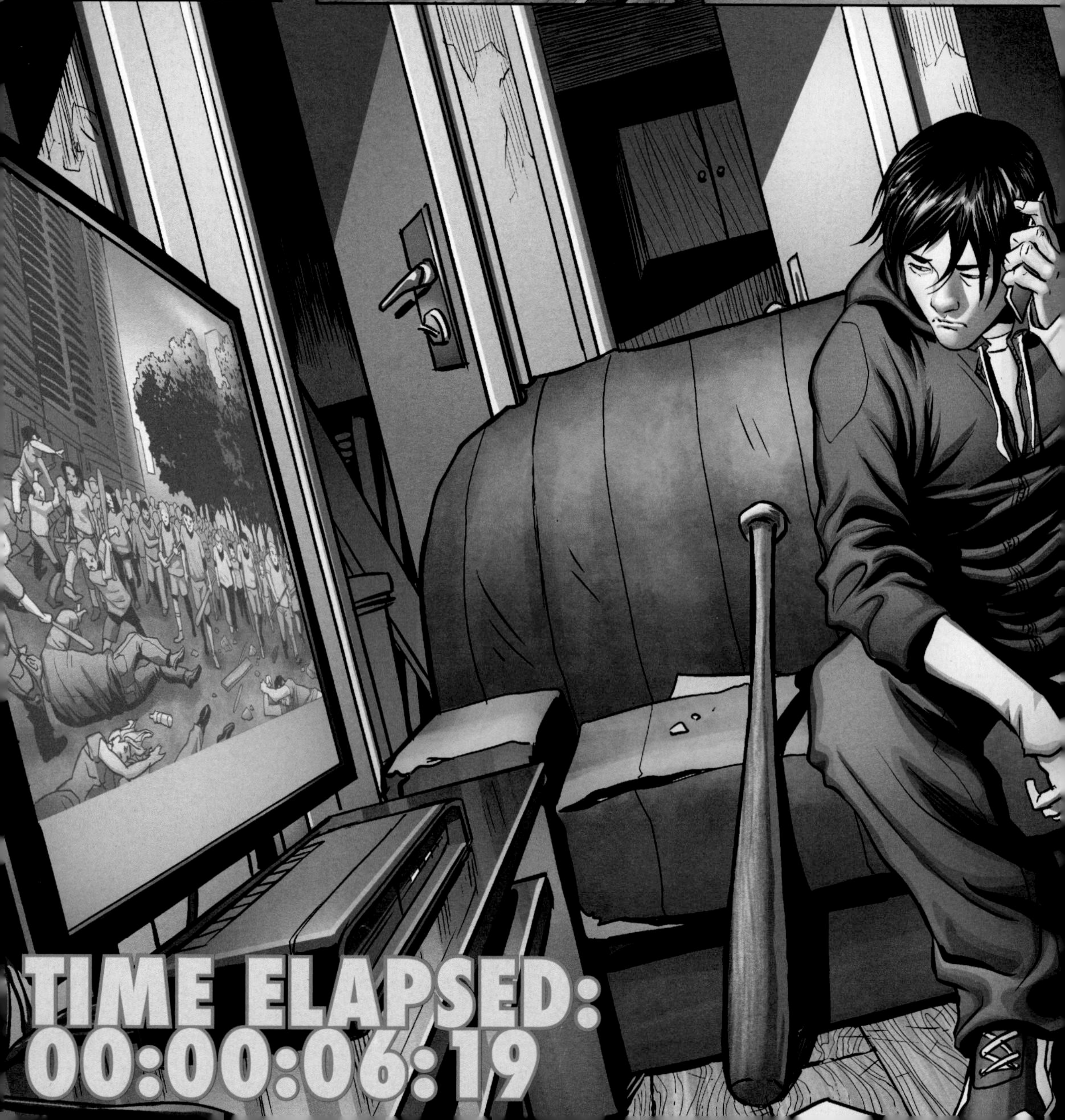
TIME ELAPSED:
00:00:06:19

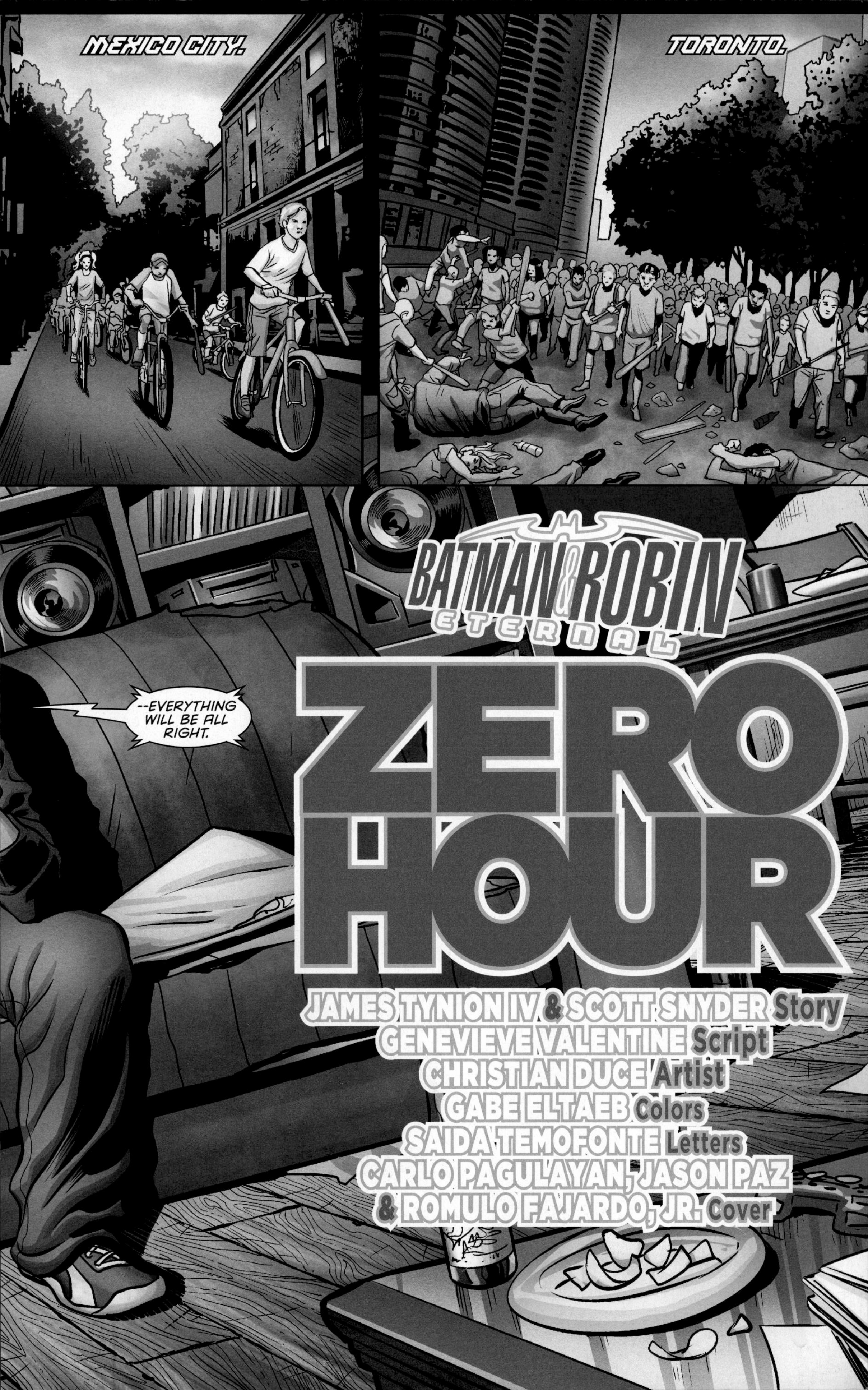
MEXICO CITY.
TORONTO.
--EVERYTHING WILL BE ALL RIGHT.
BATMAN & ROBIN ETERNAL
ZERO HOUR
JAMES TYNION IV & SCOTT SNYDER Story
GENEVIEVE VALENTINE Script
CHRISTIAN DUCE Artist
GABE ELTAEB Colors
SAIDA TEMOFONTE Letters
CARLO PAGULAYAN, JASON PAZ & ROMULO FAJARDO, JR. Cover

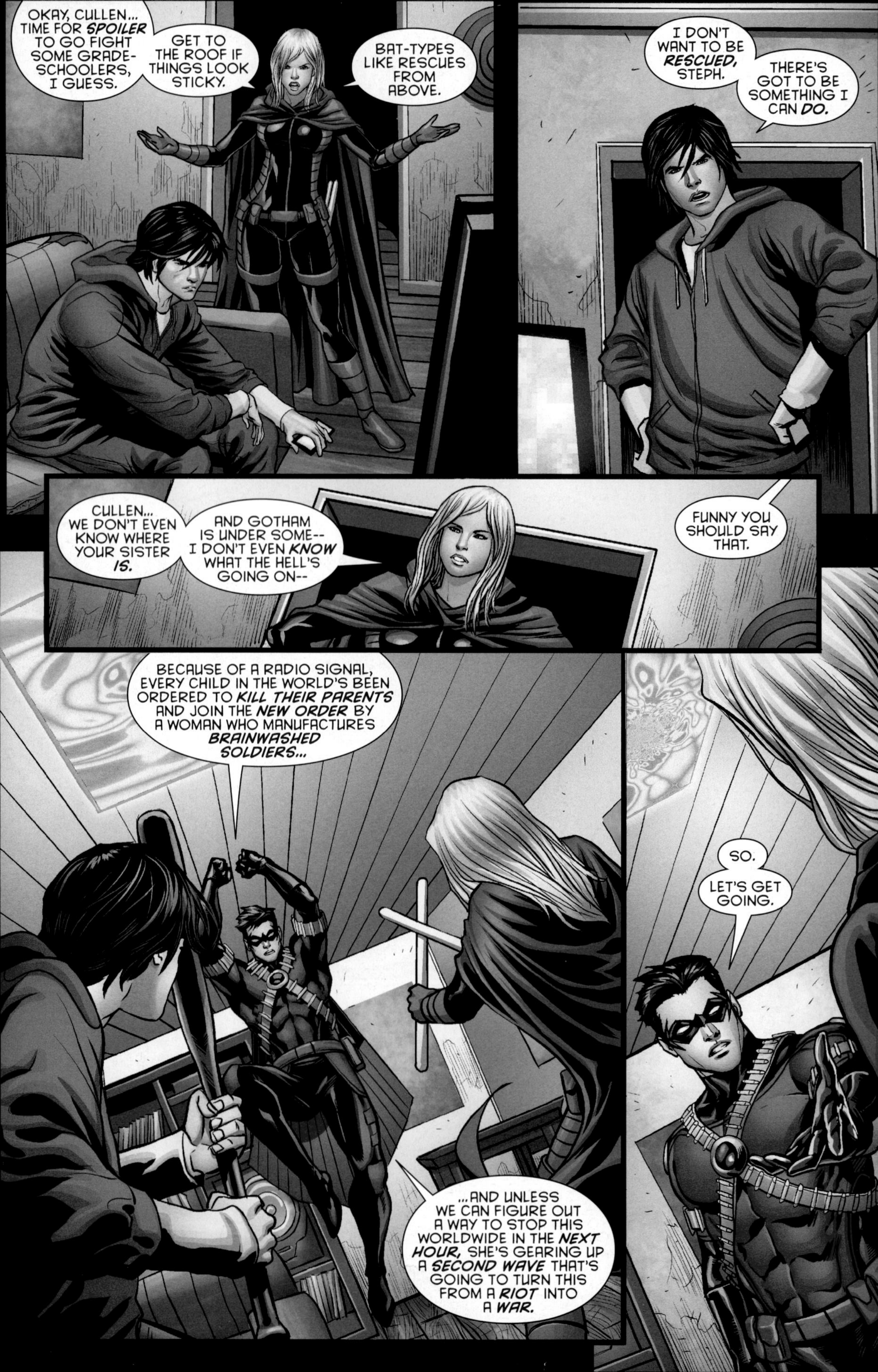
OKAY, CULLEN... TIME FOR SPOILER TO GO FIGHT SOME GRADE-SCHOOLERS, I GUESS.
GET TO THE ROOF IF THINGS LOOK STICKY.
BAT-TYPES LIKE RESCUES FROM ABOVE.
I DON'T WANT TO BE RESCUED, STEPH.
THERE'S GOT TO BE SOMETHING I CAN DO.
CULLEN... WE DON'T EVEN KNOW WHERE YOUR SISTER IS.
AND GOTHAM IS UNDER SOME-- I DON'T EVEN KNOW WHAT THE HELL'S GOING ON--
FUNNY YOU SHOULD SAY THAT.
BECAUSE OF A RADIO SIGNAL, EVERY CHILD IN THE WORLD'S BEEN ORDERED TO KILL THEIR PARENTS AND JOIN THE NEW ORDER BY A WOMAN WHO MANUFACTURES BRAINWASHED SOLDIERS...
...AND UNLESS WE CAN FIGURE OUT A WAY TO STOP THIS WORLDWIDE IN THE NEXT HOUR, SHE'S GEARING UP A SECOND WAVE THAT'S GOING TO TURN THIS FROM A RIOT INTO A WAR.
SO.
LET'S GET GOING.

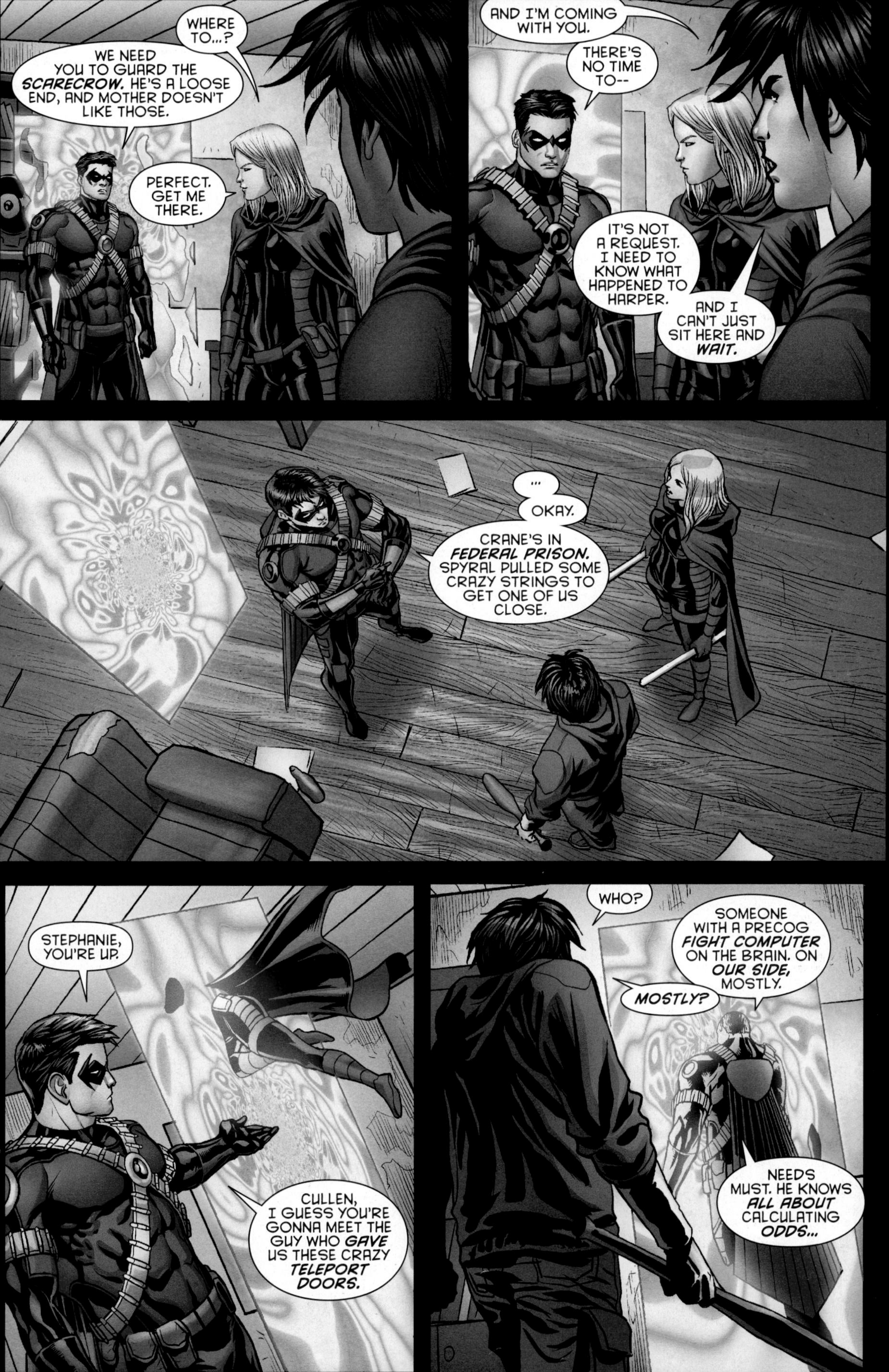
WHERE TO...?
WE NEED YOU TO GUARD THE SCARECROW. HE'S A LOOSE END, AND MOTHER DOESN'T LIKE THOSE.
PERFECT. GET ME THERE.
AND I'M COMING WITH YOU.
THERE'S NO TIME TO--
IT'S NOT A REQUEST. I NEED TO KNOW WHAT HAPPENED TO HARPER.
AND I CAN'T JUST SIT HERE AND WAIT.
...
OKAY.
CRANE'S IN FEDERAL PRISON. SPYRAL PULLED SOME CRAZY STRINGS TO GET ONE OF US CLOSE.
STEPHANIE, YOU'RE UP.
CULLEN, I GUESS YOU'RE GONNA MEET THE GUY WHO GAVE US THESE CRAZY TELEPORT DOORS.
WHO?
SOMEONE WITH A PRECOG FIGHT COMPUTER ON THE BRAIN. ON OUR SIDE, MOSTLY.
MOSTLY?
NEEDS MUST. HE KNOWS ALL ABOUT CALCULATING ODDS...

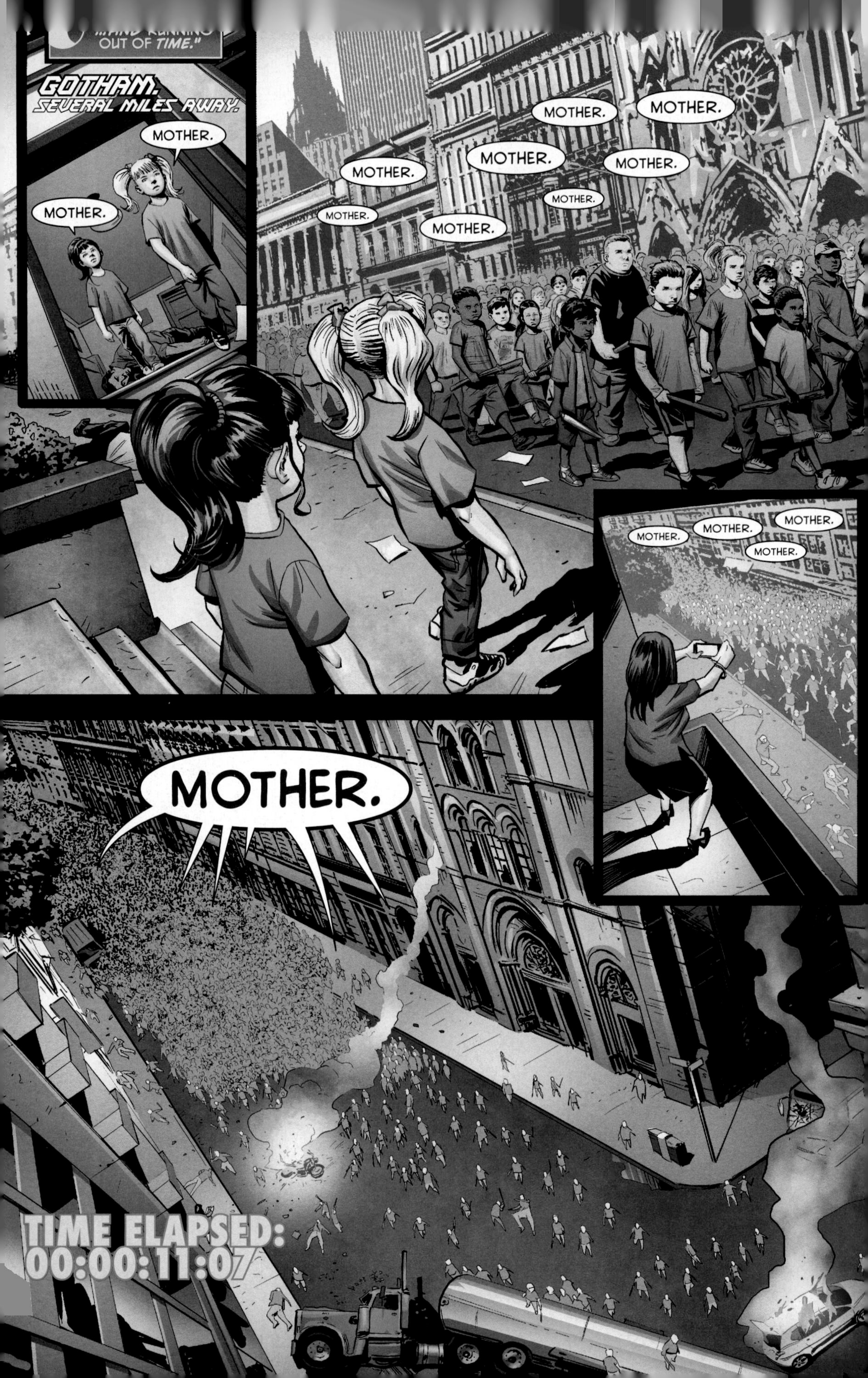
OUT OF TIME."
GOTHAM.
SEVERAL MILES AWAY.
MOTHER.
MOTHER.
MOTHER.
MOTHER.
MOTHER.
MOTHER.
MOTHER.
MOTHER.
MOTHER.
MOTHER.
MOTHER.
MOTHER.
MOTHER.
MOTHER.
MOTHER.
TIME ELAPSED:
00:00:11:07

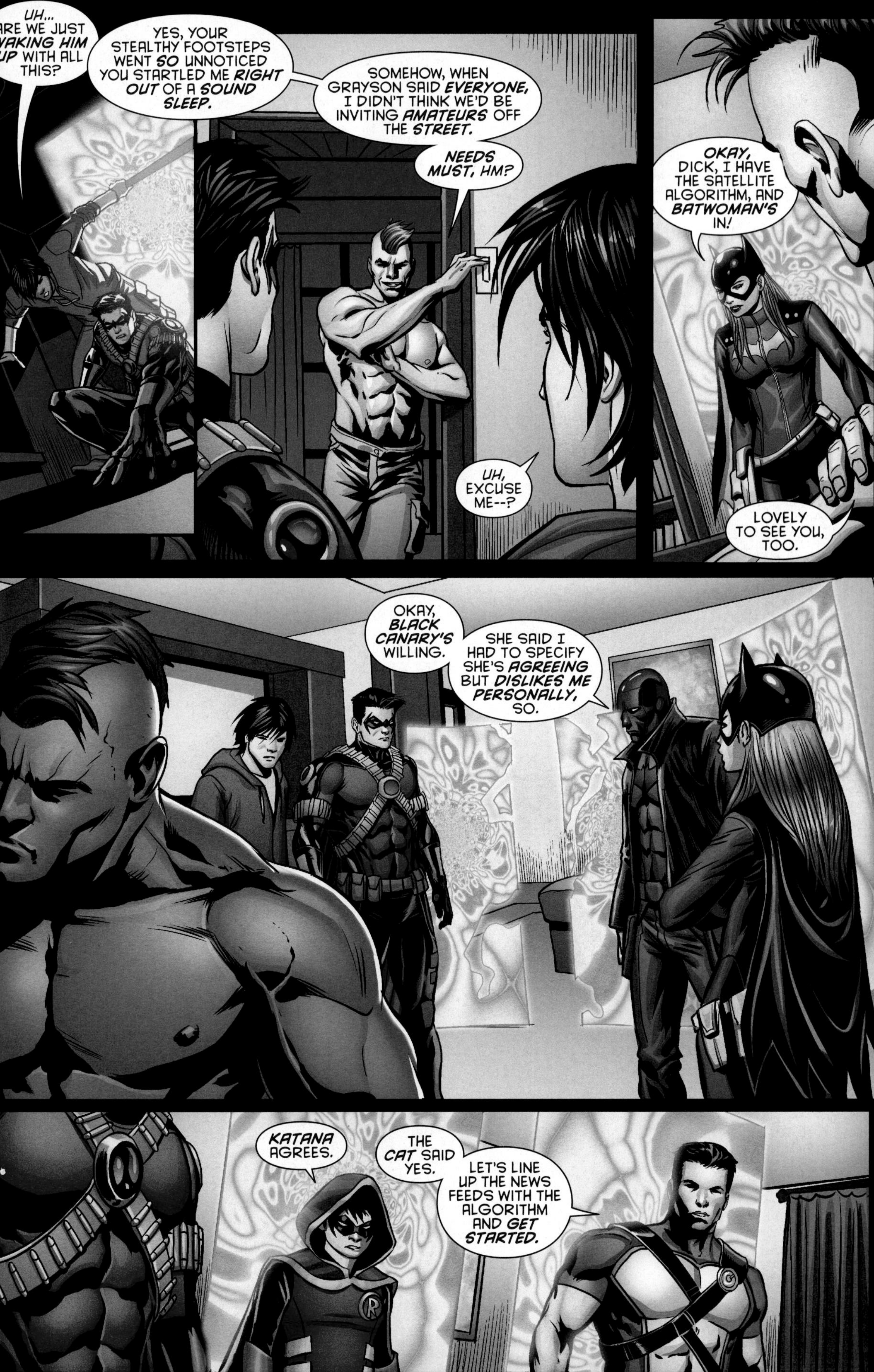
UH... ARE WE JUST WAKING HIM UP WITH ALL THIS?
YES, YOUR STEALTHY FOOTSTEPS WENT SO UNNOTICED YOU STARTLED ME RIGHT OUT OF A SOUND SLEEP.
SOMEHOW, WHEN GRAYSON SAID EVERYONE, I DIDN'T THINK WE'D BE INVITING AMATEURS OFF THE STREET.
NEEDS MUST, HM?
UH, EXCUSE ME--?
OKAY, DICK, I HAVE THE SATELLITE ALGORITHM, AND BATWOMAN'S IN!
LOVELY TO SEE YOU, TOO.
OKAY, BLACK CANARY'S WILLING.
SHE SAID I HAD TO SPECIFY SHE'S AGREEING BUT DISLIKES ME PERSONALLY, SO.
KATANA AGREES.
THE CAT SAID YES.
LET'S LINE UP THE NEWS FEEDS WITH THE ALGORITHM AND GET STARTED.

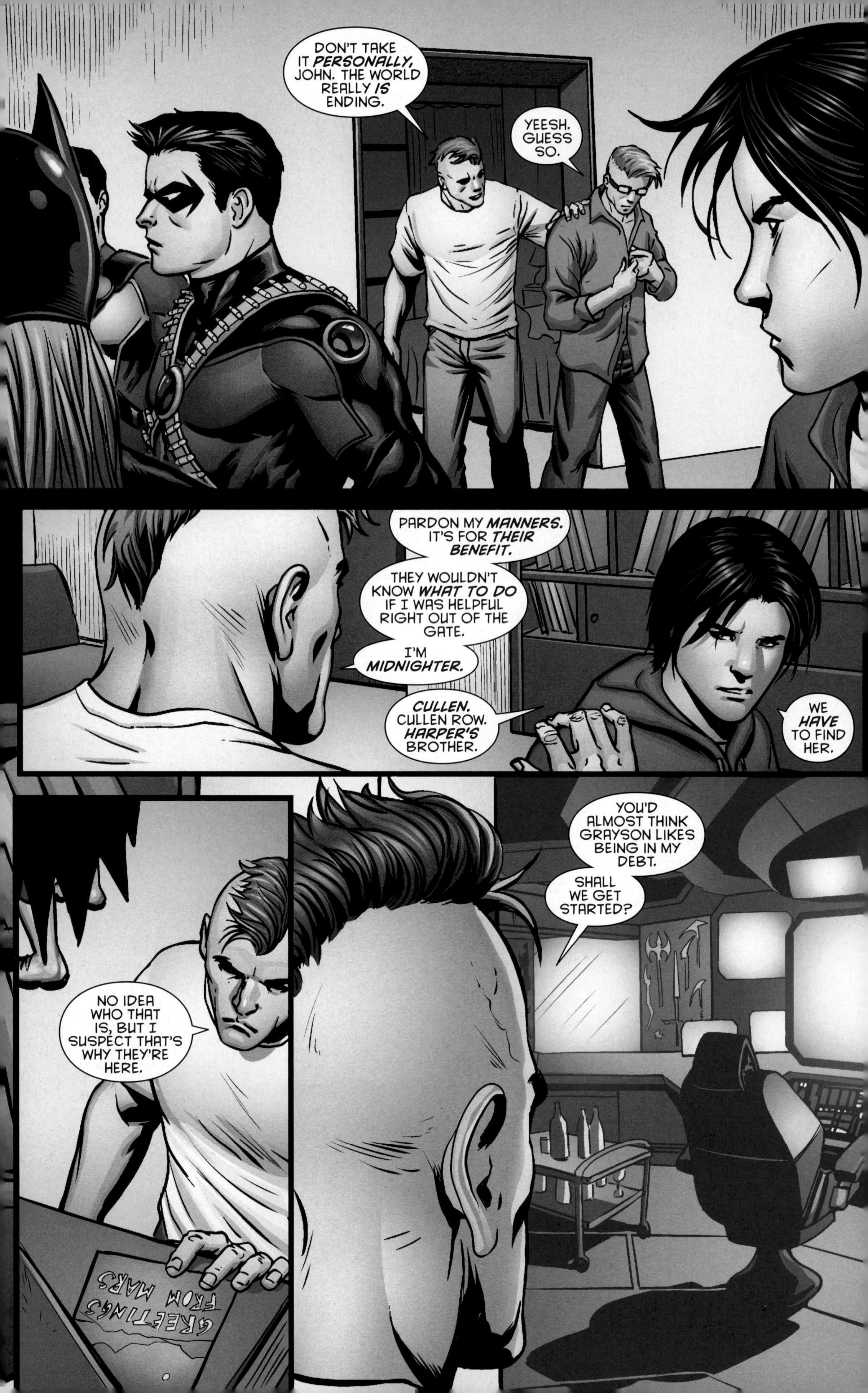
DON'T TAKE IT PERSONALLY, JOHN. THE WORLD REALLY IS ENDING.
YEESH. GUESS SO.
PARDON MY MANNERS. IT'S FOR THEIR BENEFIT.
THEY WOULDN'T KNOW WHAT TO DO IF I WAS HELPFUL RIGHT OUT OF THE GATE.
I'M MIDNIGHTER.
CULLEN. CULLEN ROW. HARPER'S BROTHER.
WE HAVE TO FIND HER.
NO IDEA WHO THAT IS, BUT I SUSPECT THAT'S WHY THEY'RE HERE.
GREETINGS FROM MARS
YOU'D ALMOST THINK GRAYSON LIKES BEING IN MY DEBT.
SHALL WE GET STARTED?

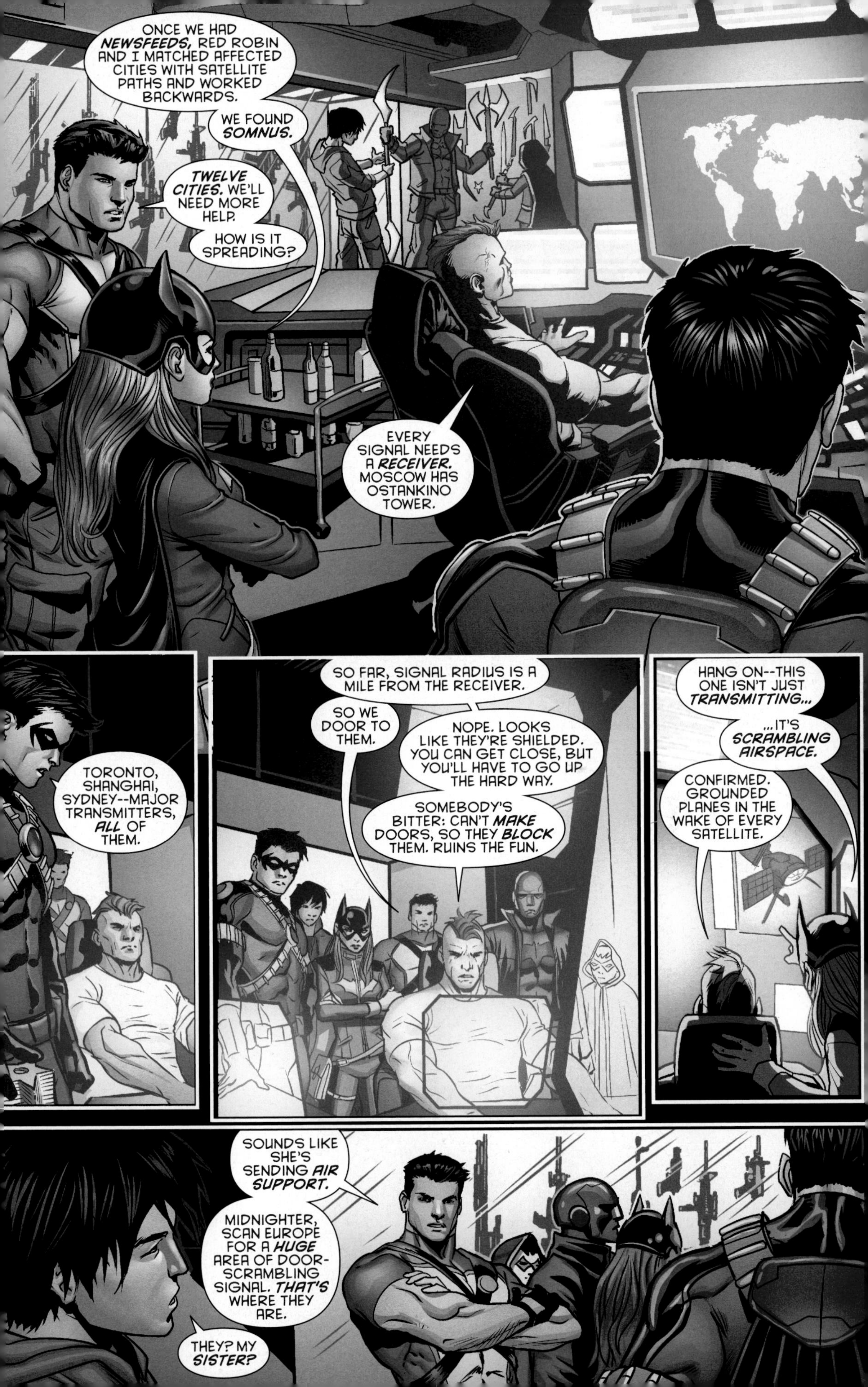
ONCE WE HAD NEWSFEEDS, RED ROBIN AND I MATCHED AFFECTED CITIES WITH SATELLITE PATHS AND WORKED BACKWARDS.
WE FOUND SOMNUS.
TWELVE CITIES. WE'LL NEED MORE HELP.
HOW IS IT SPREADING?
EVERY SIGNAL NEEDS A RECEIVER. MOSCOW HAS OSTANKINO TOWER.
TORONTO, SHANGHAI, SYDNEY--MAJOR TRANSMITTERS, ALL OF THEM.
SO FAR, SIGNAL RADIUS IS A MILE FROM THE RECEIVER.
SO WE DOOR TO THEM.
NOPE. LOOKS LIKE THEY'RE SHIELDED. YOU CAN GET CLOSE, BUT YOU'LL HAVE TO GO UP THE HARD WAY.
SOMEBODY'S BITTER: CAN'T MAKE DOORS, SO THEY BLOCK THEM. RUINS THE FUN.
HANG ON--THIS ONE ISN'T JUST TRANSMITTING...
...IT'S SCRAMBLING AIRSPACE.
CONFIRMED. GROUNDED PLANES IN THE WAKE OF EVERY SATELLITE.
SOUNDS LIKE SHE'S SENDING AIR SUPPORT.
MIDNIGHTER, SCAN EUROPE FOR A HUGE AREA OF DOOR-SCRAMBLING SIGNAL. THAT'S WHERE THEY ARE.
THEY? MY SISTER?

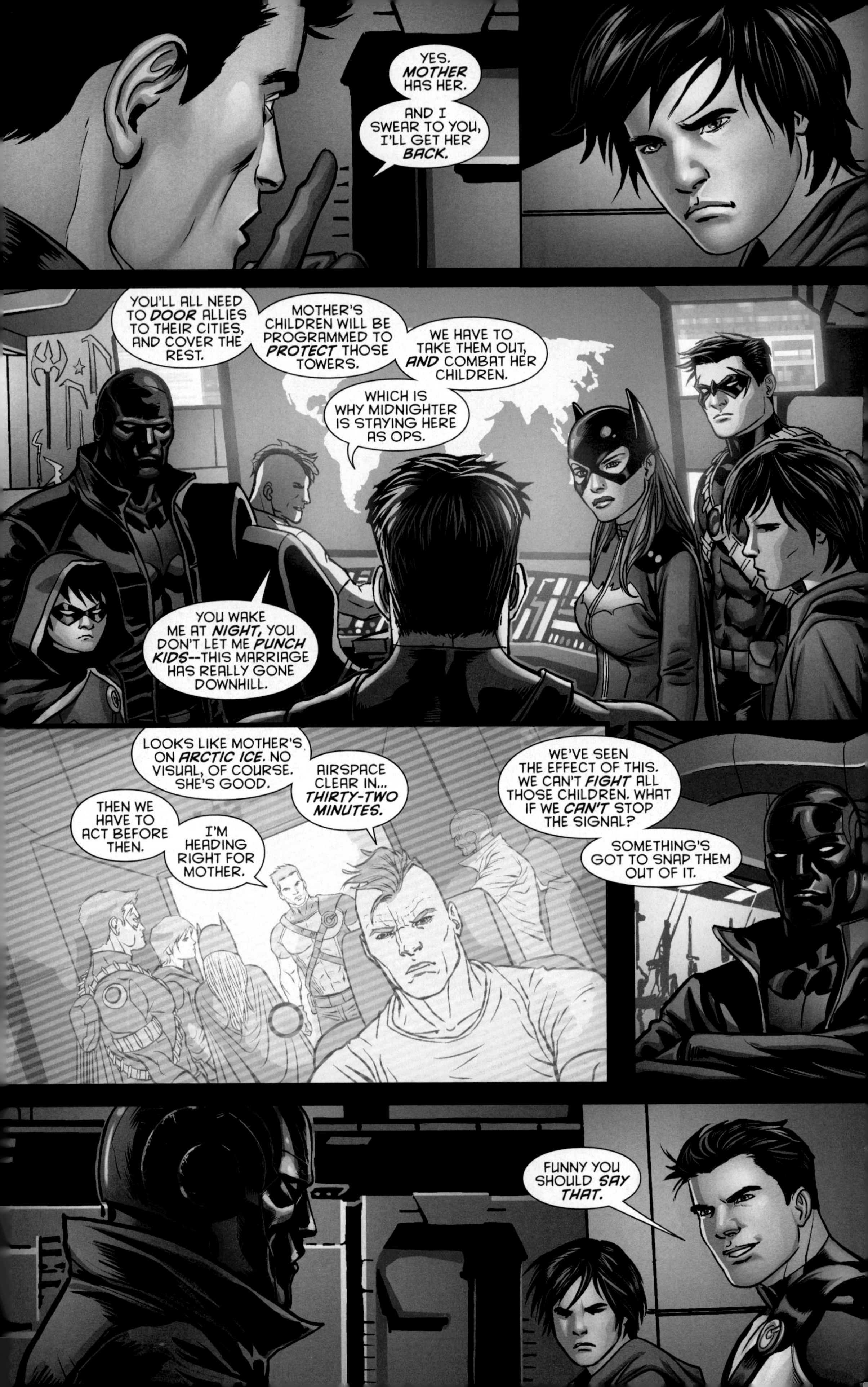

YES. MOTHER HAS HER.
AND I SWEAR TO YOU, I'LL GET HER BACK.
YOU'LL ALL NEED TO DOOR ALLIES TO THEIR CITIES, AND COVER THE REST.
MOTHER'S CHILDREN WILL BE PROGRAMMED TO PROTECT THOSE TOWERS.
WE HAVE TO TAKE THEM OUT, AND COMBAT HER CHILDREN.
WHICH IS WHY MIDNIGHTER IS STAYING HERE AS OPS.
YOU WAKE ME AT NIGHT, YOU DON'T LET ME PUNCH KIDS--THIS MARRIAGE HAS REALLY GONE DOWNHILL.
LOOKS LIKE MOTHER'S ON ARCTIC ICE. NO VISUAL, OF COURSE. SHE'S GOOD.
AIRSPACE CLEAR IN... THIRTY-TWO MINUTES.
THEN WE HAVE TO ACT BEFORE THEN.
I'M HEADING RIGHT FOR MOTHER.
WE'VE SEEN THE EFFECT OF THIS. WE CAN'T FIGHT ALL THOSE CHILDREN. WHAT IF WE CAN'T STOP THE SIGNAL?
SOMETHING'S GOT TO SNAP THEM OUT OF IT.
FUNNY YOU SHOULD SAY THAT.

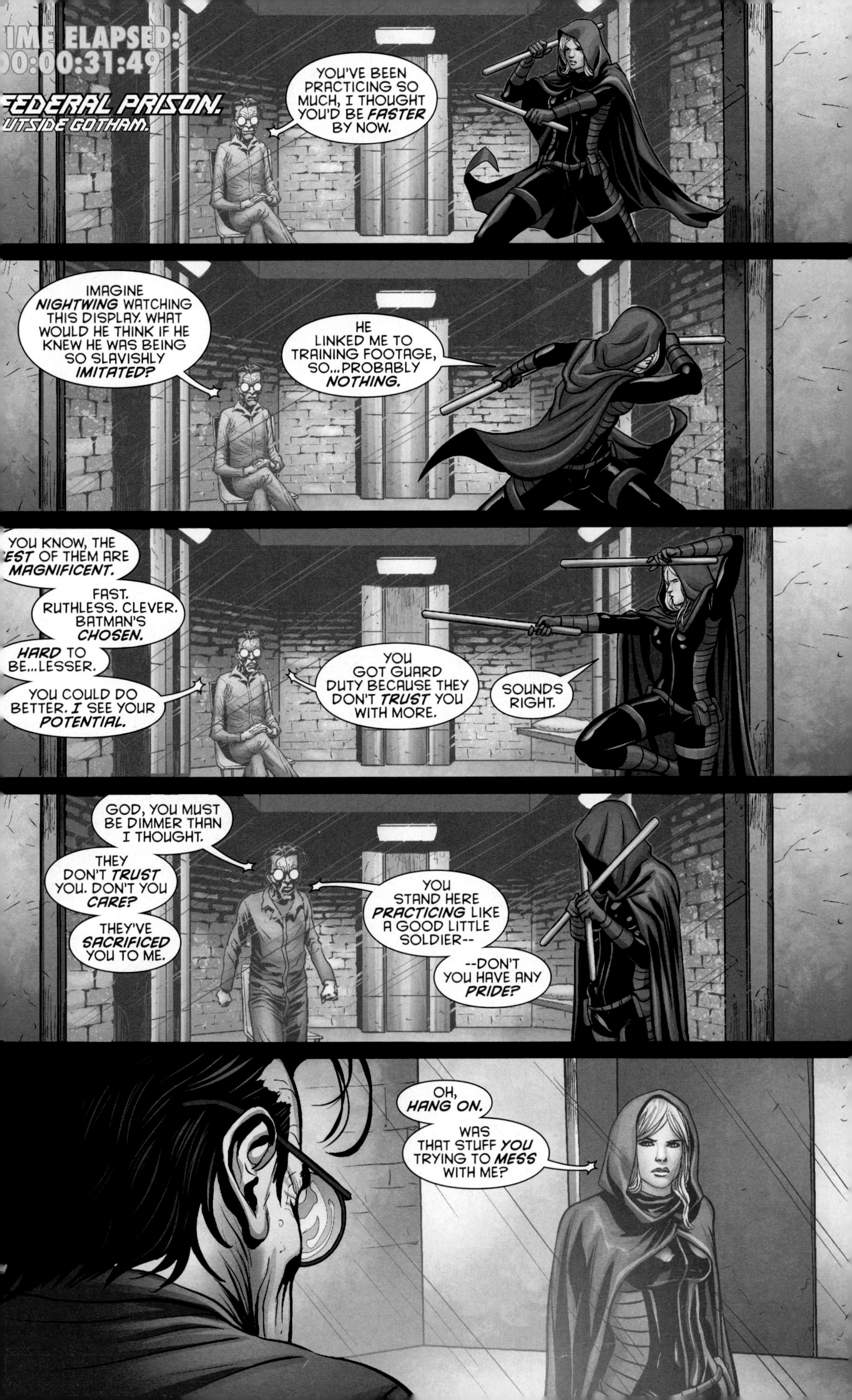
IME ELAPSED:
00:00:31:49
EDERAL PRISON.
UTSIDE GOTHAM.
YOU'VE BEEN PRACTICING SO MUCH, I THOUGHT YOU'D BE FASTER BY NOW.
IMAGINE NIGHTWING WATCHING THIS DISPLAY. WHAT WOULD HE THINK IF HE KNEW HE WAS BEING SO SLAVISHLY IMITATED?
HE LINKED ME TO TRAINING FOOTAGE, SO...PROBABLY NOTHING.
YOU KNOW, THE EST OF THEM ARE MAGNIFICENT.
FAST. RUTHLESS. CLEVER. BATMAN'S CHOSEN.
HARD TO BE...LESSER.
YOU COULD DO BETTER. I SEE YOUR POTENTIAL.
YOU GOT GUARD DUTY BECAUSE THEY DON'T TRUST YOU WITH MORE.
SOUNDS RIGHT.
GOD, YOU MUST BE DIMMER THAN I THOUGHT.
THEY DON'T TRUST YOU. DON'T YOU CARE?
THEY'VE SACRIFICED YOU TO ME.
YOU STAND HERE PRACTICING LIKE A GOOD LITTLE SOLDIER--
--DON'T YOU HAVE ANY PRIDE?
OH, HANG ON.
WAS THAT STUFF YOU TRYING TO MESS WITH ME?

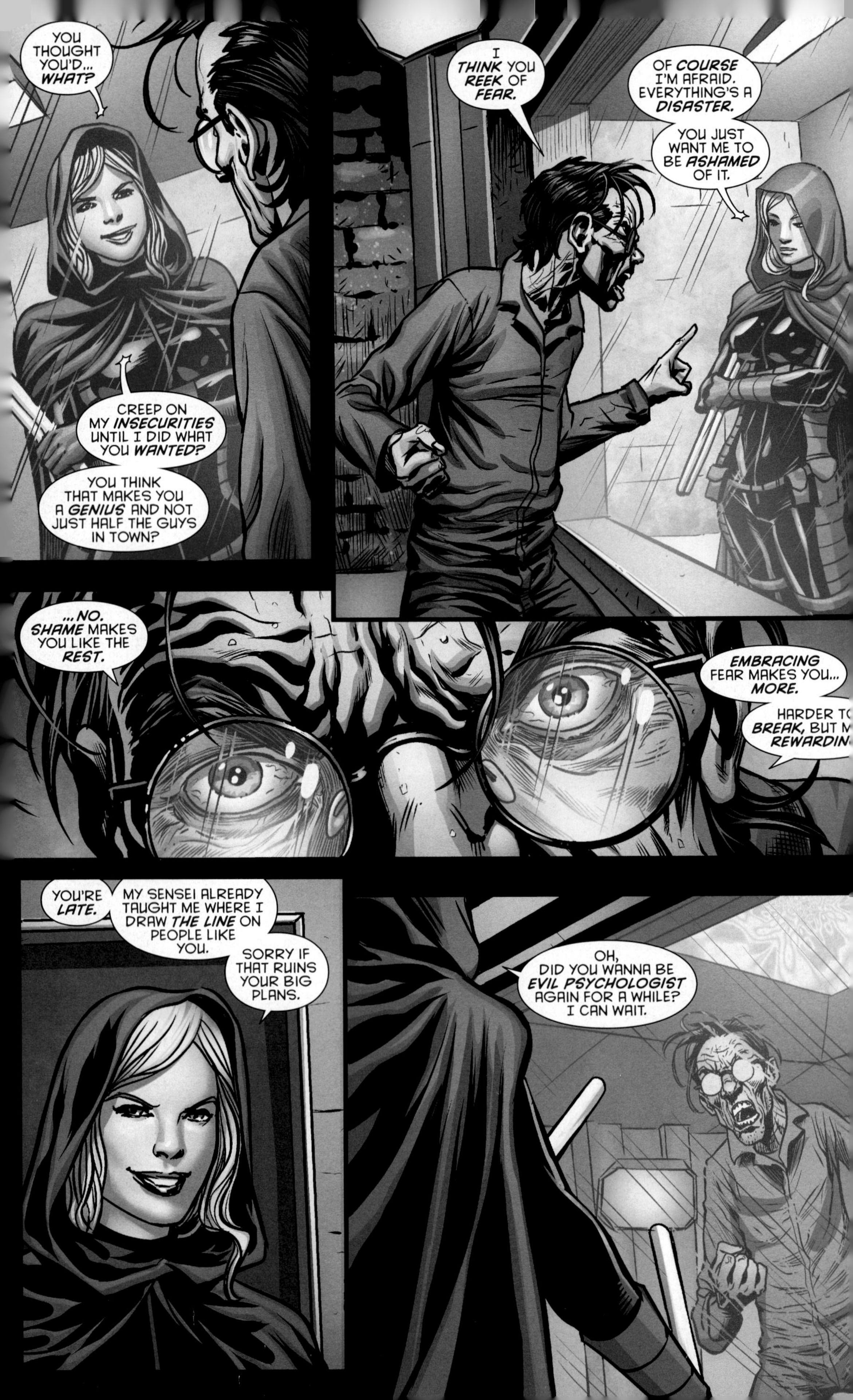

YOU THOUGHT YOU'D... WHAT?
CREEP ON MY INSECURITIES UNTIL I DID WHAT YOU WANTED?
YOU THINK THAT MAKES YOU A GENIUS AND NOT JUST HALF THE GUYS IN TOWN?
I THINK YOU REEK OF FEAR.
OF COURSE I'M AFRAID. EVERYTHING'S A DISASTER.
YOU JUST WANT ME TO BE ASHAMED OF IT.
...NO. SHAME MAKES YOU LIKE THE REST.
EMBRACING FEAR MAKES YOU... MORE.
YOU'RE LATE.
MY SENSEI ALREADY TAUGHT ME WHERE I DRAW THE LINE ON PEOPLE LIKE YOU.
SORRY IF THAT RUINS YOUR BIG PLANS.
OH, DID YOU WANNA BE EVIL PSYCHOLOGIST AGAIN FOR A WHILE? I CAN WAIT.

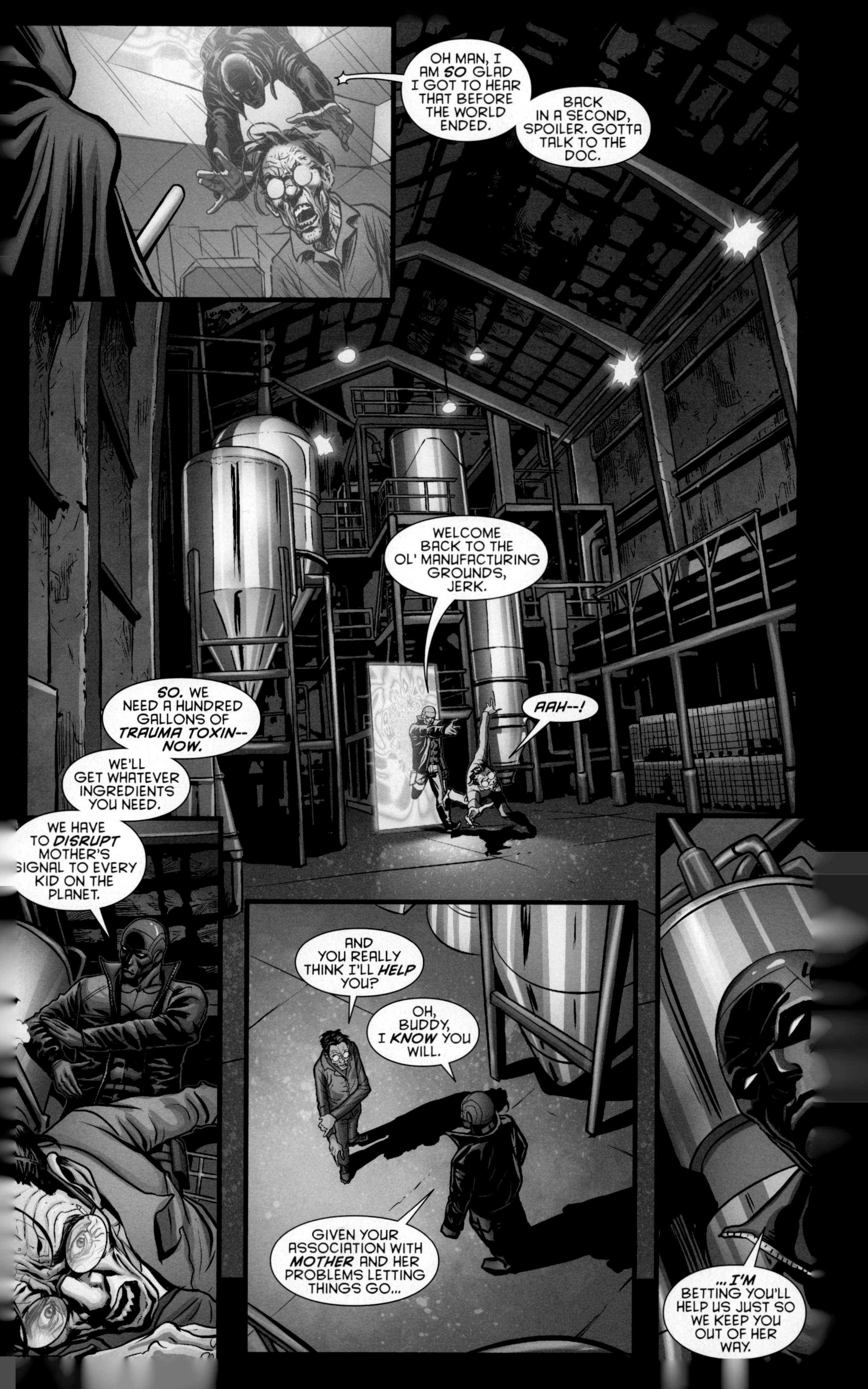
OH MAN, I AM SO GLAD I GOT TO HEAR THAT BEFORE THE WORLD ENDED.
BACK IN A SECOND, SPOILER. GOTTA TALK TO THE DOC.
WELCOME BACK TO THE OL' MANUFACTURING GROUNDS, JERK.
AAH--!
SO. WE NEED A HUNDRED GALLONS OF TRAUMA TOXIN-- NOW.
WE'LL GET WHATEVER INGREDIENTS YOU NEED.
WE HAVE TO DISRUPT MOTHER'S SIGNAL TO EVERY KID ON THE PLANET.
AND YOU REALLY THINK I'LL HELP YOU?
OH, BUDDY, I KNOW YOU WILL.
GIVEN YOUR ASSOCIATION WITH MOTHER AND HER PROBLEMS LETTING THINGS GO...
...I'M BETTING YOU'LL HELP US JUST SO WE KEEP YOU OUT OF HER WAY.

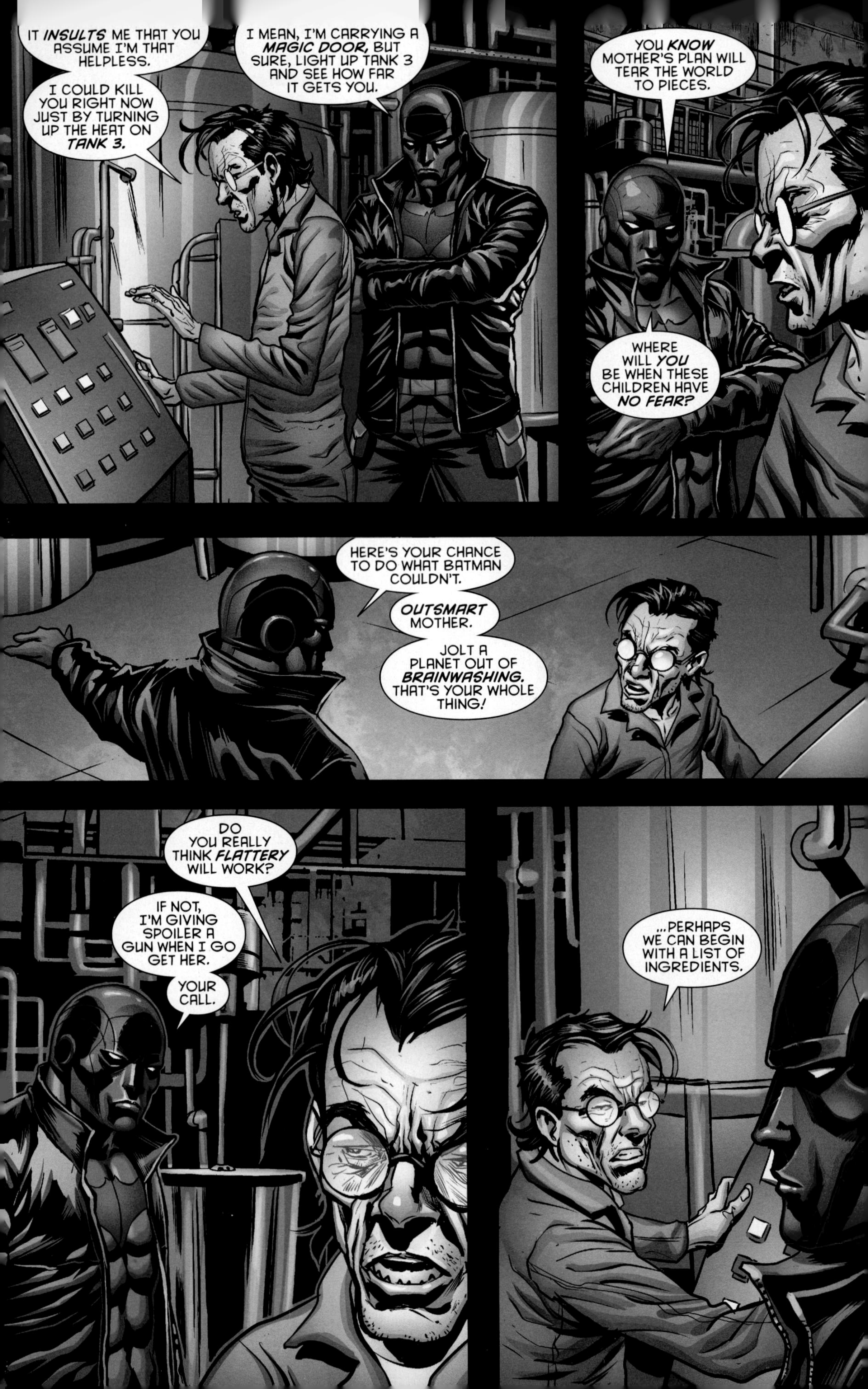
IT INSULTS ME THAT YOU ASSUME I'M THAT HELPLESS.
I COULD KILL YOU RIGHT NOW JUST BY TURNING UP THE HEAT ON TANK 3.
I MEAN, I'M CARRYING A MAGIC DOOR, BUT SURE, LIGHT UP TANK 3 AND SEE HOW FAR IT GETS YOU.
YOU KNOW MOTHER'S PLAN WILL TEAR THE WORLD TO PIECES.
WHERE WILL YOU BE WHEN THESE CHILDREN HAVE NO FEAR?
HERE'S YOUR CHANCE TO DO WHAT BATMAN COULDN'T.
OUTSMART MOTHER.
JOLT A PLANET OUT OF BRAINWASHING. THAT'S YOUR WHOLE THING!
DO YOU REALLY THINK FLATTERY WILL WORK?
IF NOT, I'M GIVING SPOILER A GUN WHEN I GO GET HER.
YOUR CALL.
...PERHAPS WE CAN BEGIN WITH A LIST OF INGREDIENTS.

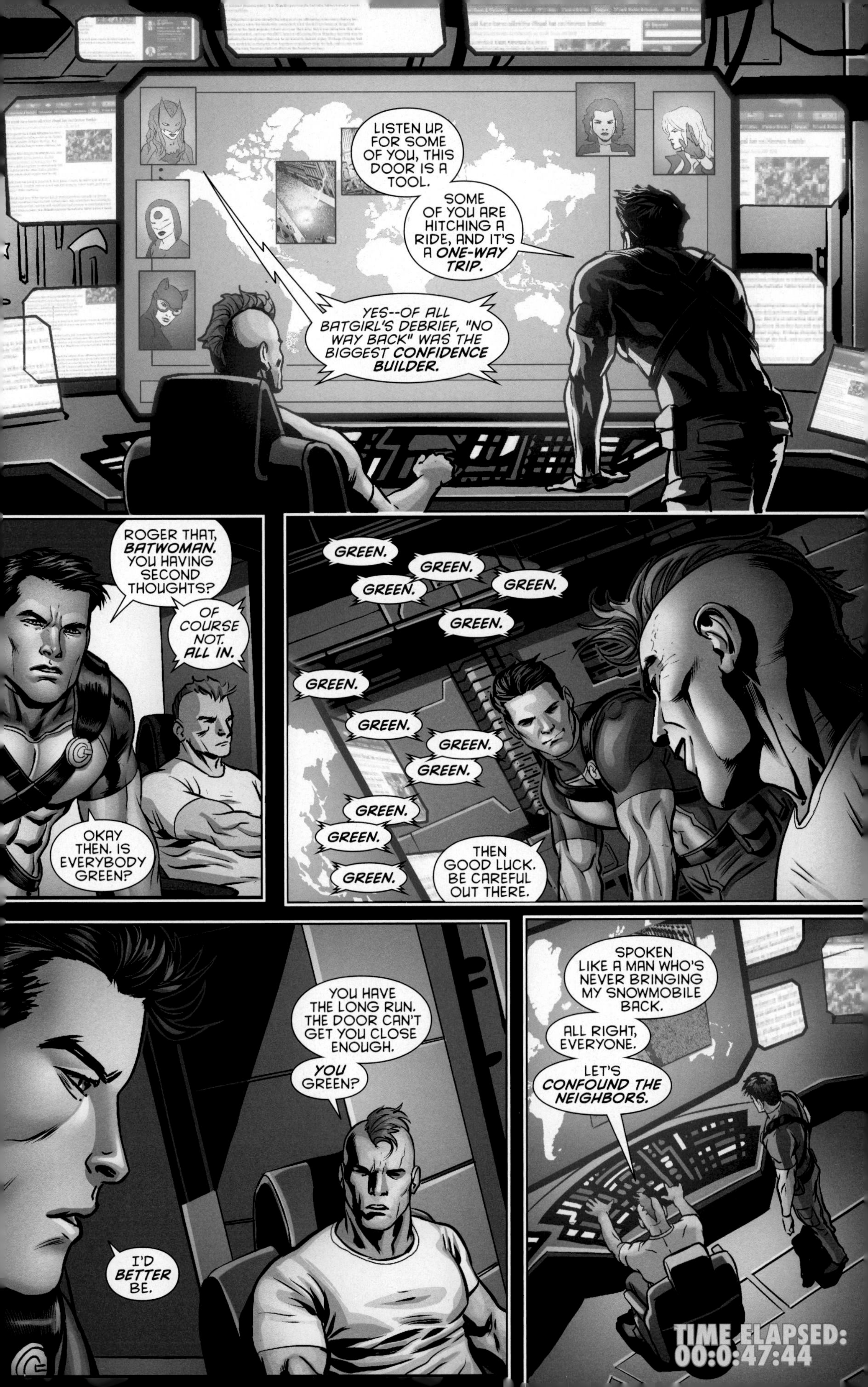
LISTEN UP. FOR SOME OF YOU, THIS DOOR IS A TOOL.
SOME OF YOU ARE HITCHING A RIDE, AND IT'S A ONE-WAY TRIP.
YES--OF ALL BATGIRL'S DEBRIEF, "NO WAY BACK" WAS THE BIGGEST CONFIDENCE BUILDER.
ROGER THAT, BATWOMAN. YOU HAVING SECOND THOUGHTS?
OF COURSE NOT. ALL IN.
OKAY THEN. IS EVERYBODY GREEN?
GREEN.
GREEN.
GREEN.
GREEN.
GREEN.
GREEN.
GREEN.
GREEN.
GREEN.
GREEN.
GREEN.
GREEN.
THEN GOOD LUCK. BE CAREFUL OUT THERE.
YOU HAVE THE LONG RUN. THE DOOR CAN'T GET YOU CLOSE ENOUGH.
YOU GREEN?
I'D BETTER BE.
SPOKEN LIKE A MAN WHO'S NEVER BRINGING MY SNOWMOBILE BACK.
ALL RIGHT, EVERYONE.
LET'S CONFOUND THE NEIGHBORS.
TIME ELAPSED: 00:0:47:44

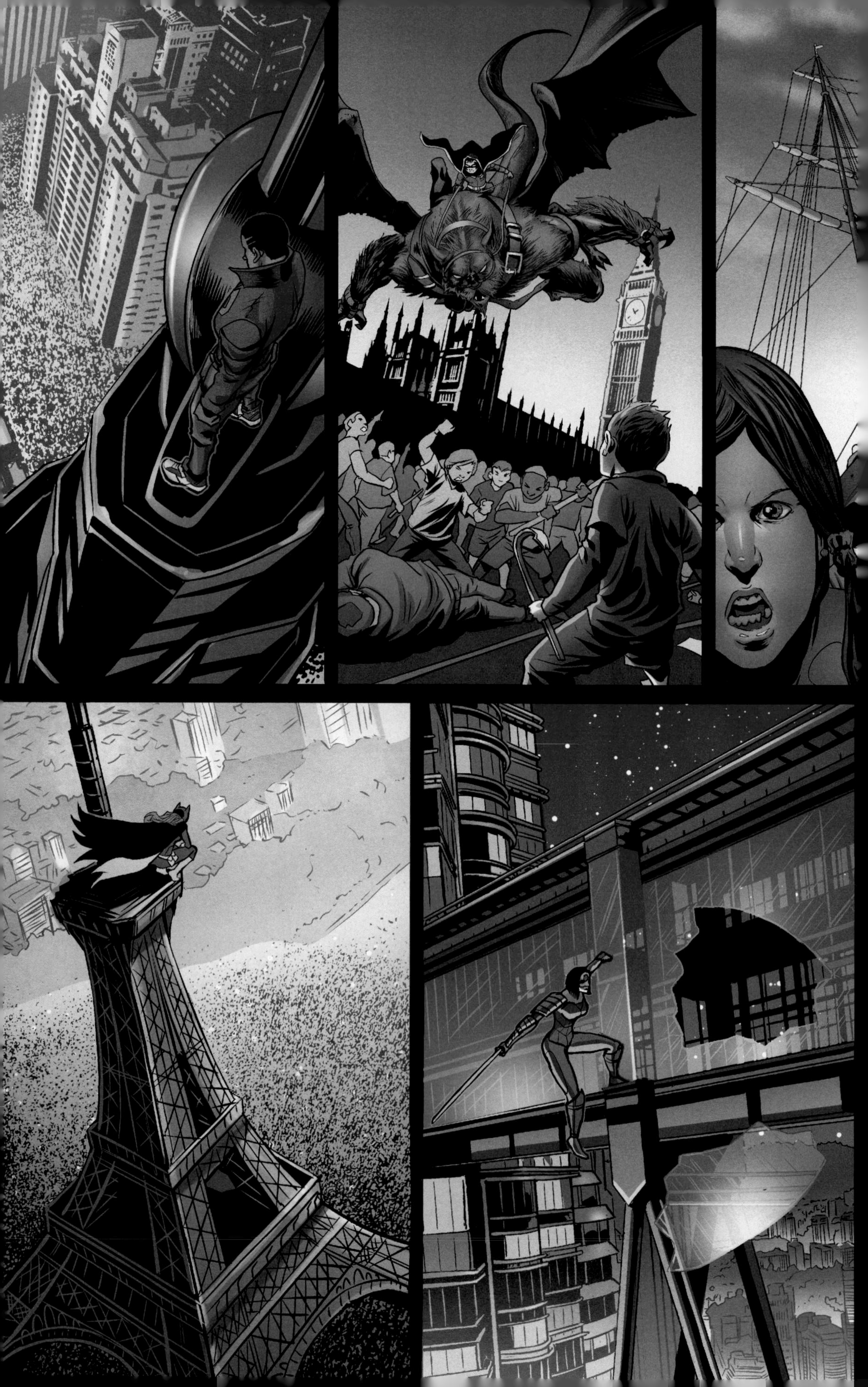

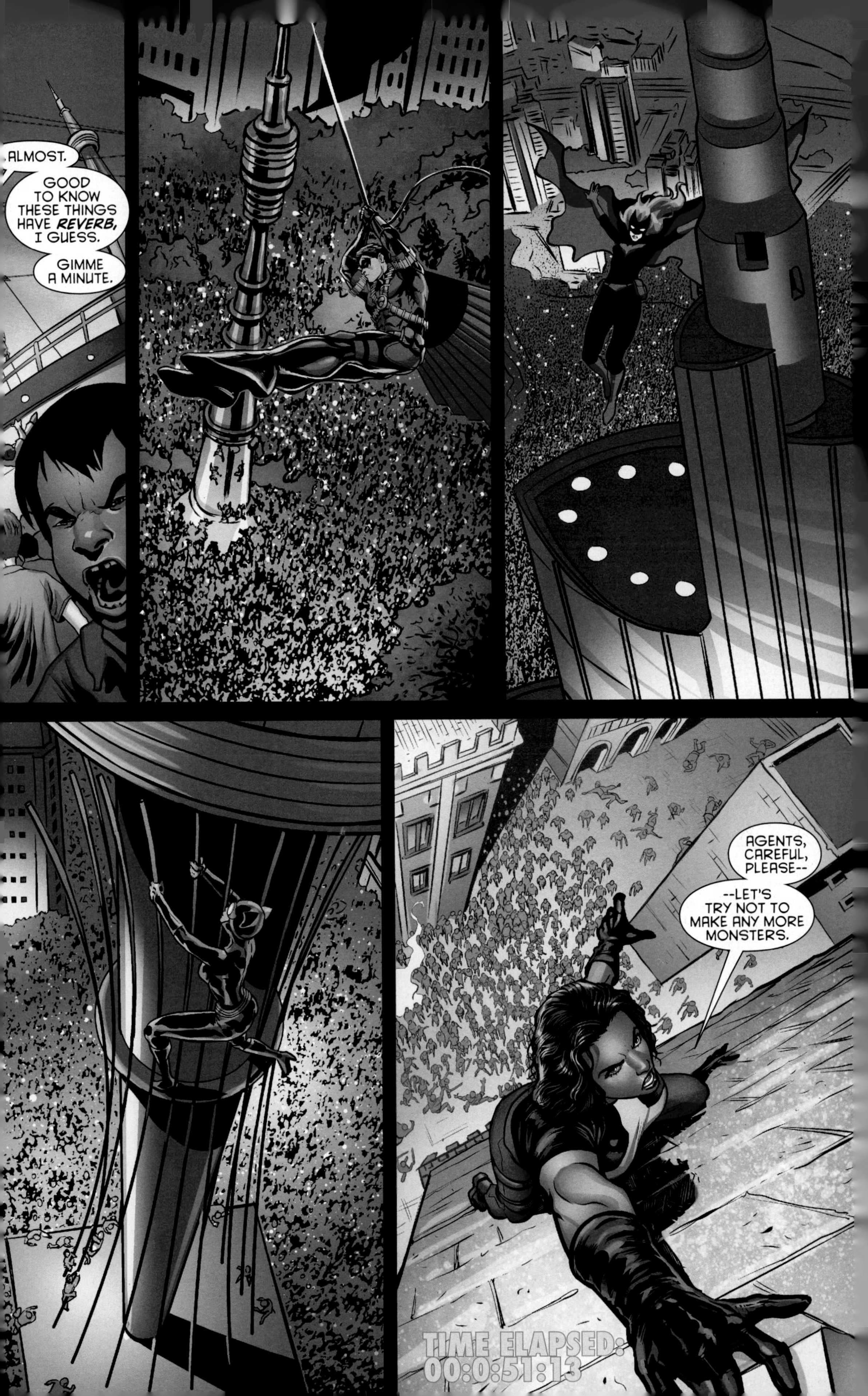
ALMOST.
GOOD TO KNOW THESE THINGS HAVE REVERB, I GUESS.
GIMME A MINUTE.
AGENTS, CAREFUL, PLEASE--
--LET'S TRY NOT TO MAKE ANY MORE MONSTERS.
TIME ELAPSED:
00:0:51:13

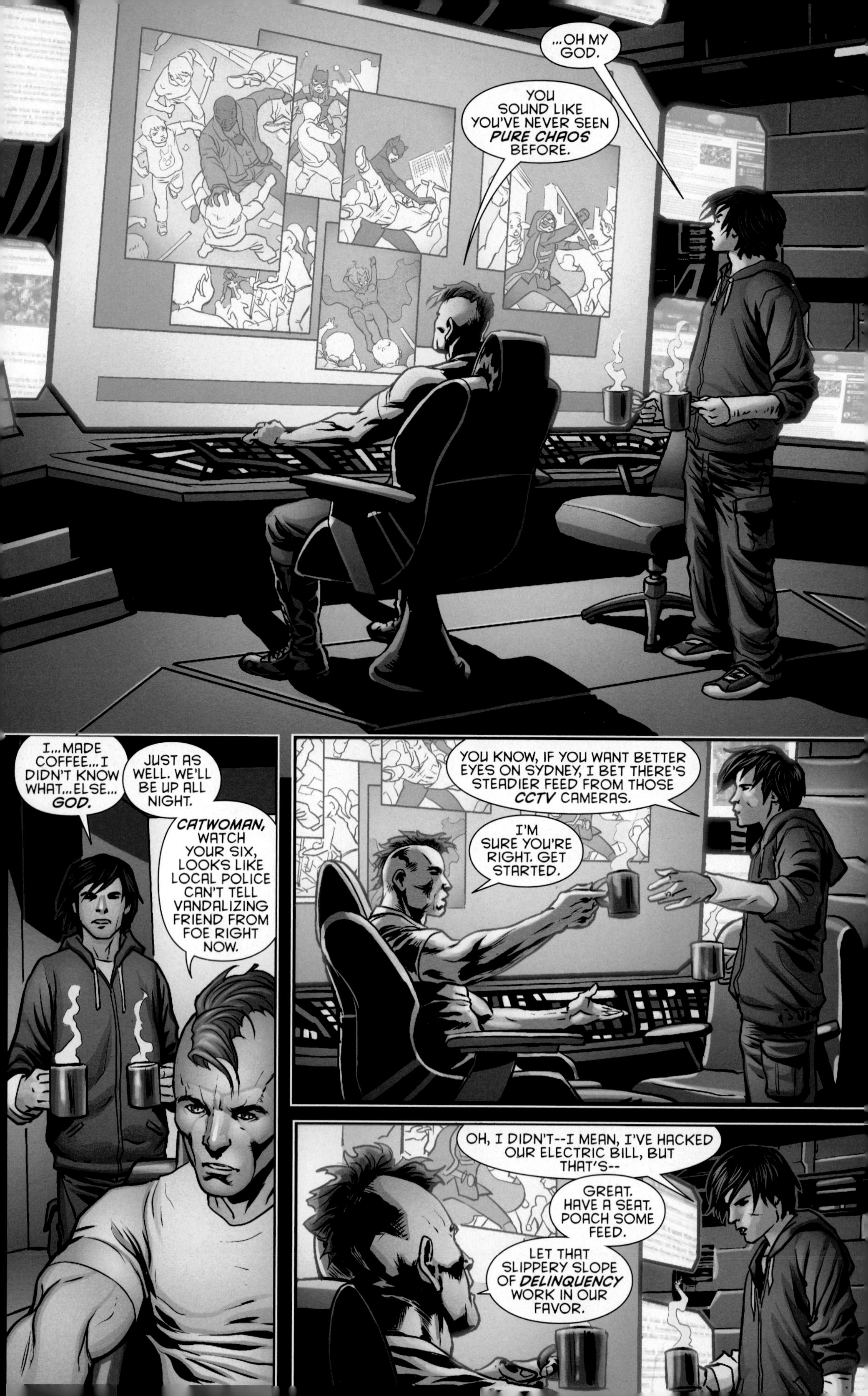
...OH MY GOD.
YOU SOUND LIKE YOU'VE NEVER SEEN PURE CHAOS BEFORE.
I...MADE COFFEE...I DIDN'T KNOW WHAT...ELSE... GOD.
JUST AS WELL. WE'LL BE UP ALL NIGHT.
CATWOMAN, WATCH YOUR SIX, LOOKS LIKE LOCAL POLICE CAN'T TELL VANDALIZING FRIEND FROM FOE RIGHT NOW.
YOU KNOW, IF YOU WANT BETTER EYES ON SYDNEY, I BET THERE'S STEADIER FEED FROM THOSE CCTV CAMERAS.
I'M SURE YOU'RE RIGHT. GET STARTED.
OH, I DIDN'T--I MEAN, I'VE HACKED OUR ELECTRIC BILL, BUT THAT'S--
GREAT. HAVE A SEAT. POACH SOME FEED.
LET THAT SLIPPERY SLOPE OF DELINQUENCY WORK IN OUR FAVOR.

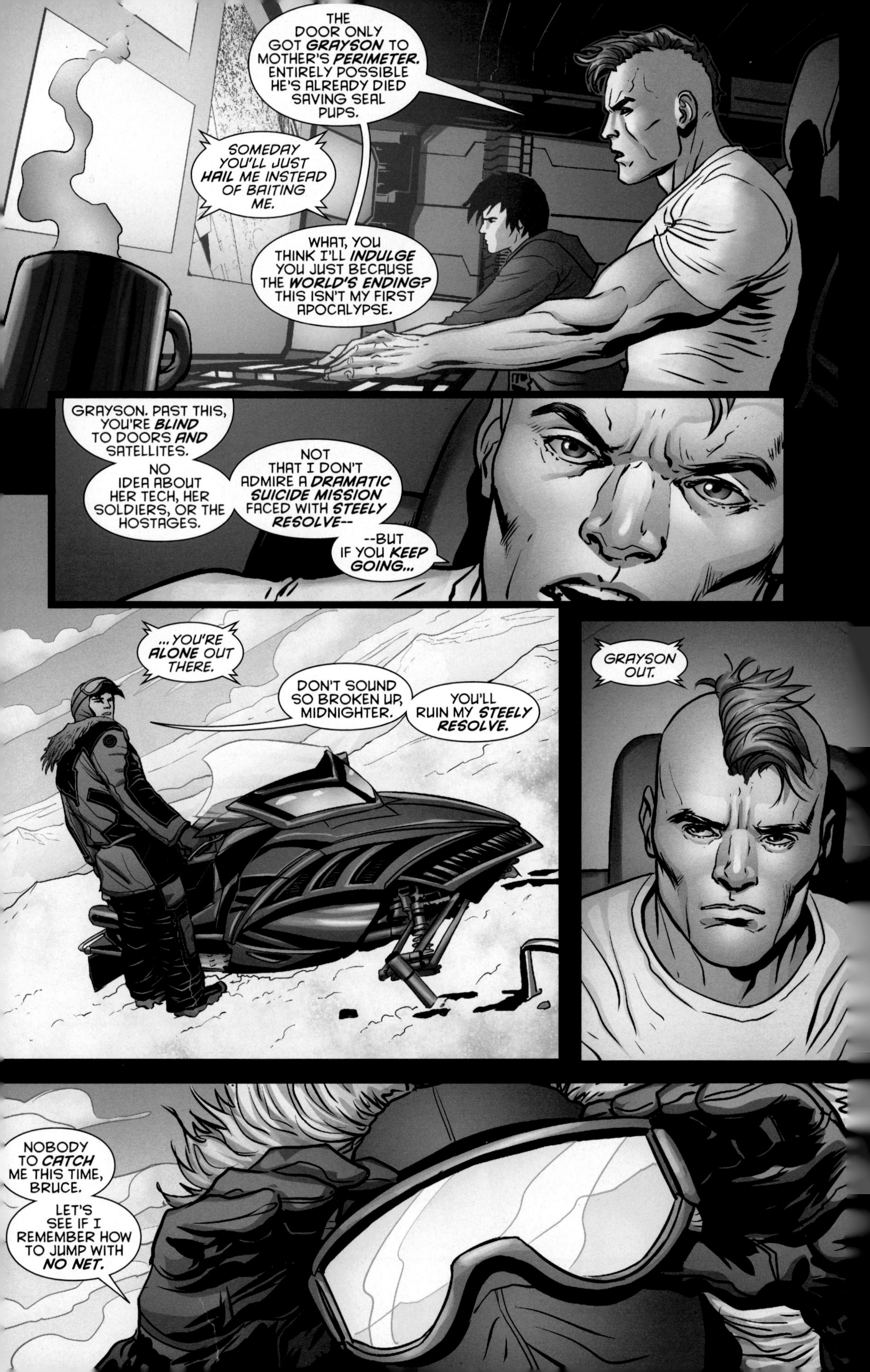
THE DOOR ONLY GOT GRAYSON TO MOTHER'S PERIMETER. ENTIRELY POSSIBLE HE'S ALREADY DIED SAVING SEAL PUPS.
SOMEDAY YOU'LL JUST HAIL ME INSTEAD OF BAITING ME.
WHAT, YOU THINK I'LL INDULGE YOU JUST BECAUSE THE WORLD'S ENDING? THIS ISN'T MY FIRST APOCALYPSE.
GRAYSON. PAST THIS, YOU'RE BLIND TO DOORS AND SATELLITES.
NO IDEA ABOUT HER TECH, HER SOLDIERS, OR THE HOSTAGES.
NOT THAT I DON'T ADMIRE A DRAMATIC SUICIDE MISSION FACED WITH STEELY RESOLVE--
--BUT IF YOU KEEP GOING...
...YOU'RE ALONE OUT THERE.
DON'T SOUND SO BROKEN UP, MIDNIGHTER.
YOU'LL RUIN MY STEELY RESOLVE.
GRAYSON OUT.
NOBODY TO CATCH ME THIS TIME, BRUCE.
LET'S SEE IF I REMEMBER HOW TO JUMP WITH NO NET.

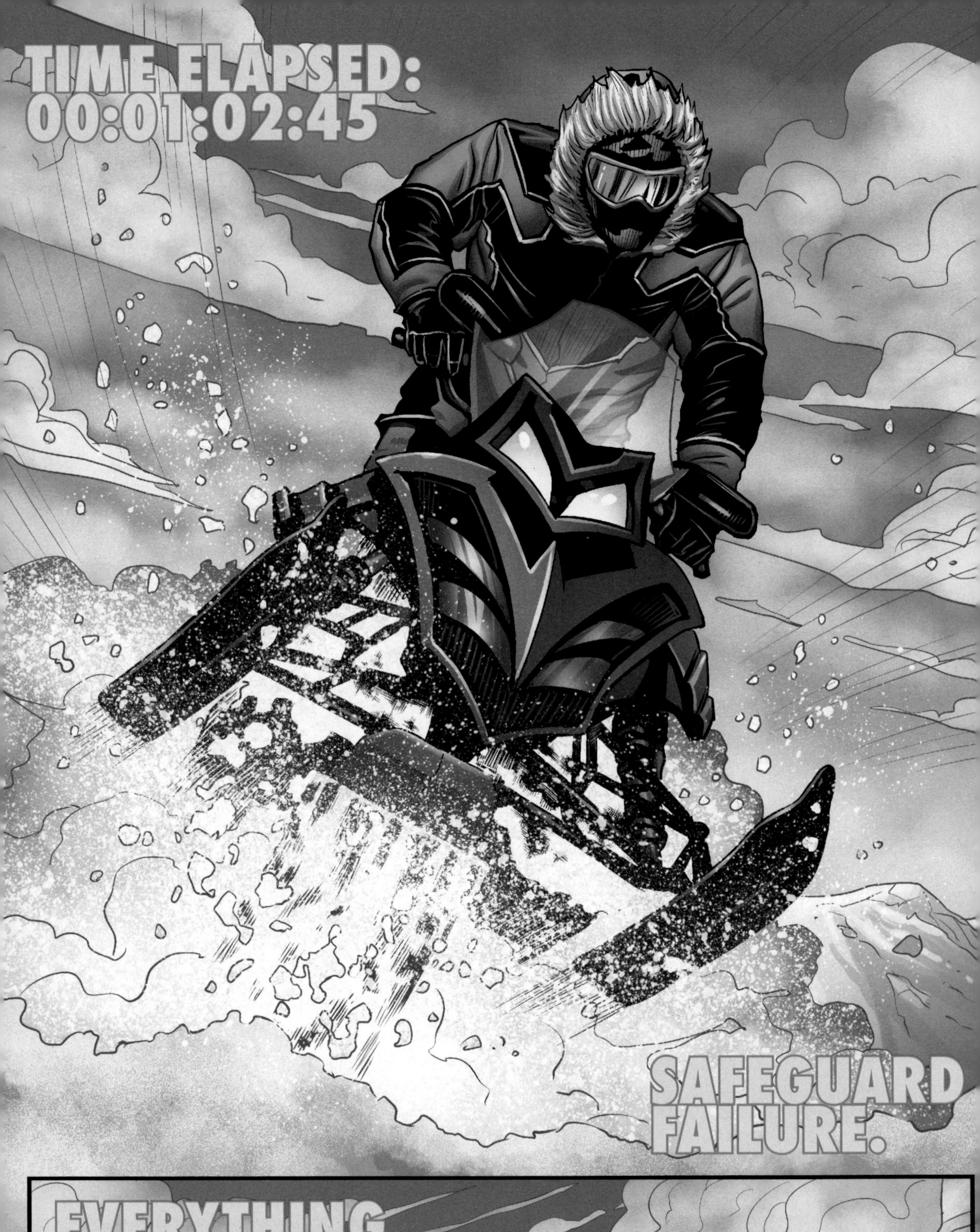
TIME ELAPSED:
00:01:02:45
SAFEGUARD FAILURE.

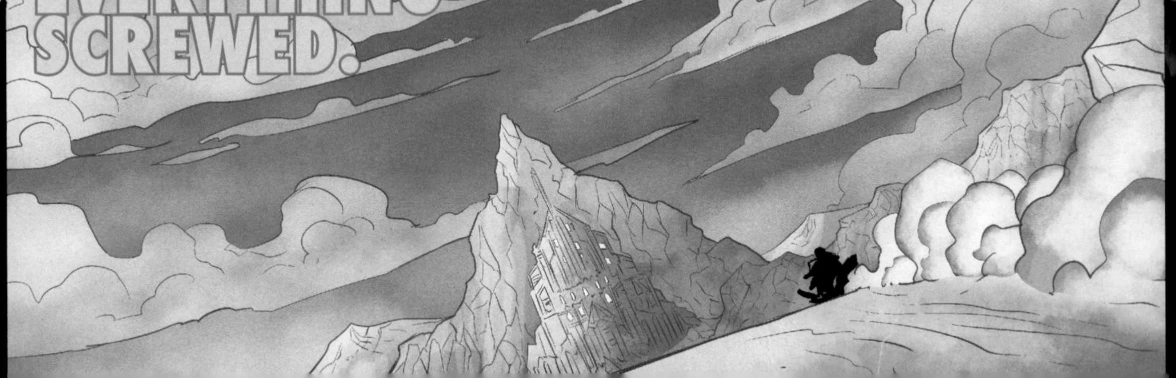
EVERYTHING SCREWED.

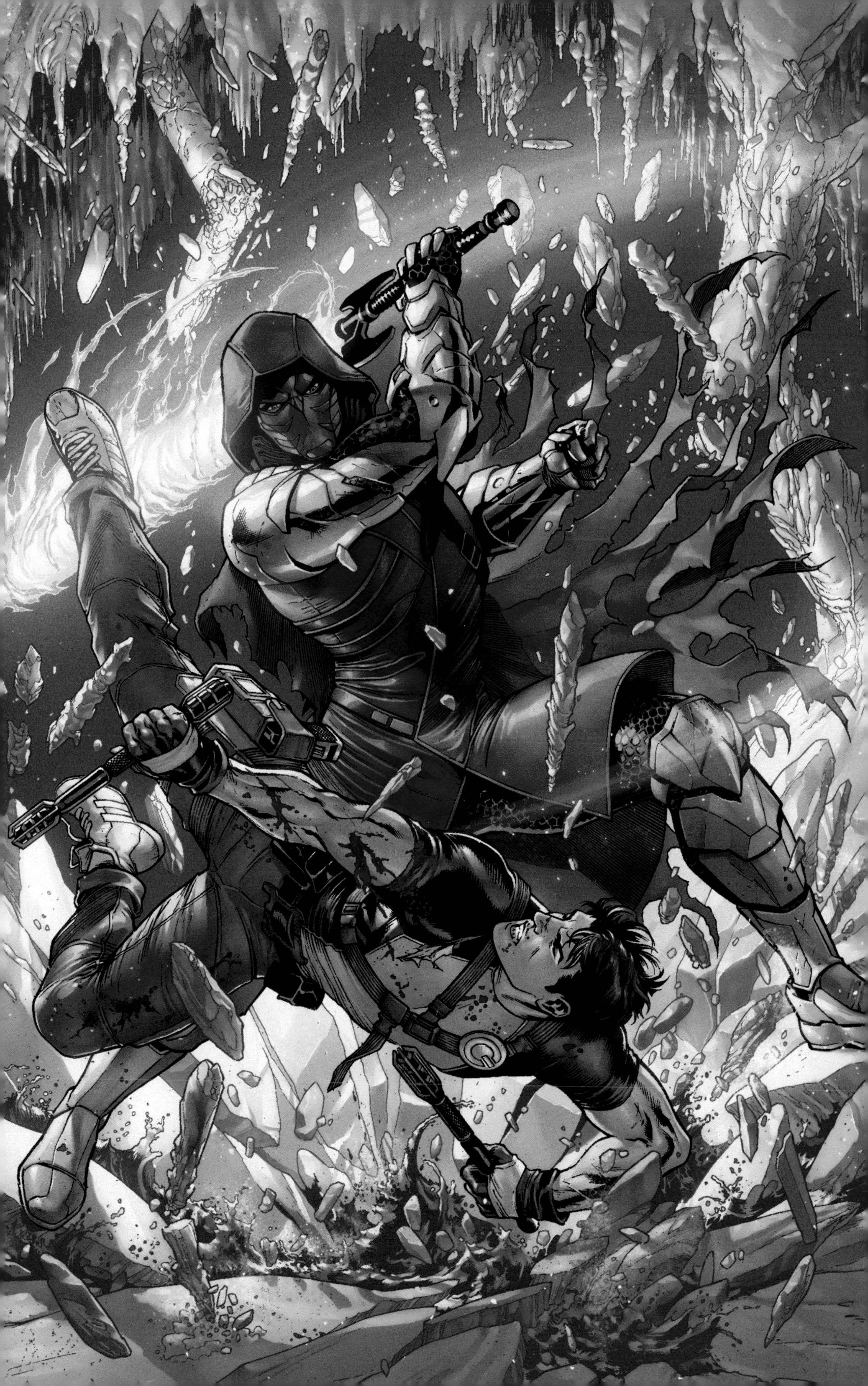

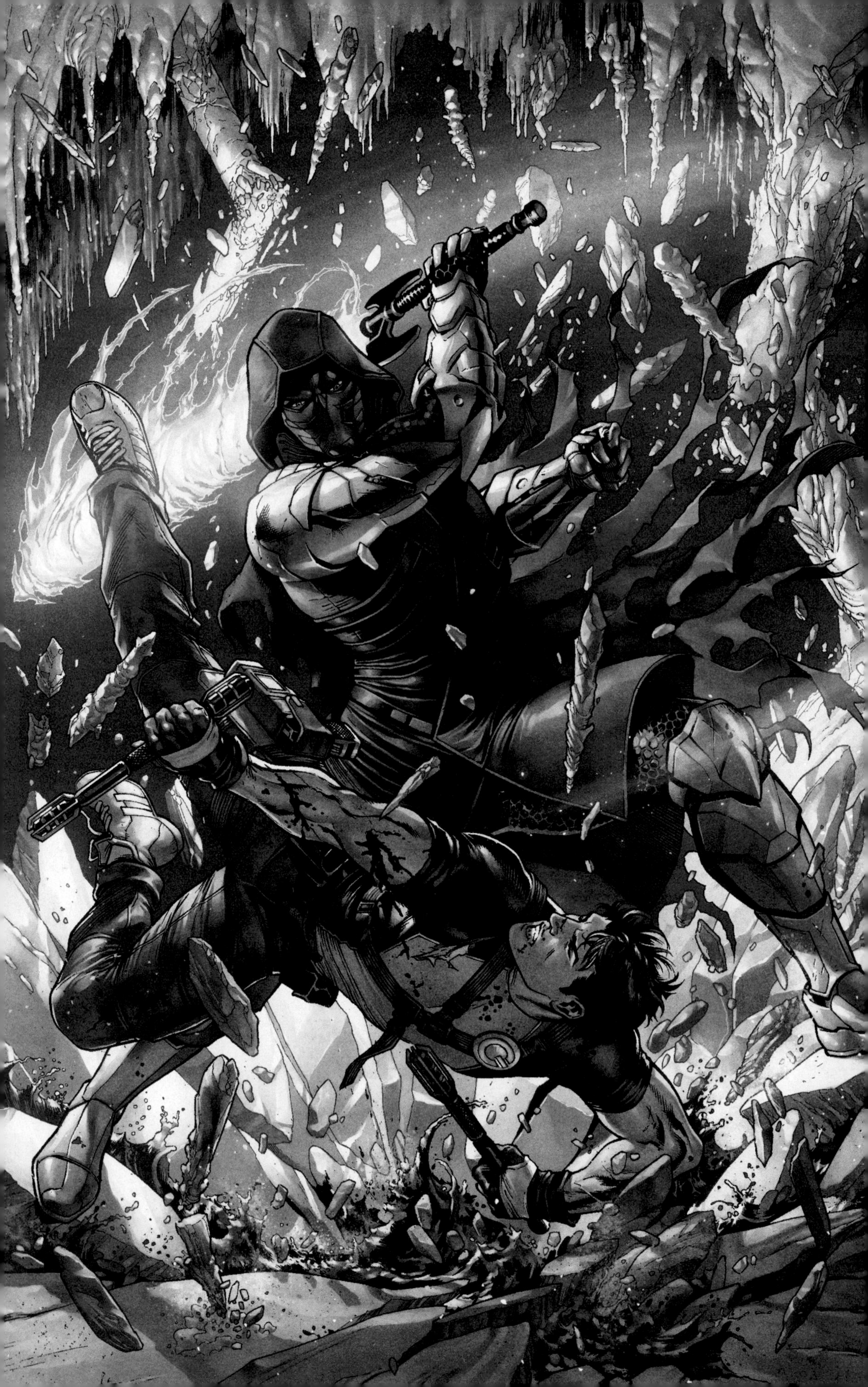

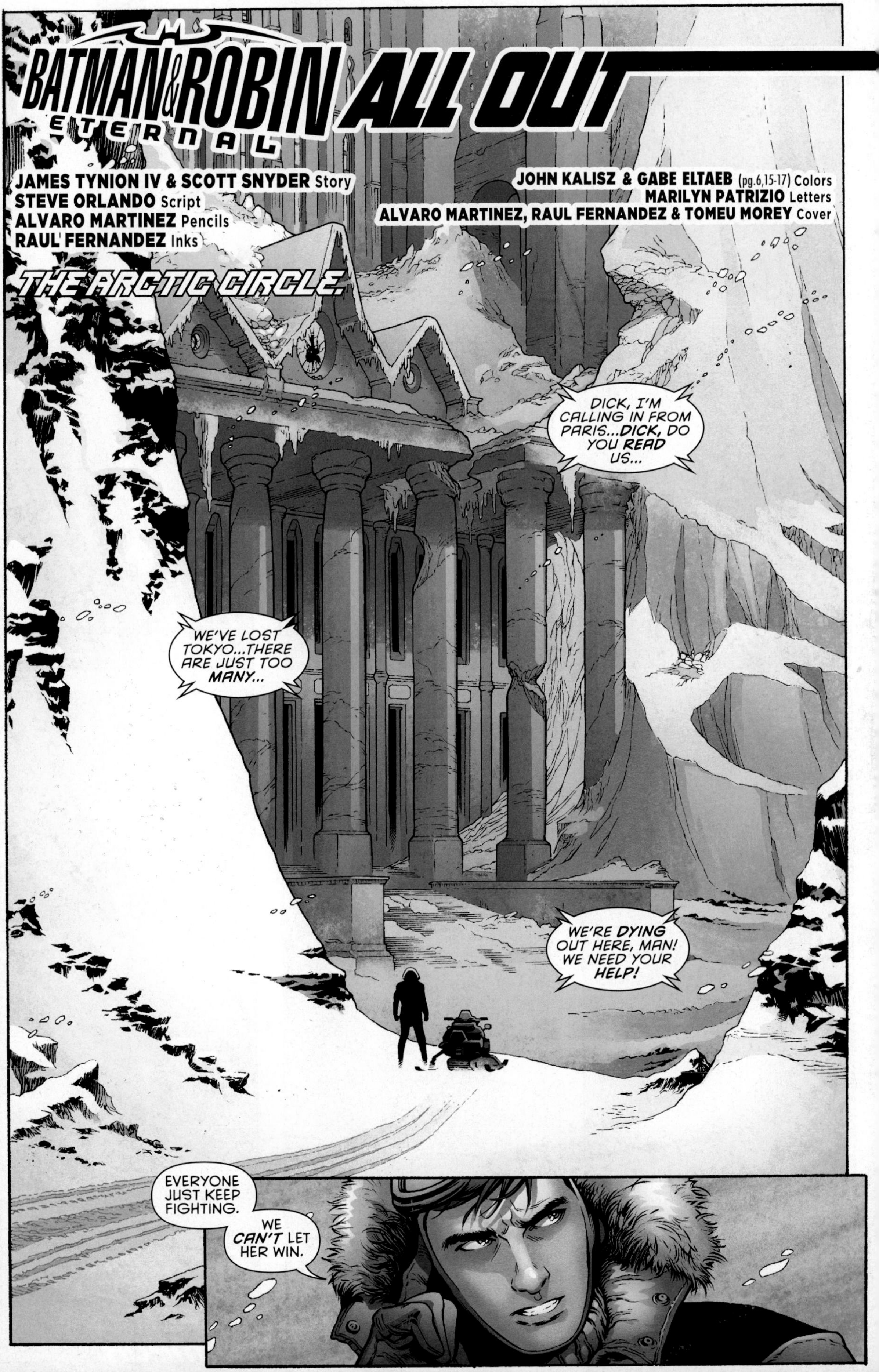
BATMAN & ROBIN ETERNAL
ALL OUT
JAMES TYNION IV & SCOTT SNYDER Story
STEVE ORLANDO Script
ALVARO MARTINEZ Pencils
RAUL FERNANDEZ Inks
JOHN KALISZ & GABE ELTAEB (pg.6,15-17) Colors
MARILYN PATRIZIO Letters
ALVARO MARTINEZ, RAUL FERNANDEZ & TOMEU MOREY Cover
THE ARCTIC CIRCLE.
DICK, I'M CALLING IN FROM PARIS...DICK, DO YOU READ US...
WE'VE LOST TOKYO...THERE ARE JUST TOO MANY...
WE'RE DYING OUT HERE, MAN! WE NEED YOUR HELP!
EVERYONE JUST KEEP FIGHTING.
WE CAN'T LET HER WIN.

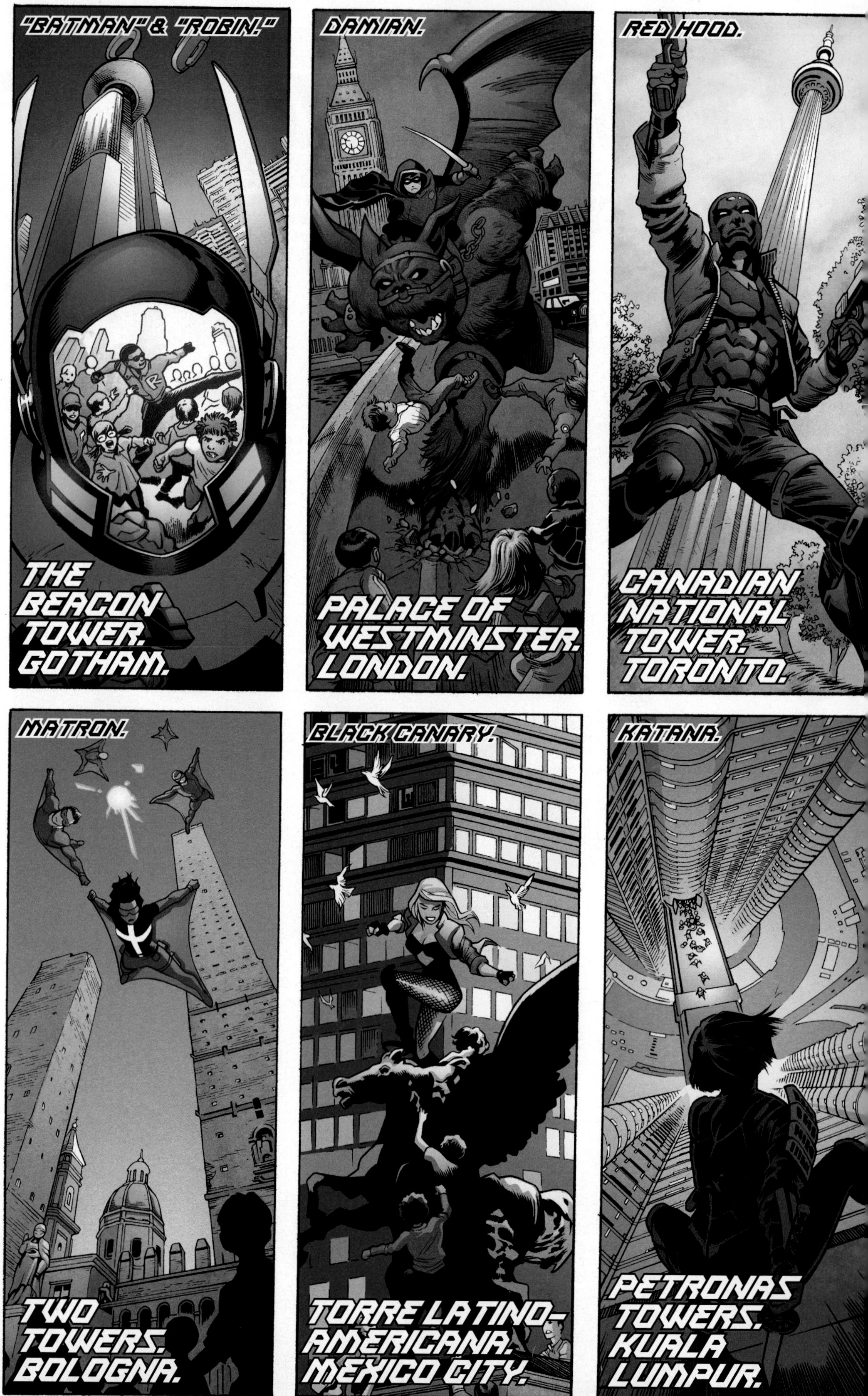
"BATMAN" & "ROBIN."
THE BEACON TOWER. GOTHAM.
DAMIAN.
PALACE OF WESTMINSTER. LONDON.
RED HOOD.
CANADIAN NATIONAL TOWER. TORONTO.
MATRON.
TWO TOWERS. BOLOGNA.
BLACK CANARY.
TORRE LATINO-AMERICANA. MEXICO CITY.
KATANA.
PETRONAS TOWERS. KUALA LUMPUR.

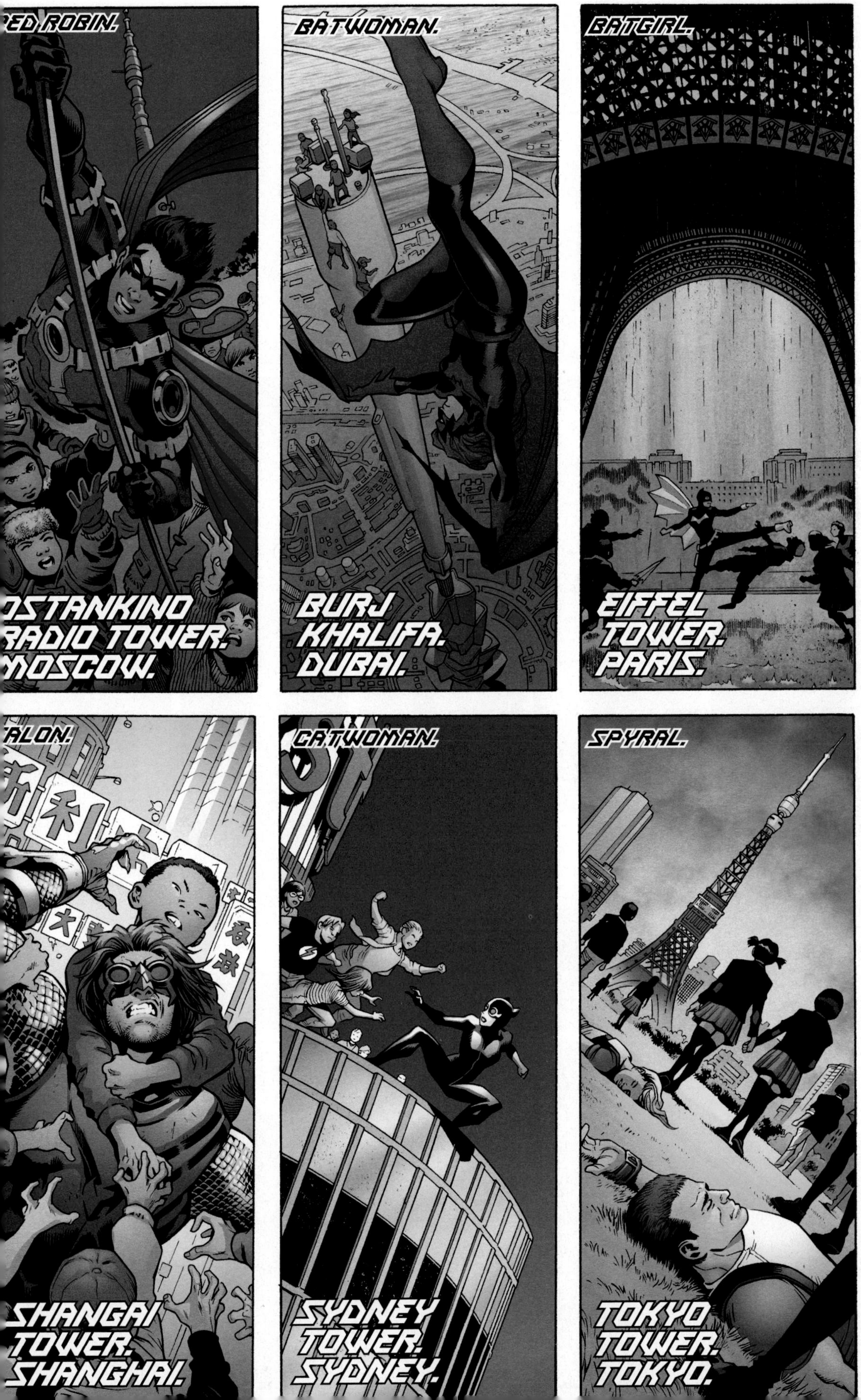
ED ROBIN.
OSTANKINO
RADIO TOWER.
OSCOW.
BATWOMAN.
BURJ
KHALIFA.
DUBAI.
BATGIRL.
EIFFEL
TOWER.
PARIS.
ALON.
SHANGAI
TOWER.
SHANGHAI.
CATWOMAN.
SYDNEY
TOWER.
SYDNEY.
SPYRAL.
TOKYO
TOWER.
TOKYO.

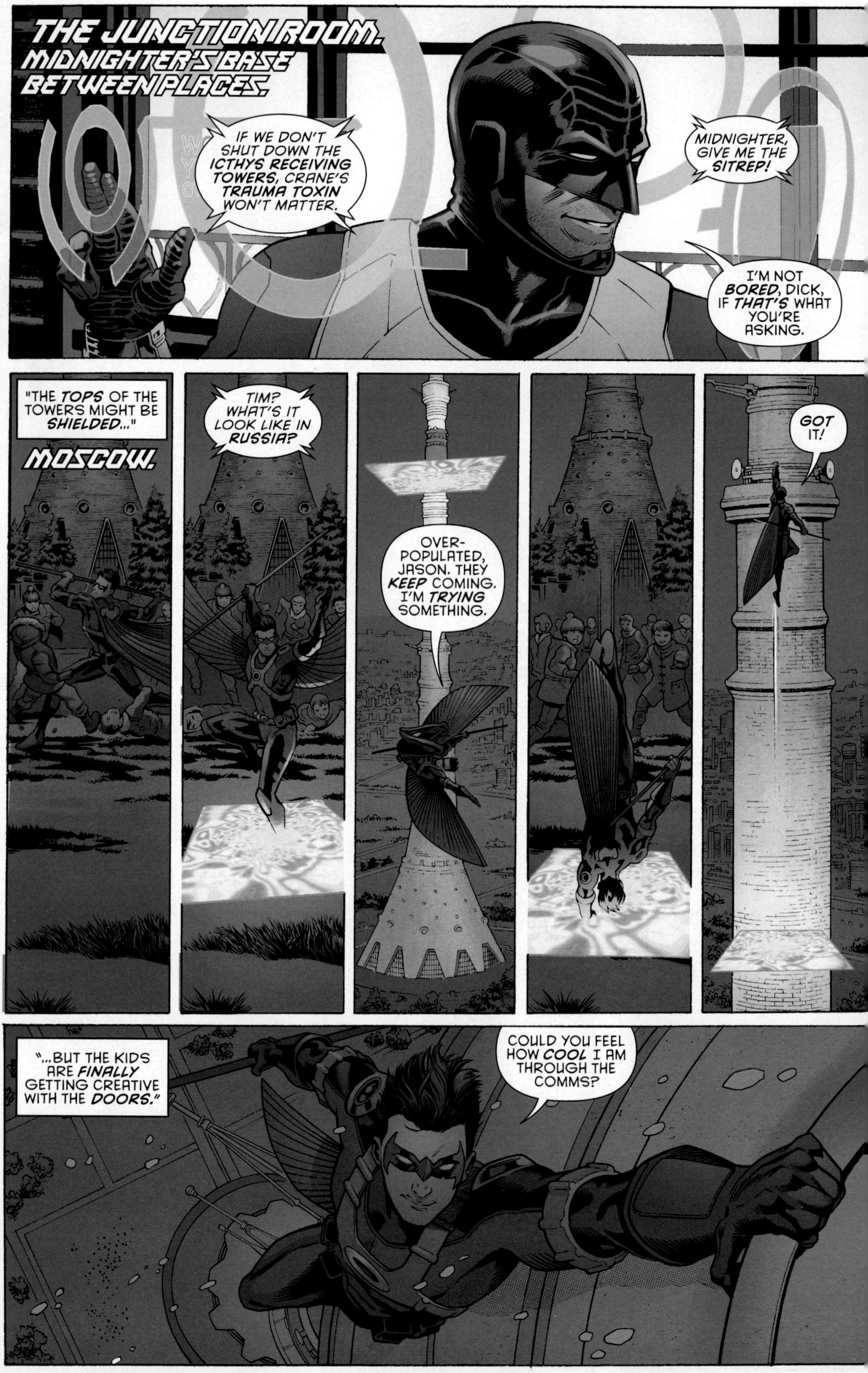
THE JUNCTION ROOM. MIDNIGHTER'S BASE BETWEEN PLACES.
IF WE DON'T SHUT DOWN THE ICTHYS RECEIVING TOWERS, CRANE'S TRAUMA TOXIN WON'T MATTER.
MIDNIGHTER, GIVE ME THE SITREP!
I'M NOT BORED, DICK, IF THAT'S WHAT YOU'RE ASKING.
"THE TOPS OF THE TOWERS MIGHT BE SHIELDED..."
MOSCOW.
TIM? WHAT'S IT LOOK LIKE IN RUSSIA?
OVER-POPULATED, JASON. THEY KEEP COMING. I'M TRYING SOMETHING.
GOT IT!
"...BUT THE KIDS ARE FINALLY GETTING CREATIVE WITH THE DOORS."
COULD YOU FEEL HOW COOL I AM THROUGH THE COMMS?

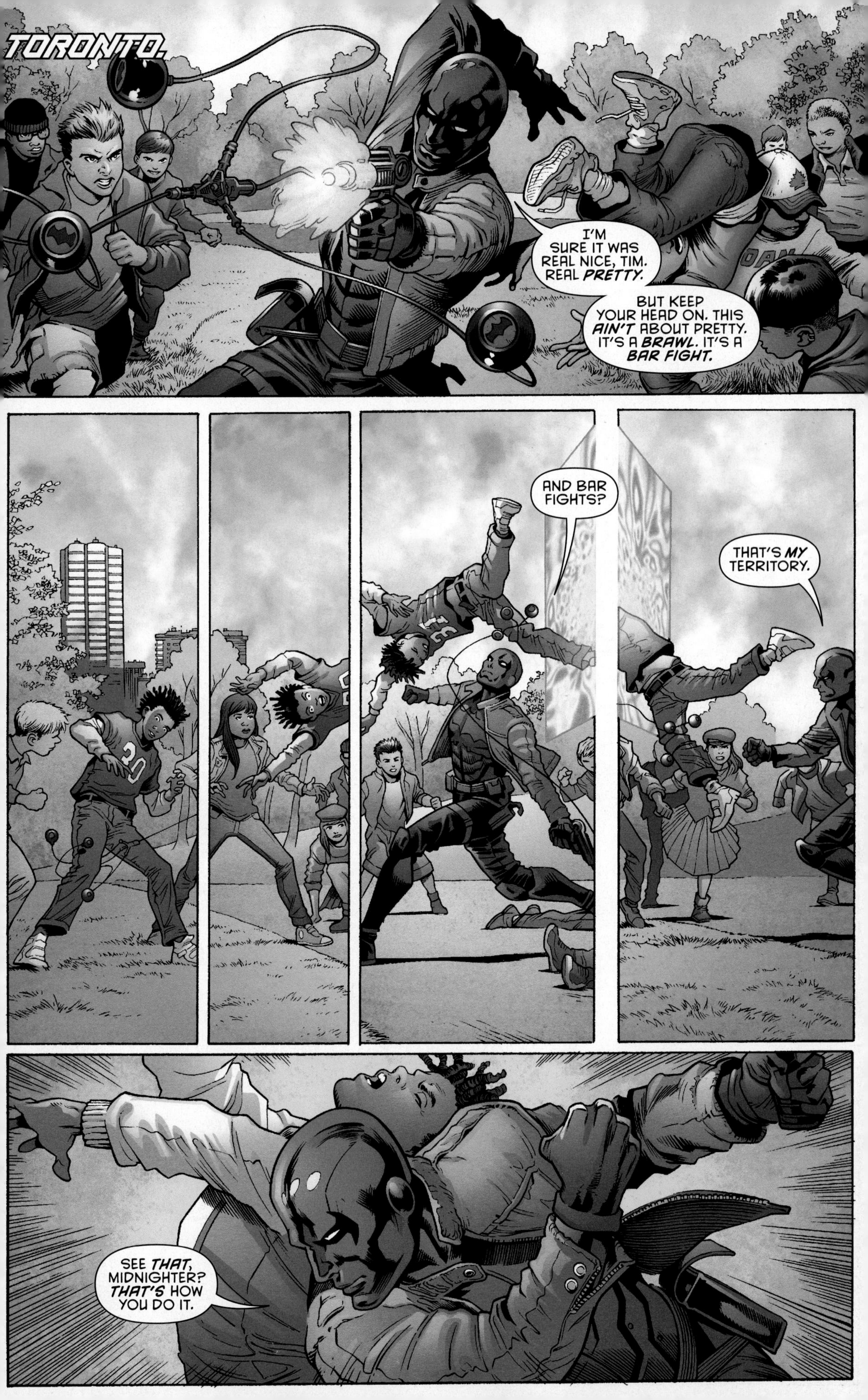
TORONTO.
I'M SURE IT WAS REAL NICE, TIM. REAL PRETTY.
BUT KEEP YOUR HEAD ON. THIS AIN'T ABOUT PRETTY. IT'S A BRAWL. IT'S A BAR FIGHT.
AND BAR FIGHTS?
THAT'S MY TERRITORY.
SEE THAT, MIDNIGHTER? THAT'S HOW YOU DO IT.

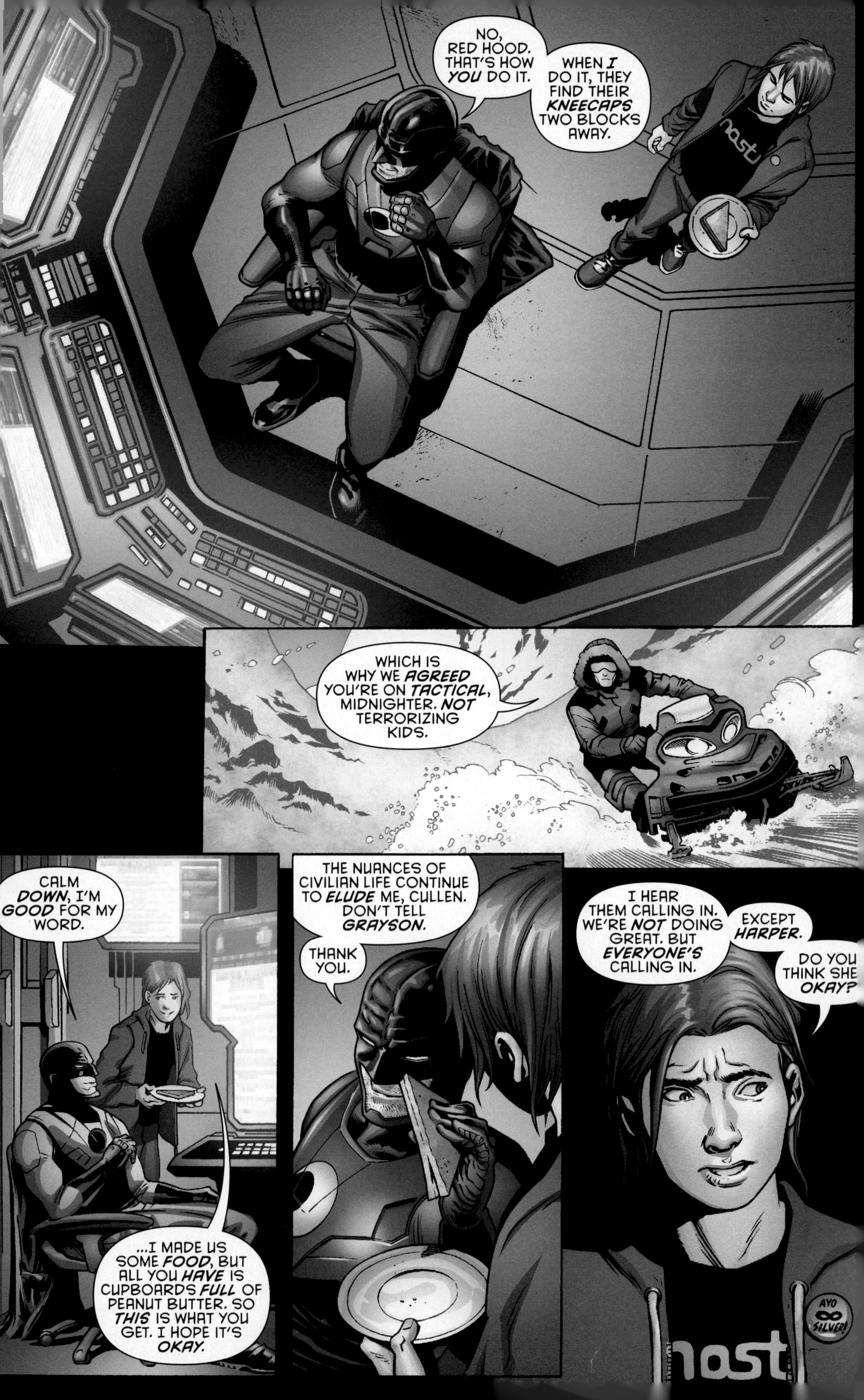
NO, RED HOOD. THAT'S HOW YOU DO IT.
WHEN I DO IT, THEY FIND THEIR KNEECAPS TWO BLOCKS AWAY.
WHICH IS WHY WE AGREED YOU'RE ON TACTICAL, MIDNIGHTER. NOT TERRORIZING KIDS.
CALM DOWN, I'M GOOD FOR MY WORD.
...I MADE US SOME FOOD, BUT ALL YOU HAVE IS CUPBOARDS FULL OF PEANUT BUTTER. SO THIS IS WHAT YOU GET. I HOPE IT'S OKAY.
THE NUANCES OF CIVILIAN LIFE CONTINUE TO ELUDE ME, CULLEN. DON'T TELL GRAYSON.
THANK YOU.
I HEAR THEM CALLING IN. WE'RE NOT DOING GREAT. BUT EVERYONE'S CALLING IN.
EXCEPT HARPER.
DO YOU THINK SHE OKAY?
AYO SILVER!

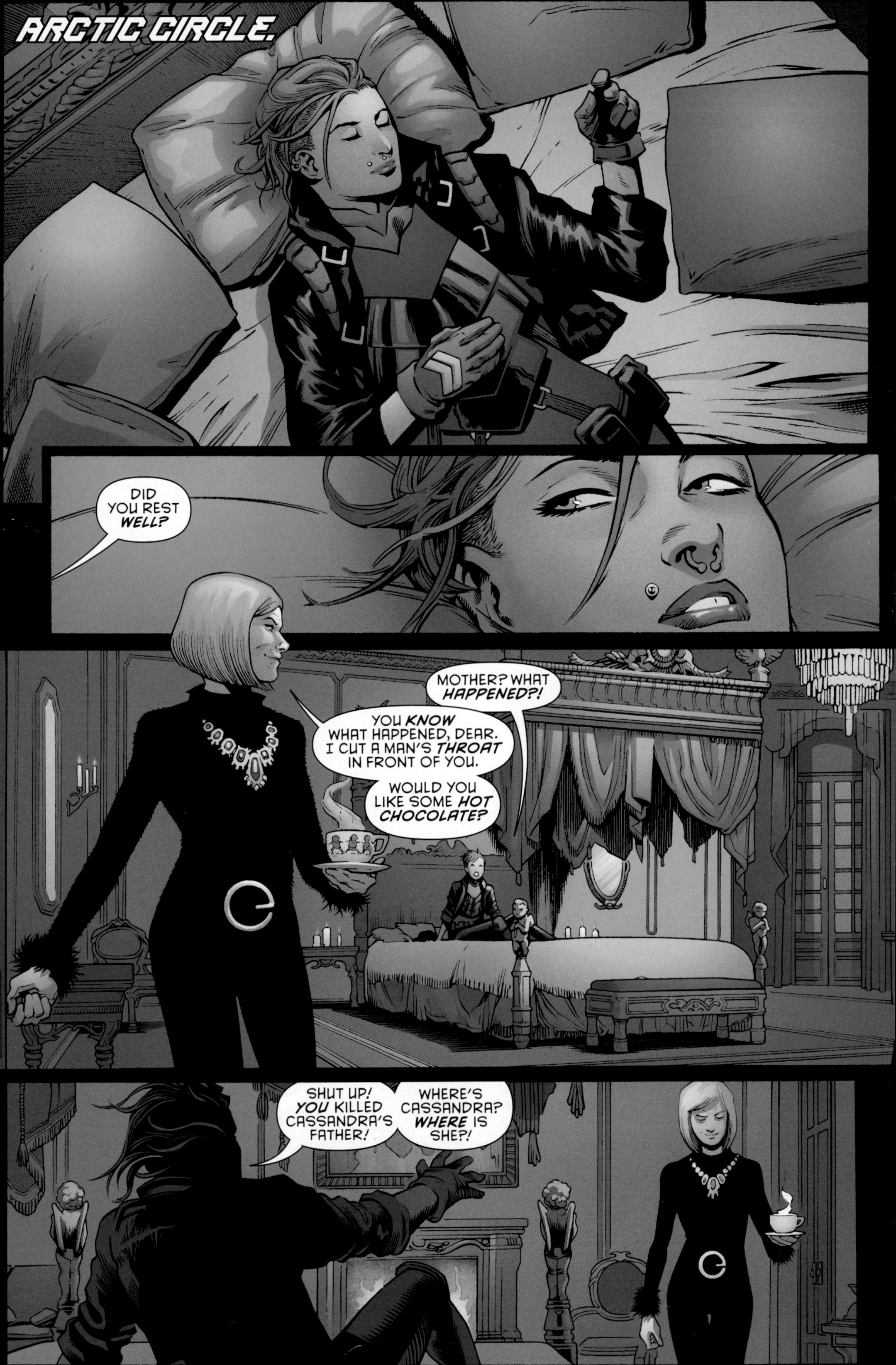
ARCTIC CIRCLE.
DID YOU REST WELL?
MOTHER? WHAT HAPPENED?!
YOU KNOW WHAT HAPPENED, DEAR. I CUT A MAN'S THROAT IN FRONT OF YOU.
WOULD YOU LIKE SOME HOT CHOCOLATE?
SHUT UP! YOU KILLED CASSANDRA'S FATHER!
WHERE'S CASSANDRA? WHERE IS SHE?!

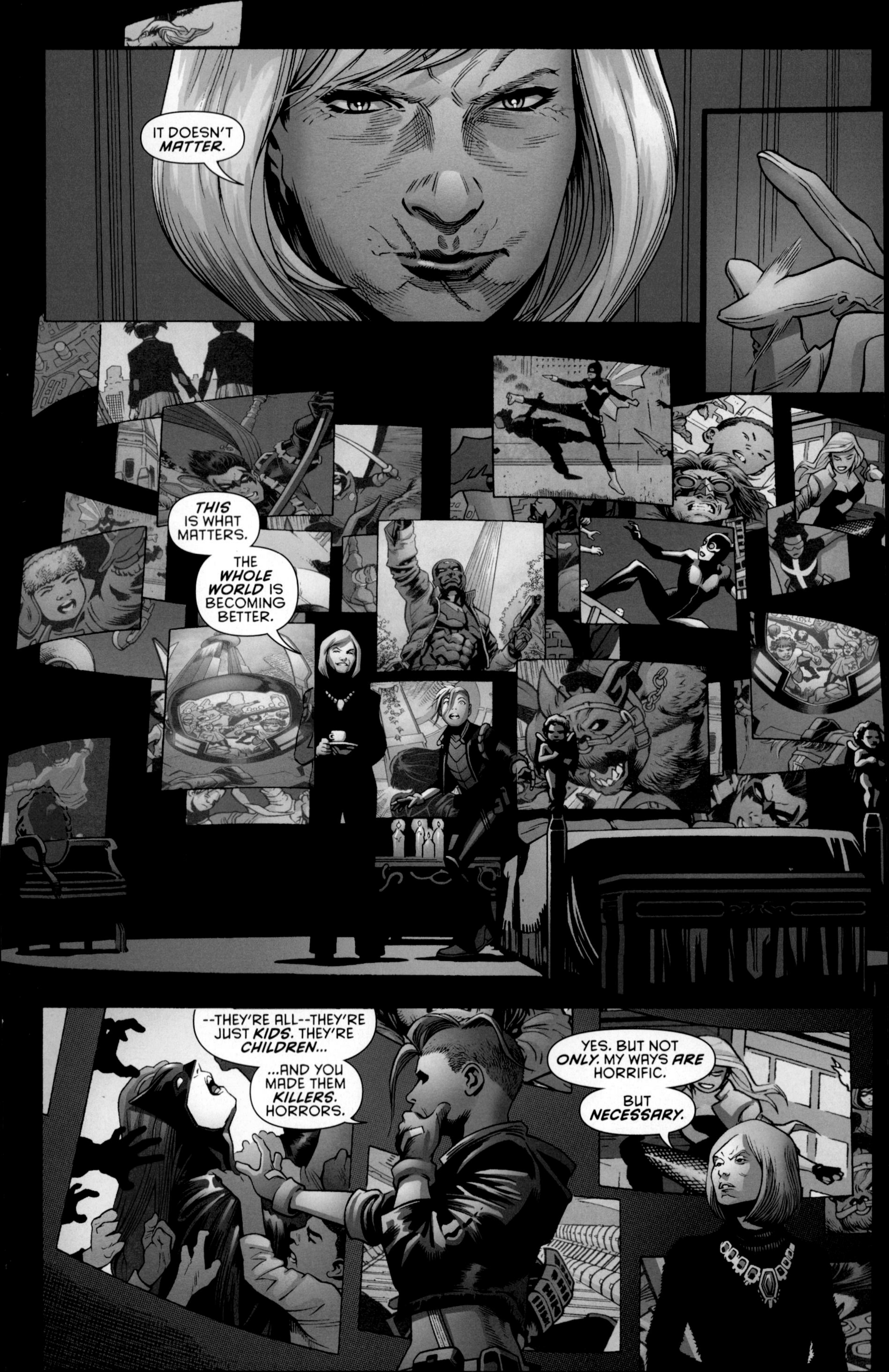
IT DOESN'T MATTER.
THIS IS WHAT MATTERS.
THE WHOLE WORLD IS BECOMING BETTER.
--THEY'RE ALL--THEY'RE JUST KIDS. THEY'RE CHILDREN...
...AND YOU MADE THEM KILLERS. HORRORS.
YES. BUT NOT ONLY. MY WAYS ARE HORRIFIC.
BUT NECESSARY.

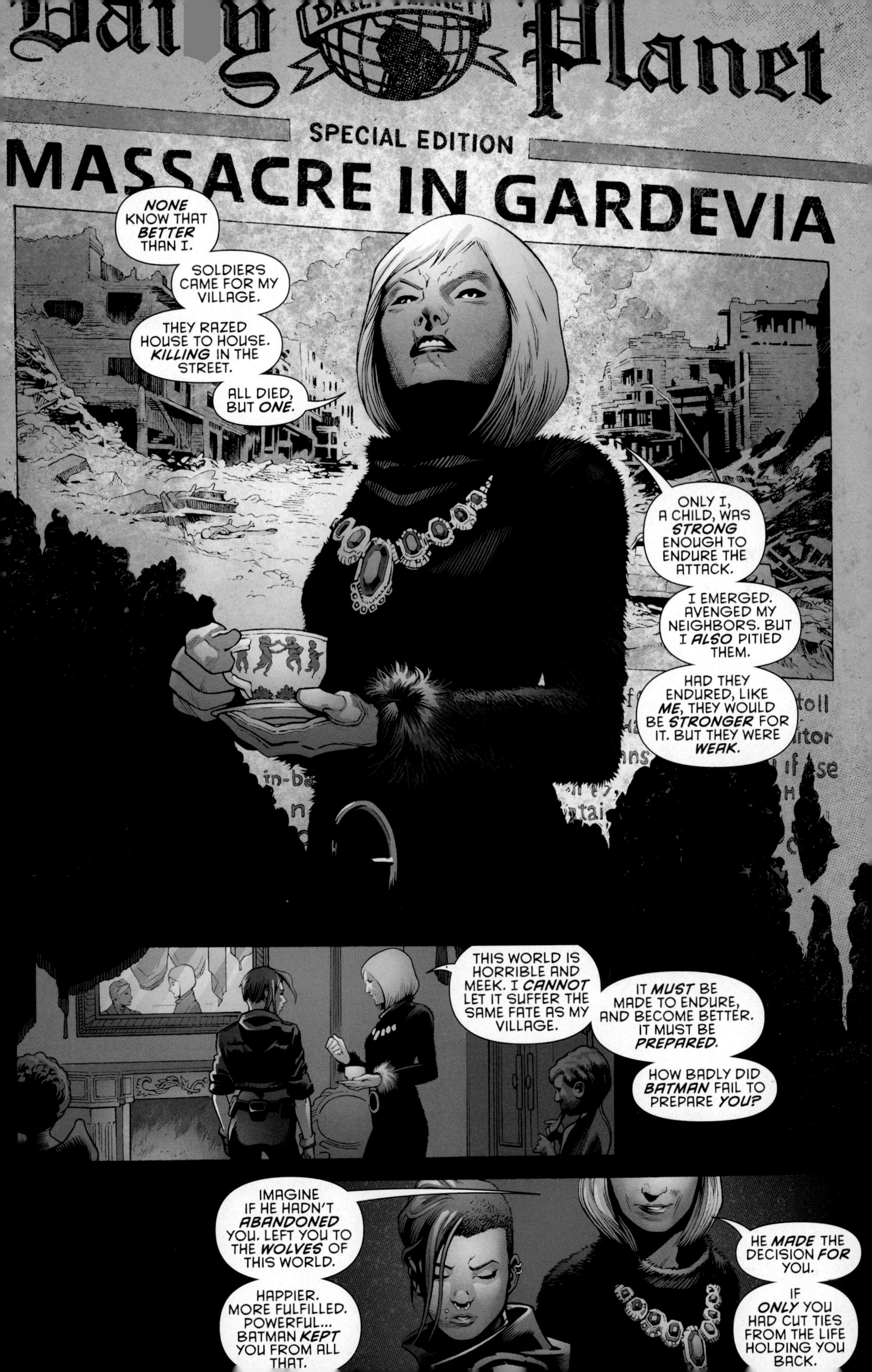

Planet
SPECIAL EDITION
MASSACRE IN GARDEVIA
NONE KNOW THAT BETTER THAN I.
SOLDIERS CAME FOR MY VILLAGE.
THEY RAZED HOUSE TO HOUSE. KILLING IN THE STREET.
ALL DIED, BUT ONE.
ONLY I, A CHILD, WAS STRONG ENOUGH TO ENDURE THE ATTACK.
I EMERGED. AVENGED MY NEIGHBORS. BUT I ALSO PITIED THEM.
HAD THEY ENDURED, LIKE ME, THEY WOULD BE STRONGER FOR IT. BUT THEY WERE WEAK.
THIS WORLD IS HORRIBLE AND MEEK. I CANNOT LET IT SUFFER THE SAME FATE AS MY VILLAGE.
IT MUST BE MADE TO ENDURE, AND BECOME BETTER. IT MUST BE PREPARED.
HOW BADLY DID BATMAN FAIL TO PREPARE YOU?
IMAGINE IF HE HADN'T ABANDONED YOU. LEFT YOU TO THE WOLVES OF THIS WORLD.
HAPPIER. MORE FULFILLED. POWERFUL... BATMAN KEPT YOU FROM ALL THAT.
HE MADE THE DECISION FOR YOU.
IF ONLY YOU HAD CUT TIES FROM THE LIFE HOLDING YOU BACK.

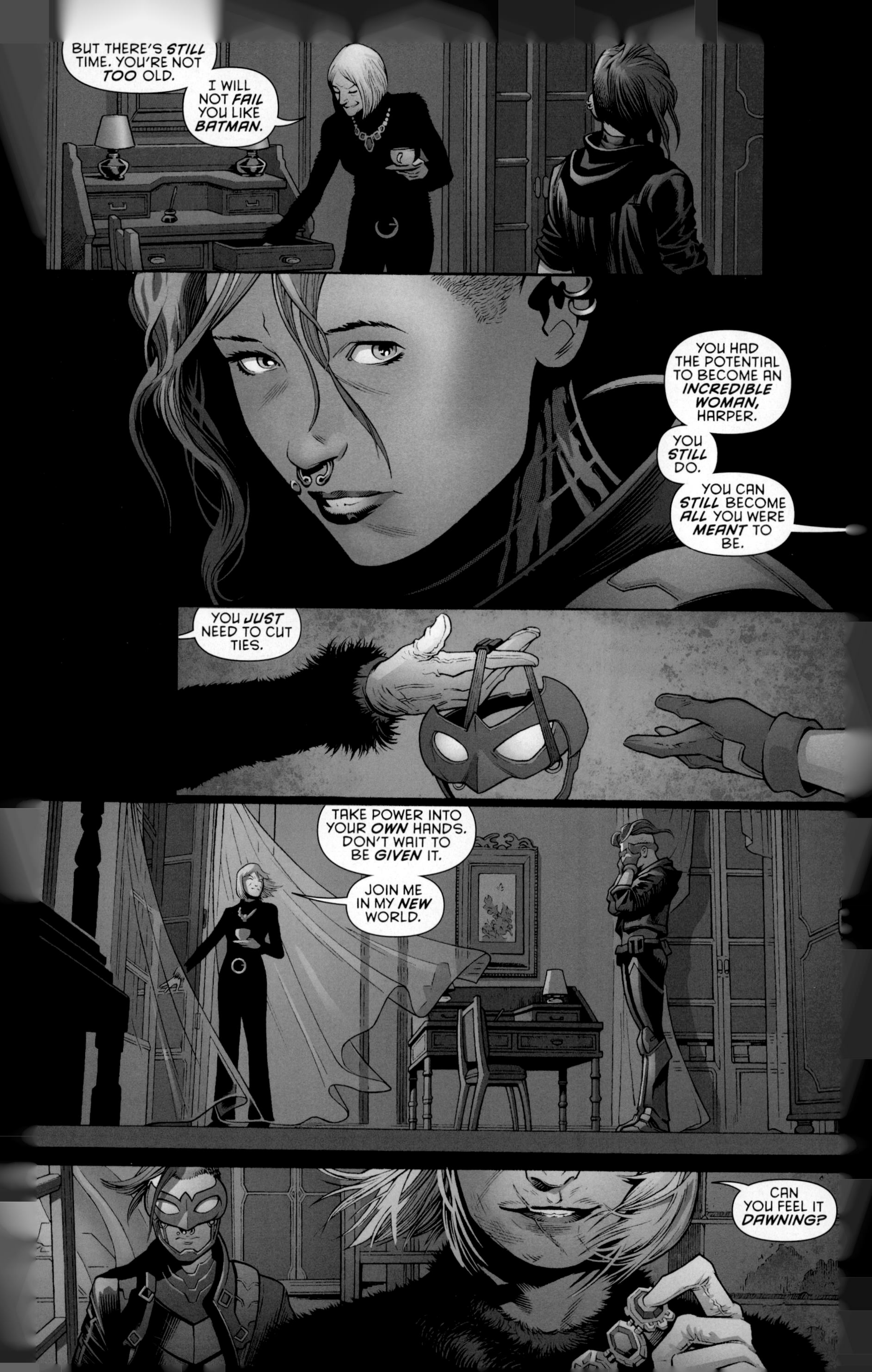
BUT THERE'S STILL TIME. YOU'RE NOT TOO OLD.
I WILL NOT FAIL YOU LIKE BATMAN.
YOU HAD THE POTENTIAL TO BECOME AN INCREDIBLE WOMAN, HARPER.
YOU STILL DO.
YOU CAN STILL BECOME ALL YOU WERE MEANT TO BE.
YOU JUST NEED TO CUT TIES.
TAKE POWER INTO YOUR OWN HANDS. DON'T WAIT TO BE GIVEN IT.
JOIN ME IN MY NEW WORLD.
CAN YOU FEEL IT DAWNING?

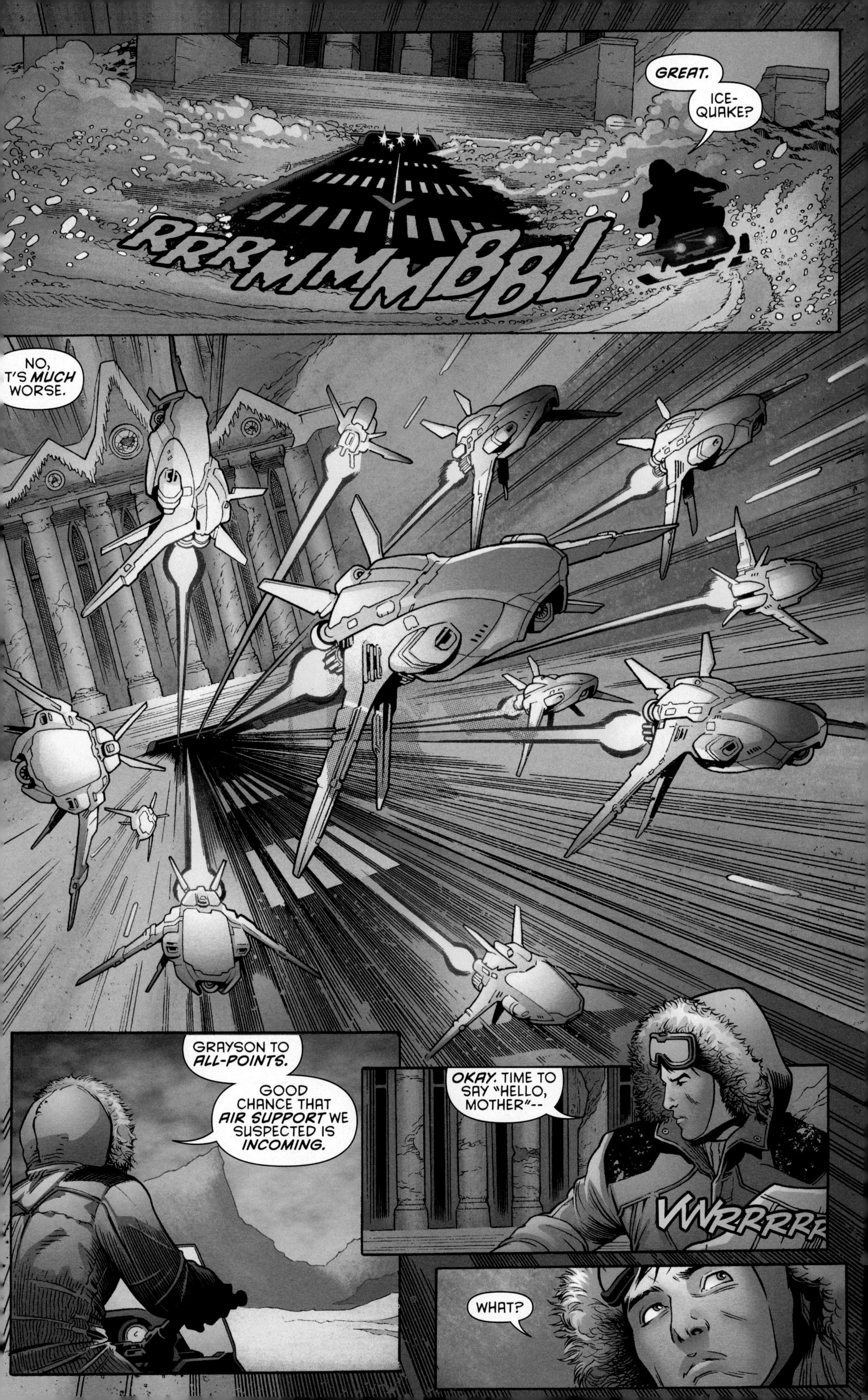
GREAT.
ICE-QUAKE?
RRRMMMBBL
NO, I'T'S MUCH WORSE.
GRAYSON TO ALL-POINTS.
GOOD CHANCE THAT AIR SUPPORT WE SUSPECTED IS INCOMING.
OKAY. TIME TO SAY "HELLO, MOTHER"--
VWRRRRR
WHAT?

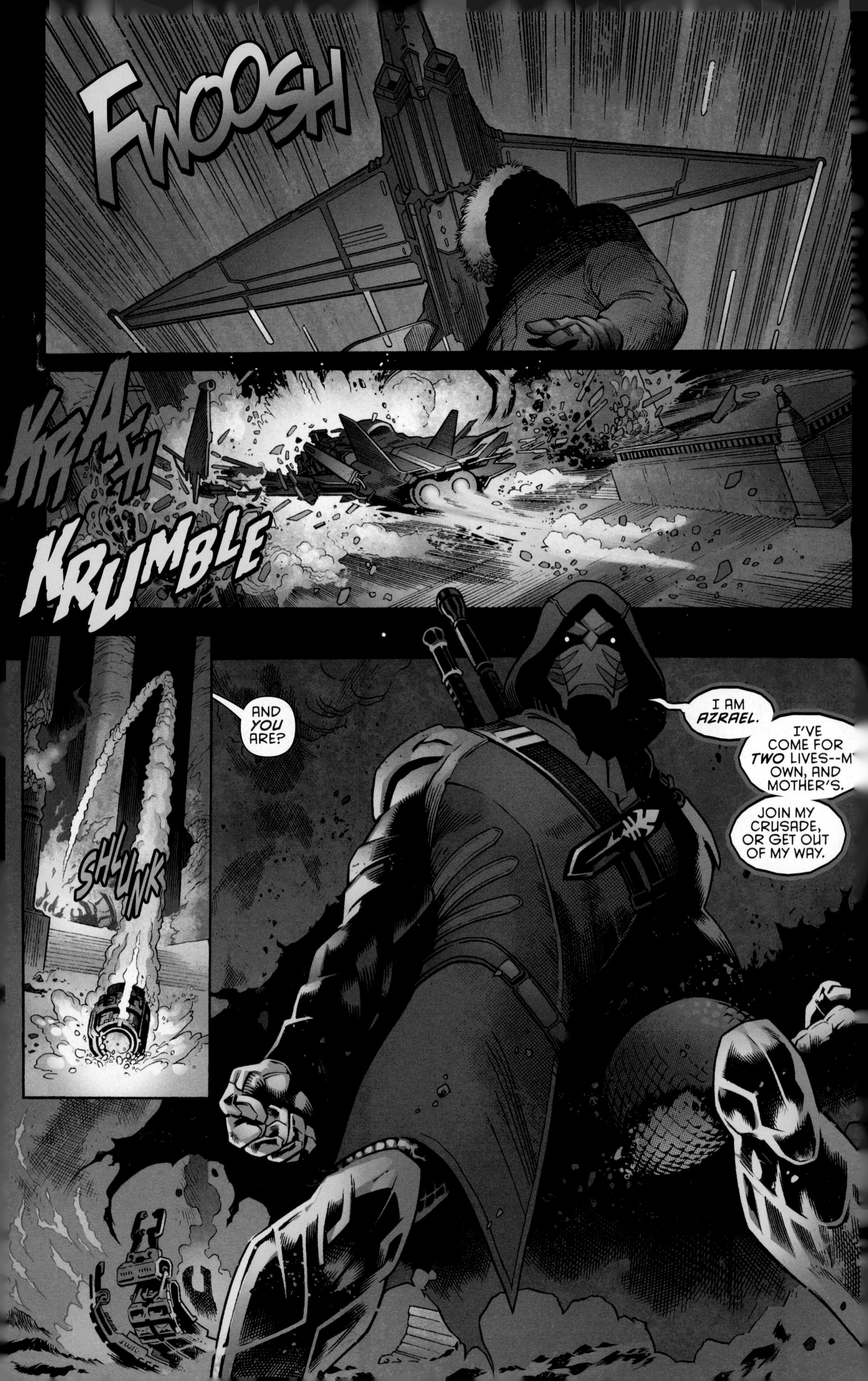
FWOOSH
KRASH
KRUMBLE
SHLUNK
AND YOU ARE?
I AM AZRAEL.
I'VE COME FOR TWO LIVES--MY OWN, AND MOTHER'S.
JOIN MY CRUSADE, OR GET OUT OF MY WAY.

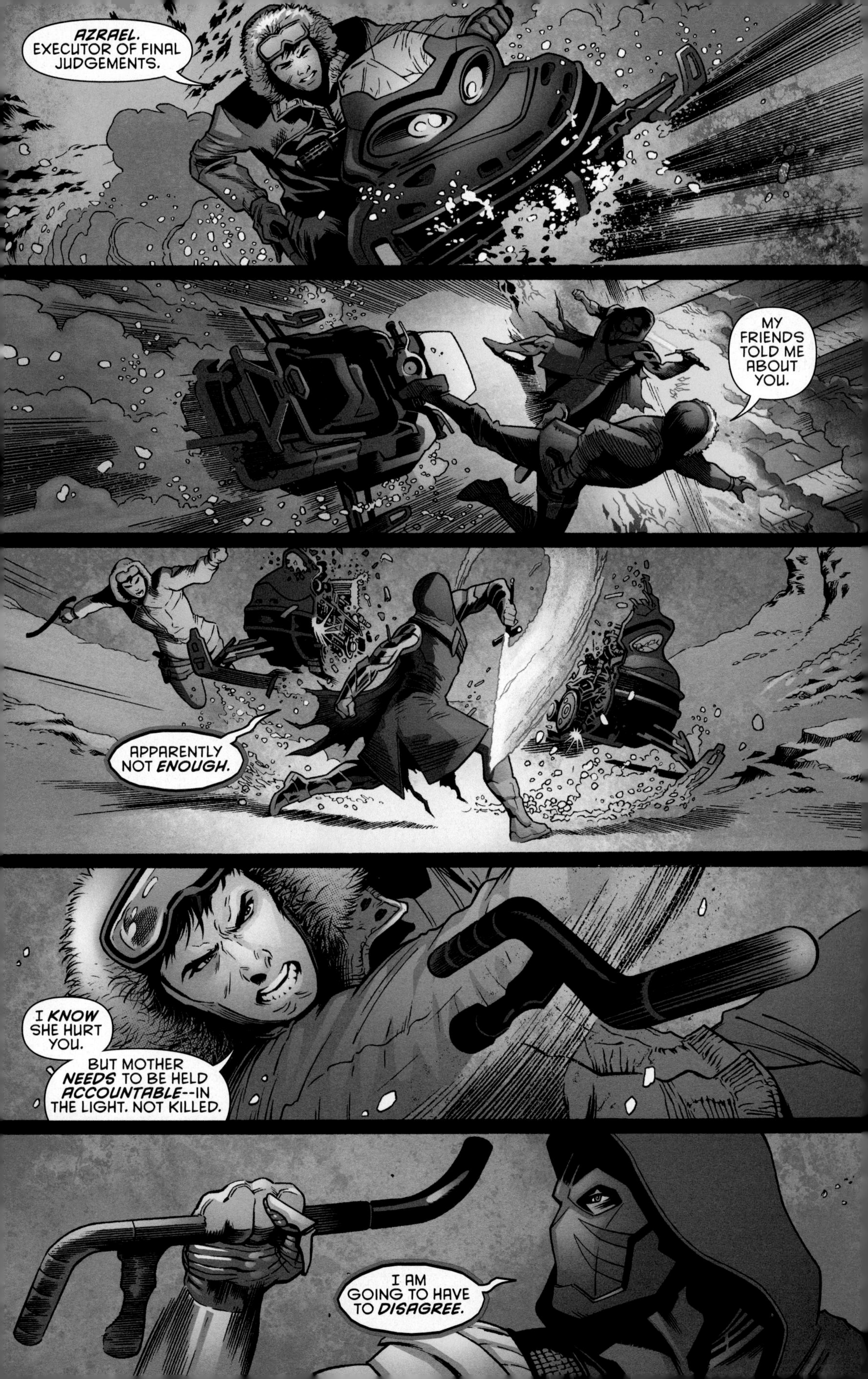
AZRAEL. EXECUTOR OF FINAL JUDGEMENTS.
MY FRIENDS TOLD ME ABOUT YOU.
APPARENTLY NOT ENOUGH.
I KNOW SHE HURT YOU.
BUT MOTHER NEEDS TO BE HELD ACCOUNTABLE--IN THE LIGHT. NOT KILLED.
I AM GOING TO HAVE TO DISAGREE.

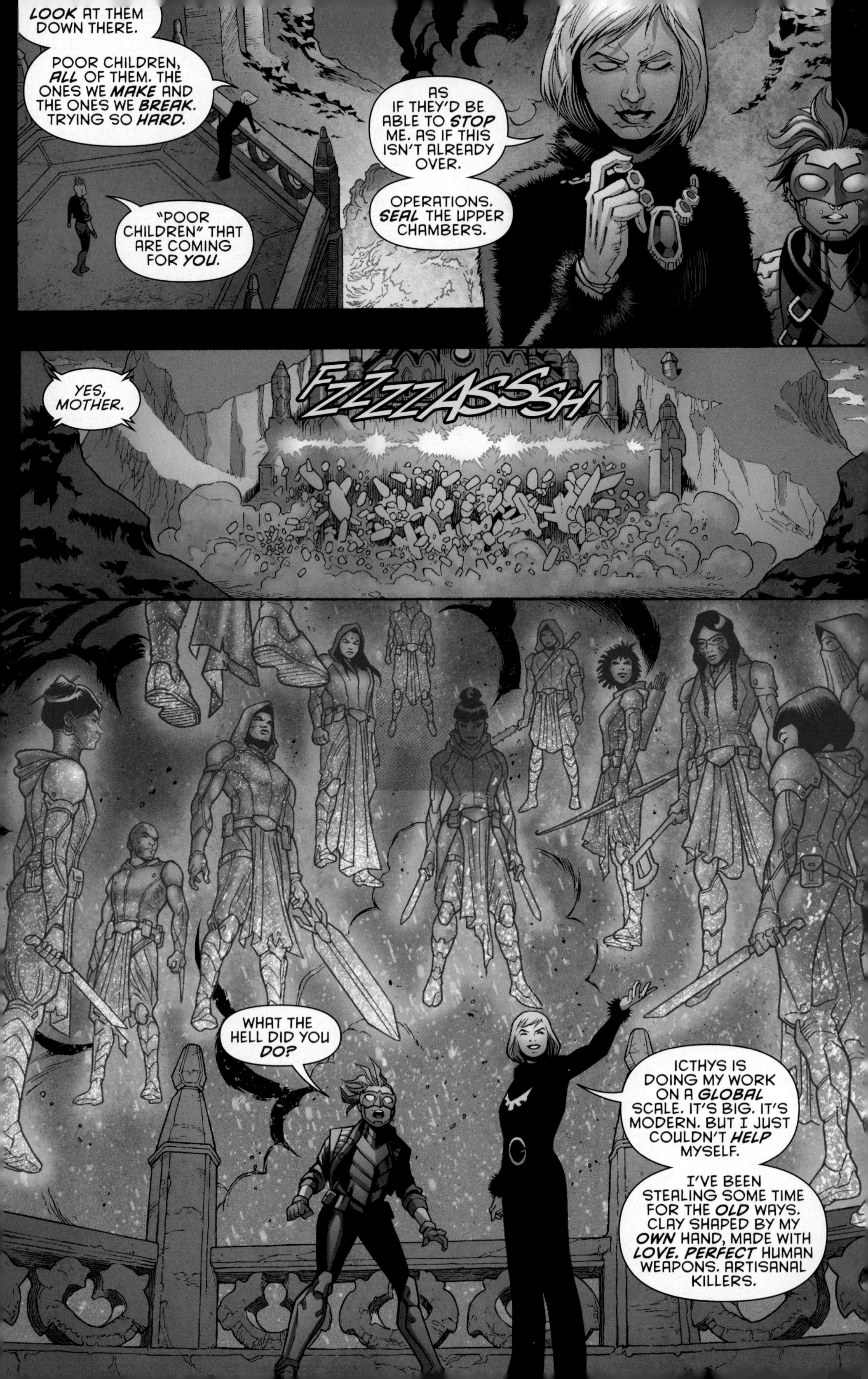
LOOK AT THEM DOWN THERE.
POOR CHILDREN, ALL OF THEM. THE ONES WE MAKE AND THE ONES WE BREAK. TRYING SO HARD.
"POOR CHILDREN" THAT ARE COMING FOR YOU.
AS IF THEY'D BE ABLE TO STOP ME. AS IF THIS ISN'T ALREADY OVER.
OPERATIONS. SEAL THE UPPER CHAMBERS.
YES, MOTHER.
FZZZZASSSH
WHAT THE HELL DID YOU DO?
ICTHYS IS DOING MY WORK ON A GLOBAL SCALE. IT'S BIG. IT'S MODERN. BUT I JUST COULDN'T HELP MYSELF.
I'VE BEEN STEALING SOME TIME FOR THE OLD WAYS. CLAY SHAPED BY MY OWN HAND, MADE WITH LOVE. PERFECT HUMAN WEAPONS. ARTISANAL KILLERS.

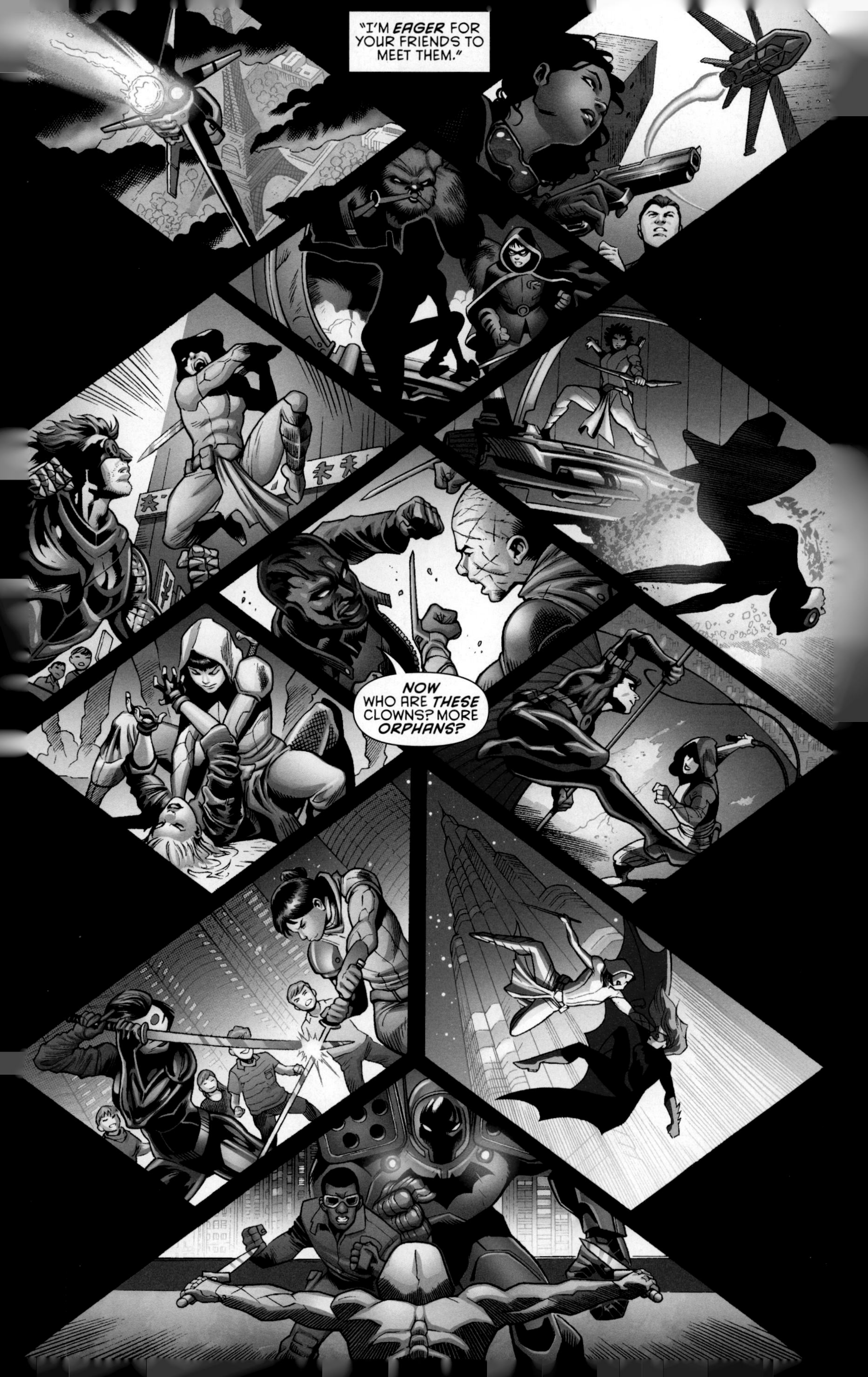
"I'M EAGER FOR YOUR FRIENDS TO MEET THEM."
NOW WHO ARE THESE CLOWNS? MORE ORPHANS?

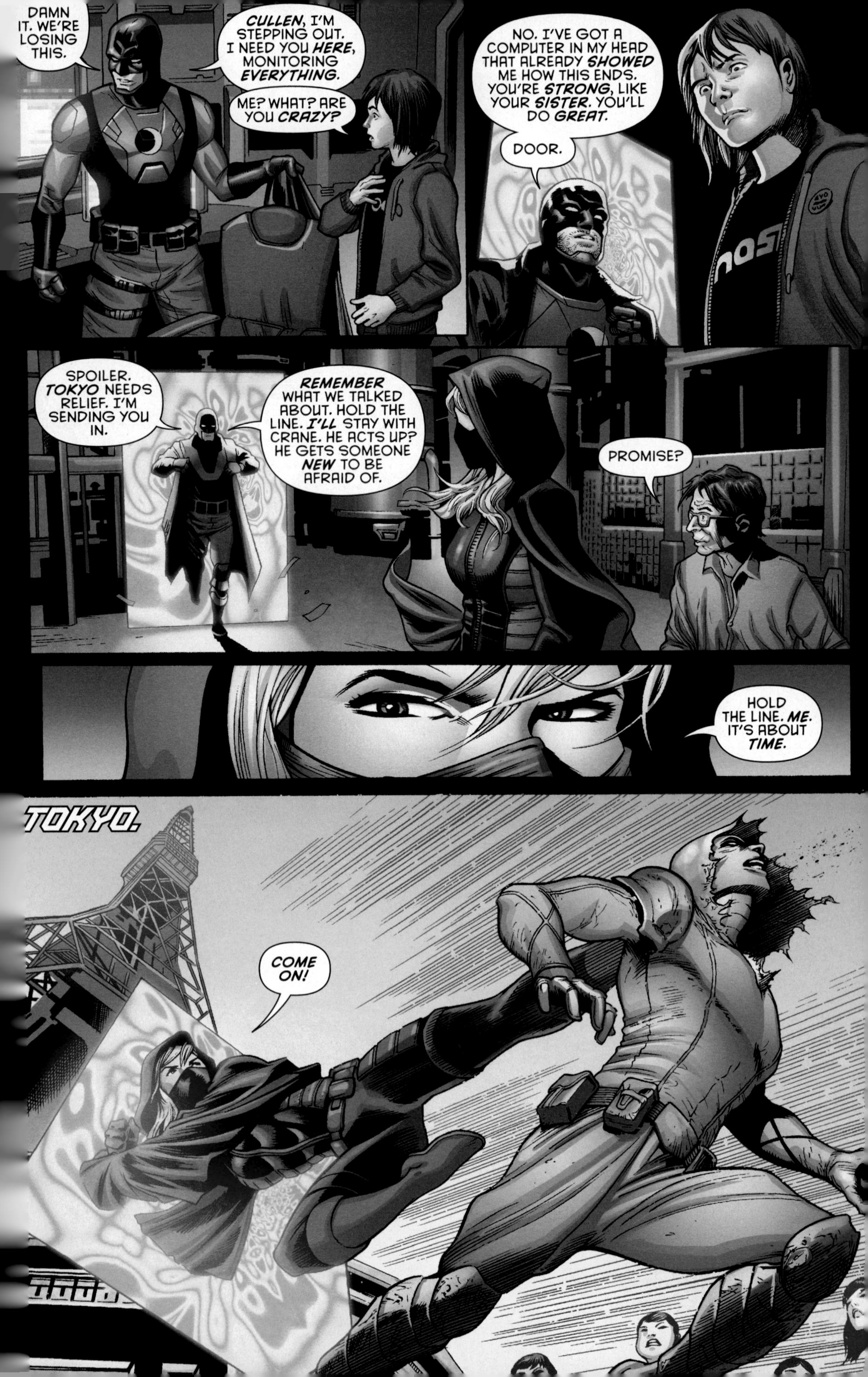
DAMN IT. WE'RE LOSING THIS.
CULLEN, I'M STEPPING OUT. I NEED YOU HERE, MONITORING EVERYTHING.
ME? WHAT? ARE YOU CRAZY?
NO. I'VE GOT A COMPUTER IN MY HEAD THAT ALREADY SHOWED ME HOW THIS ENDS. YOU'RE STRONG, LIKE YOUR SISTER. YOU'LL DO GREAT.
DOOR.
SPOILER. TOKYO NEEDS RELIEF. I'M SENDING YOU IN.
REMEMBER WHAT WE TALKED ABOUT. HOLD THE LINE. I'LL STAY WITH CRANE. HE ACTS UP? HE GETS SOMEONE NEW TO BE AFRAID OF.
PROMISE?
HOLD THE LINE. ME. IT'S ABOUT TIME.
TOKYO.
COME ON!

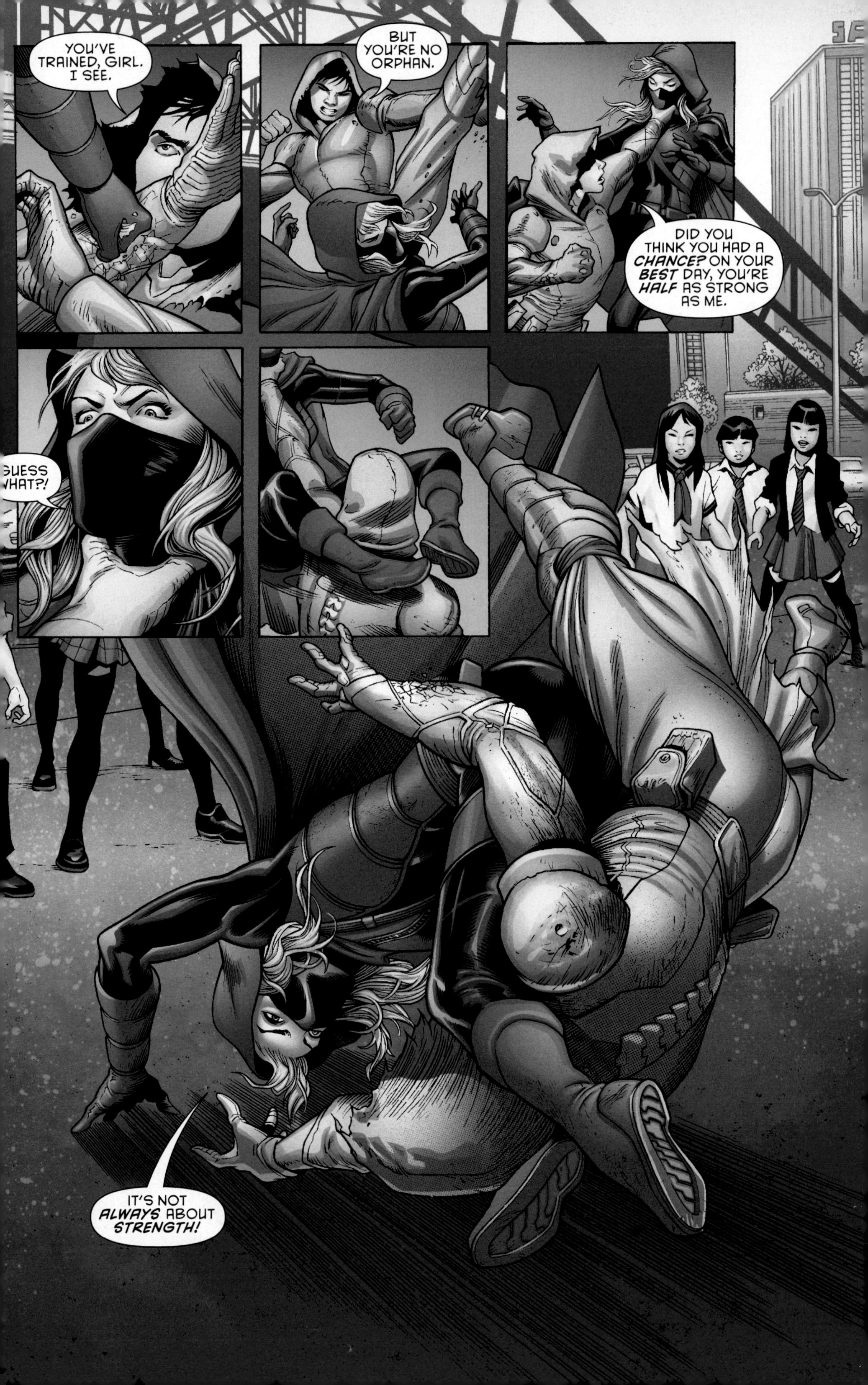
YOU'VE TRAINED, GIRL. I SEE.
BUT YOU'RE NO ORPHAN.
DID YOU THINK YOU HAD A CHANCE? ON YOUR BEST DAY, YOU'RE HALF AS STRONG AS ME.
GUESS WHAT?!
IT'S NOT ALWAYS ABOUT STRENGTH!

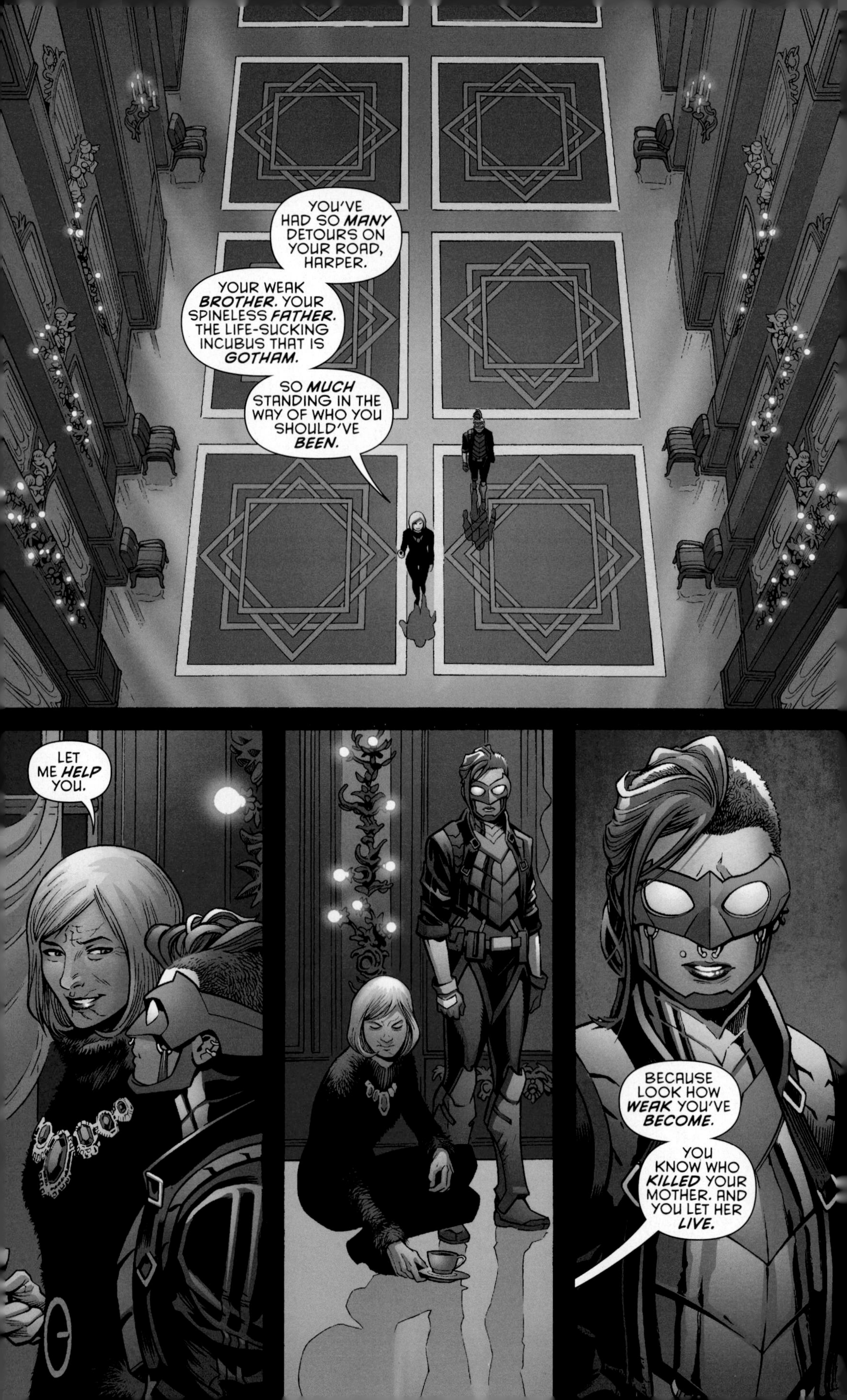
YOU'VE HAD SO MANY DETOURS ON YOUR ROAD, HARPER.
YOUR WEAK BROTHER. YOUR SPINELESS FATHER. THE LIFE-SUCKING INCUBUS THAT IS GOTHAM.
SO MUCH STANDING IN THE WAY OF WHO YOU SHOULD'VE BEEN.
LET ME HELP YOU.
BECAUSE LOOK HOW WEAK YOU'VE BECOME.
YOU KNOW WHO KILLED YOUR MOTHER. AND YOU LET HER LIVE.

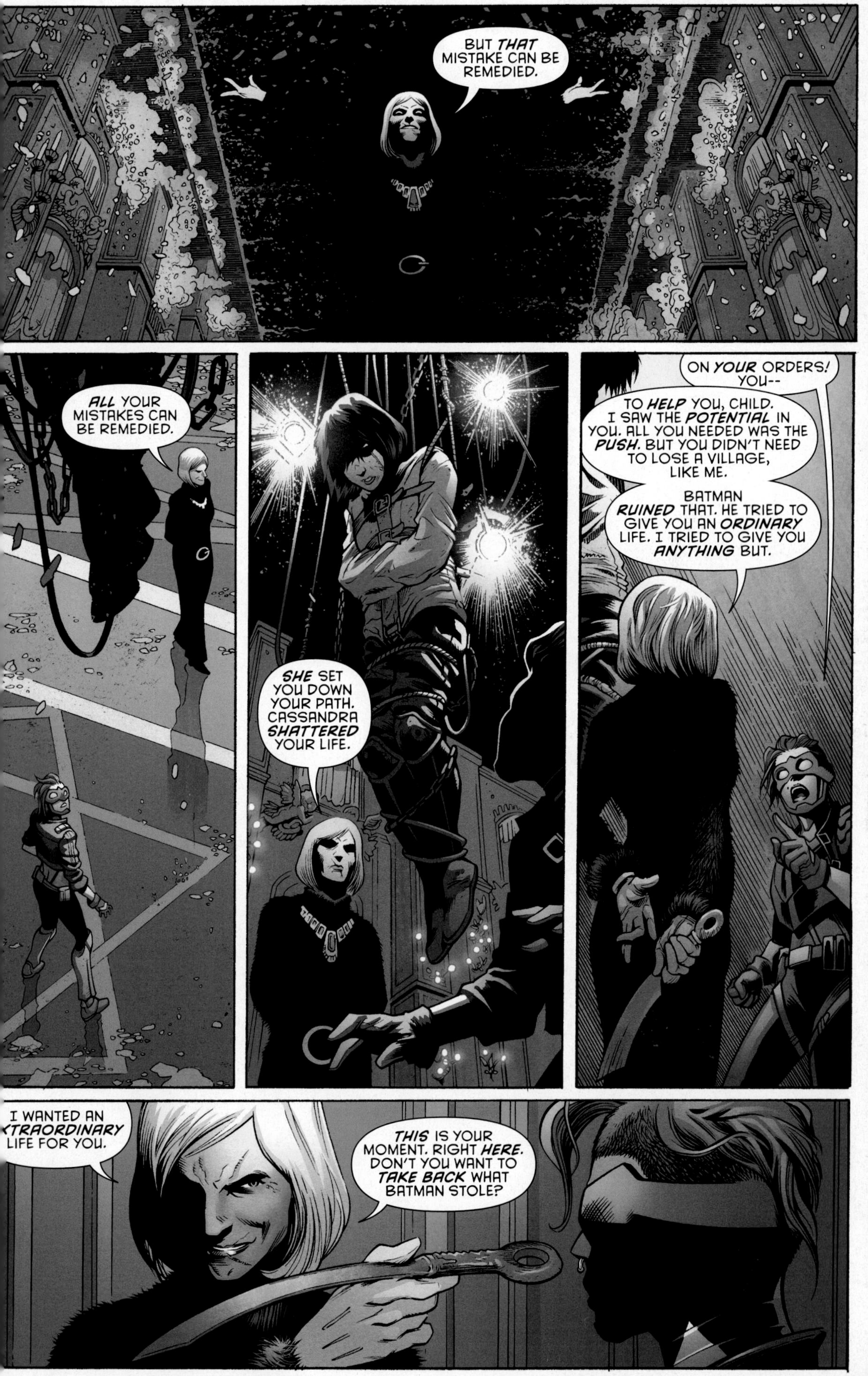
BUT THAT MISTAKE CAN BE REMEDIED.
ALL YOUR MISTAKES CAN BE REMEDIED.
SHE SET YOU DOWN YOUR PATH. CASSANDRA SHATTERED YOUR LIFE.
ON YOUR ORDERS! YOU--
TO HELP YOU, CHILD. I SAW THE POTENTIAL IN YOU. ALL YOU NEEDED WAS THE PUSH. BUT YOU DIDN'T NEED TO LOSE A VILLAGE, LIKE ME.
BATMAN RUINED THAT. HE TRIED TO GIVE YOU AN ORDINARY LIFE. I TRIED TO GIVE YOU ANYTHING BUT.
I WANTED AN XTRAORDINARY LIFE FOR YOU.
THIS IS YOUR MOMENT. RIGHT HERE. DON'T YOU WANT TO TAKE BACK WHAT BATMAN STOLE?

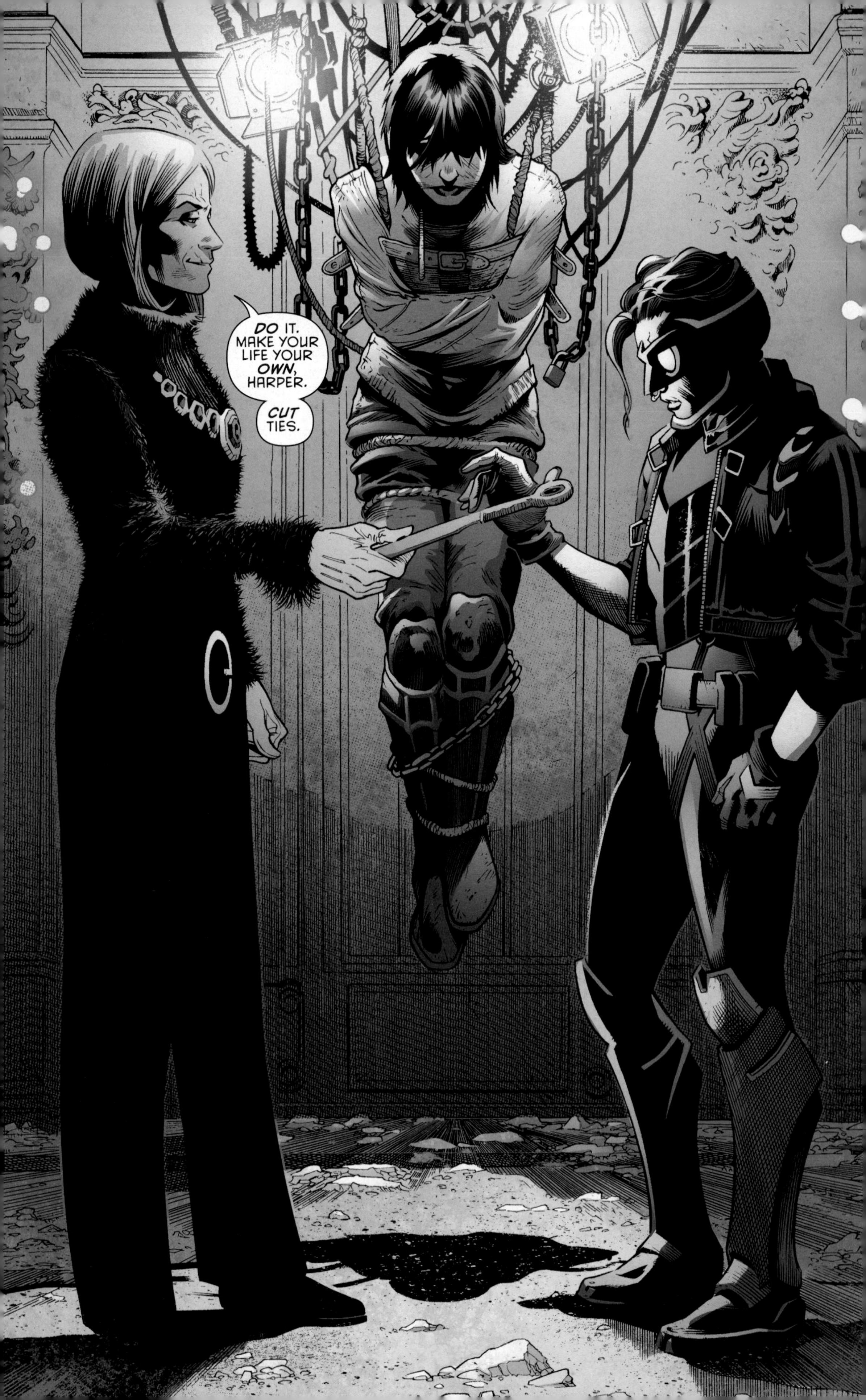
DO IT. MAKE YOUR LIFE YOUR OWN, HARPER.
CUT TIES.

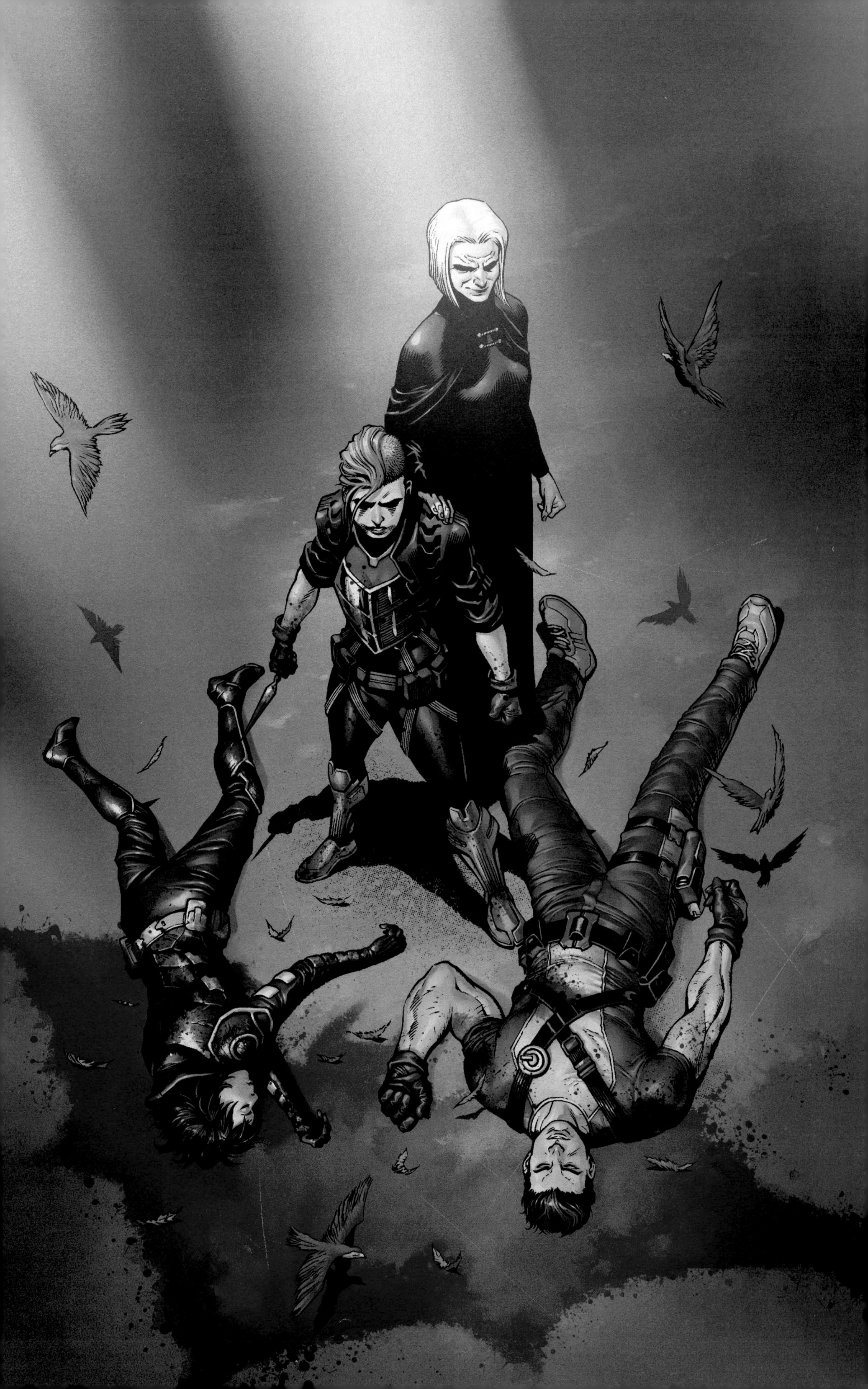

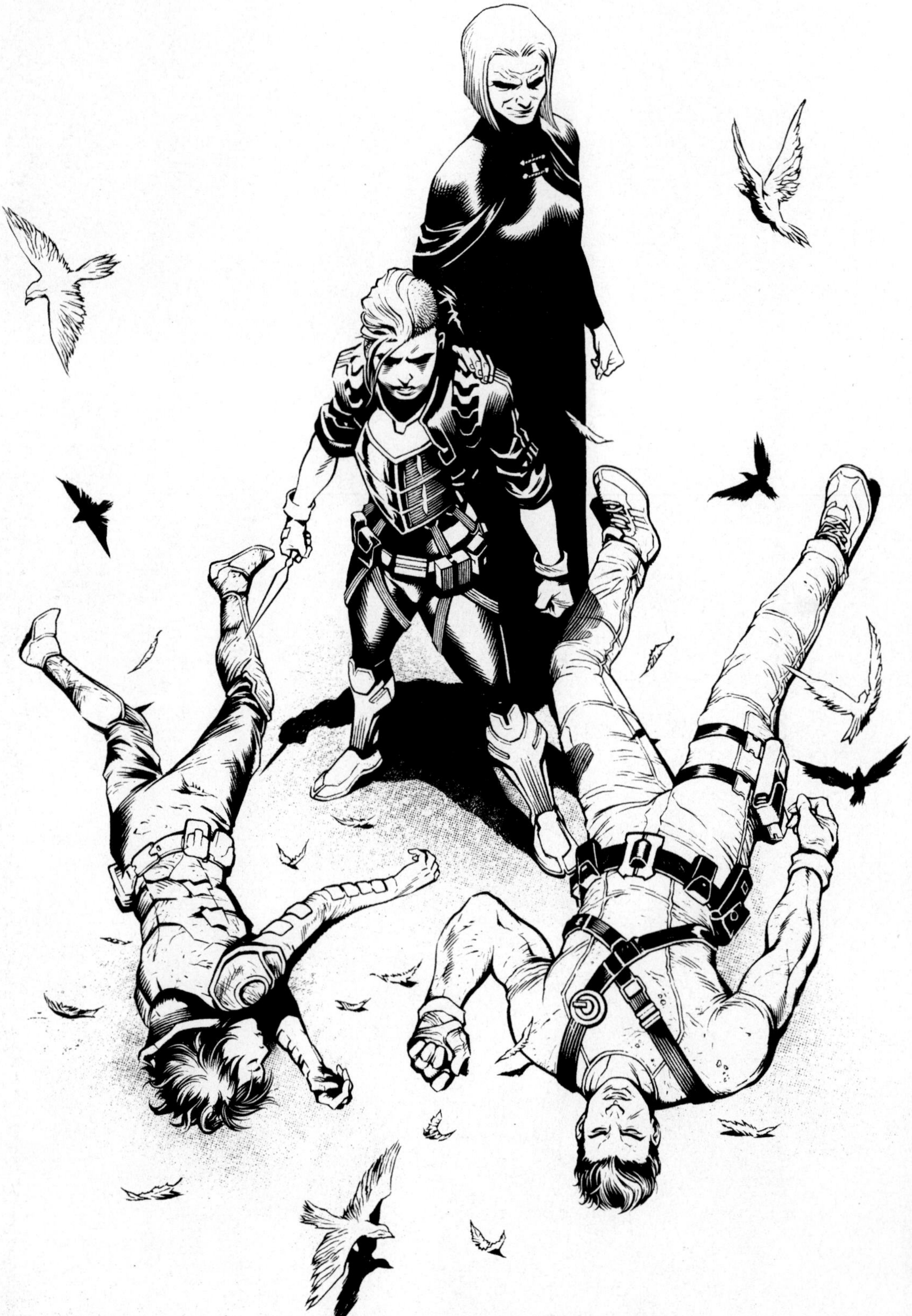

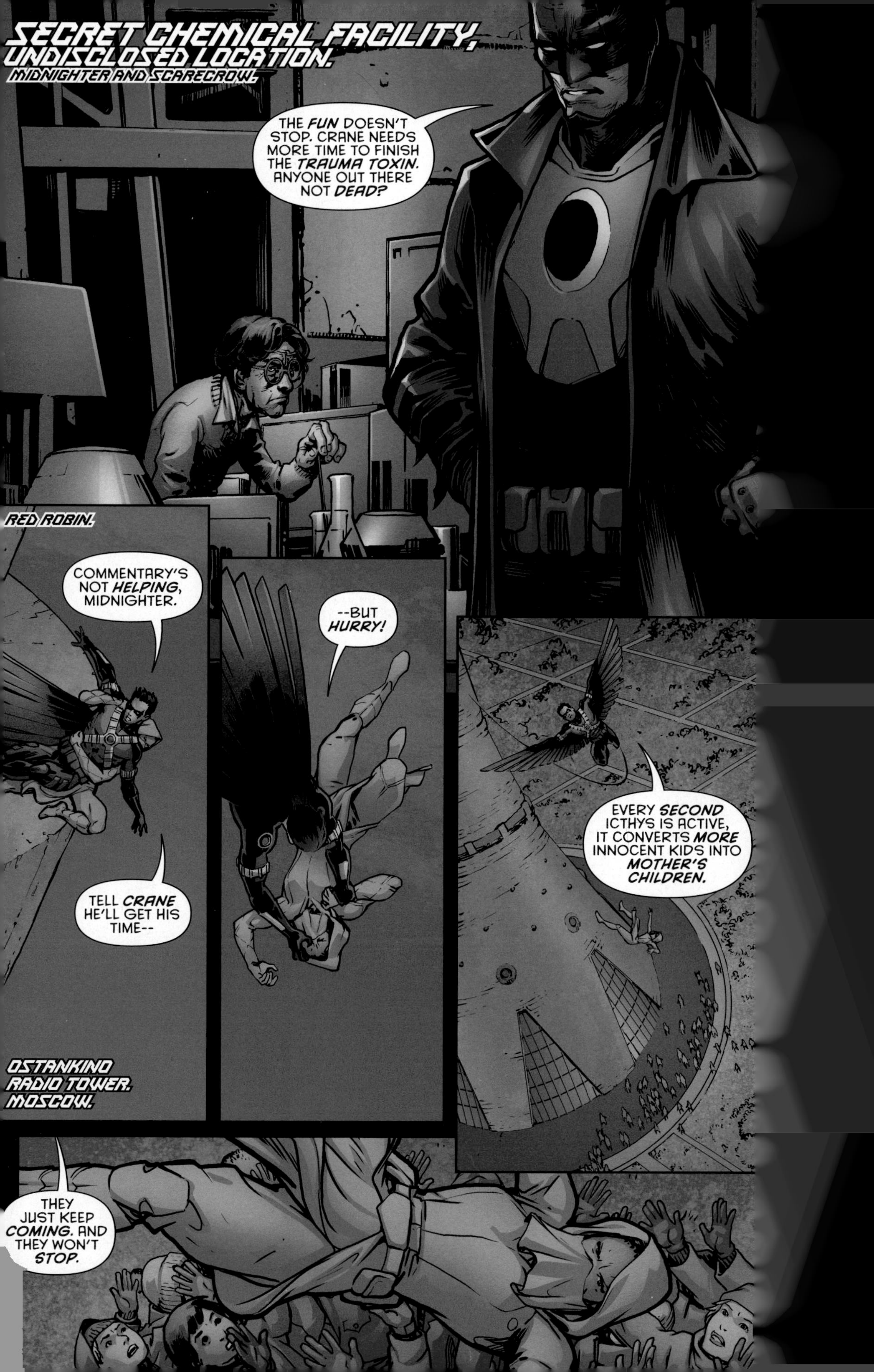
SECRET CHEMICAL FACILITY, UNDISCLOSED LOCATION.
MIDNIGHTER AND SCARECROW.
THE FUN DOESN'T STOP. CRANE NEEDS MORE TIME TO FINISH THE TRAUMA TOXIN. ANYONE OUT THERE NOT DEAD?
RED ROBIN.
COMMENTARY'S NOT HELPING, MIDNIGHTER.
TELL CRANE HE'LL GET HIS TIME--
--BUT HURRY!
EVERY SECOND ICTHYS IS ACTIVE, IT CONVERTS MORE INNOCENT KIDS INTO MOTHER'S CHILDREN.
OSTANKINO RADIO TOWER. MOSCOW.
THEY JUST KEEP COMING. AND THEY WON'T STOP.

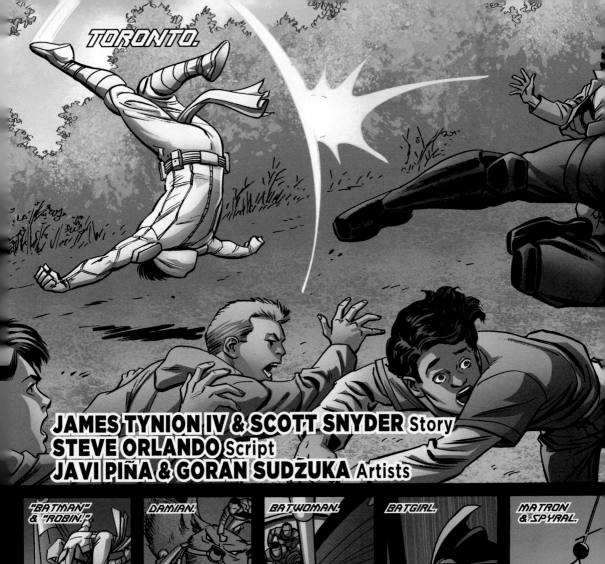

TORONTO.

JAMES TYNION IV & SCOTT SNYDER Story
STEVE ORLANDO Script
JAVI PIÑA & GORAN SUDŽUKA Artists

"BATMAN" & "ROBIN."

DAMIAN.

BATWOMAN.

BATGIRL.

MATRON & SPYRAL.

THE BEACON TOWER. GOTHAM.

PALACE OF WESTMINSTER. LONDON.

BURJ KHALIFA. DUBAI.

EIFFEL TOWER. PARIS.

TWO TOWERS. BOLOGNA.

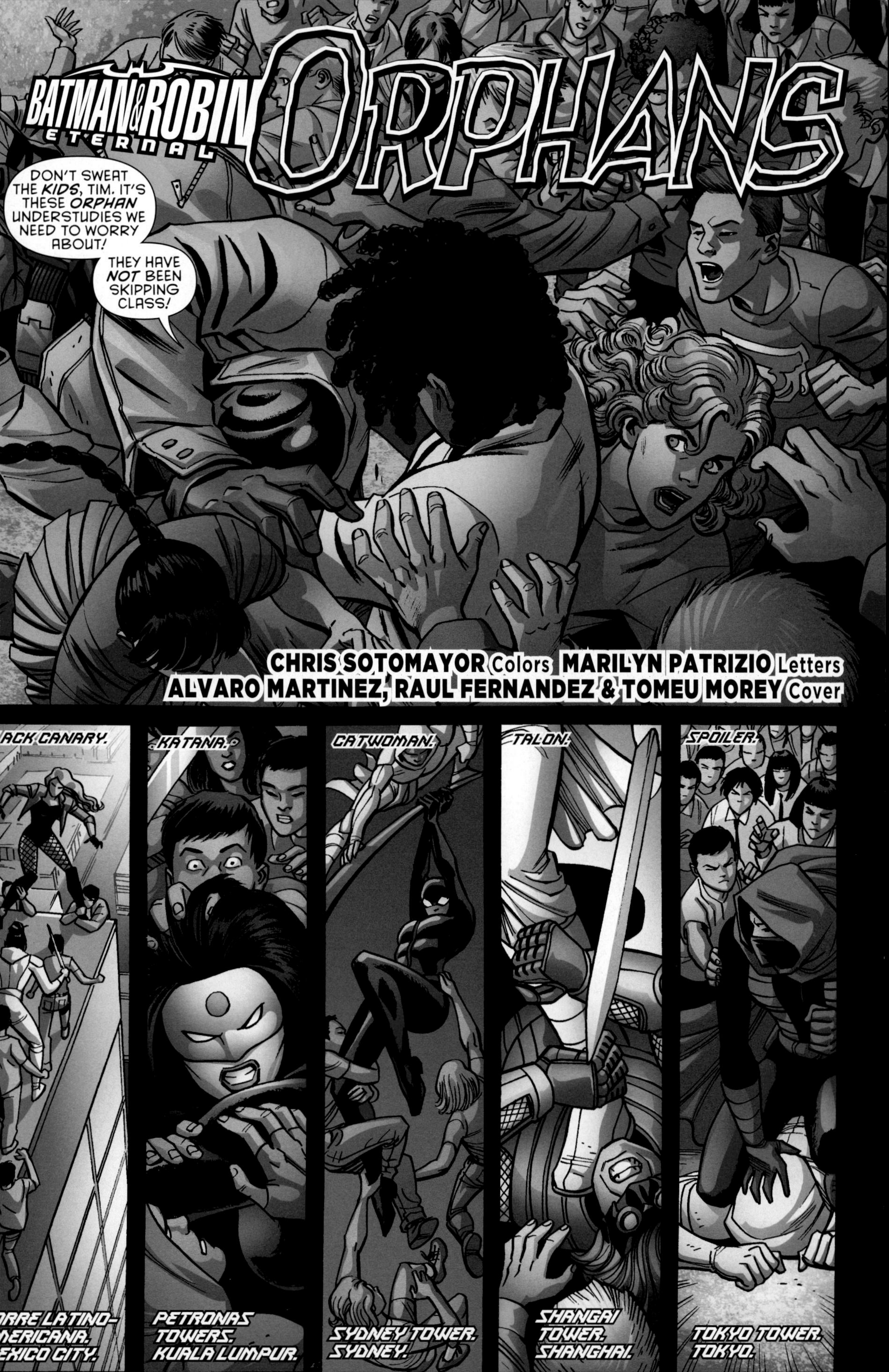
BATMAN & ROBIN ETERNAL
ORPHANS
DON'T SWEAT THE *KIDS*, TIM. IT'S THESE *ORPHAN* UNDERSTUDIES WE NEED TO WORRY ABOUT!
THEY HAVE *NOT* BEEN SKIPPING CLASS!
CHRIS SOTOMAYOR Colors MARILYN PATRIZIO Letters
ALVARO MARTINEZ, RAUL FERNANDEZ & TOMEU MOREY Cover
ACK CANARY.
KATANA.
CATWOMAN.
TALON.
SPOILER.
RRE LATINO–
MERICANA.
EXICO CITY.
PETRONAS TOWERS. KUALA LUMPUR.
SYDNEY TOWER. SYDNEY.
SHANGAI TOWER. SHANGHAI.
TOKYO TOWER. TOKYO.

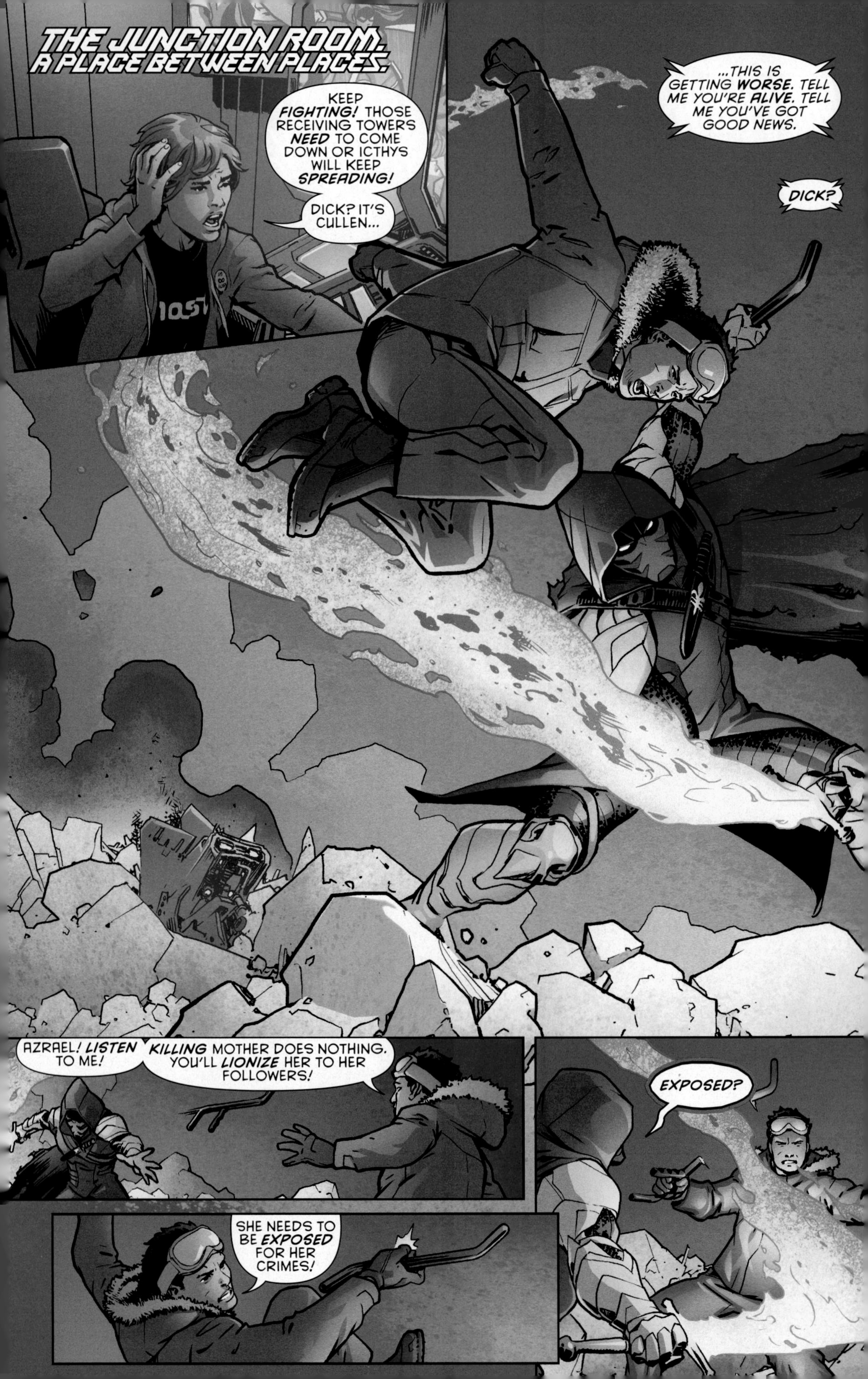
THE JUNCTION ROOM. A PLACE BETWEEN PLACES.
KEEP FIGHTING! THOSE RECEIVING TOWERS NEED TO COME DOWN OR ICTHYS WILL KEEP SPREADING!
DICK? IT'S CULLEN...
...THIS IS GETTING WORSE. TELL ME YOU'RE ALIVE. TELL ME YOU'VE GOT GOOD NEWS.
DICK?
AZRAEL! LISTEN TO ME!
KILLING MOTHER DOES NOTHING. YOU'LL LIONIZE HER TO HER FOLLOWERS!
EXPOSED?
SHE NEEDS TO BE EXPOSED FOR HER CRIMES!

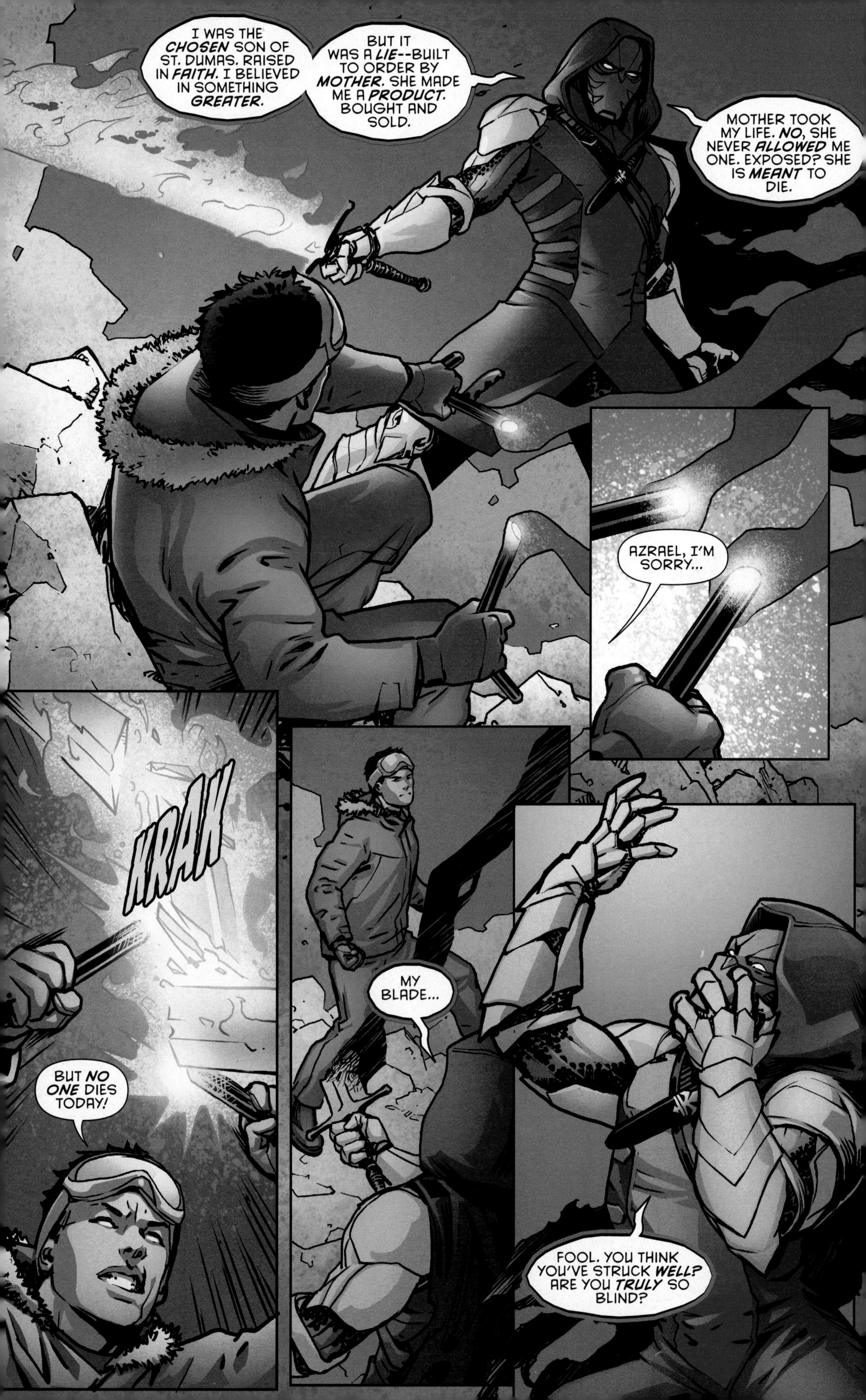
I WAS THE CHOSEN SON OF ST. DUMAS. RAISED IN FAITH. I BELIEVED IN SOMETHING GREATER.
BUT IT WAS A LIE--BUILT TO ORDER BY MOTHER. SHE MADE ME A PRODUCT. BOUGHT AND SOLD.
MOTHER TOOK MY LIFE. NO, SHE NEVER ALLOWED ME ONE. EXPOSED? SHE IS MEANT TO DIE.
AZRAEL, I'M SORRY...
KRAK
BUT NO ONE DIES TODAY!
MY BLADE...
FOOL. YOU THINK YOU'VE STRUCK WELL? ARE YOU TRULY SO BLIND?

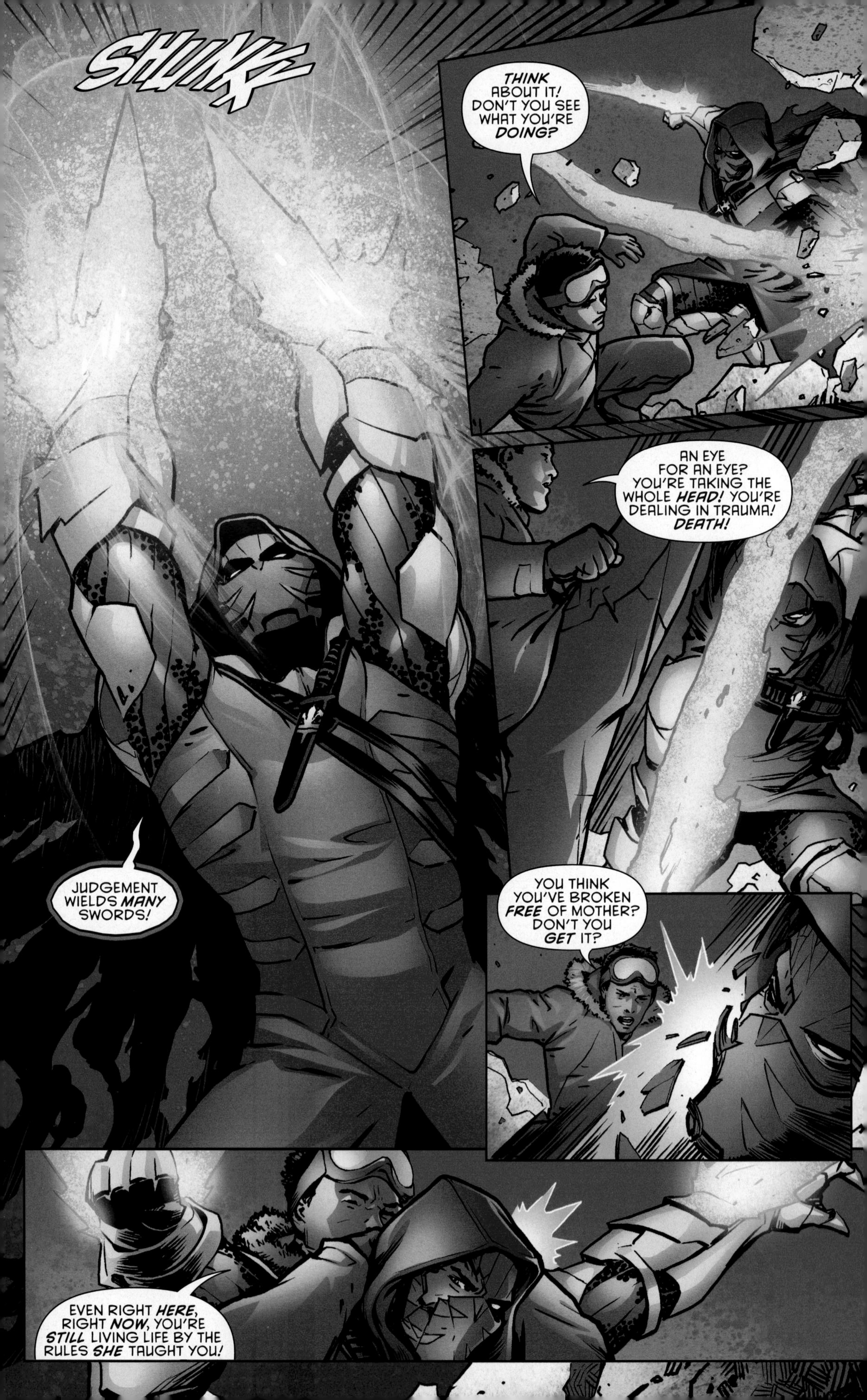
SHUNK
THINK ABOUT IT! DON'T YOU SEE WHAT YOU'RE DOING?
AN EYE FOR AN EYE? YOU'RE TAKING THE WHOLE HEAD! YOU'RE DEALING IN TRAUMA! DEATH!
JUDGEMENT WIELDS MANY SWORDS!
YOU THINK YOU'VE BROKEN FREE OF MOTHER? DON'T YOU GET IT?
EVEN RIGHT HERE, RIGHT NOW, YOU'RE STILL LIVING LIFE BY THE RULES SHE TAUGHT YOU!

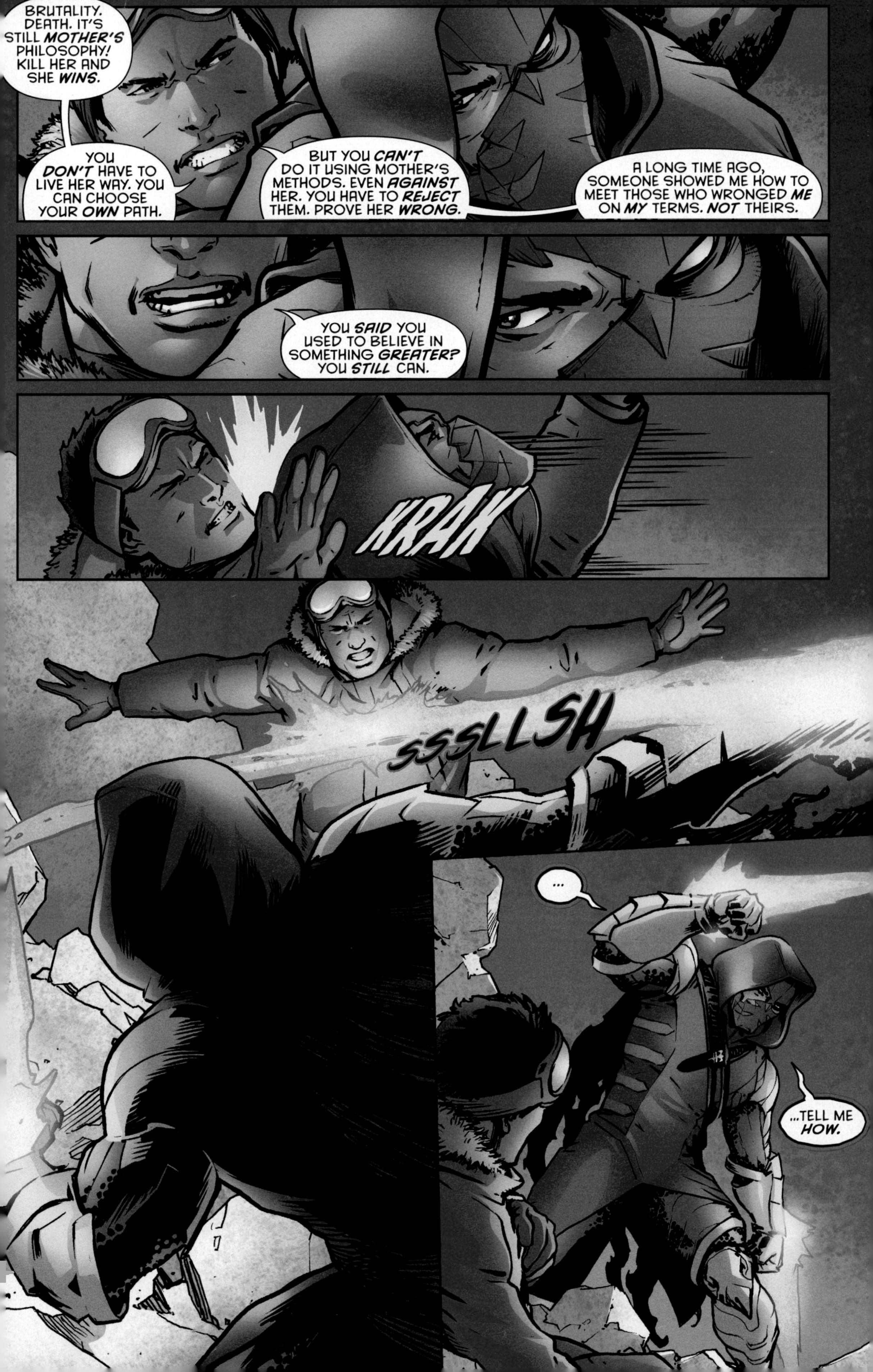
BRUTALITY. DEATH. IT'S STILL MOTHER'S PHILOSOPHY! KILL HER AND SHE WINS.
YOU DON'T HAVE TO LIVE HER WAY. YOU CAN CHOOSE YOUR OWN PATH.
BUT YOU CAN'T DO IT USING MOTHER'S METHODS. EVEN AGAINST HER. YOU HAVE TO REJECT THEM. PROVE HER WRONG.
A LONG TIME AGO, SOMEONE SHOWED ME HOW TO MEET THOSE WHO WRONGED ME ON MY TERMS. NOT THEIRS.
YOU SAID YOU USED TO BELIEVE IN SOMETHING GREATER? YOU STILL CAN.
KRAK
SSSLLSH
...
...TELL ME HOW.

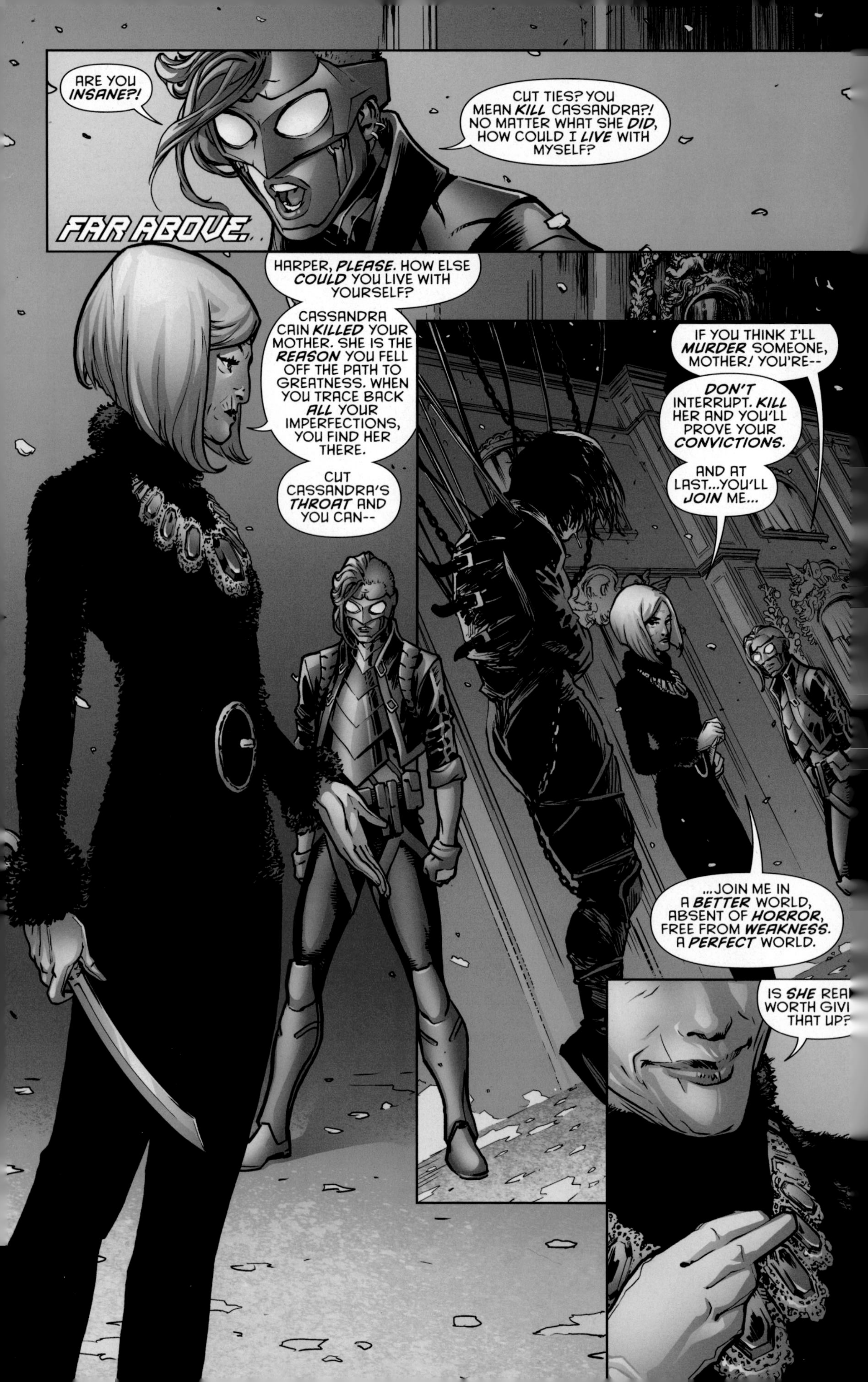
ARE YOU INSANE?!
CUT TIES? YOU MEAN KILL CASSANDRA?! NO MATTER WHAT SHE DID, HOW COULD I LIVE WITH MYSELF?
FAR ABOVE.
HARPER, PLEASE. HOW ELSE COULD YOU LIVE WITH YOURSELF?
CASSANDRA CAIN KILLED YOUR MOTHER. SHE IS THE REASON YOU FELL OFF THE PATH TO GREATNESS. WHEN YOU TRACE BACK ALL YOUR IMPERFECTIONS, YOU FIND HER THERE.
CUT CASSANDRA'S THROAT AND YOU CAN--
IF YOU THINK I'LL MURDER SOMEONE, MOTHER! YOU'RE--
DON'T INTERRUPT. KILL HER AND YOU'LL PROVE YOUR CONVICTIONS.
AND AT LAST...YOU'LL JOIN ME...
...JOIN ME IN A BETTER WORLD, ABSENT OF HORROR, FREE FROM WEAKNESS. A PERFECT WORLD.
IS SHE REA
WORTH GIVI
THAT UP?

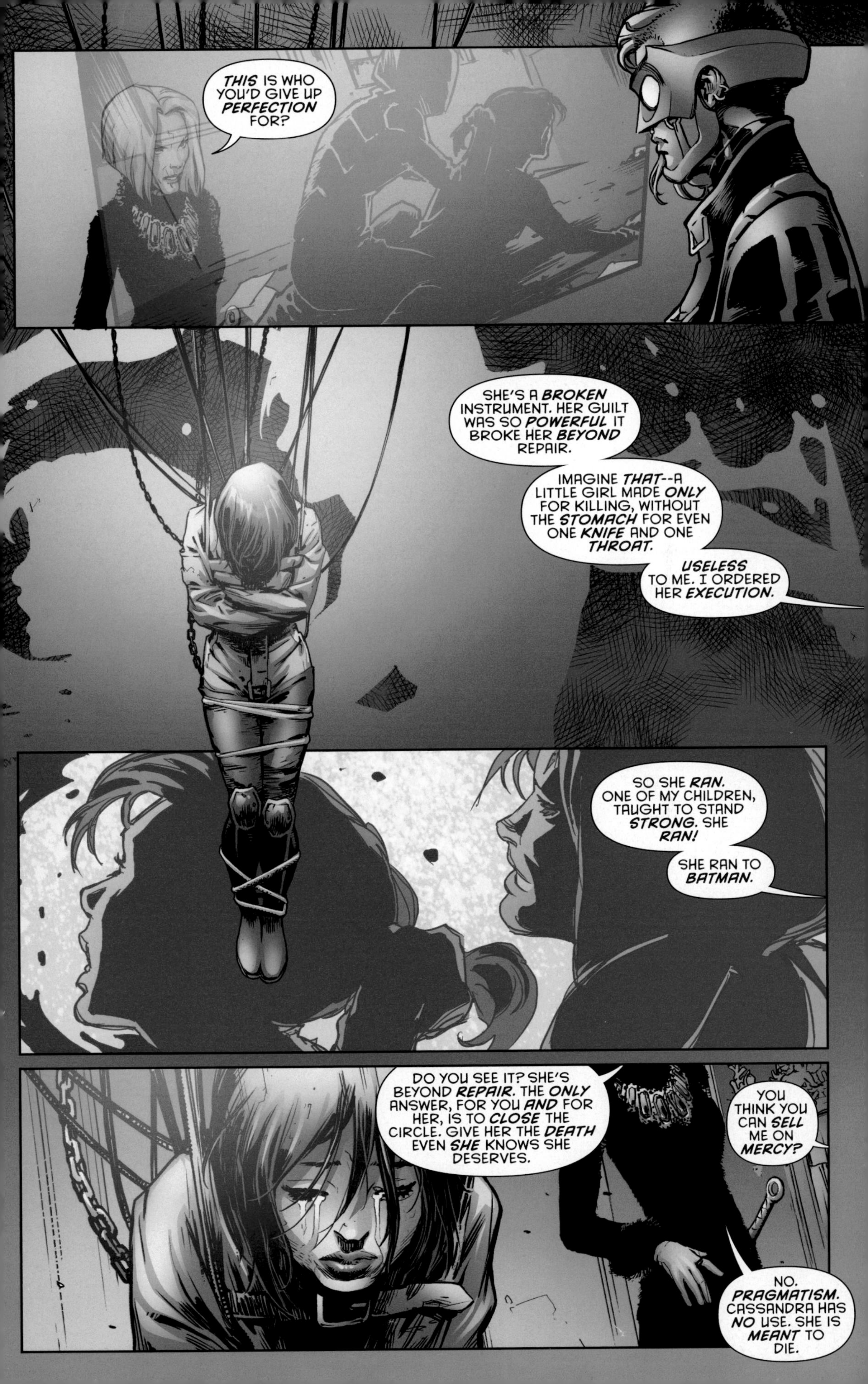
THIS IS WHO YOU'D GIVE UP PERFECTION FOR?
SHE'S A BROKEN INSTRUMENT. HER GUILT WAS SO POWERFUL IT BROKE HER BEYOND REPAIR.
IMAGINE THAT--A LITTLE GIRL MADE ONLY FOR KILLING, WITHOUT THE STOMACH FOR EVEN ONE KNIFE AND ONE THROAT.
USELESS TO ME. I ORDERED HER EXECUTION.
SO SHE RAN. ONE OF MY CHILDREN, TAUGHT TO STAND STRONG. SHE RAN!
SHE RAN TO BATMAN.
DO YOU SEE IT? SHE'S BEYOND REPAIR. THE ONLY ANSWER, FOR YOU AND FOR HER, IS TO CLOSE THE CIRCLE. GIVE HER THE DEATH EVEN SHE KNOWS SHE DESERVES.
YOU THINK YOU CAN SELL ME ON MERCY?
NO. PRAGMATISM. CASSANDRA HAS NO USE. SHE IS MEANT TO DIE.

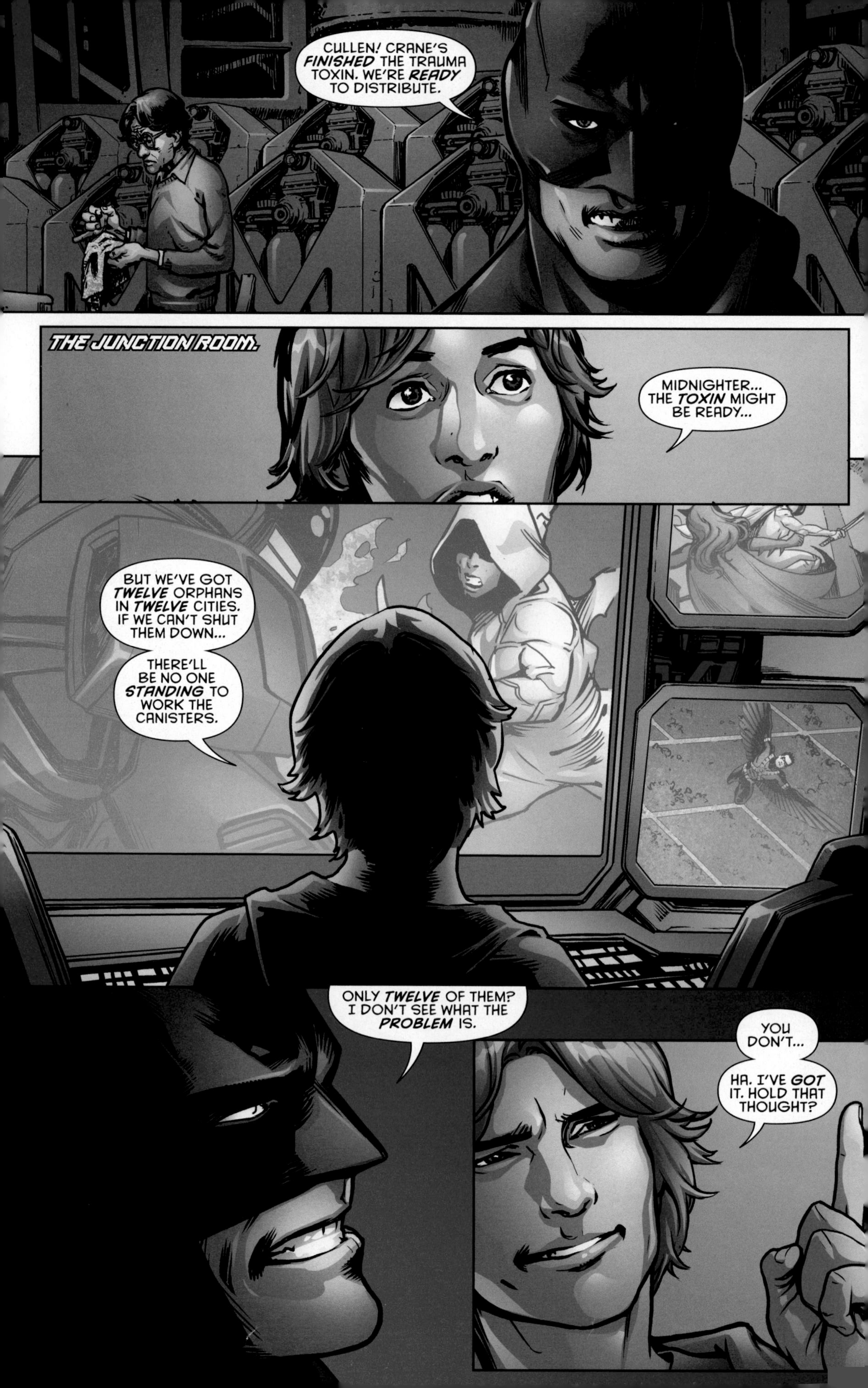
CULLEN! CRANE'S FINISHED THE TRAUMA TOXIN. WE'RE READY TO DISTRIBUTE.
THE JUNCTION ROOM.
MIDNIGHTER... THE TOXIN MIGHT BE READY...
BUT WE'VE GOT TWELVE ORPHANS IN TWELVE CITIES. IF WE CAN'T SHUT THEM DOWN...
THERE'LL BE NO ONE STANDING TO WORK THE CANISTERS.
ONLY TWELVE OF THEM? I DON'T SEE WHAT THE PROBLEM IS.
YOU DON'T...
HA. I'VE GOT IT. HOLD THAT THOUGHT?

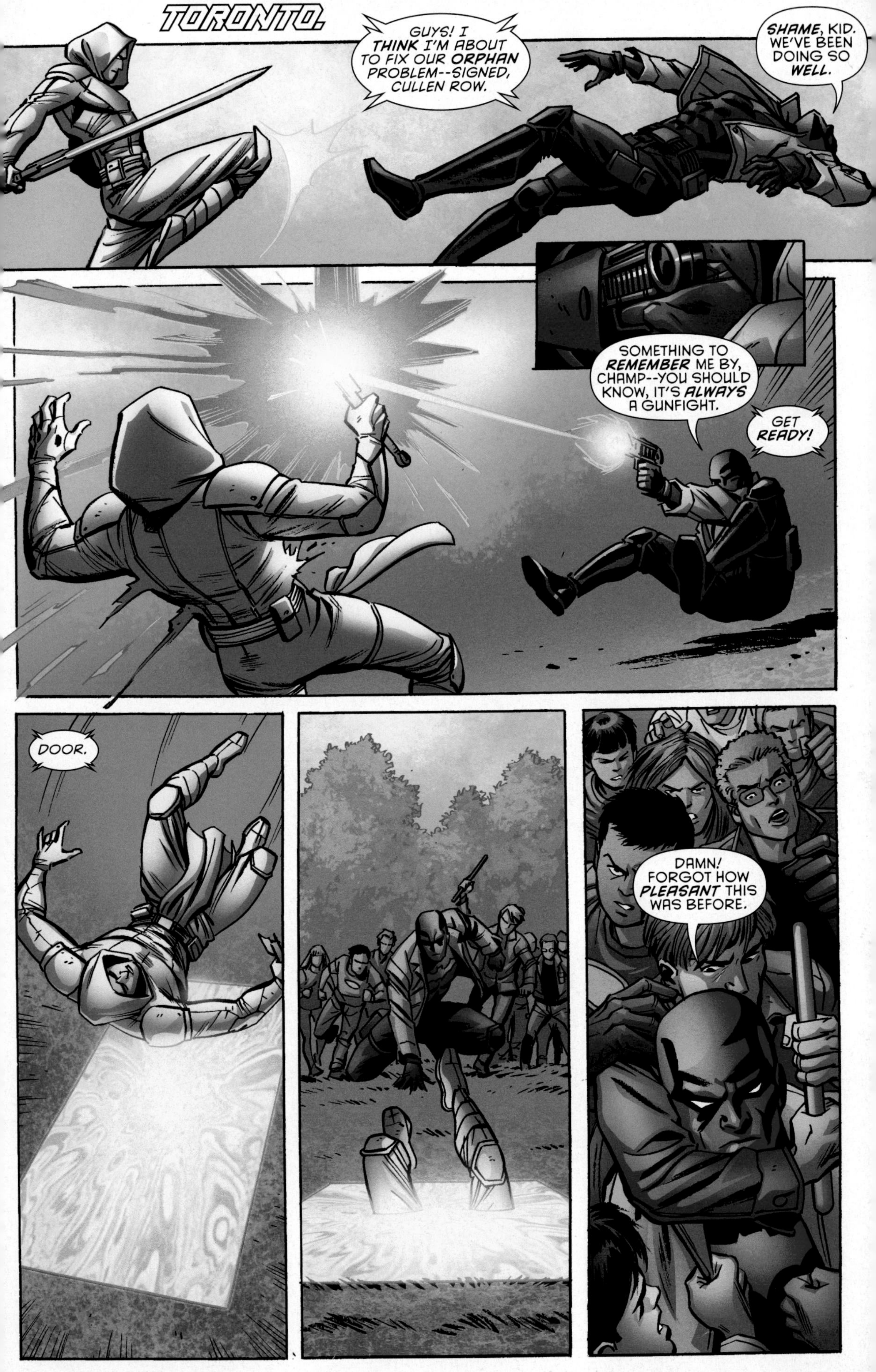
TORONTO.
GUYS! I THINK I'M ABOUT TO FIX OUR ORPHAN PROBLEM--SIGNED, CULLEN ROW.
SHAME, KID. WE'VE BEEN DOING SO WELL.
SOMETHING TO REMEMBER ME BY, CHAMP--YOU SHOULD KNOW, IT'S ALWAYS A GUNFIGHT.
GET READY!
DOOR.
DAMN! FORGOT HOW PLEASANT THIS WAS BEFORE.

GET THEM INTO THE DOORS!

SHANGHAI.

PARIS.

MOSCOW.

TOKYO.

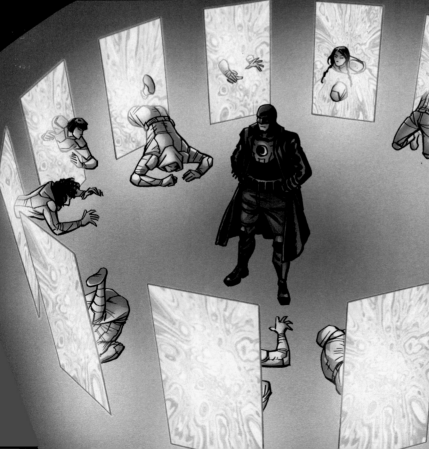

WELL, HELLO THERE.

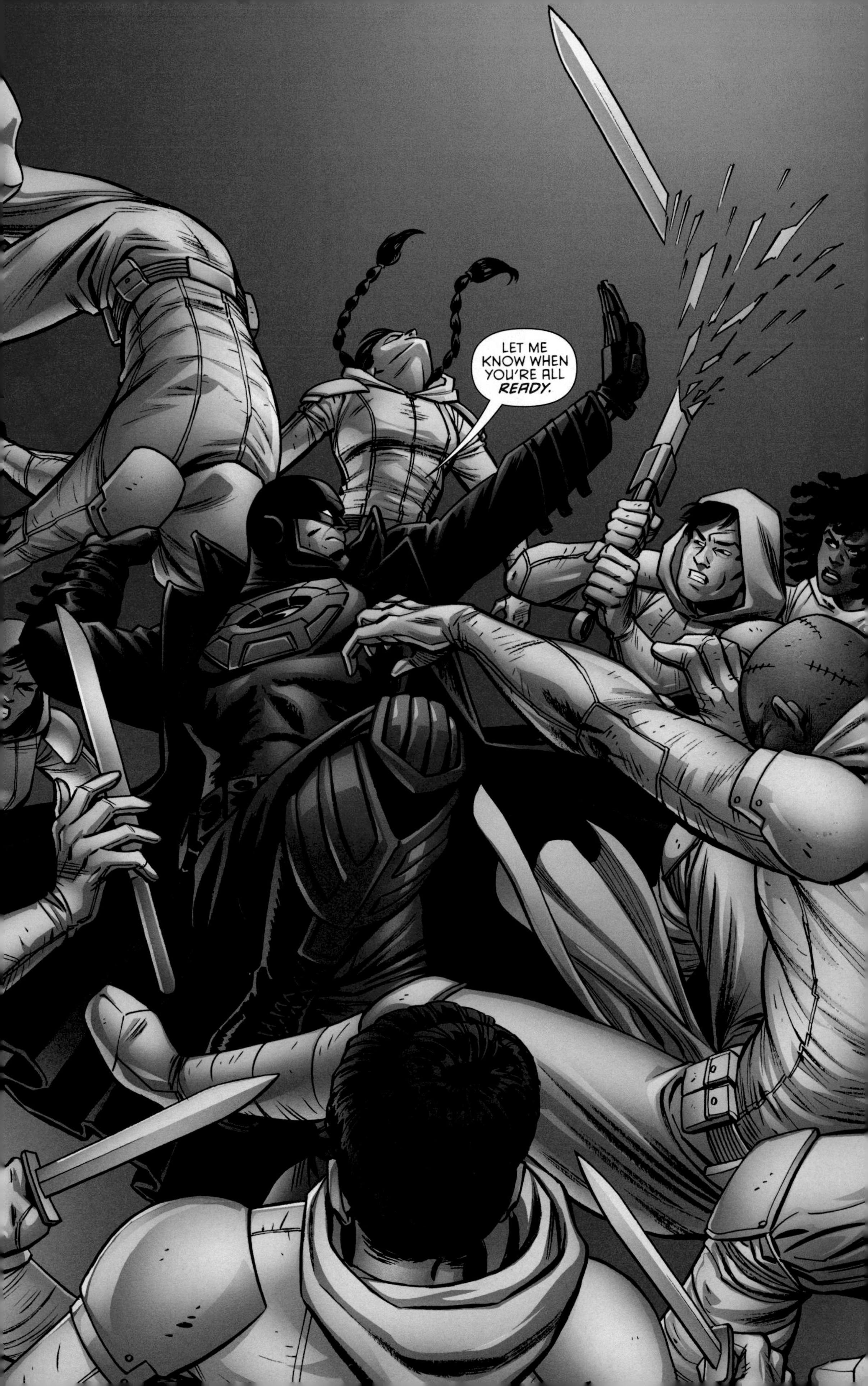
LET ME KNOW WHEN YOU'RE ALL *READY*.

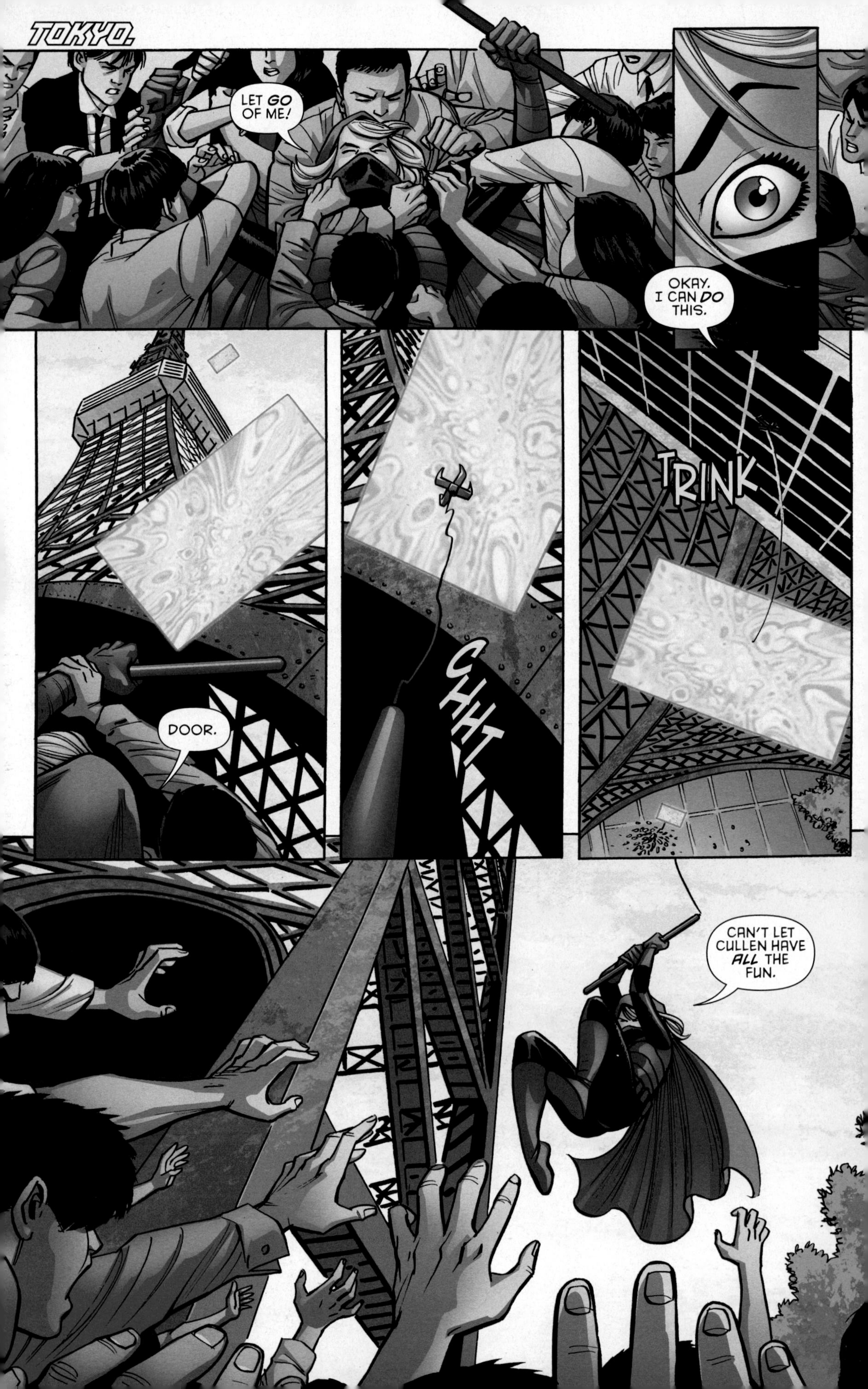
TOKYO.
LET GO OF ME!
OKAY. I CAN DO THIS.
DOOR.
CHHT
TRINK
CAN'T LET CULLEN HAVE ALL THE FUN.

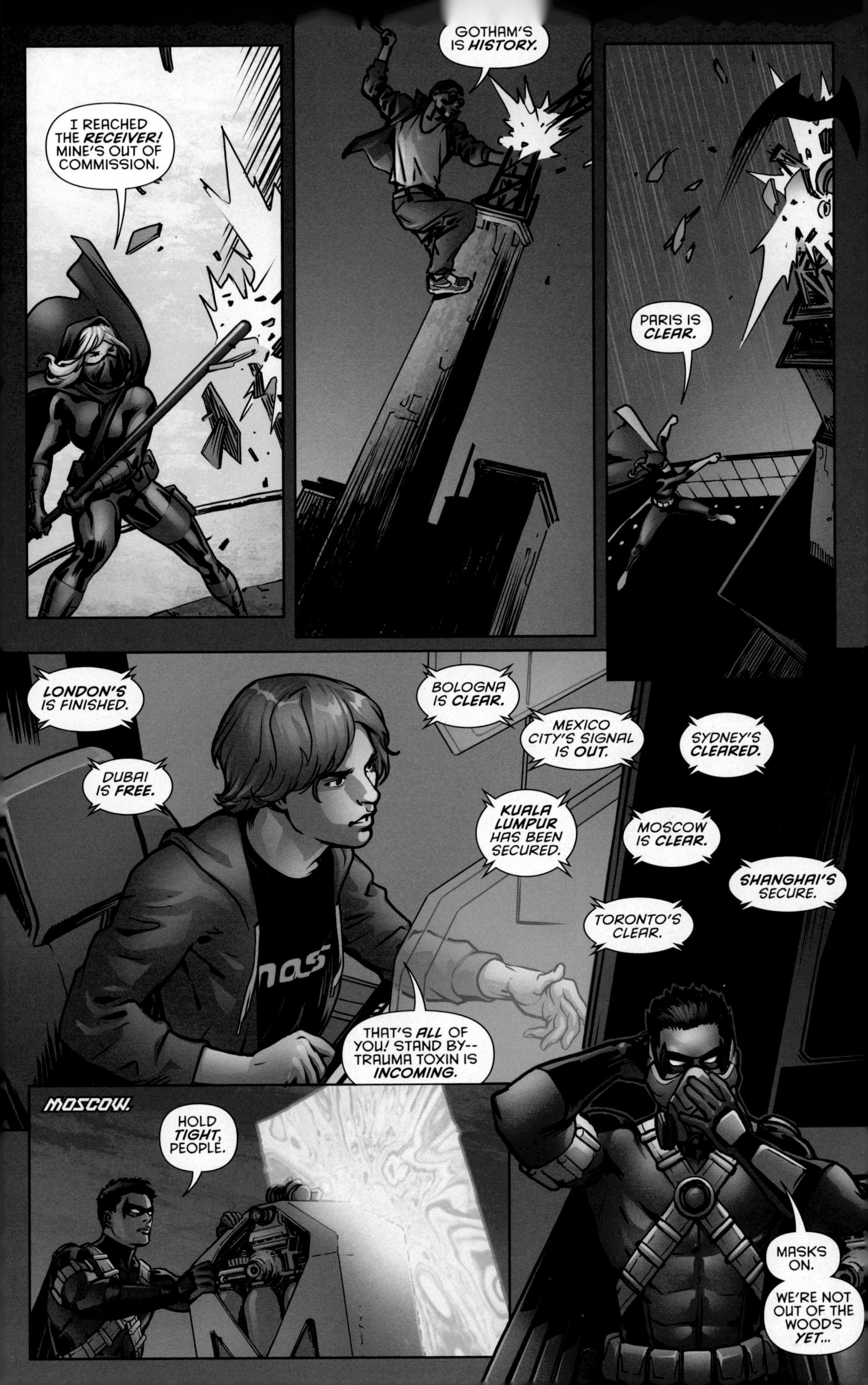
I REACHED THE RECEIVER! MINE'S OUT OF COMMISSION.
GOTHAM'S IS HISTORY.
PARIS IS CLEAR.
LONDON'S IS FINISHED.
DUBAI IS FREE.
BOLOGNA IS CLEAR.
MEXICO CITY'S SIGNAL IS OUT.
KUALA LUMPUR HAS BEEN SECURED.
SYDNEY'S CLEARED.
MOSCOW IS CLEAR.
SHANGHAI'S SECURE.
TORONTO'S CLEAR.
THAT'S ALL OF YOU! STAND BY-- TRAUMA TOXIN IS INCOMING.
MOSCOW.
HOLD TIGHT, PEOPLE.
MASKS ON.
WE'RE NOT OUT OF THE WOODS YET...

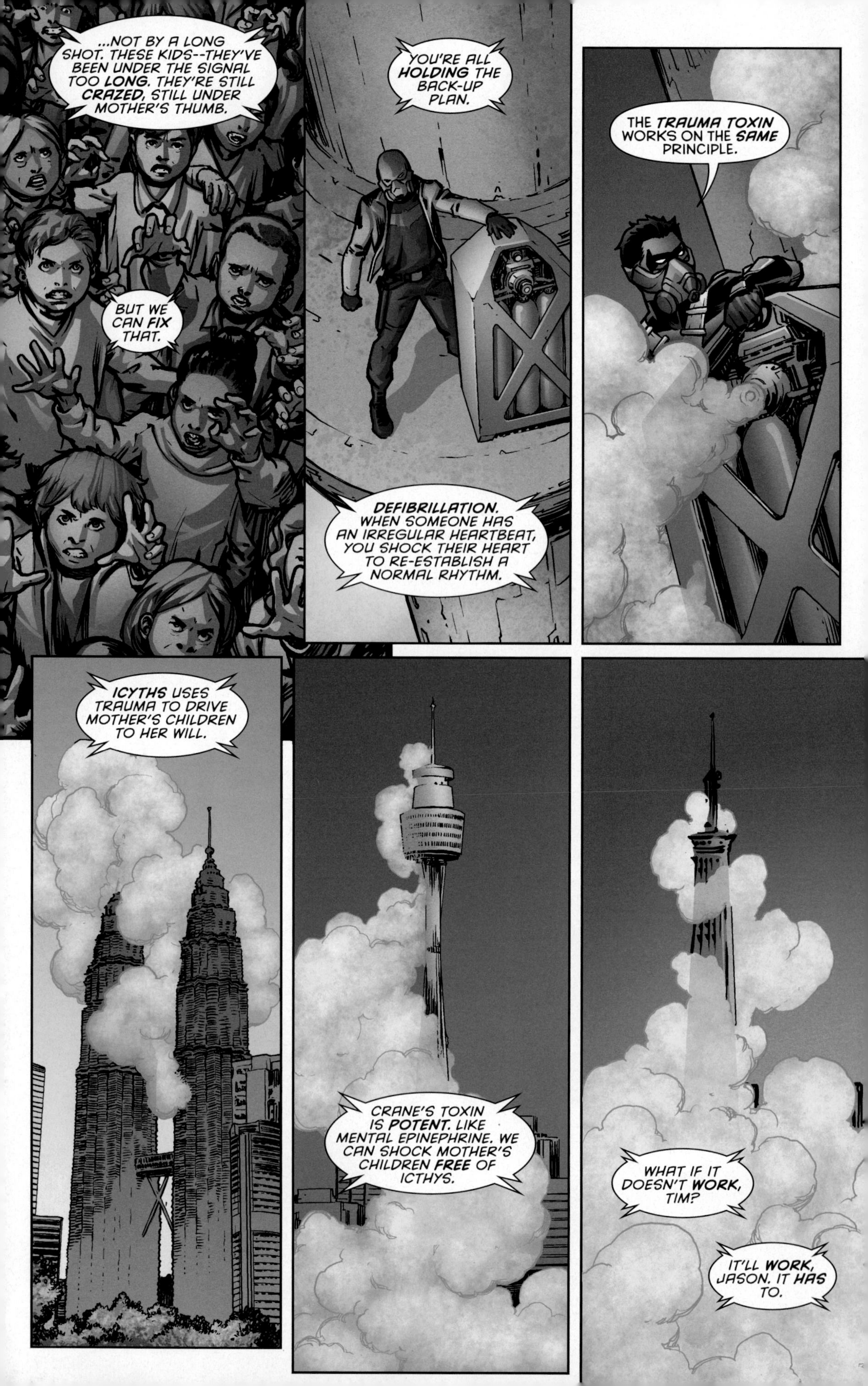
...NOT BY A LONG SHOT. THESE KIDS--THEY'VE BEEN UNDER THE SIGNAL TOO LONG. THEY'RE STILL CRAZED, STILL UNDER MOTHER'S THUMB.
BUT WE CAN FIX THAT.
YOU'RE ALL HOLDING THE BACK-UP PLAN.
DEFIBRILLATION. WHEN SOMEONE HAS AN IRREGULAR HEARTBEAT, YOU SHOCK THEIR HEART TO RE-ESTABLISH A NORMAL RHYTHM.
THE TRAUMA TOXIN WORKS ON THE SAME PRINCIPLE.
ICYTHS USES TRAUMA TO DRIVE MOTHER'S CHILDREN TO HER WILL.
CRANE'S TOXIN IS POTENT. LIKE MENTAL EPINEPHRINE. WE CAN SHOCK MOTHER'S CHILDREN FREE OF ICTHYS.
WHAT IF IT DOESN'T WORK, TIM?
IT'LL WORK, JASON. IT HAS TO.

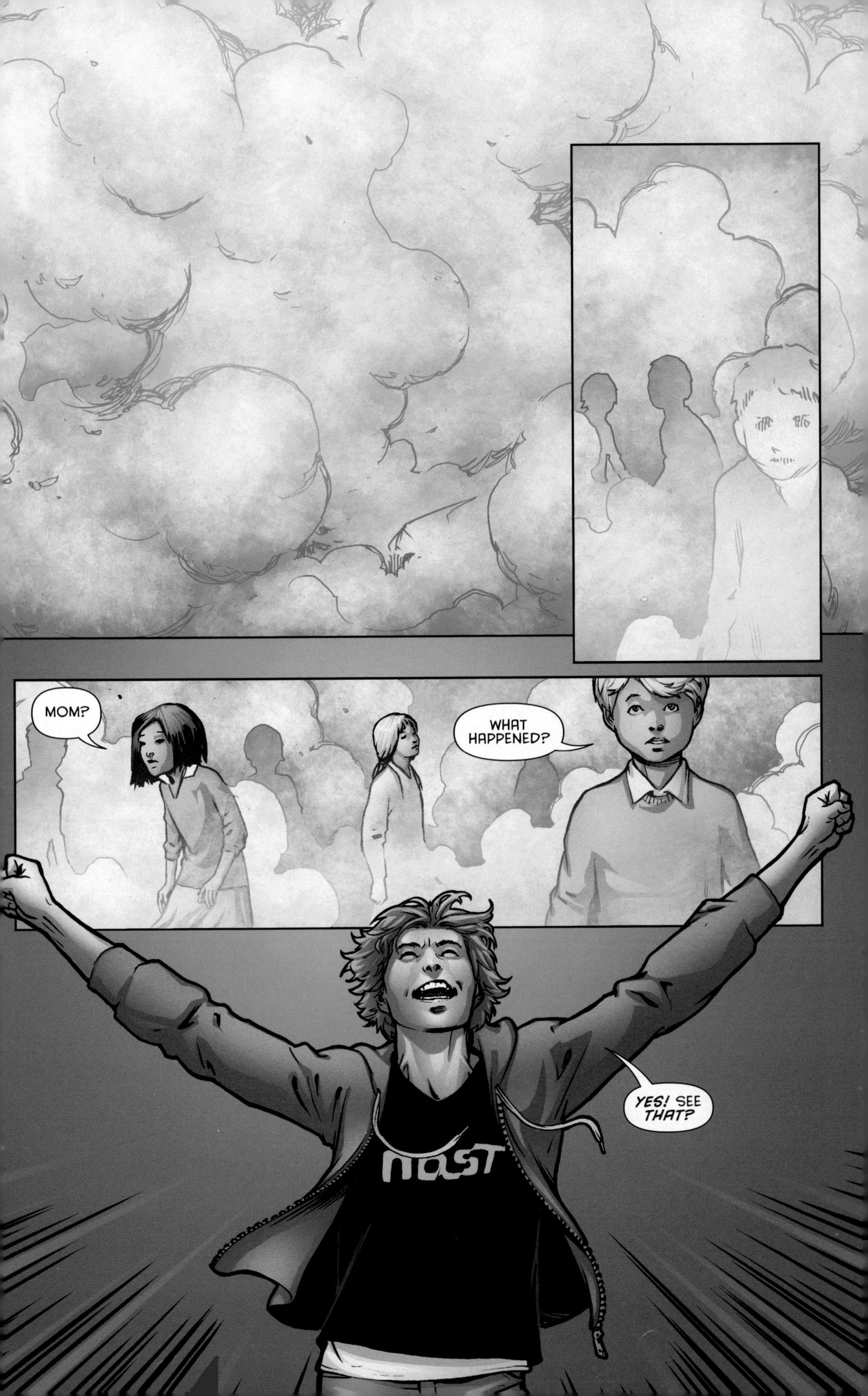
MOM?
WHAT HAPPENED?
YES! SEE THAT?
NOST

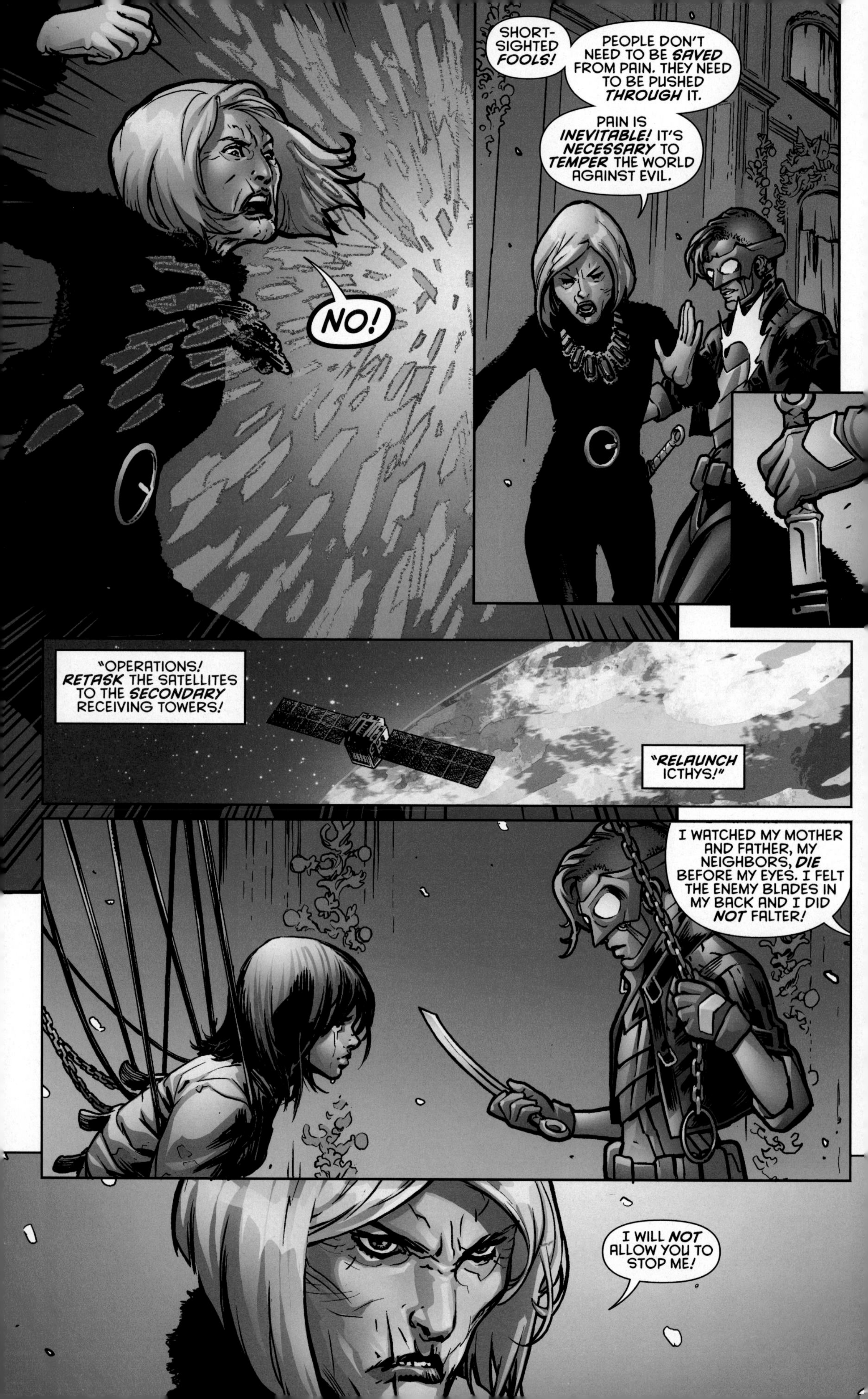
NO!
SHORT-SIGHTED FOOLS!
PEOPLE DON'T NEED TO BE SAVED FROM PAIN. THEY NEED TO BE PUSHED THROUGH IT.
PAIN IS INEVITABLE! IT'S NECESSARY TO TEMPER THE WORLD AGAINST EVIL.
"OPERATIONS! RETASK THE SATELLITES TO THE SECONDARY RECEIVING TOWERS!
"RELAUNCH ICTHYS!"
I WATCHED MY MOTHER AND FATHER, MY NEIGHBORS, DIE BEFORE MY EYES. I FELT THE ENEMY BLADES IN MY BACK AND I DID NOT FALTER!
I WILL NOT ALLOW YOU TO STOP ME!

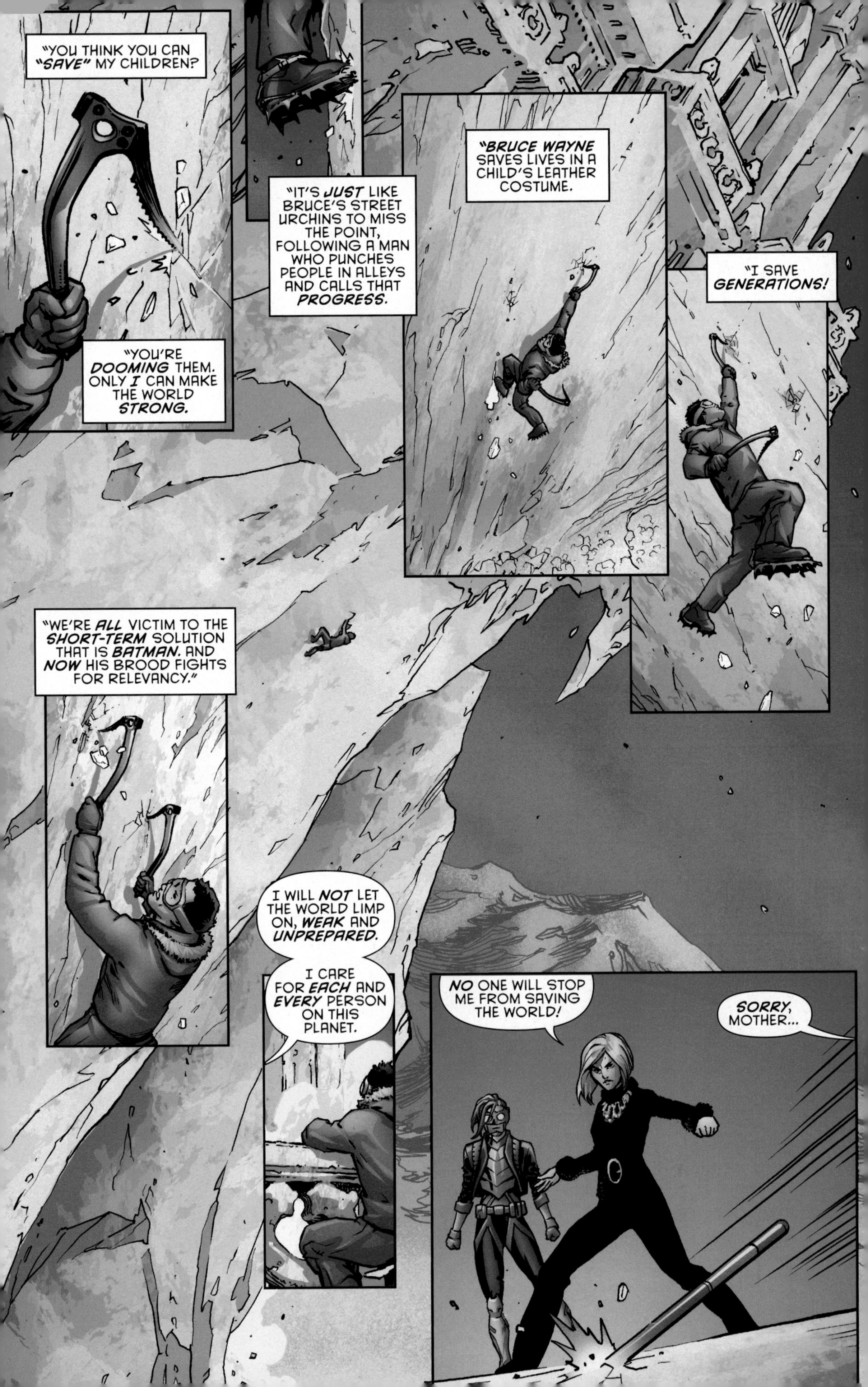
"YOU THINK YOU CAN "SAVE" MY CHILDREN?
"YOU'RE DOOMING THEM. ONLY I CAN MAKE THE WORLD STRONG.
"IT'S JUST LIKE BRUCE'S STREET URCHINS TO MISS THE POINT, FOLLOWING A MAN WHO PUNCHES PEOPLE IN ALLEYS AND CALLS THAT PROGRESS.
"BRUCE WAYNE SAVES LIVES IN A CHILD'S LEATHER COSTUME.
"I SAVE GENERATIONS!
"WE'RE ALL VICTIM TO THE SHORT-TERM SOLUTION THAT IS BATMAN. AND NOW HIS BROOD FIGHTS FOR RELEVANCY."
I WILL NOT LET THE WORLD LIMP ON, WEAK AND UNPREPARED.
I CARE FOR EACH AND EVERY PERSON ON THIS PLANET.
NO ONE WILL STOP ME FROM SAVING THE WORLD!
SORRY, MOTHER...

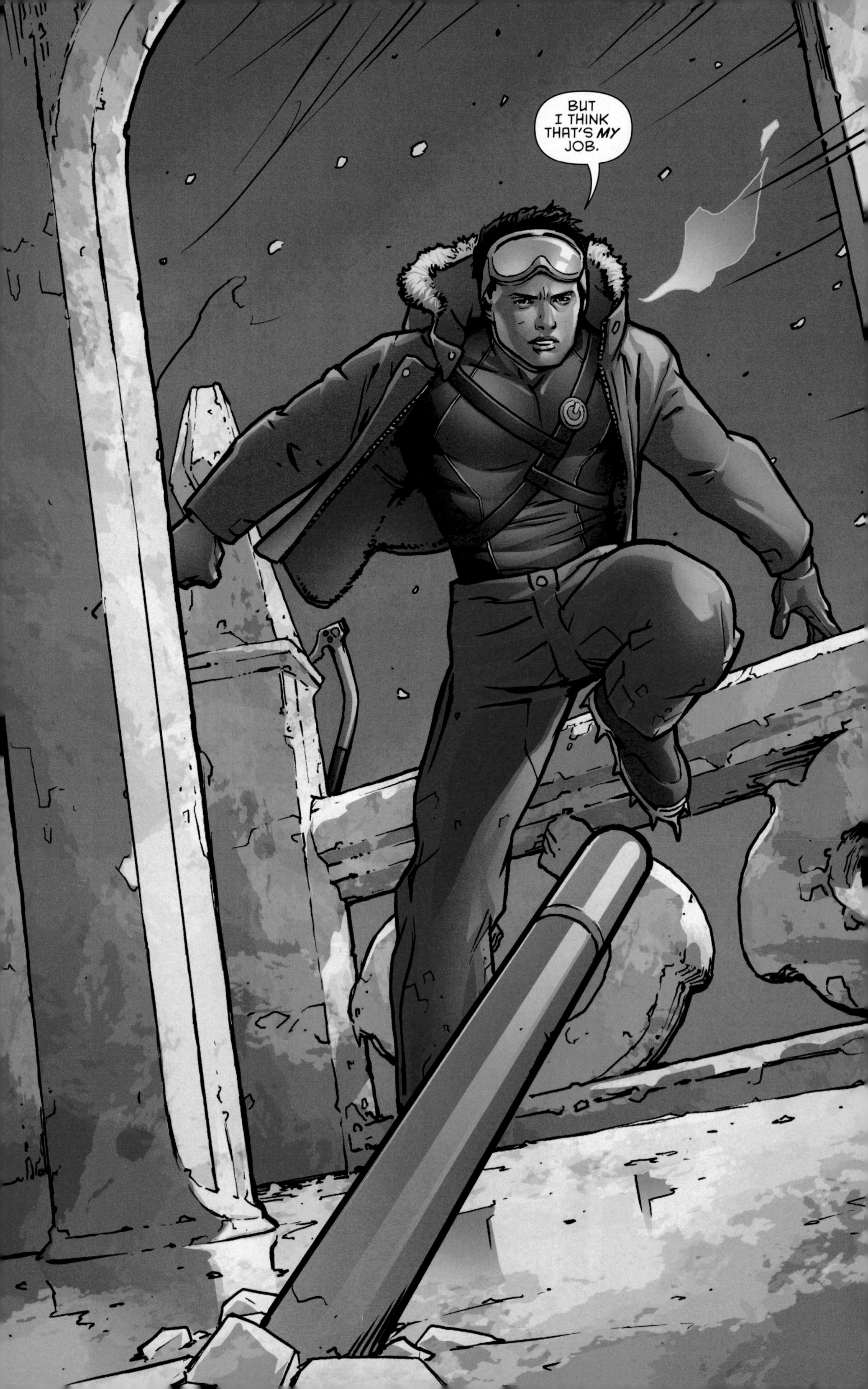
BUT I THINK THAT'S MY JOB.

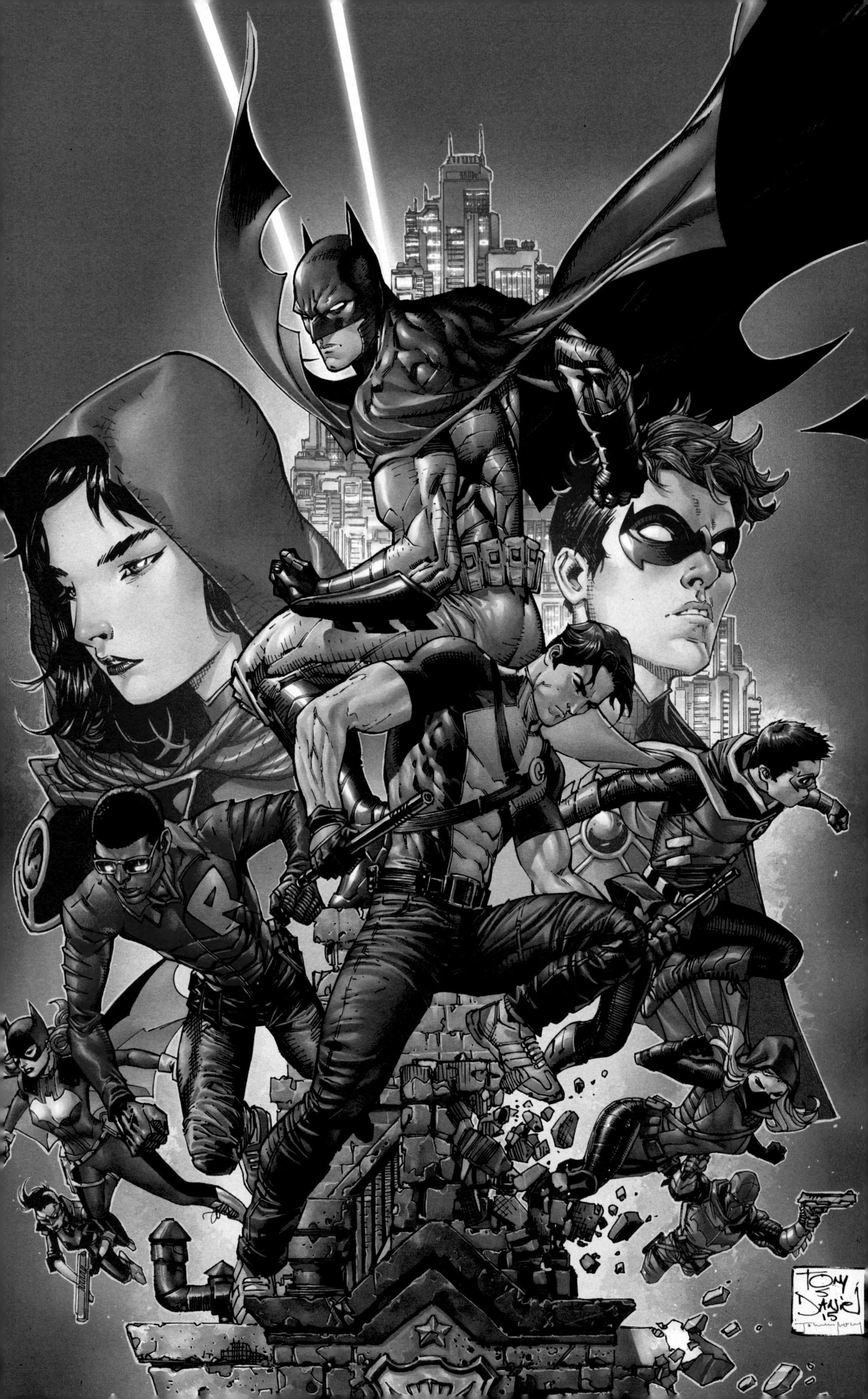
TONY S DANIEL 15

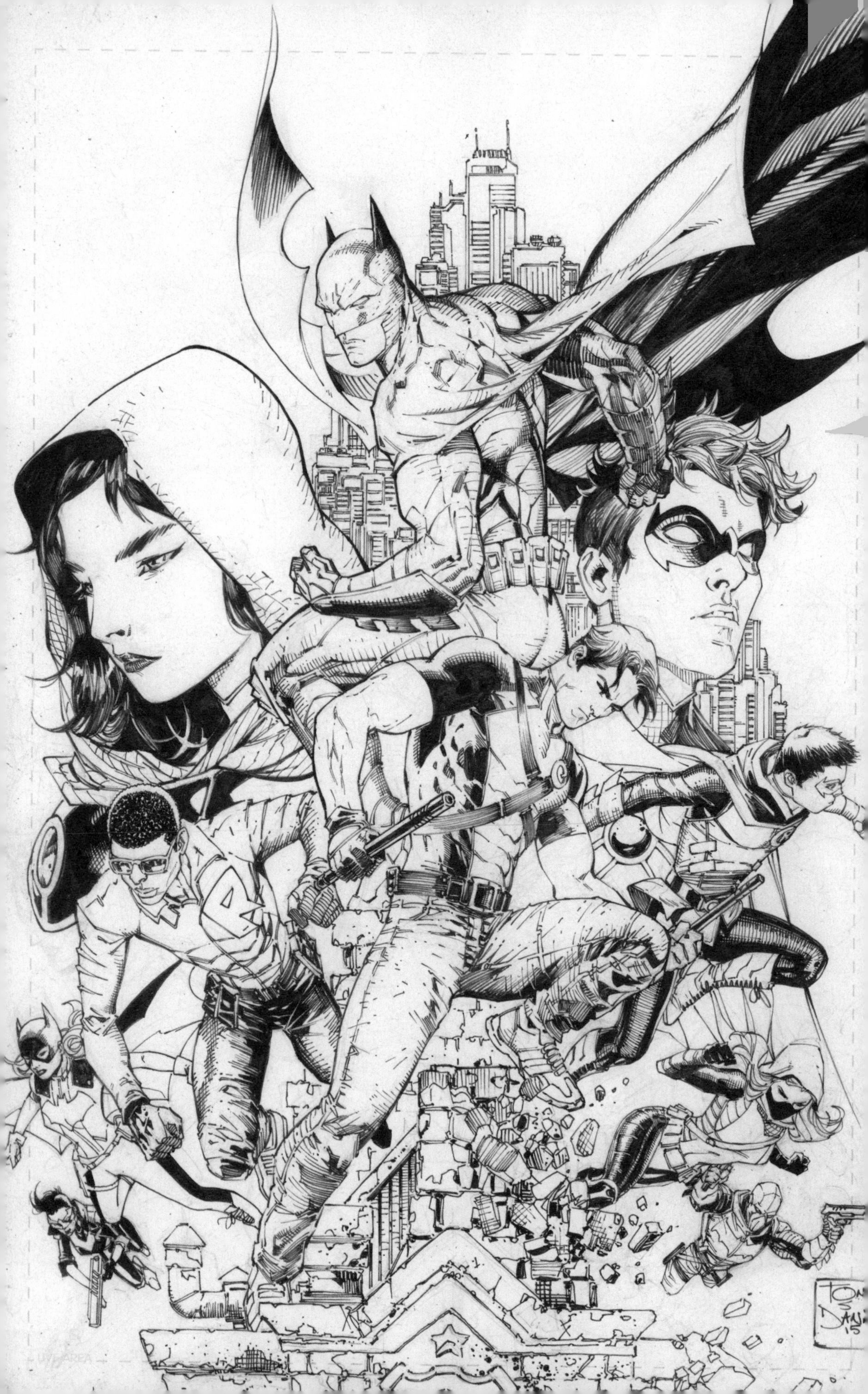

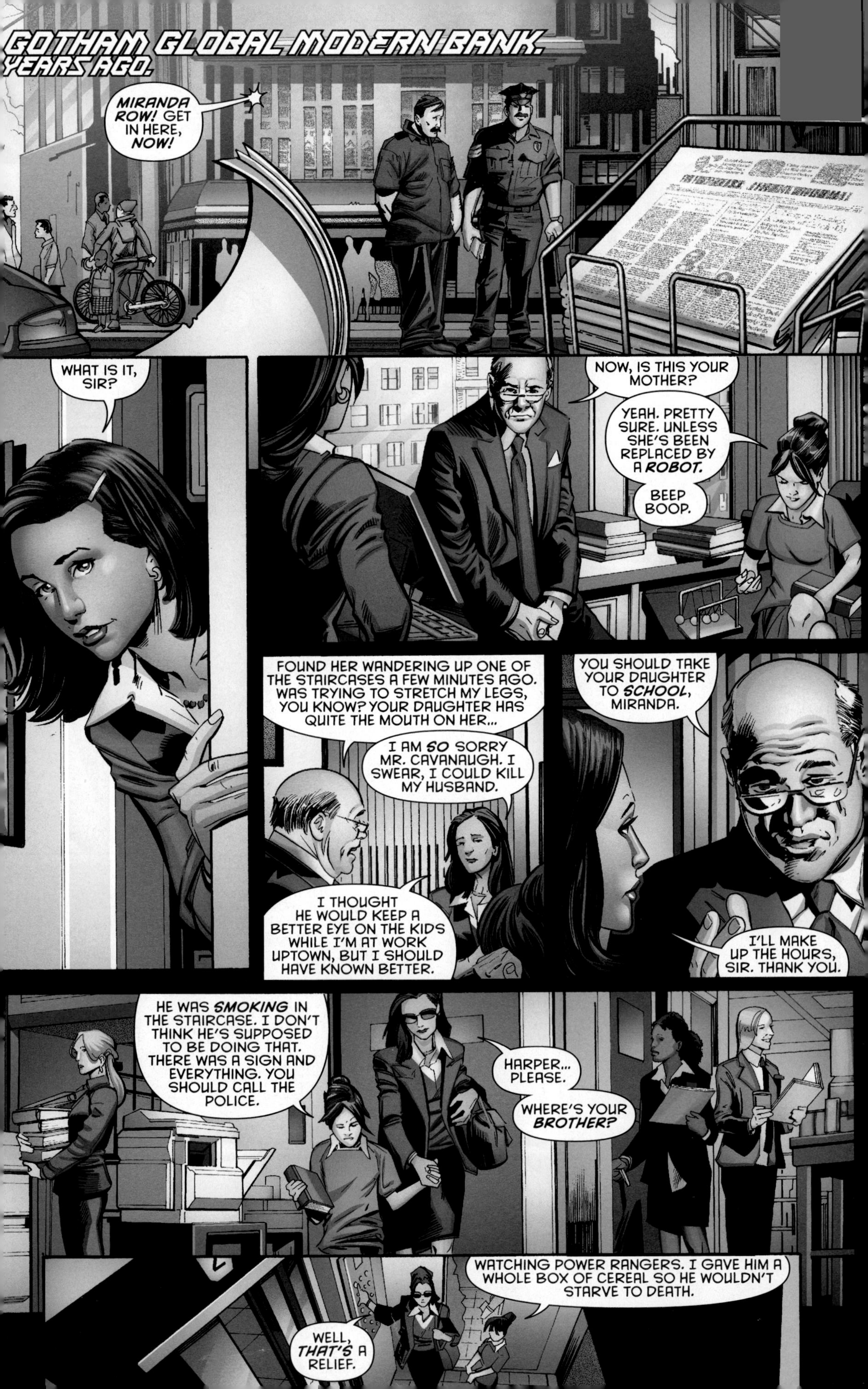
GOTHAM GLOBAL MODERN BANK. YEARS AGO.
MIRANDA ROW! GET IN HERE, NOW!
WHAT IS IT, SIR?
NOW, IS THIS YOUR MOTHER?
YEAH. PRETTY SURE. UNLESS SHE'S BEEN REPLACED BY A ROBOT.
BEEP BOOP.
FOUND HER WANDERING UP ONE OF THE STAIRCASES A FEW MINUTES AGO. WAS TRYING TO STRETCH MY LEGS, YOU KNOW? YOUR DAUGHTER HAS QUITE THE MOUTH ON HER...
I AM SO SORRY MR. CAVANAUGH. I SWEAR, I COULD KILL MY HUSBAND.
I THOUGHT HE WOULD KEEP A BETTER EYE ON THE KIDS WHILE I'M AT WORK UPTOWN, BUT I SHOULD HAVE KNOWN BETTER.
YOU SHOULD TAKE YOUR DAUGHTER TO SCHOOL, MIRANDA.
I'LL MAKE UP THE HOURS, SIR. THANK YOU.
HE WAS SMOKING IN THE STAIRCASE. I DON'T THINK HE'S SUPPOSED TO BE DOING THAT. THERE WAS A SIGN AND EVERYTHING. YOU SHOULD CALL THE POLICE.
HARPER... PLEASE.
WHERE'S YOUR BROTHER?
WATCHING POWER RANGERS. I GAVE HIM A WHOLE BOX OF CEREAL SO HE WOULDN'T STARVE TO DEATH.
WELL, THAT'S A RELIEF.

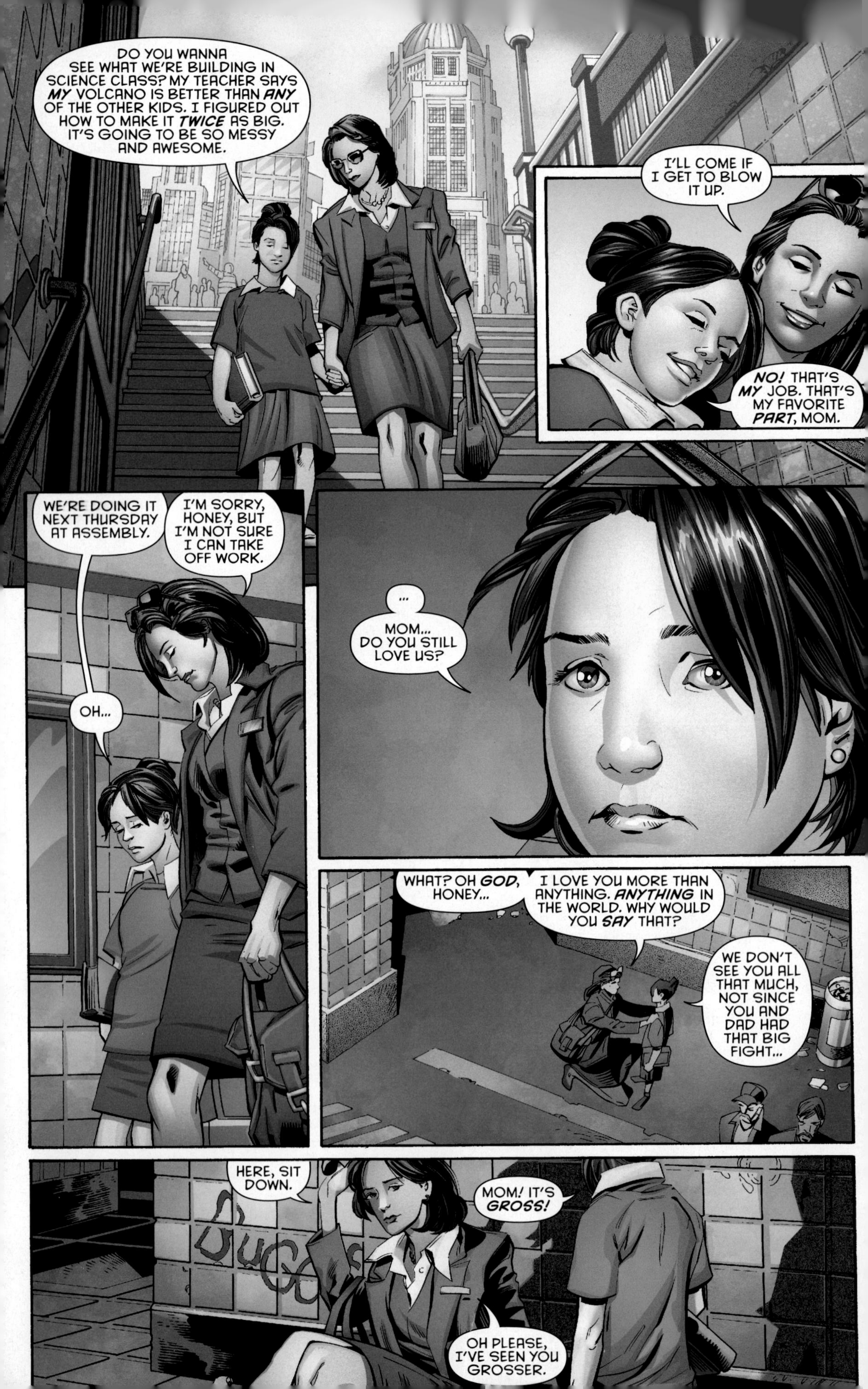
DO YOU WANNA SEE WHAT WE'RE BUILDING IN SCIENCE CLASS? MY TEACHER SAYS MY VOLCANO IS BETTER THAN ANY OF THE OTHER KIDS. I FIGURED OUT HOW TO MAKE IT TWICE AS BIG. IT'S GOING TO BE SO MESSY AND AWESOME.
I'LL COME IF I GET TO BLOW IT UP.
NO! THAT'S MY JOB. THAT'S MY FAVORITE PART, MOM.
WE'RE DOING IT NEXT THURSDAY AT ASSEMBLY.
I'M SORRY, HONEY, BUT I'M NOT SURE I CAN TAKE OFF WORK.
OH...
...
MOM... DO YOU STILL LOVE US?
WHAT? OH GOD, HONEY...
I LOVE YOU MORE THAN ANYTHING. ANYTHING IN THE WORLD. WHY WOULD YOU SAY THAT?
WE DON'T SEE YOU ALL THAT MUCH, NOT SINCE YOU AND DAD HAD THAT BIG FIGHT...
HERE, SIT DOWN.
MOM! IT'S GROSS!
OH PLEASE, I'VE SEEN YOU GROSSER.

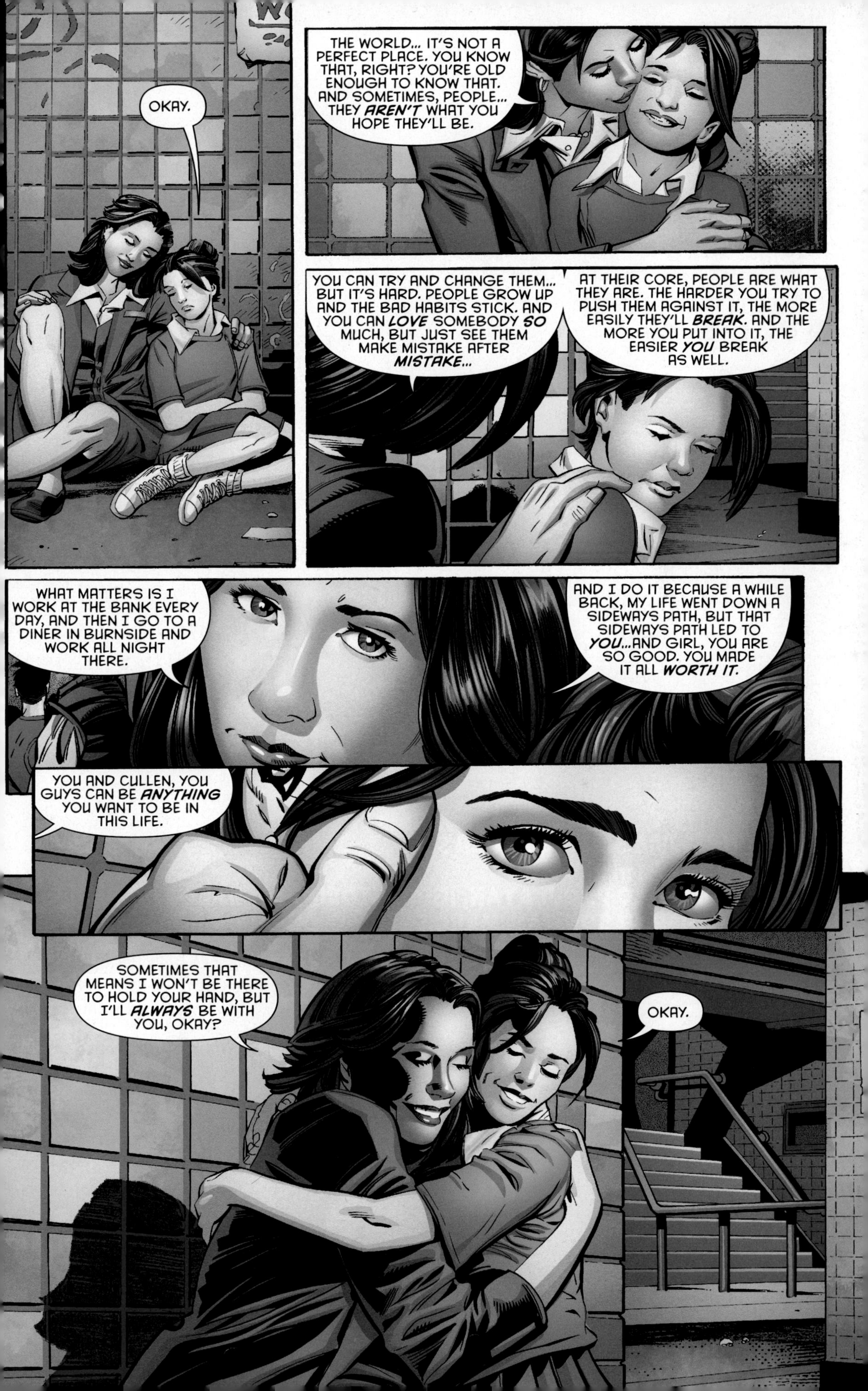
OKAY.
THE WORLD... IT'S NOT A PERFECT PLACE. YOU KNOW THAT, RIGHT? YOU'RE OLD ENOUGH TO KNOW THAT. AND SOMETIMES, PEOPLE... THEY AREN'T WHAT YOU HOPE THEY'LL BE.
YOU CAN TRY AND CHANGE THEM... BUT IT'S HARD. PEOPLE GROW UP AND THE BAD HABITS STICK. AND YOU CAN LOVE SOMEBODY SO MUCH, BUT JUST SEE THEM MAKE MISTAKE AFTER MISTAKE...
AT THEIR CORE, PEOPLE ARE WHAT THEY ARE. THE HARDER YOU TRY TO PUSH THEM AGAINST IT, THE MORE EASILY THEY'LL BREAK. AND THE MORE YOU PUT INTO IT, THE EASIER YOU BREAK AS WELL.
WHAT MATTERS IS I WORK AT THE BANK EVERY DAY, AND THEN I GO TO A DINER IN BURNSIDE AND WORK ALL NIGHT THERE.
AND I DO IT BECAUSE A WHILE BACK, MY LIFE WENT DOWN A SIDEWAYS PATH, BUT THAT SIDEWAYS PATH LED TO YOU...AND GIRL, YOU ARE SO GOOD. YOU MADE IT ALL WORTH IT.
YOU AND CULLEN, YOU GUYS CAN BE ANYTHING YOU WANT TO BE IN THIS LIFE.
SOMETIMES THAT MEANS I WON'T BE THERE TO HOLD YOUR HAND, BUT I'LL ALWAYS BE WITH YOU, OKAY?
OKAY.

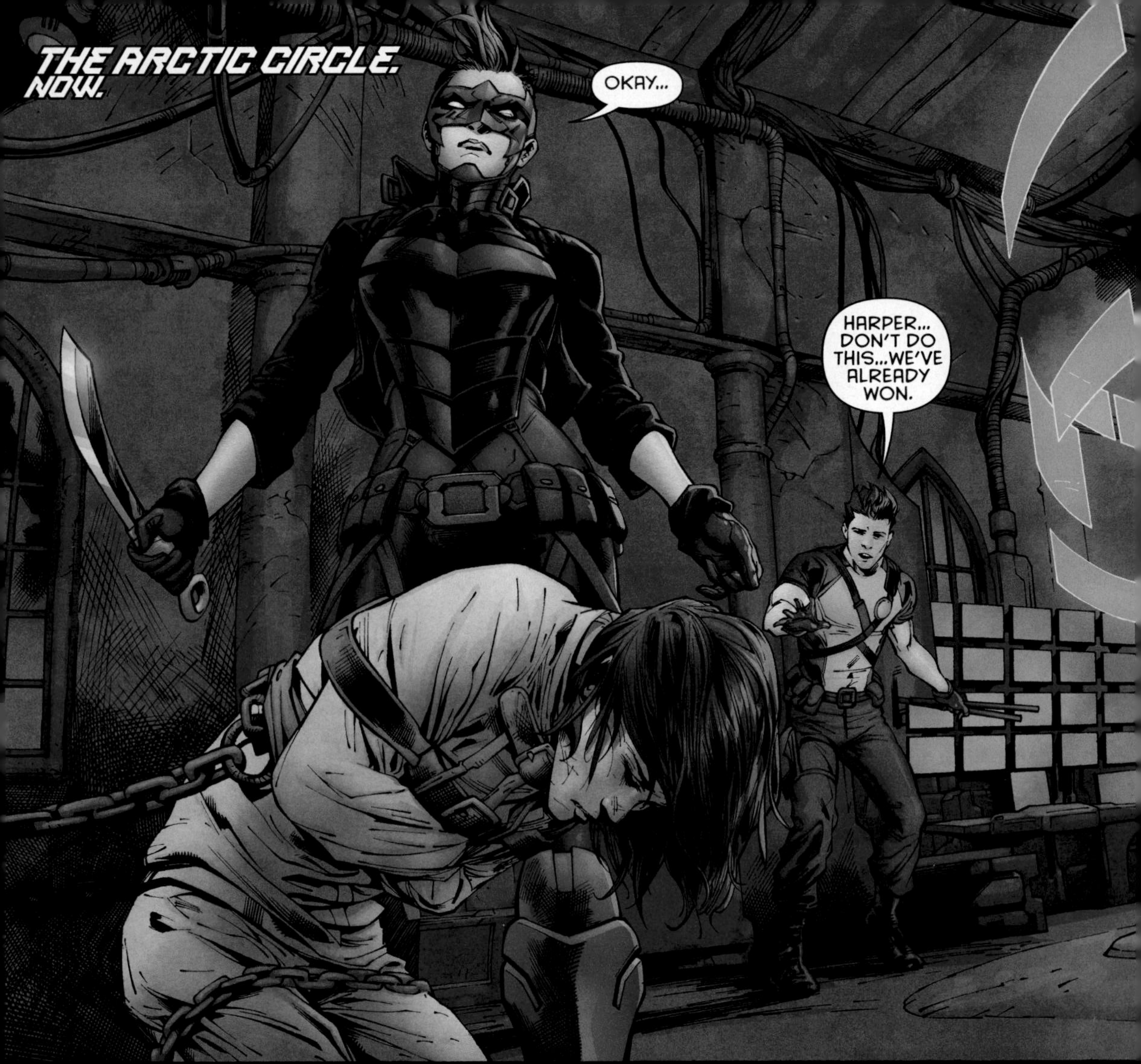
THE ARCTIC CIRCLE. NOW.
OKAY...
HARPER... DON'T DO THIS...WE'VE ALREADY WON.

JAMES TYNION IV & SCOTT SNYDER Story
JAMES TYNION IV Script
SCOT EATON, CARLO PAGULAYAN, IGOR VITORINO, GERALDO BORGES Pencils
WAYNE FAUCHER, JASON PAZ, MARC DEERING, GERALDO BORGES Inks

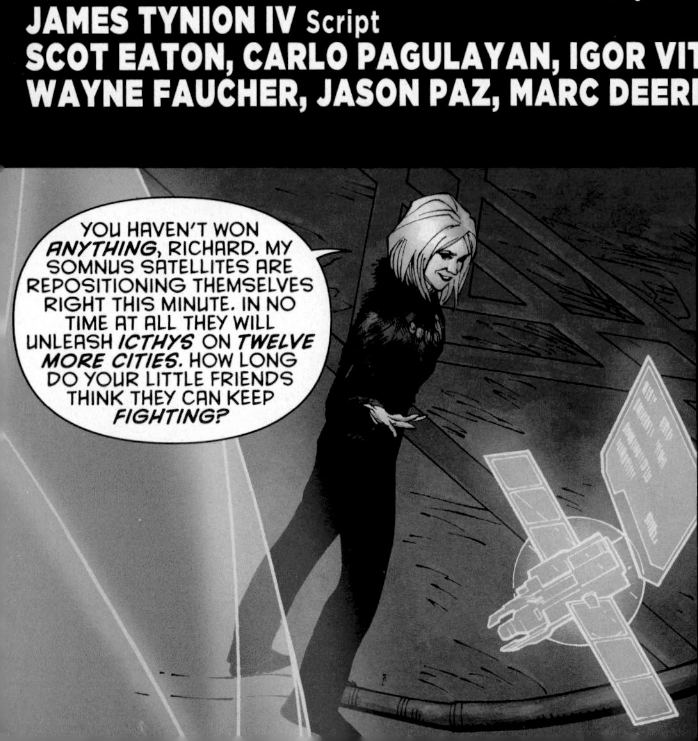
YOU HAVEN'T WON ANYTHING, RICHARD. MY SOMNUS SATELLITES ARE REPOSITIONING THEMSELVES RIGHT THIS MINUTE. IN NO TIME AT ALL THEY WILL UNLEASH ICTHYS ON TWELVE MORE CITIES. HOW LONG DO YOUR LITTLE FRIENDS THINK THEY CAN KEEP FIGHTING?

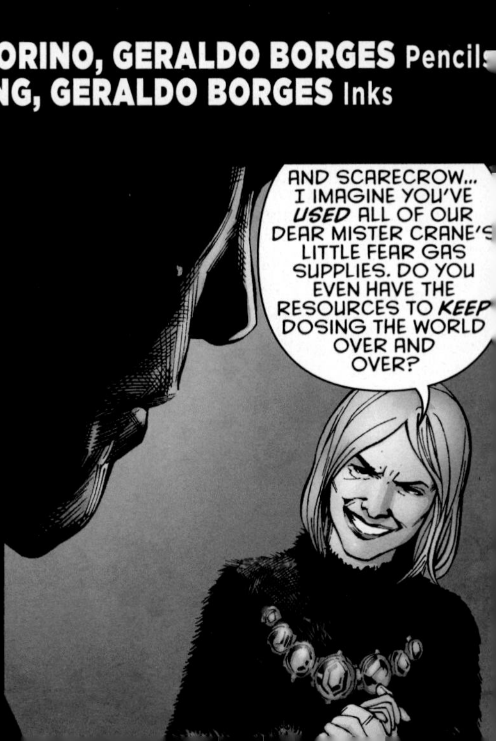
AND SCARECROW... I IMAGINE YOU'VE USED ALL OF OUR DEAR MISTER CRANE'S LITTLE FEAR GAS SUPPLIES. DO YOU EVEN HAVE THE RESOURCES TO KEEP DOSING THE WORLD OVER AND OVER?

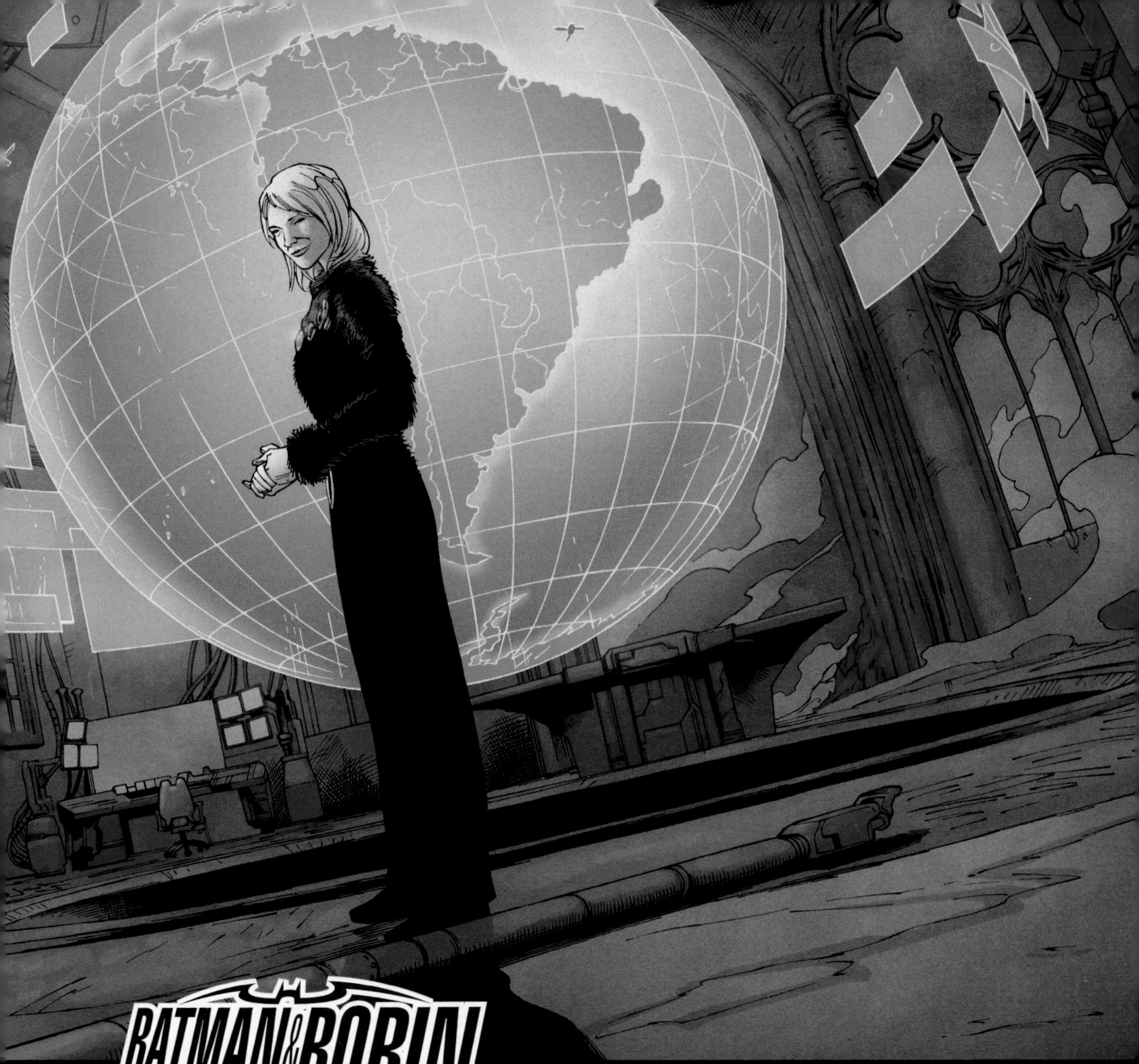

BATMAN & ROBIN ETERNAL

NEW WORLD

ALLEN PASSALAQUA & GABE ELTAEB Colors
MARILYN PATRIZIO Letters
TONY S. DANIEL & TOMEU MOREY Cover

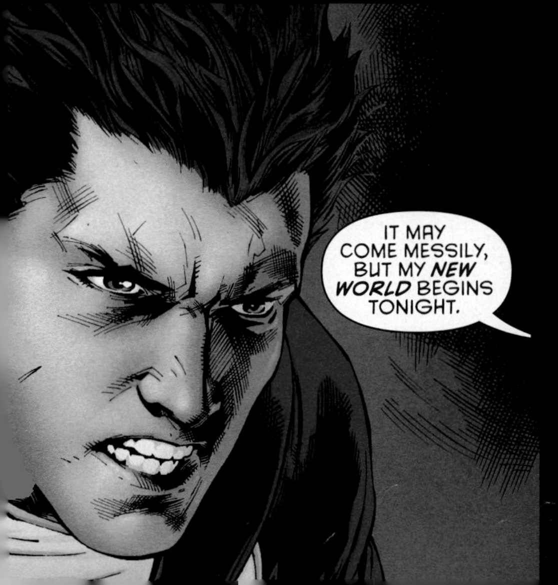
IT MAY COME MESSILY, BUT MY *NEW WORLD* BEGINS TONIGHT.

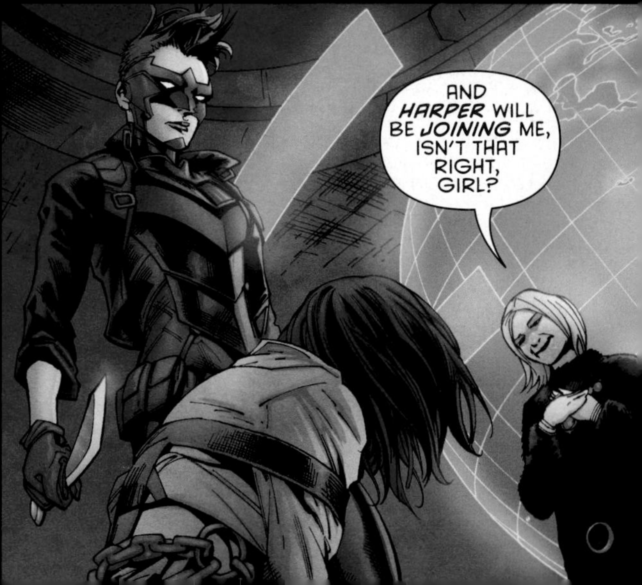
AND *HARPER* WILL BE *JOINING* ME, ISN'T THAT RIGHT, GIRL?

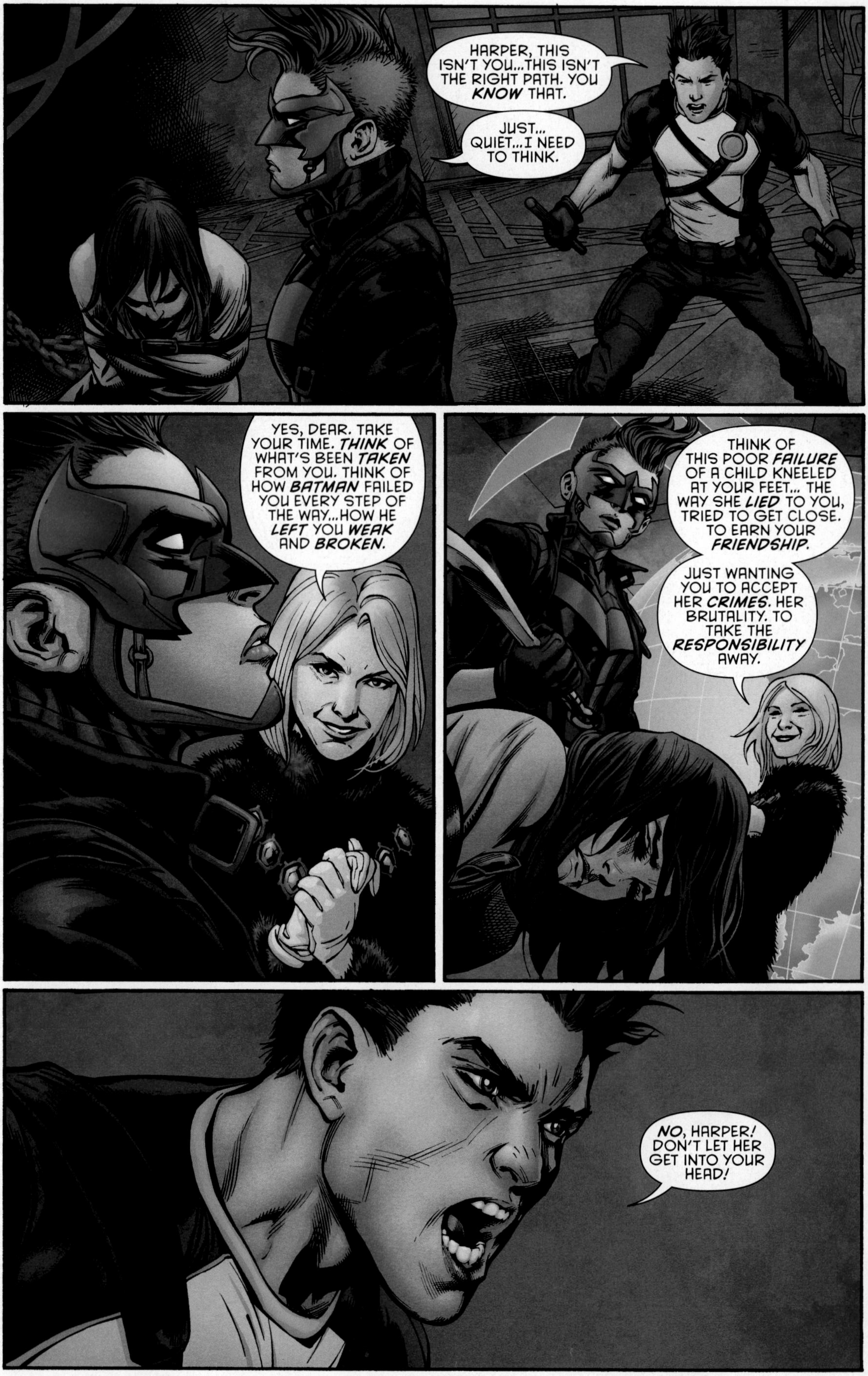
HARPER, THIS ISN'T YOU...THIS ISN'T THE RIGHT PATH. YOU *KNOW* THAT.
JUST... QUIET...I NEED TO THINK.
YES, DEAR. TAKE YOUR TIME. *THINK* OF WHAT'S BEEN *TAKEN* FROM YOU. THINK OF HOW *BATMAN* FAILED YOU EVERY STEP OF THE WAY...HOW HE *LEFT* YOU *WEAK* AND *BROKEN*.
THINK OF THIS POOR *FAILURE* OF A CHILD KNEELED AT YOUR FEET... THE WAY SHE *LIED* TO YOU, TRIED TO GET CLOSE. TO EARN YOUR *FRIENDSHIP*.
JUST WANTING YOU TO ACCEPT HER *CRIMES*. HER BRUTALITY. TO TAKE THE *RESPONSIBILITY* AWAY.
NO, HARPER! DON'T LET HER GET INTO YOUR HEAD!

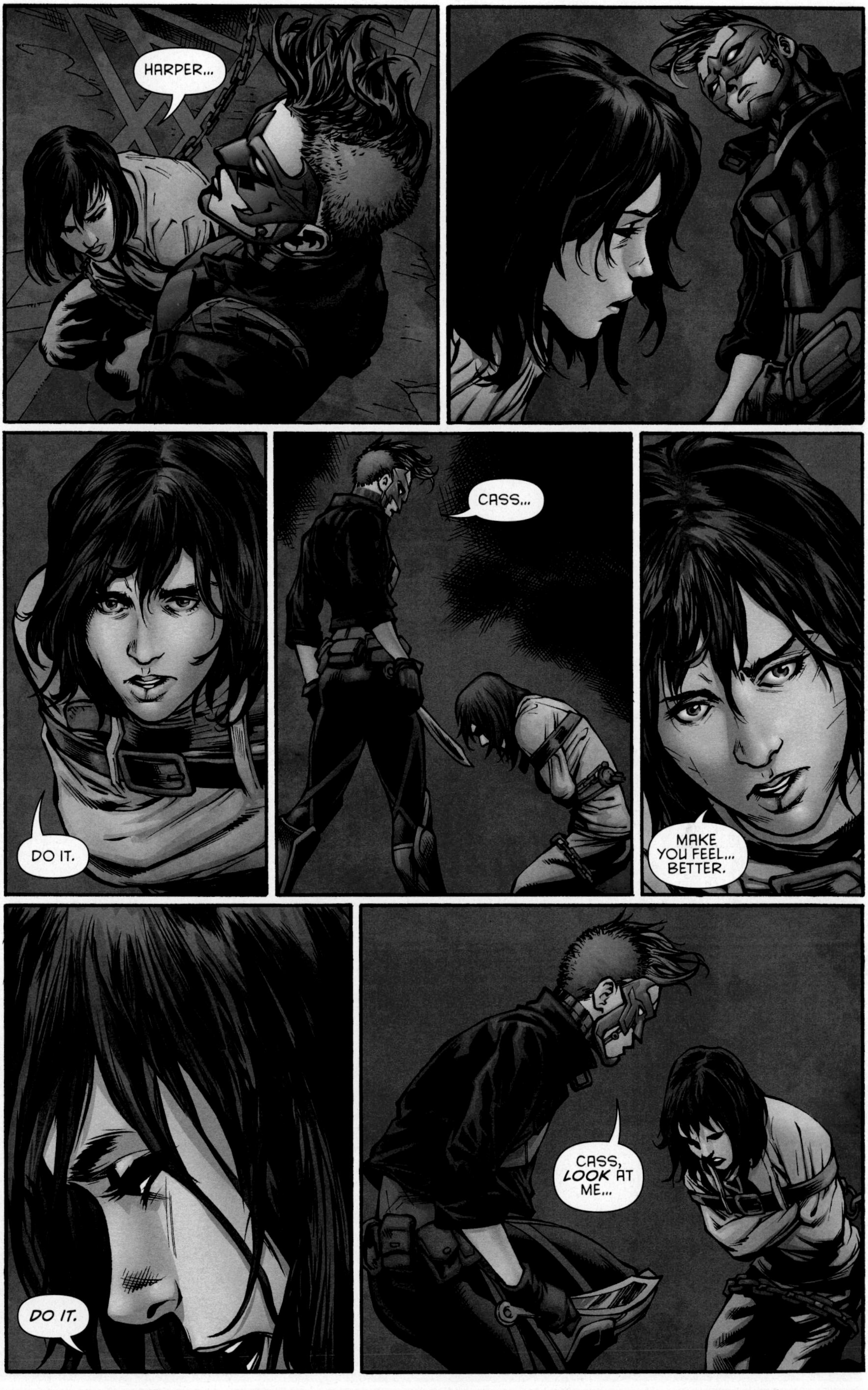
HARPER...
CASS...
DO IT.
MAKE YOU FEEL... BETTER.
DO IT.
CASS, *LOOK* AT ME...

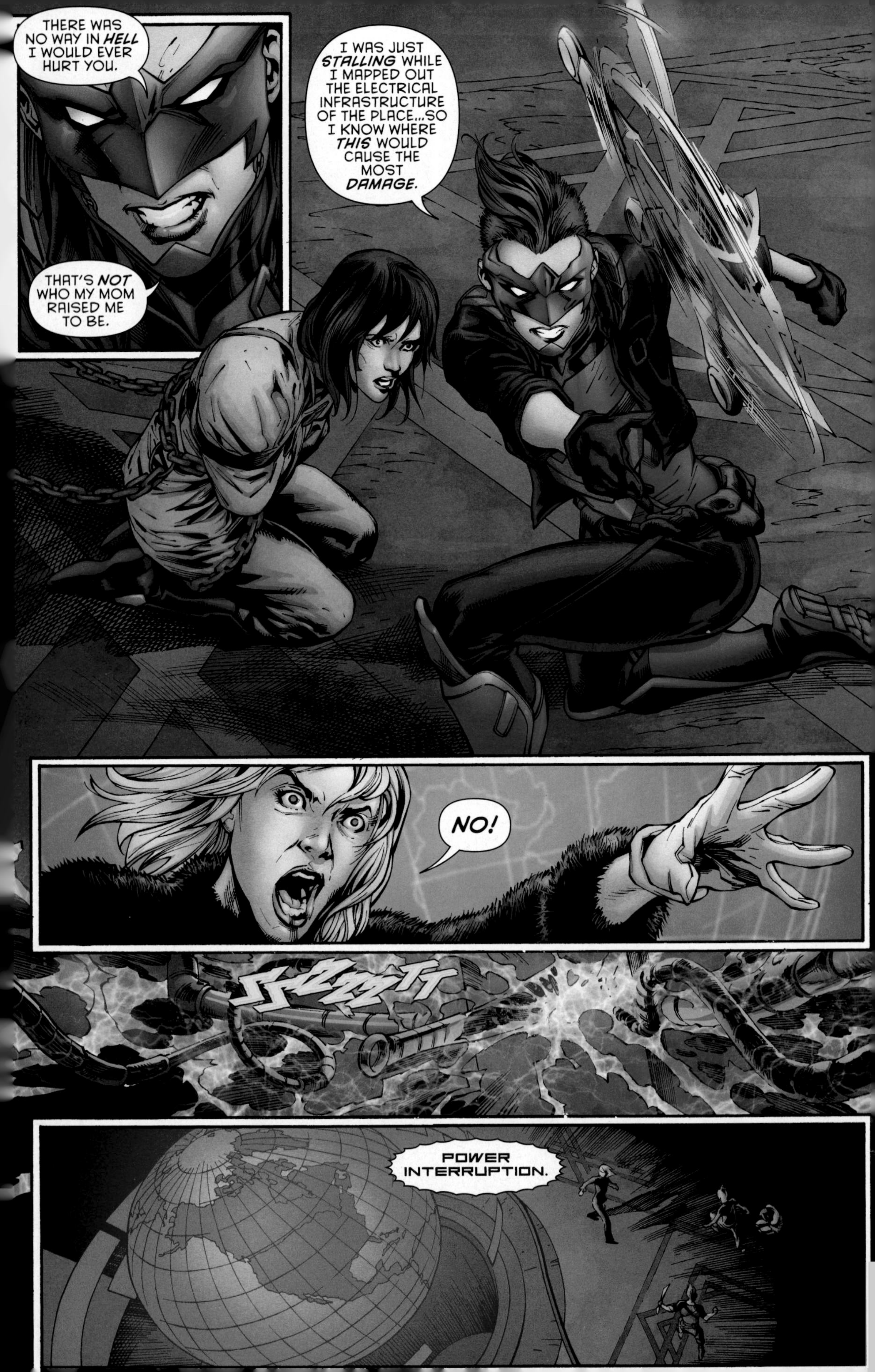
THERE WAS NO WAY IN *HELL* I WOULD EVER HURT YOU.
THAT'S *NOT* WHO MY MOM RAISED ME TO BE.
I WAS JUST *STALLING* WHILE I MAPPED OUT THE ELECTRICAL INFRASTRUCTURE OF THE PLACE...SO I KNOW WHERE *THIS* WOULD CAUSE THE MOST *DAMAGE*.
NO!
SSZZZTT
POWER INTERRUPTION.

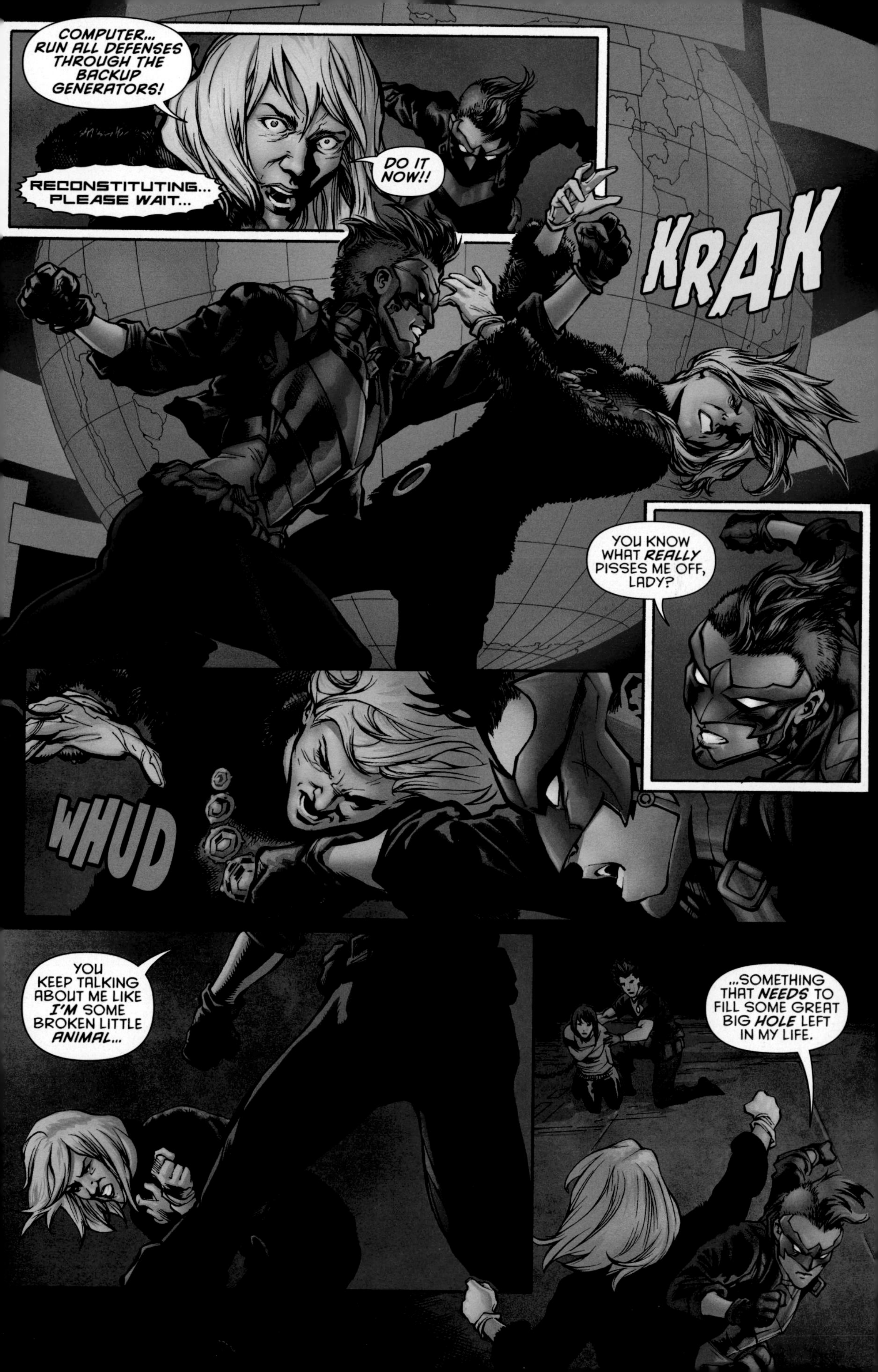

COMPUTER... RUN ALL DEFENSES THROUGH THE BACKUP GENERATORS!
DO IT NOW!!
RECONSTITUTING... PLEASE WAIT...
KRAK
YOU KNOW WHAT REALLY PISSES ME OFF, LADY?
WHUD
YOU KEEP TALKING ABOUT ME LIKE I'M SOME BROKEN LITTLE ANIMAL...
...SOMETHING THAT NEEDS TO FILL SOME GREAT BIG HOLE LEFT IN MY LIFE.

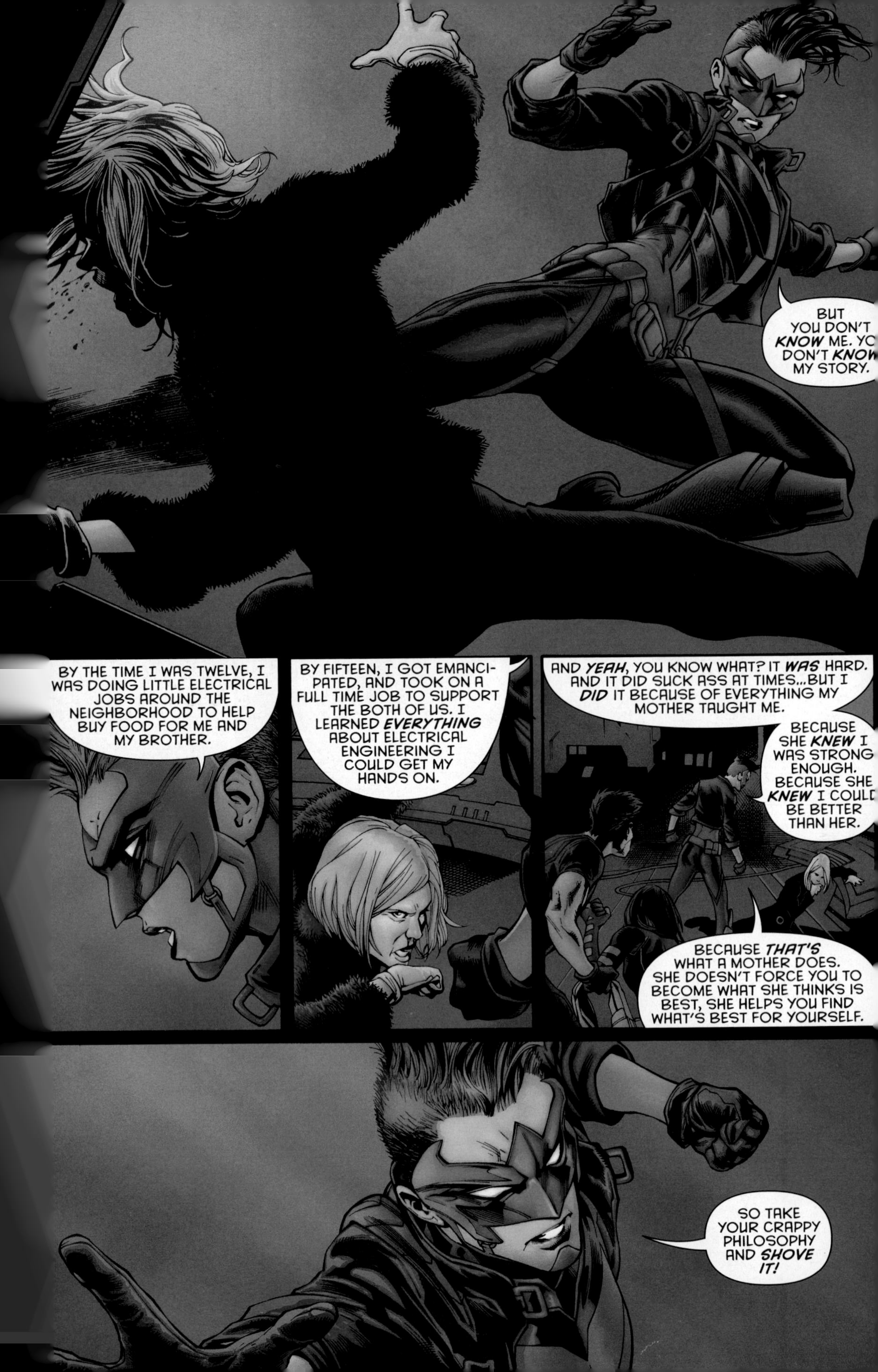
BUT YOU DON'T *KNOW* ME. YO DON'T *KNOW* MY STORY.
BY THE TIME I WAS TWELVE, I WAS DOING LITTLE ELECTRICAL JOBS AROUND THE NEIGHBORHOOD TO HELP BUY FOOD FOR ME AND MY BROTHER.
BY FIFTEEN, I GOT EMANCIPATED, AND TOOK ON A FULL TIME JOB TO SUPPORT THE BOTH OF US. I LEARNED *EVERYTHING* ABOUT ELECTRICAL ENGINEERING I COULD GET MY HANDS ON.
AND *YEAH*, YOU KNOW WHAT? IT *WAS* HARD. AND IT DID SUCK ASS AT TIMES...BUT I *DID* IT BECAUSE OF EVERYTHING MY MOTHER TAUGHT ME.
BECAUSE SHE *KNEW* I WAS STRONG ENOUGH. BECAUSE SHE *KNEW* I COULD BE BETTER THAN HER.
BECAUSE *THAT'S* WHAT A MOTHER DOES. SHE DOESN'T FORCE YOU TO BECOME WHAT SHE THINKS IS BEST, SHE HELPS YOU FIND WHAT'S BEST FOR YOURSELF.
SO TAKE YOUR CRAPPY PHILOSOPHY AND *SHOVE IT!*

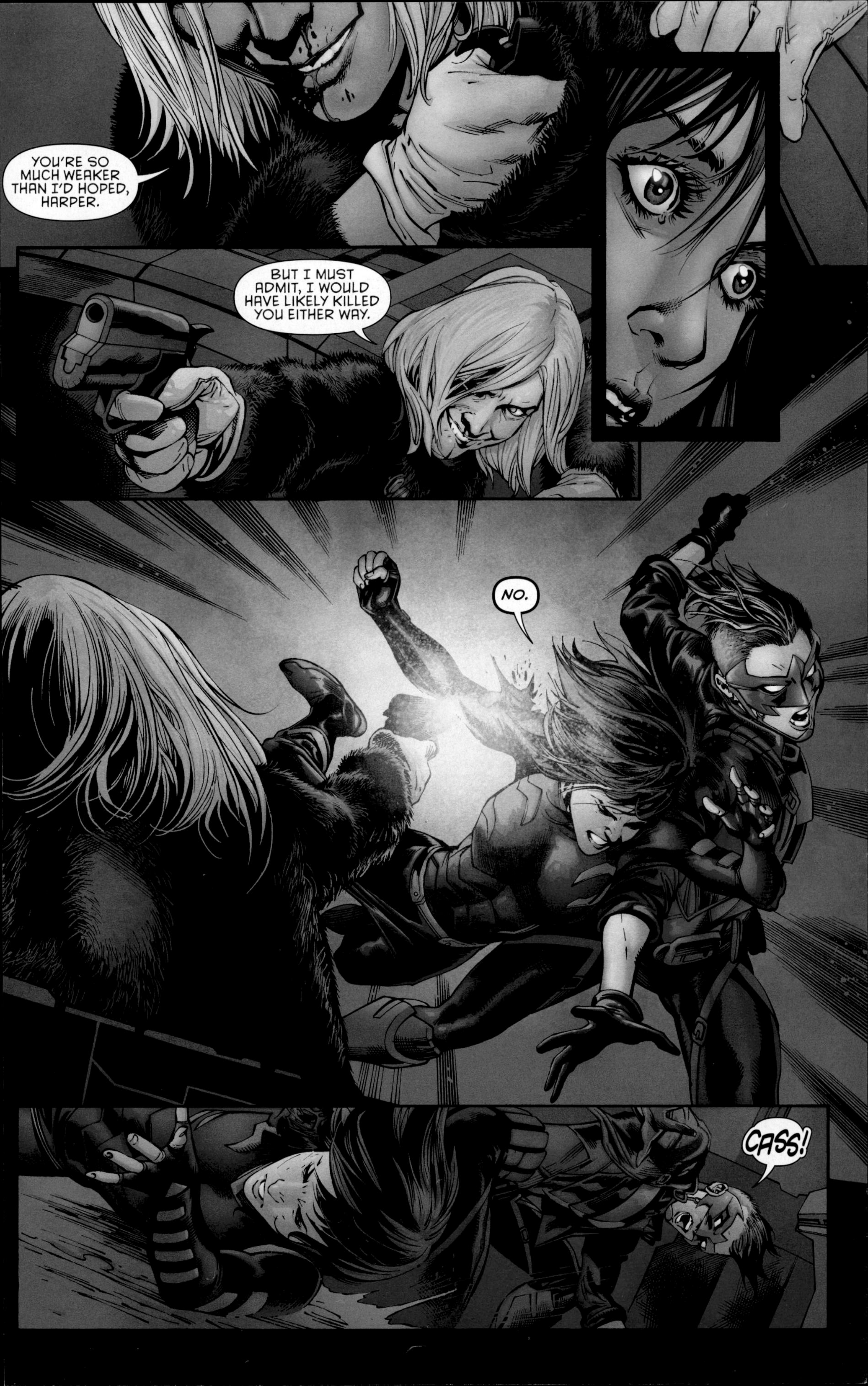
YOU'RE SO MUCH WEAKER THAN I'D HOPED, HARPER.
BUT I MUST ADMIT, I WOULD HAVE LIKELY KILLED YOU EITHER WAY.
NO.
CASS!

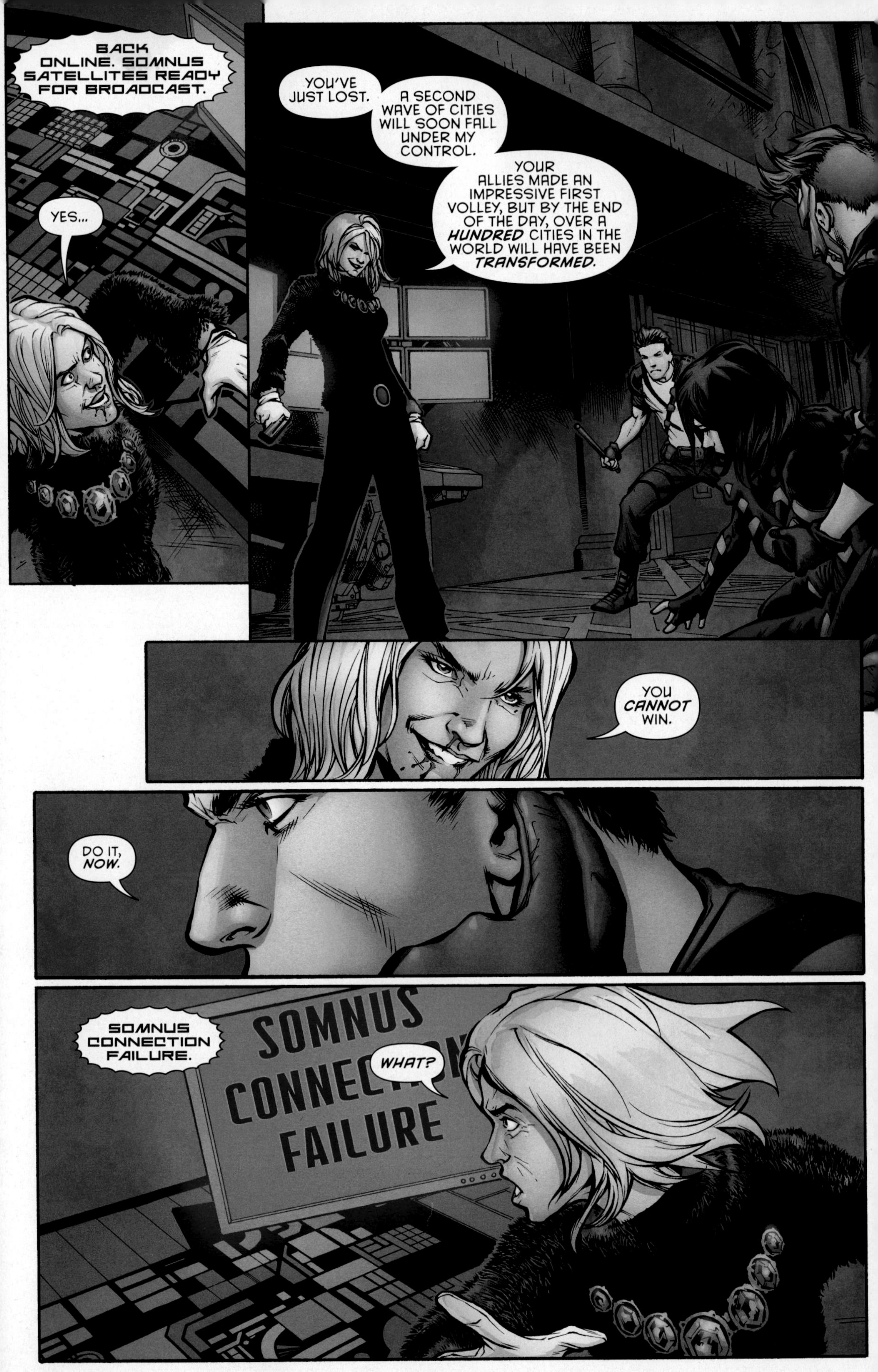
BACK ONLINE. SOMNUS SATELLITES READY FOR BROADCAST.
YES...
YOU'VE JUST LOST.
A SECOND WAVE OF CITIES WILL SOON FALL UNDER MY CONTROL.
YOUR ALLIES MADE AN IMPRESSIVE FIRST VOLLEY, BUT BY THE END OF THE DAY, OVER A HUNDRED CITIES IN THE WORLD WILL HAVE BEEN TRANSFORMED.
YOU CANNOT WIN.
DO IT, NOW.
SOMNUS CONNECTION FAILURE.
SOMNUS CONNECTI
FAILURE
WHAT?

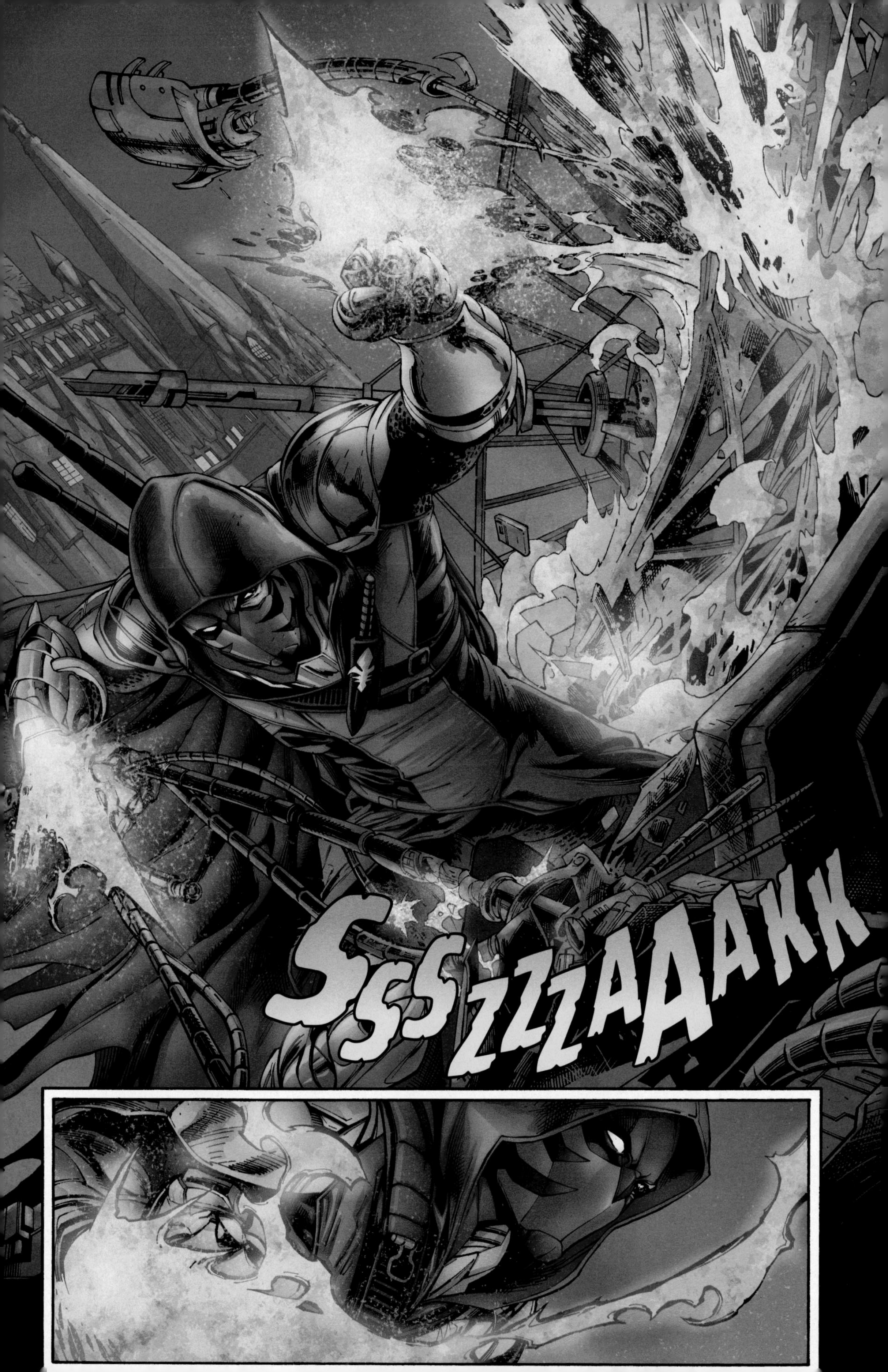
SSSZZZAAAKK

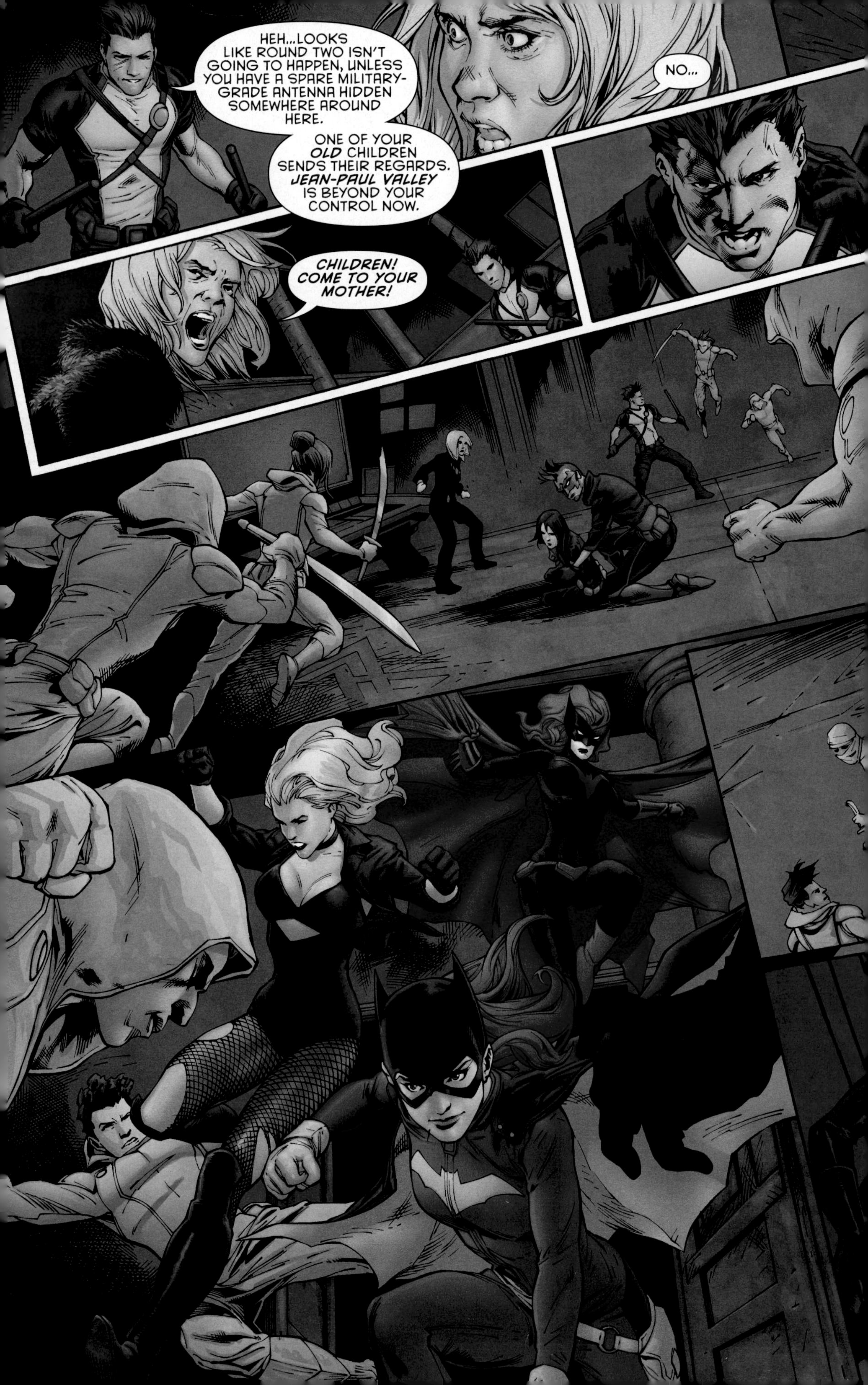
HEH...LOOKS LIKE ROUND TWO ISN'T GOING TO HAPPEN, UNLESS YOU HAVE A SPARE MILITARY-GRADE ANTENNA HIDDEN SOMEWHERE AROUND HERE.
ONE OF YOUR OLD CHILDREN SENDS THEIR REGARDS. JEAN-PAUL VALLEY IS BEYOND YOUR CONTROL NOW.
NO...
CHILDREN! COME TO YOUR MOTHER!

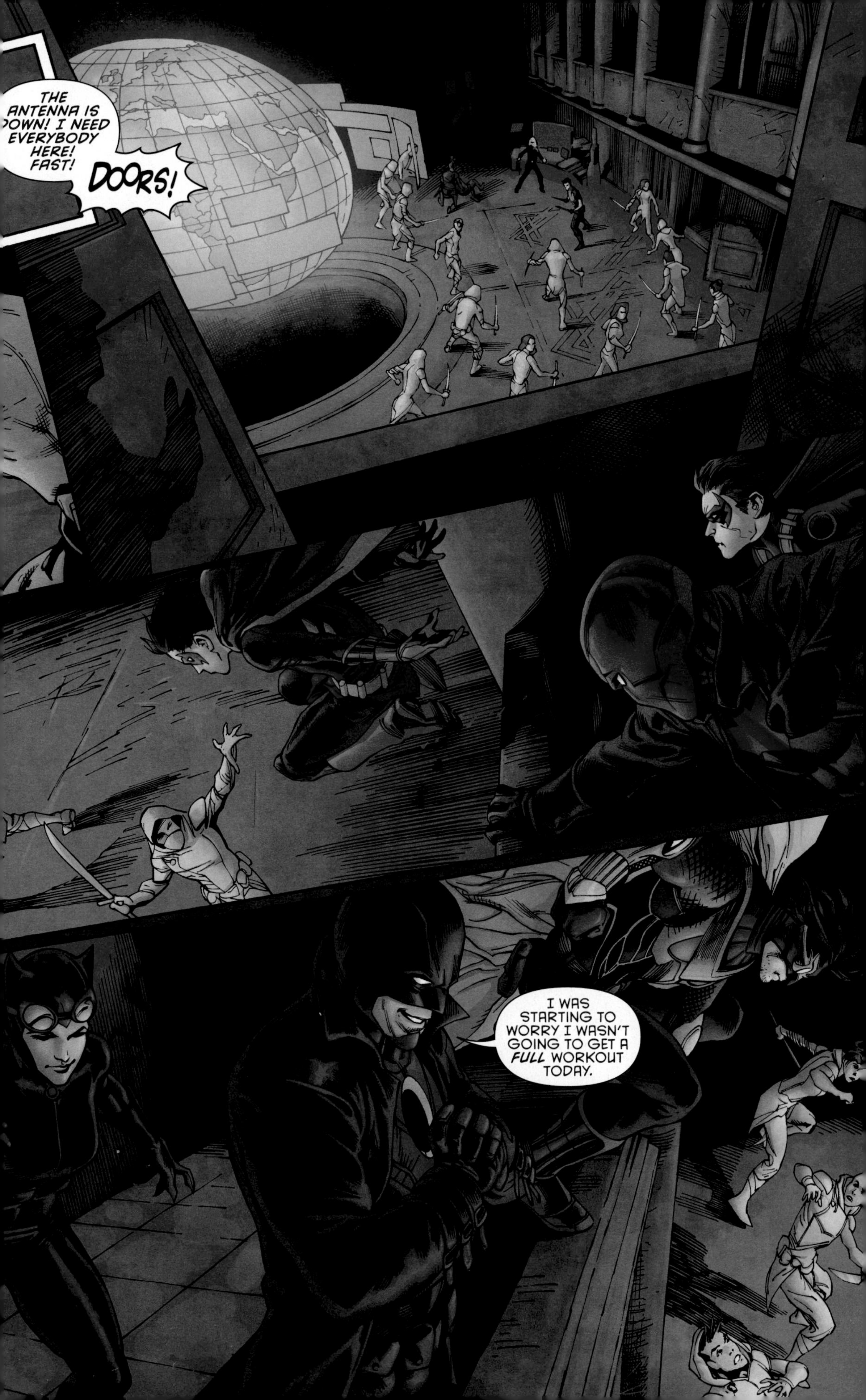
THE ANTENNA IS DOWN! I NEED EVERYBODY HERE! FAST!
DOORS!
I WAS STARTING TO WORRY I WASN'T GOING TO GET A FULL WORKOUT TODAY.

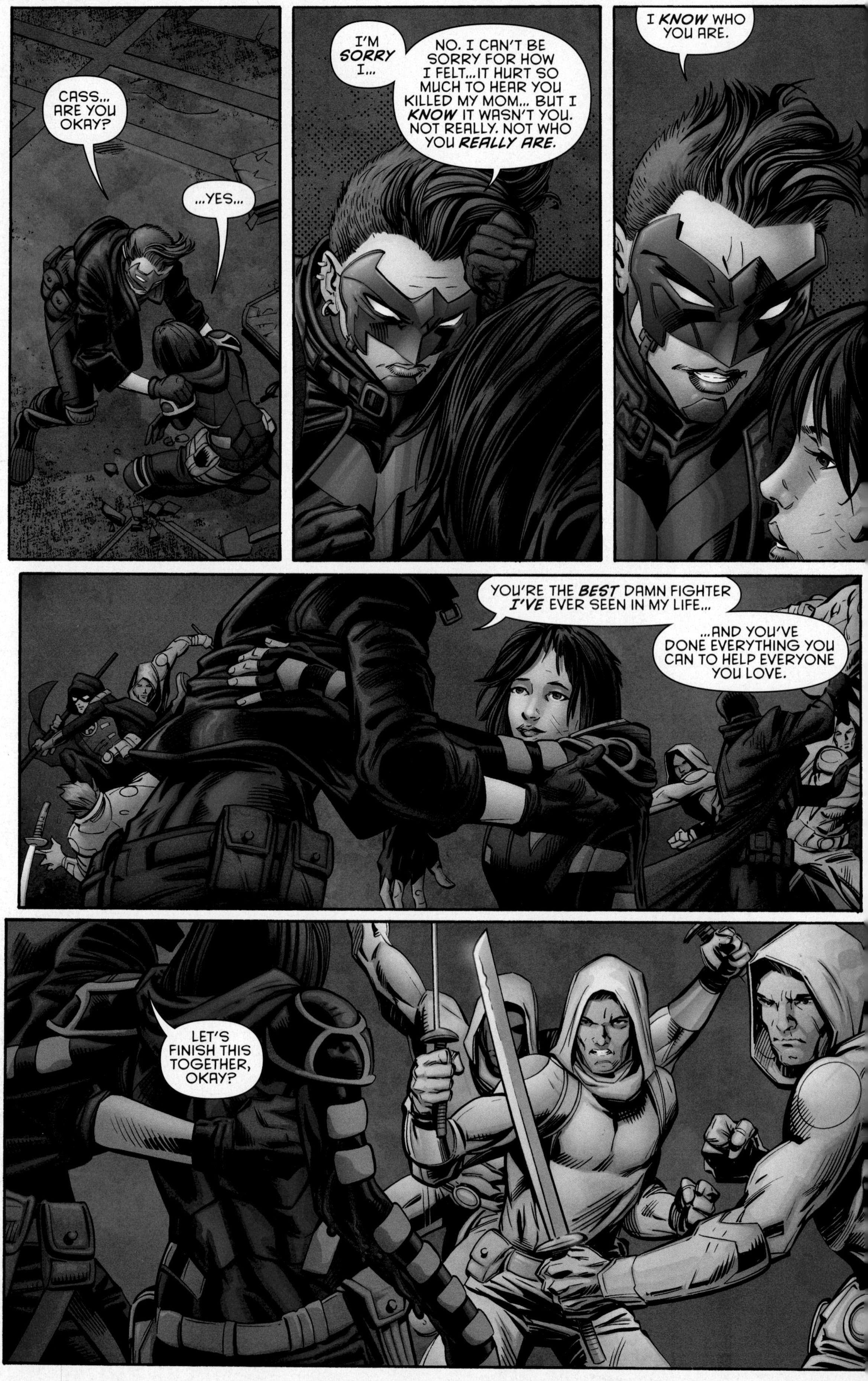
CASS... ARE YOU OKAY?
...YES...
I'M SORRY I...
NO. I CAN'T BE SORRY FOR HOW I FELT...IT HURT SO MUCH TO HEAR YOU KILLED MY MOM... BUT I KNOW IT WASN'T YOU. NOT REALLY. NOT WHO YOU REALLY ARE.
I KNOW WHO YOU ARE.
YOU'RE THE BEST DAMN FIGHTER I'VE EVER SEEN IN MY LIFE...
...AND YOU'VE DONE EVERYTHING YOU CAN TO HELP EVERYONE YOU LOVE.
LET'S FINISH THIS TOGETHER, OKAY?

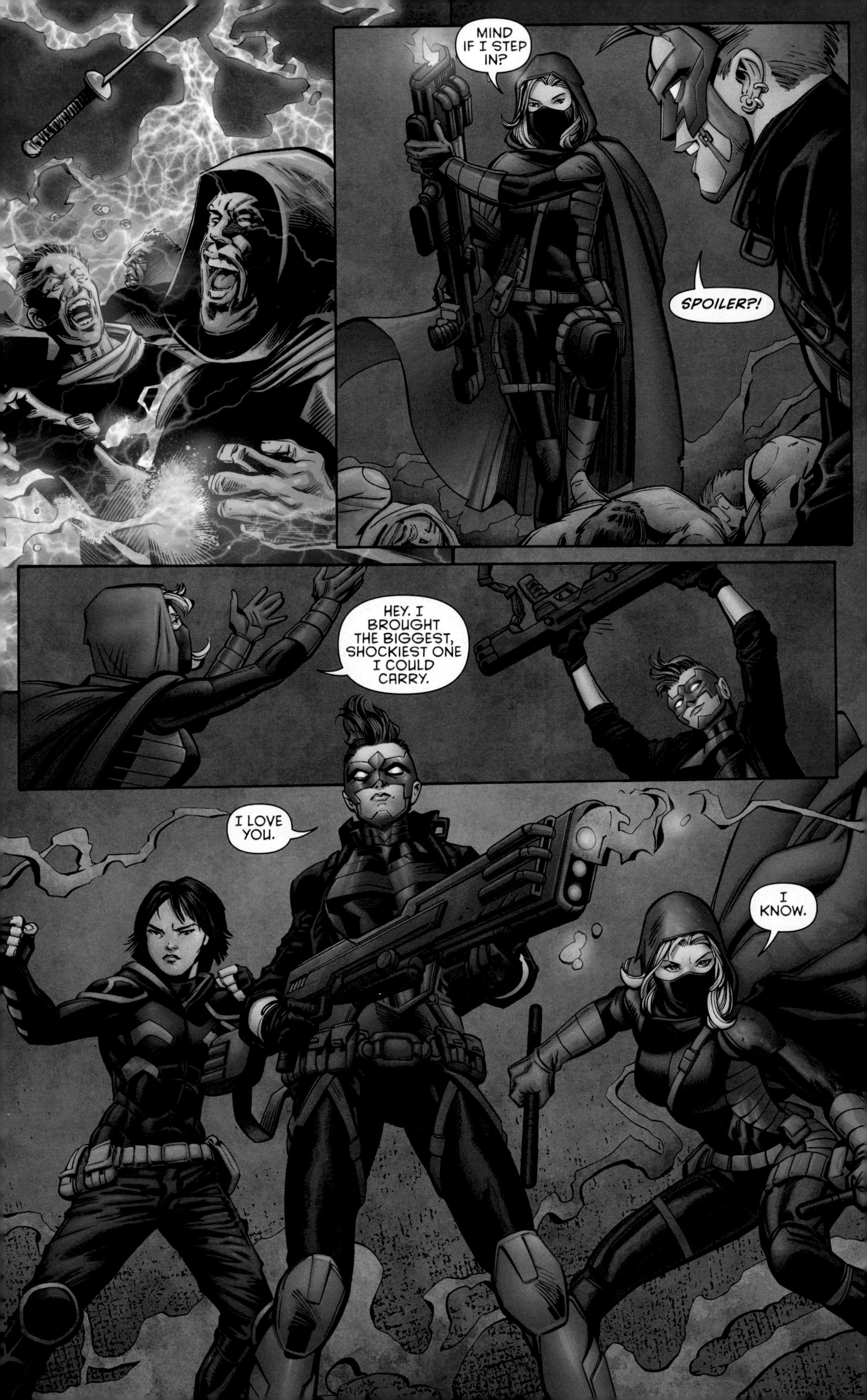
MIND IF I STEP IN?
SPOILER?!
HEY. I BROUGHT THE BIGGEST, SHOCKIEST ONE I COULD CARRY.
I LOVE YOU.
I KNOW.

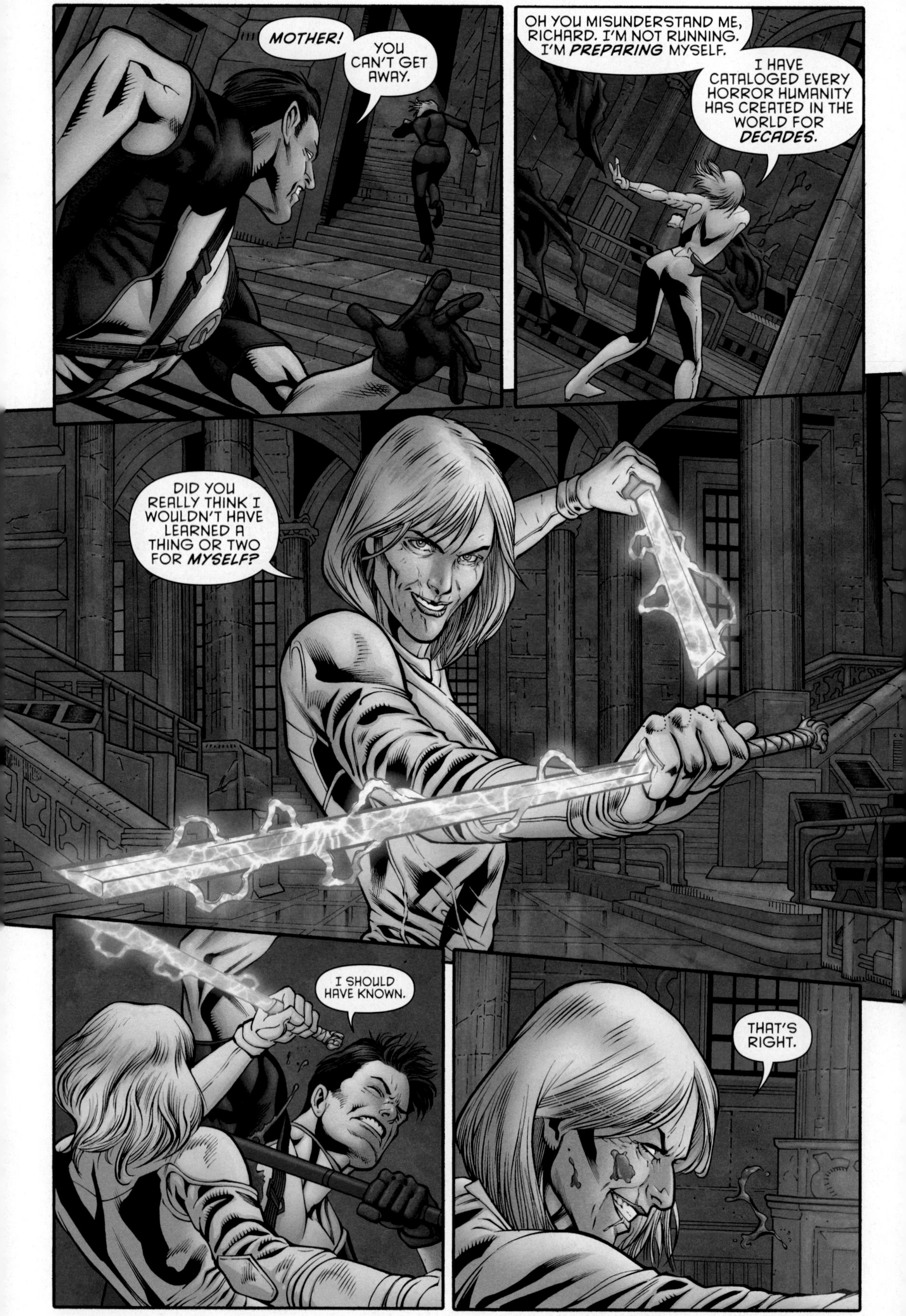
MOTHER!
YOU CAN'T GET AWAY.
OH YOU MISUNDERSTAND ME, RICHARD. I'M NOT RUNNING. I'M PREPARING MYSELF.
I HAVE CATALOGED EVERY HORROR HUMANITY HAS CREATED IN THE WORLD FOR DECADES.
DID YOU REALLY THINK I WOULDN'T HAVE LEARNED A THING OR TWO FOR MYSELF?
I SHOULD HAVE KNOWN.
THAT'S RIGHT.

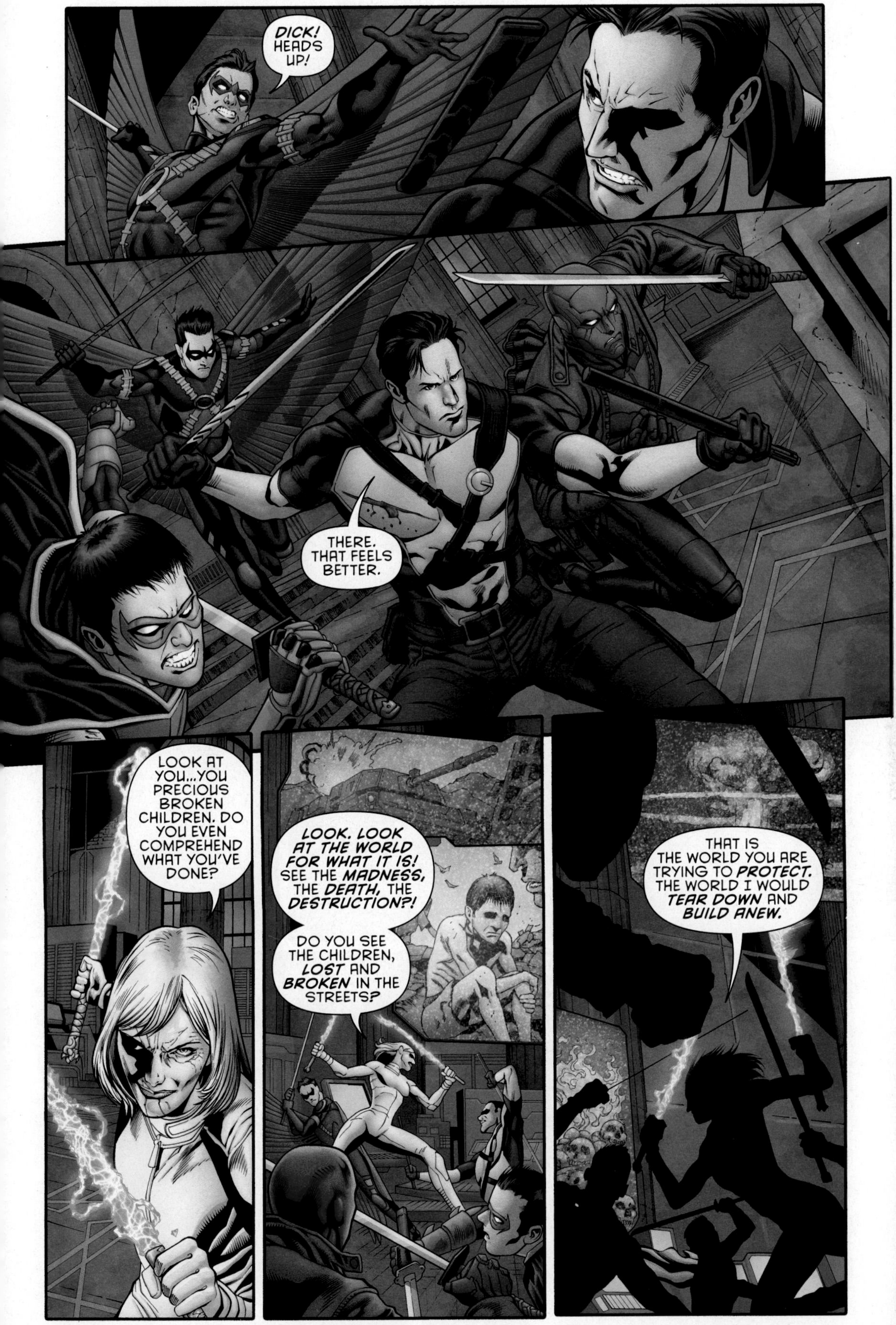
DICK! HEADS UP!
THERE. THAT FEELS BETTER.
LOOK AT YOU...YOU PRECIOUS BROKEN CHILDREN. DO YOU EVEN COMPREHEND WHAT YOU'VE DONE?
LOOK. LOOK AT THE WORLD FOR WHAT IT IS! SEE THE MADNESS, THE DEATH, THE DESTRUCTION?!
DO YOU SEE THE CHILDREN, LOST AND BROKEN IN THE STREETS?
THAT IS THE WORLD YOU ARE TRYING TO PROTECT. THE WORLD I WOULD TEAR DOWN AND BUILD ANEW.

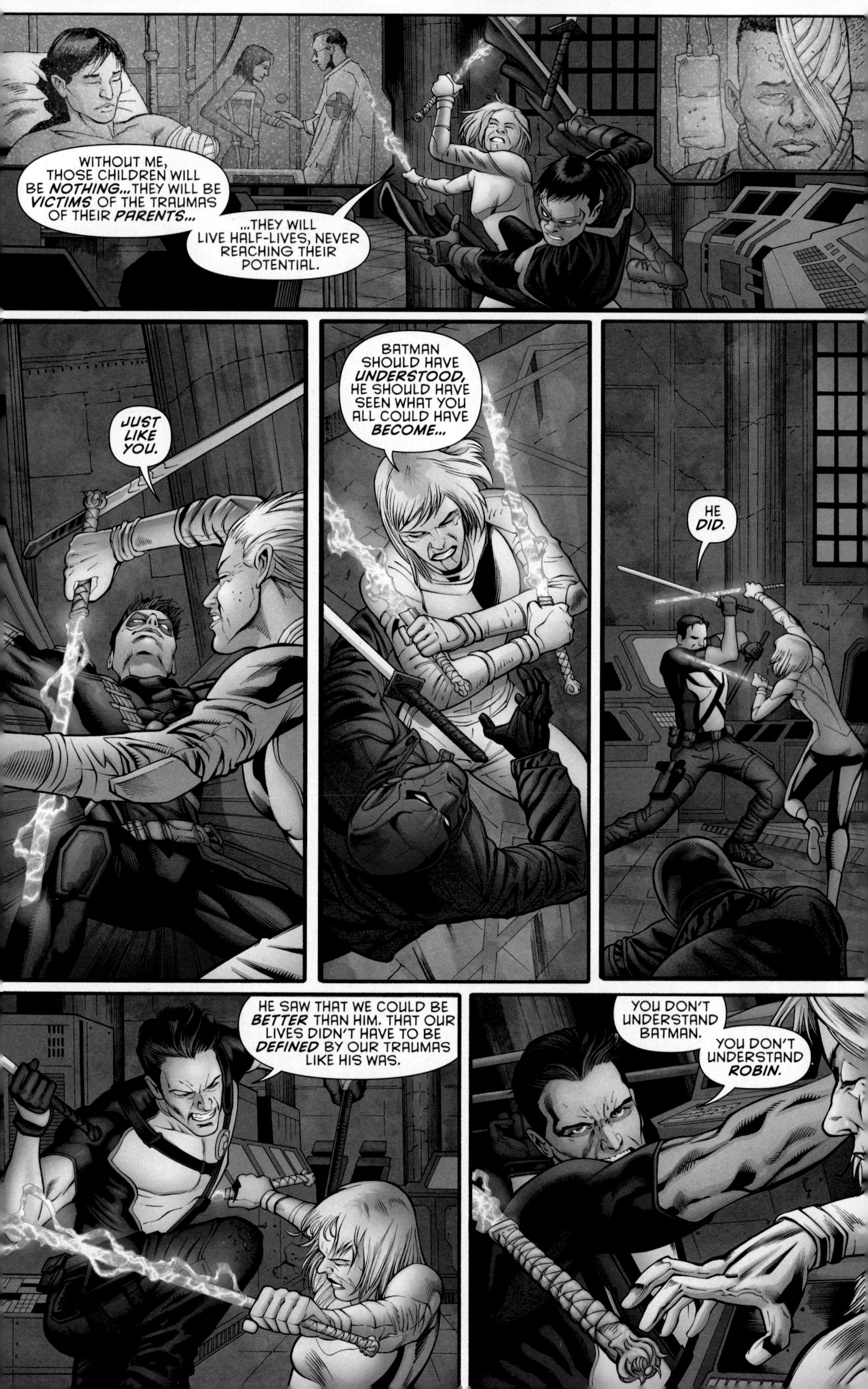
WITHOUT ME, THOSE CHILDREN WILL BE NOTHING... THEY WILL BE VICTIMS OF THE TRAUMAS OF THEIR PARENTS...
...THEY WILL LIVE HALF-LIVES, NEVER REACHING THEIR POTENTIAL.
JUST LIKE YOU.
BATMAN SHOULD HAVE UNDERSTOOD, HE SHOULD HAVE SEEN WHAT YOU ALL COULD HAVE BECOME...
HE DID.
HE SAW THAT WE COULD BE BETTER THAN HIM. THAT OUR LIVES DIDN'T HAVE TO BE DEFINED BY OUR TRAUMAS LIKE HIS WAS.
YOU DON'T UNDERSTAND BATMAN.
YOU DON'T UNDERSTAND ROBIN.

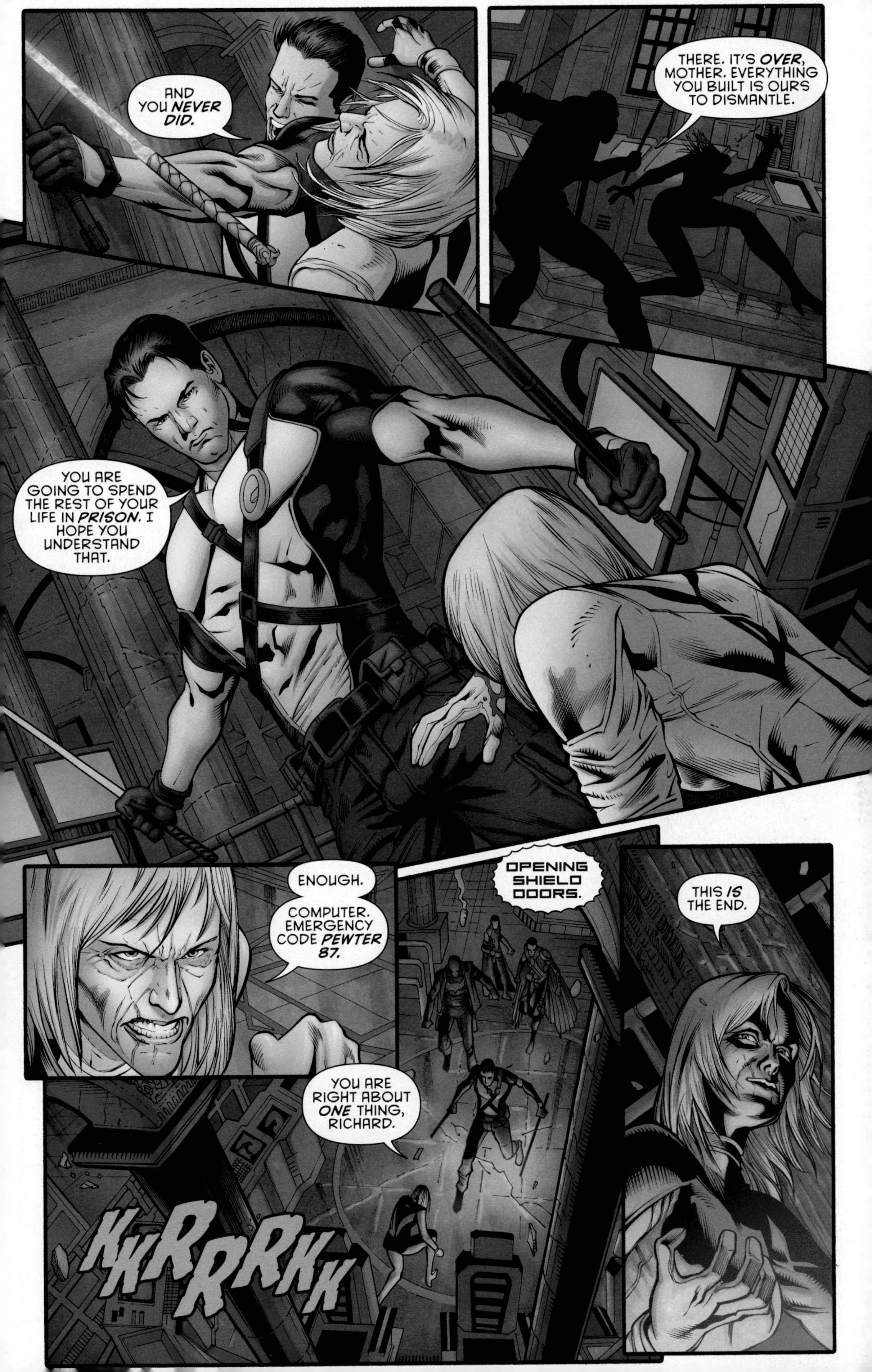
AND YOU NEVER DID.
THERE. IT'S OVER, MOTHER. EVERYTHING YOU BUILT IS OURS TO DISMANTLE.
YOU ARE GOING TO SPEND THE REST OF YOUR LIFE IN PRISON. I HOPE YOU UNDERSTAND THAT.
ENOUGH.
COMPUTER. EMERGENCY CODE PEWTER 87.
OPENING SHIELD DOORS.
YOU ARE RIGHT ABOUT ONE THING, RICHARD.
KKRRRRKK
THIS IS THE END.

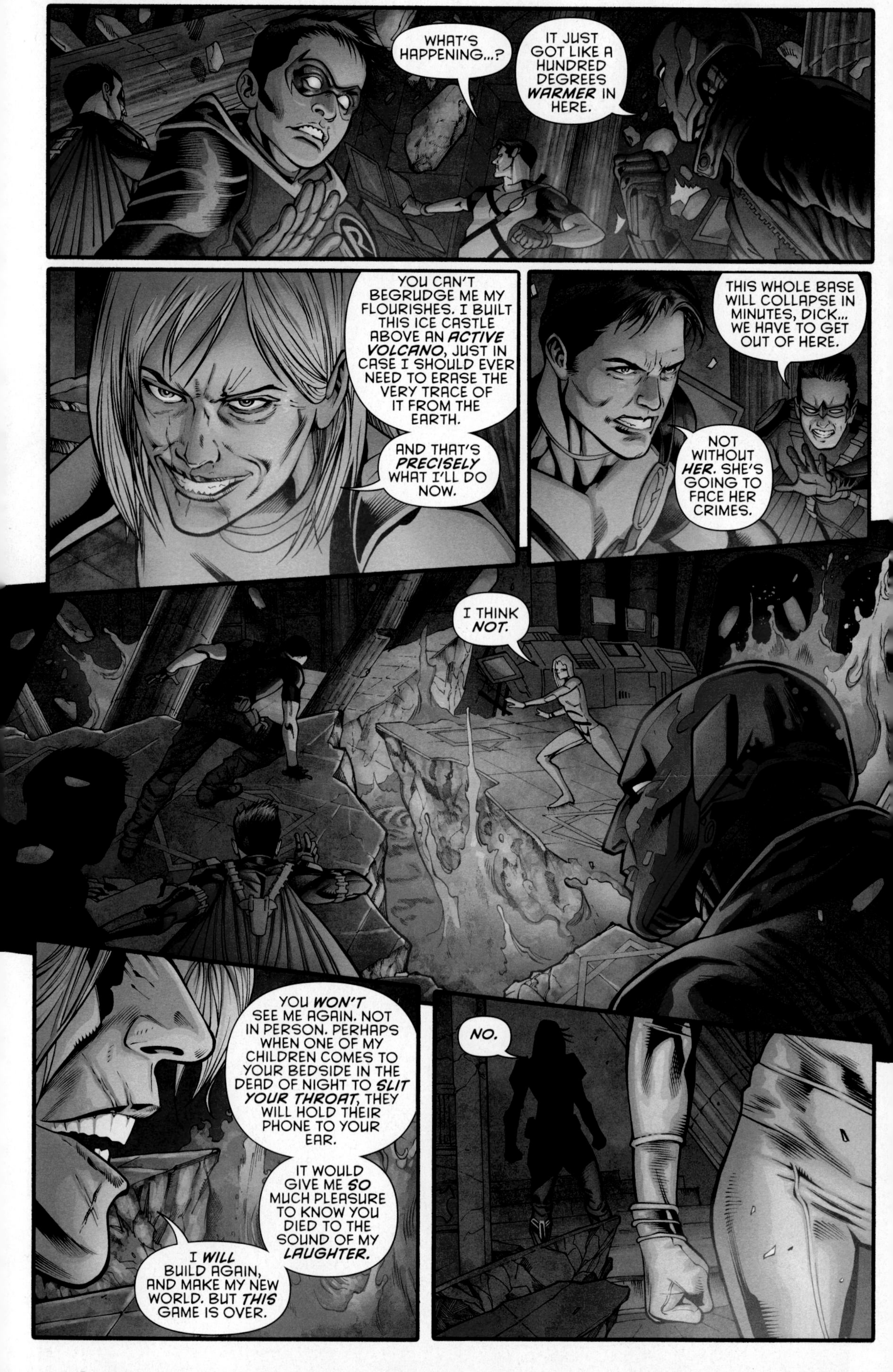
WHAT'S HAPPENING...?
IT JUST GOT LIKE A HUNDRED DEGREES WARMER IN HERE.
YOU CAN'T BEGRUDGE ME MY FLOURISHES. I BUILT THIS ICE CASTLE ABOVE AN ACTIVE VOLCANO, JUST IN CASE I SHOULD EVER NEED TO ERASE THE VERY TRACE OF IT FROM THE EARTH.
AND THAT'S PRECISELY WHAT I'LL DO NOW.
THIS WHOLE BASE WILL COLLAPSE IN MINUTES, DICK... WE HAVE TO GET OUT OF HERE.
NOT WITHOUT HER. SHE'S GOING TO FACE HER CRIMES.
I THINK NOT.
YOU WON'T SEE ME AGAIN. NOT IN PERSON. PERHAPS WHEN ONE OF MY CHILDREN COMES TO YOUR BEDSIDE IN THE DEAD OF NIGHT TO SLIT YOUR THROAT, THEY WILL HOLD THEIR PHONE TO YOUR EAR.
IT WOULD GIVE ME SO MUCH PLEASURE TO KNOW YOU DIED TO THE SOUND OF MY LAUGHTER.
I WILL BUILD AGAIN, AND MAKE MY NEW WORLD. BUT THIS GAME IS OVER.
NO.

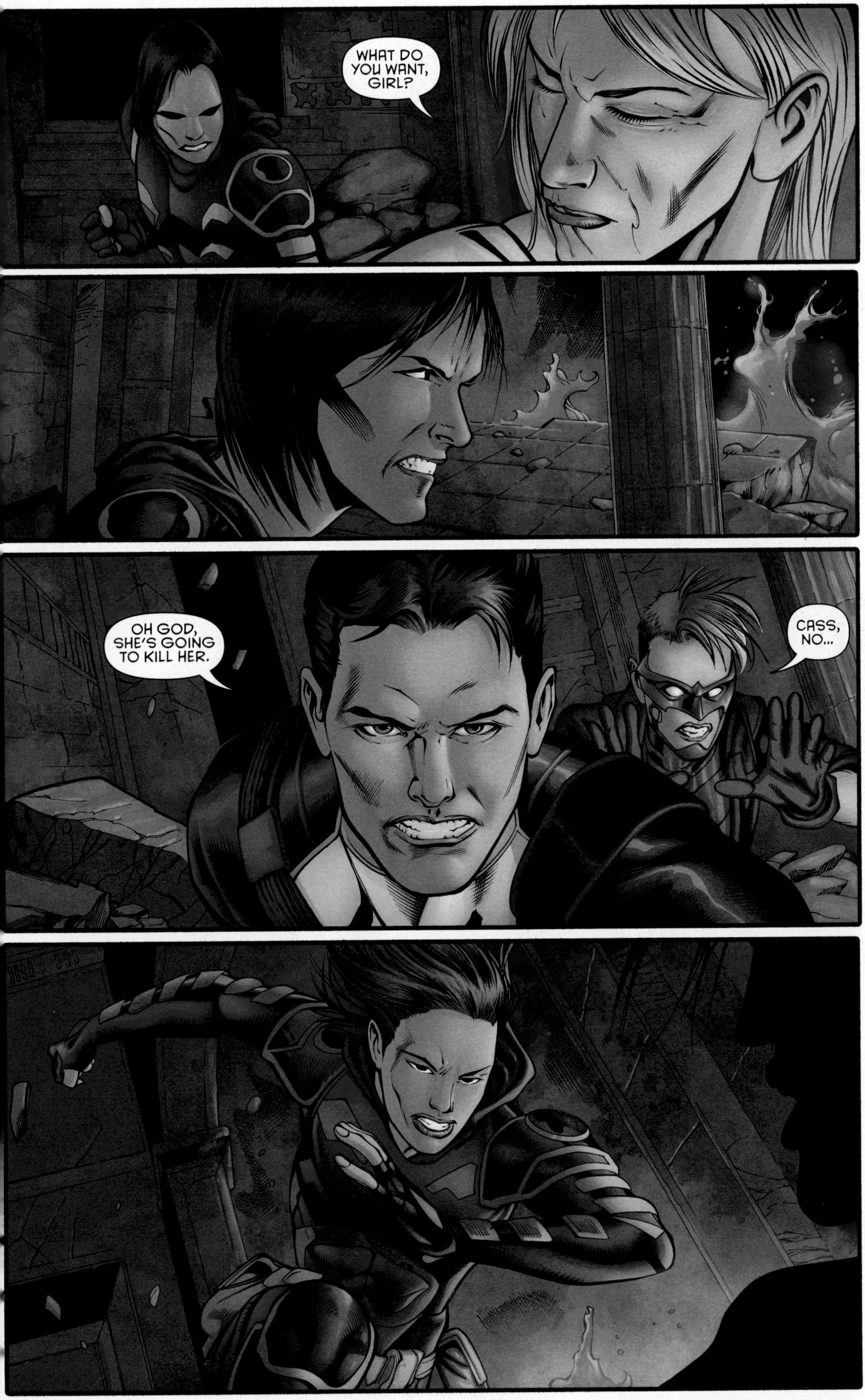
WHAT DO YOU WANT, GIRL?
OH GOD, SHE'S GOING TO KILL HER.
CASS, NO...

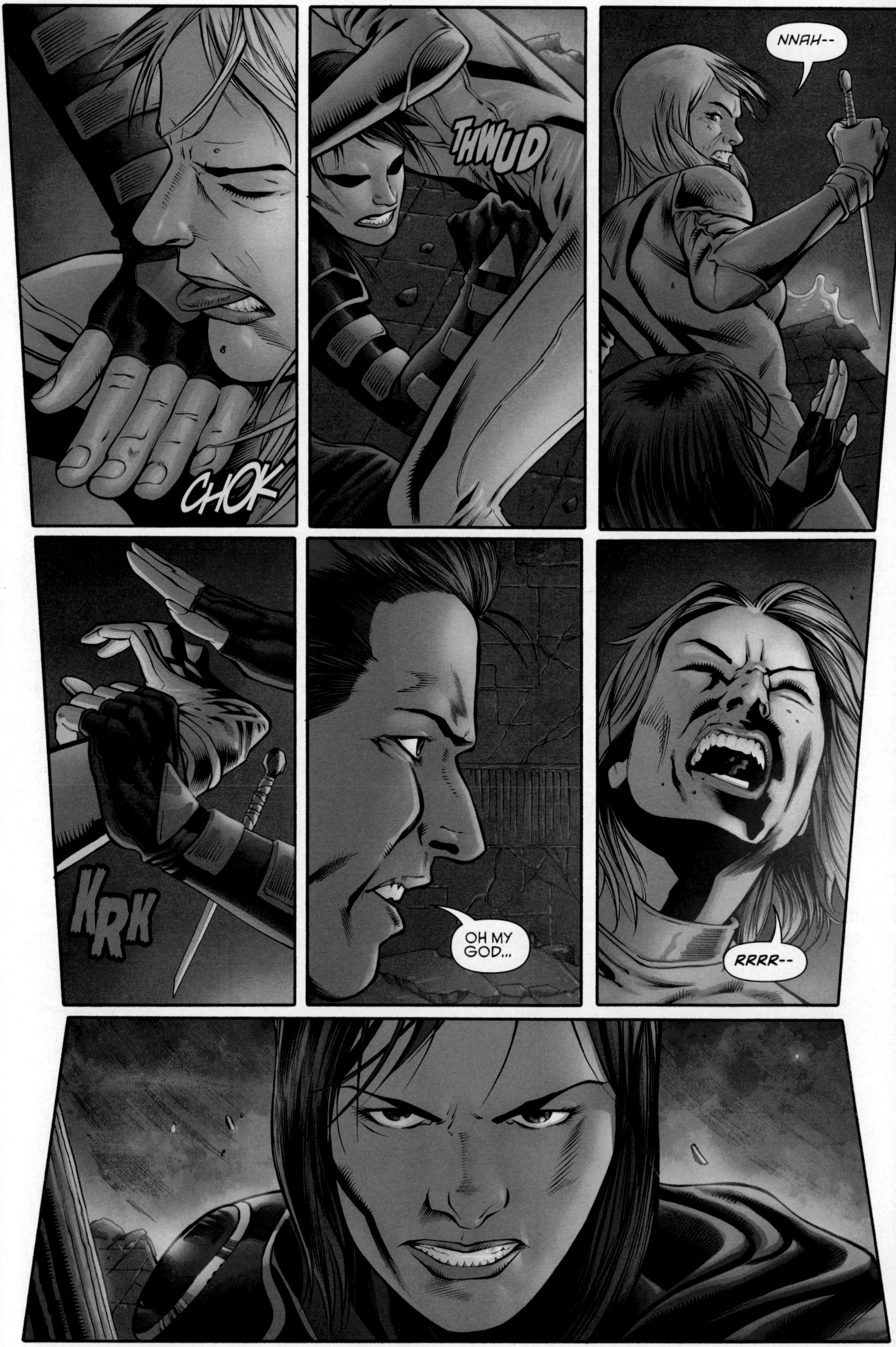
CHOK
THWUD
NNAH--
KRK
OH MY GOD...
RRRR--

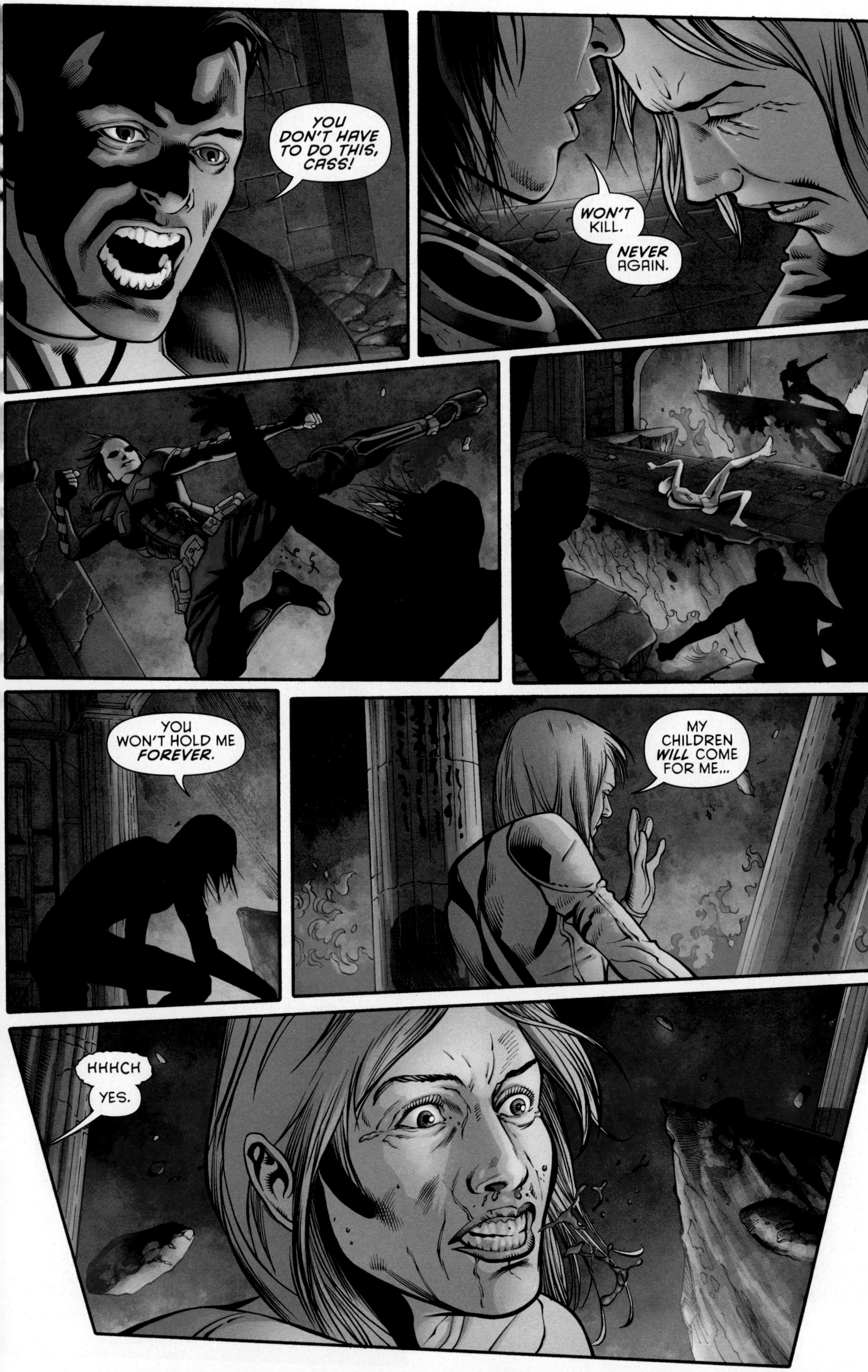
YOU DON'T HAVE TO DO THIS, CASS!
WON'T KILL.
NEVER AGAIN.
YOU WON'T HOLD ME FOREVER.
MY CHILDREN WILL COME FOR ME...
HHHCH
YES.

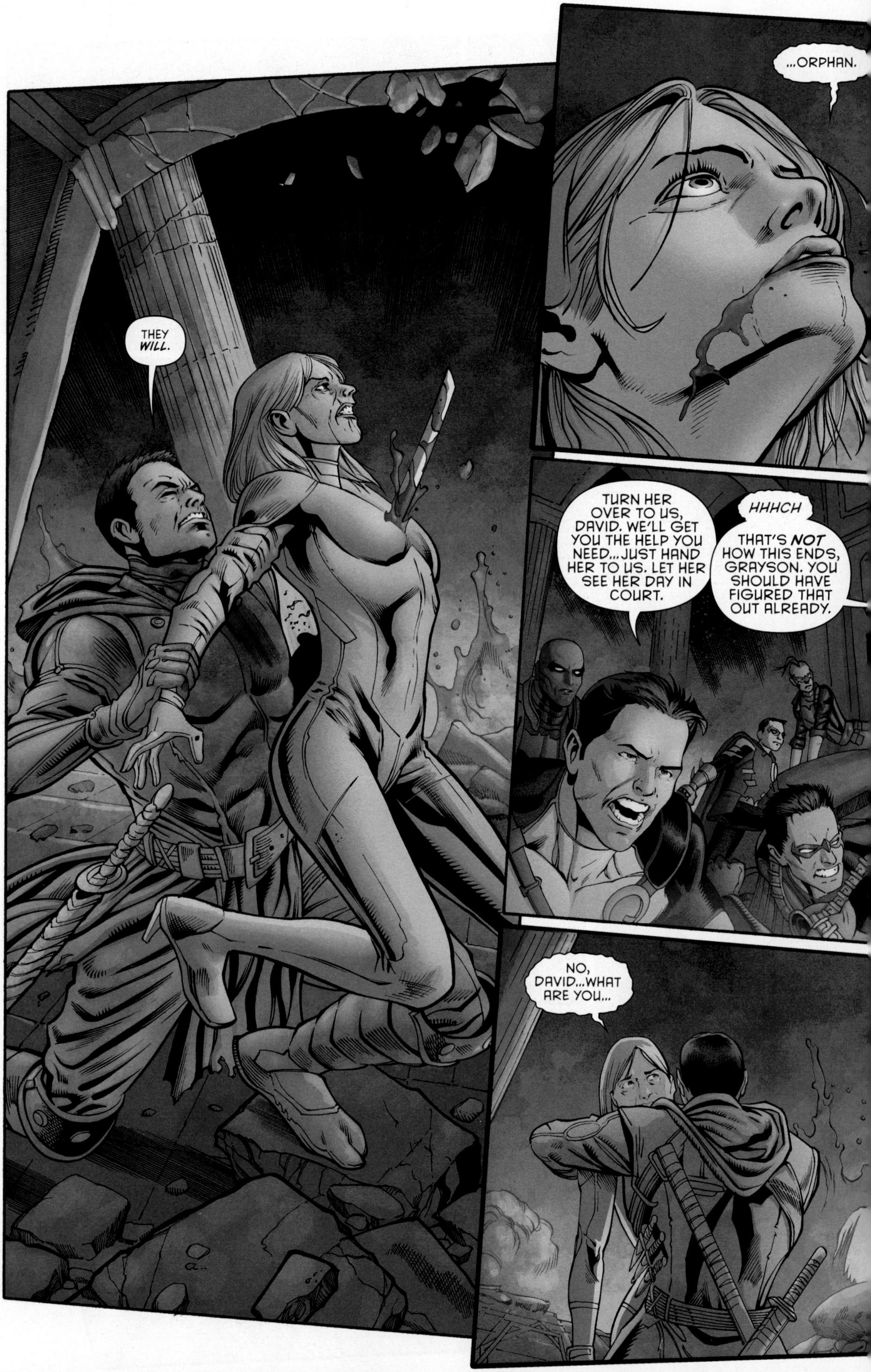
THEY WILL.
...ORPHAN.
TURN HER OVER TO US, DAVID. WE'LL GET YOU THE HELP YOU NEED... JUST HAND HER TO US. LET HER SEE HER DAY IN COURT.
HHHCH
THAT'S NOT HOW THIS ENDS, GRAYSON. YOU SHOULD HAVE FIGURED THAT OUT ALREADY.
NO, DAVID... WHAT ARE YOU...

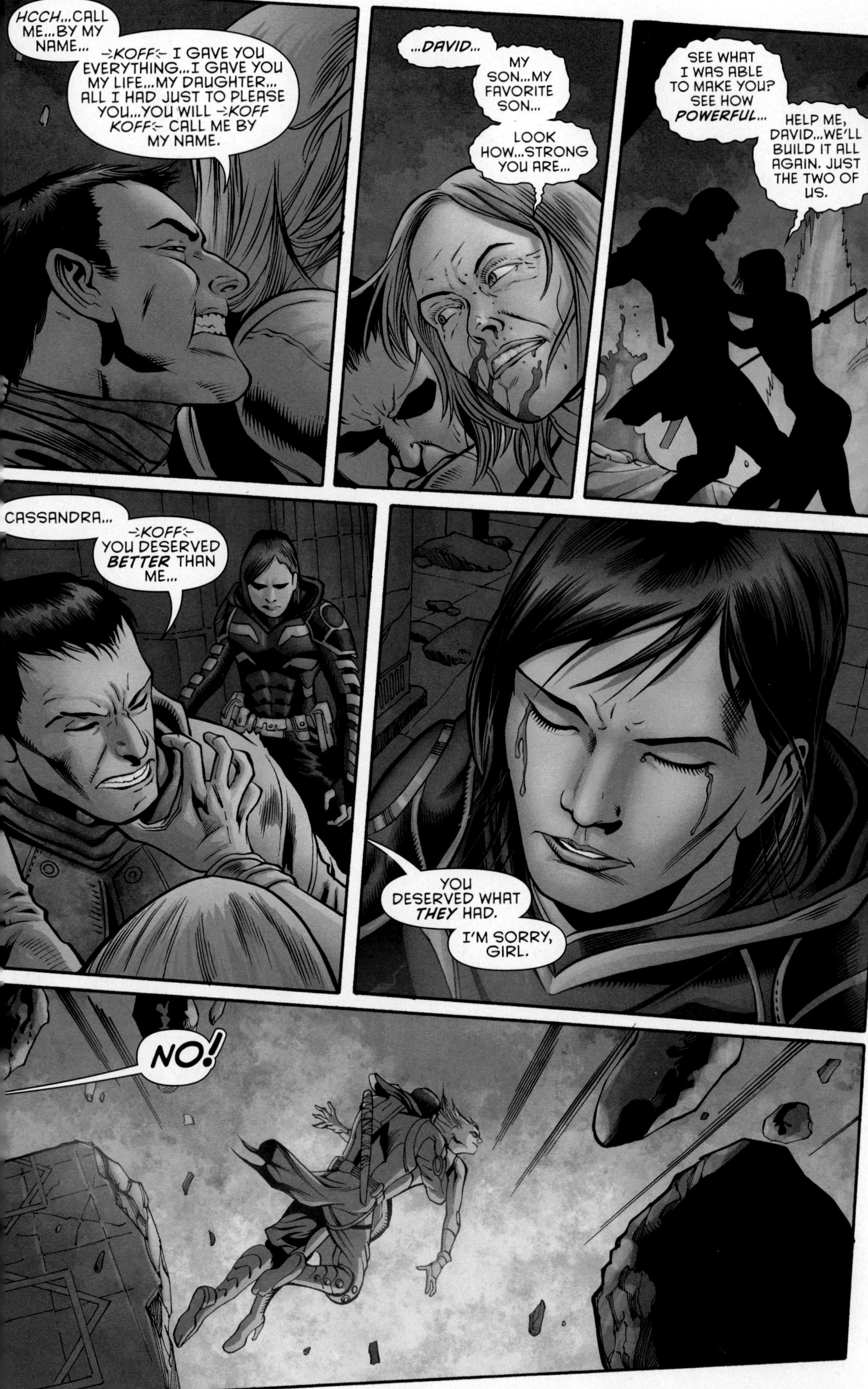
HCCH...CALL ME...BY MY NAME...
⇒KOFF⇐ I GAVE YOU EVERYTHING...I GAVE YOU MY LIFE...MY DAUGHTER... ALL I HAD JUST TO PLEASE YOU...YOU WILL ⇒KOFF KOFF⇐ CALL ME BY MY NAME.
...DAVID...
MY SON...MY FAVORITE SON...
LOOK HOW...STRONG YOU ARE...
SEE WHAT I WAS ABLE TO MAKE YOU? SEE HOW POWERFUL...
HELP ME, DAVID...WE'LL BUILD IT ALL AGAIN. JUST THE TWO OF US.
CASSANDRA...
⇒KOFF⇐ YOU DESERVED BETTER THAN ME...
YOU DESERVED WHAT THEY HAD.
I'M SORRY, GIRL.
NO!

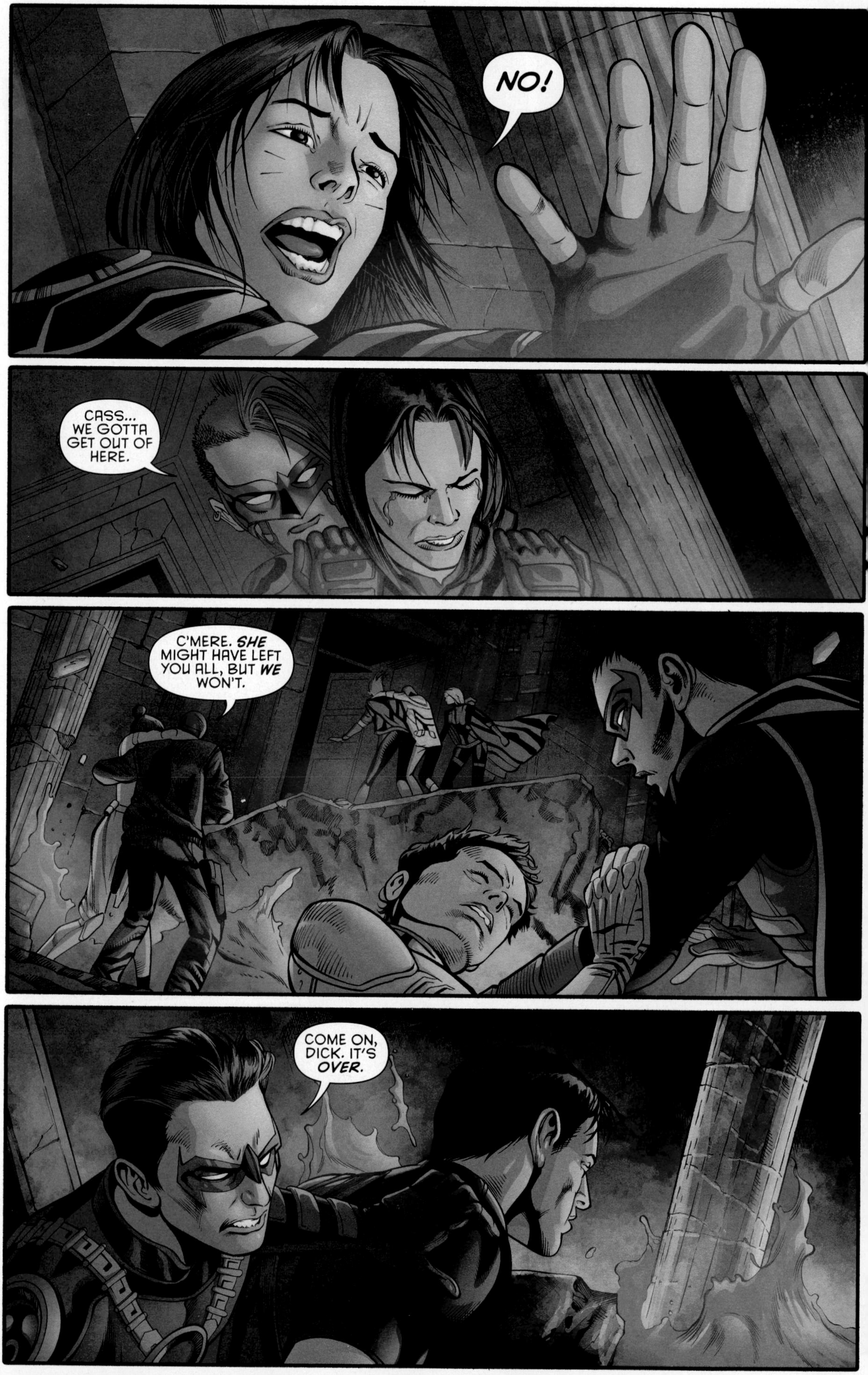
NO!
CASS... WE GOTTA GET OUT OF HERE.
C'MERE. *SHE* MIGHT HAVE LEFT YOU ALL, BUT *WE* WON'T.
COME ON, DICK. IT'S *OVER*.

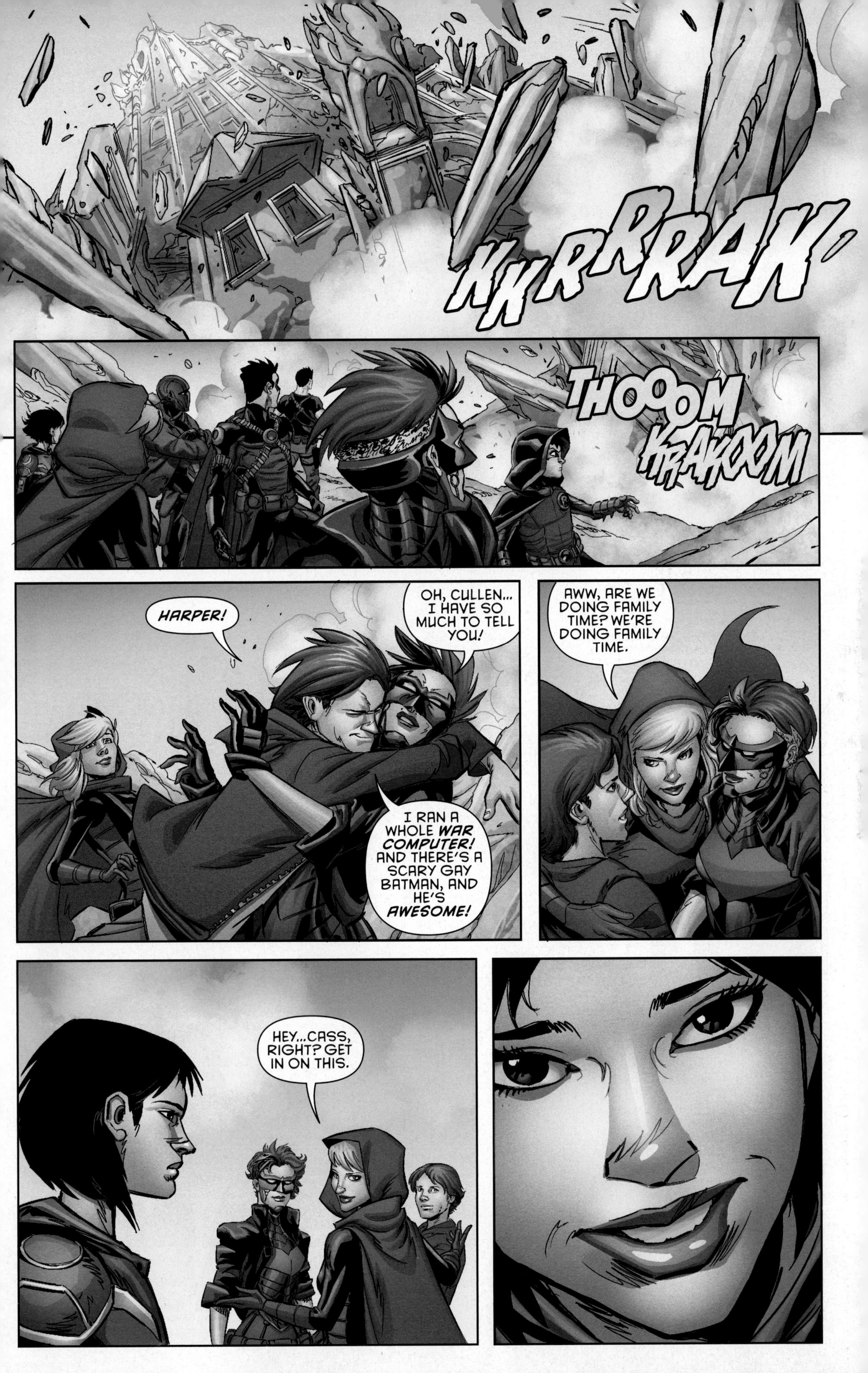
KKRRRAK
THOOOM
KRAKOOM
HARPER!
OH, CULLEN... I HAVE SO MUCH TO TELL YOU!
I RAN A WHOLE WAR COMPUTER! AND THERE'S A SCARY GAY BATMAN, AND HE'S AWESOME!
AWW, ARE WE DOING FAMILY TIME? WE'RE DOING FAMILY TIME.
HEY...CASS, RIGHT? GET IN ON THIS.

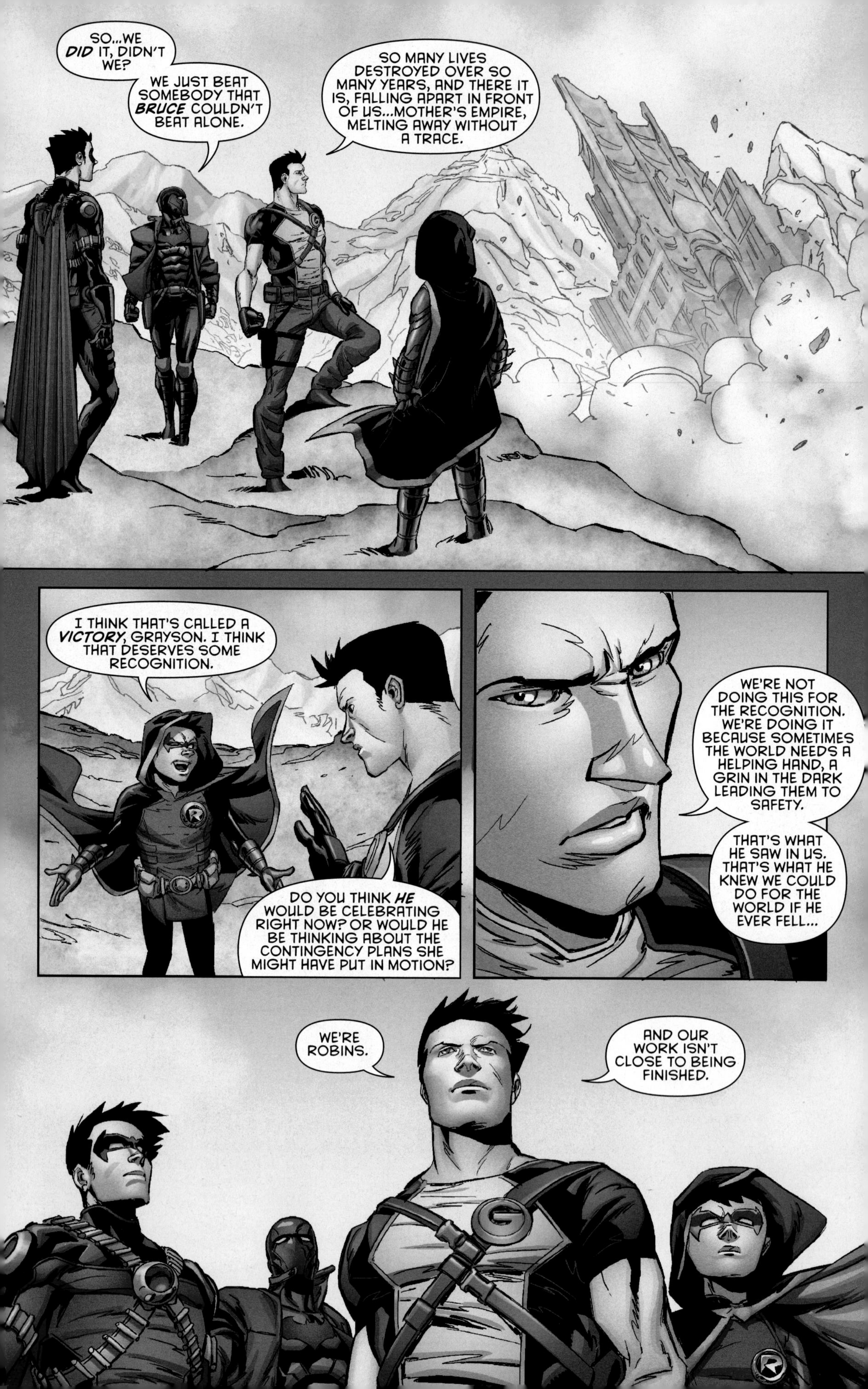
SO...WE DID IT, DIDN'T WE?
WE JUST BEAT SOMEBODY THAT BRUCE COULDN'T BEAT ALONE.
SO MANY LIVES DESTROYED OVER SO MANY YEARS, AND THERE IT IS, FALLING APART IN FRONT OF US...MOTHER'S EMPIRE, MELTING AWAY WITHOUT A TRACE.
I THINK THAT'S CALLED A VICTORY, GRAYSON. I THINK THAT DESERVES SOME RECOGNITION.
DO YOU THINK HE WOULD BE CELEBRATING RIGHT NOW? OR WOULD HE BE THINKING ABOUT THE CONTINGENCY PLANS SHE MIGHT HAVE PUT IN MOTION?
WE'RE NOT DOING THIS FOR THE RECOGNITION. WE'RE DOING IT BECAUSE SOMETIMES THE WORLD NEEDS A HELPING HAND, A GRIN IN THE DARK LEADING THEM TO SAFETY.
THAT'S WHAT HE SAW IN US. THAT'S WHAT HE KNEW WE COULD DO FOR THE WORLD IF HE EVER FELL...
WE'RE ROBINS.
AND OUR WORK ISN'T CLOSE TO BEING FINISHED.

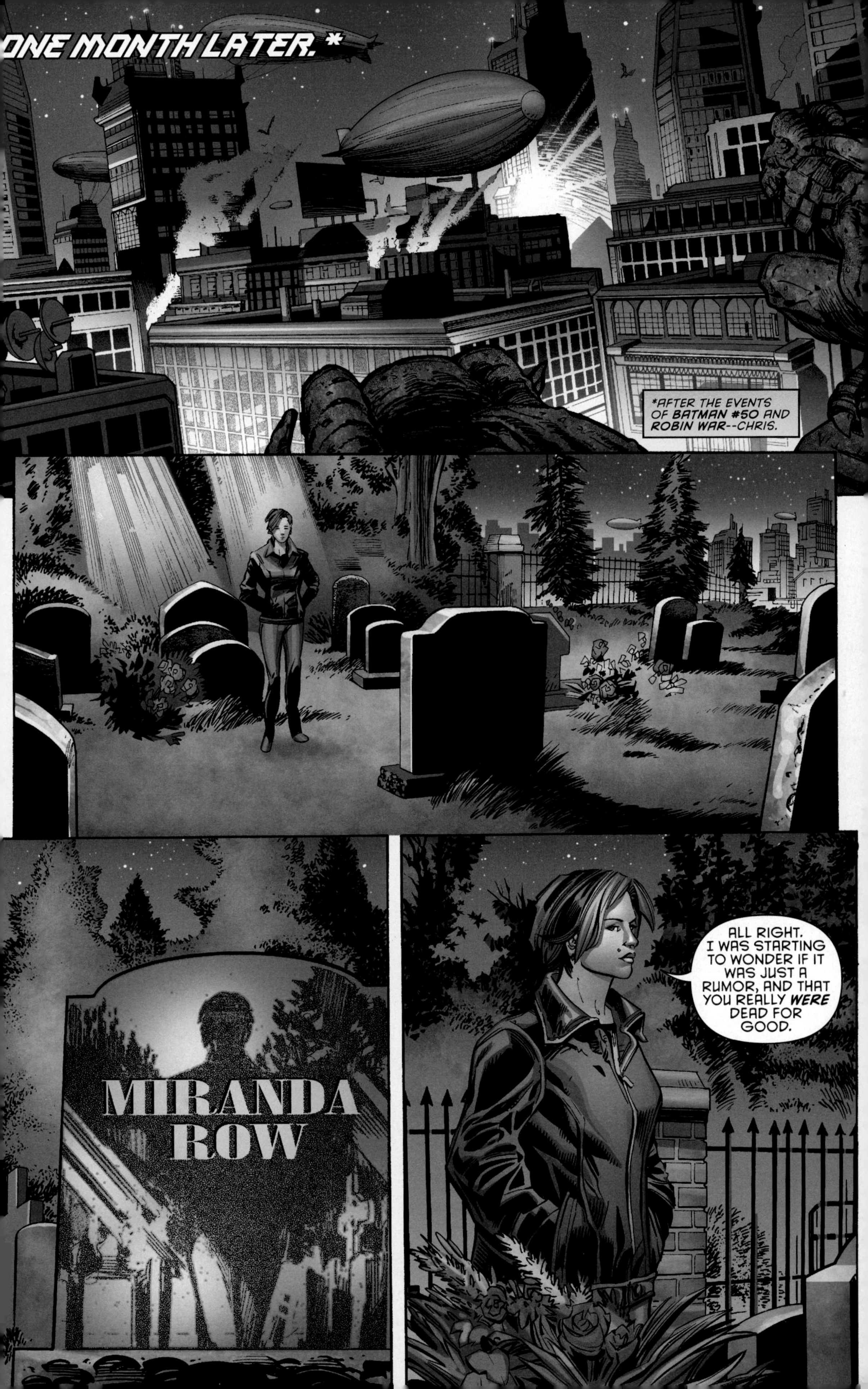
ONE MONTH LATER.*
*AFTER THE EVENTS OF BATMAN #50 AND ROBIN WAR--CHRIS.
MIRANDA ROW
ALL RIGHT. I WAS STARTING TO WONDER IF IT WAS JUST A RUMOR, AND THAT YOU REALLY WERE DEAD FOR GOOD.

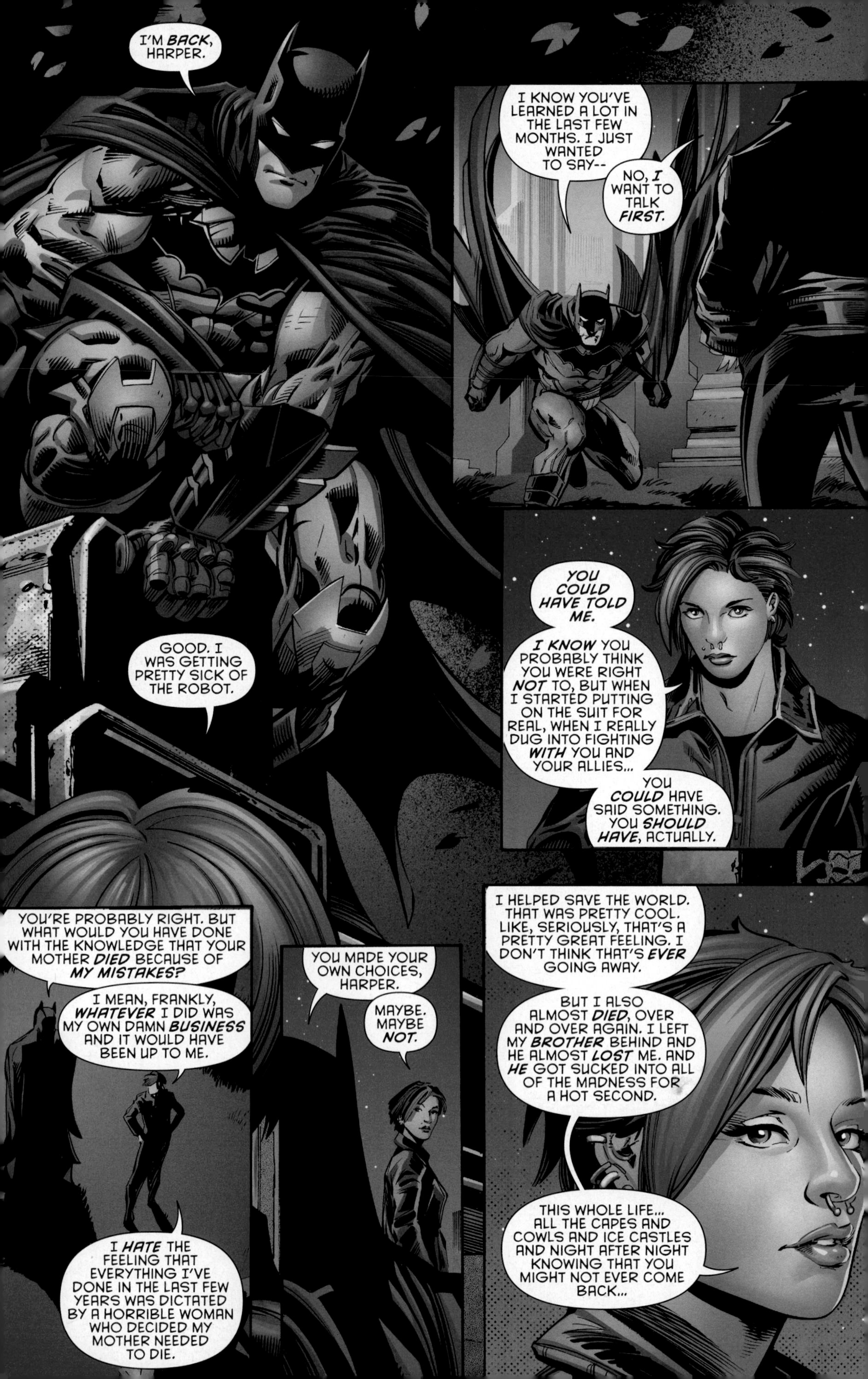
I'M BACK, HARPER.
I KNOW YOU'VE LEARNED A LOT IN THE LAST FEW MONTHS. I JUST WANTED TO SAY--
NO, I WANT TO TALK FIRST.
GOOD. I WAS GETTING PRETTY SICK OF THE ROBOT.
YOU COULD HAVE TOLD ME.
I KNOW YOU PROBABLY THINK YOU WERE RIGHT NOT TO, BUT WHEN I STARTED PUTTING ON THE SUIT FOR REAL, WHEN I REALLY DUG INTO FIGHTING WITH YOU AND YOUR ALLIES...
YOU COULD HAVE SAID SOMETHING. YOU SHOULD HAVE, ACTUALLY.
YOU'RE PROBABLY RIGHT. BUT WHAT WOULD YOU HAVE DONE WITH THE KNOWLEDGE THAT YOUR MOTHER DIED BECAUSE OF MY MISTAKES?
I MEAN, FRANKLY, WHATEVER I DID WAS MY OWN DAMN BUSINESS AND IT WOULD HAVE BEEN UP TO ME.
I HATE THE FEELING THAT EVERYTHING I'VE DONE IN THE LAST FEW YEARS WAS DICTATED BY A HORRIBLE WOMAN WHO DECIDED MY MOTHER NEEDED TO DIE.
YOU MADE YOUR OWN CHOICES, HARPER.
MAYBE. MAYBE NOT.
I HELPED SAVE THE WORLD. THAT WAS PRETTY COOL. LIKE, SERIOUSLY, THAT'S A PRETTY GREAT FEELING. I DON'T THINK THAT'S EVER GOING AWAY.
BUT I ALSO ALMOST DIED, OVER AND OVER AGAIN. I LEFT MY BROTHER BEHIND AND HE ALMOST LOST ME. AND HE GOT SUCKED INTO ALL OF THE MADNESS FOR A HOT SECOND.
THIS WHOLE LIFE... ALL THE CAPES AND COWLS AND ICE CASTLES AND NIGHT AFTER NIGHT KNOWING THAT YOU MIGHT NOT EVER COME BACK...

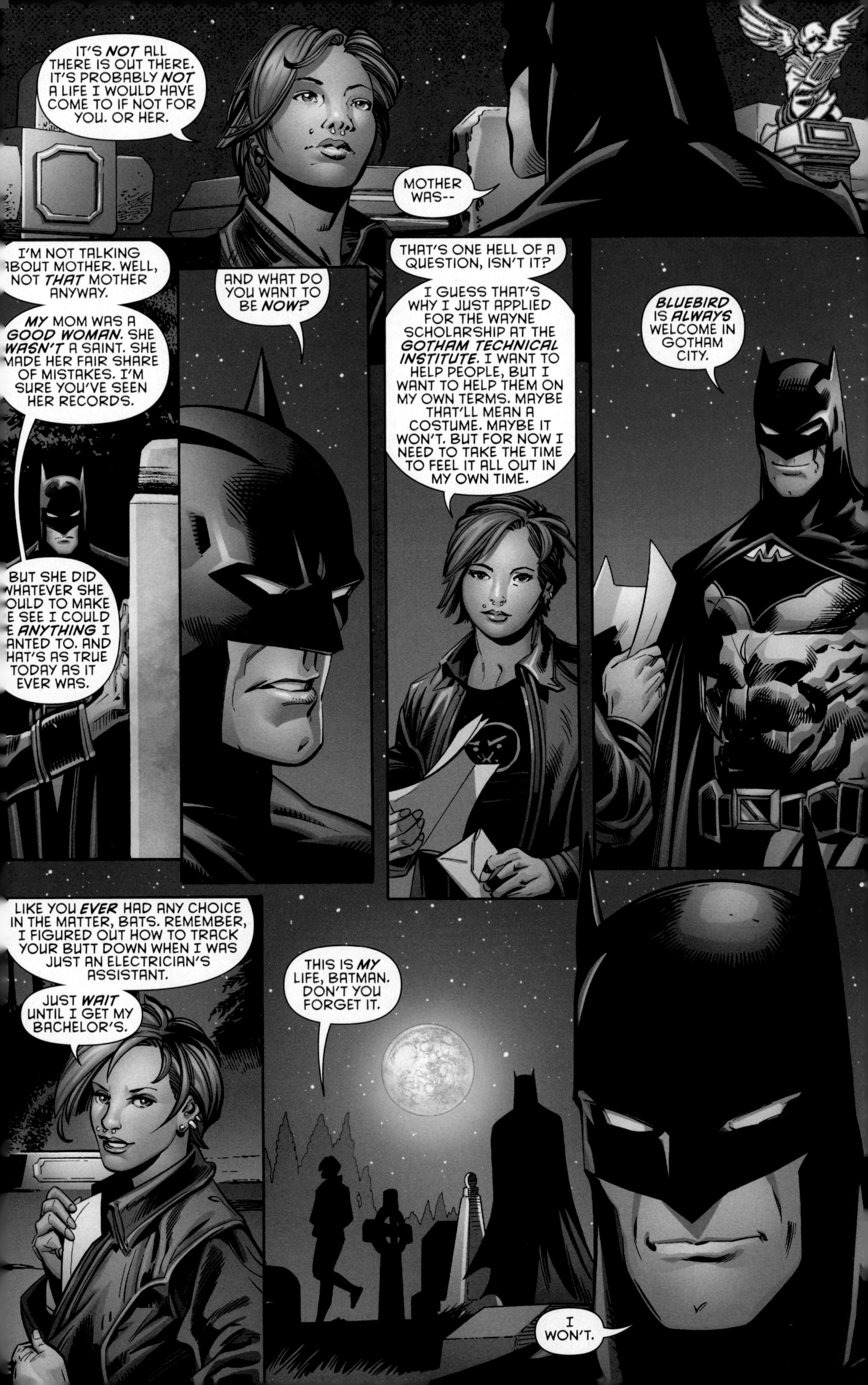
IT'S NOT ALL THERE IS OUT THERE. IT'S PROBABLY NOT A LIFE I WOULD HAVE COME TO IF NOT FOR YOU. OR HER.
MOTHER WAS--
I'M NOT TALKING ABOUT MOTHER. WELL, NOT THAT MOTHER ANYWAY.
MY MOM WAS A GOOD WOMAN. SHE WASN'T A SAINT. SHE MADE HER FAIR SHARE OF MISTAKES. I'M SURE YOU'VE SEEN HER RECORDS.
BUT SHE DID WHATEVER SHE COULD TO MAKE ME SEE I COULD BE ANYTHING I WANTED TO. AND THAT'S AS TRUE TODAY AS IT EVER WAS.
AND WHAT DO YOU WANT TO BE NOW?
THAT'S ONE HELL OF A QUESTION, ISN'T IT?
I GUESS THAT'S WHY I JUST APPLIED FOR THE WAYNE SCHOLARSHIP AT THE GOTHAM TECHNICAL INSTITUTE. I WANT TO HELP PEOPLE, BUT I WANT TO HELP THEM ON MY OWN TERMS. MAYBE THAT'LL MEAN A COSTUME. MAYBE IT WON'T. BUT FOR NOW I NEED TO TAKE THE TIME TO FEEL IT ALL OUT IN MY OWN TIME.
BLUEBIRD IS ALWAYS WELCOME IN GOTHAM CITY.
LIKE YOU EVER HAD ANY CHOICE IN THE MATTER, BATS. REMEMBER, I FIGURED OUT HOW TO TRACK YOUR BUTT DOWN WHEN I WAS JUST AN ELECTRICIAN'S ASSISTANT.
JUST WAIT UNTIL I GET MY BACHELOR'S.
THIS IS MY LIFE, BATMAN. DON'T YOU FORGET IT.
I WON'T.

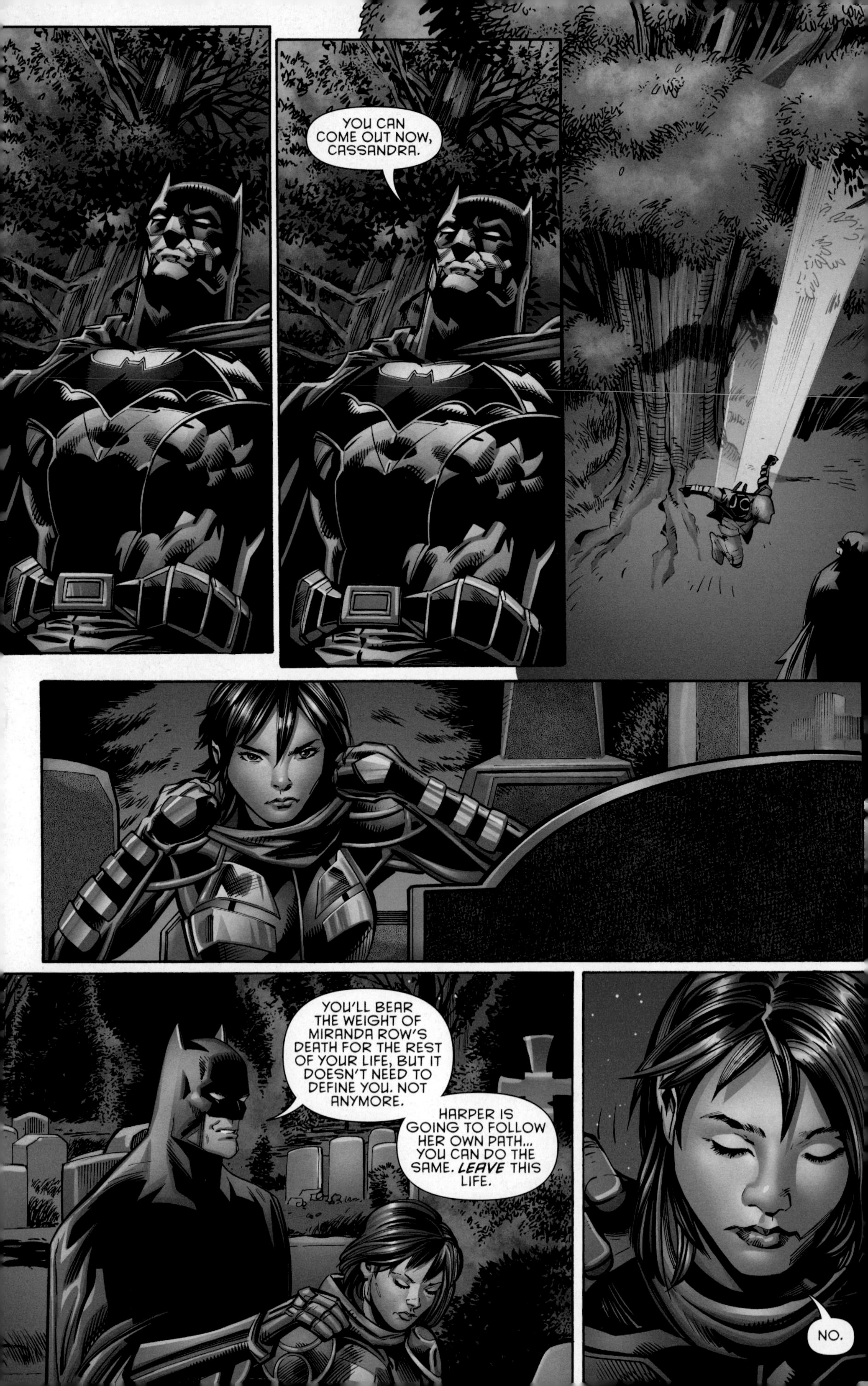
YOU CAN COME OUT NOW, CASSANDRA.
YOU'LL BEAR THE WEIGHT OF MIRANDA ROW'S DEATH FOR THE REST OF YOUR LIFE, BUT IT DOESN'T NEED TO DEFINE YOU. NOT ANYMORE.
HARPER IS GOING TO FOLLOW HER OWN PATH... YOU CAN DO THE SAME. *LEAVE* THIS LIFE.
NO.

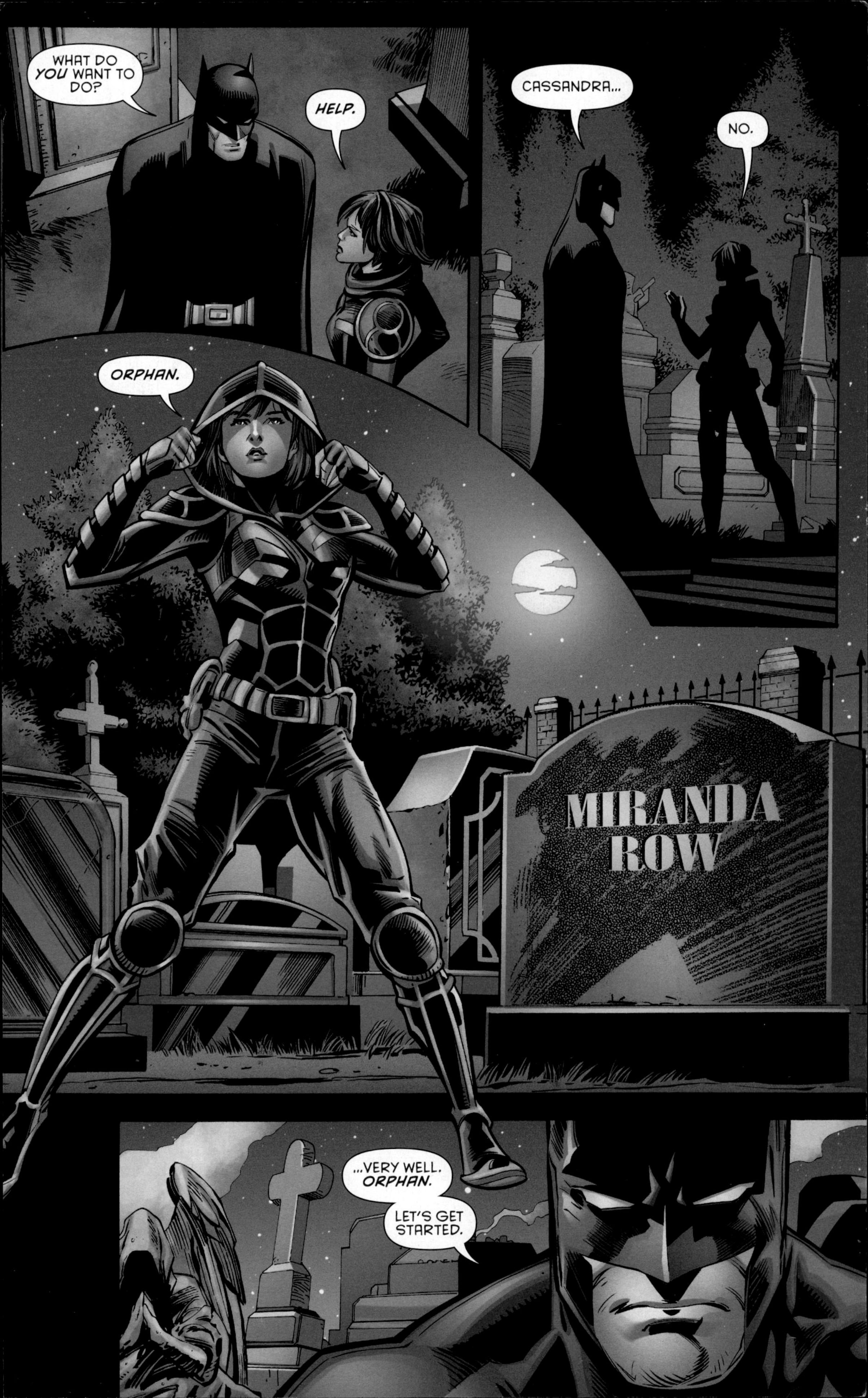
WHAT DO *YOU* WANT TO DO?
HELP.
CASSANDRA...
NO.
ORPHAN.
MIRANDA ROW
...VERY WELL. *ORPHAN.*
LET'S GET STARTED.

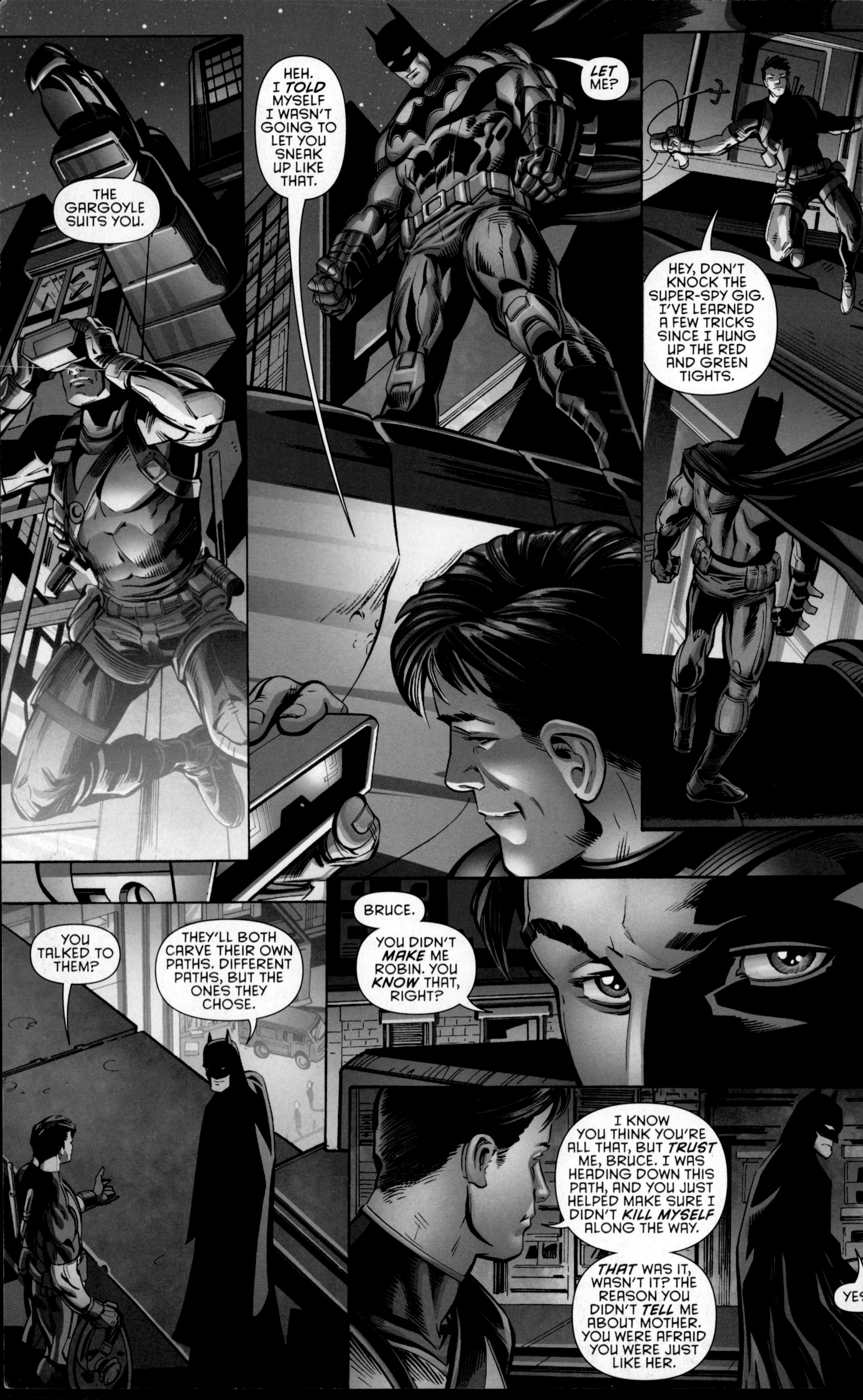
THE GARGOYLE SUITS YOU.
HEH. I TOLD MYSELF I WASN'T GOING TO LET YOU SNEAK UP LIKE THAT.
LET ME?
HEY, DON'T KNOCK THE SUPER-SPY GIG. I'VE LEARNED A FEW TRICKS SINCE I HUNG UP THE RED AND GREEN TIGHTS.
YOU TALKED TO THEM?
THEY'LL BOTH CARVE THEIR OWN PATHS. DIFFERENT PATHS, BUT THE ONES THEY CHOSE.
BRUCE.
YOU DIDN'T MAKE ME ROBIN. YOU KNOW THAT, RIGHT?
I KNOW YOU THINK YOU'RE ALL THAT, BUT TRUST ME, BRUCE. I WAS HEADING DOWN THIS PATH, AND YOU JUST HELPED MAKE SURE I DIDN'T KILL MYSELF ALONG THE WAY.
THAT WAS IT, WASN'T IT? THE REASON YOU DIDN'T TELL ME ABOUT MOTHER. YOU WERE AFRAID YOU WERE JUST LIKE HER.

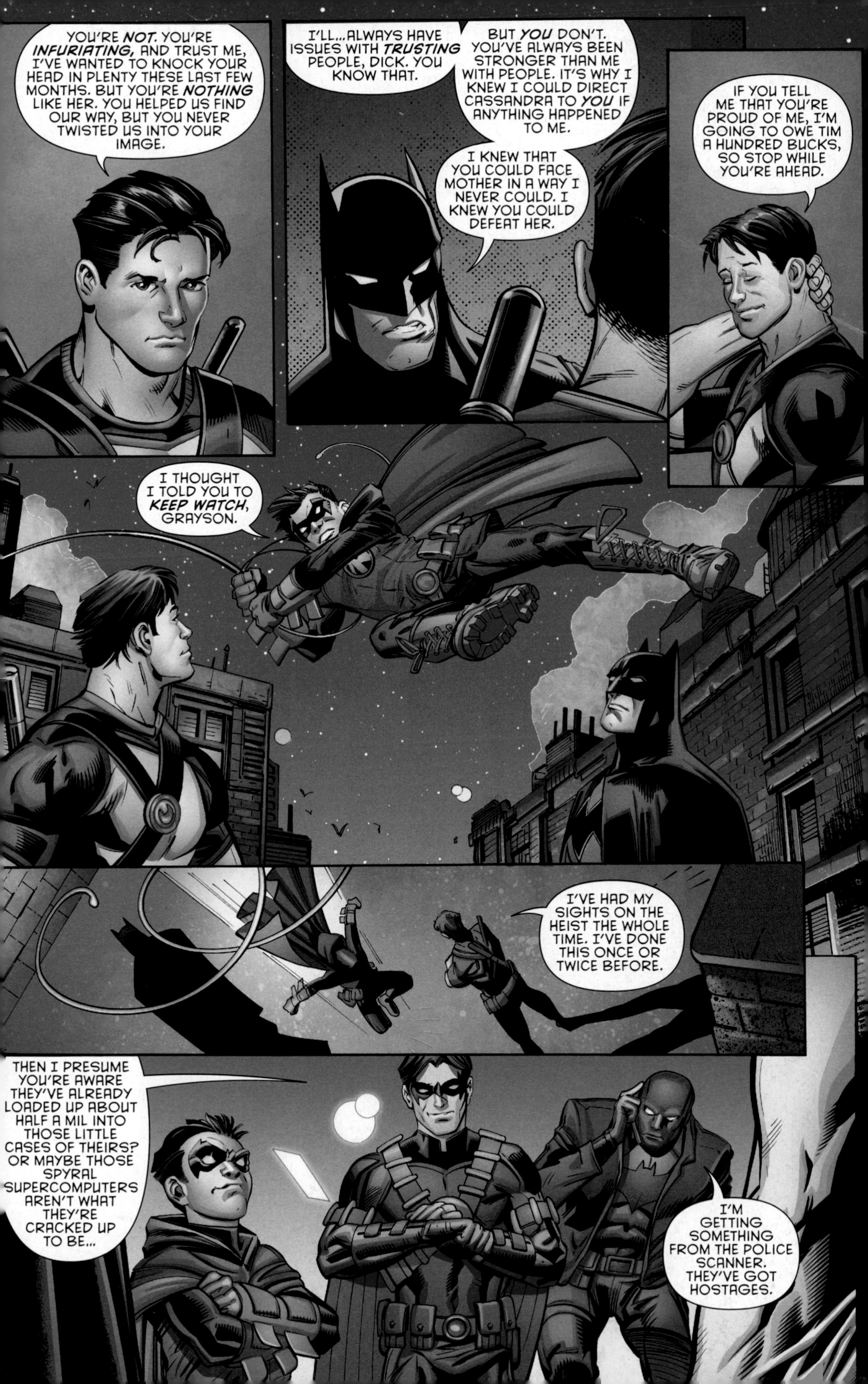
YOU'RE NOT. YOU'RE INFURIATING, AND TRUST ME, I'VE WANTED TO KNOCK YOUR HEAD IN PLENTY THESE LAST FEW MONTHS. BUT YOU'RE NOTHING LIKE HER. YOU HELPED US FIND OUR WAY, BUT YOU NEVER TWISTED US INTO YOUR IMAGE.
I'LL...ALWAYS HAVE ISSUES WITH TRUSTING PEOPLE, DICK. YOU KNOW THAT.
BUT YOU DON'T. YOU'VE ALWAYS BEEN STRONGER THAN ME WITH PEOPLE. IT'S WHY I KNEW I COULD DIRECT CASSANDRA TO YOU IF ANYTHING HAPPENED TO ME.
I KNEW THAT YOU COULD FACE MOTHER IN A WAY I NEVER COULD. I KNEW YOU COULD DEFEAT HER.
IF YOU TELL ME THAT YOU'RE PROUD OF ME, I'M GOING TO OWE TIM A HUNDRED BUCKS, SO STOP WHILE YOU'RE AHEAD.
I THOUGHT I TOLD YOU TO KEEP WATCH, GRAYSON.
I'VE HAD MY SIGHTS ON THE HEIST THE WHOLE TIME. I'VE DONE THIS ONCE OR TWICE BEFORE.
THEN I PRESUME YOU'RE AWARE THEY'VE ALREADY LOADED UP ABOUT HALF A MIL INTO THOSE LITTLE CASES OF THEIRS? OR MAYBE THOSE SPYRAL SUPERCOMPUTERS AREN'T WHAT THEY'RE CRACKED UP TO BE...
I'M GETTING SOMETHING FROM THE POLICE SCANNER. THEY'VE GOT HOSTAGES.

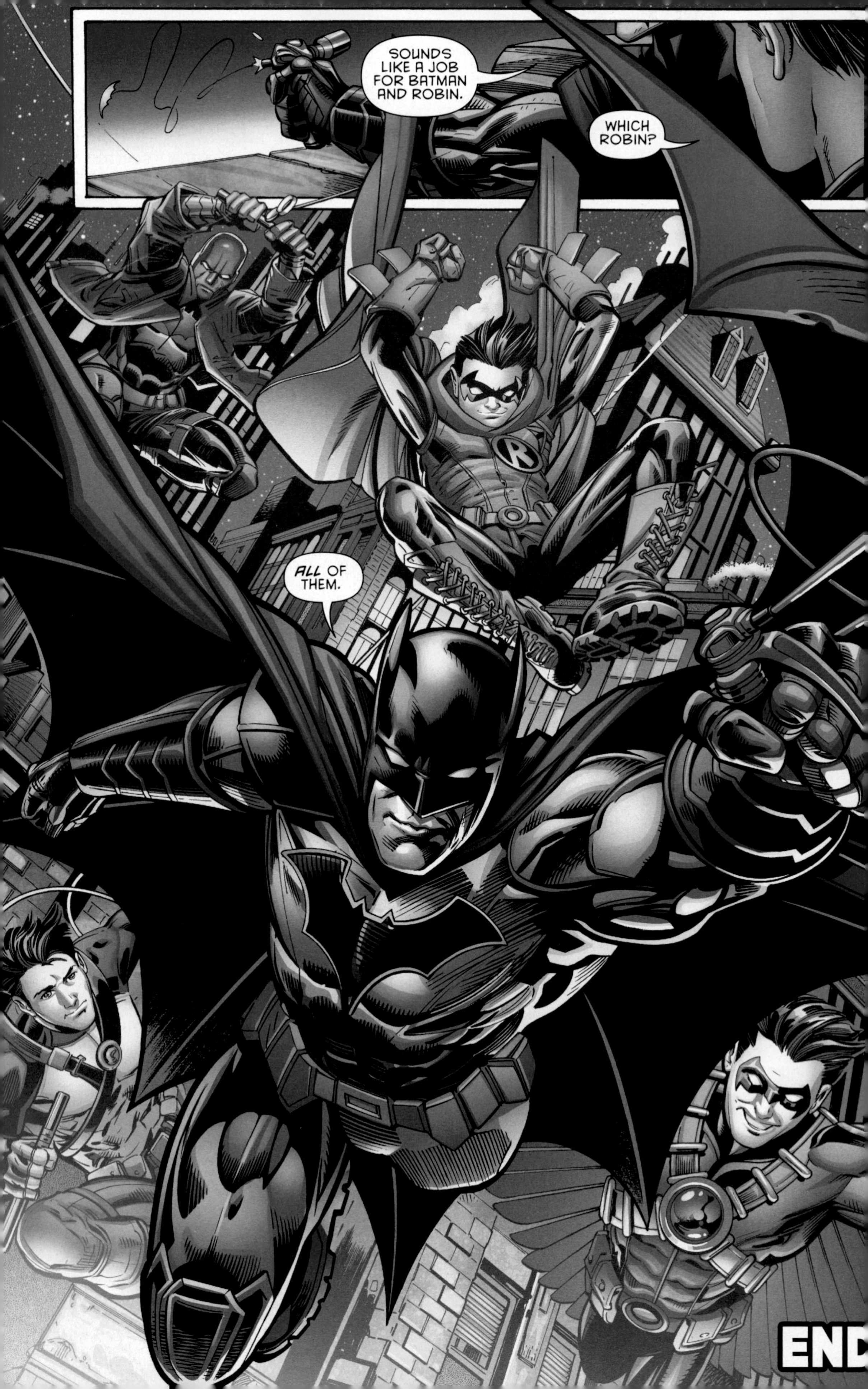
SOUNDS LIKE A JOB FOR BATMAN AND ROBIN.
WHICH ROBIN?
ALL OF THEM.
END

"[Writer Scott Snyder] pulls from the oldest aspects of the Batman myth, combines it with sinister-comic elements from the series' best period, and gives the whole thing terrific forward-spin."—ENTERTAINMENT WEEKLY

START AT THE BEGINNING!

BATMAN VOLUME 1: THE COURT OF OWLS

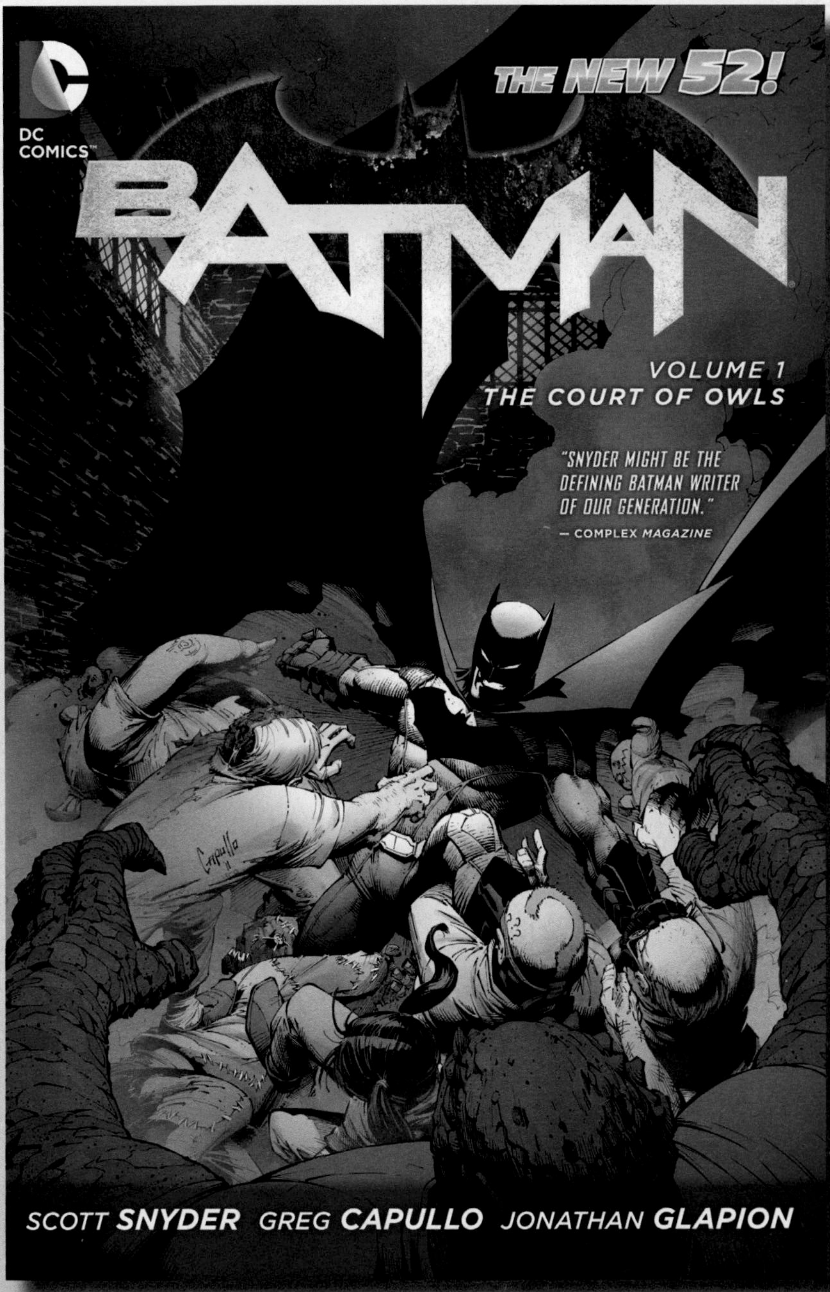

DC COMICS
THE NEW 52!
BATMAN
VOLUME 1
THE COURT OF OWLS
"SNYDER MIGHT BE THE DEFINING BATMAN WRITER OF OUR GENERATION."
— COMPLEX MAGAZINE
SCOTT SNYDER GREG CAPULLO JONATHAN GLAPION

BATMAN VOL. 2: THE CITY OF OWLS

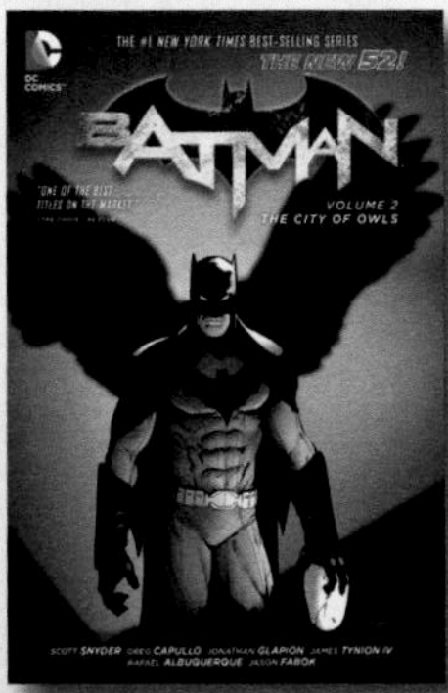

THE NEW 52!
BATMAN
VOLUME 2
THE CITY OF OWLS

with SCOTT SNYDER and GREG CAPULLO

BATMAN VOL. 3: DEATH OF THE FAMILY

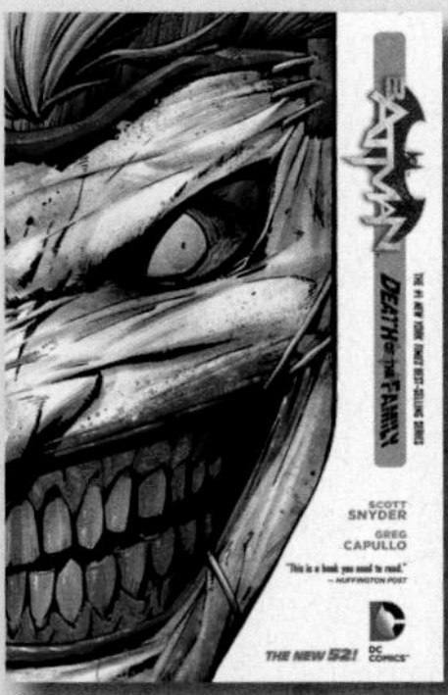

BATMAN
SCOTT SNYDER
GREG CAPULLO
THE NEW 52!

with SCOTT SNYDER and GREG CAPULLO

BATMAN: NIGHT OF THE OWLS

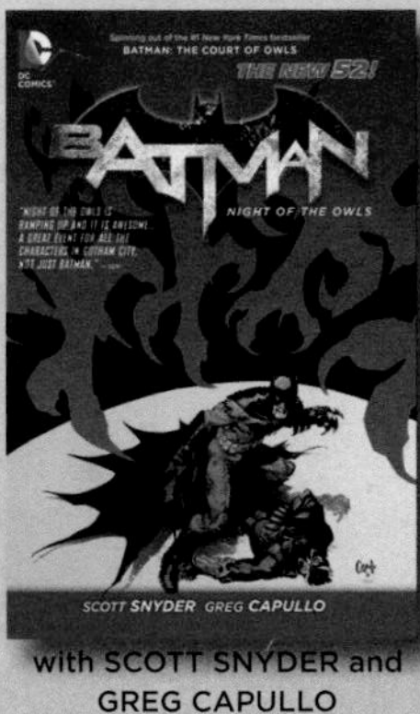

THE NEW 52!
BATMAN
NIGHT OF THE OWLS
SCOTT SNYDER GREG CAPULLO

with SCOTT SNYDER and GREG CAPULLO

START AT THE BEGINNING!

BATMAN & ROBIN
VOLUME 1: BORN TO KILL

BATMAN & ROBIN VOL. 2: PEARL

BATMAN & ROBIN VOL. 3: DEATH OF THE FAMILY

BATMAN INCORPORATED VOL. 1: DEMON STAR

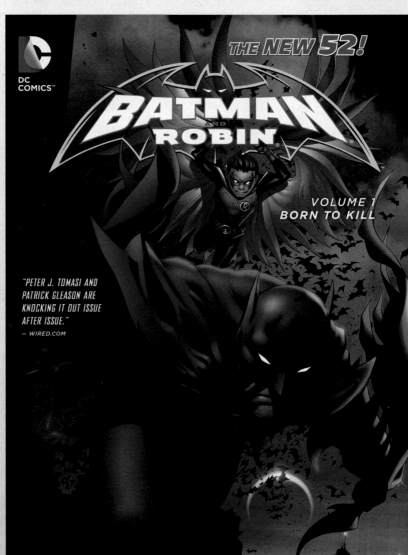

PETER J. **TOMASI** PATRICK **GLEASON** MICK **GRAY**

"This is your go-to book."—ENTERTAINMENT WEEKLY

"DETECTIVE COMICS is head-spinningly spectacular from top to bottom."—MTV GEEK

START AT THE BEGINNING!

BATMAN: DETECTIVE COMICS VOLUME 1: FACES OF DEATH

BATMAN: DETECTIVE COMICS VOL. 2: SCARE TACTICS

BATMAN: DETECTIVE COMICS VOL. 3: EMPEROR PENGUIN

THE JOKER: DEATH OF THE FAMILY

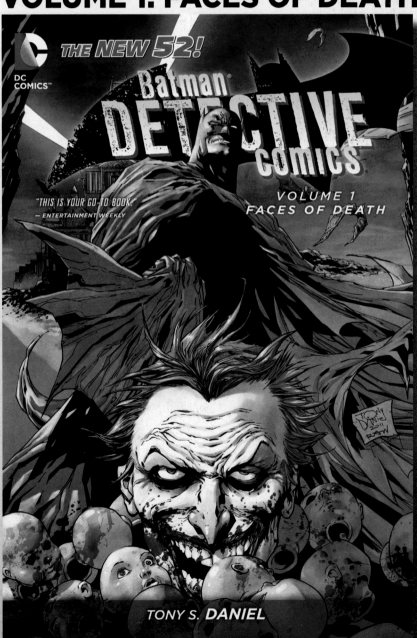

"Stellar. A solid yarn that roots itself in Grayson's past, with
gorgeous artwork by artist Eddy Barrows."—IGN

"Dynamic."—The New York Times

"A new generation is going to fall in love with Nightwing.'
—MTV Geek

START AT THE BEGINNING!

NIGHTWING
VOLUME 1: TRAPS AND TRAPEZES

**NIGHTWING VOL. 2:
NIGHT OF THE OWLS**

**NIGHTWING VOL. 3:
DEATH OF THE FAMILY**

**BATMAN:
NIGHT OF THE OWLS**

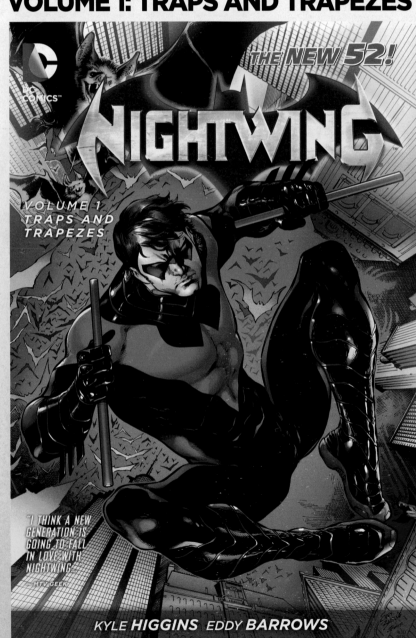

KYLE **HIGGINS** EDDY **BARROWS**

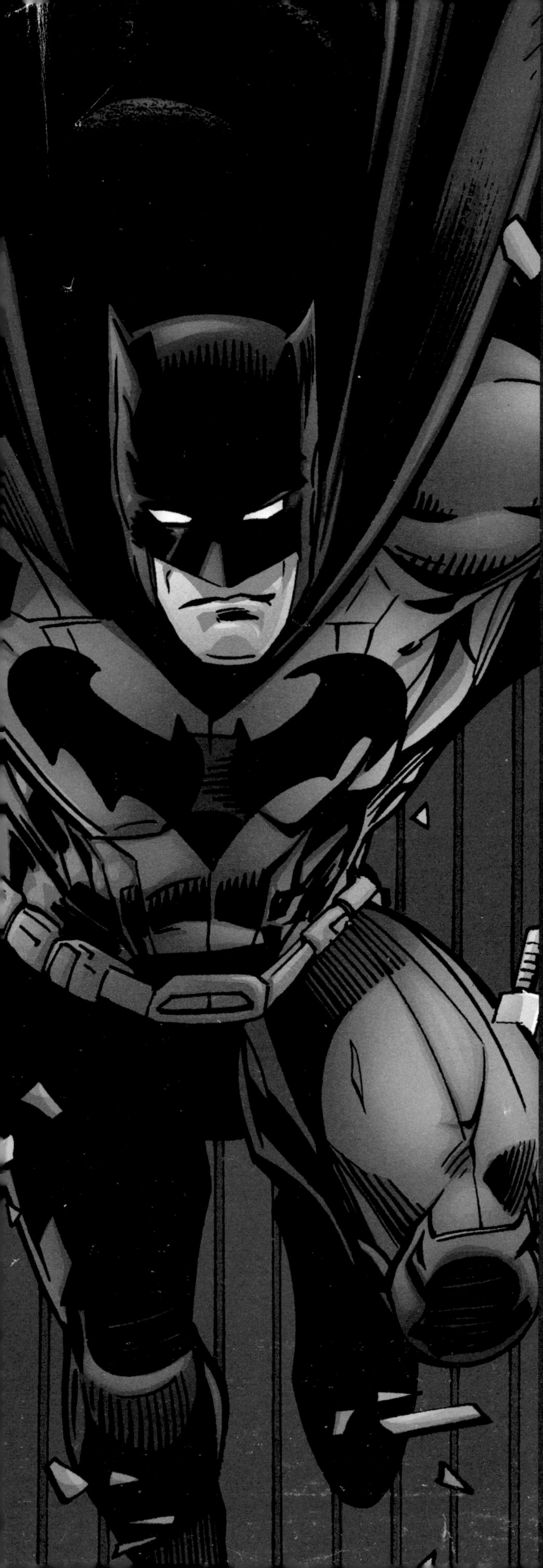

VOLUME 2

BATMAN AND ROBIN ETERNAL

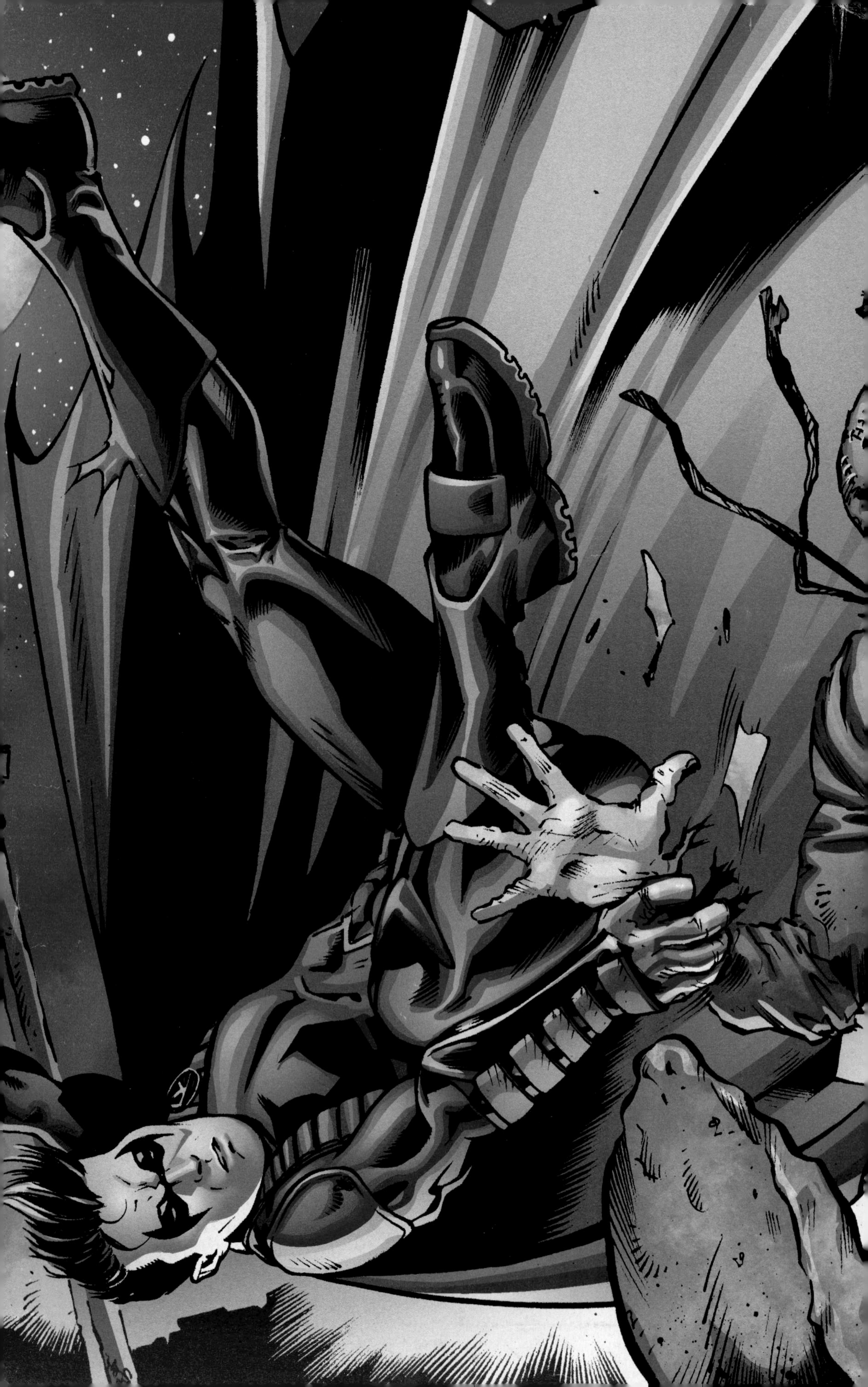

VOLUME 2

STORY BY
JAMES TYNION IV
SCOTT SNYDER

SCRIPT BY
JAMES TYNION IV JACKSON LANZING
COLLIN KELLY ED BRISSON
TIM SEELEY GENEVIEVE VALENTINE
STEVE ORLANDO

ART BY
SCOT EATON CHRISTIAN DUCE
TONY S. DANIEL MARCIO TAKARA
FERNANDO BLANCO ROGER ROBINSON
GORAN SUDŽUKA PAUL PELLETIER
TONY KORDOS WAYNE FAUCHER
SANDU FLOREA ANDREA MUTTI
ROGE ANTONIO GERALDO BORGES
ALVARO MARTINEZ RAUL FERNANDEZ
JAVI PIÑA CARLO PAGULAYAN
IGOR VITORINO JASON PAZ
MARC DEERING

COLORS BY
ALLEN PASSALAQUA GABE ELTAEB
JOHN RAUCH DEAN WHITE
RAIN BEREDO TOMEU MOREY
JOHN KALISZ CHRIS SOTOMAYOR

LETTERS BY
SAIDA TEMOFONTE MARILYN PATRIZIO
COREY BREEN TOM NAPOLITANO
A LARGER WORLD CARLOS M. MANGUAL
DAVE SHARPE

COLLECTION COVER ART BY
TONY S. DANIEL,
SANDU FLOREA & TOMEU MOREY

BATMAN CREATED BY
BOB KANE with BILL FINGER

AZRAEL CREATED BY
DENNIS O'NEIL & JOE QUESADA

BATMAN AND ROBIN ETERNAL

CHRIS CONROY Editor – Original Series
DAVE WIELGOSZ Assistant Editor – Original Series
JEB WOODARD Group Editor – Collected Editions
ROBIN WILDMAN Editor – Collected Edition
STEVE COOK Design Director – Books
DAMIAN RYLAND Publication Design

BOB HARRAS Senior VP – Editor-in-Chief, DC Comics

DIANE NELSON President
DAN DIDIO and JIM LEE Co-Publishers
GEOFF JOHNS Chief Creative Officer
AMIT DESAI Senior VP – Marketing & Global Franchise Management
NAIRI GARDINER Senior VP – Finance
SAM ADES VP – Digital Marketing
BOBBIE CHASE VP – Talent Development
MARK CHIARELLO Senior VP – Art, Design & Collected Editions
JOHN CUNNINGHAM VP – Content Strategy
ANNE DEPIES VP – Strategy Planning & Reporting
DON FALLETTI VP – Manufacturing Operations
LAWRENCE GANEM VP – Editorial Administration & Talent Relations
ALISON GILL Senior VP – Manufacturing & Operations
HANK KANALZ Senior VP – Editorial Strategy & Administration
JAY KOGAN VP – Legal Affairs
DEREK MADDALENA Senior VP – Sales & Business Development
JACK MAHAN VP – Business Affairs
DAN MIRON VP – Sales Planning & Trade Development
NICK NAPOLITANO VP – Manufacturing Administration
CAROL ROEDER VP – Marketing
EDDIE SCANNELL VP – Mass Account & Digital Sales
COURTNEY SIMMONS Senior VP – Publicity & Communications
JIM (SKI) SOKOLOWSKI VP – Comic Book Specialty & Newsstand Sales
SANDY YI Senior VP – Global Franchise Management

BATMAN AND ROBIN ETERNAL VOLUME 2

DC Comics, 2900 West Alameda Ave., Burbank, CA 91505
Printed by RR Donnelley, Salem, VA, USA. 5/27/16. First Printing.
ISBN: 978-1-4012-6248-8

Library of Congress Cataloging-in-Publication Data is available.

PEFC Certified
Printed on paper from
sustainably managed
forests and controlled
sources
PEFC/29-31-75   www.pefc.org